the ultimate
extraordinary
uses for
ordinary things

Reader's
Digest

The Reader's Digest Association, Inc.
New York, NY | Montreal

A READER'S DIGEST BOOK
Extraordinary Uses for Ordinary Things
Copyright © 2005 The Reader's Digest Association, Inc.

More Extraordinary Uses for Ordinary Things
Copyright © 2009 The Reader's Digest Association, Inc.
Previously published in hardcover as *Baking Soda, Banana Peels, Baby Oil and Beyond*

ISBN: 978-1-60652-496-1

PROJECT STAFF

Extraordinary Uses for Ordinary Things
Editor: Don Earnest
Designers: Richard Kershner and Michele Laseau
Contributing Copy Editor: Jeanette Gingold
Humor Illustration: © Chuck Rekow
How-to Illustration: © Bryon Thomspon

NAILHAUS PUBLICATIONS, INC.
Publishing Director: David Schiff
Writers: Marilyn Bader, Serena Harding, Beth Kalet,
Kathryn Kasturas, Michael Kaufman, Steven Schwartz,
Anita Seline, Angelique B. Sharps, Delilah Smittle, and
Amy Ziffer

More Extraordinary Uses for Ordinary Things
Associate Editorial Director: Elissa Altman
Project Editor: Fred DuBose
Writers: Stephen Brewer, Martha Hailey, Robert V.
Huber, Beth Kalet, Steven Schwartz, Sharon Fass Yates
Designers: Michele Laseau, Richard Kershner
Copy Editor: Marcia Mangum Cronin
Photography: © Ellen Silverman, Kevin Norris
Prop Stylist: Paul Lowe
Illustrations: © Tania Lee

READER'S DIGEST TRADE PUBLISHING
U.S. Project Editor: Kim Casey
Project Designer: Rich Kershner
Senior Art Director: George McKeon
Editor-in-Chief, Books & Home Entertainment: Neil Wertheimer
Associate Publisher, Trade Publishing: Rosanne McManus
President and Publisher, Trade Publishing: Harold Clarke

We are committed to both the quality of our products and the service we provide to our customers. We value your comments, so please feel free to contact us.

The Reader's Digest Association, Inc.
Adult Trade Publishing
44 South Broadway
White Plains, NY 10601

For more Reader's Digest products and information, visit our website: www.rd.com (in the United States)

Printed in China

1 3 5 7 9 10 8 6 4 2

NOTE TO READERS
The information in this book should not be substituted for, or used to alter, medical therapy without your doctor's advice. For a specific health problem, consult your physician for guidance. The mention of any products, retail businesses, or websites in this book does not imply or constitute an endorsement by the authors or by The Reader's Digest Association, Inc.

contents

extraordinary uses for ordinary things

{ FEATURING **Vinegar**, Baking Soda, **Salt**, Toothpaste, **String**, Plastic Cups, **Mayonnaise**, Nail Polish, **Tape**, and More Than 200 Other Common Household Items }

2,317 WAYS TO SAVE MONEY AND TIME

Reader's Digest

The Reader's Digest Association, Inc.
New York, NY | Montreal

{Yes, Extraordinary}

Welcome to *Extraordinary Uses for Ordinary Things!* Inside you'll find thousands of ingenious, money-saving tips just like these. Jump in, raid your pantry, and start saving money today!

CLEAN YOUR DISHWASHER WITH KOOL-AID

Don't buy special powder to get rid of dishwasher iron deposits. Just dump in a packet of unsweetened Kool-Aid. It's a much cheaper way to make the inside of your dishwasher sparkle.

MAKE FLUFFY PANCAKES WITH CLUB SODA

Substitute club soda for the liquid called for in your favorite pancake or waffle recipe. You'll be amazed at how light and fluffy the breakfast treats will be.

REMOVE LIPSTICK STAINS WITH HAIR SPRAY

Got lipstick on your shirt? Apply hair spray and let it sit for a few minutes. When you wipe the spray off, the stain will come off with it.

HAVE A FACIAL WITH CAT LITTER

Make a deep-cleaning mud mask for your face with a couple of handfuls of cat litter. The clay in the litter detoxifies your skin by absorbing dirt and oil from the pores.

MELT SIDEWALK ICE WITH BAKING SODA

For an effective way to melt ice on steps and walkways, sprinkle them with generous amounts of baking soda mixed with sand. It won't stain or damage concrete surfaces.

GIVE CUT FLOWERS A LONGER LIFE WITH SODA POP

Pour about a quarter cup of soda pop into the water in that vase of flowers and the sugar in the drink will make the blossoms last longer.

TABLE OF CONTENTS

YOUR COMPLETE A-Z Guide

✳ Denotes a SUPER ITEM: A household item with an amazingly large number of uses.

DISCOVER WHAT'S HIDING IN
{ Your Cupboard }

Once upon a time, in the days before computers, cable television, drive-through coffee bars, and carpet-sweeping robots, washing windows was a simple affair. Our parents poured a little vinegar or ammonia in a pail of water, grabbed a cloth, and in no time had a clear view of the outside world through gleaming glass. Then they would use the same combination to banish grime and grit from countertops, walls, shelves, fixtures, floors, and a good bit else of the house.

Some things, like window washing, shouldn't ever get more complicated. But somehow, they did. Today, store shelves are laden with a dazzling array of cleaning products, each with a unique use, a special formula, and a multimillion-dollar advertising campaign. Window cleaners alone take up shelves and shelves of space. The bottles are filled with colorful liquids and have labels touting their orange power, berry bouquet, or lemon or apple herbal scent. Ironically, many boast the added power of vinegar or ammonia as their "secret" ingredient.

This is the way of the world today. Every problem, every mess, every hobby, every daily task seems to require special tools, unique products, and extensive know-how. Why use a knife to chop garlic when there are 48 varieties of garlic presses available? Why use a rag for cleaning when you have specialized sponges, wipes, Swiffers, magnetically charged dusters, and HEPA-filter vacuums?

Which brings us to the point of this book: Why *not* just use a solution of vinegar or ammonia like our grandparents did to clean the windows? It works just as well as those fancy products—if not better. And it costs only about a quarter as much, sometimes less.

204 Everyday Items with Over 2,300 Uses

Making do with what you've already got. It's an honorable, smart, money-saving approach to life. And in fact, it can be downright fun. Sure you can buy a fancy lint brush to remove cat hairs from pants, but it's pretty

amazing how a penny's worth of tape does the job even better. Yes, you can use strong kitchen chemicals to clean the inside of a vase that held its flower water a bit too long. But isn't it more entertaining—and easier—to use a couple of Alka-Seltzer tablets instead to fizz away the mess?

Welcome to *Extraordinary Uses for Ordinary Things*. On the following pages, we'll show you more than 2,300 ingenious ways to use 204 ordinary household products to restore, replace, repair, or revive practically everything in and around your home or to pamper yourself or entertain your kids. You'll save time and money—and you'll save shelf space because you won't need all those different kinds of specialized commercial preparations. You'll even save on gasoline, because you won't need to speed off to the mall every time you run out of a staple such as air freshener, shampoo, oven cleaner, or wrapping paper.

The household items featured in this book are not costly commercial concoctions. Rather, they are everyday items that you're likely to find in your home—in your kitchen, medicine cabinet, desk, garage, and even your wastebasket. And you'll be amazed by how much you can actually accomplish using just a few of the most versatile of these items, such as baking soda, duct tape, pantyhose, salt, vinegar, and WD-40. In fact, there's a popular maxim among handymen that whittles the list to a pair of basic necessities: "To get through life," the saying goes, "you only need two tools: WD-40 and duct tape. If it doesn't move, but should, reach for the WD-40. If it moves, but shouldn't, grab the duct tape."

Less Toxic and More Earth-Friendly Items

In addition to saving you time and money, there are other, less tangible advantages to using these everyday household products. For one thing, many of the items are safer to use and considerably more environmentally friendly than their off-the-shelf counterparts. Consider, for example, using vinegar and baking soda to clear a clogged bathroom or kitchen drain (page 64). It's usually just as effective as a commercial drain cleaner. The only difference is that the baking-soda-and-vinegar combination is far less caustic on your plumbing. Plus, you don't have to worry about getting it on your skin or in your eyes.

The hints in this book will also help you reduce household waste by giving you hundreds of delightful and surprising suggestions for reusing many of the items that you would otherwise toss in the trash or recycling bin. To name a few, these include lemon rinds and banana peels, used tea bags and coffee grinds, orphaned socks and worn-out pantyhose, plastic bags, empty bottles and jugs, cans, and newspapers.

At the end of the day, you'll experience the distinct pleasure that can only come from learning creative, new ways to use those familiar objects around your house that you always thought you knew so well. Even if you'll never use Alka-Seltzer tablets to lure fish onto your line, or need to plug a hole in your car radiator with black pepper, isn't it great to know you can?

Folk Wisdom for the 21st Century

As we noted earlier, much of the advice you'll find in *Extraordinary Uses for Ordinary Things* is not really new—it's just new to us. After all, "Waste not, want not" isn't merely a quaint adage from a bygone era; it actually defined a way of life for generations. In the days before mass manufacturing and mass marketing transformed us into a throwaway society, most folks knew perfectly well that salt and baking soda (or bicarbonate of soda, as it was commonly referred to in those times) had dozens upon dozens of uses.

Now, as landfills swell, and we realize that the earth's resources aren't really endless, there are signs of a shift back to thrift, so to speak. From recycling programs to energy-efficient appliances to hybrid cars, we're constantly looking for new ways to apply the old, commonsense values of our forebears. Even the International Space Station is an example of thrifty technologies at work today. When the station is completed, nearly every waste product and used item onboard the craft will be recycled for another purpose.

How We Put This Book Together

Of course, our number one priority was to provide you with the most reliable information available. To meet that goal, we conducted countless interviews with experts on everything from acne cures to yard care and scrutinized stacks of research materials. We also performed numerous hands-on tests in our own kitchens, living rooms, bathrooms, and other areas around our homes.

The result, we believe, is the most comprehensive and dependable guide to alternative uses for household products you can find. Like a great stew, we've combined some time-honored, traditional tips (such as using apple cider vinegar to kill weeds in your garden) with new tips given to us by various reliable sources (like recycling used fabric softener sheets to clean PC and TV screens), and a few tips that we came up with on our own (such as using bathtub appliqués to steady a legless PC case).

As in any comprehensive compilation such as this, the practical wisdom contained in this book is as much art as it is science. That is to say, although we employed trial-and-error methods wherever possible to provide you with specific amounts and clear directions for using household products and objects to obtain the desired results, we can't guarantee that these solutions will work in all situations. In other words, your mileage may vary.

Moreover, while we're confident that every one of the 204 products used for all the tips included here is generally safe and effective when used as directed, please pay close attention to our "Take Care" warnings about using, storing, and especially combining certain products, particularly *bleach* and *ammonia*. Under no conditions should you ever mix these two chemicals, or use them in poorly ventilated areas.

What's on the Following Pages

The main part of this book is arranged like an encyclopedia, with the 204 product categories organized in A-Z fashion (running from Adhesive Tape to Zucchini), to provide instant access to information as well as entertaining reading. But before that, in the first part of this book, you'll find a guide to the items that are most useful for certain areas, such as the garden or for cooking.

Scattered throughout, you'll also find hundreds of fascinating asides and anecdotes. Some highlight specific warnings and safety precautions, or offer advice about buying or using certain items. But many are just plain fun—providing quirky historical information about the invention or origins of products. Haven't you always wondered who invented the Band-Aid or how Scotch tape got its name? We've also included dozens of engaging and enlightening activities and simple science experiments you can do with your children or grandchildren (and not a single one requires a visit to the local toy store).

Whether you delight in discovering new ways to use commonplace household items, or if you simply hate to throw things away, we're sure you'll find the ideas in this book entertaining and enlightening. So, pull up a comfortable chair, settle back, and get ready to be dazzled by the incredible number of everyday problems that you'll soon be able to solve with ease. We're confident this is one book you'll return to over and over again for helpful hints, trustworthy advice, and even some good, old-fashioned inspiration.

—*The Editors*

MOST

{Useful Items*}

FOR JUST ABOUT ANYTHING

If you have a special interest, such as cooking or health and beauty, you'll soon discover that certain household items are especially useful. There are, for example, close to a dozen uses for plastic bottles in the garden. On these pages, you'll find these helpful items listed for most everyday areas of interest.

10 Most Useful Items for around the

house

pad a package with a disposable diaper …

p. 152

Carpet scraps
{ PAGE 115 }

Make an exercise mat, car mat, or knee pad. • Muffle appliance noise. • Protect floor under plants. • Cushion kitchen shelves. • Give your car traction. • Protect tools.

Compact discs
{PAGE 138}

Use as holiday ornaments, driveway reflectors, or a circle template. • Catch candle drips. • Make an artistic bowl, decorative sun catcher, or clock.

Duct tape
{PAGE 153}

Remove lint. • Repair toilet seats, screens, vacuum hoses, and frames. • Cover a book, pocket folder, or present. • Make a bandage or bumper sticker. • Catch flies. • Replace a grommet. • Reinforce a book binding. • Hem pants. • Hang Christmas lights. • Make Halloween costumes.

Fabric softener sheets
{PAGE 167}

Freshen air and deodorize cars, dogs, gym bags, suitcases, and sneakers. • Pick up pet hairs. • Repel mosquitoes. • Stop static cling. • Make sheets smell good. • End tangled sewing thread.

Nail polish

{PAGE 217}

Mark hard-to-see items. • Mark thermostat and shower settings and levels in measuring cups and buckets. • Label sports gear and poison containers. • Seal envelopes and labels. • Stop shoe scuffs and keep laces, ribbons, and fabric from unraveling. • Make needle-threading easier. • Keep buckles and jewelry shiny. • Stop a stocking run. • Temporarily repair glasses. • Fix nicks in floors and glass. • Repair lacquered items. • Plug a hole in a cooler. • Fill washtub nicks.

Pantyhose

{PAGE 236}

Find and pick up small objects. • Buff shoes. • Keep hairbrush clean. • Remove nail polish. • Keep spray bottles clog-free. • Organize suitcases. Hang-dry sweaters. • Secure trash bags. • Dust under fridge. • Prevent soil erosion in houseplants.

Paper bags

{PAGE 242}

Pack on trips for souvenirs. • Dust off mops. • Carry laundry. • Cover textbooks. • Create a table decoration. • Use as gift bags and wrapping paper. • Reshape knits after washing. • Use as a pressing cloth. • Bag newspapers for recycling.

Plastic bags

{PAGE 261}

Keep mattresses dry. • Bulk curtains and stuff crafts. • Drain bath toys. • Clean pockets in the laundry. • Make bibs and a high-chair drop cloth. • Line a litter box. • Dispose of a Christmas tree.

Rubber bands

{PAGE 276}

Reshape your broom. • Childproof cabinets. • Keep thread from tangling. • Make a holder for car visor. • Use to grip paper. • Extend a button. • Use as a bookmark. • Cushion a remote control. • Secure bed slats and tighten furniture casters.

Sandwich and freezer bags

{PAGE 292}

Protect pictures and padlocks. • Dispense fabric softener. • Display baby teeth. • Carry baby wipes. • Mold soap. • Starch craft items. • Feed birds. • Make a funnel.

TOP
12 Most Useful Items for the
cook

*the secret to perfect
poached eggs is vinegar …*

p. 354

Aluminum foil
{PAGE 39}

Bake a perfect piecrust. • Soften brown sugar.
• Decorate a cake and create special-shaped pie pans.
• Keep rolls and bread warm. • Make an extra-
large salad bowl. • Make a toasted cheese
sandwich with an iron.

Apples
{PAGE 53}

Keep a roast chicken moist and cakes fresh. • Ripen
green tomatoes. • Fluff up hardened
brown sugar. • Absorb excess salt in soups.

Baking soda
{PAGE 62}

Clean fruits and vegetables. • Remove fish smells.
• Reduce the acidity of coffee and tomato-based sauces.
• Reduce the gas-producing properties of beans.
• Make fluffy omelets. • Replace yeast.

Coffee filters
{PAGE 133}

Cover food in microwave. • Filter cork crumbs from
wine or food remnants from cooking oil. • Hold a
taco, ice cream bar, or ice pop.

Ice cube trays
{PAGE 187}

Freeze eggs, pesto, chopped vegetables and herbs,
chicken soup—even leftover wine—for
future use.

Lemons

{PAGE 198}

Prevent potatoes from turning brown or rice from sticking. • Keep guacamole green. • Make soggy lettuce crisp. • Freshen the fridge and cutting boards.

Paper towels

{PAGE 248}

Microwave bacon, clean corn, and strain broth. • Keep vegetables crisp and vegetable bin clean. • Prevent soggy bread and rusty pots.

Plastic bags

{PAGE 264}

Cover a cookbook. • Bag hands to answer phone. • Crush graham crackers. • Use as mixing bowl or salad spinner. • Ripen fruit.

Rubber bands

{PAGE 276}

Keep spoons from sliding into bowls. • Secure casserole lids for travel. • Anchor a cutting board. • Get a better grip on twist-off lids and glasses.

Salt

{PAGE 283}

Prevent grease from splattering. • Speed cooking. • Shell hard-boiled eggs or pecans easier. • Test eggs for freshness and poach eggs perfectly. • Wash spinach better. • Keep salad crisp. • Revive wrinkled apples and stop cut fruit from browning. • Use to whip cream, beat eggs, and keep milk fresh. • Prevent mold on cheese.

Sandwich and freezer bags

{PAGE 293}

Store grater with cheese. • Make a pastry bag. • Dispose of cooking oil. • Color cookie dough. • Keep ice cream from forming crystals. • Soften marshmallows, melt chocolate, and save soda. • Grease pans.

Toothpicks

{PAGE 336}

Mark steaks for doneness. • Retrieve garlic cloves from marinade. • Prevent pots from boiling over. • Microwave potatoes faster. • Limit salad dressing. • Fry sausages better.

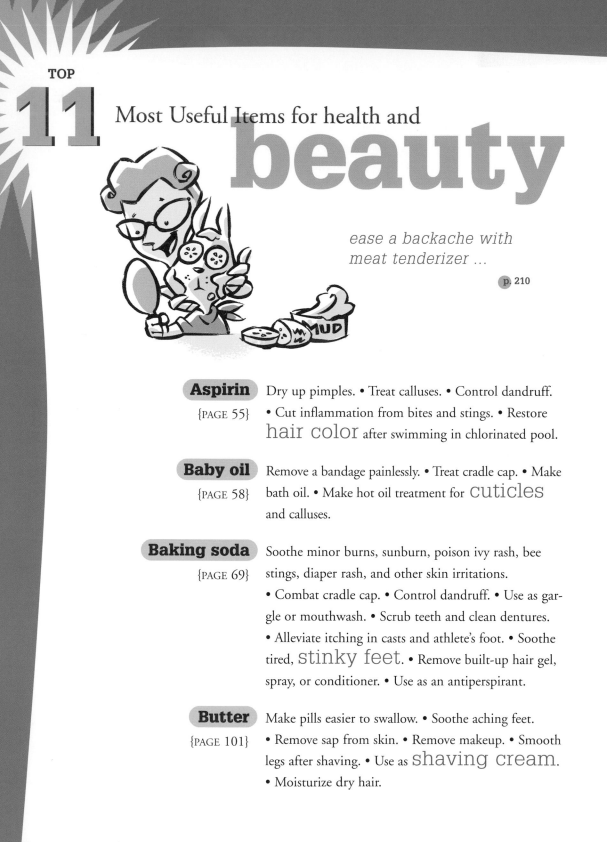

TOP

11

Most Useful Items for health and

beauty

*ease a backache with
meat tenderizer ...*

p. 210

Aspirin
{PAGE 55}
Dry up pimples. • Treat calluses. • Control dandruff.
• Cut inflammation from bites and stings. • Restore
hair color after swimming in chlorinated pool.

Baby oil
{PAGE 58}
Remove a bandage painlessly. • Treat cradle cap. • Make
bath oil. • Make hot oil treatment for cuticles
and calluses.

Baking soda
{PAGE 69}
Soothe minor burns, sunburn, poison ivy rash, bee
stings, diaper rash, and other skin irritations.
• Combat cradle cap. • Control dandruff. • Use as gargle or mouthwash. • Scrub teeth and clean dentures.
• Alleviate itching in casts and athlete's foot. • Soothe
tired, stinky feet. • Remove built-up hair gel,
spray, or conditioner. • Use as an antiperspirant.

Butter
{PAGE 101}
Make pills easier to swallow. • Soothe aching feet.
• Remove sap from skin. • Remove makeup. • Smooth
legs after shaving. • Use as shaving cream.
• Moisturize dry hair.

20

Chest rub

{PAGE 122}

Make calluses disappear. • Sooth aching feet. • Stop insect-bite itch. • Treat toenail fungus. • Repel biting insects.

Lemons

{PAGE 200}

Disinfect cuts and scrapes. • Soothe poison ivy rash. • Relieve rough hands and sore feet. • Remove warts. • Lighten age spots. • Create blond highlights. • Clean and whiten nails. • Cleanse and exfoliate your face. • Treat dandruff. • Soften dry elbows.

Mayonnaise

{PAGE 204}

Relieve sunburn pain. • Remove dead skin. • Condition hair. • Make a facial. • Strengthen fingernails.

Mustard

{PAGE 216}

Soothe aching back pain. • Relax stiff muscles. • Relieve congestion. • Make a facial mask.

Petroleum jelly

{PAGE 254}

Heal windburn. • Help diaper rash. • Protect baby's eyes from shampoo. • Moisturize lips. • Remove makeup. • Moisturize your face. • Create makeup. • Strengthen perfume. • Soften hands. • Do a professional manicure. • Smooth eyebrows.

Tea

{PAGE 327}

Relieve tired eyes. • Soothe bleeding gums. • Cool sunburn. • Relieve baby's pain from injection. • Reduce razor burn. • Condition dry hair and get the gray out. • Tan your skin. • Drain a boil. • Soothe nipples sore from nursing. • Soothe mouth pain.

Vinegar

{PAGE 355}

Control dandruff and condition hair. • Protect blond hair from chlorine. • Apply as antiperspirant. • Soak aching muscles. • Freshen breath. • Ease sunburn and itching. • Banish bruises. • Soothe sore throat. • Clear congestion. • Heal cold sores and athlete's foot. • Pamper skin. • Erase age or sun spots. • Soften cuticles. • Treat jellyfish or bee stings.

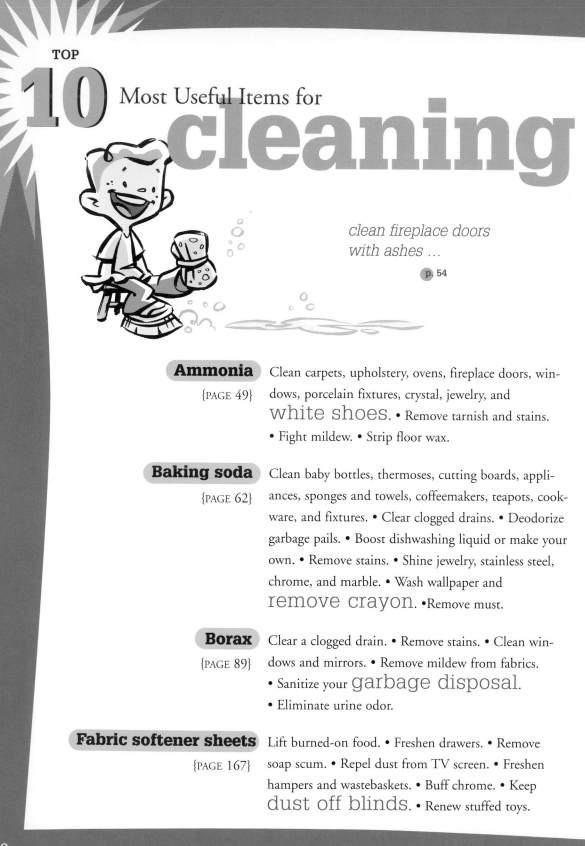

TOP

10 Most Useful Items for
cleaning

*clean fireplace doors
with ashes ...*

p. 54

Ammonia

{PAGE 49}

Clean carpets, upholstery, ovens, fireplace doors, windows, porcelain fixtures, crystal, jewelry, and white shoes. • Remove tarnish and stains. • Fight mildew. • Strip floor wax.

Baking soda

{PAGE 62}

Clean baby bottles, thermoses, cutting boards, appliances, sponges and towels, coffeemakers, teapots, cookware, and fixtures. • Clear clogged drains. • Deodorize garbage pails. • Boost dishwashing liquid or make your own. • Remove stains. • Shine jewelry, stainless steel, chrome, and marble. • Wash wallpaper and remove crayon. • Remove must.

Borax

{PAGE 89}

Clear a clogged drain. • Remove stains. • Clean windows and mirrors. • Remove mildew from fabrics. • Sanitize your garbage disposal. • Eliminate urine odor.

Fabric softener sheets

{PAGE 167}

Lift burned-on food. • Freshen drawers. • Remove soap scum. • Repel dust from TV screen. • Freshen hampers and wastebaskets. • Buff chrome. • Keep dust off blinds. • Renew stuffed toys.

22

Lemons

{PAGE 196}

Get rid of tough stains on marble. • Polish metals. • Clean the microwave. • Deodorize cutting boards, fridge, and garbage disposal.

Rubbing alcohol

{PAGE 278}

Clean fixtures, venetian blinds, windows, and phones. • Remove hair spray from mirrors. • Prevent ring around the collar. • Remove ink stains.

Salt

{PAGE 280}

Clean vases, discolored glass, flowerpots, artificial flowers, percolators, refrigerators, woks, and wicker. • Give brooms long life. • Ease fireplace or flour cleanup. Make metal polish. • Remove wine and grease from carpet, water marks from wood, and lipstick from glasses. • Restore a sponge. • Freshen the garbage disposal. • Remove baked-on food. • Soak up oven spills. • Remove stains from pans and clean cast iron.

Toothpaste

{PAGE 334}

Clean piano keys and sinks. • Polish metal and jewelry. • Deodorize baby bottles. • Remove ink or lipstick from fabric, crayon from walls, and water marks from furniture.

Vinegar

{PAGE 343}

Clean blinds, bricks, tile, paneling, carpets, piano keys, computers, appliances, and cutting boards. • Clean china, crystal, glassware, coffeemakers, and cookware. • Banish kitchen grease. • Deodorize drains and closets. • Polish metal. • Erase ballpoint pen marks. • Remove water rings and wax from furniture. • Revitalize leather. • Clean fixtures and purge bugs.

WD-40

{PAGE 377}

Remove carpet stains and floor scuffs. • Remove tea and tomato stains. • Clean toilet bowls. • Condition leather furniture. • Clean a chalkboard. • Remove marker and crayon from walls.

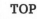

TOP

11

Most Useful Items for the

garden

keep aphids off rosebushes with banana peels ...

p. 85

Aluminum foil

{PAGE 43}

Create a sun box for window plants or an incubator for seedlings. • Mix with mulch to deter insects. • Hang strips to scare crows and other birds. • Wrap tree trunks to prevent sunscald or to keep nibbling mice and rabbits away. • Keep cuttings from getting tangled.

Bottles

{PAGE 93}

Make a bird feeder, a gutter scoop, a watering can, or an individual drip irrigator for a plant. • Secure netting over flowerbeds. • Isolate weeds when spraying. • Cover seed-packet markers or make plant tags from cut strips. • Use as trash can on mower. • Use to space seeds. • Trap bugs.

Coffee cans

{PAGE 131}

Make a sprinkler to spread seeds and fertilizer. • Measure rain to ensure your garden is getting enough water • Make a bird feeder.

Milk cartons

{PAGE 212}

Make a bird feeder. • Use as a seed starter. • Make a collar to protect vegetables. • Collect kitchen scraps for compost.

Newspaper
{PAGE 224}

Protect and ripen end-of-season tomatoes. • Use as mulch or add to compost to remove odor. • Block weeds in flower and vegetable beds. • Get rid of earwigs.

Pantyhose
{PAGE 240}

Tie up tomatoes and beans. • Fill with hair clippings to repel deer. • Make a hammock for growing melons. • Store onions and off-season bulbs. • Prevent soil lost in houseplants. • Fill with soap scraps for cleaning hands at garden spigot.

Plastic bags
{PAGE 265}

Protect plants from frost and shoes from mud. • Speed budding of poinsettias and Christmas cactus. • Keep bugs off fruit on trees. • Store outdoor equipment manuals. • Bring a favorite cracked vase back into use. • Make disposable work aprons.

Plastic containers
{PAGE 267}

Make traps for slugs and wasps. • Stop ants from crawling up picnic table legs. • Use to start seedlings.

Salt
{PAGE 287}

Kill snails and slugs. • Inhibit the growth of weeds in walkway cracks. • Extend the life of cut flowers. • Clean flowerpots.

Tea
{PAGE 330}

Spur growth of rosebushes. • Water acid-loving plants. • Nourish houseplants. • Prepare a planter for potting. • Speed the decomposition of compost.

WD-40
{PAGE 379}

Keep animals out of flowerbeds and squirrels off bird feeders. • Keep tool handles from splintering. • Stop snow from sticking on shovel or snow thrower. Prevent wasps from building nests and repel pigeons. • Kill thistle plants.

TOP

11

Most Useful Items for

outdoors

lubricate skate wheels with hair conditioner ...

p. 181

Aluminum foil

{PAGE 44}

Improve outdoor lighting. • Keep bees away from beverages. • Make an impromptu picnic platter or improvise a frying pan. • Make a drip pan for your barbecue and clean the grill. • Warm your toes when camping and keep your sleeping bag and matches dry. • Make a fishing lure.

Baking soda

{PAGE 74}

Keep weeds out of concrete cracks. • Clean plastic resin lawn furniture. • Feed your flowering plants. • Maintain proper pool alkalinity. • Scour the barbecue grill.

Bottles

{PAGE 93}

Use a plastic jug to make a scoop or bailer for your boat. • Make a plastic jug into an anchor for your boat and for landlubber jobs. • Make a bird feeder. • Fill a plastic jug with sand or cat litter for winter traction. • Keep your cooler cold.

Bubble pack

{PAGE 98}

Keep soft drinks cold. • Sleep on air while camping. • Cushion bleachers and benches.

Buckets
{PAGE 99}

Boil lobster over the campfire. • Use as a footlocker. • Build a camp washing machine or make a camp shower.

Cat litter
{PAGE 118}

Give your car traction on ice. • Prevent barbecue grease fires. • Keep tents and sleeping bags must-free. • Remove grease spots from driveway.

Cooking spray
{PAGE 140}

Prevent grass from sticking to your mower. • Spray on fishing line for quicker casting. • Prevent snow from sticking to your shovel or your snow-thrower chute.

Duct tape
{PAGE 157}

Seal out ticks. • Create a clothesline. • Stash a secret car key. • Patch a canoe or a pool. • Repair outdoor cushions and replace lawn furniture webbing. • Make bike streamers. • Tighten hockey shin guards and revive your hockey stick. • Preserve skateboarders' shoes. • Repair your ski gloves or a tent. • Waterproof your footwear.

Sandwich and freezer bags
{PAGE 296}

Inflate to make valuables float when boating. • Make a hand cleaner for the beach. • Apply bug spray with ease.

Vinegar
{PAGE 363}

Keep water fresh. • Clean outdoor furniture and decks. • Repel insects. • Trap flying insects. • Get rid of ants. • Clean off bird droppings.

WD-40
{PAGE 381}

Repel pigeons and wasps. • Waterproof shoes. • Remove wax from skis and snowboards. • Remove barnacles from boat and protect it from corrosion. • Untangle your fishing line and lure fish. • Clean and protect golf clubs. • Remove burrs from a horse's mane and protect hooves in winter. • Keep flies off cows.

TOP 13

Most Useful Items for
storage

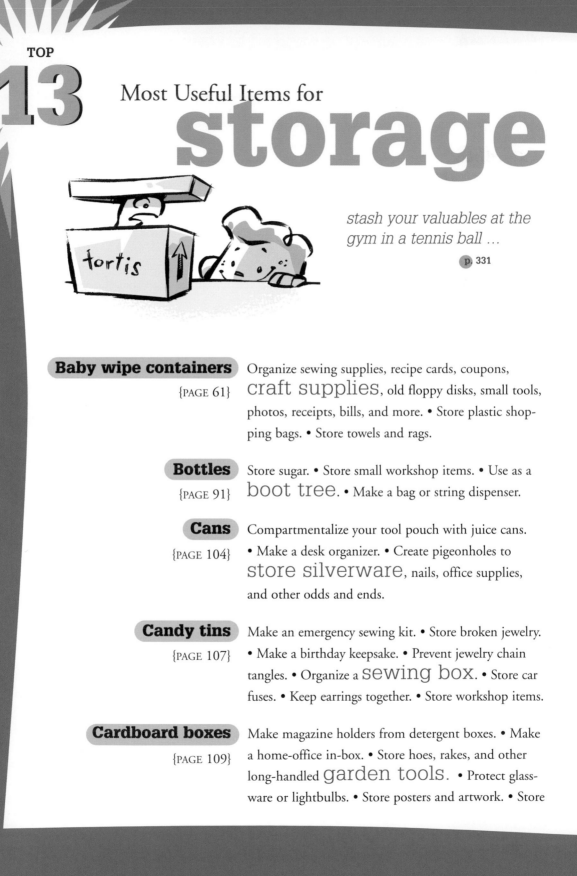

stash your valuables at the gym in a tennis ball ...

p. 331

Baby wipe containers
{PAGE 61}
Organize sewing supplies, recipe cards, coupons, craft supplies, old floppy disks, small tools, photos, receipts, bills, and more. • Store plastic shopping bags. • Store towels and rags.

Bottles
{PAGE 91}
Store sugar. • Store small workshop items. • Use as a boot tree. • Make a bag or string dispenser.

Cans
{PAGE 104}
Compartmentalize your tool pouch with juice cans. • Make a desk organizer. • Create pigeonholes to store silverware, nails, office supplies, and other odds and ends.

Candy tins
{PAGE 107}
Make an emergency sewing kit. • Store broken jewelry. • Make a birthday keepsake. • Prevent jewelry chain tangles. • Organize a sewing box. • Store car fuses. • Keep earrings together. • Store workshop items.

Cardboard boxes
{PAGE 109}
Make magazine holders from detergent boxes. • Make a home-office in-box. • Store hoes, rakes, and other long-handled garden tools. • Protect glassware or lightbulbs. • Store posters and artwork. • Store

Christmas ornaments. • Organize dowels, moldings, furring strips, 2x2s, and metal rods.

Cardboard tubes
{PAGE 112}

Store knitting needles and fabric scraps. • Keep Christmas lights tidy. • Preserve kids' artwork, important documents, and posters. • Keep linens crease-free, pants wrinkle-free, and electrical cords tangle-free. • Protect fluorescent lights. • Store string.

Clothespins
{PAGE 125}

Keep snacks fresh. • Organize workshop, kitchen, bathroom, and closets. • Keep gloves in shape.

Coffee cans
{PAGE 131}

Make a kids' bank. • Hold kitchen scraps. • Carry toilet paper when camping. • Store screws, nuts, and nails. • Organize and store belts. • Collect pocket stuff in the laundry.

Egg cartons
{PAGE 161}

Store and sort coins. • Organize buttons, safety pins, threads, bobbins, and fasteners. • Store golf balls or Christmas ornaments.

Film canisters
{PAGE 169}

Make a stamp dispenser or a sewing kit. • Organize pills. • Store fishing flies. • Carry change for tolls. • Stash jewelry at the gym. • Carry dressings, cooking spices, and condiments. • Carry nail polish remover.

Pantyhose
{PAGE 236}

Store wrapping paper. • Bundle blankets. • Store onions or flower bulbs.

Plastic bags
{PAGE 261}

Store wipes. • Collect used clothes. • Protect clothes. • Store skirts. • Keep purses in shape.

Sandwich and freezer bags
{PAGE 292}

Store breakables. • Save sweaters. • Create a sachet. • Add cedar to a closet. • Make a pencil bag. • De-clutter the bath.

TOP 15

Most Useful Items for

kids

make finger paints from yogurt ...

p. 386

Aluminum pie pans
{PAGE 47}

Use as mold for ice ornaments. • Minimize glitter mess and make trays for craft supplies.

Baking soda
{PAGE 66}

Make watercolor paints or invisible ink. • Produce gas to blow up a balloon. • Clean crayon marks from walls and baby spit-up from clothing. • Combat cradle cap and diaper rash. • Wash chemicals out of new baby clothes.

Bathtub appliqués
{PAGE 81}

Stick to bottom of kiddie pool. • Affix to sippy cups and high-chair seats.

Cardboard boxes
{PAGE 110}

Make a medieval castle, a puppet theater, or a sundial. • Make a garage for toy vehicles. • Store tennis rackets, baseball bats, fishing poles, and other sporting goods. • Use as an impromptu sled. • Play beverage-box ski-ball.

Cardboard tubes
{PAGE 112}

Make a kazoo or a megaphone. • Preserve your kids' artwork. • Build a toy log cabin. • Make no-gunpowder "English" firecrackers.

30

31

TOP
14

Most Useful Items for quick

repairs

repair your garden hose with a toothpick …

p. 338

Adhesive tape
{PAGE 36}

Remove broken window glass safely. • Hang caulk tubes for storage. • Get a better grip on tools.

Aluminum foil
{PAGE 45}

Make flexible funnel for hard-to-reach places. • Reflect light for photography. • Reattach vinyl floor. • Make an artist's palette. • Prevent paint from skinning over. • Line roller pans and keep paint off doorknobs.

Baking soda
{PAGE 73}

Clean car-battery terminals and remove tar from car. • Use as a walkway de-icer. • Tighten cane chair seats. • Give deck a weathered look. • Clean air conditioner filters • Keep humidifier odor-free.

Basters
{PAGE 78}

Cure musty air conditioner. • Transfer paints and solvents. • Fix leaky refrigerator.

Bottles
{PAGE 78}

Make a neater paint bucket. • Store paints. • Make a workshop organizer. • Use as a level. • Make an anchor for weighting tarps and patio umbrellas.

Bubble pack
{PAGE 78}

Prevent toilet-tank condensation. • Insulate windows. • Cushion work surface and protect tools.

Buckets

{PAGE 99}

Hold paint and supplies when painting on a ladder and use lids to contain paint drips • Make stilts for painting ceiling. • Organize extension cords. • Soak your saw to clean. • Use as a Christmas tree stand.

Cardboard boxes

{PAGE 111}

Make a temporary roof repair. • Protect fingers while hammering small nails. • Make an oil drip pan. • Identify fluid leaking from your car. • Make a bed tray. • Make an in-box. • Organize workshop. • Keep upholstery tacks straight.

Clothespins

{PAGE 125}

Clamp thin objects. • Make a clipboard. • Grip a nail to protect fingers. • Float paintbrushes in solvent.

Duct tape

{PAGE 155}

Temporarily fix a car taillight or water hose. • Repair siding. • Make a short-term roof shingle. • Create a clothesline. • Stash a secret car key. • Patch a canoe. • Repair a garbage can.

Garden hose

{PAGE 176}

Protect handsaw. • Make a rounded sanding block. • Make a paint-can grip.

Pantyhose

{PAGE 241}

Test a sanding job. • Apply stain in tight corners. • Patch holes in screens. • Strain paint.

Plastic bags

{PAGE 267}

Protect ceiling fan when painting ceiling. • Store paintbrushes. • Contain paint overspray.

Vinegar

{PAGE 369}

Wash concrete off skin. • Remove paint fumes. • Degrease grates, fans, and air-conditioner grilles. • Disinfect filters. • Help paint adhere to concrete. • Remove rust from tools. • Peel off wallpaper. • Slow plaster hardening. • Revive hardened paintbrushes.

YOUR COMPLETE
A-Z Guide*

*On the following pages you'll find 204 common household items that altogether have more than 2,300 unexpected uses—uses that are not just surprising and clever but can save you time, money, and effort. Some of the items, such as aluminum foil and vinegar, are labeled Super Items because they have so many extraordinary uses.

✱ Adhesive Tape

Remove a splinter Is a splinter too tiny or too deep to remove with tweezers? Avoid the agony of digging it out with a needle. Instead, cover the splinter with adhesive tape. After about three days, pull the tape off and the splinter should come out with it.

Stop ants in their tracks Is an army of ants marching toward the cookie jar on your countertop or some sweet prize in your pantry? Create a "moat" around the object by surrounding it with adhesive tape placed sticky side up.

Make a lint-lifter To lift lint and pet hair off clothing and upholstery, you don't need a special lint remover. Just wrap your hand with adhesive tape, sticky side out.

Reduce your hat size Got a hat that's a bit too big for your head? Wrap adhesive tape around the sweatband—it might take two or three layers depending on the size discrepancy. As a bonus, the adhesive tape will absorb brow sweat on hot days.

Clean a comb To remove the gunk that builds up between the teeth of your comb, press a strip of adhesive tape along the comb's length, and lift it off. Then dip the comb in a solution of alcohol and water, or ammonia and water, to sanitize it. Let dry.

Cover casters Prevent your furniture from leaving marks on your wood or vinyl floor by wrapping the furniture's caster wheels with adhesive tape.

Hang glue and caulk tubes Got an ungainly heap of glue and caulk tubes on your workbench? Cut a strip of adhesive or duct tape several inches long and fold it over the bottom of each tube, leaving a flap at the end. Punch a hole in the flap with a paper hole punch and hang the tube on a nail or hook. You'll free up counter space, and you'll be able to find the right tube fast.

Safely remove broken window glass Removing a window sash to fix a broken pane of glass can be dangerous; there's always the possibility that a sharp shard will fall out and cut you. To prevent this, crisscross both sides of the broken pane with adhesive tape before removing the sash. And don't forget to wear heavy leather gloves when you pull the glass shards out of the frame.

Get a grip on tools Adhesive tape has just the right texture for wrapping tool handles. It gives you a positive, comfortable grip, and it's highly absorbent so that tools won't become slippery if your hand sweats. When you wrap tool handles, overlap each wrap by about half a tape width and use as many layers as needed to get the best grip. Here are some useful applications:

- Screwdriver handles are sometimes too narrow and slippery to grip well when you drive or remove stubborn screws. Wrap layers of adhesive tape around the handle until the tool feels comfortable in your hand—this is especially useful if you have arthritis in your fingers.

- Take a tip from carpenters who wrap wooden hammer handles that can get slippery with sweat. Wrap the whole gripping area of the tool. A few wraps just under the head will also protect the handle from damage caused by misdirected blows.

- Plumbers also keep adhesive tape in their tool kits: When they want to cut a pipe in a spot that's too tight for their hacksaw frame, they make a mini-hacksaw by removing the blade and wrapping one end of the blade to form a handle.

 DID *You* KNOW?

In the 1920s, Josephine Dickson, an accident-prone New Jersey housewife, inspired the invention of the Band-Aid bandage. Her husband, Earle, who tended her various burns and wounds, hit upon the idea of sticking small squares of sterile gauze onto adhesive tape, covering it with a layer of crinoline, then rolling it back up so that Josephine could cut off and apply the ready-made bandages herself.

Earle's employer, Johnson & Johnson, soon began producing the first Band-Aids. By the time Earle died in 1961—by then a member of the company's board of directors—Band-Aid sales exceeded $30 million a year.

✳ Alka-Seltzer

Clean your coffeemaker Fill your percolator or the water chamber of your drip coffeemaker with water and plop in four Alka-Seltzer tablets. When the Alka-Seltzer has dissolved, put the coffeemaker through a brew cycle to clean the tubes. Rinse the chamber out two or three times, then run a brew cycle with plain water before making coffee.

Clean a vase That stuck-on residue at the bottom of narrow-neck vases may seem impossible to scrub out, but you can easily bubble it away. Fill the vase halfway with water and drop in two Alka-Seltzer tablets. Wait until the fizzing stops, then rinse the vase clean. The same trick works for cleaning glass thermoses.

Clean glass cookware Say so long to scouring those stubborn stains off your ovenproof glass cookware. Just fill the container with water, add up to six Alka-Seltzer tablets, and let it soak for an hour. The stains should easily scrub away.

Clean your toilet The citric acid in Alka-Seltzer combined with its fizzing action is an effective toilet bowl cleaner. Simply drop a couple of tablets into the bowl and find something else to do for 20 minutes or so. When you return, a few swipes with a toilet brush will leave your bowl gleaming.

Clean jewelry Drop your dull-looking jewelry in a glass of fizzing Alka-Seltzer for a couple of minutes. It will sparkle and shine when you pull it out.

Unclog a drain Drain clogged again? Get almost instant relief: Drop a couple of Alka-Seltzer tablets down the opening, then pour in a cup of vinegar. Wait a few minutes and then run the hot water at full force to clear the clog. This is also a good way to eliminate kitchen drain odors.

Soothe insect bites Mosquito or other insect bite driving you nuts? To ease the itch, drop two Alka-Seltzer tablets in half a glass of water. Dip a cotton ball in

SCIENCE FAIR

Turn plop, plop, fizz, fizz into whoosh, whoosh, gee whiz with this **Alka-Seltzer rocket.** The rocket gets its thrust from the gas created when you drop a couple of Alka-Seltzer tablets into some water inside a film canister.

The type of film canister is key: Use a **Fuji 35mm plastic canister** that has a lid that fits inside the canister. Canisters with lids that fit around an outside lip won't work. You'll also need a couple of pieces of **construction paper, transparent tape,** and **scissors.**

To form the body of the rocket, wrap a piece of construction paper

around the canister with the canister's open end facing out the bottom end of the tube. Then tape the paper in place. Form a quarter-sheet of construction paper into a nose cone. Then trim it even on the bottom and tape it onto the top of the rocket body.

To launch the rocket, fill the canister about halfway with refrigerated water—cold water is vital to a successful liftoff. Plop in two Alka-Seltzer tablets. Quickly pop on the lid, set the rocket on the ground, and stand back. The gas will quickly build up pressure in the canister, causing the canister lid to pop off and the rocket to launch several feet into the air.

the glass and apply it to the bite. *Caution:* Don't do this if you are allergic to aspirin, which is a key ingredient in Alka-Seltzer.

Attract fish All avid anglers know fish are attracted to bubbles. If you are using a hollow plastic tube jig on your line, just break off a piece of Alka-Seltzer and slip it into the tube. The jig will produce an enticing stream of bubbles as it sinks.

Aluminum Foil

Bake a perfect piecrust Keep the edges of your homemade pies from burning by covering them with strips of aluminum foil. The foil prevents the edges from getting overdone while the rest of your pie gets perfectly browned.

Create special-shaped cake pans Make a teddy bear birthday cake, a Valentine's Day heart cake, a Christmas tree cake, or whatever shaped cake the occasion may call for. Just form a double thickness of heavy-duty aluminum foil into the desired shape inside a large cake pan.

Soften up brown sugar To restore your hardened brown sugar to its former powdery glory, chip off a piece, wrap it in aluminum foil, and bake it in the oven at 300°F (150° C) for five minutes.

Decorate a cake No pastry bag handy? No problem. Form a piece of heavy-duty aluminum foil into a tube and fill it with free-flowing frosting. Bonus: There's no pastry bag to clean—simply toss out the foil when you're done.

Make an extra-large salad bowl You've invited half the neighborhood over for dinner, but don't have a bowl big enough to toss that much salad. Don't panic. Just line the kitchen sink with aluminum foil and toss away!

Keep rolls and breads warm Want to lock in the oven-fresh warmth of your homemade rolls or breads for a dinner party or picnic? Before you load up your basket, wrap your freshly baked goods in a napkin and place a layer of aluminum foil underneath. The foil will reflect the heat and keep your bread warm for quite some time.

Catch ice-cream cone drips Keep youngsters from making a mess of their clothes or your house by wrapping the bottom of an ice-cream cone (or a wedge of watermelon) with a piece of aluminum foil before handing it to them.

Toast your own cheese sandwich Next time you pack for a trip, include a couple of cheese sandwiches wrapped in aluminum foil. That way if you check into a hotel after the kitchen has closed, you won't have to resort to the cold, overpriced snacks in the mini-bar. Instead, use the hotel-room iron to press both sides of the wrapped sandwich and you'll have a tasty hot snack.

Polish your silver Is your silverware looking a bit dull these days? Try an ion exchange, a molecular reaction in which aluminum acts as a catalyst. All you have to do is line a pan with a sheet of aluminum foil, fill it with cold water, and add two teaspoons of salt. Drop your tarnished silverware into the solution, let it sit for two to three minutes, then rinse off and dry.

Keep silverware untarnished Store freshly cleaned silverware on top of a sheet of aluminum foil to deter tarnishing. For long-term storage of silverware, first tightly cover each piece in cellophane wrap—be sure to squeeze out as much air as possible—then wrap in foil and seal the ends.

Preserve steel-wool pads It's maddening. You use a steel-wool pad once, put it in a dish by the sink, and the next day you find a rusty mess fit only for the trash. To prevent rust and get your money's worth from a pad, wrap it in foil and toss it into the freezer. You can also lengthen the life of your steel-wool soap pads by crumpling up a sheet of foil and placing it under the steel wool in its dish or container. (Don't forget to periodically drain off the water that collects at the bottom.)

Scrub your pots Don't have a scrub pad? Crumple up a handful of aluminum foil and use it to scrub your pots.

Tip Foil-Eating Acidic Foods

Think twice before ripping off a sheet of aluminum foil to wrap up your leftover meat loaf—particularly one that's dripping with tomato sauce. Highly acidic or salty foods such as lemons, grapefruits, ketchup, and pickles accelerate the oxidation of aluminum and can actually "eat" through foil with prolonged exposure. This can also leach aluminum into the food, which can affect its flavor and may pose a health risk. If you want to use foil for that meat loaf, however, cover it first with a layer or two of plastic wrap or wax paper to prevent the sauce from coming into contact with the foil.

Keep the oven clean Are you baking a bubbly lasagna or casserole? Keep messy drips off the bottom of the oven by laying a sheet or two of aluminum foil over the rack below. *Do not* line the bottom of the oven with foil; it could cause a fire.

Improve radiator efficiency Here's a simple way to get more heat out of your old cast-iron radiators without spending one cent more on your gas or oil bill: Make a heat reflector to put behind them. Tape heavy-duty aluminum foil to cardboard with the shiny side of the foil facing out. The radiant heat waves will bounce off the foil into the room instead of being absorbed by the wall behind the radiator. If your radiators have covers, it also helps to attach a piece of foil under the cover's top.

Keep pets off furniture Can't keep Snoopy off your brand-new sofa? Place a piece of aluminum foil on the seat cushions, and after one try at settling down on the noisy surface, your pet will no longer consider it a comfy place to snooze.

Protect a child's mattress As any parent of a potty-trained youngster knows, accidents happen. When they happen in bed, however, you can spare the mattress—even if you don't have a plastic protector available. First, lay several sheets of aluminum foil across the width of the mattress. Then, cover them with a good-sized beach towel. Finally, attach the mattress pad and bottom sheet.

Hide worn spots in mirrors Sometimes a worn spot adds to the charm of an old mirror; sometimes it's a distraction. You can easily disguise small flaws on a mirror's reflective surface by putting a piece of aluminum foil, shiny side facing out, on the back of the glass. To hold the foil in place, attach it to the backing behind the mirror or to the frame with masking tape. Don't tape it to the mirror itself.

Kids' Stuff Mixing **finger paints** is a great way for kids to learn first-hand how colors combine while also expressing their creativity. Unfortunately, their learning experience can be your "Excedrin moment."

To **contain the mess,** cut down the sides of a **wide cardboard box** so that they are about three inches high. Line the inside of the box with **aluminum foil** and let the kids pour in the paint. With any luck, the paint should stay within the confines of the box, keeping splatters off walls and the floor.

Sharpen your scissors What can you do with those clean pieces of leftover foil you have hanging around? Use them to sharpen up your dull scissors! Smooth them out if necessary, and then fold the strips into several layers and start cutting. Seven or eight passes should do the trick. Pretty simple, huh? (See page 43 to find out how you can use the resulting scraps of foil for mulching or keeping birds off your fruit trees.)

Clean jewelry To clean your jewelry, simply line a small bowl with aluminum foil. Fill the bowl with hot water and mix in one tablespoon of bleach-free powdered laundry detergent (not liquid), such as Tide. Put the jewelry in the solution and let it soak for one minute. Rinse well and air-dry. This procedure makes use of the chemical process known as ion exchange, which can also be used to clean silverware (see page 40).

Move furniture with ease To slide big pieces of furniture over a smooth floor, place small pieces of aluminum foil under the legs. Put the dull side of the foil down—the dull side is actually more slippery than the shiny side.

Fix loose batteries Is your flashlight, Walkman, or your kid's toy working intermittently? Check the battery compartment. Those springs that hold the batteries in place can lose their tension after a while, letting the batteries loosen. Fold a small piece of aluminum foil until you have a pad that's thick enough to take up the slack. Place the pad between the battery and the spring.

Don't dye your glasses You want to catch up on your reading during the time it takes to color your hair. But you can't read without your specs, and if you put them on, hair dye can stain them. Solution: Wrap the temples of your glasses with aluminum foil.

Clean out your fireplace Looking for an easy way to clean the ashes out of your fireplace? Place a double layer of heavy-duty aluminum foil across the bottom of the fireplace or under the wood grate. The next day—or once you're sure all the ashes have cooled—simply fold it up and throw it away or, even better, use the ashes as described on pages 54-55.

✻ ALUMINUM FOIL **IN THE LAUNDRY ROOM**

Speed your ironing When you iron clothing, a lot of the iron's heat is sucked up by the board itself—requiring you to make several passes to remove wrinkles. To speed things up, put a piece of aluminum foil under your ironing board cover. The foil will reflect the heat back through the clothing, smoothing wrinkles quicker.

DID *You* KNOW?

Have you ever wondered why aluminum foil has one side that's shinier than the other? The answer has to do with how it's manufactured. According to Alcoa, the maker of Reynolds Wrap, the different shades of silver result during the final rolling process, when two layers of foil pass through the rolling mill simultaneously. The sides that contact the mill's heavy, polished rollers come out shiny, while the inside layers retain a dull, or matte, finish. Of course, the shiny side is better for reflecting light and heat, but when it comes to wrapping foods or lining grills, both sides are equally good.

Attach a patch An iron-on patch is an easy way to fix small holes in clothing—but only if it doesn't get stuck onto your ironing board. To avoid this, put a piece of aluminum foil under the hole. It won't stick to the patch, and you can just slip it out when you're finished.

Clean your iron Is starch building up on your clothes iron and causing it to stick? To get rid of it, run your hot iron over a piece of aluminum foil.

✶ ALUMINUM FOIL **IN THE GARDEN**

Put some bite in your mulch To keep hungry insects and slugs away from your cucumbers and other vegetables, mix strips of aluminum foil in with your garden mulch. As a bonus benefit, the foil will reflect light back up onto your plants.

Protect tree trunks Mice, rabbits, and other animals often feed on the bark of young trees during winter. A cheap and effective deterrent is to wrap the tree trunks with a double layer of heavy-duty aluminum foil in late fall. Be sure to remove the foil in spring.

Tip **Prevent Sunscald on Trees**

> Wrapping young tree trunks with a couple of layers of aluminum foil during the winter can help prevent sunscald, a condition widely known as southwest disease, since it damages the southwest side of some young thin-barked trees—especially fruit trees, ashes, lindens, maples, oaks, and willows. The problem occurs on warm winter days when the sun's rays reactivate some dormant cells underneath the tree's bark. The subsequent drop in nighttime temperatures kills the cells and can injure the tree. In most regions, you can remove the aluminum wrapping in early spring.

Scare crows and other birds Are the birds eating the fruit on your trees? To foil them, dangle strips of aluminum foil from the branches using monofilament fishing line. Even better, hang some foil-wrapped seashells, which will add a bit of noise to further startle your fine-feathered thieves.

Create a sun box for plants A sunny window is a great place for keeping plants that love a lot of light. However, since the light always comes from the same direction, plants tend to bend toward it. To bathe your plants in light from all sides, make a sun box: Remove the top and one side from a cardboard box and line the other three sides and bottom with aluminum foil, shiny side out, taping or gluing it in place. Place plants in the box and set it near a window.

Build a seed incubator To give plants grown from seeds a healthy head start, line a shoe box with aluminum foil, shiny side up, allowing about two inches of foil to extend out over the sides. Poke several drainage holes in the bottom—penetrating the foil—then fill the box slightly more than halfway with potting soil, and plant the seeds. The foil inside the box will absorb heat to keep the seeds warm as they germinate, while the foil outside the box will reflect light onto the young sprouts. Place the box near a sunny window, keep the soil moist, and watch 'em grow!

Grow untangled cuttings Help plant cuttings grow strong and uncluttered by starting them in a container covered with a sheet of aluminum foil. Simply poke a few holes in the foil and insert the cuttings through the holes. There's even an added bonus: The foil slows water evaporation, so you'll need to add water less frequently.

✳ ALUMINUM FOIL **IN THE GREAT OUTDOORS**

Keep bees away from beverages You're about to relax in your backyard with a well-deserved glass of lemonade or soda pop. Suddenly bees start buzzing around your drink—which they view as sweet nectar. Keep them away by tightly covering the top of your glass with aluminum foil. Poke a straw through it, and then enjoy your drink in peace.

Make a barbecue drip pan To keep meat drippings off your barbecue coals, fashion a disposable drip pan out of a couple of layers of heavy-duty aluminum foil. Shape it freehand, or use an inverted baking pan as a mold (remember to remove the pan once your creation is finished). Also, don't forget to make your drip pan slightly larger than the meat on the grill.

Clean your barbecue grill After the last steak is brought in, and while the coals are still red-hot, lay a sheet of aluminum foil over the grill to burn off any remaining foodstuffs. The next time you use your barbecue, crumple up the foil and use it to easily scrub off the burned food before you start cooking.

Improve outdoor lighting Brighten up the electrical lighting in your backyard or campsite by making a foil reflector to put behind the light. Attach the reflector to the fixture with a few strips of electrical tape or duct tape—*do not* apply tape directly to the bulb.

DID **You** KNOW?

"Hand me the tinfoil, will ya?" To this day, it's not uncommon for folks to ask for tinfoil when they want to wrap leftovers. Household foil *was* made only of tin until 1947, when aluminum foil was introduced into the home, eventually replacing tinfoil in the kitchen drawer.

Make an impromptu picnic platter When you need a convenient disposable platter for picnics or church suppers, just cover a piece of cardboard with heavy-duty aluminum foil.

Improvise a frying pan Don't feel like lugging a frying pan along on a camping trip? Form your own by centering a forked stick over two layers of heavy-duty aluminum foil. Wrap the edges of the foil tightly around the forked branches but leave some slack in the foil between the forks. Invert the stick and depress the center to hold food for frying.

Warm your toes when camping Keep your tootsies toasty at night while cold-weather camping. Wrap some stones in aluminum foil and heat them by the campfire while you are toasting marshmallows. At bedtime, wrap the stones in towels and put them in the bottom of your sleeping bag.

Keep your sleeping bag dry Place a piece of heavy-duty aluminum foil under your sleeping bag to insulate against moisture.

Keep matches dry It's a tried-and-true soldier's trick worth remembering: Wrap your kitchen matches in aluminum foil to keep them from getting damp or wet on camping trips.

Lure a fish None of your fancy fishing lures working? You can make one in a jiffy that just might do the trick: Wrap some aluminum foil around a fishhook. Fringe the foil so that it covers the hook and wiggles invitingly when you reel in the line.

✻ ALUMINUM FOIL **FOR THE DO-IT-YOURSELFER**

Make a funnel Can't find a funnel? Double up a length of heavy-duty aluminum foil and roll it into the shape of a cone. This impromptu funnel has an advantage over a permanent funnel—you can bend the aluminum foil to reach awkward holes, like the oil filler hole tucked against the engine of your lawn tractor.

Re-attach a vinyl floor tile Don't become unglued just because a vinyl floor tile does. Simply reposition the tile on the floor, lay a piece of aluminum foil over it, and run a hot clothes iron over it a few times until you can feel the glue melting underneath. Put a pile of books or bricks on top of the tile to weight it down while the glue resets. This technique also works well to smooth out bulges and straighten curled seams in sheet vinyl flooring.

Make an artist's palette Tear off a length of heavy-duty aluminum foil, crimp up the edges, and you've got a ready-to-use palette for mixing paints. If you want to get a little fancier, cut a piece of cardboard into the shape of a palette, complete with thumb hole, and cover it with foil. Or if you already have a wooden palette, cover it with foil before each use and then just strip off the foil instead of cleaning the palette.

Prevent paint from skinning over When you open a half-used can of paint, you'll typically find a skin of dried paint on the surface. Not only is this annoying to remove, but dried bits can wind up in the paint. You can prevent this by using a two-pronged attack when you close a used paint can: First, put a piece of aluminum foil under the can and trace around it. Cut out the circle and drop the aluminum foil disk onto the paint surface. Then take a deep breath, blow into the can, and quickly put the top in place. The carbon dioxide in your breath replaces some of the oxygen in the can, and helps keep the paint from drying.

Line roller pans Cleaning out paint roller pans is a pain, which is why a lot of folks buy disposable plastic pans or liners. But lining a metal roller pan with aluminum foil works just as well—and can be a lot cheaper.

Keep paint off doorknobs When you're painting a door, aluminum foil is great for wrapping doorknobs to keep paint off them. Overlap the foil onto the door when you wrap the knob, then run a sharp utility knife around the base of the knob to trim the foil. That way you can paint right up to the edge of the knob. In addition to wrapping knobs on the doors that you'll paint, wrap all the doorknobs that are along the route to where you will clean your hands and brushes.

Keep a paintbrush wet Going to continue painting tomorrow morning? Don't bother to clean the brush—just squeeze out the excess paint and wrap the brush tightly in aluminum foil (or plastic wrap). Use a rubber band to hold the foil tightly at the base of the handle. For extended wet-brush storage, think paintbrush Popsicle, and toss the wrapped brush in the freezer. But don't forget to defrost the brush for an hour or so before you paint.

Reflect light for photography Professional photographers use reflectors to throw extra light on dark areas of their subject and to even out the overall lighting. To make a reflector, lightly coat a piece of mat board or heavy cardboard with rubber cement and cover it with aluminum foil, shiny side out. You can make one single reflector, as large as you want, but it's better to make three panels and join them together with duct tape so that they stand up by themselves and fold up for handy storage and carrying.

Shine your chrome For sparkling chrome on your appliances, strollers, golf club shafts, and older car bumpers, crumple up a handful of aluminum foil with the shiny side out and apply some elbow grease. If you rub real hard, the foil will even remove rust spots. *Note:* Most "chrome" on new cars is actually plastic—don't rub it with aluminum foil.

✳ Aluminum Pie Pans

Make an instant colander Your pot of linguine is almost done when you realize you forgot to replace your broken colander. No need to panic. Just grab a clean aluminum pie pan and a small nail, and start poking holes. When you're done, bend the pan to fit comfortably over a deep bowl. Rinse your new colander clean, place it over the bowl, and *carefully* pour out your pasta.

Rein in splatters when frying Why risk burning yourself or anyone else with oil splatters from a hot frying pan? A safer way to fry is to poke a few holes in the bottom of an aluminum pie pan and place it upside down over the food in your frying pan. Use a pair of tongs or a fork to lift the pie pan and don't forget to wear a cooking glove.

Create a centerpiece Here's how to make a quick centerpiece for your table: Secure a pillar candle or a few votive candles to an aluminum pie pan by melting some wax from the bottom of the candles onto the pan. Add a thin layer of water or sand, and put in several rose petals or seashells.

Contain the mess from kids' projects Glitter is notorious for turning up in the corners and crevices of your home long after your youngster's masterpiece has been mailed off to Grandma. But you can minimize some messes by using an aluminum pie pan to encase projects involving glitter, beads, spray paint, feathers ...well, you get the picture.

Kids' Stuff Looking for a way to keep the kids busy indoors on a cold, wintry day? How about making an ice ornament that you can hang on a tree outside your house as a **homemade winter decoration?** All you'll need is an **aluminum pie pan,** some **water,** a piece of heavy **string** or a shoelace, and a mix of decorative—preferably biodegradable—materials, such as **dried flowers, dried leaves,** pinecones, seeds, shells, and twigs.

Let the children arrange the materials in the pie pan to their liking. Then fold the string or shoelace in half and place it in the pan. The fold should hang over the edges of the pan, while the two ends meet in the center. Slowly fill the pan with water, stopping just shy of the rim. You may have to place an object on the string to keep it from floating to the top.

If the temperatures outside your home are indeed below freezing, you can simply put the pan on your doorstep to freeze. Otherwise just pop it into your **freezer.** Once the water has frozen solid, slide off the pan and let your children choose the optimal outdoor location to display their artwork in ice.

Make trays for craft supplies Bring some order to your children's—or your own—inventory of crayons, beads, buttons, sequins, pipe cleaners, and such by sorting them in aluminum pie pans. To secure materials when storing the pans, cover each pan with a layer of plastic wrap.

Keep bugs out of pet dishes Use an aluminum pie pan filled with about a half-inch of water to create a metal moat around your pet's food dish. It should keep those marauding ants and roaches at bay.

Train your dog If Rover has a tendency to leap up on the sofa or kitchen counter, leave a few aluminum pie pans along the counter edges or the sofa back when you're not home. The resulting noise will give him a good scare when he jumps and hits them.

Keep squirrels and birds off your fruit trees Are furry and feathered fiends stealing the fruit off your trees? There's nothing better to scare off those pesky intruders than a few dangling aluminum pie pans. String them up in pairs (to make some noise), and you won't have to worry about finding any half-eaten apples or peaches come harvest time.

Make a mini-dustpan If you need a spare dustpan for your workplace or bathroom, an aluminum pie pan can fit the bill quite nicely. Simply cut one in half, and you're ready to go.

Use as a drip catcher under paint can Next time you have something that needs painting, place an aluminum pie pan under the paint can as a ready-made drip catcher. You'll save a lot of time cleaning up, and you can just toss the pan in the trash when you're done. Even better, rinse it off and recycle it for future paint jobs.

Store sanding disks and more Since they're highly resistant to corrosion, aluminum pie pans are especially well suited for storing sanding disks, hacksaw blades, and other hardware accessories in your workshop. Cut a pan in half and attach it (with staples or duct tape around the edges) open side up to a pegboard. Now get organized!

Use as an impromptu ashtray No ashtray on hand when you host a smoker in your home? No sweat. An aluminum pie pan—or even a piece of heavy-duty aluminum foil folded into a square with the sides turned up—should suffice.

Protect fingers during cookouts There's nothing like a cookout in the great outdoors. Whether you're planning a day trip or a longer excursion, be sure to pack a few aluminum pie pans. Put a small hole in the middle of each pan, then push them up the sticks used for roasting hot dogs or marshmallows. The pans deflect the heat of the fire, protecting your hands and your children's hands.

super item *25 uses!* **Ammonia**

Clean your oven Here's a practically effortless way to clean an electric oven: First, turn the oven on, let it warm to 150°F (65°C), and then turn it off. Place a small bowl containing 1/2 cup ammonia on the top shelf and a large pan of boiling water on the bottom shelf. Close the oven door, and let it sit overnight. The next morning, remove the dish and pan, and let the oven air out awhile. Then wipe it clean using the ammonia and a few drops of dishwashing liquid diluted in a quart of warm water—even old burned-on grease should wipe right off. *Warning: Do not use this cleaning method with a gas oven unless the pilot lights are out and the main gas lines are shut off.*

TAKE CARE Never mix ammonia with bleach or any product containing chlorine. The combination produces toxic fumes that can be deadly. Work in a well-ventilated space and avoid inhaling the vapors. Wear rubber gloves and avoid getting ammonia on your skin or in your eyes. Always store ammonia out of the reach of children.

Clean oven racks Get the cooked-on grime off your oven racks by laying them out on an old towel in a large washtub. You can also use your bathtub, though you might need to clean it afterward. Fill the tub with warm water and add 1/2 cup ammonia. Let the racks soak for at least 15 minutes, then remove, rinse off, and wipe clean.

Make crystal sparkle Has the twinkle gone out of your good crystal? Bring back its lost luster by mixing several drops of ammonia in 2 cups water and applying

 DID *You* KNOW?

During the Middle Ages, ammonia was made in northern Europe by heating the scrapings of deer antlers, and was known as spirits of hartshorn. Before the start of World War I, it was chiefly produced by the dry distillation of nitrogenous vegetable and animal products.

Today most ammonia is made synthetically using the Haber process, in which hydrogen and nitrogen gases are combined under extreme pressures and medium temperatures. The technique was developed by Fritz Haber and Carl Bosch in 1909, and was first used on a

large-scale basis by the Germans during World War I, primarily for the production of munitions.

AMMONIA*

49

with a soft cloth or brush. Rinse it off with clean water, then dry with a soft, dry cloth.

Repel moths Pesky kitchen moths seem to come out of nowhere! Send them back to wherever they came from by washing your drawers, pantry shelves, or cupboards with 1/2 cup ammonia diluted in 1 quart (1 liter) water. Leave drawers and cabinets open to thoroughly air-dry.

✳ AMMONIA **AROUND THE HOUSE**

Eliminate paint odors Your freshly painted home interior sure looks great, but that paint smell is driving you up the wall! There's no need to prolong your suffering, though. Absorb the odor by placing small dishes of ammonia in each room that's been painted. If the smell persists after several days, replenish the dishes. Vinegar or onion slices will also work.

Clean fireplace doors Think you'll need a blowtorch to remove that blackened-on soot from your glass fireplace doors? Before you get out the goggles, try mixing 1 tablespoon ammonia, 2 tablespoons vinegar, and 1 quart (1 liter) warm water in a spray bottle. Spray on some of the solution; let it sit for several seconds, then wipe off with an absorbent cloth. Repeat if necessary—it's worth the extra effort.

Clean gold and silver jewelry Brighten up your gold and silver trinkets by soaking them for 10 minutes in a solution of 1/2 cup clear ammonia mixed in 1 cup warm water. Gently wipe clean with a soft cloth and let dry. Note: Do not do this with jewelry containing pearls, because it could dull or damage their delicate surface.

Remove tarnish from brass or silver How can you put that sunny shine back in your tarnished silver or lacquered brass? Gently scrub it with a soft brush dipped

 DID *You* KNOW?

AMMONIA*

in a bit of ammonia. Wipe off any remaining liquid with a soft cloth—or preferably chamois.

Remove grease and soap scum To get rid of those ugly grease and soap-scum buildups in your porcelain enamel sink or tub, scrub it with a solution of 1 tablespoon ammonia in 1 gallon (3.7 liters) hot water. Rinse thoroughly when done.

Restore white shoes Brighten up your dingy white shoes or tennis sneakers by rubbing them with a cloth dipped in half-strength ammonia—that is, a solution made of half ammonia and half water.

 Testing Ammonia

Not sure if it's safe to put ammonia solution, or any other stain remover, on a particular fabric or material? Always test a drop or two on an inconspicuous part of the garment or object first. After applying, rub the area with a white terry-cloth towel to test colorfastness. If any color rubs off on the towel or if there is any noticeable change in the material's appearance, try another approach.

Remove stains from clothing Ammonia is great for cleaning clothes. Here are some ways you can use it to remove a variety of stains. Be sure to dilute ammonia with at least 50 percent water before applying it to silk, wool, or spandex.

- Rub out perspiration, blood, and urine stains on clothing by dabbing the area with a half-strength solution of ammonia and water before laundering.

- Remove most non-oily stains by making a mixture of equal parts ammonia, water, and dishwashing liquid. Put it in an empty spray bottle, shake well, and apply directly to the stain. Let it set for two or three minutes, and then rinse out.

- To erase pencil marks from clothing, use a few drops of undiluted ammonia and then rinse. If that doesn't work, put a little laundry detergent on the stain and rinse again.

- You can even remove washed-in paint stains from clothes by saturating them several times with a half-ammonia, half-turpentine solution, and then tossing them into the wash.

Clean carpets and upholstery Lift out stains from carpeting and upholstery by sponging them with 1 cup clear ammonia in 1/2 gallon (2 liters) warm water. Let dry thoroughly, and repeat if needed.

Brighten up windows Dirty, grimy windows can make any house look dingy. But it's easy to wipe away the dirt, fingerprints, soot, and dust covering your windows. Just wipe them down with a soft cloth dampened with a solution of 1 cup clear ammonia in 3 cups water. Your windows will not only be crystal-clear, but streak-free to boot.

Strip wax from resilient flooring Wax buildup on resilient flooring causes it to yellow in time. Remove old wax layers and freshen up your floor by washing it with a mixture of 1 cup ammonia in 1/2 gallon (2 liters) water. Let the solution sit for three to five minutes, then scrub with a nylon or plastic scouring pad to remove the old wax. Wipe away leftover residue with a clean cloth or sponge, then give the floor a thorough rinsing.

Clean bathroom tiles Make bathroom tiles sparkle again—and kill mildew on them—by sponging them with 1/4 cup ammonia in 1 gallon (3.7 liters) water.

✳ AMMONIA **IN THE GARDEN**

Use as plant food Give the alkaline-loving flowering plants and vegetables in your garden—such as clematis, lilac, hydrangea, and cucumbers—an occasional special treat with a shower of 1/4 cup ammonia diluted in 1 gallon (3.7 liters) water. They'll especially appreciate the boost in nitrogen.

Stop mosquito bites from itching If you forget to put on your insect repellent and mosquitoes make a meal of you, stop the itching instantly by applying a drop or two of ammonia directly to the bites. Don't use ammonia on a bite you've already scratched open, though; the itch will be replaced by a nasty sting.

Keep stray animals out of your trash Few things can be quite as startling as a raccoon leaping out of your garbage pail just as you're about to make your nightly trash deposit. Keep away those masked scavengers and other strays by spraying the outside and lids of your garbage bins with half-strength ammonia or by spraying the bags inside.

Remove stains from concrete Tired of those annoying discolorations on your concrete work? To get rid of them, scrub with 1 cup ammonia diluted in 1 gallon (3.7 liters) water. Hose it down well when you're done.

Fight mildew Ammonia and bleach are equally effective weapons in the battle against mold and mildew. However, each has its own distinct applications, and under no conditions should the two ever be combined.

Reach for the ammonia for the following chores, but be sure you use it in a well-ventilated area, and don't forget to wear rubber gloves:

● Clean the mildew off unfinished wooden patio furniture and picnic tables with a mixture of 1 cup ammonia, 1/2 cup vinegar, 1/4 cup baking soda, and 1 gallon (3.7 liters) water. Rinse off thoroughly and use an old terry-cloth towel to absorb excess moisture.

● To remove mildew from painted outdoor surfaces, use the same combination of ingredients.

● To remove mildew from wicker furniture, wash it down with a solution of 2 tablespoons ammonia in 1 gallon (3.7 liters) water. Use an old toothbrush to get into hard-to-reach twists and turns. Rinse well and let air-dry.

✱ Apples

Roast a juicy chicken If your roasted chicken tends to emerge from the oven as dry as a snow boot on a summer's day, don't fret. The next time you roast a chicken, stuff an apple inside the bird before placing it in the roasting pan. When it's done cooking, toss the fruit in the trash, and get ready to sit down to a delicious—and juicy—main course.

Keep cakes fresh Want a simple and effective way to extend the shelf life of your home-made or store-bought cakes? Store them with a half an apple. It helps the cake maintain its moisture considerably longer than merely popping it in the fridge.

Ripen green tomatoes How's that? You just became the proud owner of a bunch of green tomatoes? No sweat. You can quickly ripen them up by placing them—along with an already-ripe apple—in a paper bag for a couple of days. For best results, maintain a ratio of about five or six tomatoes per apple.

Fluff up hardened brown sugar Brown sugar has the irritating habit of hardening up when exposed to humidity. Fortunately, it doesn't take much to make this a temporary condition. Simply place an apple wedge in a self-sealing plastic bag with the chunk of hardened brown sugar. Tightly seal the bag and put it in a dry place for a day or two. Your sugar will once again be soft enough to use.

Absorb salt in soups and stews Salting to taste is one thing, but it is possible to overdo it. When you find yourself getting heavy-handed with the saltshaker, simply drop a few apple (or potato) wedges in your pot. After cooking for another 10 minutes or so, remove the wedges—along with the excess salt.

Use as decorative candleholders Add a cozy, country feel to your table setting by creating a natural candleholder. Use an apple corer to carve a hole three-quarters of the way down into a pair of large apples, insert a tall decorative candle into each hole, surround the apples with a few leaves, branches, or flowers, and voilà! You have a lovely centerpiece.

* Ashes

Clean fireplace doors You normally wouldn't think of using dirty wood ashes to clean glass fireplace doors, but it works. Mix some ashes with a bit of water, and apply them with a damp cloth, sponge, or paper towel, or simply dip a wet sponge into the ashes. Rub the mixture over the doors' surfaces. Rinse with a wet paper towel or sponge, then dry with a clean cloth. The results will amaze you, but remember—wood ash was a key ingredient in old-fashioned lye soap.

Tip Selecting Firewood

For a hot-burning and long-lasting fire, you can't do much better than well-seasoned sugar maple. Green or wet wood burns poorly and builds up heaps of creosote (the leading cause of chimney fires) in your chimney; pine is another major producer of creosote. Never burn scraps of pressure-treated wood; it contains chemicals that can be extremely harmful when burned.

Don't be a fanatic about cleaning ashes from your fireplace. Leave a 1- to 2-inch (2.5 to 5 centimeters) layer of ash under the andiron to reflect heat back up to the burning wood and protect your fireplace floor against hot embers. Just be sure not to let the ashes clog up the space under the grate and block the airflow a good fire needs.

Reduce sun glare Pro ball players often wear that black stuff under their eyes to cut down glare from the sun or bright stadium lights. If you're troubled by sun glare while driving or hiking, you may want to try it too. Just put a drop or two of baby oil on your finger, dip it in some wood ashes, and apply under your eyes.

Use as plant food Wood ashes have a high alkaline content and trace amounts of calcium and potassium, which encourage blooms. If your soil tends to be acidic, sprinkle the ashes in spring around alkaline-loving plants such as clematis, hydrangea, lilac, and roses (but avoid acid-lovers like rhododendrons, blueberries, and azaleas). Avoid using ashes from easy-to-ignite, pre-formed logs, which may contain chemicals harmful to plants. And be sparing when adding ashes to your compost pile; they can counteract the benefits of manure and other high-nitrogen materials.

Repel insects Scatter a border of ashes around your garden to deter cutworms, slugs, and snails—it sticks to their bodies and draws moisture out of them. Also sprinkle small amounts of ashes over garden plants to manage infestations of soft-bodied insects. Wear eye protection and gloves; getting ashes in your eyes can be quite painful.

Clean pewter Restore the shine to your pewter by cleaning it with cigarette ashes. Dip a dampened piece of cheesecloth into the ashes and rub it well over the item. It will turn darker at first, but the shine will come out after a good rinsing.

Remove water spots and heat marks from wood furniture Use cigar and or cigarette ashes to remove those white rings left on your wooden furniture by wet glasses or hot cups. Mix the ashes with a few drops of water to make a paste, and rub lightly over the mark to remove it. Then shine it with your favorite furniture polish.

Aspirin

Revive dead car batteries If you get behind the wheel only to discover that your car's battery has given up the ghost—and there's no one around to give you a jump—you may be able to get your vehicle started by dropping two aspirin tablets into the battery itself. The aspirin's acetylsalicylic acid will combine with the battery's sulfuric acid to produce one last charge. Just be sure to drive to your nearest service station.

 DID *You* KNOW?

The bark of the willow tree is rich in salicin, a natural painkiller and fever reducer. In the third century B.C. Hippocrates used it to relieve headaches and pain, and many traditional healers, including Native Americans, used salicin-containing herbs to treat cold and flu symptoms. But it wasn't until 1899 that Felix Hoffmann, a chemist at the German company Bayer, developed a modified derivative, acetylsalicylic acid, better known as aspirin.

Remove perspiration stains Before you give up all hope of ever getting that perspiration stain out of your good white dress shirt, try this: Crush two aspirins and mix the powder in 1/2 cup warm water. Soak the stained part of the garment in the solution for two to three hours.

> **TAKE CARE** About 10 percent of people with severe asthma are also allergic to aspirin—and, in fact, to all products containing salicylic acid, aspirin's key ingredient, including some cold medications, fruits, and food seasonings and additives. That percentage skyrockets to 30 to 40 percent for older asthmatics who also suffer from sinusitis or nasal polyps. Acute sensitivity to aspirin is also seen in a small percentage of the general population without asthma—particularly people with ulcers and other bleeding conditions.
>
> Always consult your doctor before using any medication, and do not apply aspirin externally if you are allergic to taking it in internally.

Restore hair color Swimming in a chlorinated pool can have a noticeable, and often unpleasing, effect on your hair coloring if you have light-colored hair. But you can usually return your hair to its former shade by dissolving six to eight aspirins in a glass of warm water. Rub the solution thoroughly into your hair, and let it set for 10-15 minutes.

Dry up pimples Even those of us who are well past adolescence can get the occasional pimple. Put the kibosh on those annoying blemishes by crushing one aspirin and moistening it with a bit of water. Apply the paste to the pimple, and let it sit for a couple of minutes before washing off with soap and water. It will reduce the redness and soothe the sting. If the pimple persists, repeat the procedure as needed until it's gone.

Treat hard calluses Soften hard calluses on your feet by grinding five or six aspirins into a powder. Make a paste by adding 1/2 teaspoon each of lemon juice and water. Apply the mixture to the affected areas, then wrap your foot in a warm towel and cover it with a plastic bag. After staying off your feet for at least ten minutes, remove the bag and towel, and file down the softened callus with a pumice stone.

Control dandruff Is your dandruff problem getting you down? Keep it in check by crushing two aspirins to a fine powder and adding it to the normal amount of shampoo you use each time you wash your hair. Leave the mixture on your hair for 1-2 minutes, then rinse well and wash again with plain shampoo.

Apply to insect bites and stings Control the inflammation caused by mosquito bites or bee stings by wetting your skin and rubbing an aspirin over the spot. Of course, if you are allergic to bee stings—and have difficulty breathing, develop abdominal pains, or feel nauseated following a bee sting—get medical attention at once.

Help cut flowers last longer It's a tried-and-true way to keep roses and other cut flowers fresh longer: Put a crushed aspirin in the water before adding your flowers. Other household items that you can put in the water to extend the life of your flower arrangements include: a multivitamin, a teaspoon of sugar, a pinch of salt and baking soda, and even a copper penny. Also, don't forget to change the vase water every few days.

Use as garden aid Aspirin is not only a first-aid essential for you, but for your garden as well. Some gardeners grind it up for use as a rooting agent, or mix it with water to treat fungus conditions in the soil. But be careful when using aspirin around plants; too much of it can cause burns or other damage to your greenery. When treating soil, the typical dosage should be a half or a full aspirin tablet in 1 quart (1 liter) water.

Remove egg stains from clothes Did you drop some raw egg on your clothing while cooking or eating? First, scrape off as much of the egg as you can, and then try to sponge out the rest with lukewarm water. Don't use hot water—it will set the egg. If that doesn't completely remove the stain, mix water and cream of tartar into a paste and add a crushed aspirin. Spread the paste on the stain and leave it for 30 minutes. Rinse well in warm water and the egg will be gone.

✳ Baby Oil

Remove a bandage You can eliminate—or at least, significantly lessen—the "ouch" factor, and subsequent tears, when removing a youngster's bandage by first rubbing some baby oil into the adhesive parts on top and around the edges. If you see the bandage working loose, let the child finish the job to help him overcome his fear. Adults who have sensitive or fragile skin may also want to try this.

Make your own bath oil Do you have a favorite perfume or cologne? You can literally bathe in it by making your own scented bath oil. Simply add a few drops of your scent of choice to 1/4 cup baby oil in a small plastic bottle. Shake well, and add it to your bath.

Buff up your golf clubs Don't waste your money on fancy cleaning kits for your chrome-plated carbon steel golf club heads. Just keep a small bottle filled with baby oil in your golf bag along with a chamois cloth or towel. Dab a few drops of oil on the cloth and polish the head of your club after each round of golf.

Slip off a stuck ring Is that ring jammed on your finger again? First lubricate the ring area with a generous amount of baby oil. Then swivel the ring around to spread the oil under it. You should be able to slide the ring off with ease.

Clean your bathtub or shower Remove dirt and built-up soap scum around your bathtub or shower stall by wiping surfaces with 1 teaspoon baby oil on a moist cloth. Use another cloth to wipe away any leftover oil. Finally, spray the area with a disinfectant cleaner to kill any remaining germs. This technique is also great for cleaning soap film and watermarks off glass shower doors.

Shine stainless steel sinks and chrome trim Pamper your dull-looking stainless steel sinks by rubbing them down with a few drops of baby oil on a soft, clean cloth. Rub dry with a towel, and repeat if necessary. This is also a terrific way to remove stains on the chrome trim of your kitchen appliances and bathroom fixtures.

Polish leather bags and shoes Just a few drops of baby oil applied with a soft cloth can add new life to an old leather bag or pair of patent-leather shoes. Don't forget to wipe away any oil remaining on the leather when you're done.

Get scratches off dashboard plastic You can disguise scratches on the plastic lens covering the odometer and other indicators on your car's dashboard by rubbing over them with a bit of baby oil.

Remove latex paint from skin Did you get almost as much paint on your face and hands as you did on the bathroom you just painted? You can quickly get latex paint off your skin by first rubbing it with some baby oil, followed by a good washing with soap and hot water.

Treat cradle cap Cradle cap may be unsightly, but it is a common, usually harmless, phase in many babies' development. To combat it, gently rub in a little baby oil, and lightly comb it through your baby's hair. If your child gets upset, comb it a bit at a time, but do not leave the oil on for more than 24 hours. Then, thoroughly wash the hair to remove all of the oil. Repeat the process in persistent cases. *Note:* If you notice a lot of yellow crusting, or if the cradle cap has spread behind the ears or on the neck, contact your pediatrician instead.

✳ Baby Powder

Give sand the brush-off How many times have you had a family member return from a day at the beach only to discover that a good portion of the beach has been brought back into your living room? Minimize the mess by sprinkling some baby powder over sweaty, sand-covered kids (and adults) before they enter the house. In addition to soaking up excess moisture, the powder makes sand incredibly easy to brush off.

Cool sheets in summer Are those sticky, hot bed sheets giving you the summertime blues when you should be deep in dreamland? Cool things down by sprinkling a bit of baby powder between your sheets before hopping into the sack on warm summer nights.

 DID *You* KNOW?

Dry-shampoo your pet Is the pooch's coat in need of a pick-me-up? Vigorously rub a handful or two of baby powder into your pet's fur. Let it settle in for a couple of minutes, and follow up with a thorough brushing. Your dog will both look and *smell* great! You can even occasionally "dry shampoo" your own, or someone else's, hair by following the same technique.

Absorb grease stains on clothing Frying foods can be dangerous business—especially for your clothes. If you get a grease splatter on your clothing, try dabbing the stain with some baby powder on a powder puff. Make sure you rub it in well, and then brush off any excess powder. Repeat until the mark is gone.

Clean your playing cards Here's a simple way to keep your playing cards from sticking together and getting grimy: Loosely place the cards in a plastic bag along with a bit of baby powder. Seal the bag and give it a few good shakes. When you remove your cards, they should feel fresh and smooth to the touch.

Slip on your rubber gloves Don't try jamming and squeezing your fingers into your rubber gloves when the powder layer inside the gloves wears out. Instead, give your fingers a light dusting with baby powder. Your rubber gloves should slide on good as new.

Remove mold from books If some of your books have been stored in a less than ideal environment and have gotten a bit moldy or mildewed, try this: First, let them thoroughly air-dry. Then, sprinkle some baby powder between the pages and stand the books upright for several hours. Afterward, gently brush out the remaining powder from each book. They may not be as good as new, but they should be in a lot better shape than they were.

Dust off your flower bulbs Many savvy gardeners use medicated baby powder to dust flower bulbs before planting them. Simply place 5-6 bulbs and about 3 tablespoons baby powder in a sealed plastic bag and give it a few gentle shakes. The medicated-powder coating helps both reduce the chance of rot and keep away moles, voles, grubs, and other bulb-munching pests.

✳ Baby Wipes

Use for quick, on-the-move cleanups Baby wipes can be used for more than just cleaning babies' bottoms. They're great for wiping your hands after pumping gas, mopping up small spills in the car, and cooling your sweaty brow after a run. In fact, they make ideal travel companions. So, next time you set off on the road, pack a small stack of wipes in a tightly closed self-sealing sandwich bag and put it in the glove compartment of your car or in your purse or knapsack.

Shine your shoes Most moms know that a baby wipe does a pretty good job of brightening Junior's white leather shoes. But did you ever think of using one to put the shine back in *your* leather pumps—especially with that 10 a.m. meeting fast approaching?

Recycle as dust cloths Believe it or not, some brands of baby wipes—Huggies, for instance—can be laundered and reused as dust cloths and cleaning rags for when you straighten up. It probably goes without saying, but only "mildly" soiled wipes should be considered candidates for laundering.

Buff up your bathroom Do you have company coming over and not much time to tidy up the house? Don't break out in a sweat. Try this double-handed trick: Take a baby wipe in one hand and start polishing your bathroom surfaces. Keep a dry washcloth in your other hand to shine things up as you make your rounds.

Remove stains from carpet, clothing, and upholstery Use a baby wipe to blot up coffee spills from your rug or carpet; it absorbs both the liquid *and* the stain. Wipes can also be effectively deployed when attacking various spills and drips on your clothing and upholstered furniture.

Clean your PC keyboard Periodically shaking out your PC's keyboard is a good way to get rid of the dust and debris that gathers underneath and in between the keys. But that's just half the job. Use a baby wipe to remove the dirt, dried spills, and unspecified gunk that builds up on the keys themselves. Make sure to turn off the computer or unplug the keyboard before you wipe the keys.

Soothe your skin Did you get a bit too much sun at the beach? You can temporarily cool a sunburn by gently patting the area with a baby wipe. Baby wipes can also be used to treat cuts and scrapes. Although most wipes don't have any antiseptic properties, there's nothing wrong with using one for an initial cleansing before applying the proper topical treatment.

Remove makeup It's one of the fashion industry's worst-kept secrets: Many models consider a baby wipe to be their best friend when it comes time to remove that stubborn makeup from their faces, particularly black eyeliner. Try it and see for yourself.

✳ Baby Wipes Containers

Organize your stuff Don't toss those empty wipes containers. These sturdy plastic boxes are incredibly useful for storing all sorts of items. And the rectangular ones are stackable to boot! Give the containers a good washing and let them dry thoroughly, then fill them with everything from sewing supplies, recipe cards, coupons, and craft and office supplies to old floppy disks, small tools, photos, receipts, and bills. Label the contents with a marker on masking tape, and you're set!

Make a first-aid kit Every home needs a first-aid kit. But you don't have to buy a ready-made one. Gather up your own choice of essentials (such as bandages, sterile gauze rolls and pads, adhesive tape, scissors, and triple-antibiotic ointment) and use a rectangular baby wipes container to hold it all. Before you add your supplies, give the container a good washing—and rub the inside with alcohol on a cotton ball after it dries.

Use as a decorative yarn or twine dispenser A clean cylindrical wipes container makes a perfect dispenser for a roll of yarn or twine. Simply remove the container's cover, insert the roll, and thread it through the slot in the lid, then reattach the cover. Paint or paper over the container to give it a more decorative look.

Tip **Removing Labels**

> Use a blow-dryer on a high setting to heat up the labels on baby wipes containers to make them easier to pull off. You can get rid of any leftover sticky stuff by applying a little WD-40 oil or orange citrus cleaner.

Store your plastic shopping bags Do you save plastic shopping bags for lining the small wastebaskets (or perhaps for pooper-scooper duty)? If so, bring order to the puffed-up chaos they create by storing the bags in cleaned, rectangular wipes containers. Each container can hold 40 to 50 bags—once you squeeze the air out of them. You can also use an empty 250-count tissue box—the kind with a perforated cutout dispenser—in a similar manner.

Make a piggy bank Well, maybe not a "piggy" bank, per se, but a bank nonetheless, and one that gives you a convenient place to dump your pocket change. Take a clean rectangular container and use a knife to cut a slot—be sure to make it wide enough to easily accommodate a quarter—on the lid. If you're making the bank for a child, you can either decorate it or let her put her own personal "stamp" on it.

Hold workshop towels or rags A used baby wipes container can be a welcome addition in the workshop for storing rags and paper towels—and to keep a steady supply on hand as needed. You can easily keep a full roll of detached paper towels or six or seven good-sized rags in each container.

Baking Soda

* BAKING SODA **IN THE KITCHEN**

Clean your produce You can't be too careful when it comes to food handling and preparation. Wash fruits and vegetables in a pot of cold water with 2-3 tablespoons baking soda; the baking soda will remove some of the impurities tap water leaves behind. Or put a small amount of baking soda on a wet sponge or vegetable brush and scrub your produce. Give everything a thorough rinsing before serving.

Tenderize meat Got a tough cut of meat on your hands? Soften it up by giving it rub-down in baking soda. Let it sit (in the refrigerator, of course) for three to five hours, then rinse it off well before cooking.

Soak out fish smells Get rid of that fishy smell from your store-bought flounder filets and fish steaks by soaking the raw fish for about an hour (inside your refrigerator) in 1 quart (1 liter) water with 2 tablespoons baking soda. Rinse the fish well and pat dry before cooking.

Reduce acids in recipes If you or someone in your family is sensitive to the high-acid content of tomato-based sauces or coffee, you can lower the overall acidity by sprinkling in a pinch of baking soda while cooking (or, in the case of coffee, before brewing). A bit of baking soda can also counteract the taste of vinegar if you happen to pour in a bit too much. Be careful not to overdo it with the soda, though—if you add too much, the vinegar-baking soda combination will start foaming.

Bake better beans Do you love baked beans but not their aftereffects? Adding a pinch of baking soda to baked beans as they're cooking will significantly reduce their gas-producing properties.

Fluff up your omelets Want to know the secret to making fluffier omelets? For every three eggs used, add 1/2 teaspoon baking soda. Shhhh! Don't let it get around.

Tip **Out of Baking Powder?**

> If you are out of baking powder, you can usually substitute 2 parts baking soda mixed with 1 part each cream of tartar and cornstarch. To make the equivalent of 1 teaspoon baking powder, for instance, mix 1/2 teaspoon baking soda with 1/4 teaspoon cream of tartar and 1/4 teaspoon cornstarch. The cornstarch slows the reaction between the acidic cream of tartar and the alkaline baking soda so that, like commercial baking powder, it maintains its leavening power longer.

Use as yeast substitute Need a stand-in for yeast when making dough? If you have some powdered vitamin C (or citric acid) and baking soda on hand, you can use a mixture of the two instead. Just mix in equal parts to equal the quantity of yeast required. What's more, the dough you add it to won't have to rise before baking.

Rid hands of food odors Chopping garlic or cleaning a fish can leave their "essence" on your fingers long after the chore is done. Get those nasty food smells off your hands by simply wetting them and vigorously rubbing with about 2 teaspoons baking soda instead of soap. The smell should wash off with the soda.

Clean baby bottles and accessories Here's some great advice for new parents: Keep all your baby bottles, nipples, caps, and brushes "baby fresh" by soaking them overnight in a container filled with hot water and half a box of baking soda. Be sure to give everything a good rinsing afterward, and to dry thoroughly before using. Baby bottles can also be boiled in a full pot of water and 3 tablespoons baking soda for three minutes.

Clean a cutting board Keep your wooden or plastic cutting board clean by occasionally scrubbing it with a paste made from 1 tablespoon each baking soda, salt, and water. Rinse thoroughly with hot water.

Clear a clogged drain Most kitchen drains can be unclogged by pouring in 1 cup baking soda followed by 1 cup hot vinegar (simply heat it up in the microwave for 1 minute). Give it several minutes to work, then add 1 quart (1 liter) boiling water. Repeat if necessary. If you know your drain is clogged with grease, use 1/2 cup each of baking soda and salt followed by 1 cup boiling water. Let the mixture work overnight; then rinse with hot tap water in the morning.

Boost potency of dishwashing liquid Looking for a more powerful dishwashing liquid? Try adding 2 tablespoons baking soda to the usual amount of liquid you use, and watch it cut through grease like a hot knife!

Make your own dishwashing detergent The dishwasher is fully loaded when you discover that you're out of your usual powdered dishwashing detergent. What do you do? Make your own: Combine 2 tablespoons baking soda with 2 tablespoons borax. You may be so pleased with the results you'll switch for good.

Deodorize your dishwasher Eliminate odors inside your automatic dishwasher by sprinkling 1/2 cup baking soda on the bottom of the dishwasher between loads. Or pour in half a box of baking soda and run the empty machine through its rinse cycle.

DID *You* KNOW?

Baking soda is the main ingredient in many commercial fire extinguishers. And you can use it straight out of the box to extinguish small fires throughout your home. For quick access, keep baking soda in buckets placed strategically around the house.

Keep baking soda near your stove and barbecue so you can toss on a few handfuls to quell a flare-up. In the case of a grease fire, first turn off the heat, if possible, and try to cover the fire with a pan lid. Be careful not to let the hot grease splatter you.

Keep a box or two in your garage and inside your car to quickly extinguish any mechanical or car-interior fires.

Baking soda will also snuff out electrical fires and flames on clothing, wood, upholstery, and carpeting.

Clean your refrigerator To get rid of smells and dried-up spills inside your refrigerator, remove the contents, then sprinkle some baking soda on a damp sponge and scrub the sides, shelves, and compartments. Rinse with a clean, wet sponge. Don't forget to place a fresh box of soda inside when you're done.

Clean your microwave To clean those splatters off the inside of your microwave, put a solution of 2 tablespoons baking soda in 1 cup water in a microwave-safe container and cook on High for 2-3 minutes. Remove the container, then wipe down the microwave's moist interior with a damp paper towel.

Remove coffee and tea stains from china Don't let those annoying coffee and/or tea stains on your good china spoil another special occasion. Remove them by dipping a moist cloth in baking soda to form a stiff paste and gently rubbing your cups and saucers. Rinse clean and dry, then set your table with pride.

Clean a thermos To remove residue on the inside of a thermos, mix 1/4 cup baking soda in 1 quart (1 liter) water. Fill the thermos with the solution—if necessary, give it a going-over with a bottle brush to loosen things up—and let it soak overnight. Rinse clean before using.

Freshen a sponge or towel When a kitchen sponge or dish towel gets that distinctly sour smell, soak it overnight in 2 tablespoons baking soda and a couple of drops of antibacterial dish soap dissolved in 1 pint (450 milliliters) warm water. The following morning, squeeze out the remaining solution and rinse with cold water. It should smell as good as new.

Remove stains and scratches on countertops Is your kitchen countertop covered with stains or small knife cuts? Use a paste of 2 parts baking soda to 1 part water to "rub out" most of them. For stubborn stains, add a drop of chlorine bleach to the paste. Immediately wash the area with hot, soapy water to prevent the bleach from causing fading.

Shine up stainless steel and chrome trim To put the shine back in your stainless steel sink, sprinkle it with baking soda, then give it a rubdown—moving in the direction of the grain—with a moist cloth. To polish dull chrome trim on your appliances, pour a little baking soda onto a damp sponge and rub over the chrome. Let it dry for an hour or so, then wipe down with warm water and dry with a clean cloth.

Get rid of grease stains on stovetops Say good-bye to cooked-on grease stains on your stovetop or backsplash. First wet them with a little water and cover them with a bit of baking soda. Then rub them off with a damp sponge or towel.

Clean an automatic coffeemaker Properly caring for your automatic coffeemaker means never having to worry about bitter or weak coffee. Every two weeks or so, brew a pot of 1 quart (1 liter) water mixed with 1/4 cup baking soda, followed by a pot of clean water. Also, sweeten your coffeemaker's plastic basket by using an old toothbrush to give it an occasional scrubbing with a paste of 2 tablespoons baking soda and 1 tablespoon water. Rinse thoroughly with cold water when done.

Care for your coffeepots and teapots Remove mineral deposits in metal coffeepots and teapots by filling them with a solution of 1 cup vinegar and 4 tablespoons baking soda. Bring the mixture to a boil, then let simmer for five minutes. Or try boiling 5 cups water with 2 tablespoons soda and the juice of half a lemon. Rinse with cold water when done. To get off annoying exterior stains, wash your pots with a plastic scouring pad in a solution of 1/4 cup baking soda in 1 quart (1 liter) warm water. Follow up with a cold-water rinse.

Remove stains from nonstick cookware It may be called nonstick cookware, but a few of those stains seem to be stuck on pretty well. Blast them away by boiling 1 cup water mixed with 2 tablespoons baking soda and 1/2 cup vinegar for 10 minutes. Then wash in hot, soapy water. Rinse well and let dry, then season with a bit of salad oil.

Clean cast-iron cookware Although it's more prone to stains and rust than the nonstick variety, many folks swear by their iron cookware. You can remove even the toughest burned-on food remnants in your iron pots by boiling 1 quart (1 liter) water with 2 tablespoons baking soda for five minutes. Pour off most of the liquid, then lightly scrub it with a plastic scrub pad. Rinse well, dry, and season with a few drops of peanut oil.

Clean burned or scorched pots and pans It usually takes heavy-duty scrubbing to get scorched-on food off the bottom of a pot or pan. But you can make life much easier for yourself by simply boiling a few cups of water (enough to get the pan about 1/4 full) and adding 5 tablespoons baking soda. Turn off the heat, and let the soda settle in for a few hours or overnight. When you're ready, that burned-on gunk will practically slip right off.

Deodorize your garbage pail Does something smell "off" in your kitchen? Most likely, it's emanating from your trash can. But some smells linger even after you dispose of the offending garbage bag. So, be sure to give your kitchen garbage pail an occasional cleaning with a wet paper towel dipped in baking soda (you may want to wear rubber gloves for this). Rinse it out with a damp sponge, and let it dry before inserting a new bag. You can also ward off stinky surprises by sprinkling a little baking soda into the bottom of your pail before inserting the bag.

Remove crayon marks from walls Has Junior redecorated your walls or wallpaper with some original artworks in crayon? Don't lose your cool. Just grab a damp rag, dip it in some baking soda, and lightly scrub the marks. They should come off with a minimal amount of effort.

Wash wallpaper Is your wallpaper looking a bit dingy? Brighten it up by wiping it with a rag or sponge moistened in a solution of 2 tablespoons baking soda in 1 quart (1 liter) water. To remove grease stains from wallpaper, make a paste of 1 tablespoon baking soda and 1 teaspoon water. Rub it on the stain, let it set for 5-10 minutes, then rub off with a damp sponge.

Clean baby spit-ups Infants do tend to spit up—and usually not at opportune moments. Never leave home without a small bottle of baking soda in your diaper bag. If your tyke spits up on his or her (or your) shirt after feeding, simply brush off any solid matter, moisten a washcloth, dip it in a bit of baking soda, and dab the spot. The odor (and the potential stain) will soon be gone.

Deodorize rugs and carpets How's this for a simple way to freshen up your carpets or rugs? Lightly sprinkle them with baking soda, let it settle in for 15 minutes or so, then vacuum up. Nothing to it!

Remove wine and grease stains from carpet What's that? Someone just dropped a slab of butter or a glass of cabernet on your beautiful white carpeting! Before you scream, get a paper towel, and blot up as much of the stain as possible. Then sprinkle a liberal amount of baking soda over the spot. Give the soda at least an hour to absorb the stain, then vacuum up the remaining powder. Now ... exhale!

> *Kids' Stuff* Make **watercolor paints** for your kids using ingredients in your kitchen. In a small bowl, combine 3 tablespoons each of **baking soda, cornstarch,** and **vinegar** with 1 1/2 teaspoons **light corn syrup.** Wait for the fizzing to subside, then separate the mixture into several small containers or jar lids. Add eight drops of **food coloring** to each batch and mix well. Put a different color in each batch or combine colors to make new shades. Kids can either use the paint right away, or wait for them to harden, in which case, they'll need to use a wet brush before painting.

Freshen up musty drawers and closets Put baking soda sachets to work on persistent musty odors in dresser drawers, cabinet hutches, or closets. Just fill the toe of a clean sock or stocking with 3-4 tablespoons soda, put a knot about an inch above the bulge, and either hang it up or place it away in an unobtrusive corner. Use a few sachets in large spaces like closets and attic storage areas. Replace them every other month if needed. This treatment can also be used to rid closets of mothball smells.

Remove musty odor from books If those books you just took out of storage emerge with a musty smell, place each one in a brown paper bag with 2 tablespoons baking soda. No need to shake the bag, just tie it up and let it sit in a dry environment for about one week. When you open the bag, shake any remaining powder off the books, and the smell should be gone.

Polish silver and gold jewelry To remove built-up tarnish from your silver, make a thick paste with 1/4 cup baking soda and 2 tablespoons water. Apply with a damp sponge and gently rub, rinse, and buff dry. To polish gold jewelry, cover with a light coating of baking soda, pour a bit of vinegar over it, and rinse clean. *Note:* Do not use this technique with jewelry containing pearls or gemstones, as it could damage their finish and loosen the glue.

Get yellow stains off piano keys That old upright may still play great, but those yellowed keys definitely hit a sour note. Remove age stains on your ivories by mixing a solution of 1/4 cup baking soda in 1 quart (1 liter) warm water. Apply to each key with a dampened cloth (you can place a thin piece of cardboard between the keys to avoid seepage). Wipe again with a cloth dampened with plain water, and then buff dry with a clean cloth. (You can also clean piano keys with lemon juice and salt.)

Remove stains from fireplace bricks You may need to use a bit of elbow grease, but you can clean the smoke stains off your fireplace bricks by washing them with a solution of 1/2 cup baking soda in 1 quart (1 liter) warm water.

Remove white marks on wood surfaces Get those white marks—caused by hot cups or sweating glasses—off your coffee table or other wooden furniture by making a paste of 1 tablespoon baking soda and 1 teaspoon water. Gently rub the spot in a circular motion until it disappears. Remember not to use too much water.

Remove cigarette odors from furniture To eliminate that lingering smell of cigarette or cigar smoke on your upholstered furniture, simply lightly sprinkle your chairs or sofas with some baking soda. Let it sit for a few hours, then vacuum it off.

Shine up marble-topped furniture Revitalize the marble top on your coffee table or counter by washing it with a soft cloth dipped in a solution of 3 tablespoons baking soda and 1 quart (1 liter) warm water. Let it stand for 15 minutes to a half hour, then rinse with plain water and wipe dry.

Clean bathtubs and sinks Get the gunk off old enameled bathtubs and sinks by applying a paste of 2 parts baking soda and 1 part hydrogen peroxide. Let the paste set for about half an hour. Then give it a good scrubbing and rinse well; the paste will also sweeten your drain as it washes down.

Remove mineral deposits from showerheads Say so long to hard-water deposits on your showerhead. Cover the head with a thick sandwich-size bag filled with 1/4 cup baking soda and 1 cup vinegar. Loosely fasten the bag—you need to let some of the gas escape—with adhesive tape or a large bag tie. Let the solution work its magic for about an hour.

Then remove the bag and turn on your shower to wash off any remaining debris. Not only will the deposits disappear, but your showerhead will be back to its old shining self!

Absorb bathroom odors Keep your bathroom smelling fresh and clean by placing a decorative dish filled with 1/2 cup baking soda either on top of the toilet tank or on the floor behind the bowl. You can also make your own bathroom deodorizers by setting out dishes containing equal parts baking soda and your favorite scented bath salts.

Tidy up your toilet bowl You don't need all those chemicals to get your toilet bowl clean. Just pour half a box of baking soda into your toilet tank once a month. Let it stand overnight, then give it a few flushes in the morning. This actually cleans both the tank and the bowl. You can also pour several tablespoons of baking soda directly into your toilet bowl and scrub it on any stains. Wait a few minutes, then flush away the stains.

✳ BAKING SODA **IN THE MEDICINE CABINET**

Treat minor burns The next time you grab the wrong end of a frying pan or forget to use a pot holder, quickly pour some baking soda into a container of ice water, soak a cloth or gauze pad in it, and apply it to the burn. Keep applying the solution until the burn no longer feels hot. This treatment will also prevent many burns from blistering.

Cool off sunburn and other skin irritations For quick relief of sunburn pain, soak gauze pads or large cotton balls in a solution of 4 tablespoons baking soda mixed in 1 cup water and apply it to the affected areas. For a bad sunburn on your legs or torso—or to relieve the itching of chicken pox—take a lukewarm bath with a half to a full box of baking soda added to the running water. To ease the sting of razor burns, dab your skin with a cotton ball soaked in a solution of 1 tablespoon baking soda in 1 cup water.

Soothe poison ivy rashes Did you have an unplanned encounter with poison ivy when gardening or camping recently? To take away the itch, make a thick paste from 3 teaspoons baking soda and 1 teaspoon water and apply it to the affected areas. You can also use baking soda to treat oozing blisters caused by the rash. Mix 2 teaspoons baking soda in 1 quart (1 liter) water and use it to saturate a few sterile gauze pads. Cover the blisters with the wet pads for 10 minutes, four times a day. *Note:* Do not apply on or near your eyes.

Make a salve for bee stings Take the pain out of that bee sting—fast. Make a paste of 1 teaspoon baking soda mixed with several drops of cool water, and let it dry on the afflicted area. *Warning*: Many people have severe allergic reactions to bee stings. If you have difficulty breathing or notice a dramatic swelling, get medical attention at once. (You can also treat bee stings with meat tenderizer. See page 210.)

BAKING SODA*

69

Fight diaper rash Soothe your baby's painful diaper rash by adding a couple of table-spoons of baking soda to a lukewarm—not hot—bath. If the rash persists or worsens after several treatments, however, consult your pediatrician.

Combat cradle cap Cradle cap is a commonplace, and typically harmless, condition in many infants. An old but often effective way to treat it is to make a paste of about 3 teaspoons baking soda and 1 teaspoon water. Apply it to your baby's scalp about an hour before bedtime and rinse it off the following morning. Do not use with shampoo. You may need to apply it several consecutive nights before the cradle cap recedes. (You can also treat cradle cap with baby oil. See page 59.)

Tip **Baking Soda Shelf Life**

How can you tell if the baking soda you've had stashed away in the back of your pantry is still good? Just pour out a small amount—a little less than a teaspoon—and add a few drops of vinegar or fresh lemon juice. If it doesn't fizz, it's time to replace it. By the way, a sealed box of baking soda has an average shelf life of 18 months, while an opened box lasts 6 months.

Control your dandruff Got a bit of a "flaky" problem? To get dandruff under control, wet your hair and then rub a handful of baking soda vigorously into your scalp. Rinse thoroughly and dry. Do this every time you normally wash your hair, but only use baking soda, no shampoo. Your hair may get dried out at first. But after a few weeks your scalp will start producing natural oils, leaving your hair softer and free of flakes.

Clean combs and brushes Freshen up your combs and hairbrushes by soaking them in a solution of 3 cups warm water and 2 teaspoons baking soda. Swirl them around in the water to loosen up all the debris caught between the teeth, then let them soak for about half an hour. Rinse well and dry before using.

Use as gargle or mouthwash Did the main course you ordered include a few too many onions or a bit too much garlic? Try gargling with 1 teaspoon baking soda in a half glass of water. The baking soda will neutralize the odors on contact. When used as a mouthwash, baking soda will also relieve canker-sore pain.

Scrub teeth and clean dentures If you run out of your regular toothpaste, or if you're looking for an all-natural alternative to commercial toothpaste, just dip your wet toothbrush in some baking soda and brush and rinse as usual. You can also use baking soda to clean retainers, mouthpieces, and dentures. Use a solution of 1 tablespoon baking soda dissolved in 1 cup warm water. Let the object soak for a half hour and rinse well before using.

Clean and sweeten toothbrushes Keep your family's toothbrushes squeaky clean by immersing them in a solution of 1/4 cup baking soda and 1/4 cup water. Let the brushes soak overnight about once every week or two. Be sure to give them a good rinsing before using.

Remove built-up gel, hair spray, or conditioner from hair When it comes to personal grooming, too much of a good thing can spell bad news for your hair. But a thorough cleansing with baking soda at least once a week will wash all of the gunk out of your hair. Simply add 1 tablespoon soda to your hair while shampooing. In addition to removing all the chemicals you put in your hair, it will wash away water impurities, and may actually lighten your hair.

Use as antiperspirant Looking for an effective, all-natural deodorant? Try applying a small amount—about a teaspoon's worth—of baking soda with a powder puff under each arm. You won't smell like a flower or some exotic spice. But then, you won't smell like anything from the opposite extreme, either.

Relieve itching inside a cast Wearing a plaster cast on your arm or leg is a misery any time of year, but wearing one in the summertime can be torture. The sweating and itchiness you feel underneath your "shell" can drive you nearly insane. Find temporary relief by using a hair dryer—on the coolest setting—to blow a bit of baking soda down the edges of the cast. *Note:* Have someone help you, to avoid getting the powder in your eyes.

Alleviate athlete's foot You can deploy wet or dry baking soda to combat a case of athlete's foot. First, try dusting your feet (along with your socks and shoes) with dry baking soda to dry out the infection. If that doesn't work, try making a paste of 1 teaspoon baking soda and 1/2 teaspoon water and rubbing it

SCIENCE FAIR

Use the gas produced by mixing **baking soda** and **vinegar** to blow up a balloon. First, pour 1/2 cup vinegar into the bottom of a narrow-neck **bottle** (such as an empty water bottle) or **jar**. Then insert a **funnel** into the mouth of an average-sized **balloon**, and fill it with 5 tablespoons baking soda. Carefully stretch the mouth of the

balloon over the opening of the bottle, then gently lift it up so that the baking soda empties into the vinegar at the bottom of the bottle. The fizzing and foaming you see is actually a chemical reaction between the two ingredients. This reaction results in the release of **carbon dioxide gas**—which will soon **inflate the balloon!**

between your toes. Let it dry, and wash off after 15 minutes. Dry your feet thoroughly before putting on your shoes.

Soothe tired, stinky feet When your dogs start barking, treat them to a soothing bath of 4 tablespoons baking soda in 1 quart (1 liter) warm water. Besides relaxing your aching tootsies, the baking soda will remove the sweat and lint that gathers between your toes. Regular footbaths can also be an effective treatment for persistent foot odor.

Deodorize shoes and sneakers A smelly shoe or sneaker is no match for the power of baking soda. Liberally sprinkle soda in the offending loafer or lace-up and let it sit overnight. Dump out the powder in the morning. (Be careful when using baking soda with leather shoes, however; repeated applications can dry them out.) You can also make your own reusable "odor eaters" by filling the toes of old socks with 2 table-spoons baking soda and tying them up in a knot. Stuff the socks into each shoe at night before retiring. Remove the socks in the morning and breathe easier.

✴ BAKING SODA **IN THE LAUNDRY**

Boost strength of liquid detergent and bleach It may sound like a cliché, but adding 1/2 cup baking soda to your usual amount of liquid laundry detergent really will give you "whiter whites" and brighter colors. The baking soda also softens the water, so you can actually use less detergent. Adding 1/2 cup baking soda in top-loading machines (1/4 cup for front-loaders) also increases the potency of bleach, so you need only half the usual amount of bleach.

Remove mothball smell from clothes If your clothes come out of storage reeking of mothballs, take heed: Adding 1/2 cup baking soda during your washer's rinse cycle will get rid of the smell.

Wash new baby clothes Get all of the chemicals out of your newborn's clothing—without using any harsh detergents. Wash your baby's new clothes with some mild soap and 1/2 cup baking soda.

Rub out perspiration and other stains Pretreating clothes with a paste made from 4 tablespoons baking soda and 1/4 cup warm water can help vanquish a variety of stains. For example, rub it into shirts to remove perspiration stains; for really bad stains, let the paste dry for about two hours before washing. Rub out tar stains by applying the paste and washing in plain baking soda. For collar stains, rub in the paste and add a bit of vinegar as you're putting the shirt in the wash.

Wash mildewed shower curtains Just because your plastic shower curtain or liner gets dirty or mildewed doesn't mean you have to throw it away. Try cleaning it in your washing machine with two bath towels on the gentle setting. Add 1/2 cup baking soda to your detergent during the wash cycle and 1/2 cup vinegar during the rinse cycle. Let it drip-dry; don't put it in the dryer.

✳ BAKING SODA **FOR THE DO-IT-YOURSELFER**

Clean battery terminals Eliminate the corrosive buildup on your car's battery terminals. Scrub them clean using an old toothbrush and a mixture of 3 tablespoons baking soda and 1 tablespoon warm water. Wipe them off with a wet towel and dry with another towel. Once the terminals have completely dried, apply a bit of petroleum jelly around each terminal to deter future corrosive buildup.

Use as deicer in winter Salt and commercial ice-melt formulations can stain—or actually eat away—the concrete around your house. For an equally effective, but completely innocuous, way to melt the ice on your steps and walkways during those cold winter months, try sprinkling them with generous amounts of baking soda. Add some sand for improved traction.

Tighten cane chair seats The bottoms of cane chairs can start to sag with age, but you can tighten them up again easily enough. Just soak two cloths in a solution of 1/2 cup baking soda in 1 quart (1 liter) hot water. Saturate the top surface of the caning with one cloth, while pushing the second up against the bottom of the caning to saturate the underside. Use a clean, dry cloth to soak up the excess moisture, then put the chair in the sun to dry.

Kids' Stuff Spies use it and so can you. Send a message or draw a picture with **invisible ink.** Here's how you do it: Mix 1 tablespoon each of **baking soda** and **water.** Dip a **toothpick** or **paintbrush** in the mixture and write your message or draw a picture or design on a piece of **plain white paper.** Let the paper and the "ink" dry completely. To reveal your message or see your picture, mix 6 drops **food coloring** with 1 tablespoon water. Dip a clean **paintbrush** in the solution, and lightly paint over the paper. Use different food-coloring combinations for a cool effect.

Remove tar from your car It may look pretty bad, but it's not that hard to get road tar off your car without damaging the paint. Make a soft paste of 3 parts baking soda to 1 part water and apply to the tar spots with a damp cloth. Let it dry for five minutes, then rinse clean.

Give your deck the weathered look You can instantly give your wooden deck a weathered look by washing it in a solution of 2 cups baking soda in 1 gallon (3.7 liters) water. Use a stiff straw brush to work the solution into the wood, then rinse with cool water.

Clean air-conditioner filters Clean washable air-conditioner filters each month they're in use. First vacuum off as much dust and dirt as possible, then wash in a solution of 1 tablespoon baking soda in 1 quart (1 liter) water. Let the filters dry thoroughly before replacing.

Keep your humidifier odor-free Eliminate musty smells from a humidifier by adding 2 tablespoons baking soda to the water each time you change it. *Note:* Check your owner's manual or consult the unit's manufacturer before trying this.

✳ BAKING SODA **IN THE GREAT OUTDOORS**

Keep weeds out of cement cracks Looking for a safe way to keep weeds and grasses from growing in the cracks of your paved patios, driveways, and walkways? Sprinkle handfuls of baking soda onto the concrete and simply sweep it into the cracks. The added sodium will make it much less hospitable to dandelions and their friends.

Clean resin lawn furniture Most commercial cleaners are too abrasive to be used on resin lawn furniture. But you won't have to worry about scratching or dulling the surface if you clean your resin furniture with a wet sponge dipped in baking soda. Wipe using circular motions, then rinse well.

Use as plant food Give your flowering, alkaline-loving plants, such as clematis, delphiniums, and dianthus, an occasional shower in a mild solution of 1 tablespoon baking soda in 2 quarts (2 liters) water. They'll show their appreciation with fuller, healthier blooms.

Maintain proper pool alkalinity Add 1 1/2 pounds (680 grams) baking soda for every 10,000 gallons (38,000 liters) of water in your swimming pool to raise the total alkalinity by 10 ppm (parts per million). Most pools require alkalinity in the 80-150 ppm range. Maintaining the proper pool alkalinity level is vital for minimizing changes in pH if acidic or basic pool chemicals or contaminants are introduced to the water.

Scour barbecue grills Keep your barbecue grill in top condition by making a soft paste of 1/4 cup baking soda and 1/4 cup water. Apply the paste with a wire brush and let dry for 15 minutes. Then wipe it down with a dry cloth and place the grill over the hot coals for at least 15 minutes to burn off any residue before placing any food on top.

Make deodorizing dog shampoo The next time Rover rolls around in your compost heap, pull out the baking soda to freshen him up. Just rub a few handfuls of the powder into his coat and give it a thorough brushing. In addition to removing the smell, it will leave his coat shiny and clean.

Wash insides of pets' ears If your pet is constantly scratching at his ears, it could indicate the presence of an irritation or ear mites. Ease the itch (and wipe out any mites) by using a cotton ball dipped in a solution of 1 teaspoon baking soda in 1 cup warm water to gently wash the inside of his ears.

Keep bugs away from pets' dishes Placing a border of baking soda around your pet's food bowls will keep away six-legged intruders. And it won't harm your pet if he happens to lap up a little (though most pets aren't likely to savor soda's bitter taste).

Deodorize the litter box Don't waste money on expensive deodorized cat litter. Just put a thin layer of baking soda under the bargain-brand litter to absorb the odor. Or mix baking soda with the litter as you're changing it.

✳ Balloons

Protect a bandaged finger Bandaging an injury on your finger is easy; keeping the bandage dry as you go about your day can be a different story. But here's the secret to skipping those wet-bandage changes: Just slip a small balloon over your finger when doing dishes, bathing, or even simply washing your hands.

Keep track of your child Those inexpensive floating helium-filled balloons sold in most shopping malls can be more than just a treat for a youngster; they could be invaluable in locating a child who wanders off into a crowd. Even if you keep close tabs on your kids, you can buy a little peace of mind by simply tying (though not too tightly) a balloon to your child's wrist on those weekend shopping trips.

Make a party invitation How's this for an imaginative invitation? Inflate a balloon (for sanitary purposes, use an electric pump, if possible). Pinch off the end, but don't tie a knot in it. Write your invitation details on the balloon with a bright permanent marker; make sure the ink is dry before you deflate it. Place the balloon in an envelope, and mail one out to each guest. When your guests receive it, they'll have to blow it up to see what it says.

Transport cut flowers Don't bother with awkward, water-filled plastic bags and such when traveling with freshly cut flowers. Simply fill up a balloon with about 1/2 cup water and slip it over the cut ends of your flowers. Wrap a rubber band several times around the mouth of the balloon to keep it from slipping off.

Use as a hat mold To keep the shape in your freshly washed knit cap or cloth hat, fit it over an inflated balloon while it dries. Use a piece of masking tape to keep the balloon from tilting over or falling onto the ground.

Mark your campsite Bring along several helium-filled balloons on your next camping trip to attach to your tent or a post. They'll make it easier for the members of your party to locate your campsite when hiking or foraging in the woods.

Make an ice pack Looking for a flexible ice pack you can use for everything from icing a sore back to keeping food cold in your cooler? Fill a large, durable balloon with as much water as you need and put it in your freezer. You can even mold it to a certain extent into specific shapes—for example, put it under something flat like a box of pizza if you want a flat ice pack for your back. Use smaller latex balloons for making smaller ice packs for lunch boxes, etc.

Freeze for cooler punch To keep your party punch bowl cold and well filled, pour juice in several balloons (use a funnel) and place them in your freezer. When it's party time, peel the latex off the ice, and periodically drop a couple into the punch bowl.

Repel unwanted garden visitors Put those old deflated shiny metallic balloons—the ones lying around your house from past birthday parties—to work in your garden. Cut them into vertical strips and hang them from poles around your vegetables and on fruit trees to scare off invading birds, rabbits, and squirrels.

Protect your rifle A dirty rifle can jam up and just be downright dangerous to use. But you can keep dust and debris from accumulating in your rifle barrel by putting a sturdy latex balloon over the barrel's front end.

SCIENCE FAIR

You experience a discharge of **static electricity** when you touch a doorknob after shuffling across a carpet. But you rarely see this phenomenon, with the exception of lightning, which is static electricity on a grand scale. Here's an experiment that offers a dazzling display of static electricity in action:

Empty the contents of a package of nonflavored **gelatin** powder onto a piece of **paper.** Blow up a **balloon,** rub it on a **woolen sweater,** and then hold it about an inch over the powder. The **gelatin particles will arch up** toward the balloon. The slightly negatively charged electrons—the built-up static electricity on the balloon—are attracting the positively charged protons in the gelatin powder.

* Bananas

Make a face mask Who needs Botox when you have bananas? That's right: You can use a banana as an all-natural face mask that moisturizes your skin and leaves it looking and feeling softer. Mash up a medium-sized ripe banana into a smooth paste, then gently apply it to your face and neck. Let it set for 10-20 minutes, then rinse it off with cold water. Another popular mask recipe calls for 1/4 cup plain yogurt, 2 tablespoons honey, and 1 medium banana.

Eat a frozen "banana-sicle" As a summer treat for friends and family, peel and cut four ripe bananas in half (across the middle). Stick a wooden ice-cream stick into the flat end of each piece. Place them all on a piece of wax paper, and then put it in the freezer. A few hours later, serve them up as simply yummy frozen banana-sicles. If you want to go all-out, quickly dip your frozen bananas in 6 ounces (170 grams) melted butterscotch or chocolate morsels (chopped nuts or shredded coconut are optional), then refreeze.

Tenderize a roast Banana leaves are commonly used in many Asian countries to wrap meat as it's cooking to make it more tender. Some folks in these areas say the banana itself also has this ability. So the next time you fear the roast you're cooking will turn tough on you, try softening it up by adding a ripe, peeled banana to the pan.

Polish silverware and leather shoes It may sound a bit like a lark, but using a banana peel is actually a great way to put the shine back into your silverware and leather shoes. First, remove any of the leftover stringy material from the inside of the peel, then just start rubbing the inside of the peel on your shoes or silver. When you're done, buff up the object with a paper towel or soft cloth. You might even want to use this technique to restore your leather furniture. Test it on a small section first before you take on the whole chair.

Brighten up houseplants Are the leaves on your houseplants looking dingy or dusty? Don't bother misting them with water—that just spreads the dirt around. Rather, wipe down each leaf with the inside of a banana peel. It'll remove all the gunk on the surface and replace it with a lustrous shine.

Deter aphids Are aphids attacking your rosebushes or other plants? Bury dried or cut-up banana peels an inch or two deep around the base of the aphid-prone plants, and soon the little suckers will pack up and leave. Don't use whole peels or the bananas themselves, though; they tend to be viewed as tasty treats by raccoons, squirrels, gophers, rabbits, and other animals, who will just dig them up.

Use as fertilizer or mulch Banana peels, like the fruit itself, are rich in potassium—an important nutrient for both you and your garden. Dry out banana peels on screens during the winter months. In early spring, grind them up in a food processor or blender and use it as a mulch to give new plants and seedlings a healthy start. Many cultivars of roses and other plants, like staghorn ferns, also benefit from the nutrients found in banana peels; simply cut up some peels and use them as plant food around your established plants.

Add to compost pile With their high content of potassium and phosphorus, whole bananas and peels are welcome additions to any compost pile—particularly in so-called compost tea recipes. The fruit breaks down especially fast in hot temperatures. But don't forget to remove any glued-on tags from the peels, and be sure to bury bananas deep within your pile—otherwise they may simply turn out to be a meal for a four-legged visitor.

Attract butterflies and birds Bring more butterflies and various bird species to your backyard by putting out overripe bananas (as well as other fruits such as mangos, oranges, and papayas) on a raised platform. Punch a few holes in the bananas to make the fruit more accessible to the butterflies. Some enthusiasts swear by adding a drop of Gatorade to further mush things up. The fruit is also likely to attract more bees and wasps as well, so make sure that the platform is well above head level and not centrally located. Moreover, you'll probably want to clear it off before sunset, to discourage visits from raccoons and other nocturnal creatures.

✳ Basters

Pour perfect batter To make picture-perfect pancakes, cookies, and muffins, simply fill your baster with batter so that you can pour just the right amount onto a griddle or cookie sheet or into a muffin pan.

Remove excess water from coffeemaker The perfect cup of coffee is determined by using the proper balance of water and ground coffee in your automatic coffeemaker. If you pour in too much water, however, you typically have to add more coffee or suffer through a weak pot. But there's another, often overlooked option: Simply use your kitchen baster to remove the excess water to bring it in at just the right level.

Water hard-to-reach plants Do you get drips all over yourself, the floor, or furniture when trying to water hanging plants or other difficult-to-reach houseplants? Instead, fill a baster with water and squeeze it directly into the pot. You can also use a baster to water a Christmas tree and to add small, precise amounts of water to cups containing seedlings or germinating seeds.

Refresh water in flower arrangements It's a fact: Cut flowers last longer with periodic water changes. But pouring out the old water and adding the new is not a particularly easy or pleasant task. Unless, that is, you use a baster to suck out the old water and then to squirt in fresh water.

> **TAKE CARE** Never use your kitchen baster for tasks such as cleaning out a fish tank or spreading or transferring chemicals.
>
> Basters are staples at discount stores, and it's worth a visit to pick up a few to keep around the house specifically for noncooking chores. Label them with a piece of masking tape to make sure you always use the same baster for the same task.

Place water in pet's bowl Are you getting tired of chasing the bunny, hamster, or other caged pet around the house whenever you change its water? Use a baster to fill the water dish. You can usually fit the baster between the slats without having to open the cage.

Clean your aquarium A baster makes it incredibly easy to change the water in your fish tank or to freshen it up a bit. Simply use the utensil to suck up the gunk that collects in the corners and in the gravel at the bottom of your tank.

Blow away roaches and ants If you've had it with sharing your living quarters with roaches or ants, give them the heave-ho by sprinkling boric acid along any cracks or crevices where you've spotted the intruders. Use a baster to blow small amounts of the powder into hard-to-reach corners and any deep voids you come across. *Note:* Keep in mind that boric acid can be toxic if ingested by young children or pets.

Transfer paints and solvents The toughest part of any touchup paint job is invariably pouring the paint from a large can into a small cup or container. To avoid the inevitable spills, and just to make life easier in general, use a baster to take the paint out of the can. In fact, it's a good idea to make a baster a permanent addition to your workshop for transferring any solvents, varnishes, and other liquid chemicals.

Cure a musty-smelling air conditioner If you detect a musty odor blowing out of the vents of your room air-conditioner, chances are it's caused by a clogged drain hole. First, unscrew the front of the unit and locate the drain hole. It's usually located under the barrier between the evaporator and compressor, or underneath the evaporator. Use a bent wire hanger to clear away any obstacles in the hole or use a baster to flush it clean. You may also need to use the baster to remove any water that may be pooling up at the bottom of the unit to gain access to the drain.

Fix a leaky refrigerator Is water leaking inside your refrigerator? The most likely cause is a blocked drain tube. This plastic tube runs from a drain hole in the back of the freezer compartment along the back of your fridge and drains into an evaporation pan underneath. Try forcing hot water through the drain hole in the freezer with a baster. If you can't access the drain hole, try disconnecting the tube on the back to blow water through it. After clearing the tube, pour a teaspoon of ammonia or bleach into the drain hole to prevent a recurrence of algae spores, the probable culprit.

* Bath Oil

Remove glue from labels or bandages Get rid of those sticky leftover adhesive marks from bandages, price tags, and labels. Rub them away with a bit of bath oil applied to a cotton ball. It works great on glass, metal, and most plastics.

Use as a hot-oil treatment Heat 1/2 cup bath oil mixed with 1/2 cup water on High in your microwave for 30 seconds. Place the solution in a deep bowl and soak your fingers or toes in it for 10-15 minutes to soften cuticles or calluses. After drying, use a pumice stone to smooth over calluses or a file to push down cuticles. Follow up by rubbing in hand cream until fully absorbed.

Pry apart stuck drinking glasses When moisture seeps in between stacked glasses, separating them can get mighty tough—not to mention dangerous. But you can break the "ties that bond" by applying a few drops of bath oil along the sides of the glasses. Give the oil a few minutes to work its way down, then simply slide your glasses apart.

Loosen chewing gum from hair and carpeting If your child comes home with chewing gum in his or her hair—or tracks a wad onto your rug or carpet—

DID You KNOW?

It appears we *Homo sapiens* have had a penchant for perfumed body oils since the beginning of history. The first use of such oils is believed to have occurred in the Neolithic period (7000-4000 B.C.), when Stone Age people began combining olive and sesame seed oils with fragrant plants. The ancient Egyptians also used scented oils, primarily in religious rituals. And the use of body oils, such as myrrh and frankincense, for both religious and secular uses is documented in the Bible. Indeed, fragrant oils have been an integral part of most cultures—including those of Native Americans and many Asian peoples.

hold off on reaching for the scissors. Instead, rub a liberal amount of bath oil into the gum. It should loosen it up enough to comb out. On a carpet, test the oil on an inconspicuous area before applying to the spot.

Remove scuff marks You can get those annoying scuff marks off your patent-leather shoes or handbags. Apply a bit of bath oil to a clean, soft cloth or towel. Gently rub in the oil, then polish with another dry towel.

Soften a new baseball glove Apply several drops of bath oil in the midsection of the glove and a few more drops under each finger. Lightly spread the oil around with a soft cloth. Place a baseball in the pocket of the glove and fold the glove over the ball, keeping it in place with one or two belts or an Ace bandage. Let it sit for a couple of days, then release the constraints and remove any excess oil with a clean cloth. The glove should be noticeably more pliable.

Clean grease or oil from skin It doesn't take much tinkering around the inside of a car or mower engine to get your hands coated in grease or oil. But before you reach for any heavy-duty grease removers, try this: Rub a few squirts of bath oil onto your hands, then wash them in warm, soapy water. It works, and it's a lot easier on the dermis than harsh chemicals.

Revitalize vinyl upholstery Give your car's dreary-looking vinyl upholstery a makeover by using a small amount of bath oil on a soft cloth to wipe down the seats, dashboard, armrests, and other surfaces. Polish with a clean cloth to remove any excess oil. As an added bonus, a scented bath oil will make the interior smell better, too.

Slide together pipe joints Can't find the all-purpose lubricating oil or the WD-40 when you're trying to join pipes together? No problem. A few drops of bath oil should provide sufficient lubrication to fit pipe joints together with ease.

✳ Bathtub Appliqués

Place on the bottom of PC case Has your desktop computer case lost its "legs" (those four small rubber feet that invariably fall off over time from moving your PC around)? To steady your case, and to minimize vibrations, cut small squares from a bathtub appliqué, and apply them to the corners of your case where the feet used to be.

Apply to dance slippers, shoes, and pajamas Avoid nasty falls caused by slippery plastic dance slippers—and even new shoes. Cut small pieces of bathtub appliqués and apply them to the sole of each slipper or shoe. You can also sew cut

81

pieces of an appliqué on the soles of your children's "feet" pajamas to prevent slips (and tears).

Stick to bottom of kids' wading pool A few bathtub appliqués applied to the floor of a kiddie pool will make it a lot less slippery for little feet and help prevent falls—especially when the water play turns rowdy. Also put a couple of appliqués along the edges of the pool to give kids easy places to grip onto.

Affix to sippy cups and high-chair seats Cut pieces of a bathtub appliqué and put them on toddlers' sippy cups to minimize spills. Also attach appliqués to high-chair seats to keep Junior from sliding down—or out.

✳ Beans (Dried)

Use for playing pieces We know you had your heart set on being the racing car in the next game of Monopoly, but if the car has taken a trip to parts unknown, would you settle for a bean? Beans work fine as replacement pieces for everything from checkers to Chutes and Ladders to bingo.

Treat sore muscles Is your bad back or tennis elbow acting up again? A hot beanbag may be just the cure you need. Place a couple of handfuls of dried beans in a cloth shoe bag, an old sock, or a folded towel (tie the ends tightly) and microwave it on High for 30 seconds to 1 minute. Let it cool for a minute or two, then apply it to your aching muscles.

Make a beanbag Pour 3/4 to 1 1/2 cups dried beans in an old sock, shaking them down to the toe section. Tie a loose knot and tighten it up as you work it down against the beans. Then cut off the remaining material about 1 inch (2.5 centimeters) above the knot. You now have a beanbag for tossing around or juggling. Or use it as a squeeze bag for exercising your hand muscles.

Practice your percussion Make a homemade percussion shaker or maraca for yourself or your youngster. Add 1/2 cup dried beans to a small plastic jar, or a soda or juice can—even an empty coconut shell. Cover any openings with adhesive or duct tape. You can use this noisemaker at sporting events or as a dog-training tool (give it a couple of shakes when the pooch misbehaves).

Decorate a jack-o'-lantern Embellish the fright potential of your Halloween jack-o'-lantern by gluing on various dried beans for the eyes and teeth.

Recycle a stuffed animal Make your own beanie creation by removing the stuffing from one of your child's old, unused stuffed animals. Replace the fluff with dried beans, and sew it closed. It's bound to rekindle your youngster's interest.

* Beer

Use as setting lotion Put some life back into flat hair with some flat beer. Before you get into the shower, mix 3 tablespoons beer in 1/2 cup warm water. After you shampoo your hair, rub in the solution, let it set for a couple of minutes, then rinse it off. You may be so pleased by what you see, you'll want to keep a six-pack in the bathroom.

Soften up tough meat Who needs powdered meat tenderizer when you have some in a can? You guessed it: Beer makes a great tenderizer for tough, inexpensive cuts of meat. Pour a can over the meat, and let it soak in for about an hour before cooking. Even better, marinate it overnight in the fridge or put the beer in your slow cooker with the meat.

Polish gold jewelry Get the shine back in your solid gold (i.e., minus any gemstones) rings and other jewelry by pouring a bit of beer (*not* dark ale!) onto a soft cloth and rubbing it gently over the piece. Use a clean second cloth or towel to dry.

Clean wood furniture Have you got some beer that's old or went flat? Use it to clean wooden furniture. Just wipe it on with a soft cloth, and then off with another dry cloth.

Make a trap for slugs and snails Like some people, some garden pests find beer irresistible—especially slugs and snails. If you're having problems with these slimy invaders, bury a container, such as a clean, empty juice container cut lengthwise in half, in the area where you've seen the pests, pour in about half a can of warm, leftover beer, and leave it overnight. You're likely to find a horde of them, drunk and drowned, the next morning.

Remove coffee or tea stains from rugs Getting that coffee or tea stain out your rug may seem impossible, but you can literally lift it out by pouring a bit of beer right on top. Rub the beer lightly into the material, and the stain should disappear. You may have to repeat the process a couple of times to remove all traces of the stain.

 DID *You* KNOW?

Some popular brands of beer proclaim their New England or Rocky Mountain pedigrees, or boast being "Milwaukee's finest." But, in fact, Pennsylvania has been home to more breweries throughout its history than any other state. One of its earliest breweries was opened in 1680 by none other than William Penn, the state's founder. And the Keystone State is still the home of the U.S.'s oldest active brewery, D. G. Yuengling & Son of Pottsville, Pennsylvania, founded in 1829.

✱ Berry Baskets

Keep peels out of drain Don't clog up your kitchen drain with peelings from potatoes or carrots. Use a berry basket as a sink strainer to catch those vegetable shavings as they fall.

Store soap pads and sponges Are you tired of throwing away prematurely rusted steel wool soap pads or smelly sponges? Place a berry basket near the corner of your kitchen sink and line the bottom with a layer of heavy-duty aluminum foil. Fashion a spout on a corner of the foil closest to the sink that can act as a drain to keep water from pooling up at the bottom of the basket. Now sit back and enjoy the added longevity of your soap pads and sponges.

Use as a colander Need a small colander to wash individual servings of fruits and vegetables or to drain off that child's portion of hot macaroni shells? Get your hands on an empty berry basket. It makes a dandy colander for these chores.

> *Kids' Stuff* **Berry baskets** can be particularly useful for all sorts of children's crafts. For example, you can cut apart the panels, and carve out geometric shapes for kids to use as **stencils.** You can also turn one into an **Easter basket** by adding some **cellophane grass** and a (preferably pink) **pipe cleaner** for a handle. Or use one as a multiple **bubble maker;** simply dip it in some **water** mixed with **dishwashing liquid** and wave it through the air to create swarms of bubbles. Lastly, let kids decorate the baskets with **ribbons** or **construction paper** and use them to store their own little trinkets and toys.

Hold recycled paper towels Don't toss out those lightly used paper towels in your kitchen. You can reuse them to wipe down countertops or to soak up serious spills. Keep a berry basket in a convenient location in your kitchen to have your recycled towels at the ready when needed.

Use as dishwasher basket If the smaller items you place in your dishwasher (such as baby bottle caps, jar lids, and food-processor accessories) won't stay put, try putting them in a berry basket. Place the items inside one basket, then cover over with a second basket. Fasten them together with a thick rubber band and place on your dishwasher's upper rack.

Organize your meds A clean berry basket could be just what the doctor ordered for organizing your vitamins and medicine bottles. If you're taking several medications, a berry basket offers a convenient way to place them all—or prepackaged individual doses—in one, easy-to-remember location. You can also use baskets to organize medications in your cupboard or medicine cabinet according to their expiration dates or uses.

Arrange flowers Droopy or lopsided flower arrangements just don't cut it. That's why the pros use something known as a frog to keep cut flowers in place. To make your own, insert an inverted berry basket into a vase (cut the basket to fit, if necessary). It will keep your stalks standing tall.

Protect seedlings Help young plants thrive in your garden by placing inverted berry baskets over them. The baskets will let water, sunlight, and air in, but keep raccoons and squirrels out. Make sure the basket is buried below ground level and tightly secured (placing a few good-sized stones around it may suffice).

Make a bulb cage Squirrels and other rodents view freshly planted flower bulbs as nothing more than tasty morsels and easy pickings. But you can put a damper on their meal by planting bulbs in berry baskets. Be sure to place the basket at the correct depth, then insert the bulb and cover with soil.

Build a hanging orchid planter Orchids are said to be addictive: Once you start collecting them, you can't stop. If you've got the bug, you can at least save yourself a bit of money by making your own hanging baskets for your orchids. Fill up a berry basket with sphagnum moss mixed with a bit of potting soil and suspend it with a length of monofilament fishing line.

Fashion a string dispenser or screwdriver holder If you don't want to bother untangling knots every time you need a piece of string, twine, or yarn, build your own string dispenser with two berry baskets. Place the ball inside one berry basket. Feed the cord through the top of a second, inverted basket, then tie the two baskets together with twist ties. You can also mount an inverted berry basket on your workshop's pegboard and use it to hold and organize your screwdrivers; they'll fit neatly between the slats.

✳ Binder Clips

Strengthen your grip Does a weak grip or arthritis make it hard for you to open jars and do other tasks with your hands? Use a large binder clip to add some zip to your grip. Squeeze the folded-back wings of the clip, hold for a count of five, and relax. Do this a dozen or so times with each hand a few times a day. It will strengthen your grip and release tension too.

Mount a picture Here's a neat way to mount and hang a picture so that it has a clean frameless look. Sandwich the picture between a sheet of glass or clear plastic and piece of hardboard or stiff cardboard. Then use tiny binder clips along the edges to clamp the pieces together. Use two or three clips on each side. After the clips are in place, remove the clip handles at front. Tie picture wire to the rear handles for hanging the picture.

Keep your place A medium-sized binder clip makes an ideal bookmark. If you don't want to leave impression marks on the pages, tape a soft material like felt, or even just some adhesive tape, to the inside jaws of the clip before using.

Make a money clip To keep paper money in a neat bundle in your pocket or purse, stack the bills, fold them in half, and put a small binder clip over the fold.

Keep ID handy You're at the airport and you know you'll be asked to show your ID a few times. Instead of fishing in your wallet or trying to figure out which pocket you stuck your driver's license in, use a binder clip to firmly and conveniently attach your ID and other documents to your belt. You can also use a small binder clip to secure your office ID to your belt or a breast pocket.

✳ Bleach

Clean off mold and mildew Bleach and ammonia are both useful for removing mold and mildew both inside and outside your home. However, the two should *never* be used together. Bleach is especially suited for the following chores:

● Wash mildew out of washable fabrics. Wet the mildewed area and rub in some powdered detergent. Then wash the garment in the hottest water setting permitted by the clothing manufacturer using 1/2 cup chlorine bleach. If the garment can't be washed in hot water and bleach, soak it in a solution of 1/4 cup oxygen bleach (labeled "all fabric" or "perborate") in 1 gallon (3.7 liters) warm water for 30 minutes before washing.

● Remove mold and mildew from the grout between your bathroom tiles. Mix equal parts of chlorine bleach and water in a spray bottle, and spray it over grout. Let it sit for 15 minutes, then scrub with a stiff brush and rinse off. You can also do this just to make your grout look whiter.

● Get mold and mildew off your shower curtains. Wash them—along with a couple of bath towels (to prevent the plastic curtains from crinkling)—in warm water with 1/2 cup chlorine bleach and 1/4 cup laundry detergent. Let the washer run for a couple of minutes before loading. Put the shower curtain and towels in the dryer on the lowest temperature setting for 10 minutes, then immediately hang-dry.

- Rid your rubber shower mat of mildew. Soak in a solution of 1/8 cup chlorine bleach in 1 gallon (3.7 liters) water for 3-4 hours. Rinse well.

- Get mildew and other stains off unpainted cement, patio stones, or stucco. Mix a solution of 1 cup chlorine bleach in 2 gallons (7.5 liters) water. Scrub vigorously with a stiff or wire brush and rinse. If any stains remain, scrub again using 1/2 cup washing soda (this is sodium carbonate, not baking soda) dissolved in 2 gallons (7.5 liters) warm water.

- Remove mildew from painted surfaces and siding. Make a solution of 1/4 cup chlorine bleach in 2 cups water and apply with a brush to mildewed areas. Let the solution set for 15 minutes, then rinse. Repeat as necessary.

Sterilize secondhand items Remember Mom saying, "Put that down. You don't know where it's been"? She had a point—especially when it comes to toys or kitchen utensils picked up at thrift shops and yard sales. Just to be on the safe side, take your used, waterproof items and soak them for 5-10 minutes in a solution containing 3/4 cup bleach, a few drops of antibacterial dishwashing liquid, and 1 gallon warm water. Rinse well, then air-dry, preferably in sunlight.

Clean butcher block cutting boards and countertops Don't even think about using furniture polish or any other household cleaner to clean a butcher block cutting board or countertop. Rather, scrub the surface with a brush dipped in a solution of 1 teaspoon bleach diluted in 2 quarts (2 liters) water. Scrub in small circles, and be careful not to saturate the wood. Wipe with a slightly damp paper towel, then immediately buff dry with a clean cloth.

TAKE CARE Never mix bleach with ammonia, lye, rust removers, oven or toilet-bowl cleaners, or vinegar. Any combination can produce toxic chlorine gas fumes, which can be deadly. Some people are even sensitive to the fumes of undiluted bleach itself. Always make sure you have adequate ventilation in your work area before you start pouring.

Brighten up glass dishware Put the sparkle back in your glasses and dishes by adding a teaspoon of bleach to your soapy dishwater as you're washing your glassware. Be sure to rinse well, and dry with a soft towel.

Shine white porcelain Want to get your white porcelain sink, candleholder, or pottery looking as good as new? In a well-ventilated area on a work surface protected by heavy plastic, place several paper towels over the item (or across the bottom of the sink) and carefully saturate them with undiluted bleach. Let soak for 15 minutes to a half hour, then rinse and wipe dry with a clean towel. *Note:*

Do not try this with antiques; you can diminish their value or cause damage. And never use bleach on colored porcelain, because the color will fade.

Make a household disinfectant spray Looking for a good, all-purpose disinfectant to use around the house? Mix 1 tablespoon bleach in 1 gallon (3.7 liters) hot water. Then fill a clean, empty spray bottle and use it on a paper towel to clean countertops, tablecloths, lawn furniture—basically, wherever it's needed. Just be sure not to use it in the presence of ammonia or other household cleaners.

TAKE CARE Some folks skip the bleach when cleaning their toilets, fearing that lingering ammonia from urine—especially in households with young children—could result in toxic fumes. Unless you are sure there is no such problem, you may want to stick with ammonia for this job.

Disinfect trash cans Even the best housekeepers must confront a gunked-up kitchen garbage pail every now and then. On such occasions, take the pail outside, and flush out any loose debris with a garden hose. Then add 1/2 to 1 cup bleach and several drops of dishwashing liquid to 1 gallon (3.7 liters) warm water. Use a toilet brush or long-handled scrub brush to splash and scour the solution on the bottom and sides of the container. Empty, then rinse with the hose, empty it again, and let air-dry.

Increase cut flowers' longevity Freshly cut flowers will stay fresh longer if you add 1/4 teaspoon bleach per quart (1 liter) of vase water. Another popular recipe calls for 3 drops bleach and 1 teaspoon sugar in 1 quart (1 liter) water. This will also keep the water from getting cloudy and inhibit the growth of bacteria.

Clean plastic lawn furniture Is your plastic-mesh lawn furniture looking dingy? Before you place it curbside, try washing it with some mild detergent mixed with 1/2 cup bleach in 1 gallon (3.7 liters) water. Rinse it clean, then air-dry.

Kill weeds in walkways Do weeds seem to thrive in the cracks and crevices of your walkways? Try pouring a bit of undiluted bleach over them. After a day or two, you can simply pull them out, and the bleach will keep them from coming back. Just be careful not to get bleach on the grass or plantings bordering the walkway.

Get rid of moss and algae To remove slippery and unsightly moss and algae on your brick, concrete, or stone walkways, scrub them with a solution of 3/4 cup bleach in 1 gallon (3.7 liters) water. Be careful not to get bleach on your grass or ornamental plants.

Sanitize garden tools You cut that diseased stalk off your rosebush with your branch clipper. Unless you want to spread the disease the next time you use the tool, sterilize it by washing it with 1/2 cup bleach in 1 quart (1 liter) water. Let the tool air-dry in the sun, then rub on a few drops of oil to prevent rust.

✳ Blow-Dryer

Get wax off wood furniture It may have been a romantic evening, but that hardened candle wax on your wooden table or bureau is not the sort of lingering memory you had in mind. Melt it with a blow-dryer on its slowest, hottest setting. Remove the softened wax with a paper towel, then wipe the area with a cloth dipped in equal parts vinegar and water. Repeat if necessary. You can also remove wax from silver candlestick holders with a blow-dryer: Use the blow-dryer to soften the wax, then just peel it off.

Clean off radiators Are those dusty cast-iron radiators around your house becoming something of an eyesore? To clean them, hang a large, damp cloth behind each radiator. Then use your blow-dryer on its highest, coolest setting to blow dust and hidden dirt onto the cloth.

Remove bumper stickers Want to remove those cutesy stickers your kids used to decorate your car bumper to "surprise" you? Use a blow-dryer on its hottest setting to soften the adhesive. Move the dryer slowly back and forth for several minutes, then use your fingernail or credit card to lift up a corner and slowly peel off.

Dust off silk flowers and artificial houseplants They may require less care than their living counterparts, but silk flowers and artificial houseplants are apt to collect dust and dirt. Use your blow-dryer on its highest, coolest setting for a quick, efficient way to clean them off. Since this will blow the dust onto the furniture surfaces and floor around the plant, do this just before you vacuum those areas.

✳ Borax

Clear a clogged drain Before you reach for a caustic drain cleaner to unclog that kitchen or bathroom drain, try this much gentler approach: Use a funnel to insert 1/2 cup borax into the drain, then slowly pour in 2 cups boiling water. Let the mixture set for 15 minutes, then flush with hot water. Repeat for stubborn clogs.

Rub out heavy sink stains Get rid of those stubborn stains—even rust—in your stainless steel or porcelain sink. Make a paste of 1 cup borax and 1/4 cup lemon juice. Put some of the paste on a cloth or sponge and rub it into the stain, then rinse with running warm water. The stain should wash away with the paste.

Clean windows and mirrors Want to get windows and mirrors spotless *and* streakless? Wash them with a clean sponge dipped in 2 tablespoons borax dissolved in 3 cups water.

Remove mildew from fabric To remove mildew from upholstery and other fabrics, soak a sponge in a solution of 1/2 cup borax dissolved in 2 cups hot water, and rub it into the affected areas. Let it soak in for several hours until the stain disappears, then rinse well. To remove mildew from clothing, soak it in a solution of 2 cups borax in 2 quarts (2 liters) water.

Kids' Stuff Help your children brew up some **slime**—that gooey, stretchy stuff kids love to play with. First, mix 1 cup water, 1 cup **white glue,** and 10 drops **food coloring** in a medium bowl. Then, in a second, larger bowl, stir 4 teaspoons **borax** into 1 1/3 cups **water** until the powder is fully dissolved. Slowly pour the contents of the first bowl into the second. Use a wooden **mixing spoon** to roll (don't mix) the glue-based solution around in the borax solution four or five times. Lift out the globs of glue mixture, then knead it for 2-3 minutes. Store your homemade slime in an **airtight container** or a **self-sealing plastic storage bag.**

Get out rug stains Remove stubborn stains from rugs and carpets. Thoroughly dampen the area, then rub in some borax. Let the area dry, then vacuum or blot it with a solution of equal parts vinegar and soapy water and let dry. Repeat if necessary. Don't forget to first test the procedure on an inconspicuous corner of the rug or on a carpet scrap before applying it to the stain.

Sanitize your garbage disposal A garbage disposal is a great convenience but can also be a great breeding ground for mold and bacteria. To maintain a more sanitary disposal, every couple of weeks pour 3 tablespoons borax down the drain and let it sit for 1 hour. Then turn on the disposal and flush it with hot water from the tap.

Clean your toilet Want a way to disinfect your toilet bowl *and* leave it glistening without having to worry about dangerous or unpleasant fumes? Use a stiff brush to scrub it using a solution of 1/2 cup borax in 1 gallon (3.7 liters) water.

Eliminate urine odor on mattresses Toilet training can be a rough experience for all the parties involved. If your child has an "accident" in bed, here's how to get rid of any lingering smell: Dampen the area, then rub in some borax. Let it dry, then vacuum up the powder.

Make your own dried flowers Give your homemade dried flowers the look of a professional job. Mix 1 cup borax with 2 cups cornmeal. Place a 3/4-inch (2-centimeter) coating of the mixture in the bottom of an airtight container, like a large flat plastic food storage container. Cut the stems off the flowers you want to dry, then lay them on top of the powder, and lightly sprinkle more of the mixture on top of the flowers (be careful not to bend or crush the petals or other flower parts). Cover the container, and leave it alone for

7-10 days. Then remove the flowers and brush off any excess powder with a soft brush.

Keep away weeds and ants Get the jump on those weeds that grow in the cracks of the concrete outside your house by sprinkling borax into all the crevices where you've seen weeds grow in the past. It will kill them off before they have a chance to take root. When applied around the foundation of your home, it will also keep ants and other six-legged intruders from entering your house. But be very careful when applying borax—it is toxic to plants (see Take Care warning).

> **TAKE CARE** Borax, like its close relative, boric acid, has relatively low toxicity levels, and is considered safe for general household use, but the powder can be harmful if ingested in sufficient quantities by young children or pets. Store it safely out of their reach.
>
> Borax is toxic to plants, however. In the yard, be very careful when applying borax onto or near soil. It doesn't take much to leach into the ground to kill off nearby plants and prevent future growth.

Control creeping Charlie Is your garden being overrun by that invasive perennial weed known as creeping Charlie (*Glechoma hederacea*, also known as ground ivy, creeping Jenny and gill-over-the-ground)? You may be able to conquer Charlie with borax. First, dissolve 8-10 ounces (230-280 grams) borax in 4 ounces (120 milliliters) warm water. Then pour the solution into 2 1/2 gallons (9.5 liters) warm water—this is enough to cover 1,000 square feet (93 square meters). Apply this treatment only one time in each of two years. If you still have creeping Charlie problems, consider switching to a standard herbicide. (See Take Care warning about using borax in the garden.)

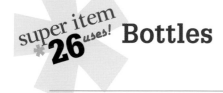

super item *26 uses! Bottles

✳ BOTTLES **AROUND THE HOUSE**

Make a foot warmer Walking around on harsh winter days can leave you with cold and tired tootsies. But you don't need to shell out your hard-earned money on a heating pad or a hot-water bottle to ease your discomfort. Just fill up a 1- or 2-liter soda bottle with hot water, then sit down and roll it back and forth under your feet.

Use as a boot tree Want to keep your boot tops from getting wrinkled or folded over when you put them in storage? Insert a clean empty 1-liter soda bottle into each boot. For added tautness, put a couple of old socks on the bottles or wrap them in towels.

BOTTLES*

91

Recycle as a chew toy If Lassie has been chewing on your slippers instead of fetching them, maybe she's in need of some chew toys. A no-cost way to amuse your dog is to let her chew on an empty plastic 1-liter soda bottle. Maybe it's the crunchy sound they make, but dogs love them! Just be sure to remove the label and bottle cap (as well as the loose plastic ring under it). And replace it before it gets too chewed up—broken pieces of plastic are choke hazards.

Make a bag or string dispenser An empty 2-liter soda bottle makes the perfect container for storing and dispensing plastic grocery bags. Just cut off the bottom and top ends of the bottle, and mount it with screws upside down inside a kitchen cabinet or closet. Put washers under the screw heads to keep them from pulling through the plastic. Fill it with your recycled bags (squeeze the air out of them first) and pull them out as needed. You can make a twine dispenser the same way, using a 1-liter bottle and letting the cord come out the bottom.

Place in toilet tank Unless your house was built relatively recently, chances are you have an older toilet that uses a lot of water each flush. To save a bit of money on your water bills, fill an empty 1-liter soda bottle with water (remove any labels first) and put it in the toilet tank to cut the amount of water in each flush.

Cut out a toy carryall If you're fed up with Lego or erector-set pieces underfoot, make a simple carryall to store them in by cutting a large hole in the side of a clean gallon jug with a handle. Cut the hole opposite the handle so you or your youngster can easily carry the container back to the playroom after putting the pieces away. For an easy way to store craft materials, crayons, or small toys, just cut the containers in half and use the bottom part to stash your stuff.

Store your sugar The next time you bring home a 5-pound (2.2-kilogram) bag of sugar from the supermarket, try pouring it into a clean, dry 1-gallon (3.7-liter) jug with a handle. The sugar is less likely to harden, and the handle makes it much easier to pour it out.

𝒯ip Safe Rotary Cutter

> Cutting plastic containers can be a tricky, dangerous business—especially when you reach for your sharpest kitchen knife. But you can greatly minimize the risk by visiting your local fabric or crafts store and picking up a rolling cutter knife (this is not the same device used to slice pizza, by the way). The device shown in the picture in the hint "Make a scoop or boat bailer," facing page, usually sells for between $6 and $10. Be careful, though. These knives use blades that are razor sharp, but they make life much easier when it's time to cut into a hard plastic container.

Fashion a funnel To make a handy, durable funnel, cut a cleaned milk jug, bleach, or liquid detergent container with a handle in half across its midsection. Use the top portion (with the spout and handle) as a funnel for easy pouring of paints, rice, coins, and so on.

Make a scoop or boat bailer Cut a clean plastic half-gallon (2-liter) jug with a handle diagonally from the bottom so that you have the top three-quarters of the jug intact. You now have a handy scoop that can be used for everything from removing leaves and other debris from your gutters, to cleaning out the litter box and poop-scooping up after your dog. Use it to scoop dog food from the bag, spread sand or ice-melt on walkways in winter, or bail water out of your boat (you might want to keep the cap on for this last application).

Keep the cooler cold Don't let your cooler lose its cool while you're on the road. Fill a few clean plastic jugs with water or juice and keep them in the freezer for use when transporting food in your cooler. This is not only good for keeping food cold; you can actually drink the water or juice as it melts. It's also not a bad idea to keep a few frozen jugs in your freezer if you have extra space; a full freezer actually uses less energy and can save money on your electric bill. When filling a jug, leave a little room at the top for the water to expand as it freezes.

Use for emergency road kit in winter Don't get stuck in your car the next time a surprise winter storm hits. Keep a couple of clean gallon (3.7-liter) jugs with handles filled with sand or kitty litter in the trunk of your car. Then you'll be prepared to sprinkle the material on the road surface to add traction under your wheels when you need to get moving on a slippery road. The handle makes it easier to pour them.

Feed the birds Why spend money on a plastic bird feeder when you probably have one in your recycling bin? Take a clean 1/2-gallon (2-liter) juice or milk jug and carve a large hole on its side to remove the handle. (You might even drill a small hole under the large one to insert a sturdy twig or dowel for a perch.) Then poke a hole in the middle of the cap and suspend it from a tree with a piece of strong string or monofilament fishing line. Fill it up to the opening with birdseed, and enjoy the show.

Make a watering can No watering can? It's easy to make one from a clean 1-gallon (3.7-liter) juice, milk, or bleach jug with a handle. Drill about a dozen tiny (1/16-inch or 1.5-millimeter is good) holes just below the spout of the jug on the side opposite the handle. Or carefully punch the holes with an ice pick. Fill it with water, screw the cap on, and start sprinkling.

Create a drip irrigator for plants During dry spells, a good way to get water to the roots of your plants is to place several drip irrigators around your garden. You can make them from clean 1-gallon (3.7-liter) juice or detergent jugs. Cut a large hole in the bottom of a jug, then drill 2-5 tiny (about 1/16-inch or 1.5-millimeter) holes in or around the cap. Bury the capped jugs upside down about three-quarters submerged beneath the soil near the plants you need to water, and fill with water through the hole on top. Refill as often as needed.

Mark your plants Want an easy way to make ID badges for all the vegetables, herbs, and flowers in your garden? Cut vertical strips from a couple of clear 1-gallon (3.7-liter) water jugs. Make the strips the same width as your seed packets but double their length. Fold each strip over an empty packet to protect it from the elements, and staple it to a strong stick or chopstick.

Secure garden netting If you find yourself having to constantly re-stake the loose netting or plastic lining over your garden bed, place water-filled large plastic jugs around the corners to keep the material in place.

Use as an attachable trash can or harvest basket Here's a great tip for weekend gardeners and pros alike: Cut a large hole opposite the handle of a 1/2- or 1-gallon (2-or 3.7-liter) container, and loop the handle through a belt or rope on your waist. Use it to collect the debris—rocks, weeds, broken stems—you encounter as you mow the lawn or stroll through your garden. Use the same design to make an attachable basket for harvesting berries, cherries, and other small fruits or vegetables.

Space seeds in garden Want an easy way to perfectly space seeds in your garden? Use an empty soda bottle as your guide. Find the distance that the seed company recommends between seeds and then cut off the tapered top of the bottle so its diameter equals that distance. When you start planting, firmly press your bottle, cut edge down, into the soil and place a seed in the center of the circle it makes. Then line up the bottle so that its edge touches the curve of the first impression, and press down again. Plant a seed in the center, and repeat until you've filled your rows.

B

Build a bug trap Do yellow jackets, wasps, or moths swarm around you every time you set foot in the yard? Use an empty 2-liter soda bottle to make an environment-friendly trap for them. First, dissolve 1/2 cup sugar in 1/2 cup water in the bottle. Then add 1 cup apple cider vinegar and a banana peel (squish it up to fit it through). Screw on the cap and give the mixture a good shake before filling the bottle halfway with cold water. Cut or drill a 3/4-inch (2-centimeter) hole near the top of the bottle, and hang it from a tree branch where the bugs seem especially active. When the trap is full, toss it into the garbage and replace it with a new one.

Isolate weeds when spraying herbicides When using herbicides to kill weeds in your garden, you have to be careful not to also spray and kill surrounding plants. To isolate the weed you want to kill, cut a 2-liter soda bottle in half and place the top half over the weed you want to spray. Then direct your pump's spraying wand through the regular opening in the top of the bottle and blast away. After the spray settles down, pick up the bottle and move on to your next target. Always wear goggles and gloves when spraying chemicals in the garden.

Set up a backyard sprayer When temperatures soar out-doors, keep your kids cool with a homemade backyard sprayer. Just cut three 1-inch (2.5-centimeter) vertical slits in one side of a clean 2-liter soda bottle. Or make the slits at different angles so the water will squirt in different directions. Attach the nozzle of the hose to the bottle top with duct tape (make sure it's fastened on tight). Turn on the tap, and let the fun begin!

✳ BOTTLES **FOR THE DO-IT-YOURSELFER**

Build a paint bucket Tired of splattering paint all over as you work? Make a neater paint dispenser by cutting a large hole opposite the handle of a clean 1-gallon (3.7 liter) jug. Pour in the paint so that it's about an inch below the edge of the hole, and use the edge to remove any excess paint from your brush before you lift your brush. You can also cut jugs in half and use the bottom halves as disposable paint buckets when several people work on the same job.

Store your paints Why keep leftover house paints in rusted or dented cans when you can keep them clean and fresh in plastic jugs? Use a funnel to pour the paint into a clean, dry milk or water jug, and add a few marbles (they help mix the paint when you shake the container before your next paint job). Label each container with a piece of masking tape, noting the paint manufacturer, color name, and the date.

Use as workshop organizers Are you always searching for the right nail to use for a particular chore, or for a clothespin, picture hook, or small fastener? Bring some organization to your workshop with a few 1- or 1/2-gallon (3.7- or 2-liter) jugs. Cut out a section near the top of each jug on the side opposite the handle. Then use the containers to store and sort all the small items that seem to "slip through the cracks" of your workbench. The handle makes it easy to carry a jug to your worksite.

Use as a level substitute How can you make sure that shelf you're about to put up is straight if you don't have a level on hand? Easy. Just fill a 1-liter soda bottle about three-quarters full with water. Replace the cap, then lay the bottle on its side. When the water is level, so is the shelf.

Make a weight for anchoring or lifting Fill a clean, dry gallon (3.7-liter) jug with a handle with sand and cap it. You now have an anchor that is great for holding down a paint tarp, securing a shaky patio umbrella, or steadying a table for repair. The handle makes it easy to move or attach a rope. Or use a pair of sand-filled bottles as exercise weights, varying the amount of sand to meet your lifting capacity.

✳ Bottle Openers

Remove chestnut shells An easy way to remove the shells from chestnuts is to use the pointed end of a bottle opener to pierce the tops and bottoms of the shells and then boil the chestnuts for 10 minutes.

Cut packing tape on cartons Can't wait to open that long-awaited package on your doorstep? If you don't have a penknife handy, just run the sharp end of a bottle opener along the tape. It should do the job quite nicely.

Deploy as a shrimp de-veiner If you don't have a small paring knife on hand when you're getting ready to de-vein a batch of shrimp, don't worry. Just use the sharp end of a bottle opener. It just happens to be the perfect shape to make this messy chore a breeze.

DID You KNOW?

The old-fashioned bottle opener with one flat end and one pointed end is often referred to as a "church key." Although no one is exactly sure how or when this association came into being, it originated years ago in the brewery industry and was used to describe a flat opener with a hooked cutout used to lever off bottle caps—it is widely believed that the term derived from the early openers' resemblance to the heavy, ornate keys used to unlock big, old doors, such as those found on churches. Ironically, the term is now applied only to openers with both flat and pointed ends.

Scrape barbecue grill Looking for an easy way to clean off the burned remnants of last weekend's meal from your barbecue grill? If you have a bottle opener and a metal file, you're in luck. Simply file a notch about 1/8-inch (3 millimeters) wide into the flat end of the opener and you're ready to go.

Loosen plaster or remove grout It may not be the carpenter's best friend, but the sharp end of a bottle opener can be handy for removing loose plaster from a wall before patching it. It's great for running along cracks, and you can use to undercut a hole—that is, make it wider at the bottom than at the surface—so that the new plaster will "key" into the old. The sharp end of the opener is equally useful for removing old grout between your bathroom tiles before regrouting.

✳ Bread

Remove scorched taste from rice Did you leave the rice cooking too long and let it get burned? To get rid of the scorched taste, place a slice of white bread on top of the rice while it's still hot. Replace the pot lid and wait several minutes. When you remove the bread, the burned taste should be gone.

Soften up hard marshmallows You reach for your bag of marshmallows only to discover that they've gone stale. Put a couple of slices of fresh bread in the bag and seal it shut (you may want to transfer the marshmallows to a self-sealing plastic bag). Leave it alone for a couple of days. When you reopen the bag, your marshmallows should taste as good as new.

Absorb vegetable odors Love cabbage or broccoli, but hate the smell while it's cooking? Try putting a piece of white bread on top of the pot when cooking up a batch of "smelly" vegetables. It will absorb most of the odor.

Soak up grease and stop flare-ups To paraphrase a famous bear: Only you can prevent grease fires. One of the best ways to prevent a grease flare-up when broiling meat is to place a couple of slices of white bread in your drip pan to absorb the grease. It will also cut down on the amount of smoke produced.

Clean walls and wallpaper Most kids have a hard time understanding how easily the dirt on their hands can be transferred to walls. But you can remove most dirty or greasy fingerprints from painted walls by rubbing the area with a slice of white bread. Bread does a good job cleaning nonwashable wallpaper as well. Just cut off the crusts first to minimize the chance of scratching the paper.

Pick up glass fragments Picking up the large pieces of a broken glass or dish is usually easy enough, but getting up those tiny slivers can be a real pain (figuratively if not literally). The easiest way to make sure you don't miss any is to press a slice of bread over the area. Just be careful not to prick yourself when you toss the bread into the garbage.

Dust oil paintings You wouldn't want to try this with an original Renoir, or with any museum-quality painting for that matter, but you can clean off everyday dust and grime that collects on an oil painting by gently rubbing the surface with a piece of white bread.

✳ Bubble Pack

Prevent toilet-tank condensation If your toilet tank sweats in warm, humid weather, bubble pack could be just the right antiperspirant. Lining the inside of the tank with bubble pack will keep the outside of the tank from getting cold and causing condensation when it comes in contact with warm, moist air. To line the tank, shut off the supply valve under the tank and flush to drain the tank. Then wipe the inside walls clean and dry. Use silicone sealant to glue appropriate-sized pieces of bubble pack to the major flat surfaces.

Protect patio plants Keep your outdoor container plants warm and protected from winter frost damage. Wrap each container with bubble pack and use duct tape or string to hold the wrap in place. Make sure the wrap extends a couple of inches above the lip of the container. The added insulation will keep the soil warm all winter long.

DID *You* KNOW?

Bubble Wrap wallpaper? Yep, that's what inventors Alfred Fielding and Marc Chavannes had in mind when they began developing the product in Saddle Brook, New Jersey, in the late 1950s. Perhaps they had the padded-cell market in mind. In any case, they soon realized their invention had far greater potential as packaging material. In 1960 they raised $85,000 and founded the Sealed Air Corporation. Today Sealed Air is a Fortune 500 company with $3.5 billion in annual revenues. The company produces Bubble Wrap cushioning in a multitude of sizes, colors, and properties, along with other protective packaging materials such as Jiffy padded mailers.

Keep cola cold Wrap soft-drink cans with bubble pack to keep beverages refreshingly cold on hot summer days. Do the same for packages of frozen or chilled picnic foods. Wrap ice cream just before you leave for the picnic to help keep it firm en route.

Protect produce in the fridge Line your refrigerator's crisper drawer with bubble pack to prevent bruises to fruit and other produce. Cleanup will be easier, too—when the lining gets dirty, just throw it out and replace it with fresh bubble pack.

Add insulation Cut window-size pieces of wide bubble pack and duct-tape them to inside windows for added warmth and savings on fuel bills in winter. Lower the blinds to make it less noticeable.

Make a bedtime buffer Keep cold air from creeping into your bed on a chilly night by placing a large sheet of bubble pack between your bedspread or quilt and your top sheet. You'll be surprised at how effective it is in keeping warm air in and cold air out.

Cushion your work surface When repairing delicate glass or china, cover the work surface with bubble pack to help prevent breakage.

Protect tools Reduce wear and tear on your good-quality tools and extend their lives. Line your toolbox with bubble pack. Use duct tape to hold it in place.

Sleep on air while camping Get a better night's sleep on your next camping trip: Carry a 6-foot (2-meter) roll of wide bubble pack to use as a mat under your sleeping bag. No sleeping bag? Just fold a 12-foot-long (3.6-meter-long) piece of wide bubble pack in half, bubble side out, and duct-tape the edges. Then slip in and enjoy a restful night in your makeshift padded slumber bag.

Cushion bleachers and benches Take some bubble pack out to the ballgame with you to soften those hard stadium seats or benches. Or stretch a length along a picnic bench for more comfy dining.

✳ Buckets

Make a lobster pot If you don't have a large kettle, boil lobsters in an old metal bucket. Make sure to use pot holders and tongs when cooking and removing the lobster. Let the bucket cool before handling it again.

> *Kids' Stuff* Add the beat of bucket **tom-toms** to create an exciting, fun atmosphere at your next family campfire. Cut **plastic buckets** to different lengths to create a distinct tone for each drum or use a mix of various-sized **plastic** and **galvanized buckets.** For more musical accompaniment, make a **broom-handle string bass** using a bucket as the sound box.

Create a food locker A tightly sealed 5-gallon (19-liter) bucket is an ideal waterproof (and animal-proof) food locker to bring with you on canoe trips.

Build a camp washing machine Here's a great way to wash clothes while camping. Make a hole in the lid of a 5-gallon (19-liter) plastic bucket and insert a new toilet plunger. Put in clothes and laundry detergent. Snap on the lid and move the plunger up and down as an agitator. You can safely clean even delicate garments.

Camp shower A bucket perforated with holes on the bottom makes an excellent campsite shower. Hang it securely from a sturdy branch, fill it using another bucket or jug, and then take a quick shower as the water comes out. Want to shower in warm water? Paint the outside of another bucket matte black. Fill it with water and leave it out in the sun all day.

Paint high Avoid messy paint spills when painting on a scaffold or ladder. Put your paint can and brush in a large bucket and use paint-can hooks to hang the bucket *and* the brush. If the bucket is large enough, you'll even have room for your paint scraper, putty knife, rags, or other painting tools you may need. A 5-gallon (19-liter) plastic bucket is ideal.

Paint low Use the lids from 5-gallon (19-liter) plastic buckets as trays for 1-gallon (3.78-liter) cans of paint. The lids act as platforms for the paint cans and are also large enough to hold a paintbrush.

Make stilts Make working on a ceiling less of a stretch. Use two sturdy buckets (minus handles) and a pair of old shoes to make your own mini-stilts. Drive screws through the shoe soles and into wood blocks inside the buckets. Or punch holes in the bucket bottoms and tie or strap down the shoes.

Keep extension cords tangle-free A 5-gallon (19-liter) bucket can help you keep a long extension cord free of tangles. Just cut or drill a hole near the bottom of the pail, making sure it is large enough for the cord's pronged end to pass through. Then coil the rest of the cord into the bucket. The cord will come right out when pulled and is easy to coil back in. Plug the ends of the cord together when it's not in use. You can use the center space to carry tools to a worksite.

Soak your saw The best way to clean saw blades is to soak them in acetone or turpentine in a shallow pan, with a lid on the pan to contain the fumes. You can make your own shallow pan by cutting the bottom two inches or so off a plastic 5-gallon (19-liter) bucket with a utility knife. The bucket's lid can serve as the cover. Remember to wear rubber gloves and use a stick to lever out the sharp blades.

Garden in a bucket Use a 5-gallon (19-liter) plastic bucket as a minigarden or planter. Use another as a composter for scraps and cuttings. Bucket gardens are just the right size for apartment balconies.

Tip Where to Find Five-Gallon Buckets

Five-gallon (19-liter) plastic buckets are versatile, virtually indestructible, and offer a myriad of handy uses. And you can usually get them for free. Ask nicely and your local fast-food restaurant or supermarket deli section may be happy to give you the buckets shortening or coleslaw came in. Or check with neighborhood plasterers, who use 5-gallon buckets of drywall compound. Also keep an eye open for neighbors doing home improvements. Don't forget to get the lids, too. Wash a bucket with water and household bleach, then let it dry in the sun for a day or two. Put some scented kitty litter, charcoal, or a couple of drops of vanilla inside to remove any lingering odors.

Make a Christmas tree stand Fill a bucket partway with sand or gravel and insert the base of the tree in it. Then fill it the rest of the way and pour water on the sand or gravel to help keep the tree from drying out.

✳ Butter

Keep mold off cheese Why waste good cheese by letting the cut edges get hard or moldy? Give semi-hard cheeses a light coat of butter to keep them fresh and free of mold. Each time you use the cheese, coat the cut edge with butter before you rewrap it and put it back in the fridge.

Make cat feel at home Is the family feline freaked out by your move to a new home? Moving is often traumatic for pets as well as family members. Here's a good way to help an adult cat adjust to the new house or apartment: Spread a little butter on the top of one of its front paws. Cats love the taste of butter so much they'll keep coming back for more.

Get rid of fishy smell Your fishing trip was a big success, but now your hands reek of fish. What to do? Just rub some butter on your hands, wash with warm water and soap, and your hands will smell clean and fresh again.

Swallow pills with ease If you have difficulty getting pills to go down, try rolling them in a small amount of butter or margarine first. The pills will slide down your throat more easily.

101

Soothe aching feet To soothe tired feet, massage them with butter, wrap in a damp, hot towel, and sit for 10 minutes. Your feet will feel revitalized … and they'll smell like popcorn too.

Remove sap from skin You've just gotten home from a pleasant walk in the woods, but your hand is still covered with sticky tree sap that feels like it will never come off. Don't worry. Just rub butter on your hand and the gunky black sap will wash right off with soap and water.

Keep leftover onion fresh The recipe calls for half an onion and you want to keep the remaining half fresh as long as possible. Rub butter on the cut surface and wrap the leftover onion in aluminum foil before putting it in the fridge. The butter will keep it fresh longer.

Zap ink stain on doll's face Uh-oh, one of the kids used a pen to draw a new smile on that favorite doll's face. Try eliminating the kiddy graffiti by rubbing butter on it and leaving the doll face-up in the sun for a few days. Wash it off with soap and water.

Cut sticky foods with ease Rub butter on your knife or scissor blades before cutting sticky foods like dates, figs, or marshmallows. The butter will act as a lubricant and keep the food from sticking to the blades.

Emergency shave cream If you run out of shaving cream, try slathering some butter onto your wet skin for a smooth, close shave.

Prevent pots from boiling over You take your eye off the pasta for two seconds, and the next thing you know, the pot is boiling over onto the stovetop. Keep the boiling water in the pot next time by adding a tablespoon or two of butter.

 DID *You* KNOW?

Butter is the semi-solid material that results from churning cream—a process that is depicted on a Sumerian tablet from 2500 B.C. A butter-filled churn was found in a 2,000-year-old Egyptian grave, and butter was plentiful in King Tut's day, when it was made from the milk of water buffaloes and camels. The Bible also contains many references to butter—as the product of cow's milk. Later, the Vikings are believed to have introduced butter to Normandy, a region world-renowned for its butter.

In the U.S.A., butter was the only food ever defined by an Act of Congress prior to the enactment of the Food, Drug, and Cosmetic Act of 1938. Butter made in North America must contain at least 80 percent milk fat. The remaining 20 percent is composed of water and milk solids. It may be salted or unsalted (sweet). The salt adds flavor and also acts as a preservative. It takes 21 pounds of fresh cow's milk to make a pound of butter (10 kilograms to make 500 grams).

Kids' Stuff Making **butter** is fun and easy, especially when there are several kids around to take turns churning. All you need is a **jar**, a **marble**, and 1 to 2 cups of heavy **whipping cream** or double cream (preferably without carrageenan or other stabilizers added). Use the freshest cream possible and leave it out of the refrigerator until it reaches a temperature of about 60°F (15°C). Pour the cream into the jar, add the marble, close the lid, and let the kids take turns shaking (churning), about one shake per second. It may take anywhere from 5 to 30 minutes, but the kids will see the cream go through various stages from sloshy to coarse whipped cream. When the whipped cream suddenly seizes and collapses, fine-grained bits of butter will be visible in the liquid buttermilk. Before long a glob of yellowish **butter** will appear. Drain off the **buttermilk** and enjoy the delightful taste of fresh-made butter.

Treat dry hair Is your hair dry and brittle? Try buttering it up for a luxuriant shine. Massage a small chunk of butter into your dry hair, cover it with a shower cap for 30 minutes, then shampoo and rinse thoroughly.

✳ Buttons

Decorate a dollhouse Use buttons as sconces, plates, and wall hangings in a child's dollhouse. The more variety, the better.

Beanbag filler Use small buttons the next time you make beanbags and save the dried beans for the soup.

Make a necklace String attractive buttons on two strands of heavy-duty thread or dental floss. Make an attractive design by alternating large and small buttons of various colors.

Decorate a Christmas tree Give your Christmas tree an old-fashioned look. Make a garland by knotting large buttons on a sturdy length of string or dental floss.

Use as game pieces or poker chips Don't let lost pieces stop you from playing games like backgammon, bingo, or Parcheesi. Substitute buttons for the lost pieces and keep playing to your heart's content. For an impromptu game of poker, use buttons as chips, with each color representing a different value.

Keep tape unstuck You're trying to wrap a present and you can't find the end of the tape roll. Instead of scratching in frustration trying to find that elusive end every time you use the tape, stick a button on the end of the tape. As you use the tape, keep moving the button.

C

✱ Cans

Keep tables together When you're having a large dinner party, lock card tables together by setting adjacent pairs of legs into empty cans. You won't have to clean up any spills caused by the tables moving this way and that.

Make light reflectors It's simple to make reflectors for your campsite or backyard lights. Just remove the bottom of a large empty can with a can opener and take off any label. Then use tin snips to cut the can in half lengthwise. You've just made two reflectors.

Quick floor patch Nail can lids to a wooden floor to plug knotholes and keep rodents out. If you can get access to the hole from the basement, nail the lid in place from underneath so the patch won't be obvious.

Tuna can egg poacher An empty 6-ounce (170-gram) tuna can is the perfect size to use as an egg poacher. Remove the bottom of the can as well as the top and remove any paper label. Then place the metal ring in a skillet of simmering water, and crack an egg into it.

Make a miniature golf course Arrange cans with both ends removed so the ball must go through them, go up a ramp into them, or ricochet off a board through them.

DID **You** KNOW?

Tin cans are often described as "hermetically sealed," but do you know the origin of the term? The word *hermetic* comes from Hermes Trismegistus, a legendary alchemist who is reputed to have lived sometime in the first three centuries A.D. and to have invented a magic seal that keeps a vessel airtight.

The hermetically sealed can was invented in 1810 by British merchant Peter Durand. His cans were so thick they had to be hammered open! Two years later, Englishman Thomas Kensett set up America's first cannery on the New York waterfront to can oysters, meats, fruits, and vegetables.

Feed the birds A bird doesn't care if the feeder is plain or fancy as long as it is filled with suet. For a feeder that's about as basic as you can get, wedge a small can filled with suet between tree branches or posts.

Create decorative snowman Wrap an old soda can with white paper and tape with transparent tape. For a head use a styrene foam ball and tape it to the top of the can. Cover the body with cotton batting or cotton bandaging material and tape or glue it in place. Make a cone-shaped paper hat. Make eyes and a nose with buttons. To add arms, punch holes in the sides of the can and insert twigs. Use dots from a black marker pen to make buttons down the snowman's front. Make a scarf from a scrap of wooly fabric.

Make planters more portable Don't strain your back moving a planter loaded with heavy soil. Reduce the amount of soil and lighten the load by first filling one-third to one-half of the bottom of the planter with empty, upside-down aluminum cans. Finish filling with soil and add your plants. In addition to making the planter lighter, the rustproof aluminum cans also help it to drain well.

Protect young plants Remove both ends of an aluminum can and any paper label. Then push it into the earth to serve as a collar to protect young garden plants from cutworms. Use a soup can or a coffee can, depending on the size you need.

Make a tool tote Tired of fumbling around in your tool pouch to find the tool you need? Use empty frozen juice cans to transform the deep, wide pockets of a nail pouch into a convenient tote for wrenches, pliers, and screwdrivers. Make sure to remove the bottom of the can as well as the top. Glue or tape the cylinders together to keep them from shifting around, and slip them into the pouches to create dividers.

Make a pedestal Fill several wide identical-sized cans with rocks or sand and glue them together, one atop another. Screw a piece of wood into the bottom of the topmost can before attaching it, upside down, to the others. Paint your pedestal and place a potted plant, lamp, or statue on top. See the Tip on the following page for suggestions on the type of glue to use for this project.

Organize your desk If your office desk is a mess, a few empty cans can be the start of a nifty solution. Just attach several tin cans of assorted sizes together in a group to make an office-supplies holder for your desk. Start by cleaning and drying the cans and removing any labels. Then spray paint them (or wrap them in felt). When the paint is dry, glue them together using a hot glue gun. Your desk organizer is now ready to hold pens, pencils, paper clips, scissors, and such.

Tip Glue for Cans

> When gluing cans and other metal pieces together, use a glue that adheres well to metal, such as polyvinyl chloride (PVC), liquid solder, or epoxy. If the joint won't be subject to stress, you can use a hot glue gun. Make sure to wash and dry the cans and to remove any labels first. Also let any paint dry thoroughly before gluing.

Make pigeonholes Assemble half a dozen or more empty cans and paint them with bright enamel. After they dry, glue the cans together and place them on their sides on a shelf. Then store silverware, nails, office supplies, or other odds and ends in them.

✳ Candles

Unstick a drawer If you have a desk or chest drawer that sticks, remove it and rub a candle on the runners. The drawer will open more smoothly when you slip it back in place.

Make a pincushion A wide candle makes an ideal pincushion. The wax will help pins and needles glide more easily through fabric too.

Weatherproof your labels After you address a package with a felt-tip pen, weatherproof the label by rubbing a white candle over the writing. Neither rain, nor sleet, nor snow will smear the label now.

Quiet a squeaky door If a squeaky door is driving you batty, take it off its hinges and rub a candle over the hinge surfaces that touch each other. The offending door will squeak no more.

DID *You* KNOW?

Beeswax—the substance secreted by honeybees to make honeycombs—didn't make its debut in candles until the Middle Ages. Until then, candles were made of the rendered animal fat called tallow that produced a smoky flame and gave off acrid odors. Beeswax candles, by contrast, burned pure and clean. But they were not widely used at the time, being far too expensive for ordinary serfs and peasants.

The growth of whaling in the late 1700s brought a major change to candle-making as spermaceti—a waxlike substance derived from sperm-whale oil—became available in bulk.

The 19th century witnessed the advent of mass-produced candles and low-cost paraffin wax. Made from oil and coal shale, paraffin burned cleanly with no unpleasant odor.

Mend shoelace ends When the plastic or metal tips come off the ends of shoelaces, don't wait for the laces to fray. Do something to prevent the annoyance that comes from having to force a scraggly shoelace end through a teeny eyelet: Just dip the end into melted candle wax and the lace will hold until you can buy a new one.

Make a secret drawing Have a child make an "invisible" drawing with a white candle. Then let him or her cover it with a wash of watercolor paint to reveal the picture. The image will show up because the wax laid down by the candle will keep the paper in the areas it covers from absorbing the paint. If you have a few kids around, they can all make secret drawings and messages to swap and reveal.

Use puff-proof candle to ignite fires Don't let a draft blow out the flame when you're trying to light your fireplace or spark up the barbecue grill. Start your fire with one of those trick puff-proof birthday candles, designed to be a practical joke aid that prevents birthday celebrants from blowing out the candles on their cakes. Once your fire is up and roaring, smother the candle flame and save the trick candle for future use.

✳ Candy Tins

Emergency sewing kit A small candy tin is just the right size to hold a handy selection of needles, thread, and buttons in your purse or briefcase for on-the-spot repairs.

Store broken jewelry Don't lose all the little pieces of that broken jewelry you plan to have repaired someday. Keep the pieces together and safe in a small candy tin.

Prevent jewelry-chain tangles Keep necklaces and chain bracelets separate and tangle-free in their own individual tins.

Keep earrings together You are late for the party but you can only find one earring from the pair that matched your dress so nicely. To prevent pairs of small earrings from going their separate ways, store them together in a little candy tin and you'll be right on time for the next party.

Make a birthday keepsake Decorate the outside of a small candy tin, line it with felt or silk, and insert a penny or, if you can find one, a silver dollar from the birth year of your friend or loved one.

Organize your sewing gear Use a small candy tin to store snaps, sequins, buttons, and beads in your sewing box. Label the lids or glue on a sample for easy identification of the contents.

Store workshop accessories Candy tins are great for storing brads, glazing points, setscrews, lock washers, and other small items that might otherwise clutter up your workshop.

Store car fuses You'll always know where to find your spare car fuses if you store them in a little candy tin in the glove compartment of your car.

Cardboard Boxes

Make a bed tray Have breakfast in bed on a tray made from a cardboard box. Just remove the top flaps and cut arches from the two long sides to fit over your lap. Decorate the bottom of the box—which is now the top of your tray—with adhesive shelf paper and you're ready for those bacon and eggs.

Shield doors and furniture Use cardboard shields to protect doors and furniture from stains when you polish doorknobs and furniture pulls. Cut out the appropriate-sized shield and slide it over the items you are going to polish. This works best when you make shields that slip over the neck of knobs or knoblike pulls. But you can also make shields for hinges and U-shaped pulls.

Create gift-wrap suspense Take a cue from the Russians and their nesting *matryoshka* dolls. Next time you are giving a small but sure-to-be appreciated gift to a friend, place the gift-wrapped little box inside a series of increasingly bigger gaily wrapped boxes.

DID *You* KNOW?

The Chinese invented cardboard in the early 1500s, thus anticipating the demand for containers for Chinese take-out food by several hundred years.

In 1871 New Yorker Albert Jones patented the idea of gluing a piece of corrugated paper between two pieces of flat cardboard to create a material rigid enough to use for shipping. But it wasn't until 1890 that another American, Robert Gair, invented the corrugated cardboard box. His boxes were pre-cut flat pieces manufactured in bulk that folded into boxes, just like the cardboard boxes that surround us today.

Make dustcovers Keep dust and dirt out of a small appliance, power tool, or keyboard. Cut the flaps off a cardboard box that fits over the item, decorate it or cover it with self-adhesive decorative paper, and use it as a dustcover.

Tip **A Good Box Source**

> Even if you don't drink alcohol, the proprietors of your local liquor store will often be happy to provide you with empty wine and liquor cartons. Don't forget to ask for the handy sections to be left intact.

Make an office in-box Making an in-box (or out-box) for your office desk is easy. Simply cut the top and one large panel off a cereal box; then slice the narrow sides at an angle. Wrap with self-adhesive decorative paper.

Make place mats Cut several 12 x 18-inch (30 x 45-centimeter) pieces of cardboard and cover them with colorful adhesive shelf paper or other decoration.

Play liquor box "ski ball" Transform your rec room or backyard into a carnival midway. Just leave the dividers in place in an empty wine or liquor carton. Place the carton at an angle and erect a small ramp in front (a rubber mat over a pile of books will do). Assign numbered values to each section of the carton, grab a few tennis or golf balls and you're ready to roll.

✳ CARDBOARD BOXES **FOR STORING THINGS**

Protect glassware or lightbulbs A good way to safely store fine crystal glassware is to put it in an empty wine or liquor carton with partitions. You can also use it for storing lightbulbs, but be sure to sort the bulbs by wattage so that it's easy to find the right one when you need a replacement.

Make a magazine holder Store your magazines in holders made from empty detergent boxes. Remove the top, then cut the box at an angle, from the top of one side to the bottom third of the other. Cover the holders with self-adhesive decorative paper.

Poster and artwork holder A clean liquor carton with its dividers intact is a great place to store rolled-up posters, drawings on paper, and canvases. Just insert the items upright between the partitions.

Store Christmas ornaments When you take down your Christmas tree, wrap each ornament in newspaper or tissue paper and store it in an empty liquor box with partitions. Each of the carton's segments can hold several of the wrapped holiday tree ornaments.

Create an impromptu sled Use a large cardboard box to pull a small child (or a load of firewood) over the snow.

Garage for toy vehicles Turn an empty large appliance box on its side and let the kids use it as a "garage" for their wheeled vehicles. They can also use a smaller box as a garage for miniature cars, trucks, and buses.

Make a puppet theater Stand a large cardboard box on end. Cut a big hole in the back for puppeteers to crouch in and a smaller one high up in the front for the stage. Decorate with markers or glue on pieces of fabric for curtains.

Organize kids' sporting goods Keep a decorated empty wine or liquor carton with partitions, and with the top cut off, in your child's room and use it for easy storage of tennis rackets, baseball bats, fishing poles, and such.

Make a play castle Turn a large appliance cardboard box into a medieval castle. Cut off the top flaps and make battlements by cutting notches along the top. To make a notch, use a utility knife to make a cut on either side of the section you want to remove, then fold the cut section forward and cut along the fold. To make a drawbridge, cut a large fold-down opening on one side that is attached at the bottom. Connect the top of the drawbridge to the sidewalls with ropes on either side, punching holes for the rope and knotting the rope on the other side. Use duct tape to reinforce the holes. Also cut

SCIENCE FAIR

Making a simple cardboard **sundial** is a great way for kids to observe how the sun's path changes every day. Just take a 10 x 10-inch (25 x 25- centimeter) piece of **cardboard** and poke a stick through the middle. If necessary, screw or nail a **small board** to the bottom of the stick to hold it upright. Place the sundial in a

sunny spot. At **each hour,** have the kids **mark** where the **stick's shadow** falls on the cardboard. Check again the next day, and sure enough, the sundial seems pretty accurate. Check a week later, though, and the shadows won't align to the marks at the right times. When the curious kids start searching the Internet for a reason, give them a hint: The earth is tilted on its axis.

out narrow window slits in the walls. Let the kids draw stones and bricks on the walls.

Repair a roof For temporary repair on your roof, put a piece of cardboard into a plastic bag and slide it under the shingles.

Organize your workshop A sectioned wine or liquor carton is a great place to store dowels, moldings, furring strips, weather stripping, and metal rods.

Store tall garden tools Turn three empty liquor cartons into a sectioned storage bin for your long-handled garden tools. Put a topless box on the floor with the dividers left in. Then cut the tops and bottoms off two similar boxes and stack them so the dividers match up. Use duct tape to attach the boxes to each other. Use the bin to store hoes, rakes, and other long-handled garden tools.

Protect work surfaces Keep work surfaces from being damaged. Flatten a large box or cut a large flat piece from a box and use it to protect your countertop, workbench, table, or desk from ink, paint, glue, or nicks from knives and scissors. Just replace it when it becomes messed up.

Protect your fingers Ouch! You just hammered your finger instead of the tiny nail you were trying to drive. To keep this from happening again, stick the little nail through a small piece of thin cardboard before you do your hammering. Hold the cardboard by an edge, position the nail, and pound it home. When you're done, use your bruise-free fingers to tear away the cardboard.

Keep upholstery tacks straight Reupholstering a chair or sofa? Here's a neat way to get a row of upholstery tacks perfectly straight and evenly spaced. Mark the spacing along the edge of a lightweight cardboard strip and press the tacks into it. After driving all of the tacks most of the way in, tug on the strip to pull the edge free before driving in the rest of the way.

Make a drip pan Prevent an oil leak from soiling your garage floor or driveway. Make a drip pan by placing a few sheets of corrugated cardboard in a cookie sheet and placing the pan under your car's drip. For better absorption, sprinkle some cat litter, sawdust, or oatmeal into the pan on top of the cardboard. Replace with fresh cardboard as needed.

Help your mechanic *Something* is dripping from your car's engine, but you don't know what. Instead of blubbering helplessly to your mechanic about it, place a large piece of cardboard under the engine overnight and bring it with you when you take the car in for service. The color and location of the leaked fluid will help the mechanic identify the problem.

✱ Cardboard Tubes

Extend vacuum cleaner reach Can't reach that cobweb on the ceiling with your regular vacuum cleaner attachment? Try using a long, empty wrapping paper tube to extend the reach. You can even crush the end of the paper tube to create a crevice tool. Use duct tape to make the connection airtight.

Make a sheath Flatten a paper towel tube, duct tape one end shut, and you have a perfect sheath for a picnic/camp knife. Use toilet paper rolls for smaller cutlery.

Keep electrical cords tangle-free Keep computer and appliance cords tangle-free. Fanfold the cord and pass it through a toilet paper tube before plugging in. You can also use the tubes to store extension cords when they're not in use. Paper towel tubes will also work. Just cut them in half before using them to hold the cords.

Make a fly and pest strip Get rid of pesky flies and mosquitoes with a homemade pest strip. Just cover an empty paper towel or toilet paper roll with transparent tape, sticky side out, and hang where needed.

Use as kindling and logs Turn toilet paper and paper towel tubes into kindling and logs for your fireplace. For fire starter, use scissors to cut the cardboard into 1/8-inch (3-millimeter) strips. Keep the strips in a bin near the fireplace so they'll be handy to use next time you make a fire. To make logs, tape over one end of the tube and pack shredded newspaper inside. Then tape the other end. The tighter you pack the newspaper, the longer your log will burn.

Make boot trees To keep the tops of long, flexible boots from flopping over and developing ugly creases in the closet, insert cardboard mailing tubes into them to help them hold their shape.

 DID *You* KNOW?

It took nearly 500 years for toilet paper to make the transition from sheets to rolls. Toilet paper was first produced in China in 1391 for the exclusive use of the emperor—in sheets that measured a whopping 2 x 3 feet (60 x 90 centimeters) each. Toilet paper in rolls was first made in the U.S.A. in 1890 by Scott Paper Company. Scott began making paper towels in 1907, thanks to a failed attempt to develop a new crepe toilet tissue. This paper was so thick it couldn't be cut and rolled into toilet paper, so Scott made larger rolls, perforated into 13 x 18-inch (33 x 45-centimeter) sheets and sold them as Sani-Towels.

Make a plant guard It's easy to accidentally scar the trunk of a young tree when you are whacking weeds around it. To avoid doing this, cut a cardboard mailing tube in half lengthwise and tie the two halves around the trunk while you work around the tree. Then slip it off and use it on another tree.

Protect important documents Before storing diplomas, marriage certificates, and other important documents in your cedar chest, roll them tightly and insert them in paper towel tubes. This prevents creases and keeps the documents clean and dry.

Start seedlings Don't go to the garden supply store to buy biodegradable starting pots for seedlings. Just use the cardboard tubes from paper towels and toilet paper. Use scissors to cut each toilet paper tube into two pots, or each paper towel tube into four. Fill a tray with the cut cylinders packed against each other so they won't tip when you water the seedlings. This will also prevent them from drying out too quickly. Now fill each pot with seed-starting mix, gently pack it down, and sow your seeds. When you plant the seedlings, make sure to break down the side of the roll and make sure all the cardboard is completely buried.

Store knitting needles To keep your knitting needles from bending and breaking, try this: Use a long cardboard tube from kitchen foil or plastic wrap. Cover one end with cellophane tape. Pinch the other end closed and secure it tightly with tape. Slide the needles in through the tape on the taped end. The tape will hold them in place for secure, organized storage.

Store fabric scraps Roll up leftover fabric scraps tightly and insert them inside a cardboard tube from your bathroom or kitchen. For easy identification, tape or staple a sample of the fabric to the outside of the tube.

Store string Nothing is more useless and frustrating than tangled string. To keep your string ready to use, cut a notch into each end of a toilet paper tube. Secure one end of the string in one notch, wrap the string tightly around the tube, and then secure the other end in the other notch.

Keep linens crease-free Wrap tablecloths and napkins around cardboard tubes after laundering to avoid the creases they would get if they were folded. Use long tubes for tablecloths and paper towel or toilet paper tubes for napkins. To guard against stains, cover the tubes with plastic wrap first.

Keep pants crease-free You go to your closet for that good pair of pants you haven't worn in a while, only to find an ugly crease at the fold site from the hanger rack. It won't happen again if you cut a paper towel tube lengthwise, fold it in half horizontally, and place it over the rack before you hang up your pants. Before hanging pants, tape the sides of the cardboard together at the bottom to keep it from slipping.

Keep Christmas lights tidy Spending more time untangling your Christmas lights than it takes to put them up? Make yuletide prep easier by wrapping your lights around a cardboard tube. Secure them with masking tape. Put small strands of lights or garlands *inside* cardboard tubes, and seal the ends of the tubes with masking tape.

Tip **Carpet Tubes**

> Carpet stores discard long, thick cardboard tubes that store workers will probably be happy to provide to you free for the asking. Because the tubes can be up to 12 feet (3.6 meters) long, you might want to ask for them to cut one to the size you want before you cart it away.

Protect fluorescent lights Keep fluorescent light tubes from breaking before you use them. They will fit neatly into long cardboard tubes sealed with tape at one end.

Make a kazoo Got a bunch of bored kids driving you crazy on a rainy day? Cut three small holes in the middle of a paper towel tube. Then cover one end of the tube with wax paper secured with a strong rubber band. Now hum into the other end, while using your fingers to plug one, two, or all three holes to vary the pitch. Make one for each kid. They may still drive you crazy, but they'll have a ball doing it!

Instant megaphone Don't shout yourself hoarse when you're calling outside for a child or pet to come home *right now*. Give your vocal cords a rest by using a wide cardboard tube as a megaphone to amplify your voice.

Make a hamster toy Place a couple of paper towel or toilet paper tubes in the hamster (or gerbil) cage. The little critters will love running and walking through them, and they like chewing on the cardboard too. When the tubes start looking ragged, just replace them with fresh ones.

Preserve kids' artwork You want to save some of your kids' precious artwork for posterity (or you don't want it to clutter up the house). Simply roll up the artwork and place it inside a paper towel tube. Label the outside with the child's name and date. The tubes are easy to store, and you can safely preserve the work of your budding young artists. Use this method to hold and store your documents, such as certificates and licenses, too.

Build a toy log cabin Notch the ends of several long tubes with a craft knife and then help the kids build log cabins, fences, or huts with them. Use different-sized tubes for added versatility. For added realism, have the kids paint or color the tubes before construction begins.

Make English crackers Keep the spirit of holiday firecrackers but cut out the dangers associated with burning explosives. Use toilet paper tubes to make English crackers, which "explode" into tiny gifts. For each cracker, tie a string about 8 inches (20 centimeters) long around a small gift such as candy, a balloon, or a figurine. After tying, the string should have about 6 inches (15 centimeters) to spare. Place the gift into the tube so the string dangles out one end. Cover the tube with bright-colored crepe paper or tissue and twist the ends. When you pull the string, out pops the gift.

✳ Car Wax

Fix skips on CDs Don't throw out that scratched compact disc. Try fixing it first with a small dab of car wax. Spread a cloth on a flat surface and place the CD on it damaged side up. Then, holding the disc with one hand, use the other to wipe the polish into the affected area with a soft cloth. Wait for it to dry and buff using short, brisk strokes along the scratch, not across it. A cloth sold to wipe eyeglasses or camera lenses will work well. When you can no longer see the scratch, wash the disc with water and let it dry before playing.

Keep bathroom mirrors fog-free Prevent your bathroom mirror from steaming up after your next hot shower. Apply a small amount of car paste wax to the mirror, let it dry, and buff with a soft cloth. Next time you step out of the shower, you'll be able to see your face in the mirror immediately. Rub the wax on bathroom fixtures to prevent water spots too.

Eliminate bathroom mildew To chase grime and mildew from your shower, follow these two simple steps: First clean the soap and water residue off the tiles or shower wall. Then rub on a layer of car paste wax and buff with a clean, dry cloth. You'll only need to reapply the wax about once a year. Don't wax the bathtub—it will become dangerously slippery.

Eradicate furniture stains Someone forgot to use a coaster and now there's an ugly white ring on the dining room table. When your regular furniture polish doesn't work, try using a dab of car wax. Trace the ring with your finger to apply the wax. Let it dry and buff with a soft cloth.

Keep snow from sticking When it's time to clear the driveway after a big snowstorm, you don't want snow sticking to your shovel. Apply two thick coats of car paste wax to the work surface of the shovel before you begin shoveling. The snow won't stick and there will be less wear and tear on your cardiovascular system. If you use a snow thrower, wax the inside of the chute.

✳ Carpet Scraps

Muffle clunky appliance noise Does your washer or dryer shake, rattle, and roll when you're doing a load? Put a piece of scrap carpet underneath it, and that may be all you need to calm things down.

115

Catch a falling sock You may never be able to stop socks and other articles of clothing from falling to the floor en route from washer to dryer. But you can make retrieval a lot easier by placing a narrow piece of carpet on the floor between the two appliances. When something falls, just pull out the strip and the article comes with it.

Keep Fido's home dry Don't let the raindrops keep falling on your dog's head. Weatherproof the doghouse: Make a rain flap by nailing a carpet remnant over the entrance to your doggy's domicile. In colder areas, you can also use small pieces of carpet to line interior walls and the floor to add insulation.

Make a scratching post If your cat is clawing up the living room sofa, this might do the trick. Make a scratching post by stapling carpet scraps to a post or board and place it near kitty's favorite target. If you want it to be freestanding, nail a board to the bottom of the post to serve as a base.

Keep garden paths weed-free Place a series of carpet scraps upside down and cover them with bark mulch or straw for a weed-free garden path. Use smaller scraps as mulch around your vegetable garden.

Exercise in comfort Make an instant exercise mat. Cut a length of old carpet around 3 feet (1 meter) wide and as long as your height. When you're not using it for yoga or sit-ups, roll it up and store it under your bed.

Make your own car mats Why buy expensive floor mats for your car when you can make your own? Cut carpet remnants to fit the floorboards of your car and drive off in comfort.

Protect your knees To protect your knees when you're washing the floor, weeding, or doing other work on all fours, make your own kneepads. Cut two pieces of carpeting 10 inches (25 centimeters) square and then cut two parallel slits or holes in each. Run old neckties or scarves through the slits and use them to tie the pads to your knees.

Keep floors dry Don't let the floor get soaked when you water your indoor plants. Place 12-inch (30-centimeter) round carpet scraps under houseplants to absorb any overwatering excess.

Prevent scratched floors Stop screeching chairs from scratching or making black marks on wood or vinyl floors. Glue small circles of carpet remnants to the bottom of chair and table legs.

Make a buffer Use epoxy resin to glue an old piece of carpet to a block of wood to make a buffer. Make several and use one to buff shoes, another to wipe blackboards, and one to clean window screens.

Cushion kitchen shelves Reduce the noisy clattering when putting away pots and pans: Cushion kitchen shelves and cabinets with pieces of carpet.

Add traction Keep good-sized carpet scraps in the trunk of your car to add traction when you're stuck in snow or ice. Keep one piece with your spare tire: When you have a flat, you won't have to kneel or lie on the dirty ground when you have to look under the carriage.

Protect workshop tools Does your workshop have a floor made of concrete or another hard material? If so, put down a few carpet remnants in the area closest to your workbench. Now when tools or containers accidentally fall to the floor, they will be far less likely to break.

✳ Castor Oil

Soften cuticles If you were ever forced to swallow castor oil as a child, this may be a pleasant surprise: The high vitamin-E content of that awful-tasting thick oil can work wonders on brittle nails and ragged cuticles. And you don't have to swallow the stuff. Just massage a small amount on your cuticles and nails each day and within three months you will have supple cuticles and healthy nails

Soothe tired eyes Before going to bed, rub odorless castor oil all around your eyes. Rub some on your eyelashes, too, to keep them shiny. Be careful not to get the oil in your eyes.

Lubricate kitchen scissors Use castor oil instead of toxic petroleum oil to lubricate kitchen scissors and other utensils that touch food.

Repel moles If moles are destroying your garden and yard, try using castor oil to get rid of them. Mix 1/2 cup castor oil and 2 gallons (7.5 liters) water and drench the molehill with it. It won't kill them, but it will get them out looking for another neighborhood to dig up.

Enjoy a massage Castor oil is just the right consistency to use as a soothing massage oil. For a real treat, warm the oil on the stovetop or on half-power in the microwave. Ahhh!

 DID *You* KNOW?

Castor oil is more than an old-fashioned medicine cabinet staple. It has hundreds of industrial uses. Large amounts are used in paints, varnishes, lipstick, hair tonic, and shampoo. Castor oil is also converted into plastics, soap, waxes, hydraulic fluids, and ink. And it is made into lubricants for jet engines and racing cars because it does not become stiff with cold or unduly thin with heat. North American manufacturers now use about 40 percent of the entire world's crop of castor oil.

Perk up ailing ferns Give your sickly ferns a tonic made by mixing 1 tablespoon castor oil and 1 tablespoon baby shampoo with 4 cups lukewarm water. Give the fern about 3 tablespoons of the tonic, then follow with plain water. Your plants should be perky by the time you use up your supply of tonic.

Condition your hair For healthy, shiny hair, mix 2 teaspoons castor oil with 1 teaspoon glycerin and one egg white. Massage it into your wet hair, wait several minutes, and wash out.

✳ Cat Litter

Make a mud mask Make a deep-cleansing mud mask. Mix two handfuls of fresh cat litter with enough warm water to make a thick paste. Smear the paste over your face, let it set for 20 minutes, and rinse clean with water. The clay from cat litter detoxifies your skin by absorbing dirt and oil from the pores. When your friends compliment you on your complexion and ask how you did it, just tell them it's your little secret.

Sneaker deodorizer If your athletic shoes reek, fill a couple of old socks with scented cat litter, tie them shut, and place them in the sneakers overnight. Repeat if necessary until the sneakers are stink-free.

Add traction on ice Keep a bag of cat litter in the trunk of your car. Use it to add traction when you're stuck in ice or snow.

Prevent grease fires Don't let a grease fire spoil your next barbecue. Pour a layer of cat litter into the bottom of your grill for worry-free outdoor cooking.

Stop musty odors Get rid of that musty smell when you open the closet door. Just place a shallow box filled with cat litter in each musty closet or room. Cat litter works great as a deodorant.

DID **You** KNOW?

Ed Lowe might not have gotten the idea for cat litter if a neighbor hadn't asked him for some sand for her cat box one day in 1947. Ed, who worked for his father's company selling industrial absorbents, suggested clay instead because it was more absorbent and would not leave tracks around the house. When she returned for more, he knew he had a winner. Soon he was criss-crossing the country, selling bags of his new Kitty Litter from the back of his Chevy Coupe. By 1990 Edward Lowe Industries, Inc., was the nation's largest producer of cat box filler with retail sales of more than $210 million annually.

Preserve flowers The fragrance and beauty of freshly cut flowers is such a fleeting thing. You can't save the smell, but you can preserve their beauty by drying your flowers on a bed of cat litter in an airtight container for 7-10 days.

Remove foul stench Just because your garbage cans hold garbage doesn't mean they have to smell disgusting. Sprinkle some cat litter into the bottom of garbage cans to keep them smelling fresh. Change the litter after a week or so or when it becomes damp. If you have a baby in the house, use cat litter the same way to freshen diaper pails.

Keep tents must-free Keep tents and sleeping bags fresh smelling and free of must when not in use. Pour cat litter into an old sock, tie the end, and store inside the bag or tent.

Repel moles Moles may hate the smell of soiled cat litter even more than you do. Pour some down their tunnels to send them scurrying to find new homes.

Make grease spots disappear Get rid of ugly grease and oil spots in your driveway or on your garage floor. Simply cover them with cat litter. If the spots are fresh, the litter will soak up most of the oil right away. To remove old stains, pour some paint thinner on the stain before tossing on the cat litter. Wait 12 hours and then sweep clean.

Freshen old books You can rejuvenate old books that smell musty by sealing them overnight in a can with clean cat litter.

✳ Chalk

Repel ants Keep ants at bay by drawing a line around home entry points. The ants will be repelled by the calcium carbonate in the chalk, which is actually made up of ground-up and compressed shells of marine animals. Scatter powdered chalk around garden plants to repel ants and slugs.

Polish metal and marble To make metal shine like new, put some chalk dust on a damp cloth and wipe. (You can make chalk dust by using a mortar to pulverize pieces of chalk.) Buff with a soft cloth for an even shinier finish. Wipe clean marble with a damp soft cloth dipped in powdered chalk. Rinse with clear water and dry thoroughly.

Keep silver from tarnishing You love serving company with your fine silver, but polishing it before each use is another story. Put one or two pieces of chalk in the drawer with your good silver. It will absorb moisture and slow tarnishing. Put some in your jewelry box to delay tarnishing there too.

C

Remove grease spots Rub chalk on a grease spot on clothing or table linens and let it absorb the oil before you brush it off. If the stain lingers, rub chalk into it again before laundering. Get rid of ring-around-the-collar stains too. Mark the stains heavily with chalk before laundering. The chalk will absorb the oils that hold dirt in.

Stop screwdriver slips Does your screwdriver slip when you try to tighten a screw? It won't slip nearly as much if you rub some chalk on the tip of the blade.

Reduce closet dampness Tie a dozen pieces of chalk together and hang them up in your damp closet. The chalk will absorb moisture and help prevent mildew. Replace with a fresh bunch every few months.

Hide ceiling marks Temporarily cover up water or scuff marks on the ceiling until you have time to paint or make a permanent repair. Rub a stick of white chalk over the mark until it lightens or disappears.

Keep tools rust-free You can eliminate moisture and prevent rust from invading your toolbox by simply putting a few pieces of chalk in the box. Your tools will be rust-free and so will the toolbox.

✳ Charcoal Briquettes

Make a dehumidifier A humid closet, attic, or basement can wreak havoc on your health as well as your clothes. Get rid of all that humidity with several home-made dehumidifiers. To make one, just put some charcoal briquettes in a coffee can, punch a few holes in the lid, and place in the humid areas. Replace the charcoal every few months.

Keep root water fresh Put a piece of charcoal in the water when you're rooting plant cuttings. The charcoal will keep the water fresh.

Banish bathroom moisture and odors Hide a few pieces of charcoal in the nooks and crannies of your bathroom to soak up moisture and cut down on unpleasant odors. Replace them every couple of months.

Keep books mold-free Professional librarians use charcoal to get rid of musty odors on old books. You can do the same. If your bookcase has glass doors, it may provide a damp environment that can cause must and mold. A piece of charcoal or two placed inside will help keep the books dry and mold-free.

 DID *You* KNOW?

Henry Ford: father of ... *charcoal briquettes?* Yes, the first mass-produced charcoal briquettes were manufactured by the Ford Motor Company. They were made from waste wood from a Ford-owned sawmill in Kingsford, Michigan, built to provide wood for the bodies of Ford's popular "Woody" station wagons. The charcoal was manufactured into briquettes and sold as Ford Charcoal Briquettes. Henry Ford II closed the sawmill in 1951 and sold the plant to a group of local businessmen, who formed the Kingsford Chemical Company. The company continues to make the charcoal briquettes that are now a household name, despite relocating to Louisville, Kentucky, in 1961.

✱ Cheesecloth

Remove turkey stuffing with ease To keep turkey dressing from sticking to the bird's insides, pack the dressing in cheesecloth before you stuff it into the turkey's cavity. When the turkey is ready to serve, pull out the cheesecloth and the stuffing will slide out with it.

Make a homemade butterfly net Just sew cheesecloth into a bag and glue or staple it to a hoop formed from a wire coat hanger—and send the kids a-hunting. Or make a smaller cheesecloth net for when you take the kids fishing and let them use it as a bait-net to catch minnows. For an inexpensive Halloween costume, wrap a child in cheesecloth from head to toe and send your mini-mummy out to collect candy.

Convert a colander into a strainer If you can't find a strainer when you need one, a colander lined with cheesecloth will serve in a pinch.

Cut vacuuming time Here is a neat, time-saving way to vacuum the contents of a drawer filled with small objects without having to remove the contents. Simply cover the nozzle of your vacuum cleaner with cheesecloth, secured with a strong rubber band, and the vacuum will pick up only the dust.

Reduce waste drying herbs When drying fresh herbs, wrap them in cheesecloth to prevent seeds and smaller crumbled pieces from falling through.

Picnic food tent Keep bugs and dirt away from your picnic food serving plates. Wrap a piece of cheesecloth around an old wire umbrella form and place it over the plates. Use a hacksaw to remove the umbrella handle and tack the cheesecloth to the umbrella ribs with a needle and thread.

Make instant festive curtains Brighten any room with inexpensive, colorful, and festive cheesecloth curtains. Dye inexpensive cheesecloth (available in bulk from fabric vendors) in bright colors and cut it to the lengths and widths you need. Attach clip-on café-curtain hooks and your new curtains are ready to hang.

✳ Chest Rub

Repel ticks and other bugs Going for a walk in the woods? Smear some chest rub on your legs and pants before you leave the house. It will keep ticks from biting and may spare you from getting Lyme disease. Pesky biting insects like gnats and mosquitoes will look elsewhere for victims if you apply chest rub to your skin before venturing outdoors. They hate the smell.

DID *You* KNOW?

Lunsford Richardson, the pharmacist who created Vick's VapoRub in 1905, also originated America's first "junk mail." Richardson was working in his brother-in-law's drugstore when he blended menthol and other ingredients into an ointment to clear sinuses and ease congestion. He called it Richardson's Croup and Pneumonia Cure Salve, but soon realized he needed something catchier to sell successfully. He changed the name to Vick's after his brother-in-law, Joshua Vick, and convinced the U.S. Post Office to institute a new policy allowing him to send advertisements addressed only to "Boxholder." Sales of Vick's first surpassed a million dollars during the Spanish flu epidemic of 1918.

Make calluses disappear Coat calluses with chest rub and then cover them with an adhesive bandage overnight. Repeat the procedure as needed. Most calluses will disappear after several days.

Soothe aching feet Are your feet aching after that long walk in the woods? Try applying a thick coat of chest rub and cover with a pair of socks before going to bed at night. When you wake up, your feet will be moisturized and rejuvenated.

Stop insect-bite itch fast Apply a generous coat of chest rub for immediate relief from itchy insect bites. The eucalyptus and menthol in the ointment are what do the trick.

Treat toenail fungus If you have a toenail fungus (onychomycosis), try applying a thick coat of chest rub to the affected nail several times a day. Many users and even some medical pros swear that it works (just check the Internet). But if you don't see results after a few weeks, consult a dermatologist or podiatrist.

❋ Chewing Gum

Retrieve valuables Oops, you just lost an earring or other small valuable down the drain. Try retrieving it with a just-chewed piece of gum stuck to the bottom of a fishing weight. Dangle it from a string tied to the weight, let it take hold, and reel it in.

DID *You* KNOW?

Humans have been chewing gum a long time. Ancient Greeks chewed *mastiche*, a chewing gum made from the resin of the mastic tree. Ancient Mayans chewed *chicle*, the sap from the sapodilla tree. North American Indians chewed the sap from spruce trees, and passed the habit on to the Pilgrims. And other early American settlers made chewing gum from spruce sap and beeswax. John B. Curtis produced the first commercial chewing gum in 1848 and called it State of Maine Pure Spruce Gum. North Americans now spend more than $2 billion per year on chewing gum.

Lure a crab You'll be eating plenty of crab cakes if you try this trick: Briefly chew a stick of gum so that it is soft but still hasn't lost its flavor, then attach it to a crab line. Lower the line and wait for the crabs to go for the gum.

Fill cracks Fill a crack in a clay flowerpot or a dog bowl with piece of well-chewed gum.

Use as makeshift window putty Worried that a loose pane of glass may tumble and break before you get around to fixing it? Hold it in place temporarily with a wad or two of fresh-chewed gum.

Repair glasses When your glasses suddenly have a lens loose, put a small piece of chewed gum in the corner of the lens to hold it in place until you can get the glasses properly repaired.

Treat flatulence and heartburn Settle stomach gases and relieve heartburn by chewing a stick of spearmint gum. The oils in the spearmint act as an antiflatulent. Chewing stimulates the production of saliva, which neutralizes stomach acid and corrects the flow of digestive juices. Spearmint also acts as a digestive aid.

✳ Chicken Wire

Repel deer Are the deer tearing up your garden again? Here's a simple method to keep them away: Stake chicken wire *flat* around the perimeter of your garden. Deer don't like to walk on it, and it is not an eyesore like a chicken-wire fence.

Crown catnip plants If you are growing catnip for your cat, put a crown of chicken wire over the plant, close to the ground. As the catnip grows through the wire and gets eaten, the roots will remain intact, growing new catnip. Make sure the edges of the wire are tucked in securely. Catnip is a hardy plant, even in frigid temperatures, so if the roots remain, you will see it year after year.

Protect bulbs from rodents Keep pesky burrowing rodents from damaging your flower bulbs. Line the bottom of a prepared bed with chicken wire, plant the bulbs, and cover with soil.

Flower holder Keep cut flowers aligned in a vase. Squish some chicken wire together and place it in the bottom of the vase before inserting the flowers.

Make a childproof corral Your garage or shed is full of dangerous tools and toxic substances. Keep kids away from these hazardous items by enclosing them in a childproof corral. Make it by first attaching standard-width chicken wire to the walls in a corner. Then staple 1 x 2s to the cut ends of the wire and install screw eyes in the wood to accommodate two padlocks.

Firmer fence posts Before setting a fence post in concrete, wrap the base with chicken wire. This will make the anchoring firmer and the post more secure.

Secure insulation After you place fiberglass batting between roof rafters or floor joists, staple chicken wire across the joists to secure it and, in the case of the rafters, to keep it from sagging.

✱ Clipboards

Makeshift pants hanger Can't find a hanger for a pair of pants? Use a clipboard instead. Just suspend the clipboard from a hook inside the closet or on the bedroom door. Hang the trousers overnight by clipping the cuffs to the board.

Keep recipes at eye level When you are following a recipe clipped from a magazine or newspaper, it's hard to read and keep clean when the clipping is lying on the counter. Solve the problem by attaching a clipboard to a wall cabinet at eye level. Just snap the recipe of the day onto the clipboard and you are ready to create your kitchen magic.

Hold place mats Hang a clipboard inside a kitchen cabinet or pantry door and use the clamp as a convenient, space-saving way to store your place mats.

Keep sheet music in place Flimsy pages of sheet music are susceptible to drafts and sometimes seem to spend more time on the floor than on the music stand. To eliminate this problem, attach the music sheets to a clipboard before placing it in the stand. The pages will remain upright and in place.

Aid road-trip navigation Before starting out on a long motor trip, fold the map to the area you will be traveling in. Attach it to a clipboard and keep it nearby to check your progress at rest stops.

Organize your sandpaper Most of the time, sandpaper is still good after the first or second time you use it. The trick is to find that used sandpaper again. Hang a clipboard on a hook on your workshop pegboard. Just clip still-usable sandpaper to the board when you are done and the sandpaper will be handy next time you need it.

✱ Clothespins

Fasten Christmas lights Keep your outdoor Christmas lights in place and ready to withstand the elements. As you affix your lights to gutters, trees, bushes (or even your spouse!) fasten them securely with clip-on clothespins.

Make a clothespin clipboard Organize your workshop, kitchen, or bathroom with a homemade rack made with straight clothespins. Space several clothespins evenly apart on a piece of wood, and screw them on with screws coming through from the back of the board (pre-drill the holes so you don't split the clothespin). Now your rack is ready to hang.

C

Keep snacks fresh Tired of biting into stale potato chips from a previously opened bag? Use clip-on clothespins to reseal bags of chips and other snacks, cereal, crackers, and seeds. The foods will stay fresh longer and you won't have as many spills in the pantry, either. Use a clothespin for added freshness insurance when you store food in a freezer bag too.

Organize your closet Okay, you found one shoe. Now, where the heck is the other one? From now on use clip-on clothespins to hold together pairs of shoes, boots, or sneakers, and put an end to those unscheduled hunting expeditions in your closets. It's a good idea for gloves, too.

Keep gloves in shape After washing wool gloves, insert a straight wooden clothespin into each finger. The clothespins will keep the gloves in their proper shape.

Prevent vacuum cord "snapback" Whoops! You're vacuuming the living room floor when suddenly the machine stops. You've accidentally pulled out the plug and the cord is automatically retracting and snapping back into the machine. To avoid similar annoyance in the future, simply clip a clothespin to the cord at the length you want.

Make an instant bib Make bibs for your child by using a clip-on clothespin to hold a dish towel around the child's neck. Use bigger towels to make lobster bibs for adults. It's much faster than tying on a bib.

Make clothespin puppets Traditional straight clothespins without the metal springs are ideal for making little puppets. Using the knob as a head, have kids paste on bits of yarn for hair, and scraps of cloth or colored paper for clothes to give each one its own personality.

Hold leaf bag open Ever try filling a large leaf bag all by your lonesome, only to see half the leaves fall to the ground because the bag won't stay open? Next time enlist a couple of clip-on clothespins as helpers. After you shake open the bag and

DID You KNOW?

Between 1852 and 1857 the U.S. Patent Office granted patents for 146 different clothespins. Today wood clothespin makers have practically disappeared. "The small family-owned, secondary wood processing companies are dying off," says Richard Penley, who closed his family's clothespin plant in Maine in 2002. The company founded by Penley's grandfather and two brothers in 1923 survives, importing and distributing clothespins made overseas. Only two wood clothespin manufacturers are left in the United States: Diamond-Forster in Maine and National Clothespin Company in Vermont.

spread it wide, use the clothespins to clip one side of the bag to a chain-link fence or other convenient site. The bag will stay open for easy filling.

Mark a bulb spot What to do when a flower that blooms in the spring … doesn't? Just push a straight clothespin into the soil at the spot where it didn't grow. In the fall you will know exactly where to plant new bulbs to avoid gaps.

Grip a nail Hammer the nail and not your fingers. Just remember to use a clip-on clothespin to hold nails when hammering in hard-to-reach places.

Clamp thin objects Use clip-on clothespins as clamps when you're gluing two thin objects together. Let the clothespin hold them in place until the glue sets.

Keep paintbrush afloat Keep your paintbrush from sinking into the solvent residue when you soak it. Clamp the brush to the container with a clothespin.

✳ Club Soda

Make pancakes and waffles fluffier If you like your pancakes and waffles on the fluffy side, substitute club soda for the liquid called for in the recipes. You'll be amazed at how light and fluffy your breakfast treats turn out.

❓ DID *You* KNOW?

Bubbling water has been associated with good health since the time of the ancient Romans, who enjoyed drinking mineral water almost as much as they liked bathing in it. The first club soda was sold in North America at the end of the 1700s. That's when pharmacists figured out how to infuse plain water with carbon dioxide, which they believed was responsible for giving natural bubbling water health-inducing qualities. Club soda and seltzer are essentially the same. However, seltzer is a natural effervescent water (named for a region in Germany where it is plentiful) whereas club soda is manufactured.

Give your plants a mineral bath Don't throw out that leftover club soda. Use it to water your indoor and outdoor plants. The minerals in the soda water help green plants grow. For maximum benefit, try to water your plants with club soda about once a week.

Remove fabric stains Clean grease stains from double-knit fabrics. Pour club soda on the stain and scrub gently. Scrub more vigorously to remove stains on carpets or less delicate articles of clothing.

Help shuck oysters If you love oysters but find shucking them to be a near-impossible chore, try soaking them in club soda before you shuck. The oysters won't exactly jump out of their shells, but they will be much easier to open.

Clean precious gems Soak your diamonds, rubies, sapphires, and emeralds in club soda to give them a bright sheen. Simply place them in a glass full of club soda and let them soak overnight.

Clean your car windshield Keep a spray bottle filled with club soda in the trunk of your car. Use it to help remove bird droppings and greasy stains from the windshield. The fizzy water speeds the cleaning process.

Restore hair color If your blond hair turns green when you swim in a pool with too much chlorine, don't panic. Rinse your hair with club soda and it will change back to its original color.

Tame your tummy Cold club soda with a dash of bitters will work wonders on an upset stomach caused by indigestion or a hangover.

Clean countertops and fixtures Pour club soda directly on stainless steel countertops, ranges, and sinks. Wipe with a soft cloth, rinse with warm water, and wipe dry. To clean porcelain fixtures, simply pour club soda over them and wipe with a soft cloth. There's no need for soap or rinsing, and the soda will not mar the finish. Give the inside of your refrigerator a good cleaning with a weak solution of club soda and a little bit of salt.

Remove rust To loosen rusty nuts and bolts, pour some club soda over them. The carbonation helps to bubble the rust away.

Eliminate urine stains Did someone have an accident? After blotting up as much urine as possible, pour club soda over the stained area and immediately blot again. The club soda will get rid of the stain and help reduce the foul smell.

Ease cast-iron cleanup Food tastes delicious when it's cooked in cast iron, but cleaning those heavy pots and pans with the sticky mess inside is no fun at all. You can make the cleanup a lot easier by pouring some club soda in the pan while it's still warm. The bubbly soda will keep the mess from sticking.

✳ Coat Hangers

Stop caulk-tube ooze To prevent caulk from oozing from the tube once the job is done, cut a 3-inch (7.5-centimeter) piece of coat hanger wire; shape one end into a hook and insert the other, straight end into the tube. Now you can easily pull out the stopper as needed.

Secure a soldering iron Keeping a hot soldering iron from rolling away and burning something on your workbench is a real problem. To solve this, just twist a wire coat hanger into a holder for the iron to rest in. To make the holder, simply bend an ordinary coat hanger in half to form a large **V**. Then bend each half in half so that the entire piece is shaped like a **W**.

Extend your reach Can't reach that utensil that has fallen behind the refrigerator or stove? Try straightening a wire coat hanger (except for the hook at the end), and use it to fish for the object.

Make a giant bubble wand Kids will love to make giant bubbles with a homemade bubble wand fashioned from a wire coat hanger. Shape the hanger into a hoop with a handle and dip it into a bucket filled with 1 part liquid dish-washing detergent in 2 parts water. Add a few drops of food coloring to make the bubbles more visible.

Create arts and crafts Make mobiles for the kids' room using wire coat hangers; paint them in bright colors. Or use hangers to make wings and other accessories for costumes.

Unclog toilets and vacuum cleaners If your toilet is clogged by a foreign object, fish out the culprit with a straightened wire coat hanger. Use a straightened hanger to unclog a jammed vacuum cleaner hose.

Make a mini-greenhouse To convert a window box into a mini-greenhouse, bend three or four lengths of coat hanger wire into **U**'s and place the ends into the soil. Punch small holes in a dry-cleaning bag and wrap it around the box before putting it back in the window.

SCIENCE FAIR

Here's a fun way to demonstrate **Newton's first law of motion.** Bend a wire **coat hanger** into a large loopy **M**, as shown. Holding the wire in the middle, attach a same-sized **modeling-clay ball** to each of the hooks. Then place the low center point of the **M** on top of your head. If you **turn your head** to the left or right, the **inertia** of the balls will be enough to **keep them in place,** demonstrating Newton's law that "objects at rest tend to stay at rest." With practice, you can actually turn all the way around and the balls will remain still.

Hang a plant Wrap a straightened wire coat hanger around a 6- to 8-inch (15- to 20-centimeter) flowerpot, just below the lip; twist it back on itself to secure it, then hang.

Make plant markers Need some waterproof markers for your outdoor plants? Cut up little signs from a milk jug or similar rigid but easy-to-cut plastic. Write the name of the plant with an indelible marker. Cut short stakes from wire hangers. Make two small slits in each marker and pass the wire stakes through the slits. Neither rain nor sprinkler will obscure your signs.

Make a paint can holder When you are up on a ladder painting your house, one hand is holding on while the other is painting. How do you hold the paint can? Grab a pair of wire snips and cut the hook plus 1 inch (2.5 centimeters) of wire from a wire hanger. Use a pair of pliers to twist the 1-inch section firmly around the handle of your paint can. Now you have a handy hanger.

Light a hard-to-reach pilot light The pilot light has gone out way inside your stove or furnace. You'd rather not risk a burn by lighting a match and sticking your hand all the way in there. Instead, open up a wire hanger and tape the match to one end. Strike the match and use the hanger to reach the pilot.

DID **You** KNOW?

All Albert J. Parkhouse wanted to do when he arrived at work was to hang up his coat and get busy doing his job. It was 1903, and Albert worked at Timberlake Wire and Novelty Company in Jackson, Michigan. But when he went to hang his clothes on the hooks the company provided for workers, all were in use. Frustrated, Albert picked up a piece of wire, bent it into two large oblong hoops opposite each other, and twisted both ends at the center into a hook. He hung his coat on it and went to work. The company thought so much of the idea they patented it and made a fortune.

Alas, Albert never got a penny for inventing the wire coat hanger.

✳ Coffee Beans

Freshen your breath What to do when you're all out of breath mints? Just suck on a coffee bean for a while and your mouth will smell clean and fresh again.

Remove foul odor from hands If your hands smell of garlic, fish or other strong foods you've been handling, a few coffee beans may be all you need to get rid of the odor. Put the beans in your hands and rub them together. The oil released from the coffee beans will absorb the foul smell. When the odor is gone, wash your hands in warm, soapy water.

Fill a beanbag They don't call them beanbags for nothing. Coffee beans are ideal as beanbag filler, but with the price of coffee nowadays it's a good idea to wait for a sale and then buy the cheapest beans available.

✱ Coffee Cans

Bake perfectly round bread Use small coffee cans to bake perfectly cylindrical loaves of bread. Use your favorite recipe but put the dough in a well-greased coffee can instead of a loaf pan. For yeast breads use two cans and fill each only half full. Grease the inside of the lids and place them on the cans. For yeast breads, you will know when it is time to bake when the rising dough pushes the lids off. Place the cans—without the lids—upright in the oven to bake.

Separate hamburgers Before you put those hamburger patties in the freezer, stack them with a coffee-can lid between each and put them in a plastic bag. Now, when the patties are frozen you'll be able to easily peel off as many as you need.

Hold kitchen scraps Line a coffee can with a small plastic bag and keep it near the sink to hold kitchen scraps and peelings. Instead of walking back and forth to the garbage can, you'll make one trip to dump all the scraps at the same time.

Make a bank To make a bank for the kids or a collection can for a favorite charity, use a utility knife to cut a 1/8-inch (3-millimeter) slit in the center of the plastic lid of a coffee can. Tape decorative paper or adhesive plastic to the sides of the kids' bank; for a collection can, use the sides of the can to highlight the charity you are helping.

Create a toy holder Make a decorative container for kids' miniature books and small toys. Wash and dry a coffee can and file off any sharp edges. Sponge on two coats of white acrylic paint, letting it dry between coats. Cut out a design from an old sheet or pillowcase to wrap around the can. Mix 4 tablespoons white glue with enough water to the consistency of paint. Paint on the glue mixture and gently press the fabric onto the can. Trim the bottom and tuck top edges

?? DID *You* KNOW?

Ground coffee loses its flavor immediately unless it is specially packaged or brewed. Freshly roasted and ground coffee is often sealed in combination plastic-and-paper bags, but the coffee can is by far the most common container in North America. Vacuum-sealed cans keep coffee fresh for up to three years. The U.S. is the world's largest consumer of coffee, importing up to 2.5 million pounds (1.1 million kilograms) each year. More than half the U.S. population consumes coffee. The typical coffee drinker has 3.4 cups of coffee per day. That translates into 350 million cups of coffee guzzled daily.

inside the can. Apply two coats of glue mixture over the fabric overlay, letting it dry between coats.

Store belts If you have more belts than places to hang them up, just roll them up and store them in a cleaned-out coffee can with a clear lid. Coffee cans are just the right size to keep belts from creasing, and clear lids will let you find each belt easily.

Keep the laundry room neat Have an empty coffee can nearby as you're going through the kids' pockets before putting up a load of wash. Use it to deposit gum and candy wrappers, paper scraps, and other assorted items that kids like to stuff into their pockets. Keep another can handy for coins and bills.

Make a dehumidifier If your basement is too damp, try this easy-to-make dehumidifier. Fill an empty coffee can with salt and leave it in a corner where it will be undisturbed. Replace the salt at monthly intervals or as needed.

Keep carpets dry Place plastic coffee-can lids under houseplants as saucers. They will protect carpets or wood floors and catch any excess water.

Keep toilet paper dry when camping Bring a few empty coffee cans with you on your next camping trip. Use them to keep toilet paper dry in rainy weather or when you're carrying supplies in a canoe or boat.

Gauge rainfall or sprinkler coverage Find out if your garden is getting enough water from the rain. Next time it starts to rain, place empty coffee cans in several places around the garden. When the rain stops, measure the depth of the water in the cans. If they measure at least an inch, there's no need for additional watering. This is also a good way to test if your sprinkler is getting sufficient water to the areas it is supposed to cover.

Make a coffee-can bird feeder To fashion a coffee can into a sturdy bird feeder, begin with a full can and open the top only halfway. (Pour the coffee into an airtight container.) Then open the bottom of the can halfway the same way. Carefully bend the cut ends down inside the can so the edges are not exposed to cut you. Punch a hole in the side of the can at both ends, where it will be the "top" of the feeder, and put some wire through each end to make a hanger.

Make a spot lawn seeder When it's time to reseed bare spots on your lawn, don't use a regular spreader. It wastes seed by throwing it everywhere. For precision seeding, fashion a spot seeder from an empty coffee can and a pair of plastic lids. Drill small holes in the bottom of the can, just big enough to let grass seeds pass through. Put one lid over the bottom of the can, fill the can with seeds, and cap it with the other lid. When you're ready to spread the seeds, take off the bottom lid. When you're finished, replace it to seal in any unused seed for safe storage.

Eliminate workshop clutter You want small items like screws, nuts, and nails to be handy, but you don't want them to take up workbench space. Here's a way to get the small stuff up out of the way. Drill a hole near the top of empty coffee cans so you can hang them on nails in your workshop wall. Label the cans with masking tape so you will know what's inside.

Soak a paintbrush An empty coffee can is perfect for briefly soaking a paintbrush in thinner before continuing a job the next day. Cut an **X** into the lid and insert the brush handles so the bristles clear the bottom of the can by about 1/2 inch (12 millimeters). If the can has no lid, attach a stick to the brush handle with a rubber band to keep the bristles off the bottom of the can.

Catch paint drips Turn the plastic lids from old coffee cans into drip catchers under paint cans and under furniture legs when you're painting. Protect cupboard shelves by putting them under jars of cooking oil and syrup too.

❋ Coffee Filters

Cover food in the microwave Coffee filters are microwave-safe. Use them to cover bowls or dishes to prevent splatter when cooking or baking in your microwave oven.

Filter cork crumbs from wine Don't let cork droppings ruin your enjoyment of a good glass of wine. If your attempt at opening the bottle results in floating cork crumbs, just decant the wine through a coffee filter.

DID *You* KNOW?

The coffee filter was invented in 1908 by a housewife from Dresden, Germany. Melitta Bentz was looking for a way to brew a perfect cup of coffee without the bitterness often caused by overbrewing. She decided to try making a fil- tered coffee, pouring boiling water over ground coffee, and filtering out the grinds. Melitta experimented with different materials, until she found that the blotter paper that her son used for school worked best. She cut a round piece of blotting paper, put it in a metal cup, and the first Melitta coffee filter was born. Shortly thereafter, Melitta and her husband, Hugo, launched the company that still bears her name.

Line a sieve If you save your cooking oil for reuse after deep-fat frying, line your sieve with a basket-style coffee filter to remove smaller food remnants and impurities.

Hold a taco Serve tacos, hot dogs, popcorn, and other messy foods in cone or basket-style coffee filters. The filter is a perfect sleeve and will help keep fingers clean and cleanup a snap.

Catch ice-cream drips Next time the kids scream for ice-cream bars or ice pops, serve it to them with a drip catcher made from basket-style coffee filters. Just poke the stick through the center of two filters and the drips will fall into the paper, not on the child or your carpet.

Make an instant funnel Cut the end off a cone-style coffee filter to make an instant funnel. Keep a few in your car and use them to avoid spillage when you add a quart of oil or two.

Clean your specs Next time you clean your glasses, try using a coffee filter instead of a tissue. Good-quality coffee filters are made from 100 percent virgin paper, so you can use them to clean your glasses without leaving lint. You can also use them safely to polish mirrors and TV and computer-monitor screens.

Keep skillets rust-free Prolong the life of your good cast-iron cookware. Put a coffee filter in the skillet when it's not in use. The filter will absorb moisture and prevent rusting.

Prevent soil leakage When you're repotting a plant, line the pot with a coffee filter to keep the soil from leaking out through the drain hole.

Make an air freshener Fill a coffee filter with baking soda, twist-tie it shut, and you have just made an air freshener. Make several and tuck them into shoes, closets, the fridge, or wherever else they may be needed.

✱ Coffee Grounds

Don't raise any dust Before you clean the ashes out of your fireplace, sprinkle them with wet coffee grounds. They'll be easier to remove, and the ash and dust won't pollute the atmosphere of the room.

Deodorize a freezer Get rid of the smell of spoiled food after a freezer failure. Fill a couple of bowls with used or fresh coffee grounds and place them in the freezer overnight. For a flavored-coffee scent, add a couple of drops of vanilla to the grounds.

Fertilize plants Don't throw out those old coffee grounds. They're chock-full o' nutrients that your acidic-loving plants crave. Save them to fertilize rosebushes, azaleas, rhododendrons, evergreens, and camellias. It's better to use grounds from a drip coffeemaker than the boiled grounds from a percolator. The drip grounds are richer in nitrogen.

Keep worms alive A cup of used coffee grounds will keep your bait worms alive and wiggling all day long. Just mix the grounds into the soil in your bait box before you dump in the worms. They like coffee almost as much as we do, and the nutrients in the grounds will help them live longer.

Keep cats out of the garden Kitty won't think of your garden as a latrine anymore if you spread a pungent mixture of orange peels and used coffee grounds around your plants. The mix acts as great fertilizer too.

Boost carrot harvest To increase your carrot harvest, mix the seeds with fresh-ground coffee before sowing. Not only does the extra bulk make the tiny seeds easier to sow, but the coffee aroma may repel root maggots and other pests. As an added bonus, the grounds will help add nutrients to the soil as they decompose around the plants. You might also like to add a few radish seeds to the mix before sowing. The radishes will be up in a few days to mark the rows, and when you cultivate the radishes, you will be thinning the carrot seedlings and cultivating the soil at the same time.

DID *You* KNOW?

Coffee grows on trees that reach a height of up to 20 feet (6 meters), but growers keep them pruned to about 6 feet (2 meters) to simplify picking and encourage heavy berry production. The first visible sign of a coffee tree's maturity is the appearance of small white blossoms, which fill the air with a heady aroma reminiscent of jasmine and orange. The mature tree bears cherry-size oval berries, each containing two coffee beans with their flat sides together. A mature coffee tree will produce one pound (450 grams) of coffee per growing season. It takes 2,000 hand-picked Arabica coffee berries (4,000 beans) to make a pound of roasted coffee.

✳ Coins

Test tire tread Let old Abe Lincoln's head tell you if it's time to replace the tires on your car. Insert an American penny into the tread. If you can't cover the top of Honest Abe's head inside the tread, it's time to head for the tire store. Check tires regularly and you will avoid the danger and inconvenience of a flat tire on a busy road.

Give carpet a lift When you move a chair, sofa, table, or bed, you will notice the deep indentations in your carpet made by the legs. To fluff it up again, simply hold a coin on its edge and scrape it against the flattened pile. If it still doesn't pop back up, hold a steam iron a couple of inches (5 centimeters) above the affected spot. When the area is damp, try fluffing again with the coin.

Keep cut flowers fresh Your posies and other cut flowers will stay fresh longer if you add a copper penny and a cube of sugar to the vase water.

Instant measure If you need to measure something but you don't have a ruler, just reach into your pocket and pull out a quarter. It measures exactly 1 inch (2.54 centimeters) in diameter. Just line up quarters to measure the length of a small object.

Make a noisemaker Drop a few coins into an empty aluminum soda can, seal the top with duct tape, and head for the stadium to root for your favorite team. Take your noisemaker with you when you walk the dog and use it as a training aid. When the pooch is naughty, just shake the noisemaker.

Decorate a barrette Use shiny pennies to decorate a barrette for a little girl. Gather enough pennies to complete the project (5 pennies for each large barrette; fewer for smaller barrettes). Arrange pennies as you like on the barrette and use hot-melt glue to attach them. Allow 24 hours to dry.

Hang doors perfectly Next time you hang an entry door, nickel-and-dime it to ensure proper clearance between the outside of the door and the inside of the frame. When the door is closed, the gap at the top should be the thickness of a nickel, and the gap at the sides should be that of a dime. If you do it right, you will keep the door from binding and it won't let in drafts.

SCIENCE FAIR

Scientists use **optical illusions** to show how the brain can be tricked. This simple experiment uses **two coins**, but you'll think you are seeing three. Hold two coins on top of each other between your **thumb and index finger**. Quickly slide the coins back and forth and you will see a third coin!

How it works: Scientists say that everything we see is actually light reflected from objects. Our eyes use the light to create images on our retinas, the light-sensitive linings in our eyeballs. Because images don't disappear instantly, when something moves quickly you may see both an object and an afterimage of it at the same time.

Make a paperweight If you have ever traveled abroad, you have probably come home with a few odd-looking coins from foreign lands. Instead of leaving them lying around in a desk drawer, use them to make an interesting paperweight. Just put the coins into a small glass jar with a closable lid and cover the lid with decorative cloth or paper.

DID **You** KNOW?

Coins were first produced around 700 B.C. by Lydians, a people who lived in what is now Turkey. From there, they spread to ancient Greece and Rome. However, worldwide use of coins (and paper money) took centuries to occur. Even in early America, bartering remained the popular way to exchange goods and services. On April 2, 1792, after the ratification of the U.S. Constitution, Congress passed the Mint Act. This established the coinage system in the United States and the dollar as the official U.S. currency. The first U.S. coins were produced by the Philadelphia Mint in 1793.

✳ Colanders

Prevent grease splatters Sick of cleaning grease splatters on the stovetop after cooking your famous burgers? Prevent them by inverting a large metal colander over the frying pan. The holes will let heat escape but the colander will trap the splatters. Be careful! The metal colander will be hot—use an oven mitt to remove it.

Heat a pasta bowl Does your pasta get too cold too fast? To keep it warm longer, heat the bowl first. Place a colander in the bowl, pour the pasta and water into the colander, and let the hot water stand in the bowl for a few seconds to heat it. Pour out the water, add the pasta and sauce, and you're ready to serve.

Keep berries and grapes fresh Do your berries and grapes get moldy before you've had a chance to enjoy their sweet taste? To keep them fresher longer, store them in a colander, not a closed plastic container, in the refrigerator. The cold air will circulate through the holes in the colander, keeping them fresh for days.

Corral bathtub toys Don't let the bathtub look like another messy toy box. After each bath, corral your child's small playthings in a large colander and store it in the tub. The water will drain from the toys, keeping them ready for next time, and the bathtub will stay tidy.

Use as sand toy Forget spending money on expensive sand toys for your budding archeologist. A simple inexpensive plastic colander is perfect for digging at the beach or in the sandbox.

✱ Cold Cream

Erase temporary tattoos Kids love temporary tattoos, but getting them off can be a painful, scrubbing chore. To make removal easier, loosen the tattoo by rubbing cold cream on it and then gently rub it off with a facecloth. Voilà!

Remove bumper stickers Does your bumper sticker still say "Honk for Gore"? Erase the past by rubbing cold cream on the sticker and letting it soak in. Once it does, you should be able to peel it right off.

Make face paint Need a safe, easy recipe for Halloween face paint? Mix 1 teaspoon cornstarch, 1/2 teaspoon water, 1/2 teaspoon cold cream, and 2 drops food coloring (depending on the costume) together. Use a small paintbrush to paint designs on your face or your child's. Remove it with soap and water.

DID *You* KNOW?

Yes, cold cream really is cold. That's because it's made with a lot of water that evaporates and cools your warm face. Cold cream is the granddaddy of all facial ointments. It was invented by the Greek physician Galen in A.D. 157. It's not known exactly why Galen created his mixture, but according to Michael Boylan, a professor at Marymount College in Arlington, Virginia, and an expert on Galen, ancient medicine was based on treating with opposites. And Galen might have been seeking a cure for a hot and dry skin condition like eczema or psoriasis. But the women of ancient Greece soon discovered the soothing white cream was great for taking off makeup, which remains the primary use for cold cream to this day.

✱ Compact Discs

Use as holiday ornaments Decorate your Christmas tree in style! Hang CDs shiny side out to create a flickering array of lights—or paint and decorate the label side to create inexpensive personalized ornaments. For variety, cut the CDs into stars and other shapes with sharp scissors. Drill a 1/4-inch (6-millimeter) hole through the CD and thread ribbon through to hang.

Make wall art in teen's room Old CDs make inexpensive and quirky wall art for your teenager's room. Attach the CDs with thumbtacks and use them to create a border at the ceiling or halfway up the wall. Or let your teen use them to frame his or her favorite posters.

Catch candle drips You should always use a candleholder specifically designed to catch melting wax. However, if one is not available, a CD is great in a pinch. Make sure it's a short candle that can stand on its own with a flat bottom. It should also be slightly larger than the CD hole. Place the candleholder on a stable, heat-resistant surface and keep a watchful eye on it.

Make artistic bowls Looking for a funky, decorative bowl? Place a CD in the oven on low heat over a metal bowl until the CD is soft. Wearing protective gloves, gently bend the CD into the shape desired. Seal the hole by gluing the bottom edge to another surface such as a flat dish using expoxy or PVC glue. Don't use the bowl for food.

Use as sidewalk/driveway reflectors Forget those ugly orange reflectors. Instead, drill small holes in a CD and screw it onto your mailbox post or onto a wood stake and push it into the ground. Install several of them to light a nighttime path to your front door.

Kids' Stuff Use an **old CD** to make a **picture frame** for someone you love. You need a CD, a **picture** of you that is larger than the CD hole, a **large bead, ribbon,** and **glue.** Glue the picture in the middle of the CD on the shiny side. If you wish, decorate the CD with **markers** or **stickers.** Use **hot-melt glue** to attach the bead at the top of the CD, let dry, and thread ribbon through the bead.

Use as template for perfect circle Need to draw a perfect circle? Forget tracing around cups or using cumbersome compasses. Every CD provides two circle sizes— trace around the inner hole or the outer circumference.

Tip **CD Repair**

> Before throwing away or recycling a scratched-up CD, try to repair it. First, clean it thoroughly with a lint-free cloth or mild soap and a little bit of water. Hold the CD by the edge to keep from getting fingerprints on it. Polish it from the middle to the edge, not in a circular motion. If your CD still skips, try fixing it with a little non-gel toothpaste. Dab some toothpaste on the end of your finger and rub it lightly onto the entire CD. Use a damp paper towel to remove the toothpaste and dry it with a fresh paper towel. The fine abrasive in the toothpaste might smooth out the scratch. You might also want to use car wax on a scratch (see page 115).

Make a decorative sun catcher Sun catchers are attractive to watch, and all you need to make one is a couple of CDs. Glue two CDs together, shiny side out, wrap yarn or colored string through the hole, and hang them in a window. The prism will make a beautiful light show.

Create a spinning top Turn an old CD into a fun toy for the kids (and adults too!). With a knife, make two slits across from each other in the CD hole. Force a penny halfway through the hole, and then spin the CD on its edge.

Make a CD clock Old CDs can be functional! Turn a disc into a funky clock face for clockwork sold by arts-and-crafts stores. Paint and design one side of the CD and let it dry. Write or use stickers to create the numbers around its edge. Assemble the clockwork onto the CD.

Cover with felt and use as coasters CDs can help to prevent those unsightly stains from cups left on the table. Simply cut a round piece of felt to fit over the CD and glue it onto the label side of the CD so that the shiny side will face up when you use the coaster.

✳ Cooking Spray

Prevent rice and pasta from sticking Most cooks know that a little cooking oil in the boiling water will keep rice or pasta from sticking together when you drain it. If you run out of cooking oil, however, a spritz of cooking oil spray will do the job just as well.

Grating cheese Put less elbow grease into grating cheese by using a nonstick cooking spray on your cheese grater for smoother grating. The spray also makes for easier and faster cleanup.

Prevent tomato sauce stains Sick of those hard-to-clean tomato sauce stains on your plastic containers? To prevent them, apply a light coating of nonstick cooking spray on the inside of the container before you pour in the tomato sauce.

Keep car wheels clean. You know that fine black stuff that collects on the wheels of your car and is so hard to clean off? That's brake dust—it's produced every time you apply your brakes and the pads wear against the brake disks or cylinders. The

DID You KNOW?

Ever wondered where PAM, the name of the popular cooking spray, comes from? It stands for "Product of Arthur Meyerhoff." The first patent for a nonstick cooking spray was issued in 1957 to Arthur and his partner, Leon Rubin, who began marketing PAM All Natural Cooking Spray in 1959. After appearing on local Chicago TV cooking shows in the early '60s, the product developed a loyal following, and it quickly became a household world. By the way, PAM is pretty durable stuff—it has a shelf life of two years.

next time you invest the elbow grease to get your wheels shiny, give them a light coating of cooking spray. The brake dust will wipe right off.

De-bug your car When those bugs smash into your car at 55 miles (88 kilometers), per hour, they really stick. Give your grille a spritz of nonstick cooking spray so you can just wipe away the insect debris.

Lubricate your bicycle chain Is your bike chain a bit creaky and you don't have any lubricating oil handy? Give it a shot of nonstick cooking spray instead. Don't use too much—the chain shouldn't look wet. Wipe off the excess with a clean rag.

Cure door squeak Heard that door squeak just one time too many? Hit the hinge with some nonstick cooking spray. Have paper towels handy to wipe up the drips.

Remove paint and grease Forget smelly solvents to remove paint and grease from your hands. Instead, use cooking spray to do the job. Work it in well and rinse. Wash again with soap and water.

Dry nail polish Need your nail polish to dry in a hurry? Spray it with a coat of cooking spray and let dry. The spray is also a great moisturizer for your hands.

Quick casting Pack a can of cooking spray when you go fishing. Spray it on your fishing line and the line will cast easier and farther.

Prevent grass from sticking Mowing the lawn should be easy, but cleaning stuck grass from the mower is tedious. Prevent grass from sticking on mower blades and the underside of the housing by spraying them with cooking oil before you begin mowing.

Prevent snow sticks Shoveling snow is hard enough, but it can be more aggravating when the snow sticks to the shovel. Spray the shovel with nonstick cooking spray before shoveling—the snow slides right off! If you use a snow thrower, spray inside the discharge chute to prevent it from clogging.

✳ Corks

Create a fishing bobber It's an idea that's as old as Tom Sawyer, but worth remembering: A cork makes a great substitute fishing bobber. Drive a staple into the top of the cork, then pull the staple out just a bit so you can slide your fishing line through it.

Make an impromptu pincushion Need a painless place to store pins while you sew? Save corks from wine bottles—they make great pincushions!

Prevent pottery scratches Your beautiful pottery can make ugly scratches on furniture. To save your tabletops, cut thin slices of cork and glue them to the bottom of your ceramic objects.

Replace soda bottle caps Lost the cap to your soda bottle and need a replacement? Cork it! Most wine corks fit most soda bottles perfectly.

Make a pour spout Don't have one of those fancy metal pour spouts to control the flow from your oil or vinegar bottle? You don't need one. Make your own spout by cutting out a wedge of the cork along its length. Use a utility or craft knife. Stick the cork in the bottle and pour away. When you're through, cover the hole with a tab of masking tape.

Use as Halloween face paint Kids love to dress up as a hobo for Halloween. To create that scruffy look, char the end of a piece of cork by holding it over a candle. Let it cool a little, then rub it on the kid's face.

Block sun glare In the olden days of football and baseball, players would burn cork and rub it under their eyes to reduce glare from the sun and stadium lights. These days, ballplayers use commercial products to do the same, but you can still use cork to get the job done.

Prevent chair scratches The sound of a chair scraping across your beautiful floor can make your skin crawl. Solve the problem by cutting cork into thin slices and attaching them to the bottom of the chair legs with a spot of wood glue.

Create craft stamps You can use cork to create a personalized stamp. Carve the end of a cork into any shape or design you want. Use it with ink from a stamp pad to decorate note cards. Or let the kids dip carved corks in paint to create artwork.

 DID **You** KNOW?

Cork, the bark of the cork oak, has been used to seal wine bottles and other vessels for more than 400 years. The bark has a unique honeycomb cell structure—each cell is sealed, filled with air, and not connected to any other cell. This makes it waterproof and a poor conductor of heat and vibration. Plus cork contains suberin, a natural waxy substance that makes it impermeable to liquids and gases and prevents the cork from rotting. No wonder it's still the material of choice for sealing up your favorite cabernet or bubbly.

Create a cool bead curtain. Want a creative, stylish beaded curtain for a child's or teen's room? Drill a hole through corks and string them onto a cord along with beads and other decorations. Make as many strings as you need and tie them onto a curtain rod.

Fasten earrings Earring backs always get lost, and you can't always find a perfect-sized stand-in when you need it. Instead, use a snippet of cork as a temporary substitute. Slice a small piece about the size of the backing and push it on. An eraser cut off the end of a pencil will also work.

> **TAKE CARE** Should you use a corkscrew to open a bottle of wine? Yes, but don't use it on a bottle of champagne! Pushing a corkscrew down into a bottle of champagne against the pressure of the carbonation can actually make the bottle explode! If possible, wait a day before opening and let the carbonation settle a bit. Wrap the cork in a towel and twist the bottle, not the cork, slowly.
>
> To open wine, use a traditional corkscrew that twists into the stopper. Peel the top of the plastic to expose the cork. Insert the corkscrew in the center. Twist it straight down and pull the cork straight out with even pressure.

Picture-perfect frames If you're always straightening picture frames on the wall, cut some small flat pieces of cork—all the same thickness—and glue them to the back of the frame. The cork will grip the wall and stop the sliding. It will also prevent the frame from marring the wall.

Mass-produce sowing holes Here's a neat trick for quickly getting your seeds sown in straight rows of evenly spaced holes. Mark out the spacing you need on a board. Drill drywall screws through the holes, using screws that will protrude about 3/4 inch (2 centimeters) through the board. Now twist wine corks onto the screws. Just press the board, corks down, into your garden bed, and voilà—instant seed holes.

✳ Cornstarch

Dry shampoo Fido needs a bath, but you just don't have time. Rub cornstarch into his coat and brush it out. The dry bath will fluff up his coat until it's tub time.

Untangle knots Knots in string or shoelaces can be stubborn to undo, but the solution is easy. Sprinkle the knot with a little cornstarch. It will then be easy to work the segments apart.

Soak up furniture polish residue You've finished polishing your furniture, but there's still a bit left on the surface. Sprinkle cornstarch lightly on furniture after polishing. Wipe up the oil and cornstarch, then buff the surface.

Remove ink stains from carpet Oh no, ink on the carpet! In this case a little spilt milk might save you from crying. Mix the milk with cornstarch to make a paste. Apply the paste to the ink stain. Allow the concoction to dry on the carpet for a few hours, then brush off the dried residue and vacuum it up.

Give carpets a fresh scent Before vacuuming a room, sprinkle a little cornstarch on your carpeting. Wait about half an hour and then vacuum normally.

Make your own paste The next time the kids want to go wild with construction paper and paste, save money by making the paste yourself. Mix 3 teaspoons cornstarch for every 4 teaspoons cold water. Stir until you reach a paste consistency. This is especially great for applying with fingers or a wooden tongue depressor or Popsicle stick. If you add food coloring, the paste can be used for painting objects.

Make finger paints This simple recipe will keep the kids happy for hours. Mix together 1/4 cup cornstarch and 2 cups cold water. Bring to a boil and continue boiling until the mixture becomes thick. Pour your product into several small containers and add food coloring to each container. You've created a collection of homemade finger paints.

Clean stuffed animals To clean a stuffed animal toy, rub a little cornstarch onto the toy, wait about 5 minutes, and then brush it clean. Or place the stuffed animal (or a few small ones) into a bag. Sprinkle cornstarch into the bag, close it tightly, and shake. Now brush the pretend pets clean.

Separate marshmallows Ever buy a bag of marshmallows only to find them stuck together? Here's how to get them apart: Add at least 1 teaspoon cornstarch to

DID *You* KNOW?

Cornstarch has been made into biodegradable packing "peanuts" sold in bulk. If you receive an item shipped in this material, you can toss the peanuts on the lawn. They'll dissolve with water, leaving no toxic waste. To test if the peanuts are made from cornstarch, wet one in the sink to see if it dissolves.

CORNSTARCH*

the bag and shake. The cornstarch will absorb the extra moisture and force most of the marshmallows apart. Repackage the remaining marshmallows in a container and freeze them to avoid sticking in future.

Lift a scorch mark from clothing You moved the iron a little too slowly and now you have a scorch mark on your favorite shirt. Wet the scorched area and cover it with cornstarch. Let the cornstarch dry, then brush it away along with the scorch mark.

Remove grease spatters from walls Even the most careful cook cannot avoid an occasional spatter. A busy kitchen takes some wear and tear but here's a handy remedy for that unsightly grease spot. Sprinkle cornstarch onto a soft cloth. Rub the grease spot gently until it disappears.

Get rid of bloodstains The quicker you act, the better. Whether it's on clothing or table linens, you can remove or reduce a bloodstain with this method. Make a paste of cornstarch mixed with cold water. Cover the spot with the cornstarch paste and rub it gently into the fabric. Now put the cloth in a sunny location to dry. Once dry, brush off the remaining residue. If the stain is not completely gone, repeat the process.

Polish silver Is the sparkle gone from your good silverware? Make a simple paste by mixing cornstarch with water. Use a damp cloth to apply this to your silverware. Let it dry, then rub it off with cheesecloth or another soft cloth to reveal that old shine.

Make windows sparkle Create your own streak-free window cleaning solution by mixing 2 tablespoons cornstarch with 1/2 cup ammonia and 1/2 cup white vinegar in a bucket containing 3-4 quarts (3-4 liters) warm water. Don't be put off by the milky concoction you create. Mix well and put the solution in a trigger spray bottle. Spray on the windows, then wipe with a warm-water rinse. Now rub with a dry paper towel or lint-free cloth. Voilà!

Say good riddance to roaches There's no delicate way to manage this problem. Make a mixture that is 50 percent plaster of Paris and 50 percent cornstarch. Spread this in the crevices where roaches appear. It's a killer recipe.

✳ Correction Fluid

Cover scratches on appliances Daub small nicks on household appliances with correction fluid. Once it dries, cover your repair with clear nail polish for staying power. This works well on white china, too, but only for display. Now that correction fluid comes in a rainbow of colors, its uses go beyond white. You may easily find a match for your beige or yellow household stove or refrigerator.

Touch up a ceiling Hide marks on white or beige ceilings with judiciously applied brush strokes of correction fluid. You can tone down the brightness, if you need to, by buffing the repaired area with a paper towel once it has dried.

Erase scuffs Need a quick fix for scuffed white shoes? Correction fluid will camouflage the offensive marks. On leather, buff gently once the fluid dries. No need to buff on patent leather.

Paint the town Decorate your windows for any occasion. Paint snowflakes, flowers, or Welcome Home signs using correction fluid. Later you can remove your art with nail polish remover, an ammonia solution, vinegar and water, or a commercial window cleaner. Or you can scrape it off with a single-edged razor blade in a holder made for removing paint from glass.

DID *You* KNOW?

Correction fluid was invented in 1951 by Bette Nesmith Graham, mother of Michael Nesmith of the Monkees musical group. Graham was working as an executive secretary in Texas. She used water-based paint and began supplying little bottles of it to other secretaries, calling it Mistake Out. Five years later, she improved the formula and changed the name to Liquid Paper. Despite its proven use, Graham was turned down when she tried to sell it to IBM, so she marketed it on her own. In the 1960s her invention began to generate a tidy profit; by 1979, when she sold the product to the Gillette Corp, she received $47.5 million plus a royalty on every bottle sold until 2000. Today, with the ease of correcting documents on a computer, correction fluid is no longer the office essential it once was.

✳ Cotton Balls

Scent the room Saturate a cotton ball with your favorite cologne and drop it into your vacuum cleaner bag. Now, as you vacuum, the scent will be expressed and gently permeate the room.

Deodorize the refrigerator Sometimes the refrigerator just doesn't smell fresh. Dampen a cotton ball with vanilla extract and place it on a shelf. You'll find it acts as a deodorizer, offering its own pleasant scent.

Fight mildew There are always hard-to-reach spots in the bathroom, usually around the fixtures, where mildew may breed in the grout between tiles. Forget about becoming a contortionist to return the sparkle to those areas. Soak a few cotton balls in bleach and place them in those difficult spots. Leave them to work their magic for a few hours. When you remove them, you'll find your job has been done. Finish by rinsing with a warm-water wash.

Protect little fingers Pad the ends of drawer runners with a cotton ball. This will prevent the drawer from closing completely and keep children from catching their fingers as the drawer slides shut.

Rescue your rubber gloves If your long, manicured nails sometimes puncture the fingertips of your rubber dishwashing gloves, here's a solution you'll appreciate. Push a cotton ball into the fingers of your gloves. The soft barrier should prolong the gloves' life.

✳ Crayons

Use as a floor filler Crayons make great fill material for small gouges or holes in resilient flooring. Get out your crayon box and select a color that most closely matches the floor. Melt the crayon in the microwave over wax paper on medium power, a minute at a time until you have a pliant glob of color. Now, with a plastic knife or putty knife, fill the hole. Smooth it over with a rolling pin, a book, or some other flat object. You'll find the crayon cools down quickly. Now wax the floor, to provide a clear protective coating over your new fill.

Fill furniture scratches Do your pets sometimes treat your furniture like … well, a scratching post? Don't despair. Use a crayon to cover scratches on wooden furniture. Choose the color most like the wood finish. Soften the crayon with a hair dryer or in the microwave on the defrost setting. Color over the scratches, then buff your repair job with a clean rag to restore the luster.

Carpet cover-up Even the most careful among us manage to stain the carpet. If you've tried to remove a stain and nothing works, here's a remedy you might be able

 DID *You* KNOW?

Jazberry Jam and Mango Tango. Those aren't ice-cream flavors, they are recently introduced Crayola crayon colors. When Edwin Binney and C. Harold Smith introduced the first crayons safe for children to use in 1903, a box of eight sold for a nickel and included colors with more pedestrian names: black, brown, blue, red, violet, orange, yellow, and green. Since then, the manufacturer, Binney and Smith, has introduced more than 400 colors, retiring many along the way. Currently there are 120 colors available. Inch Worm and Wild Blue Yonder are other recent introductions.

to live with. Find a crayon that matches or will blend with your carpet. Soften the crayon a bit with a hair dryer or in the microwave on the defrost setting. Now color over the spot. Cover your repair with wax paper and gently iron the color in. Keep the iron on a low setting. Repeat as often as necessary.

Colorful decoration Here's a fun project to do with the kids. Make a multicolored sun catcher by shaving crayons onto a 4- or 5-inch (10- or 12-centimeter) sheet of wax paper. Use a potato peeler or grater for this task. Place another sheet of wax paper over the top and press with a hot iron until the shavings melt together. Poke a hole near the top through the layers of wax and crayon while still warm. Once your ornament cools, peel away the papers and thread a ribbon through it to hang in a window.

❋ Cream of Tartar

Tub scrubber Let this simple solution of cream of tartar and hydrogen peroxide do the hard work of removing a bathtub stain for you. Fill a small, shallow cup or dish with cream of tartar and add hydrogen peroxide drop by drop until you have a thick paste. Apply to the stain and let it dry. When you remove the dried paste, you'll find that the stain is gone too.

Brighten cookware Discolored aluminum pots will sparkle again if you clean them with a mixture of 2 tablespoons cream of tartar dissolved into 1 quart (1 liter) water. Bring the mixture to a boil inside the pot and boil for 10 minutes.

Make play clay for kids Here's a recipe for fun dough that's like the famous commercial stuff: Add together 2 tablespoons cream of tartar, 1 cup salt, 4 cups plain flour (without rising agents), and 1-2 tablespoons cooking oil. Stir well with a wooden spoon to mix together, then slowly stir while adding 4 cups water. Cook the mixture in a saucepan over a medium flame, stirring occasionally until it thickens. It's ready when it forms a ball that is not sticky. Work in food coloring, if you want. Let it cool, then let the kids get creative. It dries out quicker than the commercial variety, so store it in an airtight container in the fridge.

❋ Curtain Rings

Get hooked On a camping trip or a hike, when you don't want to carry a backpack, it's easy to lash a few items to your belt loop with the help of a curtain ring. Mountain climbers rely on expensive carabiners, which they use to hold items and to control ropes. But you don't need to carry along anything so heavy. Attach your sneakers to your sleeping bag with a metal curtain ring; your gloves and canteen can dangle from a metal shower curtain ring or a brass key ring.

Keep curiosity at bay It's a natural stage of development, but not always one you want to encourage. Curious toddlers can't help poking around in your kitchen cupboards. If you've got a toddler visiting, lock up your accessible cupboards by clicking shower curtain rings over the latches. Then when baby leaves, it's easy to remove the rings.

Hold your hammer Sometimes you need three hands when you're doing household repair jobs. Attach a sturdy metal shower curtain ring to your belt and slip your hammer through it. Now you can climb a ladder or otherwise work with both hands and just grab the hammer when needed.

Store nuts and washers Keep nuts and washers on metal shower curtain rings hung from a hook in your workshop. The ring's pear shape and latching action ensure secure storage. Put nuts and washers of similar size on their own rings so that you can find the right size quickly.

Keep track of kids' mittens "Where are my mittens, Ma?" "Where did you leave them?" "I dunno." Something as simple as a curtain ring can help you do away with this dialogue: Drive a nail in the mudroom wall. Hand Junior a curtain ring and tell him to use it to clip his mittens together and hang them on the nail.

✴ Dental Floss

Remove a stuck ring Here's a simple way to slip off a ring that's stuck on your finger. Wrap the length of your finger from the ring to the nail tightly with dental floss. Now you can slide the ring off over the floss "carpet."

Lift cookies off baking tray Ever fought with a freshly baked cookie that wouldn't come off the pan? Crumbled cookies may taste just as good as those in one piece, but they sure don't look as nice on the serving plate. Use dental floss to easily remove cookies from the baking tray. Hold a length of dental floss taut and slide it neatly between the cookie bottom and the pan.

Slice cake and cheese Use dental floss to cut cakes, especially delicate and sticky ones that tend to adhere to a knife. Just hold a length of the floss taut over the cake and then slice away, moving it slightly side to side as you cut through the cake. You can also use dental floss to cut small blocks of cheese cleanly.

Repair outdoor gear Because dental floss is strong and resilient but slender, it's the ideal replacement for thread when you are repairing an umbrella, tent, or backpack. These items take a beating and sometimes get pinhole nicks. Sew up the small holes with floss. To fix larger gouges, sew back and forth over the holes until you have covered the space with a floss patch.

Extra-strong string for hanging things Considering how thin it is, dental floss is strong stuff. Use it instead of string or wire to securely hang pictures, sun catchers, or wind chimes. Use it with a needle to thread together papers you want to attach or those you want to display, in clothesline fashion.

Secure a button permanently Did that button fall off again? This time, sew it back on with dental floss—it's much stronger than thread, which makes it perfect for reinstalling buttons on coats, jackets, and heavy shirts.

Separate photos Sometimes photos get stuck to each other and it seems the only way to separate them is to ruin them. Try working a length of dental floss between the pictures to gently pry them apart.

✳ Denture Tablets

Re-ignite your diamond's sparkle Has your diamond ring lost its sparkle? Drop a denture tablet into a glass containing a cup of water. Follow that with your ring or diamond earrings. Let it sit for a few minutes. Remove your jewelry and rinse to reveal the old sparkle and shine.

Vanish mineral deposits on glass Fresh flowers often leave a ring on your glass vases that seems impossible to remove no matter how hard you scrub. Here's the answer. Fill the vase with water and drop in a denture tablet. When the fizzing has stopped, all of the mineral deposits will be gone. Use the same method to clean thermos bottles, cruets, glasses, and coffee decanters.

Clean a coffeemaker Hard water leaves mineral deposits in the tank of your electric drip coffeemaker that not only slows the perking but also affects the taste of your brew. Denture tablets will fizz away these deposits and give the tank a bacterial clean-out too. The tablets were designed to clean and disinfect dentures, and they'll do the same job on your coffeemaker. Drop two denture tablets in the tank and fill it with water. Run the coffeemaker. Discard that potful of water and follow up with one or two rinse cycles with clean water.

Clean your toilet Looking for a way to make the toilet sparkle again? Porcelain fixtures respond to the cleaning agent in denture tablets. Here's a solution that does the job in the twinkling of an eye. Drop a denture tablet in the bowl. Wait about 20 minutes and flush. That's it!

Clean enamel cookware Stains on enamel cookware are a natural for the denture tablet cleaning solution. Fill the pot or pan with warm water and drop in a tablet or two, depending on its size. Wait a bit—once the fizzing has stopped, your cookware will be clean.

DID **You** KNOW?

Bleaching agents are a common component of denture cleaner tablets, providing the chemical action that helps the tablets to remove plaque and to whiten and bleach away stains. This is what makes them surprisingly useful for cleaning toilets, coffeemakers, jewelry, and enamel cookware, among other things.

Unclog a drain Slow drain got you down? Reach for the denture tablets. Drop a couple of tablets into the drain and run water until the problem clears. For a more stubborn clog, drop 3 tablets down the sink, follow that with 1 cup white vinegar, and wait a few minutes. Now run hot water in the drain until the clog is gone.

✳ Disposable Diapers

Make a heating pad Soothe your aching neck. Or, for that matter, your aching back or shoulder. Use a disposable diaper's high level of absorbency to your advantage by creating a soft, pliant heating pad. Moisten a disposable diaper and place it in the microwave on medium-high setting for about 2 minutes. Check that it's not too hot for comfort and then apply to your achy part.

Keep a plant watered longer Before potting a plant, place a clean disposable diaper in the bottom of the flowerpot—absorbent side up. It will absorb water that would otherwise drain out the bottom and will keep the plant from drying out too fast. You'll also cut back on how often you have to water the plant.

Pad a package You want to mail your friend that lovely piece of china you know she'll love. But you don't have any protective wrapping on hand. If you have disposable diapers, wrap the item in the diapers or insert them as padding before sealing the box. Diapers cost more than regular protective packaging wrap, but at least you will have gotten the package out today, and you can be assured your gift will arrive in one piece.

DID **You** KNOW?

It took a mother to invent disposable diapers. Looking for an alternative to messy cloth diapers, Marion Donovan first created a plastic covering for diapers. She made her prototype from a shower curtain and later parachute fabric. Manufacturers weren't interested, but when she created her own company and debuted the product in 1949 at Saks Fifth Avenue in New York City, it was an instant success. Donovan soon added disposable absorbent material to create the first disposable diaper and, in 1951, sold her company for $1 million.

Duct Tape

* DUCT TAPE **AROUND THE HOUSE**

Temporarily hem your pants You've found a terrific pair of jeans, but the length isn't right. You expect a little shrinkage anyway, so why spend time hemming? Besides, thick denim jeans are difficult to sew through. Fake the hem with duct tape. The new hem will last through a few washes too.

Remove lint on clothing You're all set to go out for the night and suddenly you notice pet hairs on your outfit. Quick, grab the duct tape and in no time, you'll be ready to go. Wrap your hand with a length of duct tape, sticky side out. Then roll the sticky tape against your clothing in a rocking motion until every last hair has been picked up. Don't wipe, since that may affect the nap.

Make a bandage in a pinch You've gotten a bad scrape. Here's how to protect it until you get a proper bandage. Fold tissue paper or paper towel to cover the wound and cover this with duct tape. It may not be attractive, but it works in a jam.

Reseal bags of chips Tired of stale potato chips? To keep a half-finished bag fresh, fold up the top and seal it tight with a piece of duct tape.

Pocket folder protector Old pocket folders may lose their resiliency but are otherwise useful. Cover your old folder with duct tape; reinforce between sections and it's as good as new.

Bumper sticker Got something you want to say? Make your own bumper sticker. Cut a length of duct tape, affix it to your bumper and with a sharp marker, pen your message.

Keep a secret car key You'll never get locked out of your car again if you affix an extra key to the undercarriage with duct tape.

Catch pesky flies You've just checked into a rustic cabin on the lake and you're ready to start your vacation. Everything would be perfect if only the flying insects were not part of the deal. Grab your roll of duct tape and roll off a few foot-long strips. Hang them from the rafters as flypaper. Soon you'll be rid of the bugs and you can roll up the tape to toss it in the trash.

Replace a shower curtain grommet How many times have you yanked the shower curtain aside only to rip through one of the delicate eyelets? Grab the duct tape to make a simple repair. Once the curtain is dry, cut a rectangular piece and fold it from front to back over the torn hole. Slit the tape with a mat knife, razor blade, or scissors, and push the shower curtain ring back in place.

Repair a vacuum hose Has your vacuum hose cracked and developed a leak? It doesn't spell the end of your vacuum. Repair the broken hose with duct tape. Your vacuum will last until the motor gives out.

Reinforce book binding Duct tape is perfect for repairing a broken book binding. Using a nice-colored tape, run the tape down the length of the spine and cut shorter pieces to run perpendicular to that if you need extra reinforcement.

Cover a book Use duct tape in an interesting color to create a durable book cover for a school textbook or a paperback that you carry to the beach. Make a pattern for the cover on a sheet of newspaper; fit the pattern to your book, then cover the pattern, one row at a time, with duct tape, overlapping the rows. The resulting removable cover will be waterproof and sturdy.

Repair a photo frame Many people enjoy displaying family photos in easel-type frames on mantels and side tables throughout the house. But sometimes the foldout leg that holds a frame upright pulls away from the back of the frame and your photo won't stand up properly. Don't despair! Just use duct tape to reattach the broken leg to the frame back.

Hang Christmas lights Festive holiday lights are fun in season, but a real chore when it's time for them to come down. Use duct tape to hang your lights and the removal job will be much easier. Tear duct tape into thin strips. At intervals, wrap strips around the wire and then tape the strand to the gutter or wherever you hang your lights.

Wrap holiday presents Here's a novel way to wrap a special gift. Don't bother with the paper. Go straight for the tape. Press duct tape directly on the gift box. Make designs or cover in stripes and then add decorative touches by cutting shapes, letters, and motifs from tape to attach to the "wrapped" surface.

 DID *You* KNOW?

Duct tape really did start as duck tape. During World War II, the U.S. military needed a flexible, durable, waterproof tape. They called on Permacell, a division of Johnson & Johnson, which used its own medical tape as a base and added a strong polycoat adhesive and a polyethylene coating laminated to a cloth backing. The resulting strong flexible tape—colored army green and easy to rip into useful strips—was used for everything from sealing ammunition cases to repairing jeep windshields. GI's nicknamed it duck tape because it was waterproof, like a duck's back.

After the war, the tape—in a new silvery color—found use joining heating and air conditioning ductwork and became known as duct tape. It's rarely used to join ducts anymore, but it lives on—now in a rainbow of colors—as the handyman's best friend.

Make Halloween costumes Want to be the Tin Man for Halloween? How about a robot? These are just two ideas that work naturally with the classic silver duct tape. Make a basic costume from brown paper grocery bags, with openings in the back so the child can easily put on and take off the costume. Cover this pattern with rows of duct tape. For the legs, cover over an old pair of pants, again giving your little robot or Tin Man an easy way to remove the outfit for bathroom breaks. Duct tape comes in an array of colors, so let your imagination lead your creativity.

Make a toy sword Got a couple of would-be swashbucklers around the house? Make toy swords for the junior Errol Flynns by sketching a kid-size sword on a piece of cardboard. Use two pieces if you haven't got one thick enough. Be sure to make a handle the child's hand can fit around comfortably once it's been increased in thickness by several layers of duct tape. Wrap the entire blade shape in silver duct tape. Wrap the handle in black tape.

Make play rings and bracelets Make rings by tearing duct tape into strips about 1/2-inch (1.2-centimeter) wide, then folding the strips in half lengthwise—sticky sides together. Continue to put more strips over the first one until the ring is thick enough to stand on its own. You can adjust the size with a scissors and tape the ends closed. To make a stone for the ring, cover a small item such as a pebble and attach it to the ring. Make a bracelet by winding duct tape around a stiff paper pattern.

Make hand puppets Duct tape is great for puppet making. Use a small paper lunch bag as the base for the body of your puppet. Cover the bag with overlapping rows of duct tape. Make armholes through which your fingers will poke out. Create a head from a tape-covered ball of wadded paper and affix buttons or beads for eyes and mouth.

Make bicycle streamers Add snazzy streamers to your kids' handlebars. Make them using duct tape in various colors. Cut the tape into strips about 1/2-inch (1.2-centimeter) wide by 10 inches (25 centimeters) long. Fold each strip in half, sticky sides together. Once you have about half a dozen for each side, stick them into the end of the handlebar and secure them with wraps of duct tape. Be sure your child will still have a good grip on the handlebar.

✳ DUCT TAPE **FOR THE DO-IT-YOURSELFER**

Repair a taillight Someone just backed into your car and smashed the taillight! Here's a quick repair that will last until you have time to get to the repair shop.

DUCT TAPE*

Depending on where the cracks lie, use yellow or red duct tape to hold the remaining parts together. In some states this repair will even pass inspection.

Short-term auto hose fix Until you can get to your mechanic, duct tape makes a strong and dependable temporary fix for broken water hoses on your automobile. But don't wait too long. Duct tape can only withstand temperatures up to 200°F (93°C). Also, don't use it to repair a leak in your car's gas line—the gasoline dissolves the adhesive.

Make a temporary roof shingle If you've lost a wooden roof shingle, make a temporary replacement by wrapping duct tape in strips across a piece of 1/4-inch (6-millimeter) plywood you've cut to size. Wedge the makeshift shingle in place to fill the space. It will close the gap and repel water until you can repair the roof.

Fix a hole in your siding Stormy weather damaged your vinyl siding? A broken tree limb tossed by the storm, hailstones, or even an errant baseball can rip your siding. Patch tears in vinyl siding with duct tape. Choose tape in a color that matches your siding and apply it when the surface is dry. Smooth your repair by hand or with a rolling pin. The patch should last at least a season or two.

Replace lawn chair webbing Summertime is here, and you go to the shed to fetch your lawn furniture, only to discover the webbing on your favorite backyard chair has worn through. Don't throw it out. Colorful duct tape makes a great, sturdy replacement webbing. Cut strips twice as long as you need. Double the tape, putting sticky sides together, so that you have backing facing out on both sides. Then screw it in place with the screws on the chair.

Tape a broken window Before removing broken window glass, crisscross the broken pane with duct tape to hold it all together. This will ensure a shard doesn't fall out and cut you.

DID **You** KNOW?

As most Canadians know, the star of *The Red Green Show* on the Canadian Broadcasting Corporation—and the Public Broadcasting System in the United States—has been known to use duct tape for everything from fixing a spare tire to re-webbing a lawn chair. Red's real-life persona, Steve Smith, admits he doesn't use "the handyman's secret weapon" as much as his screen character. "I live in a pretty nice neighborhood, where duct tape is discouraged as a renovation tool," he says. Nevertheless, when he had to prevent his front door from locking, he put a small strip of duct tape across the bolt. He points out that this was the first time he'd used duct tape "to *stop* something from working."

Repair outdoor cushions Don't let a little rip in the cushions for your outdoor furniture bother you. Repair the tear with a closely matched duct tape and it will hold up for several seasons.

Repair a trash can Plastic trash cans often split or crack along the sides. But don't toss out the can with the trash. Repair the tear with duct tape. It's strong enough to withstand the abuses a trash can takes, and easy to manipulate on the curved or ridged surface of your can. Put tape over the crack both outside and inside the can.

Quick fix for a toilet seat You're giving a party and someone taps you on the shoulder to tell you the toilet seat has broken. You don't have to make a mad dash to the home center. Grab the duct tape and carefully wrap the break for a neat repair. Your guests will thank you.

Mend a screen Have the bugs found the tear in your window or door screen? Thwart their entrance until you make a permanent fix by covering the hole with duct tape.

✻ DUCT TAPE **FOR SPORTS AND OUTDOOR GEAR**

Tighten shin guards Hockey players need a little extra protection. Use duct tape to attach shin guards firmly in place. Put on all your equipment, including socks. Now split the duct tape to the width appropriate for your size—children might need narrower strips than adults—and start wrapping around your shin guard to keep it tight to your leg.

Add life to a hockey stick Street hockey sticks take a beating. If yours is showing its age, breathe a little more life into it by wrapping the bottom of the stick with duct tape. Replace the tape as often as needed.

Extend the life of skateboard shoes Kids who perform fantastic feats on their skateboards find their shoes wear out very quickly because a lot of the jumps involve sliding the toe or side of the foot along the board. They wear holes in new shoes fast. Protect their feet and prolong the life of their shoes by putting a layer or two of duct tape on the area that scrapes along the board.

Repair your ski gloves Ski glove seams tearing open? Duct tape is the perfect solution to ripped ski gloves because it's waterproof, incredibly adhesive, strong, and can easily be torn into strips of any width. Make your repair lengthwise or around the fingers and set out on the slopes again.

Repair a tent You open your tent at the campsite and oops—a little tear. No problem as long as you've brought your duct tape along. Cover the hole with a patch; for double protection mirror the patch inside the tent. You'll keep insects and weather where they belong.

Extra insulation Make your winter boots a little bit warmer by taping the insoles with duct tape, silver side up. The shiny tape will reflect the warmth of your feet back into your boots.

Stay afloat You're out for a paddle, when you discover a small hole in your canoe. Thank goodness you thought to pack duct tape in your supply kit. Pull the canoe out of the water, dry the area around the hole, and apply a duct tape patch to the outside of the canoe. You're ready to finish your trip.

Waterproof footwear Need a waterproof pair of shoes for fishing, gardening, or pushing off the canoe into the lake? Cover an old pair of sneakers with duct tape, overlapping the edges of each row. As you round corners, cut little **V**'s in the edges of the tape so that you can lap the tape smoothly around the corner.

Pool patch Duct tape will repair a hole in your swimming pool liner well enough to stand up to water for at least a season. Be sure to cover the area thoroughly.

Protect yourself from ticks When you're out on a hike, on your way to your favorite fishing hole, or just weeding in the yard, protect your ankles from those pesky ticks. Wrap duct tape around your pant cuffs to seal out the bugs. This is a handy way to keep your pant leg out of your bicycle chain too!

Create a clothesline Whether you're out in the wilderness on a camping trip or in your own backyard, when you need a clothesline and you're without rope, think: duct tape. Twist a long piece of duct tape into a rope and bind it between trees for a clothesline. It makes a dandy jump rope as well or a basic rope sturdy enough to lash two items together. You can even use your creation to drag a child's wagon.

DID *You* KNOW?

The folks at 3M's product information lines handle a lot of calls about duct tape. Three of the most commonly asked questions are:

1. Can duct tape be used for removing warts?
2. Can it be used to secure the duct from the household dryer to the outdoors?
3. Is it waterproof?

The official answers:

1. Duct tape is not recommended for removing warts, because it hasn't been scientifically tested.
2. The company does not recommend using duct tape for the dryer duct, because the temperatures may exceed 200°F (93°C), the maximum temperature duct tape can withstand.
3. The backing of the duct tape is waterproof, but the adhesive is not. Duct tape will hold up to water for a while, but eventually the adhesive will give out.

Protect your gas grill hose For some reason, mice and squirrels love to chew on rubber, and one of their favorite snacks is often the rubber hose that connects the propane tank to your gas grill. Protect the hose by wrapping it in duct tape.

Make an emergency sneaker lace You're enjoying a game of driveway hoops when you bust a sneaker lace. Ask for a brief time-out while you grab the duct tape from the garage. Cut off a piece of tape that's as long as you need and rip off twice the width you need. Fold the tape in half along its length, sticky side in. Thread your new lace onto your sneaker, tie it up, and you are ready for your next jump shot.

Repair your ski pants Oh no, you ripped your ski pants and the wind is whipping into the nylon outer layer. No need to pay inflated lodge shop prices for a new pair if you have a roll of duct tape in the car. Just slip a piece of tape inside the rip, sticky side out, and carefully press both sides of the rip together. The repair will be barely detectable.

✳ Dustpans

Decorate your door for fall Gather dried fall foliage, such as Indian corn, bittersweet branches with orange berries, and other decorative greens. Tie them together as a bouquet with a rubber band or tape. Spread them out in a fan shape and cover the binding with a ribbon. Now set this against a copper dustpan. Use super glue or a glue gun to attach your bouquet to the pan. Hang this homage to fall on your front door.

Enlist the littlest shoveler Youngsters enjoy mimicking their elders. While you shovel snow, let the little one help by your side using a dustpan as a shovel.

Use as a sand toy Pack a clean dustpan with your beach toys. It's a great sand scoop and will really help the castle builders in their task.

Speed toy cleanup Picking up all those little toys gets tiresome. Scoop them up with a dustpan and deposit them in the toy bin. It's a real time-saver, not to mention a back-saver.

E

✱ Earrings

Use as a bulletin board tack Lend a little personal style to your bulletin board. Use mateless pierced earrings to tack up pictures, notes, souvenirs, and clippings.

Create a brooch Got a batch of mateless pierced earrings collecting dust in a box? Use wire cutters to snip off the stems and get creative: Arrange the earrings on a swatch of cardboard or foam core, and secure them with hot-melt glue. Add a pin backing and, voilà! a new brooch. Or use the same method to jazz up a plain picture frame.

Make a magnet Give your fridge some glitz. Use wire cutters to cut the stem off an orphan earring and glue it to a magnet. What a great way to emphasize how pleased you are with that perfect report card when you stick it on the refrigerator.

Clip your scarf Did you lose one of your very favorite earrings? Oh well, at least you can still work the survivor into an ensemble by using it to secure a scarf. Just tie the scarf as desired, then clip or pierce it with the earring.

Make an instant button. Oh, darn! You're dressed to go out and you discover a button missing. No need to re-invent your whole outfit. Just dip into your collection of clip-on earrings. Clip the earring on the button side of the clothing to create

?? DID *You* KNOW?

People have been wearing—and probably losing—earrings for nearly 5,000 years. According to historians who have studied jewelry, the tiny baubles were likely introduced in western Asia in about 3000 B.C. The oldest earrings that have been discovered date to 2500 B.C. and were found in Iraq. The popularity of earrings over time has grown or receded, depending on hairstyles and clothing trends. The clip-on earring was introduced in the 1930s, and by the 1950s, fashionable women simply did not pierce their ears. But twenty years later, pierced ears were back.

a new "button," then button as usual with the buttonhole. If you have time, move the top button on that favorite blouse to replace the lost one and then use the earring at the top of the blouse.

Decorate your Christmas tree Scatter clip-on earrings around the boughs of your Christmas tree as an eye-catching accent to your larger tree decorations. Or use them as the main adornment on a small tree or wreath.

✳ Eggs

Make a facial Who has time or money to spend at the local day spa, paying someone to tell you how awful your skin looks? For a little pampering, head to the refrigerator and grab an egg. If you have dry skin that needs moisturizing, separate the egg and beat the yolk. Oily skin takes the egg white, to which a bit of lemon or honey can be added. For normal skin, use the entire egg. Apply the beaten egg, relax and wait 30 minutes, then rinse. You'll love your new fresh face.

Use as glue Out of regular white glue? Egg whites can act as a glue substitute when gluing paper or light cardboard together.

Add to compost Eggshells are a great addition to your compost because they are rich in calcium—a nutrient that helps plants. Crushing them before you put them in your compost heap will help them break down faster.

Water your plants After boiling eggs, don't pour the water down the drain. Instead, let it cool; then water plants with the nutrient-filled water.

Start seeds Plant seeds in eggshells. Place the eggshell halves in the carton, fill each with soil, and press seeds inside. The seeds will draw extra nutrients from the eggshells. Once the seedlings are about 3 inches (7.5 centimeters) tall, they are ready to be transplanted into your garden. Remove them from the shell before you put them in the ground. Then crush the eggshells and put them in your compost or plant them in your garden.

✳ Egg Cartons

Use for storing and organizing With a dozen handy compartments, egg cartons are a natural for storing and organizing small items. Here are some ideas to get you going. You're sure to come up with more of your own.

- Instead of emptying the coins in your pocket into a jar for later sorting, cut off a four-section piece of an egg carton and leave it on your dresser. Sort your quarters, dimes, nickels, and pennies as you pull them out of your pockets. (Dump pennies in a larger container, such as a jar, or put them in a piggy bank.)

- Organize buttons, safety pins, threads, bobbins, and fasteners on your sewing table.

- Organize washers, tacks, small nuts and bolts, and screws on your workbench. Or use to keep disassembled parts in sequence.

- Keep small Christmas ornaments from being crushed in handy, stackable egg cartons.

Start a fire Fill a cardboard egg carton with briquettes (and a bit of leftover candle wax if it's handy), place in your barbecue grill, and light. Egg cartons can also be filled with tinder, such as small bits of wood and paper, and used as a fire starter in a fireplace or a woodstove.

Start seedlings An egg carton can become the perfect nursery for your seeds. Use a cardboard egg carton, not a polystyrene one. Fill each cell in the carton with soil and plant a few seeds in each one. Once the seeds have sprouted, divide the carton into individual cells and plant, cardboard cells and all.

Make ice Making a bunch of ice for a picnic or party? Use the bottom halves of clean polystyrene egg cartons as auxiliary ice trays.

Reinforce a trash bag Yuck! You pull the plastic trash bag out of the kitchen trash container and gunk drips out. Next time, put an opened empty egg carton at the bottom of the trash bag to prevent tears and punctures.

Create shippable homemade goodies Here's a great way to brighten the day of a soldier, student, or any faraway friend or loved one. Cover an egg carton with bright wrapping paper. Line the individual cells with candy wrappers or shredded coconut. Nestle homemade treats inside each. Include the carton in your next care package or birthday gift, and rest assured the treats will arrive intact.

Golf ball caddy An egg carton in your golf bag is a great way to keep golf balls clean and ready for teeing off.

✳ Emery Boards

Sand deep crevices If you are refinishing an elaborate piece of wood such as turned table legs or chair spindles, you can use emery boards to gently smooth those hard-to-reach crevices before applying stain or finish. These filelike nail sanders are easy to handle and provide a choice of two sanding grits.

Remove dirt from an eraser Do you have a fussy student who doesn't like dirt on the end of the pencil? Take an emery board and rub lightly over the eraser until the dirt is filed off.

Prep seeds for planting Use an emery board to remove the hard coating on seeds before you plant them. This will speed sprouting and help them absorb moisture.

Save your suede Did somebody step on your blue suede shoes? Or worse, spill some wine on them? Don't check into Heartbreak Hotel. Rub the stain lightly with an emery board, and then hold the shoe over steam from a teakettle or pan to remove the stain. This works for suede clothing too.

* Envelopes

Shred old receipts faster The best way to get rid of receipts that may have your credit card number or other personal information is to shred them. But feeding tiny receipts into a shredder is tedious. Instead, place all the old receipts into a few old envelopes and shred the envelopes.

Make a small funnel You save money by buying your spices in bulk and you want to transfer them to smaller, handier bottles for use in the kitchen, but you don't have a small funnel to do the job. Make a couple of disposable funnels from an envelope. Seal the envelope, cut it in half diagonally, and snip off one corner on each half. Now you have two funnels for pouring spices into your smaller jars.

Sort and store sandpaper You know how sheets of sandpaper love to curl themselves up into useless tubes? Prevent that problem and keep your sandpaper sheets organized by storing them in standard letter-size cardboard mailing envelopes. Use one envelope for each grit and write the grit on the envelopes.

Make bookmarks Recycle envelopes by making them into handy bookmarks of different sizes. Cut off the gummed flap and one end of the envelope. Then slip the remainder over the corner of the page where you stopped reading for a quick placeholder that doesn't damage your book. Give a batch to the kids to decorate for their own set or to give as a homemade gift.

Make file folders Don't let papers get disorganized just because you ran out of file folders. Cut the short ends off a light cardboard mailing envelope. Turn it inside out so you have a blank cardboard on the outside. Cut a 3/4-inch (2-centimeter) wide strip lengthwise off the top of one side. The other edge becomes the place where you label your file.

✳ Epsom Salt

Get rid of raccoons Are the masked night marauders poking around your trash can, creating a mess and raising a din? A few tablespoons of Epsom salt spread around your garbage cans will deter the raccoons, who don't like the taste of the stuff. Don't forget to reapply after it rains.

Deter slugs Are you tired of visiting your yard at night only to find the place crawling with slimy slugs? Sprinkle Epsom salt where they glide and say good-bye to the slugs.

Fertilize tomatoes and other plants Want those Big Boys to be big? Add Epsom salt as a foolproof fertilizer. Every week, for every foot of height of your tomato plant, add one tablespoon. Your tomatoes will be the envy of the neighborhood. Epsom salt is also a good fertilizer for houseplants, roses and other flowers, and trees.

Make your grass greener How green is your valley? Not green enough, you say? Epsom salt, which adds needed magnesium and iron to your soil, may be the answer. Add 2 tablespoons to 1 gallon (3.7 liters) of water. Spread on your lawn and then water it with plain water to make sure it soaks into the grass.

Clean bathroom tiles Is the tile in your bathroom getting that grungy look? Time to bring in the Epsom salt. Mix it in equal parts with liquid dish detergent, then dab it onto the offending area and start scrubbing. The Epsom salt works with the detergent to scrub and dissolve the grime.

Regenerate a car battery Is your car battery starting to sound as if it won't turn over? Worried that you'll be stuck the next time you try to start your car? Give your battery a little more life with this potion. Dissolve about an ounce of Epsom salt in warm water and add it to each battery cell.

Get rid of blackheads Here's a surefire way to dislodge blackheads: Mix 1 teaspoon Epsom salt and 3 drops iodine in 1/2 cup boiling water. When the mixture cools enough to stick your finger in it, apply it to the blackhead with a cotton ball. Repeat this three or four times, reheating the solution if necessary. Gently remove the blackhead and then dab the area with an alcohol-based astringent.

Frost your windows for Christmas If you are dreaming of a white Christmas, but the weather won't cooperate, at least you can make your windows look frosty. Mix Epsom salt with stale beer until the salt stops dissolving. Apply the mixture to your windows with a sponge—for a realistic look, sweep the sponge in an arc at the bottom corners. When the mixture dries, the windows will look frosted.

Kids' Stuff Here are two fun winter-inspired projects using Epsom salt for the holiday season:

Make snowflakes by folding a piece of **blue paper** several times and snipping shapes into the resulting square of paper. Unfold your snowflake. Brush one side with a thick mixture of **water** and **Epsom salt**. After it dries, turn it over and brush the other side. When it's finished, you'll have a **frosty-looking snowflake** you can hang in your window.

To make a **snowy scene**, use crayons to draw a picture on **construction paper**. Mix equal parts of **Epsom salt** and **boiling water**. Let it cool; then use a wide artist's paintbrush to paint the picture. When it dries, "snow" crystals will appear.

EPSOM SALT*

F

✳ Fabric Softener

End clinging dust on your TV Are you frustrated to see dust fly back onto your television screen, or other plastic surfaces, right after cleaning them? To eliminate the static cling that attracts dust, simply dampen your dust cloth with fabric softener straight from the bottle and dust as usual.

Remove old wallpaper Removing old wallpaper is a snap with fabric softener. Just stir 1 capful liquid softener into 1 quart (1 liter) water and sponge the solution onto the wallpaper. Let it soak in for 20 minutes, then scrape the paper from the wall. If the wallpaper has a water-resistant coating, score it with a wire-bristle brush before treating with the fabric softener solution.

Abolish carpet shock To eliminate static shock when you walk across your carpet, spray the carpet with a fabric softener solution. Dilute 1 cup softener with 2 1/2 quarts (2.5 liters) water; fill a spray bottle and lightly spritz the carpet. Take care not to saturate it and damage the carpet backing. Spray in the evening and let the carpet dry overnight before walking on it. The effect should last for several weeks.

Remove hair-spray residue Dried-on overspray from hair spray can be tough to remove from walls and vanities, but even a buildup of residue is no match for a solu-

DID **You** KNOW?

How does fabric softener reduce cling as well as soften clothes? The secret is in the electrical charges. Positively charged chemical lubricants in the fabric softener are attracted to your load of negatively charged clothes, softening the fabric. The softened fabrics create less friction, and less static, as they rub against each other in the dryer, and because fabric softener attracts moisture, the slightly damp surface of the fabrics makes them electrical conductors. As a result, the electrical charges travel through them instead of staying on the surface to cause static cling and sparks as you pull the clothing from the dryer.

tion of 1 part liquid fabric softener to 2 parts water. Stir to blend, pour into a spray bottle, spritz the surface, and polish it with a dry cloth.

Clean now, not later Clean glass tables, shower doors, and other hard surfaces, and repel dust with liquid fabric softener. Mix 1 part softener into 4 parts water and store in a squirt bottle, such as an empty dishwashing liquid bottle. Apply a little solution to a clean cloth, wipe the surface, and then polish with a dry cloth.

Float away baked-on grime Forget scrubbing. Instead, soak burned-on foods from casseroles with liquid fabric softener. Fill the casserole with water, add a squirt of liquid fabric softener, and soak for an hour, or until residue wipes easily away.

Keep paintbrushes pliable After using a paintbrush, clean the bristles thoroughly and rinse them in a coffee can full of water with a drop of liquid fabric softener mixed in. After rinsing, wipe the bristles dry and store the brush as usual.

Untangle and condition hair Liquid fabric softener diluted in water and applied after shampooing can untangle and condition fine, flyaway hair, as well as curly, coarse hair. Experiment with the amount of conditioner to match it to the texture of your hair, using a weaker solution for fine hair and a stronger solution for coarse, curly hair. Comb through your hair and rinse.

Remove hard-water stains Hard-water stains on windows can be difficult to remove. To speed up the process, dab full-strength liquid fabric softener onto the stains and let it soak for 10 minutes. Then wipe the softener and stain off the glass with a damp cloth and rinse.

Make your own fabric softener sheets Fabric softener sheets are convenient to use, but they're no bargain when compared to the price of liquid softeners. You can make your own dryer sheets and save money. Just moisten an old washcloth with 1 teaspoon liquid softener and toss it into the dryer with your next load.

✳ Fabric Softener Sheets

Pick up pet hair Pet hair can get a pretty tenacious grip on furniture and clothing. But a used fabric softener sheet will suck that fur right off the fabric with a couple of swipes. Just toss the fuzzy wipe into the trash.

End car odors Has that new-car smell gradually turned into that old-car stench? Tuck a new dryer fabric softener sheet under each car seat to counteract musty odors and cigarette smells.

Lift burned-on casserole residue Those sheets will soften more than fabric. The next time food gets burned onto your casserole dish, save the elbow grease. Instead fill the dish with hot water and toss in three or four used softener sheets. Soak overnight, remove the sheets, and you'll have no trouble washing away the residue. Be sure to rinse well.

Freshen drawers There's no need to buy scented drawer-liner paper; give your dresser drawers a fresh-air fragrance by tucking a new dryer fabric softener sheet under existing drawer liners, or tape one to the back of each drawer.

Wipe soap scum from shower door Tired of scrubbing scummy shower doors? It's easy to wipe the soap scum away with a used dryer fabric softener sheet.

> **TAKE CARE** People with allergies or chemical sensitivities may develop rashes or skin irritations when they come into contact with laundry treated with some commercial fabric softeners or fabric softener sheets. If you are sensitive to softeners, you can still soften your laundry by substituting 1/4 cup white vinegar or the same amount of your favorite hair conditioner to your washer's last rinse cycle for softer, fresher-smelling washables.

Repel dust from electrical appliances Because television and PC screens are electrically charged, they actually attract dust, making dusting them a never-ending chore, but not if you dust them with used dryer softener sheets. These sheets are designed to reduce static cling, so they remove the dust, and keep it from resettling for several days or more.

Do away with doggy odor If your best friend comes in from the rain and smells like a … well … wet dog, wipe him down with a used dryer softener sheet, and he'll smell as fresh as a daisy.

Freshen laundry hampers and wastebaskets There's still plenty of life left in used dryer fabric softener sheets. Toss one into the bottom of a laundry hamper or wastebasket to counteract odors.

Tame locker-room and sneaker smells Deodorizing sneakers and gym bags calls for strong stuff. Tuck a new dryer fabric softener sheet into each sneaker and leave overnight to neutralize odors (just remember to pull them out before wearing the sneaks). Drop a dryer sheet into the bottom of a gym bag and leave it there until your nose lets you know it's time to renew it.

Prevent musty odors in suitcases Place a single, unused dryer fabric softener sheet into an empty suitcase or other piece of luggage before storing. The bag will smell great the next time you use it.

Buff chrome to a brilliant shine After chrome is cleaned, it can still look streaky and dull, but whether it's your toaster or your hubcaps, you can easily buff up the shine with a used dryer softener sheet.

Use as a safe mosquito repellent For a safe mosquito repellent, look no farther than your laundry room. Save used dryer fabric softener sheets and pin or tie one to your clothing when you go outdoors to help repel mosquitoes.

Use an inconspicuous air freshener Don't spend hard-earned money on those plug-in air fresheners. Just tuck a few sheets of dryer fabric softener into closets, behind curtains, and under chairs.

Do away with static cling You'll never be embarrassed by static cling again if you keep a used fabric softener sheet in your purse or dresser drawer. When faced with static, dampen the sheet and rub it over your pantyhose to put an end to clinging skirts.

Keep dust off blinds Cleaning venetian blinds is a tedious chore, so make the results last by wiping them down with a used dryer fabric softener sheet to repel dust. Wipe them with another sheet whenever the effect wears off.

Renew grubby stuffed toys Wash fake-fur stuffed animals in the washing machine set on gentle cycle, then put the stuffed animals into the clothes dryer along with a pair of old tennis shoes and a fabric softener sheet, and they will come out fluffy and with silky-soft fur.

Substitute a dryer sheet for a tack cloth Sticky tack cloths are designed to pick up all traces of sawdust on a woodworking project before you paint or varnish it, but they are expensive and not always easy to find at the hardware store. If you find yourself in the middle of a project without a tack cloth, substitute an unused dryer fabric softener sheet; it will attract sawdust and hold it like a magnet.

Consolidate sheets and make them smell pretty To improve sheet storage, store the sheet set in one of the matching pillowcases, and tuck a new dryer fabric softener sheet into the packet for a fresh fragrance.

Abolish tangled sewing thread To put an end to tangled thread, keep an unused dryer fabric softener sheet in your sewing kit. After threading the needle, insert it into the sheet and pull all of the thread through to give it a nonstick coating.

✳ Film Canisters

Rattle toy for the cat Cats are amused by small objects that rattle and shake, and they really don't care what they look like. To provide endless entertainment for your cat, drop a few dried beans, a spoonful of dry rice, or other small objects that can't harm a cat, into an empty film canister, snap on the lid, and watch the fun begin.

Handy stamp dispenser To keep a roll of stamps from being damaged, make a stamp dispenser from an empty film canister. Hold the canister steady by taping it to a counter with duct tape, and use a utility knife to carefully cut a slit into the side of the canister. Drop the roll of stamps in, feed it out through the slit, snap the cap on, and it's ready to use.

Use as hair rollers You can collect all the hair rollers you'll ever need if you save your empty plastic film canisters. To use, pop the top off, roll damp hair around the canister, and hold it in place by fastening a hair clip over the open end of the canister and your hair.

Emergency sewing kit You'll never be at a loss if you pop a button or your hem unravels if you fill an empty film canister with buttons, pins, and a pre-threaded needle. Make several; tuck one into each travel bag, purse, or gym bag, and hit the road.

On-the-road pill dispensers Use empty film canisters as travel-size pill bottles for your purse or overnight bag. If you take more than one medication, use a separate canister for each. Write the medication and dosage on a peel-and-stick label and attach to each canister. For at-a-glance identification, color the labels with different-colored highlighter pens.

Tip The Vanishing Film Canister

Plastic film canisters have myriad uses, from emergency ashtrays to spice bottles. But with the rise of digital cameras, these small wonders are rapidly going the way of the rotary dial phone or the phonograph needle. A good source for free film canisters has always been the neighborhood one-hour photo shop. But these days you may find that even they have a canister shortage. If so, check the yellow pages for a professional film developer, because most high-quality, professional photographers still use film—and film canisters.

Store fishing flies You can save a lot of money and grief by storing fishing flies and hooks in film canisters. They don't take up much room in a fishing vest, and if you do drop one in a stream, the airtight lid will keep it floating long enough for you to … well … fish it out.

Carry spices for camp cooking Just because you are roughing it, doesn't mean that you have to eat bland food. You can store a multitude of seasonings in individual film canisters to take along when you go camping, and you'll still have plenty of room for the food itself in your backpack or car trunk. It's a good idea for your RV or vacation cabin too.

Carry small change for laundry and tolls Film canisters are just the right size to hold quarters and smaller change. Tuck a canister of change into your laundry bag or your car's glove compartment, and you'll never have to hunt for change when you're at a self-service laundry or a tollbooth.

Bring your own diet aids If you are on a special diet, you can easily and discreetly transport your favorite salad dressings, artificial sweetener, or other condiments to restaurants in plastic film canisters. Clean, empty canisters hold single-sized servings, have snap-on, leakproof lids, and are small enough to tuck into a purse.

Keep jewelry close at hand An empty film canister doesn't take up much room in your gym bag, and it'll come in handy for keeping your rings and earrings from being misplaced while you work out.

Emergency nail polish remover Create a small, spillproof carry case for nail polish remover by tucking a small piece of sponge into a plastic film canister. Saturate the sponge with polish remover and snap on the lid. For an emergency repair, simply insert a finger and rub the nail against the fluid-soaked sponge to remove the polish.

✳ Flour

Repel ants with flour Sprinkle a line of flour along the backs of pantry shelves and wherever you see ants entering the house. Repelled by the flour, ants won't cross over the line.

Freshen playing cards After a few games, cards can accumulate a patina of snack residue and hand oil, but you can restore them with some all-purpose flour in a paper bag. Drop the cards into the bag with enough flour to cover, shake vigorously, and remove the cards. The flour will absorb the oils, and it can be easily knocked off the cards by giving them a vigorous shuffle.

 DID *You* KNOW?

Ever wondered why the word *flour* is pronounced exactly like the word *flower?* Well, you may be surprised to learn that *flour* is actually derived from the French word for flower, which is *fleur.* The French use the word to describe the most desirable, or floury (flowery) and protein-rich, part of a grain after processing removes the hull. And, because much of our food terminology comes from the French, we still bake and make sauces with the flower of grains, such as wheat, which we call flour.

Safe paste for children's crafts Look no farther than your kitchen canister for an inexpensive, nontoxic paste that is ideal for children's paper craft projects, such as papier-mâché and scrap-booking. To make the paste, add 3 cups cold water to a saucepan and blend in 1 cup all-purpose flour. Stirring constantly, bring the mixture to a boil. Reduce heat and simmer, stirring until smooth and thick. Cool and pour into a plastic squeeze bottle to use. This simple paste will keep for weeks in the refrigerator, and cleans up easily with soap and water.

Make modeling clay Keep the kids busy on a rainy day with modeling clay—they can even help you make the stuff. Knead together 3 cups all-purpose flour, 1/4 cup salt, 1 cup water, 1 tablespoon vegetable oil, and 1 or 2 drops food coloring. If the mixture is sticky, add more flour; if it's too stiff, add more water. When the "clay" is a workable consistency, store it until needed in a self-sealing plastic bag.

Polish brass and copper No need to go out and buy cleaner for your brass and silver. You can whip up your own at much less cost. Just combine equal parts of flour, salt, and vinegar, and mix into a paste. Spread the paste onto the metal, let it dry, and buff it off with a clean, dry cloth.

Bring back luster to a dull sink To buff your stainless steel sink back to a warm glow, sprinkle flour over it and rub lightly with a soft, dry cloth. Then rinse the sink to restore its shine.

✳ Flowerpots

Container for baking bread Want to give the staff of life an interesting shape? Take a new, clean medium-sized clay flowerpot, soak it in water for about 20 minutes, and then lightly grease the inside with butter. Place your bread dough,

DID *You* KNOW?

For thousands of years people have been plopping plants into pots to transport a native plant to a new land or to bring an exotic plant home. In 1495 B.C., Egyptian queen Hatshepsut sent workers to Somalia to bring back incense trees in pots. And in 1787 Captain Bligh reportedly had more than 1,000 breadfruit plants in clay pots aboard the H.M.S. *Bounty*. The plants were destined for the West Indies, where they were to be grown as food for the slaves.

prepared as usual, in the pot and bake. The clay pot will give your bread a crusty outside and keep the inside moist.

Create a firewood container Who needs an expensive metal or brass rack to hold firewood by the fireplace? Spare yourself the expense and put an extra-large empty ceramic or clay flowerpot beside the hearth. It's a perfect—and cheap—place to keep kindling and small logs ready for when the weather outside gets frightful.

Unfurl yarn knot-free That sweater you're knitting will take forever if you're constantly stopping to pull out tangles in the yarn. To prevent this, place your ball of yarn under an upturned flowerpot and thread the end through the drain hole. Set it next to where you are sitting for more pleasurable purling.

Create an aquarium fish cave Some fish love to lurk in shadowy corners of their home aquariums, keeping themselves safe from imagined predators. Place a mini flowerpot on its side on the aquarium floor to create a cave for spelunking fish.

Kill fire ants If fire ants plague your yard or patio and you're tired of getting stung by the tiny attackers, a flowerpot can help you quench the problem. Place the flowerpot upside down over the anthill. Pour boiling water through the drain hole and you'll be burning down their house.

Help container plant roots The plants that you want to put in that beautiful new deep container you ordered for your patio have a shallow root system, and you don't want to go to the bother—and expense—of filling that huge container completely with potting soil. What do you do? When planting shallow-rooted plants in a deep container, one easy solution is to find another smaller flowerpot that will fit upside down in the base of the deeper pot and occupy a lot of that space. After you insert it, fill around it with soil before putting in your plants.

Keep soil in your flowerpot Soil from your houseplant won't slip-slide away if you place broken clay flowerpot shards in the bottom of the pot before re-planting. When watering your plants, you'll find that the water drains out, but not the soil.

✱ Foam Food Trays

Make knee pads for gardening If you find gardening is a pain in the knees when you tend your little patch of green, tape foam food trays to your knees. Or attach them to your legs using the top halves of old tube socks. The trays give you extra padding while you pull out weeds and fertilize your plants.

Release your innersoles If your tired old dogs need a little padding, grab a couple of clean meat trays and cut them to fit inside the sole of your shoes or boots. You'll have happy feet and some extra cushioning for free.

Produce a disposable serving dish If you need a quick disposable serving platter while you're on a cookout or camping trip, you can make one from a foam food tray. Wash it with soap and water, cover it entirely with foil, and load it up with food. Use these serving dishes to bring goodies to the church potluck, local bake sale, or sick neighbor. No worries about losing your own platters.

Provide an art palette Create a paint palette for your budding Picasso. A thoroughly cleaned and dried food tray is the perfect place for kids to squirt their tempera or oil paints. Are they experimenting with watercolors? Use two trays: Put watercolor paint in one and water in the other. At the end of the art session, you can just throw them away.

Protect pictures in the mail Why buy expensive padded envelopes to send photographs to loved ones? Cut foam trays slightly smaller than your mailing envelope. Insert your photographs between the trays, place in the envelope, and mail. The photos will arrive without creases or bends.

✳ Freezer

Eliminate unpopped popcorn Don't you just hate the kernels of popcorn that are left at the bottom of the bowl? Eliminate the popcorn duds by keeping your unpopped supply in the freezer.

Remove wax from candlesticks Grandma's heirloom silver candlesticks will get a new life if you place them in the freezer and then pick off the accumulated wax drippings. But don't do this if your candlesticks are made from more than one type of metal. The metals can expand and contract at different rates and damage the candlesticks.

Extend candle life Place candles in the freezer for at least two hours before burning. They will last longer.

Unstick photos Picture this: Water spills on a batch of photographs, causing them to stick together. If you pull them apart, your pictures will be ruined. Don't be so hasty. Stick them in the freezer for about 20 minutes. Then use a butter knife to gingerly separate the photos. If they don't come free, place them back in the freezer. This works for envelopes and stamps too.

Clean a pot Your favorite pot has been left on the stove too long, and now you've got a burned-on mess to clean up. Place the pot in the freezer for a couple of hours. When the burned food becomes frozen, it will be easier to remove.

Tip **Freezer Tactics**

Here are some ways to get the most out of your freezer or your refrigerator's freezer compartment:

● To prevent spoilage, keep your freezer at 0°F (-18°C). To check the temperature, stick a freezer thermometer (sold at hardware stores) between two frozen food containers.

● A full freezer runs the compressor less often and stays colder longer. Good to remember the next time there's a blackout.

● The shelves on a freezer door are a little warmer than the freezer interior, making them ideal for storing items such as bread and coffee.

● When defrosting your freezer, place a large towel or sheet on the bottom. Water drips onto it, making cleanup much easier.

● The next time you defrost your freezer, apply a thin coat of petroleum jelly to the walls to keep frost from sticking.

Remove odors Got a musty-smelling book or a plastic container with a fish odor? Place them in the freezer overnight. By morning they'll be fresh again. This works with almost any other small item that has a bad smell you want to get rid of.

✱ Funnels

Make a string dispenser Don't get yourself tied up in knots over tangled string. Nail a large funnel to the wall, with the stem pointing down. Place a ball of string in the funnel and thread the end through the funnel's stem. You have an instant knot-free string dispenser.

Separate eggs Want an egg-ceptional egg separator? Try a funnel. Simply crack the egg into the funnel. The white will slide out the spout into another container, while the yolk stays put. Of course, you have to be careful not to break the yolk when you're cracking the egg.

Make a kids' telephone Just because you choke every time you open your phone bill doesn't mean the kids have to, too. Use two small plastic funnels to make them a durable string telephone. For each funnel, tie a button to one end of a length of kite string and thread it through the large end of the funnel. Tie another button at the bottom of the spout to keep the string in place and let the kids start yakking.

✳ Garden Hose

Snake decoy to scare birds If flocks of annoying, messy birds are invading your yard, try replicating their natural predator to keep them away. Cut a short length of hose, lay it in your grass—poised like a snake—and the birds will steer clear.

Stabilize a tree A short length of old garden hose is a good way to tie a young tree to its stake. You'll find that the hose is flexible enough to bend when the tree does, but at the same time, it's strong enough to keep the tree tied to its stake until it can stand on its own. Also, the hose will not damage the bark of the young tree as it grows.

Capture earwigs Pesky garden earwigs will find their final resting place in that leaky old hose. Cut the hose into 12-inch (30-centimeter) lengths, making sure the inside is completely dry. Place the hose segments where you have seen earwigs crawling around and leave them overnight. By the morning the hoses should be filled with the earwigs and ready for disposal. One method is to dunk the hoses in a bucket of kerosene.

Tip **Buying a Hose**

> It's just a garden-variety hose, right? Actually, there are a few important points to keep in mind when you buy this important outdoor tool:
> ● To determine how long a hose you need, measure the distance from the faucet to the farthest point in your yard. Add several feet to allow for watering around corners; this will help you avoid annoying kinks that cut water pressure.
> ● Vinyl and rubber hoses are generally more sturdy and weather resistant than ones made of cheaper forms of plastic. If a hose flattens when you step on it, it is not up to gardening duties.
> ● Buy a hose with a lifetime warranty; only good-quality hoses have one.

Unclog a downspout When leaves and debris clog up your rainspout and gutters, turn to your garden hose to get things flowing again. Push the hose up the spout and poke through the blockage. You don't even have to turn the hose on, because the water in the gutters will flush out the dam.

Cover swing set chains No parent wants to see his or her child hurt on the backyard swing set. Put a length of old hose over each chain to protect little hands from getting pinched or twisted. If you have access to one end of the chains, just slip the chain through the hose. Otherwise, slit the hose down the middle, and slip it over the swing set chains. Close the slit hose with a few wraps of duct tape.

Make a play phone Transform your old garden hose into a fun new telephone for the kids. Cut any length of hose you desire. Stick a funnel at each end and attach it with glue or tape. Now the kids can talk for as long as they want, with no roaming charges.

Protect your handsaw and ice skate blades Keep your handsaw blade sharp and safe by protecting it with a length of garden hose. Just cut a piece of hose to the length you need, slit it along its length, and slip it over the teeth. This is a good way to protect the blades of your ice skates on the way to the rink and your cooking knives when you pack them for a camping trip.

Make a paint can grip You don't want that heavy paint can to slip and spill. Plus those thin wire handles can really cut into your hand. Get a better grip by cutting a short length of hose. Slit it down the middle and encase the paint can handle.

Make a sander for curves If you've got a tight concave surface to sand—a piece of cove molding, for example—grab a 10-inch (25-centimeter) length of garden hose. Split open the hose lengthwise and insert one edge of the sandpaper. Wrap it around the hose, cut it to fit, and insert the other end in the slit. Firmly close the slit with a bit of duct tape. Get stroking!

✳ Gloves

Grip a stubborn jar lid It's a jarring experience when you can't open a jar of peanut butter or olives. If the lid just won't come loose, don some rubber gloves. You'll get a better grip to unscrew the top.

Make an ice pack If you need an ice pack in a hurry, fill a kitchen rubber glove with ice. Close the wrist with a rubber band to contain water from the melting ice. When you're done, turn the glove inside out to dry.

Paper-sorting finger Don't fancy licking your finger when you riffle through a stack of papers or dollar bills? Cut off the index finger piece from an old rubber glove and you have an ideal sheath for your finger the next time you have to quickly sort through some papers.

Make strong rubber bands If you need some extra-strong rubber bands, cut up old rubber gloves. Make horizontal cuts in the finger sections for small rubber bands and in the body of the glove for large ones.

Latex surgical gloves for extra insulation You've got a good pair of gloves or mittens, but your hands still get cold while shoveling the snow or doing other outdoor activities. Try slipping on a pair of latex surgical gloves underneath your usual mittens or gloves. The rubber is a super insulator, so your hands will stay toasty, and dry too.

Clean your knickknacks Need to dust that collection of glass animals or other delicate items? Put on some fabric gloves—the softer the better—to clean your bric-a-brac thoroughly.

Dust a chandelier If your chandelier has become a haven for spiderwebs and dust, try this surefire dusting tip. Soak some old fabric gloves in window cleaner. Slip them on and wipe off the lighting fixture. You'll beam at the gleaming results.

Remove cat hair Here's a quick and easy way to remove cat hair from upholstery: Put on a rubber glove and wet it. When you rub it against fabric, the cat hair will stick to the glove. If you are worried about getting the upholstery slightly damp, test it in an inconspicuous area first.

✳ Glycerin

Make your own soap Homemade soap is a great gift and snap to make if you have glycerin and a microwave. Here's how: Cut the glycerin material, usually sold in blocks, into 2-inch (5-centimeter) cubes. Using a microwave set at half-power, zap several cubes in a glass container for 30 seconds at a time—checking and stirring as needed—until the glycerin melts. Add drops of color dye or scents at this point,

DID **You** KNOW?

Glycerin is a clear, colorless thick paste that is a by-product of the soap-making process, in which lye is combined with animal or vegetable fat. Commercial soap makers remove the glycerin when they make soap so that they can use it in more profitable lotions and creams. Glycerin works well in lotions because it is essentially a moisturizing material that dissolves in alcohol or water. Glycerin is also used to make nitroglycerin and candy and to preserve fruit and laboratory specimens. Look for glycerin in the hand lotion aisle of your local drugstore or at a craft store that carries soap-making products.

if you wish. Pour the melted glycerin into soap or candy molds. If you don't have any molds, fill the bottom 3/4 inch (2 centimeters) of a polystyrene cup. Let harden for 30 minutes.

Clean a freezer spill Spilled sticky foods that are frozen to the bottom of your freezer don't have a chance against glycerin. Unstick the spill and wipe it clean with a rag dabbed with glycerin, a natural solvent.

Remove tar stains Do you think it's impossible to remove a tar or mustard stain? It's not, if you use glycerin. Rub glycerin into the spot and leave it for about an hour. Then, with paper towels, gently remove the spot using a blot-and-lift motion. You may need to do this several times.

Make new liquid soap Wondering what to do with those little leftover slivers of soap? Add a bit of glycerin and crush them together with some warm water. Pour the mixture into a pump bottle. You'll have liquid soap on the cheap.

✱ Golf Gear

Make a golf-tee tie rack If your ties are scattered about the closet or your room, try using golf tees to get them organized. Sand and paint a length of pine board. Drill 1/8-inch (3-millimeter) holes every 2 inches (5 centimeters). Dip the tip of each tee in yellow carpenter's glue and tap it into a hole. Hang the tie rack on the closet wall or inside the door. A perfect gift for the golfer in your life.

Aerate your lawn Kill two birds with one stone by wearing your golf shoes to aerate your lawn the next time you mow. The grip that a golf shoe gives you is also a good idea if you have to push the mower up a hill.

Fill stripped screw holes You're replacing a rusty door hinge when you discover that a screw won't grip because its hole has gotten too big. The fix is easy. Dip the tip of a golf tee in yellow carpenter's glue and tap the tee into the hole. Cut the tee flush with the door frame surface with a utility knife. When the glue dries, you can drill a new pilot hole for the screw in the same spot.

✳ Hair Conditioner

Take off makeup Put your face first. Why buy expensive makeup removers when a perfectly good substitute sits in your shower stall? Hair conditioner quickly and easily removes makeup for much less money than name-brand makeup removers.

Unstick a ring Grandma's antique ring just got stuck on your middle finger. Now what? Grab a bottle of hair conditioner and slick down the finger. The ring should slide right off.

Protect your shoes in foul weather Here's a way to keep salt and chemicals off your shoes during the winter: Lather your shoes or boots with hair conditioner to protect them from winter's harsh elements. It's a good leather conditioner too.

Lubricate a zipper You're racing out the door, throwing on your jacket, and dang! Your zipper's stuck, so you yank and pull until it finally zips up. A dab of hair conditioner rubbed along the zipper teeth can help you avoid this bother next time.

Smooth shave-irritated legs After you shave your legs, they may feel rough and irritated. Rub on hair conditioner; it acts like a lotion and can soothe the hurt away.

 DID *You* KNOW?

Hair conditioner has been around for about 50 years. While researching ways to help World War II burn victims, Swiss chemists developed a compound that improved the health of hair. In the 1950s other scientists developing fabric softeners found that the same material could soften hair.

Despite our efforts to keep hair healthy with hair conditioner, we still lose on average between 50 and 100 strands a day. For most of us, thankfully, there are still many more strands left: People with blond hair have an average of 140,000 strands of hair, brown-haired people, 100,000, and redheads, 90,000.

Smooth-sliding shower curtain Tired of yanking on the shower curtain? Instead of closing smoothly, does it stutter along the curtain rod, letting the shower spray water onto the floor? Rub the rod with hair conditioner, and the curtain will glide across it.

Prevent rust on tools Every good do-it-yourselfer knows how important it is to take care of the tools in your toolbox. One way to condition them and keep rust from invading is to rub them down with hair conditioner.

Clean and shine your houseplants Do your houseplants need a good dusting? Feel like your peace lily could use a makeover? Put a bit of hair conditioner on a soft cloth and rub the plant leaves to remove dust and shine the leaves.

Oil skate wheels Do your child's skateboard wheels whine? Or are the kids complaining about their in-line and roller skates sticking? Try this trick: Rub hair conditioner on the axles of the wheels, and they'll be down the block with their rehabilitated equipment in no time.

Shine stainless steel Forget expensive stainless steel polishers. Apply hair conditioner to your faucets, golf clubs, chrome fixtures, or anything else that needs a shine. Rub it off with a soft cloth, and you'll be impressed with the gleam.

Clean silk garments Do you dare to ignore that "dry clean only" label in your silk shirt? Here's a low-cost alternative to sending it out. Fill the sink with water (warm water for whites and cold water for colors). Add a tablespoon of hair conditioner. Immerse the shirt in the water and let it sit for a few minutes. Then pull it out, rinse, and hang it up to dry. The conditioner keeps the shirt feeling silky smooth.

✳ Hair Spray

Exterminate houseflies An annoying, buzzing housefly has been bobbing and weaving around your house for two days. Make it bite the dust with a squirt of hair spray. Take aim and fire. Watch the fly drop. But make sure the hair spray is water-soluble so that, if any spray hits the walls, you'll be able to wipe it clean. Works on wasps and bees too.

Reduce runs in pantyhose Often those bothersome runs in your pantyhose or stockings start at the toes. Head off a running disaster by spraying hair spray on the toes of a new pair of pantyhose. The spray strengthens the threads and makes them last longer.

Remove lipstick from fabric Has someone been kissing your shirts? Apply hair spray to the lipstick stain and let it sit for a few minutes. Wipe off the hair spray and the stain should come off with it. Then wash your shirts as usual.

Preserve a Christmas wreath When you buy a wreath at your local Christmas tree lot, it's fresh, green, and lush. By the time a week has gone by, it's starting to shed needles and look a little dry. To make the wreath last longer, grab your can of hair spray and spritz it all over as soon as you get the fresh wreath home. The hair spray traps the moisture in the needles.

Protect children's artwork Picture this: Your preschooler has just returned home with a priceless work of art demanding that it find a place on the refrigerator door. Before you stick it up, preserve the creation with hair spray, to help it last longer. This works especially well on chalk pictures, keeping them from being smudged so easily.

Preserve your shoes' shine After you've lovingly polished your shoes to give them the just-from-the-store look, lightly spray them with hair spray. The shoe polish won't rub off so easily with this coat of protection.

Keep recipe cards splatter-free Don't let the spaghetti sauce on the stove splatter on your favorite recipe card. A good coating of hair spray will prevent the card from being ruined by kitchen eruptions. With the protection, they wipe off easily.

Keep drapes dirt-free Did you just buy new drapes or have your old ones cleaned? Want to keep that like-new look for a while? The trick is to apply several coats of hair spray, letting each coat dry thoroughly before the next one.

Remove ink marks on garments Your toddler just went wild with a ballpoint pen on your white upholstery and your new shirt. Squirt the stain with hair spray and the pen marks should come right off.

Extend the life of cut flowers A bouquet of cut flowers is such a beautiful thing, you want to do whatever you can to postpone wilting. Just as it preserves your hairstyle, a spritz of hair spray can preserve your cut flowers. Stand a foot away from the bouquet and give them a quick spray, just on the undersides of the leaves and petals.

✳ Hydrogen Peroxide

Remove stains of unknown origin Can't tell what that stain is? Still want to remove it? Try this sure-fire remover: Mix a teaspoon of 3% hydrogen peroxide with a little cream of tartar or a dab of non-gel toothpaste. Rub the paste on the stain with a soft cloth. Rinse. The stain, whatever it was, should be gone.

> **TAKE CARE** Hydrogen peroxide is considered corrosive—even in the relatively weak 3% solution sold as a household antiseptic. Don't put it in your eyes or around your nose. Don't swallow it or try to set it on fire either.

Remove wine stains Hydrogen peroxide works well to remove wine stains so don't worry if you spill while you quaff.

Remove grass stains If grass stains are ruining your kids' clothes, hydrogen peroxide may bring relief. Mix a few drops of ammonia with just 1 teaspoon 3% hydrogen peroxide. Rub on the stain. As soon as it disappears, rinse and launder.

Remove mildew The sight and smell of mildew is a bathroom's enemy. Bring out the tough ammunition: a bottle of 3% hydrogen peroxide. Don't water it down, just attack directly by pouring the peroxide on the offending area. Wipe it clean. Mildew surrender.

Remove bloodstains This works only on fresh bloodstains: Apply 3% hydrogen peroxide directly to the stain, rinse with fresh water, and launder as usual.

Sanitize your cutting board Hydrogen peroxide is a surefire bacteria-killer—just the ally you need to fight the proliferation of bacteria on your cutting board, especially after you cut chicken or other meat. To kill the germs on your cutting board, use a paper towel to wipe the board down with vinegar, then use another paper towel to wipe it with hydrogen peroxide. Ordinary 3% peroxide is fine.

 DID *You* KNOW?

Hydrogen peroxide, (H_2O_2) was discovered in 1818. The most common household use for it is as an antiseptic and bleaching agent. (It's the key ingredient in most teeth-whitening kits and all-fabric oxygen bleaches, for example). Textile manufacturers use higher concentrations of hydrogen peroxide to bleach fabric.

During World War II, hydrogen peroxide solutions fueled torpedoes and rockets.

* Ice-Cream Scoops

Scoop meatballs and cookie dough If you want uniform-size meatballs every time, use an ice-cream scoop to measure out the perfect orbs. This method works well for cookies too. Dip the scoop in the dough, and plop the ball on the cookie sheet. You'll end up with cookies all the same size—no tiffs over which one is the largest.

Make butter balls At your next large family gathering, scoop out large globes of butter or margarine to serve to your guests. A smaller scoop, or melon baller, can create individual-size balls of butter.

Create sand castles On your next trip to the beach, throw an ice-cream scoop into your bag. Your kids will have a fun tool for making their sand castles down by the shore. The scoop allows them to make interesting rounded shapes with the sand.

DID *You* KNOW?

Spade, dipper, spatula, or spoon—the styles of ice-cream scoop you can buy are almost as varied as the flavors of ice cream you'll put in them. One Web site lists 168 choices of the device! Here's some more dish on ice-cream scoops that you might not know:

- A scoop introduced during the Depression, called the slicer, helped the ice-cream parlor owner scoop out the same amount every time and not give away any extra.
- Many ways have been developed to help the ice cream plop out of a scoop. Some scoops split apart; others have a wire scraper to nudge the stuff out. Still others have antifreeze in the handle or a button on the back to make it pop out.
- Some ice-cream scoops, also called molds, can imprint symbols on the ice cream, for fraternal organizations and others.
- Most scoops come in two standard sizes—#10 and #20, indicating the number of level scoops you'll get from a quart of ice cream. But since most people make rounded scoops, it's more practical to think of a #10 as giving you about seven rounded scoops and a #20, about 12.

Plant seeds If you're out in the garden faced with a plot of earth that needs seeding, turn to your kitchen drawer for help. An ice-cream scoop will make equal-sized planting holes for the seeds for your future harvest.

Repot a houseplant Does dirt scatter everywhere when you are repotting your houseplants? An ice-cream scoop is the perfect way to add soil to the new pot without making a mess.

Pre-scoop ice cream If you're tiring of constantly being bugged by your kids for a scoop of ice cream, try this tip. Scoop several scoops of ice cream onto a wax-paper-lined cookie sheet, spaced apart. Place the sheet with the scoops back in your freezer to re-harden. Remove the scoops from the wax paper and pile them up in a self-sealing plastic bag. The next time the kids want a scoop of strawberry ice cream, they can help themselves.

✳ Ice Cubes

Water hanging plants and Christmas trees If you're constantly reaching for the step stool to water hard-to-reach hanging plants, ice cubes can help. Just toss several cubes into the pots. The ice melts and waters the plants and does it without causing a sudden downpour from the drain hole. This is also a good way to water your Christmas tree, whose base may be hard to reach with a watering can.

Remove dents in carpeting If you've recently rearranged the furniture in your living room, you know that heavy pieces can leave ugly indents in your carpet. Use ice cubes to remove them. Put an ice cube, for example, on the spot where the chair leg stood. Let it melt, then brush up the dent. Rug rehab completed.

Smooth caulk seams You're caulking around the bathtub, but the sticky caulk compound keeps adhering to your finger as you try to smooth it. If you don't do something about it, the finished job will look pretty awful. Solve the problem by running an ice cube along the caulk line. This forms the caulk into a nice even bead and the caulk will never stick to the ice cube.

Help iron out wrinkles So your ready-to-wear shirt is full of wrinkles and there's no time to wash it again. Turn on the iron and wrap an ice cube in a soft cloth. Rub over the wrinkle just before you iron and the shirt will smooth out.

Mask the taste of medicine No matter what flavor your local pharmacist offers in children's medicine, kids can still turn up their noses at the taste. Have them suck on an ice cube before taking the medicine. This numbs the taste buds and allows the medicine to go down, without the spoonful of sugar.

Pluck a splinter Parental challenge #573: removing a splinter from the hand of a screaming, squirming toddler. Before you start jabbing with that needle, grab an ice cube and numb the area. This should make splinter removal more painless and quicker.

Prevent a blister from a burn Have you burned yourself? An ice cube applied to the burn will stop it from blistering.

Cool water for your pets Imagine what it's like to wear a fur coat in the middle of summer. Your rabbits, hamsters, and gerbils will love your thoughtfulness if you place a few cubes in their water dish to cool down. This is also a good tip for your cat, who's spent the hot morning lounging on your bed, or your dog, who's just had a long romp in the park.

Unstick a sluggish disposal If your garbage disposal is not working at its optimum because of grease buildup (not something stuck inside), ice cubes may help. Throw some down the disposal and grind them up. The grease will cling to the ice, making the disposal residue-free.

Make creamy salad dressing Do you want to make your homemade salad dressing as smooth and even as the bottled variety? Try this: Put all the dressing ingredients in a jar with a lid, then add a single ice cube. Close the lid and shake vigorously. Spoon out the ice cube and serve. Your guests will be impressed by how creamy your salad dressing is.

Stop sauces from curdling Imagine this: Your snooty neighbors are over for a Sunday brunch featuring eggs Benedict. But when you mixed butter and egg yolks with lemon juice to make hollandaise sauce for the dish, it curdled. What do you do? Place an ice cube in the saucepan, stir, and watch the sauce turn back into a silky masterpiece.

 DID *You* KNOW?

Here are some cold, hard facts about ice cubes:
- To make clear ice cubes, use distilled water and boil it first. It's the air in the water that causes ice cubes to turn cloudy.

- A British Columbian company sells fake ice cubes that glow and blink in your drink.
- Those aren't ice cubes in that inviting drink in the print advertisement, because they'd never last under hot studio lights. They're plastic or glass.

- The word ice cube has been commercially co-opted over the years. To name two examples: a vintage candy (the chocolate pat wrapped in silver paper) and a well-known rapper/actor.

De-fat soup and stews Want to get as much fat as possible out of your homemade soup or stew as quickly as possible? Fill a metal ladle with ice cubes and skim the bottom of the ladle over the top of the liquid in the soup pot. Fat will collect on the ladle.

Reheat rice Does your leftover rice dry out when you reheat it in the microwave? Try this: Put an ice cube on top of the rice when you put it in the microwave. The ice cube will melt as the rice reheats, giving the rice much-needed moisture.

Remove gum from clothing You're just about to walk out the door when Junior points to the gum stuck to his pants. Keep your cool and grab an ice cube. Rub the ice on the gum to harden it, then scrape it off with a spoon.

✳ Ice Cube Trays

Divide a drawer If your junk drawer is an unsightly mess, insert a plastic ice cube tray for easy, low-cost organization. One "cube" can hold paper clips, the next, rubber bands, another, stamps. It's another small way to bring order to your life.

Organize your workbench If you're looking through your toolbox for that perfect-sized fastener that you know you have somewhere, here's the answer to your problem. An ice cube tray can help you organize and store small parts you may need at one time or another, such as screws, nails, bolts, and other diminutive hardware.

Keep parts in sequence You're disassembling your latest swap-meet acquisition that has lots of small parts and worry that you'll never be able to get them back together again in the correct sequence. Use an old plastic ice cube tray to help keep the small parts in the right order until you get around to reassembling it. If you really want to be organized, mark the sequence by putting a number on a piece of masking tape in each compartment. The bottom half of an egg carton will also work.

A painter's palette Your child, a budding Mary Cassatt or Picasso, requires a palette to mix colors. A plastic ice cube tray provides the perfect sturdy container for holding and mixing small amounts of paints and watercolors.

Freeze extra eggs Are you overstocked on bargain-priced eggs? Freeze them for future baking projects. Medium eggs are just the right size to freeze in plastic ice cube trays with one egg in each cell, with no spillover. After they freeze, pop them out into a self-sealing plastic bag. Defrost as many as you need when the time comes.

Freeze foods in handy cubes An ice cube tray is a great way to freeze small amounts of many different kinds of food for later use. The idea is to freeze the food in the tray's cells, pop out the frozen cubes, and put them in a labeled self-sealing plastic bag for future use. Some ideas:

- Your garden is brimming with basil, but your family can't eat pesto as quickly as you're making it. Make a big batch of pesto (without the cheese) and freeze it in ice cube trays. Later, when you're ready to enjoy summer's bounty in the middle of winter, defrost as many cubes as you need, add cheese, and mix with pasta.

- There's only so much sweet potato your growing baby will eat at one sitting. Freeze the rest of it in trays for a future high-chair meal.

- The recipe calls for 1/2 cup chopped celery, but you have an entire head of celery and no plans to use it soon. Chop it all, place in an ice cube tray, add a little water, and freeze. The next time you need chopped celery, it's at your fingertips. This works well for onions, carrots, or any other vegetable you'd use for stew and such.

- Are you always throwing out leftover parsley? Just chop it up, put it in an ice cube tray with a little water, and freeze for future use. Works with other fresh herbs.

- There's a bit of chicken soup left in the bottom of the pot. It's too little for another meal, but you hate to throw it out. Freeze the leftovers, and the next time you make soup or another dish that needs some seasoning, grab a cube or two.

- If you are cooking a homemade broth, make an extra-large batch and freeze the excess in ice cube trays. You'll have broth cubes to add instant flavor to future no-time-to-cook dishes. You can do the same with a leftover half-can of broth.

- Here's what to do with that half-drunk bottle of red or white wine: Freeze the wine into cubes that can be used later in pasta sauce, casseroles, or stews.

Kids' Stuff This is a great summertime project. Collect a bunch of small objects around your house: **buttons, beads, tiny toys**. Then get an **ice cube tray** and place one or more of the items in each tray cube. Fill the tray with water. Then cut a length of **yarn** (long enough to make a comfortable **necklace, bracelet, or anklet**). Lay the yarn in the ice cube tray, making sure it hits every cube and is submerged. **Freeze**. When frozen, pop out and tie on the jewelry. The kids will cool off while they see how long their creation takes to melt.

✳ Ice Scrapers

Remove splattered paint If you just painted your bathroom and have gotten paint splatters all over your acrylic bathtub, use an ice scraper to remove them without scratching the tub surface. Use ice scrapers to remove paint specks from any other nonmetallic surfaces.

Smooth wood filler Do you have small gouges in your wood floors? Want to use wood filler to make them smooth again? An ice scraper can help you do the job right. Once you've packed wood filler into a hole, the ice scraper is the perfect tool to smooth and level it.

Remove wax from skis Every experienced skier knows that old wax buildup on skis can slow you down. An ice scraper can swiftly and neatly take off that old wax and prepare your plows for the next coat.

Scrape out your freezer Your windshield isn't the only place ice and frost build up. If the frost is building up in your freezer and you want to delay the defrosting chore for a while, head out to the car and borrow the scraper.

Clean up bread dough No matter how much flour you put on your work surface, some of that sticky bread dough always seems to stick to it. A clean ice scraper is just the tool for skimming the sticky stuff off the work surface. In a pinch, a plastic scraper can also substitute for a spatula for nonstick pans.

Jars

Waterproof camping storage When you're boating or camping, keeping things like matches and paper money dry can be a challenge. Store items that you don't want to get wet in clear jars with screw tops that can't pop off. Even if you're backpacking, plastic peanut butter jars are light enough not to weigh you down, plus they provide more protection for crushable items than a resealable plastic bag.

Create workshop storage Don't let workshop hardware get mixed up. Keep all your nails, screws, nuts, and bolts organized by screwing jar lids to the underside of a wooden or melamine shelf. (Make sure the screw won't poke through the top of the shelf.) Then put each type of hardware in its own jar, and screw each jar onto its lid. You'll keep everything off the counters, and

by using clear jars, you can find what you need at a glance. Works great for storing seeds in the potting shed too!

Stamp out cookies Just about any clean, empty wide-mouthed jar is just the right size for cutting cookies out of any rolled dough.

Use to dry gloves or mittens You took a break from shoveling snow to come in for soup and a sandwich, and want to get back to work. To help your gloves or mittens dry out during lunch, pull each one over the bottom of an empty jar, then stand the jar upside down on a radiator or hot-air vent. Warm air will fill the jar and radiate out to dry damp clothing in a jiffy.

Make a piggy bank You can encourage thriftiness in your child by making a piggy bank out of any jar with a metal lid. Take the lid off the jar, place it on a flat work surface like a cutting board, and tap a screwdriver with a hammer to carefully punch a slot hole in the center. Then use the hammer or a rasp to smooth the rough edges on the underside of the slot to protect fingers from scratches. Personalizing the mini-bank with paints or collage makes a fun rainy-day project.

Collect insects Help the kids observe nature by gently collecting fireflies and other interesting bugs in clear jars. Punch a few small airholes in the lids for ventilation. Don't make the holes too large, or your bugs will escape! Don't forget to let the critters go after you've admired them.

Make baby-food portions Take advantage of the fact that baby-food jars are already the perfect size for baby's portions. Clean them thoroughly before reuse, and fill them with anything from pureed carrots to vanilla pudding. Attach a spoon with a rubber band, and you've got a perfect take-along meal when you travel with your little one.

Bring along baby's treats Dry cereal can be a nutritious snack for your baby. No need to bring the whole box when you leave the house; pack individual servings in clean, dry baby-food jars. If they get spilled, the mess is minimal.

SCIENCE FAIR

Turn a large **wide-mouthed jar** into a **miniature biosphere.** Clean the jar and lid, then place a handful of **pebbles** and **charcoal chips** in the bottom. Add several trowelfuls of slightly damp, sterilized **potting soil**. Select a few **plants** that like similar conditions (such as ferns and mosses, which both like moderate light and moisture). Add a few colorful **stones, seashells,** or a piece of **driftwood**. Add **water** to make the terrarium humid. Tighten the lid and place the jar in dim light for two days. Then display in bright light but not direct sunlight. You shouldn't need to add water— it cycles from the plants to the soil and back again.

It's important to use sterilized soil to avoid introducing unwanted organisms. The charcoal chips filter the water as it recycles.

* Jar Lids

Make safety reflectors Is your driveway difficult to maneuver after dark? With some scrap wood and jar lids you can make inexpensive reflectors to guide drivers. Spray the lids with reflective paint, screw them to the sides of stakes cut from the scrap wood, and drive the stakes into the ground. Voilà! No more dinged fenders or flattened flowers!

Save half-eaten fruit Got half a peach, apple, or orange you'd like to save for later? Wrap a jar lid in plastic wrap or wax paper and then set the fruit cut side down on it in the refrigerator. A bit of lemon juice on the cut surface of the fruit will help prevent discoloration. And why throw out the contents of a partially consumed glass of milk or juice? Just cover it with a lid and refrigerate to keep it fresh.

Cut biscuits Yum, homemade biscuits! Lids with deep rims or canning jar bands (the part with the cut-out center) make impromptu biscuit cutters. Use different-sized lids for Papa, Mama, and Baby biscuits. Dip the bottom edge of the lid in flour to keep it from sticking when you press it into the dough. Avoid lids whose rims are rolled inward; the dough can get stuck inside and be hard to extract.

Create a spoon rest Place a jar lid on the stove or the countertop next to the stove while cooking. After stirring a pot, rest the spoon on the lid, and there'll be less to clean up later.

Drip catcher under honey jar Honey is delicious, but it can be a sticky mess. At the table, place the honey jar on a plastic lid to stop drips from getting on the tabletop. Store it that way, too, and your cabinet shelf will stay cleaner.

Make coasters to protect furniture Wet drinking glasses and hot coffee mugs can really do a number on furniture finishes. The simple solution is to keep plenty of coasters on hand. Glue rounds of felt or cork to both sides of a jar lid (especially flat canning jar lids, which shouldn't be reused for canning, anyhow), and keep a stack wherever cups and glasses accumulate in your house. Your furniture will thank you!

Kids' Stuff What's on your fridge door? Probably a bunch of magnets and children's artwork. Combine the two and you've got something both useful and beautiful. For a stimulating **craft project**, set out a bunch of **fun materials**—paints, glue, fabrics, family photos, googly eyes, glitter, pompoms, or even just paper and markers—and let your child decorate several **jar lids**. Glue some strong **magnets** from the hardware store on the backs (**hot-melt glue** works well), and when they're done, have an unveiling—with refreshments, of course!

Saucers for potted plants Lids with a rim are perfect for catching excess water under small potted plants, and unlike your ceramic saucers, if they get encrusted with minerals, you won't mind throwing them out.

Organize your desk Corral those paper clips and other small office items that clutter up your desk, by putting them in jar lids with deep rims. Works great to hold loose change or earrings on your dresser or bureau too. A quick coat of matte spray paint and an acrylic sealant will make them more attractive and water-resistant.

✳ Ketchup

Get rid of chlorine green If chlorine from swimming pools is turning your blond tresses green or just giving your hair an unwanted scent, eliminate the problem with a ketchup shampoo. To avoid a mess, do it in the shower. Massage ketchup generously into your hair and leave it for fifteen minutes, then wash it out, using baby shampoo. The odor and color should be gone.

Make copper pots gleam When copper pots and pans—or decorative molds—get dull and tarnished, brighten them with ketchup. It's cheaper than commercial tarnish removers and safe to apply without gloves. Coat the copper surface with a thin layer of the condiment. Let it sit for five to thirty minutes. Acids in the ketchup will react with the tarnish and remove it. Rinse the pan and dry immediately.

Keep silver jewelry sparkling Let ketchup do the work of shining tarnished silver. If your ring, bracelet, or earring has a smooth surface, dunk it in a small bowl of ketchup for a few minutes. If it has a tooled or detailed surface, use an old toothbrush to work ketchup into the crevices. To avoid damaging the silver, don't leave the ketchup on any longer than necessary. Rinse your jewelry clean, dry it, and it's ready to wear.

DID **You** KNOW?

Ketchup originated in the Far East as a salty fish sauce. The word *ketchup* (also spelled *catsup*) probably comes from Chinese or Malay. Brought to the West, it was transformed by the 1700s into a huge variety of sauces with vegetable and animal main ingredients. To this day, you can still find banana ketchup, mushroom ketchup, and other variants. Tomato ketchup is a relative newcomer, first sold in 1837, but it is now found in more than 90 percent of North American homes.

✳ Keys

Weigh down drapery Need to keep your draperies hanging properly? Just slip a few old keys in the hems. If you are worried about them falling out, tack them in place with a few stitches going through the holes in the keys. You can also keep blind cords from tangling by using keys as weights on their bottoms.

Make fishing sinkers Old unused keys make great weights for your fishing line. Since they already have a hole in them, attaching them to the line is a cinch. Whenever you come across an unidentified key, toss it into your tackle box.

Create an instant plumb bob You are getting ready to hang wallpaper and you need to draw a perfectly vertical line on the wall to get you started. Take a length of cord or string and tie a key or two to one end. You've got a plumb bob that will give you a true vertical. You can do the same with a pair of scissors too.

✳ Kool-Aid

Clean your dishwasher Is the inside of your dishwasher rusty brown? The cause is a high iron content in your water. Dump a packet of unsweetened lemonade Kool-Aid into the soap drawer and run the washer through a hot-water cycle. When you open the door, the inside will be as white as the day you bought the machine.

Clean rust from concrete Nasty rust stains on your concrete? Mix unsweetened lemonade Kool-Aid with hot water. Scrub and the rust stain should come right out.

Color wall paints Mix any flavor of unsweetened Kool-Aid into water-based latex paint to alter its color. Or mix unsweetened Kool-Aid with water to create your own watercolors, but don't give them to the kids—Kool-Aid stains can be tough to remove.

Make play makeup lip gloss Make some tasty lip gloss for little girls playing dress-up. Let the girls pick their favorite presweetened Kool-Aid flavor. Blend a package of the drink mix with 3 tablespoons vegetable shortening, then microwave for one minute. Transfer to a 35mm film canister and refrigerate overnight.

✳ Ladders

Make display shelving Convert a short wooden stepladder to shelving for displaying plants and collectibles. It's as easy as one, two, three:

1. Remove the folding metal spreader that holds the front and rear legs of the ladder together. Then position the ladder's rear legs upright against the wall and attach two 1 x 2 cleats to fix the distance between the front and rear legs. Position the cleats so that their tops are level with the top of a rung.

2. Each shelf will be supported at front by an existing rung. To support the back of each shelf, attach a cleat between the rear legs, positioning it at the same level as a rung.

3. Cut plywood or boards to fit as shelves and screw them to the rungs and cleats. Now screw the centermost rear cleat to the wall and you're done.

Construct a rustic indoor trellis Give your vines and trailing plants something to climb on. Using wall anchors, attach vinyl-covered hooks to your wall and hang an attractive straight ladder (or a segment of one) from the hooks, positioning the ladder's legs on the floor a couple of inches from the wall. It's easy to train potted plants to grow up and around this rustic support. It looks nice on a porch too.

Display quilts and more Don't let your fancy stitching languish in the closet! For that homespun feel, a ladder is a great way to display lacework, crochet, quilts, and throws. To prevent rough surfaces from damaging delicate fabrics, smooth wooden ladder rungs with sandpaper or metal rungs with steel wool if necessary.

Create a garden focal point Got some old wooden straight ladders around that you no longer trust? Show your whimsical side by using them to create a decorative garden archway. Cut two sections of old ladder to the desired height and position them opposite one another along a path. Screw the legs of each one to two strong posts sunk deeply into the soil. Cut a third ladder section to fit across the top of the two others and tie it to them using supple grapevine, young willow twigs, or heavy jute twine. Festoon your archway with fun and fanciful stuff, such as old tools, or let climbing plants clamber up and over it. It also works well as the entryway to an enclosed area.

Plop it down and plant it When a ladder is truly on its last legs, it can still be of service lying down. On the ground, a straight ladder or the front part of a stepladder makes a shallow planter with ready-made sections that look sweet filled with annuals, herbs, or salad greens. After a couple of years of contact with soil, a wooden ladder will decompose, so don't expect to use it again.

Make a temporary table The big family picnic is a summertime staple, but where to put all the food? You can cook up a makeshift table in no time by placing a straight ladder across two sawhorses. Top it with plywood and cover it with a tablecloth. The ladder will provide strength to support your buffet, as well as any guests who might lean on it.

Make a pot rack Accessorize your country kitchen with a pot rack made from a sawed-off section of a wooden straight ladder with thin, round rungs. Sand the cut ends smooth; then tie two pieces of sturdy rope to the rungs at either end. To suspend your pot rack, screw four large metal eye hooks into the ceiling, going into the joists; then tie the other ends of the ropes to them.

Hang some S-hooks from the rungs to hold your kitchenware. Leave the rack unfinished if you want a rustic look. Or paint or stain it if you want a more finished look.

Lemons

✳LEMONS **AROUND THE HOUSE**

Eliminate fireplace odor There's nothing cozier on a cold winter night than a warm fire burning in the fireplace—unless the fire happens to smell horrible. Next time you have a fire that sends a stench into the room, try throwing a few lemon peels into the flames. Or simply burn some lemon peels along with your firewood as a preventive measure.

Get rid of tough stains on marble You probably think of marble as stone, but it is really petrified calcium (also known as old seashells). That explains why it is so porous and easily stained and damaged. Those stains can be hard to remove. If washing won't remove a stubborn stain, try this: Cut a lemon in half, dip the exposed flesh into some table salt, and rub it vigorously on the stain. But do this only as a last resort; acid can damage marble. Rinse well.

Make a room scent/humidifier Freshen and moisturize the air in your home on dry winter days. Make your own room scent that also doubles as a humidifier. If you have a wood-burning stove, place an enameled cast-iron pot or bowl on top, fill with water, and add lemon (and/or orange) peels, cinnamon sticks, cloves, and apple skins. No wood-burning stove? Use your stovetop instead and just simmer the water periodically.

Neutralize cat-box odor You don't have to use an aerosol spray to neutralize foul-smelling cat-box odors or freshen the air in your bathroom. Just cut a couple of lemons in half. Then place them, cut side up, in a dish in the room, and the air will soon smell lemon-fresh.

?? DID *You* KNOW?

With all due respect to Trini Lopez and his rendition of "Lemon Tree," a lemon tree actually isn't very pretty—and its flower isn't sweet either. The tree's straggly branches bear little resemblance to an orange tree's dense foliage, and its purplish flowers lack the pleasant fragrance of orange blossoms. Yes, the fruit of the "poor lemon" is sour—thanks to its high citric acid content—but it is hardly "impossible to eat." Sailors have been sucking on vitamin-C-rich lemons for hundreds of years to prevent scurvy. To this day, the British navy requires ships to carry enough lemons so that every sailor can have one ounce of juice daily.

Deodorize a humidifier When your humidifier starts to smell funky, deodorize it with ease: Just pour 3 or 4 teaspoons lemon juice into the water. It will not only remove the off odor but will replace it with a lemon-fresh fragrance. Repeat every couple of weeks to keep the odor from returning.

Clean tarnished brass Say good-bye to tarnish on brass, copper, or stainless steel. Make a paste of lemon juice and salt (or substitute baking soda or cream of tartar for the salt) and coat the affected area. Let it stay on for 5 minutes. Then wash in warm water, rinse, and polish dry. Use the same mixture to clean metal kitchen sinks too. Apply the paste, scrub gently, and rinse.

Polish chrome Get rid of mineral deposits and polish chrome faucets and other tarnished chrome. Simply rub lemon rind over the chrome and watch it shine! Rinse well and dry with a soft cloth.

197

Prevent potatoes from turning brown Potatoes and cauliflower tend to turn brown when boiling, especially when you're having company for dinner. You can make sure the white vegetables stay white by squeezing a teaspoon of fresh lemon juice into the cooking water.

Freshen the fridge Remove refrigerator odors with ease. Dab lemon juice on a cotton ball or sponge and leave it in the fridge for several hours. Make sure to toss out any malodorous items that might be causing the bad smell.

Brighten dull aluminum Make those dull pots and pans sparkle, inside and out. Just rub the cut side of half a lemon all over them and buff with a soft cloth.

Kids' Stuff Kids love to send and receive secret messages, and what better way to do it than by writing them in **invisible ink**? All they need is **lemon juice** (fresh-squeezed or bottled) to use as ink, a **cotton swab** to write with, and a sheet of **white paper** to write on. When the ink is dry and they are ready to read the invisible message, have them hold the paper up to bright sunlight or a lightbulb. The heat will cause the writing to darken to a pale brown and the message can be read! Make sure they don't overdo the heating and ignite the paper.

Keep rice from sticking To keep your rice from sticking together in a gloppy mass, add a spoonful of lemon juice to the boiling water when cooking. When the rice is done, let it cool for a few minutes, then fluff with a fork before serving.

Refresh cutting boards No wonder your kitchen cutting board smells! After all, you use it to chop onions, crush garlic, cut raw and cooked meat and chicken, and pre-pare fish. To get rid of the smell and help sanitize the cutting board, rub it all over with the cut side of half a lemon or wash it in undiluted juice straight from the bottle.

Keep guacamole green You've been making guacamole all day long for the big party, and you don't want it to turn brown on top before the guests arrive. The solution: Sprinkle a liberal amount of fresh lemon juice over it and it will stay fresh and green. The flavor of the lemon juice is a natural complement to the avocados in the guacamole. Make the fruit salad hours in advance too. Just squeeze some lemon juice onto the apple slices, and they'll stay snowy white.

Make soggy lettuce crisp Don't toss that soggy lettuce into the garbage. With the help of a little lemon juice you can toss it in a salad instead. Add the juice of half a lemon to a bowl of cold water. Then put the soggy lettuce in it and refrigerate for 1 hour. Make sure to dry the leaves completely before putting them into salads or sandwiches.

Keep insects out of the kitchen You don't need insecticides or ant traps to ant-proof your kitchen. Just give it the lemon treatment. First squirt some lemon juice on door thresholds and windowsills. Then squeeze lemon juice into any holes or cracks where the ants are getting in. Finally, scatter small slices of lemon peel around the outdoor entrance. The ants will get the message that they aren't welcome. Lemons are also effective against roaches and fleas: Simply mix the juice of 4 lemons (along with the rinds) with 1/2 gallon (2 liters) water and wash your floors with it; then watch the fleas and roaches flee. They hate the smell.

Clean your microwave Is the inside of your microwave caked with bits of hardened food? You can give it a good cleaning without scratching the surface with harsh cleansers or using a lot of elbow grease. Just mix 3 tablespoons lemon juice into 1 1/2 cups water in a microwave-safe bowl. Microwave on High for 5-10 minutes, allowing the steam to condense on the inside walls and ceiling of the oven. Then just wipe away the softened food with a dishrag.

Deodorize your garbage disposal If your garbage disposal is beginning to make your sink smell yucky, here's an easy way to deodorize it: Save leftover lemon and orange peels and toss them down the drain. To keep it smelling fresh, repeat once every month.

✳LEMONS **IN THE LAUNDRY**

Bleach delicate fabrics Ordinary household chlorine bleach can cause the iron in water to precipitate out into fabrics, leaving additional stains. For a mild, stain-free bleach, soak your delicates in a mixture of lemon juice and baking soda for at least half an hour before washing.

Remove unsightly underarm stains Avoid expensive dry-cleaning bills. You can remove unsightly underarm stains from shirts and blouses simply by scrubbing them with a mixture of equal parts lemon juice (or white vinegar) and water.

Tip **Before You Squeeze**

> To get the most juice out of fresh lemons, bring them to room temperature and roll them under your palm against the kitchen counter before squeezing. This will break down the connective tissue and juice-cell walls, allowing the lemon to release more liquid when you squeeze it.

Boost laundry detergent To remove rust and mineral discolorations from cotton T-shirts and briefs, pour 1 cup lemon juice into the washer during the wash

LEMONS*

199

cycle. The natural bleaching action of the juice will zap the stains and leave the clothes smelling fresh.

Rid clothes of mildew You unpack the clothes you've stored for the season and discover that some of the garments are stained with mildew. To get rid of mildew on clothes, make a paste of lemon juice and salt and rub it on the affected area, then dry the clothes in sunlight. Repeat the process until the stain is gone. This works well for rust stains on clothes too.

Whiten clothes Diluted or straight, lemon juice is a safe and effective fabric whitener when added to your wash water. Your clothes will also come out smelling lemon-fresh.

✱LEMONS **FOR HEALTH AND BEAUTY**

Lighten age spots Before buying expensive medicated creams to lighten unsightly liver spots and freckles, try this: Apply lemon juice directly to the area, let sit for 15 minutes, and then rinse your skin clean. Lemon juice is a safe and effective skin-lightening agent.

Create blond highlights For blond highlights worthy of the finest beauty salon, add 1/4 cup lemon juice to 3/4 cup water and rinse your hair with the mixture. Then sit in the sun until your hair dries. Lemon juice is a natural bleach. Don't forget to put on plenty of sunscreen before you sit out in the sun. To maximize the effect, repeat once daily for up to a week.

Clean and whiten nails Pamper your fingernails without the help of a manicurist. Add the juice of 1/2 lemon to 1 cup warm water and soak your fingertips in the mixture for 5 minutes. After pushing back the cuticles, rub some lemon peel back and forth against the nail.

SCIENCE FAIR

Turn a **lemon into a battery**! It won't start your car, but you will be able to feel the current with your tongue. Roll the lemon on a flat surface to "activate" the juices. Then cut two small slices in the lemon about 1/2 inch (1.25 centimeters) apart. Place a **penny** into one slot and a **dime** into the other. Now touch your **tongue** to the penny

and the dime at the same time. You'll feel a slight **electric tingle**. Here's how it works: The acid in the lemon reacts differently with each of the two metals. One coin contains positive electric charges, while the other contains negative charges. The charges create current. Your tongue conducts the charges, causing a small amount of electricity to flow.

Cleanse your face Clean and exfoliate your face by washing it with lemon juice. You can also dab lemon juice on blackheads to draw them out during the day. Your skin should improve after several days of treatment.

Freshen your breath Make an impromptu mouthwash using lemon juice straight from the bottle. Rinse with the juice and then swallow it for longer-lasting fresh breath. The citric acid in the juice alters the pH level in your mouth, killing the bacteria that cause bad breath. Rinse after a few minutes, because long-term exposure to the acid in the lemon can harm tooth enamel.

Treat flaky dandruff If itchy, scaly dandruff has you scratching your head, relief may be no farther away than your refrigerator. Just massage 2 tablespoons lemon juice into your scalp and rinse with water. Then stir 1 teaspoon lemon juice into 1 cup water and rinse your hair with it. Repeat this daily until your dandruff disappears. No more itchy scalp, and your hair will smell lemon-fresh.

Soften dry, scaly elbows It's bad enough that your elbows are dry and itchy, but they look terrible too. Your elbows will look and feel better after a few treatments with this regimen: Mix baking soda and lemon juice to make an abrasive paste. Then rub the paste into your elbows for a soothing, smoothing, and exfoliating treatment.

Remove berry stains Sure it was fun to pick your own berries, but now your fingers are stained with berry juice that won't come off with soap and water. Try washing your hands with undiluted lemon juice. Wait a few minutes and wash with warm, soapy water. Repeat if necessary until the stain is completely gone.

Disinfect cuts and scrapes Stop bleeding and disinfect minor cuts and scrapes. Pour a few drops of lemon juice directly on the cut or apply the juice with a cotton ball and hold firmly in place for one minute.

Soothe poison ivy rash You won't need an ocean of calamine lotion the next time poison ivy comes a-creeping around. Just apply lemon juice full-strength directly to the affected area to soothe itching and alleviate the rash.

Relieve rough hands and sore feet You don't have to take extreme measures to soothe your extremities. If you have rough hands or sore feet, rinse them in a mixture of equal parts lemon juice and water, then massage with olive oil and dab dry with a soft cloth.

Remove warts You've tried countless remedies to get rid of your warts, and nothing seems to work. Next time, try this: Apply a dab of lemon juice directly to the wart, using a cotton swab. Repeat for several days until the acids in the lemon juice dissolve the wart completely.

✳ Lighter Fluid

Wipe away rust Rust marks on stainless steel will come off in a jiffy. Just pour a little lighter fluid onto a clean rag and rub the rust spot away. Use another rag to wipe away any remaining fluid.

Get gum out of hair It happens to the best of us, not to mention the kids. Gum in the hair is a pain in the neck to remove. Here is an easy solution that really works: Apply a few drops of lighter fluid directly to the sticky area, wait a few seconds, and comb or wipe away the gum. The solvents in the fluid break down the gum, making it easy to remove from many surfaces besides hair.

Remove labels with ease Lighter fluid will remove labels and adhesives from almost any surface. Use it to quickly and easily remove the strapping tape from new appliances or to take stickers off book covers.

Take out crayon marks Did the kids leave their mark with crayons on your walls during that last visit? No problem. Dab some lighter fluid on a clean rag and wipe till the marks vanish.

> **TAKE CARE** Lighter fluid is inexpensive, easy to find (look for a small plastic bottle next to the larger bottles of barbecue starter) and has many surprising uses. But it is highly flammable and can be hazardous to your health if inhaled or ingested. Always use it in a well-ventilated area. Do not smoke around it or use it near an open flame.

Remove heel marks from floors You don't have to scrub to remove those black heel marks on the kitchen floor. Just pour a little lighter fluid on a paper towel and the marks will wipe right off.

Rid cooking-oil stain from clothes When cooking-oil stains won't wash out of clothes, try pouring a little lighter fluid directly onto the stain before washing it the next time. The stain will come out in the wash.

✳ Lip Balm

Prevent windburn You love to ski, but you hate wearing a ski mask. Next time you go snow skiing, try rubbing lip balm, such as ChapStick, on your face before you hit the slopes. The lip balm will protect your skin from windburn.

Remove a stuck ring No need to pull and tug on your poor beleaguered finger to try to remove that stuck ring. Simply coat the finger with lip balm and gently wriggle the ring loose.

Groom wild eyebrows Use lip balm as a styling wax to groom unruly mustaches, eyebrows, or other wild hairs.

Tip **Lip Balm and Lipstick**

> During the dry winter months you may be tempted to apply a layer of lip balm before you put on your lipstick. Beauty experts say this is not a good idea because the lip balm could interfere with the adherence of the lipstick. Instead of using lip balm during the day, the experts recommend that you switch to a moisturizing lipstick. Save the lip balm for moisturizing your lips before you go to bed.

Zap bleeding from shaving cuts Ouch! You just cut yourself shaving and you've no time to spare. Just dab a bit of lip balm directly onto the nick and the bleeding from most shaving cuts will quickly stop.

Lubricate a zipper Rub a small amount of lip balm up and down the teeth of a sticky or stuck zipper. Then zip and unzip it a few times. The lip balm will act as a lubricant to make the zipper work smoothly.

Simplify carpentry Rub some lip balm over nails and screws being drilled or pounded into wood. The lip balm will help them slide in a little easier.

Keep a lightbulb from sticking Outdoor lightbulbs, which are exposed to the elements, often get stuck in place and become hard to remove. Before screwing a lightbulb into an outdoor socket, coat the threads on the bulb with lip balm. This will prevent sticking and make removal easier.

Lubricate tracks for sliding things Apply lip balm to the tracks of drawers and windows, or to the ridges on a medicine cabinet, for easier opening and shutting.

M

✱ Magazines

No-cost gift wrap Cut out pages with colorful magazine advertisements and use them to make lovely gift wrap for small gifts.

Keep wet boots in shape Roll up a couple of old magazines and use them as boot trees inside a pair of damp boots. The magazines will help the boots maintain their shape as they dry.

Use in kids' craft projects Save up your old magazines for use in rainy-day craft projects with the kids. Let them go through the magazines to find pictures and words to use in collages. Suggest themes for the collages if you like.

Line drawers Pages from large magazines with heavy coated paper make wonderful liners for small dresser and desk drawers. Look for advertisements with especially colorful designs or pictures. Clip the page, place inside the drawer, and press around the edges to define where to trim with scissors.

✱ Magnets

Clean up a nail spill Keep a strong magnet on your workbench. Next time you spill a jar of small items like nails, screws, tacks, or washers, save time and energy and let the magnet help pick them up for you.

DID *You* KNOW?

Ancient Chinese and Greeks discovered that certain rare stones, called lodestones, seem to magically attract bits of iron and always pointed in the same direction when allowed to swing freely.

Manmade magnets come in many shapes and sizes, but every magnet has a north pole and a south pole. If you break a magnet into pieces, each piece, no matter how small, will have a north and south pole. The magnetic field, which every magnet creates, has long been used to harness energy, although scientists still don't know for sure what it is!

Prevent a frozen car lock Here's a great way to use refrigerator magnets during the bitter cold of winter. Place them over the outside door locks of your car overnight and they will keep the locks from freezing.

Keep desk drawer neat Are your paper clips all over the place? Place a magnet in your office desk drawer to keep the paper clips together.

Store a broom in a handy place Why run to the hall closet every time you need to sweep the kitchen? Instead, just use a screw to attach a magnet about halfway down the broom handle. Then store the broom attached to the side of your refrigerator between the fridge and the wall, where it will remain hidden until you are ready to use it.

✳ Margarine Tubs

Corral those odds and ends Loose thumbtacks in every room? Odd bolts and nails in a broken cup? Stray superball under the couch? These are just some of the items waiting to be organized into your extra plastic margarine tubs. Get your board game going faster and easier by storing the loose pieces in a tub until the next time. You've sorted out all the sky pieces for a puzzle, so keep them separate and safe in their own tub. With or without their lids, a few clean margarine tubs can do wonders for a junk drawer in need of organization.

Make a baby footprint paperweight Make an enduring impression of your baby's foot, using quick-drying modeling clay—which comes in lots of great colors. Put enough clay in a margarine tub to hold a good impression. Put a thin layer of petroleum jelly on baby's foot and press it firmly into the clay. Let the clay dry as directed, then flex the tub away from the edges until the clay comes free. Years from now you'll be able to show Johnny that his size 13s were once smaller than the palm of your hand! You can also preserve your pet's paw print the same way.

Use as a paint container Want to touch up the little spots here and there in the living room, but don't want to lug around a gallon of paint? Pour a little paint into a margarine tub to carry as you make your inspection. Hold it in a nest of paper towels to catch any possible drips. The tubs with lids are also perfect for storing that little bit of leftover paint for future touch-ups.

Make individual ice-cream portions Small margarine tubs are just the right size for a quick ice-cream snack. And when it comes home from the store, a gallon of ice cream is the perfect consistency to portion out into the tubs. No more time-consuming getting out the bowls, finding the scoop, and waiting for the ice cream to soften up enough to dish out. When Johnny and Janey want their ice cream *now*, they can get it themselves and everyone has an equal portion—they just go to the freezer and pull out a tub.

Mold gelatin desserts Don't buy a fancy mold for your next birthday party or barbecue. Use a large margarine tub as the mold for a gelatin or mousse centerpiece. For individual fun gelatin dessert molds, use the smaller tubs and put a surprise gummy or mini-marshmallow face on the top, which will show through from the bottom when the mold is inverted. The flexible tubs are easy to squeeze to release the dessert.

Make frugal freezer storage Reuse your clean, sturdy margarine and other plastic containers for freezing measured portions of soups and stocks, and to break up leftovers into single servings. A 2-pound (1 kilogram) container, for example, stores the perfect amount of sauce for 1 pound (.5 kilogram) of pasta. *Hint:* Before freezing, let the food cool just enough to reduce condensation.

Give kids some lunch box variety As a break from the usual sandwich, put some fruit salad, rice mix, or other interesting fare in one or two recycled margarine tubs for your child's lunch. The tubs are easy to open and will keep the food from getting crushed.

Bring fast food for baby Need to bring your home cooking for Junior on the road? Use a disposable margarine tub for a container that won't break in your baby bag. It's also a handy food bowl, and you won't have to wrap it up and bring it home for cleaning.

Make a piggy bank Use a tall tub as a homemade bank for your little one. Cut out a piece of paper that will fit wrapped around the side, tape it in place and encourage him or her to decorate it with flair. Cut a slit in the top, and start saving!

Travel light with your pet Lightweight, disposable margarine tubs make the perfect pet food containers and double as food and water bowls. And those valuable dog cookies won't get crushed if you put them in a plastic tub. If your pet is vacationing at a friend's house, make things a little easier for the caregiver by putting one serving in each container, to be used and discarded as needed.

Create thrifty seed starters Starting your seeds indoors is supposed to save you money, so don't spend your savings on lots of big seed trays. Take a margarine tub, poke a few holes in the bottom, add moistened seed-starting mix, and sow your seeds following packet instructions. Use permanent marker on the side of the tub to help you remember what you've sown, and use the tub's lid as a drip saucer. Small tubs are space savers as well, especially if you want to start only one or two of each type of plant.

✳ Marshmallows

Separate toes when applying polish Get the comfort of a salon treatment when giving yourself a home pedicure. Just place marshmallows between your toes to separate them before you apply the nail polish.

Keep brown sugar soft Ever notice how brown sugar seems to harden overnight once you've opened the bag? Next time you open a bag of brown sugar, add a few marshmallows to the bag before closing it. The marshmallows will add enough moisture to keep the sugar soft for weeks.

Stop ice-cream drips Here's an easy way to keep a leaky ice-cream cone from staining your clothes. Just place a large marshmallow in the bottom of the cone before you add the ice cream.

Keep wax off birthday cakes If one of your birthday wishes is to keep candle wax off the frosting on the cake, try this trick: Push each candle into a marshmallow and set the marshmallow atop the frosting. The wax will melt onto the marshmallow, which you can discard. Meanwhile, the marshmallows will add a festive look to the cake.

DID *You* KNOW?

Ancient Egyptians made the first marshmallow candy—a honey-based concoction flavored and thickened with the sap of the root of the marshmallow plant (*Althaea officinalis*). Marshmallow grows in salt marshes and on banks near large bodies of water. Its sap was used to make marshmallow candy and medicine until the mid-1800s. Today's commercial marshmallows are a mixture of corn syrup or sugar, gelatin, gum arabic, and flavoring.

Impromptu cupcake frosting You're already mixing the batter for the cupcakes when you realize you're out of frosting. No problem—if you happen to have some marshmallows on hand. Just pop a marshmallow on top of each cupcake about a minute or so before they come out of the oven. It will make a delicious, instant, gooey frosting.

*️ Masking Tape

Label foods and school supplies You don't need to buy labels or a fancy machine that makes them. Use inexpensive masking tape instead to mark food containers and freezer bags before putting them in the refrigerator or freezer, and don't forget to write the date! You can also use masking tape to conveniently mark kids' schoolbooks and supplies.

Fix a broken umbrella rib If a strong wind breaks a rib on your umbrella, it's easy to fix it. Use a piece of masking tape and a length of wire cut from a coat hanger to make a splint.

Reuse a vacuum cleaner bag Save money by using a vacuum cleaner bag twice. Here's how: After the bag is full the first time, do not empty it the usual way through the hole in front. Take out the bag and cut a slit down the middle of the back. After you empty the bag, hold the cut edges together, fold them closed, and seal them with masking tape. Your bag is ready to be used again. Take care not to overfill during the second use.

Hang party streamers Use masking tape instead of transparent tape to put up streamers and balloons for your next party. The masking tape won't leave a residue on the wall like transparent tape does. Always remember to remove the masking tape within a day or two. If you wait too long, it could take paint off the wall when it comes off.

Keep paint can neat To prevent paint from filling the groove at the top of a paint can, simply cover the rim of the can with masking tape.

Make a road for toy cars Make a highway for those tiny toy cars your little ones love to play with. Just tape two strips of masking tape to a floor or tabletop. Add a little handmade cardboard stop sign or two and they're off to the races. Carefully guiding a toy car along the taped roadway is more than just fun for small children, it also helps them gain motor control of their fingers for skills they will need later, such as writing.

Mayonnaise

Condition your hair Hold the mayo ... and massage it into your hair and scalp just as you would any fine conditioner! Cover your head with a shower cap, wait several minutes, and shampoo. The mayonnaise will moisturize your hair and give it a lustrous sheen.

Give yourself a facial Why waste money on expensive creams when you can treat yourself to a soothing facial with whole-egg mayonnaise from your own refrigerator? Gently spread the mayonnaise over your face and leave it on for about 20 minutes. Then wipe it off and rinse with cool water. Your face will feel clean and smooth.

Strengthen your fingernails To add some oomph to your fingernails, just plunge them into a bowl of mayonnaise every so often. Keep them bathed in the mayo for about 5 minutes and then wash with warm water.

Relieve sunburn pain Did someone forget to put on sunscreen? To treat dry, sunburned skin, slather mayonnaise liberally over the affected area. The mayonnaise will relieve the pain and moisturize the skin.

Remove dead skin Soften and remove dead skin from elbows and feet. Rub mayonnaise over the dry, rough tissue, leave it on for 10 minutes, and wipe it away with a damp cloth.

Safe way to kill head lice Many dermatologists now recommend using mayonnaise to kill and remove head lice from kids instead of toxic prescription drugs and over-the-counter preparations. What's more, lice are becoming more resistant to such chemical treatments. To treat head lice with mayonnaise, massage a liberal amount of mayonnaise into the hair and scalp before bedtime. Cover with a shower cap to maximize the effect. Shampoo in the morning and then use a fine-tooth comb to remove any remaining lice and nits. To completely eradicate the infestation, repeat the treatment in 7-10 days.

Make plant leaves shiny Professional florists use this trick to keep houseplant leaves shiny and clean. You can do the same thing at home. Just rub a little mayonnaise on the leaves with a paper towel, and they will stay bright and shiny for weeks and even months at a time.

Remove crayon marks Did the kids leave crayon marks on your wood furniture? Here's a simple way to remove them that requires hardly any elbow grease: Simply rub some mayonnaise on the crayon marks and let it soak in for several minutes. Then wipe the surface clean with a damp cloth.

Clean piano keys If the keys to your piano are starting to yellow, just tickle the ivories with a little mayonnaise applied with a soft cloth. Wait a few minutes, wipe with a damp cloth, and buff. The piano keys will look like new.

Remove bumper stickers Time to get rid of that Nixon for President bumper sticker on your car? Instead of attacking it with a razor and risk scratching the bumper, rub some mayonnaise over the entire sticker. Let it sit for several minutes and wipe it off. The mayonnaise will dissolve the glue.

Get tar off your car To get road tar or pine sap off your car with ease, slather some mayonnaise over the affected area, let it sit for several minutes, and wipe it away with a clean, soft rag.

M

✳ Meat Tenderizer

Ease backache To relieve your aching back, mix sufficient water with meat tenderizer to make a paste and rub it on your back where it hurts. The enzymes in the tenderizer will help soothe those aching back muscles.

Relieve wasp-sting pain Make a paste of meat tenderizer and water and apply it directly to the sting from a bee or wasp. Be careful not to push any remaining part of the stinger deeper into your skin. The enzymes in the meat tenderizer will break down the proteins in the insect venom.

Remove protein-based stains Try a little tenderness to remove protein-based stains like milk, chocolate, and blood from clothes. For fresh wet stains, sprinkle on enough meat tenderizer to cover the area and let it sit for an hour. Then brush off the dried tenderizer and launder as usual. For stains that are already set, mix water and meat tenderizer to make a paste and rub it into the stain. Wait an hour before laundering as usual.

 DID *You* KNOW?

When Lloyd Rigler and Lawrence Deutsch dined at Adolph Rempp's Los Angeles restaurant one night in 1949, they had no clue that their fortunes were about to change forever. But the two partners were so impressed by the tender, flavorful meat that they soon bought the rights to the product now known as Adolph's Meat Tenderizer. Rigler toured the country—visiting 63 cities in 60 days—demonstrating the product, winning over skeptical food critics by sending them home with tenderized meat to cook themselves. Rave reviews led to windfall sales and profits, allowing the partners to sell the business in 1974 and turn their attention to philanthropy and the arts for the rest of their lives.

"Tenderize" tough perspiration stains Tenderize away hard-to-remove perspiration stains. Before you wash that sweat-stained sweatshirt (or any other perspiration-stained garment) dampen the stain and then sprinkle some meat tenderizer on it. Then just wash as usual.

✳ Milk

Make frozen fish taste fresh If you want fish from your freezer to taste like it was fresh caught, try this trick: Place the frozen fish in a bath of milk until it thaws. The milk will make it taste fresher.

Boost corn on the cob flavor Here's a simple way to make corn on the cob taste sweeter and fresher. Just add 1/4 cup powdered milk to the pot of boiling water before you toss in the corn.

Repair cracked china Before you throw out that cracked plate from your grandmother's old china set, try mending it with milk. Place the plate in a pan, cover it with milk (fresh or reconstituted powdered milk), and bring to a boil. As soon as it starts to boil, lower the heat and simmer for about 45 minutes. The protein in the milk will miraculously meld most fine cracks.

Polish silverware Tarnished silverware will look like new with a little help from some sour milk. If you don't have any sour milk on hand, you can make some by adding vinegar to fresh milk. Then simply soak the silver in the milk for half an hour to loosen the tarnish, wash in warm, soapy water, and buff with a soft cloth.

Soothe sunburn and bug bites If your skin feels like it's burning up from too much sun exposure or if itchy bug bites are driving you crazy, try using a little milk paste for soothing relief. Mix one part powdered milk with two parts water and add a pinch or two of salt. Dab it on the burn or bite. The enzymes in the milk powder will help neutralize the insect-bite venom and help relieve sunburn pain.

Impromptu makeup remover When you run out of makeup remover and you can't get to the store, use powdered milk instead. Just mix 3 tablespoons powdered milk with 1/3 cup warm water in a jar and shake well. Add more water or powder as necessary to achieve the consistency of heavy cream. Now you are ready to apply your makeshift makeup remover with a facecloth. When you're done, wipe it off and rinse with water.

Give yourself a facial Here's another way to give yourself a fancy spa facial at home. Make a mask by mixing 1/4 cup powdered milk with enough water to form a thick paste. Thoroughly coat your face with the mixture, let dry completely, then rinse with warm water. Your face will feel fresh and rejuvenated.

Soften skin Treat yourself to a luxurious foamy milk bath. Toss 1/2 cup or so of powdered milk into the tub as it fills. Milk acts as a natural skin softener.

Clean and soften dirty hands You come back from the garden with stained and gritty hands. Regular soap just won't do, but this will: Make a paste of oatmeal and milk and rub it vigorously on your hands. The stains will be gone and the oatmeal-and-milk mixture will soften and soothe your skin.

Clean patent leather Make your patent-leather purses or shoes look like new again. Just dab on a little milk, let it dry, and buff with a soft cloth.

Remove ink stains from clothes To remove ink stains from colored clothes, an overnight milk bath will often do the trick. Just soak the affected garment in milk overnight and launder as usual the next day.

* Milk Cartons

Make ice blocks for parties Keep drinks cold at your next barbecue or party with ice blocks made from empty milk cartons. Just rinse out the old cartons, fill them with water, and put them in the freezer. Peel away the container when you're ready to put the blocks in the cooler or punch bowl.

Make a lacy candle Here's an easy way to make a delicate, lacy candle. Coat the inside of a milk carton with cooking spray, put a taper candle in the middle, anchoring it with a base of melted wax, then fill it with ice cubes. Pour in hot wax; when the wax cools, peel off the carton. The melting ice will form beautiful, lacy voids in the wax.

Instant kids' bowling alley Make an indoor bowling alley for the kids with pins made from empty milk and juice cartons. Just rinse the cartons (use whatever sizes you like) and let them dry. Then take two same-sized cartons and slide one upside down into the other, squeezing it a little to make it fit. Once you've made ten, set your pins up at the end of the hall and let the kids use a tennis ball to roll for strikes and spares.

Feed birds in winter To make an attractive wintertime treat for feathered visitors, combine melted suet and birdseed into an empty milk carton. Suet is beef fat; you can get it from a butcher. To render it, chop or grind the fat and heat it over a low flame until it melts. Then strain it through cheesecloth into the carton. Insert a loop of string into the mixture while it is still melted. After it hardens, tear away the carton and tie your new mass of bird food to a branch. Do this only in cold weather. Once the temperature gets above about 70°F (20°C), the suet will turn rancid and melt.

Make seed starters Milk cartons are the perfect size to use for seed starters. Simply cut off the top half of a carton, punch holes in the bottom, fill with potting mix, and sow the seeds according to instructions on the packet.

Make vegetable garden collars Use empty milk cartons to discourage grubs and cutworms from attacking your young tomato and pepper plants. Just cut off the tops and bottoms of the containers, and when the ground is soft, push them into the ground around the plants when you set them out.

Collect food scraps for compost Keep an empty milk carton handy near the kitchen sink and use it to collect food scraps for your compost heap.

Disposable paint holder If you have a small paint project and you don't want to save the leftover paint (or lug a heavy can), an empty milk carton can help. Just cut off the top of the carton and pour in the amount of paint you need. When the job is finished, throw the carton into the trash, leftover paint and all.

✳ Mothballs

Rinse woolens for storage Of course it is a good idea to store woolens with mothballs to ward off moths. To give your favorite sweaters even more protection, dissolve a few mothballs in the final rinse when you wash them before storage.

SCIENCE FAIR

Make **mothballs dance** and give children a basic science lesson too. Just fill a **glass jar** about 2/3 full with **water**. Add about 1/4 to 1/3 cup **vinegar** and 2 teaspoons **baking soda**. Stir gently, then toss in a few **mothballs** and watch them bounce up and down. The vinegar and baking

soda create carbon dioxide bubbles, which cling to the irregular surfaces of the mothballs. When enough bubbles accumulate to lift the weight of a mothball, it rises to the surface of the water. There, some of the bubbles escape into the air, and the mothball sinks to the bottom of the jar to start the cycle again. The effect will last longer if the container is sealed.

Kill bugs on potted plants To exterminate bugs on a potted plant, put the plant in a clear plastic bag, such as a cleaning bag, add a few mothballs, and seal for a week. When you take the plant out of the bag, your plant will be bug-free. It will also keep moths away for a while.

Repel mice from garage or shed Don't let mice spend their winter vacation in your garage. Place a few mothballs around the garage, and the mice will seek other quarters. To keep mice out of your potting shed, put the mothballs around the base of wrapped or covered plants.

Keep dogs and cats away from garden Don't throw out old mothballs. Scatter them around your gardens and flowerbeds to keep cats, dogs, and rodents away. Animals hate the smell!

Keep bats at bay Bats won't invade your belfry (or attic) if you scatter a few mothballs around. Add some mothballs to the boxes you store in the attic and silverfish will stay away too.

✳ Mouse Pads

Pad under table legs When you get a new mouse pad for your computer, don't throw out the old one. Use it to make pads for table legs and chairs to prevent them from scratching wood and other hard-surface floors. Just cut the foam and cloth pad into small pieces and superglue each piece to the bottom of a leg.

Make knee pads for the garden Old computer mouse pads are just the right size to cushion your knees when you're working in the garden. Kneel on them loose as is or attach them directly to your pant legs with duct tape.

Pad under houseplants Keep potted plant containers from scratching or damaging your hard floors. Just set the pot atop an old mouse pad and your floor will remain scratch-free. Use four pads for large pots.

Hot pad for the table Protect your table from hot casseroles, coffeepots, and serving dishes. Use old PC mouse pads as hot pads. The cloth-topped foam mouse pad is the perfect size to hold most hot containers you bring to the table.

✳ Mouthwash

Clean computer monitor screen Out of glass cleaner? A strong, alcohol-based mouthwash will work as well as, or better than, glass cleaner on your computer monitor or TV screen. Apply with a damp, soft cloth and buff dry. Remember to use only on glass screens, not liquid crystal displays! The alcohol can damage the material used in LCDs.

Cleanse your face An antiseptic mouthwash makes a wonderful astringent for cleansing your face. Check the ingredients to make sure it does not contain sugar, then use as follows. Wash your face with warm, soapy water and rinse. Dab a cotton ball with mouthwash and gently wipe your face as you would with any astringent. You should feel a pleasant, tingling sensation. Rinse with warm water followed by a splash of cold water. Your face will look and feel clean and refreshed.

Treat athlete's foot A sugarless antiseptic mouthwash may be all you need to treat mild cases of athlete's foot or toenail fungus. Use a cotton ball soaked in mouthwash to apply to the affected area several times a day. Be prepared: It will sting a bit! Athlete's foot should respond after a few days. Toenail fungus may take up to several months. If you do not see a response by then, make an appointment with a dermatologist or podiatrist.

Add to wash water Smelly gym socks are often full of bacteria and fungi that may not all come out in the wash—unless you add a cup of alcohol-based, sugarless mouthwash during the regular wash cycle.

Tip **Homemade Mouthwash**

> Freshen your breath with your own alcohol-free mouthwash. Place 1 ounce (30 grams) whole cloves and/or 3 ounces (85 grams) fresh rosemary in a pint-size (half-liter) jar and pour in 2 cups boiling water. Cover the jar tightly and let it steep overnight before straining. Need a mouthwash immediately? Dissolve 1/2 teaspoon baking soda in 1/2 cup warm water.

Cure underarm odor Regular deodorants mask unpleasant underarm odors with a heavy perfume smell but do little to attack the cause of the problem. To get rid of the bacteria that cause perspiration odor, dampen a cotton ball with a sugarless, alcohol-based mouthwash and swab your armpits. If you've just shaved your armpits, it's best to wait for another day to try this.

Disinfect a cut When you need to clean out a small cut or wound, use an alcohol-based mouthwash to disinfect your skin. Remember that before it became a mouthwash, it was successfully used as an antiseptic to prevent surgical infections.

Get rid of dandruff To treat a bad case of dandruff, wash your hair with your regular shampoo; then rinse with an alcohol-based mouthwash. You can follow with your regular conditioner.

Clean your toilet All out of your regular toilet bowl cleaner? Try pouring 1/4 cup alcohol-based mouthwash into the bowl. Let it stand in the water for 1/2 hour, then swish with a toilet brush before flushing. The mouthwash will disinfect germs as it leaves your toilet bowl sparkling and clean.

* Mustard

Soothe an aching back Take a bath in yellow mustard to relieve an aching back or arthritis pain. Simply pour a regular 6- to 8-ounce (175- to 240-milliliter) bottle of mustard into the hot water as the tub fills. Mix well and soak yourself for 15 minutes. If you don't have time for a bath, you can rub some mustard directly on the affected areas. Use only mild yellow mustard and make sure to apply it to a small test area first. Undiluted mustard may irritate your skin.

Relax stiff muscles Next time you take a bath in Epsom salt, throw in a few tablespoons yellow mustard too. The mustard will enhance the soothing effects of the Epsom salt and also help to relax stiff, sore muscles.

Relieve congestion Relieve congestion with a mustard plaster just like Grandma used to make. Rub your chest with prepared mustard, soak a washcloth in hot water, wring it out, and place it over the mustard.

Make a facial mask Pat your face with mild yellow mustard for a bracing facial that will soothe and stimulate your skin. Try it on a small test area first to make sure it will not be irritating.

Remove skunk smell from car You didn't see the skunk in the road until it was too late, and now your car exudes that foul aroma. Use mustard powder to get rid of those awful skunk odors. Pour 1 cup dry mustard into a bucket of warm water, mix well, and splash it on the tires, wheels, and underbody of the car. Your passengers will thank you.

Remove odor from bottles You've got some nice bottles you'd like to keep, but after washing them, they still smell like whatever came in them. Mustard is a sure way to kill the smell. After washing, just squirt a little mustard into the bottle, fill with warm water, and shake it up. Rinse well, and the smell will be gone.

? DID *You* KNOW?

Ancient Romans brought mustard back from Egypt and used the seeds to flavor unfermented grape juice, called *must*. This is believed to be how the mustard plant got its name. The Romans also made a paste from the ground seeds for medicinal purposes and may have used it as a condiment. But the mustard we use today was first prepared in Dijon, France, in the 13th century. Dijon-style mustard is made from darker seeds than yellow mustard.

N

super item
38 uses!

Nail Polish

✳NAIL POLISH **AROUND THE HOUSE**

Make buttons glow in the dark It happens all the time. The lights are dimmed, you grab the remote control to increase the TV volume, and darn, you hit the wrong button and change the channel instead. To put an end to video flubs, dab glow-in-the-dark nail polish onto frequently used remote buttons. You can also use phosphorescent polish to mark keys and keyholes and other hard-to-spot items.

Mark your thermostat setting When you wake up with a chill and don't have your glasses, it's easy to return to your comfort zone if you've marked your dial-type thermostat. Simply set it to your preferred temperature and then make a thin mark with colored nail polish from the dial into the outside ring.

𝒯ip **Using Nail Polish**

> • To keep nail polishes fresh and easy to use, store them in the refrigerator. Keep them together in a little square plastic container.
> • Shaking a polish bottle to mix the color can cause bubbles. Roll the bottle between your palms instead.
> • Wipe the inside threads of your nail polish bottle and cap with a cotton swab dipped in polish remover before closing them. It'll open more easily.

Mark temperature settings on shower knobs Don't waste precious shower time fiddling with the water temperature. With the shower on, select your ideal settings, then turn off the flow to the shower and make a small mark with bright nail polish onto the stationary lip of both the hot and cold knob indicating the handle position that's best. Once it's set, no sweat!

Make cup measurements legible Find your measuring cup markings faster, especially if you like to measure "on the fly" while cooking. Use a very visible color of nail polish to trace over the basic measurement levels. This also works great for those dimly lit, late-night bottle feedings, when you need to see how well

NAIL POLISH✳

217

Junior has tanked up. And you won't have to squint to find the correct dosage on little plastic medicine cups if you first mark them with a thin line of dark polish.

Mark levels inside a bucket When you're mixing in a big bucket, you don't typically have the opportunity to lift the bucket to check the quantity. Besides, the bucket you use for mixing might not have the measurements clearly marked at all. Make sure you know you're using the right amounts by marking pint, quart, and gallon (or half, full, and other liter) levels with lines of nail polish. Use a color that stands out against the bucket's color.

Label your sports gear You share a lot of interests with your golf partner, including the same brand of golf balls. Make it clear who got on the green first, by putting a dot of bright nail polish on your ball supply. This also works well with batting gloves and other items that don't have enough room to fit your name.

Label poison containers If everyone in your home has easy access to your cupboard, prevent someone from grabbing dangerous items in haste. Use dark red or other easily visible nail polish to label the poisons. Draw an unmistakable X on the label as well as the lid or spout.

Seal an envelope Do you have a mild distrust of those self-sealing envelopes? Brush a little nail polish along the underside of the flap, seal it, and it won't even open over a teakettle! Add some flair to a special card by brushing your initial (or any design) in nail polish over the sealed flap tip, as a modern type of sealing wax that doesn't need to be melted first.

Smudgeproof important drug labels Preserve the important information on your prescription medicine and other important medicine labels with a coat of clear polish, and they won't be smudged as you grab them after getting your glass of water.

Waterproof address labels When you're sending a parcel on a rainy day, a little clear polish brushed over the address information will make sure your package goes to the right place.

Prevent rust rings from metal containers If your guests are going to peek into your medicine cabinet, you don't want them to see rust rings on your shelves. Brush nail lacquer around the bottom of shaving cream cans and other metal containers to avoid those unsightly stains.

Make a gleaming paperweight To create paperweights that look like gemstones, or interesting rocks for the base of your potted cactus, try this: Find some palm-size, smooth clean rocks. Put about 1/2 inch (1.25 centimeters) water into a pie pan, and put 1 drop clear nail polish onto the water. The polish will spread out over the water surface. Holding a rock with your fingertips, slowly roll it in the water to coat it with the polish. Set the rock on newspaper to dry.

Prevent rusty toilet seat screws If you're installing a new toilet seat, keep those screws from quickly rusting. Paint them with a coat or two of clear nail lacquer; it will also help prevent seat wobble by keeping the screws in place.

Paint shaker holes to restrict salt If your favorite saltshaker dispenses a little too generously, paint a few of the holes shut with nail polish. It is a good idea for those watching their salt.

Tarnish-proof costume jewelry Inexpensive costume jewelry can add sparkle and color to an everyday outfit, but not if it tarnishes and the tarnish rubs off the jewelry and onto your skin. To keep your fake jewelry and your skin sparkling clean, brush clear nail polish onto the back of each piece and allow it to dry before wearing.

Protect your belt buckle's shine Cover new or just-shined belt buckles with a coat of clear polish. You'll prevent oxidation and guarantee a gleaming first impression.

Seal out scuffs on shoes On leather shoes, it's the back and toes that really take the brunt of the wear and tear that leaves scratches on the surface. Next time you buy a new pair of shoes—especially ones for a kid or an active adult—give these areas the extra measure of protection they need. Paint a little clear nail polish on the outside of the back seam and over the toes. Rub the polish in a little to feather out the shine of the polish. After it dries, you'll be a step ahead of those perennial shoe problems "driver's heel" and "jump rope toe."

Keep laces from unraveling Neaten the appearance of frayed shoelaces, and extend their life. Dip the ends in clear nail polish and twist the raveled ends together. Repair laces in the evening so that the polish will dry overnight.

 DID **You** KNOW?

Nail polish is certainly not a recent concept. As early as 3000 B.C., ancient Chinese nobility are believed to have colored their long nails with polishes, made from gum arabic, beeswax, gelatin, and pigments. The nobility wore shades of gold, silver, red, or black, while lesser classes were restricted to pastel shades. Colored nails were also popular with ancient Egyptians, who often dyed their nails with henna or stained them with berries. Polish wasn't just for women. In Egypt and Rome, military commanders painted their nails red before going into battle.

Get rid of a wart Warts are unsightly, embarrassing, and infectious. In order to get rid of warts and prevent spreading the virus to others, cover them with nail polish. The wart should be gone or greatly diminished in one week.

Protect pearl buttons Delicate pearl buttons will keep their brand-new sparkle with a protective coat of clear nail polish. It will keep costume pearl buttons from peeling as well.

Prevent loss of buttons Keep that brand-new shirt in good shape by putting a drop of clear nail polish on the thread in the buttons. It prevents the thread from fraying, so taking this precaution in advance could save you some embarrassment later. Put a dab on just-repaired buttons as well.

DID **You** KNOW?

Unless you work in a lab, you probably don't know that clear nail polish is the respected workhorse used in mounting microscopic slides. Officially referred to as NPM (nail polish mountant) it is the preferred and inexpensive substance used around a cover glass to seal it onto a slide, protecting the specimen from air and moisture.

Make needle threading easier Do you fumble with your needle and thread, licking and re-licking the frayed thread end until it's too floppy to go through the eye? Try dragging the cut thread end through the application brush of nail polish once or twice, and then roll the thread end between your thumb and forefinger. It will dry in a second, and your thread end stays stiff enough to thread in a flash. Your sewing box is a great retirement home for a nail color you no longer use.

Prevent frayed fabric from unraveling Do you have wisps peeking out from the bottom of your skirt? Is the nylon lining of your jacket fraying at the cuffs? You can tame those fraying strays by brushing them into place with some clear nail polish.

Keep ribbons from fraying The gift is perfect, so make sure the wrapping is just as nice. Brush the cut ends of ribbon with a little clear nail polish to stop them from unraveling. This is also the perfect solution for your little girl's hair ribbons on special occasions; at least one part of her will stay together all day!

Stop a run in your hose It's a helpless feeling, realizing that a small run in your stocking is about to turn into a big embarrassment. Happily you can stop runs permanently and prolong the life of fragile stockings with a dab of clear nail polish. Simply apply polish to each end of a run (no need to remove hose), and let it dry. This invisible fix stops runs, and lasts through many hand launderings.

Mend a fingernail You just split a nail, but don't have a nail repair kit handy? Grab an unused tea bag instead. Cut the bag open, dump the tea, cut a piece of the bag into the shape of your nail, and cover it with clear nail polish. Press it onto your nail, then apply colored nail polish. You'll be good to go until the break grows out.

Temporarily repair eyeglasses So you sat on your glasses and one lens has a small crack, but you can't get to the optometrist right away? Seal the crack on both sides with a thin coat of clear nail polish. That will hold it together until you can see your way to the doctor's office.

Stop a windshield crack from spreading If you've developed a small crack in your windshield, stop it cold with some clear polish. Working in the shade, brush the crack on both sides of the glass with polish to fill it well. Move the car into the sun so the windshield can dry. You will eventually need to repair your windshield, but this will give you time to shop around for the best estimate.

Fill small nicks on floors and glass Have the children been playing hockey on your hardwood floors? Fill those little nicks by dabbing them with some clear nail polish. It will dry shiny, so sand the spot gently with some 600-grit sandpaper. A thick coat of clear nail polish also helps to soften the sharp edge of a nicked mirror or glass pane.

Reset loose jewelry stones If your jewelry has popped a stone or two, you don't have to put it in the "play dress-up" box yet. The stone can be reset using a little drop of clear nail polish as the "glue." It dries quickly, and the repair will be invisible.

Repair lacquered items Did you chip a favorite lacquered vase or other lacquered item? Try mixing colors of nail polish to match the piece. Paint over the chipped area to make it less noticeable. *Caution:* You may lower the value of an antique by doing this, so you probably only want to try this with inexpensive items.

Plug a hole in your cooler A small hole inside your cooler doesn't make it trash-worthy yet. Seal the hole with two coats of nail polish to hold in ice and other melted substances.

Fill washtub nicks It's a mystery how they got there, but your washing machine tub has one or two nicks near the holes, and now you're concerned about snags in your clothes or even rust spots. Seal those nicks with some nail polish, feathering the edges so there is no lip.

Keep chipped car paint from rusting If your car suffers small dings and chips, you can keep them from rusting or enlarging by dabbing clear nail polish onto the damaged areas.

Smooth wooden hangers If you've noticed a few splinters or nicks in your wooden hangers, no need to toss them out. Brush some nail polish over the rough edges to smooth the surface again and keep your coat linings safe.

Tighten loose screws You're not rough with your drawers and cabinets, but you find yourself tightening certain pull screws once too often. Keep them in place by brushing a little clear polish on the screw threads, insert the screws, and let dry before using again. This is also a great solution if you've been keeping a Phillips screwdriver in the kitchen for loose pot handles. You can also use clear nail polish to keep nuts on machine screws or bolts from coming loose, and if you need to take the nuts off, a twist with a wrench will break the seal.

Mend holes in window screens You notice a small hole has been poked in your window or door screen. If the hole is no more than about 1/4 inch (6 millimeters) in diameter, you can block the bugs and keep the hole from getting bigger by dabbing on a bit of clear nail polish.

Fix torn window shades Got a little tear in your window shade? Don't worry. You can usually seal it with a dab of clear nail polish.

✳ Nail Polish Remover

Remove stains from china Your bone china has assorted stains from years of use. Spruce up your set by rubbing soiled areas with nail polish remover. Clean spots with a cotton swab and then wash dishes as usual.

> **TAKE CARE** Frequent use of nail polish remover containing acetone—check the label—can cause dry skin and brittle nails. All nail polish removers are flammable and potentially hazardous if inhaled for a long time; use them in a well-ventilated area away from flames. And work carefully; they can damage synthetic fabrics, wood finishes, and plastics.

Eliminate ink stains If the ink stains on your skin won't come off with soap and water, they are probably not water-soluble. Try using nail polish remover instead. Take a cotton ball and wipe the affected areas with the solution. Once the ink stains are gone, wash skin with soap and water. Nail polish remover can also eliminate ink stains on the drum of your clothes dryer.

Rub paint off windows Spare your nails the next time you want to remove paint on a window. Working in a well-ventilated area, dab on nail polish remover in small sections. Let the solution remain on the painted areas for a few minutes before rubbing it off with a cloth. Once finished, take a damp cloth and go over the areas again.

Remove stickers from glass Scraping price stickers from glass objects can be messy, and it often leaves behind a gummy adhesive that attracts dirt and is sticky to the touch. Remove the stickers and clean up the residual glue by wiping the area with acetone-based nail polish remover. The same method can be used for removing stickers and sticky residue from metal surfaces.

Dissolve melted plastic Ever get too close to a hot metal toaster with a plastic bag of bread or bagels? The resulting mess can be a real cleaning challenge. But don't let a little melted plastic ruin a perfectly good appliance. Eliminate the sticky mess with nail polisher remover. First unplug the toaster and wait for it to cool. Then pour a little nail polish remover on a soft cloth and gently rub over the damaged areas. Once the melted plastic is removed, wipe with a damp cloth and dry with a paper towel. Your toaster is now ready for the next round of bagels. The same solution works for melted plastic on curling irons.

Unhinge superglue Superglue will stick tenaciously to just about anything, including your skin. And trying to peel it off your fingers can actually cause skin damage. Instead, soak a cotton ball with acetone-based nail polish remover and hold it on the skin until the glue dissolves.

Clean vinyl shoes Patent-leather shoes may not reflect up, but they *do* show off scuff marks, as will white or other light-colored vinyl shoes. To remove the marks,

SCIENCE FAIR

Some kids love to study insects, and just like the pros, your budding entomologist can kill and **preserve bugs**, using nail polish remover. Use a **nail polish remover** that contains the solvent acetone. (Check the label or sniff it for a banana-like odor.) To preserve the insects, soak some **cotton balls** with

the polish remover and place them in a **glass or plastic jar** along with several **tissues** and the selected insects. A wide-mouthed peanut butter jar works well. The tissues prevent the insects from damaging their wings. Seal the jar tightly with a lid, and the specimens will quickly dehydrate. Use a **straight pin** stuck through the insect's body to mount it on a cork-board or corrugated **cardboard**.

rub them lightly but briskly with a soft cloth or paper towel dipped in nail polish remover. Afterward, remove any residue with a damp cloth.

Keep watches clean Tired of looking at your watch and seeing unsightly scratches when you check the time? Get rid of them with nail polish remover. If the face of your watch is made from unbreakable plastic, rub the remover over the scratches until they diminish or disappear.

Clean computer keyboards You can keep computer keyboards clean with nail polish remover and an old toothbrush. Simply moisten the brush with remover and lightly rub the keys.

Dilute correction fluid To take the goop out of correction fluid or old nail polish, dilute it with nail polish remover. Pour just a few drops into the bottle and then shake. Add a little more polish remover to the solution, if needed, to attain the desired consistency.

Prep brass for re-lacquering Old or damaged lacquer coatings on brass can be safely removed with nail polish remover. Take a soft cloth and pour a small amount of remover on it. Rub the brass object until the old lacquer has been lifted. Your brass item is now ready to be polished or professionally re-lacquered.

* Newspaper

Encase your glassware for moving Are you relocating or packing up items for long-term storage? Use several sheets of soaking-wet newspapers to wrap up your glass dishes, bowls, drinking glasses, and other fragile items, and then let them thoroughly dry before packing. The newspaper will harden and form a protective cast around the glass that will dramatically improve its chances of surviving the move without breaking.

Store sweaters and blankets Don't treat moths to a fine meal of your homemade or store-bought woolen sweaters and blankets. When putting them into storage,

DID *You* KNOW?

America's first newspaper was called *Publick Occurrences, Both Foreign and Domestick*. It was a folded three-panel sheet of paper printed in Boston on September 25, 1690, by Richard Pierce and Benjamin Harris. Unfortunately, British colonial authorities closed it after its first and only issue and quickly issued a decree banning "unlicensed" publications. Ironically, the only known copy isn't found in the United States. It's in the Public Records Office in London.

wrap your woolens in a few sheets of newspaper (be sure to tape up the corners). It will keep away the moths, and keep out dust and dirt.

Clean and polish your windows If you're like most folks, you probably use a lot of absorbent paper towels for drying off your just-washed windows. Did you know that crumpled-up newspaper dries and polishes windows even better than paper towels? And it's a lot cheaper too.

Deodorize luggage and containers Do you have a plastic container or wooden box with a persistent, unpleasant odor? Stuff in a few sheets of crumpled newspaper and seal it closed for three or four days. You can also use this technique to deodorize trunks and suitcases (using more newspaper, of course).

Dry wet shoes If your shoes get soaked after walking through the rain or slogging through the snow, stuff them with dry, balled-up newspaper to prevent any long-term damage. Place the shoes on their sides at room temperature so the moisture can be thoroughly absorbed. For severe sogginess, you may need to replace the stuffing a few times.

Make an impromptu ironing board If you always take along a travel iron—just in case you end up in a motel that doesn't provide irons and ironing boards—it's a cinch to make your own on-the-road ironing board. Simply fill a pillowcase with a short stack of newspapers, keeping it as level as possible. Then place it on a countertop or the floor and get pressing.

Create an emergency splint If someone you're with takes a nasty fall—and you suspect there may be a bone injury to an arm or leg—it's important to immobilize the limb to prevent pain and additional damage. Fashion a makeshift splint by folding up several sheets of newspaper until stiff and attach it beneath the limb using a few pieces of adhesive tape. You may need to overlap a couple of folded sheets to make a splint long enough for a leg injury.

Remove oven residue They may call it a self-cleaning oven, but when it's done cleaning, you always have to contend with mopping off that ashlike residue. Don't waste a roll of paper towels on the flaky stuff; clean it up with a few sheets of moistened, crumpled newspaper.

Pick up broken glass shards Okay, so everyone breaks a big glass bowl at least once in a lifetime. It's no big thing. A safe way to get up the small shards of glass that remain after you remove the large pieces is to blot the area with wet newspapers. The tiny fragments will stick to the paper, which makes for easy disposal. Just carefully drop the newspaper in your garbage can.

Unscrew a broken lightbulb To remove a broken lightbulb, wad up several sheets of newspaper, press the paper over the bulb, and turn it counterclockwise. (Make sure you're wearing protective gloves and that the power is off.) The bulb should loosen up enough to remove from the socket. Wrap it in the paper and toss it into the garbage.

Slow-ripen tomatoes in late fall Is there an early frost predicted and you still have a bunch of tomatoes on the vine? Relax. Pick your tomatoes and wrap each one in a couple of sheets of newspaper. Store them in airtight containers inside a dark cabinet or closet at room temperature. Check each one every three to four days; they will all eventually ripen to perfection.

Line your trash compactor Putting a few layers of newspapers at the bottom of your trash compactor will not only soak up the nasty odors caused by rotting foods, it will also protect the unit against damage caused by any sharp objects that manage to squeeze through.

Use as mulch Newspaper makes terrific mulch for veggies and flowers. It's excellent at retaining moisture and does an equally fine job at fighting off and suffocating weeds. Just lay down several sheets of newspaper. Then cover the paper with about 3 inches (7.5 centimeters) of wood mulch so it doesn't blow away. *Warning:* Avoid using glossy stock and colored newsprint for mulching (or composting); color inks may contain lead or harmful dyes that can leach into the ground. To check your newsprint, contact your local paper and ask about the inks they use; many papers now use only safe vegetable-based inks.

Add to compost Adding moderate amounts of wet, shredded newsprint—printed in black ink only—to your compost heap is a good and relatively safe way to reduce odor and to give earthworms a tasty treat.

Adios, earwigs If your garden is under siege by earwigs—those creepy-looking insects with the sharp pincers on their hindquarters—get rid of them by making your own environmentally friendly traps. Tightly roll up a wet newspaper, and put a rubber band around it to keep it from unraveling. Place it in the area you've seen the insects, and leave it overnight. By morning, it will be

? DID **You** KNOW?

What we call newsprint—the type of paper used by newspapers around the world—was invented around 1838 by a Nova Scotia teenager, Charles Fenerty. After hearing frequent complaints from local paper mills about maintaining adequate supplies of rags to make rag paper, Fenerty hit upon the idea of making paper from spruce pulp. Unfortunately, Fenerty didn't go public with his discovery until 1844. By then, a consortium of European investors had already patented a process for creating paper solely from wood fiber.

standing room only for the bugs. Place the newspaper in a plastic grocery bag, tie a knot at the top of the bag, and toss it into the trash. Repeat until your traps are free of earwigs.

Winterize outdoor faucets If you live in an older home without frost-free outdoor spigots, it's a good idea to insulate the outdoor faucets. To prevent damage from ice and cold temperatures, make sure you shut off the valve to each faucet, and drain off any excess water from the spigots. Then insulate each faucet by wrapping it with a few sheets of newspaper covered with a plastic bag (keep the bag in place by wrapping it with duct tape or a few rubber bands).

Protect windows when painting Don't bother buying thick masking or carpenter tape when painting around the windows of your home. Simply wet several long strips of newspaper and place them on the glass alongside the wood you're painting. The newspaper will easily adhere to the surface and keep the paint off the glass or frames, and it is much easier to remove than tape.

Roll your own fireplace logs Bad winter on the way? Bolster your supply of fireplace logs by making a few of your own out of old newspapers. Just lay out a bunch of sheets end to end, roll them up as tightly as you can, tie up the ends with twine or wire, and wet them in a solution of slightly soapy water. Although it will take a while, let them dry thoroughly, standing on end, before using. *Note:* Do not use newspaper logs in a woodstove unless the manufacturer specifies that it is okay.

Put traction under your wheels Unless your vehicle has four-wheel drive, it's always a good idea to keep a small stack of newspapers in the trunk of your car during the winter months to prevent getting stranded on a patch of ice or slush. Placing a dozen or two sheets of newspaper under each rear wheel will often provide just the traction you need to get your car back on the road.

* Oatmeal

Treat itchy poison ivy or chicken pox Take the itch out of a case of chicken pox or a poison ivy rash with a relaxing, warm oatmeal bath. Simply grind 1 cup oatmeal in your blender until it is a fine powder, then pour it into a piece of cheesecloth, the foot section of a clean nylon stocking, or the leg of an old pantyhose. Knot the material, and tie it around the faucet of your bathtub so the bag is suspended under the running water. Fill the tub with lukewarm water and soak in it for 30 minutes. You may find additional relief by applying the oatmeal pouch directly to the rash or pox.

Add luxury to a regular bath You don't have to have itchy skin to make a luxurious bath mix with oatmeal. And it beats buying expensive bath oils. All you need is 1 cup oatmeal and your favorite scented oil, such as rose or lavender. Grind the oatmeal in a blender, put it in a cheesecloth bag, add a few drops of the scented oil, and suspend the bag under the running water as you fill your bathtub. You'll not only find it sweetly soothing, you can also use the oatmeal bag as a washcloth to exfoliate your skin.

Make a facial mask If you're looking for a quick pick-me-up that will leave you feeling *and* looking better, give yourself an oatmeal facial. Combine 1/2 cup hot—

DID *You* KNOW?

Thirty minutes. Five minutes. One minute! Oatmeal cooking times depend on how the oats were made into oatmeal. After the inedible hull is removed, the oat is called a groat. If the groats are just cut into about four pieces, the oatmeal takes up to 30 minutes to cook. If the groats are steamed and rolled but not cut, it takes about five minutes. If they are steamed, rolled, *and* cut, the cooking time drops to a minute or so. Steaming, rolling, and cooking breaks down the fiber, so if you want a lot of fiber, use 30-minute oatmeal and cook it until it is chewy, not mushy.

not boiling—water and 1/3 cup oatmeal. After the water and oatmeal have settled for two or three minutes, mix in 2 tablespoons plain yogurt, 2 tablespoons honey, and 1 small egg white. Apply a thin layer of the mixture to your face, and let it sit for 10-15 minutes. Then rinse with warm water. (Be sure to place a metal or plastic strainer in your sink to avoid clogging the drain with the granules.)

Make a dry shampoo Do you sometimes need to skip washing your hair in order to get to work on time? Keep a batch of dry shampoo on hand in an airtight container specifically for those occasions when your alarm clock "malfunctions." Put 1 cup oatmeal in the blender and grind it into a fine powder. Add 1 cup baking soda, and mix well. Rub a bit of the mixture into your hair. Give it a minute or two to soak up the oils, then brush or shake it out of your hair (preferably over a towel or bag to avoid getting it all over). This dry shampoo mixture is also ideal for cleaning the hair of bedridden people who are unable to get into a shower or bathtub. Plus, it's equally effective for deodorizing that big ol' bath-hating mutt of yours.

✳ Olive Oil

Remove paint from hair Did you get almost as much paint in your hair as you did on the walls in your last paint job? You can easily remove that undesirable tint by moistening a cotton ball with some olive oil and gently rubbing it into your hair. The same approach is also effective for removing mascara—just be sure to wipe your eyes with a tissue when done.

Make your own furniture polish Restore the lost luster of your wooden furniture by whipping up some serious homemade furniture polish that's just as good as any of the commercial stuff. Combine 2 parts olive oil and 1 part lemon juice or white vinegar in a clean recycled spray bottle, shake it up, and spritz on. Leave on the mixture for a minute or two, then wipe off with a clean terry-cloth or paper towel. In a hurry? Get fast results by applying olive oil straight from the bottle onto a paper towel. Wipe off the excess with another paper towel or an absorbent cloth.

Use as hair conditioner Is your hair as dry and brittle as sagebrush in the desert? Put the moisture back into it by heating 1/2 cup olive oil (don't boil it), and then liberally applying it to your hair. Cover your hair with a plastic grocery bag, then wrap it in a towel. Let it set for 45 minutes, then shampoo and thoroughly rinse.

Clear up acne Okay, the notion of applying oil to your face to treat acne does sound a bit wacky. Still, many folks swear this works: Make a paste by mixing 4 tablespoons salt with 3 tablespoons olive oil. Pour the mixture onto your hands and fingers and work it around your face. Leave it on for a minute or two, then rinse it off with warm, soapy water. Apply daily for one week, then cut back to two or three times weekly. You should see a noticeable improvement in your condition. (The principle is that the salt cleanses the pores by exfoliation, while the olive oil restores the skin's natural moisture.)

Substitute for shaving cream If you run out of shaving cream, don't waste your time trying to make do with soap—it could be rough on your skin. Olive oil, on the other hand, is a dandy substitute for shaving cream. It not only makes it easier for the blade to glide over your face or legs, but it will moisturize your skin as well. In fact, after trying this, you may swear off shaving cream altogether.

Tip **Buying Olive Oil**

> Expensive extra virgin olive oil is made from olives crushed soon after harvest and processed without excessive heat. It's great for culinary uses where the taste of the oil is important. But for everyday cooking and non-food applications, lower grades of olive oil—light, extra light, or just plain olive oil—work fine and save you money.

Clean your greasy hands To remove car grease or paint from your hands, pour 1 tea-spoon olive oil and 1 teaspoon salt or sugar into your palms. Vigorously rub the mixture into your hands and between your fingers for several minutes; then wash it off with soap and water. Not only will your hands be cleaner, they'll be softer as well.

Recondition an old baseball mitt If your beloved, aging baseball glove is showing signs of wear and tear—cracking and hardening of the leather—you can give it a second lease on life with an occasional olive oil rubdown. Just work the oil into the dry areas of your mitt with a soft cloth, let it set for 30 minutes, then wipe off any excess. Your game may not improve, but at least it won't be your glove's fault. Some folks prefer to use bath oil to recondition their mitts (see page 81).

* Onions

Remove rust from knives Forget about using steel wool or harsh chemicals—how's this for an easy way to get the rust off your kitchen or utility knives? Plunge your rusty knife into a large onion three or four times (if it's very rusty, it may require a few extra stabs). The only tears you shed will be ones of joy over your rust-free blade.

Eliminate new paint smell Your bedroom's new shade of paint looks great, but the smell is keeping you up all night. What to do? Place several freshly cut slices of onion in a dish with a bit of water. It will absorb the smell within a few hours.

Correct pet "mistakes" If Rover or Kitty is still not respecting your property—whether it be by chewing, tearing, or soiling—you may be able to get the message across by leaving several onion slices where the damage has been done. Neither cats nor dogs are particularly fond of *"eau de onion,"* and they'll avoid returning to the scene of their crimes.

Soothe a bee sting If you have a nasty encounter with a bee at a barbecue, grab one of the onion slices intended for your burger and place it over the area where you got stung. It will ease the soreness. (If you are severely allergic to bee or other insect stings, seek medical attention at once.)

Use as smelling salts If you happen to be with someone at a party or in a restaurant who feels faint—and you don't normally carry smelling salts in your pocket—reach for a freshly cut onion. The strong odor is likely to bring him around.

Use as a natural pesticide Whip up an effective insect and animal repellent for the flowers and vegetables in your garden. In a blender, puree 4 onions, 2 cloves garlic, 2 tablespoons cayenne pepper, and 1 quart water (1 liter). Set the mixture aside. Now dilute 2 tablespoons soap flakes in 2 gallons (7.5 liters) water. Pour in the contents of your blender, shake or stir well, and you have a potent, environment-friendly solution to spray on your plants.

DID *You* KNOW?

How can you keep your eyes from tearing when cutting onions? Suggestions range from wearing protective goggles while chopping, to placing a fan behind you to blow away the onion's tear-producing vapors, to rubbing your hands with vinegar before you start slicing. The National Onion Association, however, advises chilling onions in the freezer for 30 minutes prior to slicing them. The association also suggests cutting off the top portion and peeling off the outer layers. The idea is to leave the root end intact, because it has the highest concentrations of the sulfur compounds that cause your eyes to tear.

Make mosquito repellent Some people find that increasing their intake of onions or garlic in the summer—or rubbing a slice of onion over their exposed skin—is a good way to keep away mosquitoes and other biting insects (not to mention friends and family).

✳ Oranges

Use for kindling Dried orange and lemon peels are a far superior choice for use as kindling than newspaper. Not only do they smell better and produce less creosote than newspaper, but the flammable oils found inside the peels enable them to burn much longer than paper.

Make a pomander Pomanders have been used for centuries to fill small spaces with a delightful fragrance as well as to combat moths. They are also incredibly easy to make: Take a bunch of cloves and stick them into an orange, covering the whole surface. That's it. Pretty simple, huh? Now suspend your pomander using a piece of string, twine, or monofilament fishing line inside a closet or cupboard, and it will keep the space smelling fresh for years.

Simmer for stovetop potpourri Fill your abode with a refreshing citrus scent by simmering several orange and/or lemon peels in 1-2 cups of water in an aluminum pot for a few hours. Add water as needed during the simmering. This process freshens up the pot as well as the air in your home.

Keep kitties off your lawn Are the neighbor's cats still mistaking your lawn for their litter box? Gently point them elsewhere by making a mixture of orange peels and coffee grounds and distributing it around the cats' "old haunts." If they don't take the hint, lay down a second batch and try moistening it with a bit of water.

Apply as mosquito repellent If you're not crazy about the idea of rubbing onions all over yourself to keep away mosquitoes (see previous page), you may be happy to know that you can often get similar results by rubbing fresh orange or lemon peels over your exposed skin. It's said that mosquitoes and gnats are totally repulsed by either scent.

Show ants the door Get rid of the ants in your garden, on your patio, and along the foundation of your home. In a blender, make a smooth puree of a few orange peels in 1 cup warm water. Slowly pour the solution over and into anthills to send the little pests packing.

✳ Oven Cleaner

Put the style back in your curling iron Is your curling iron buried under a layer of caked-on styling gel or conditioner? Before the next time you use it, spray on a light coating of oven cleaner. Let it sit for one hour, then wipe it off with a damp rag, and dry with a clean cloth. *Warning:* Do not use iron until it is thoroughly dry.

Wipe away bathtub ring Got a stubborn stain or ring around your white porcelain tub that refuses to come clean? Call out the big guns by spraying it with oven cleaner. Let it sit for a few hours, then give it a thorough rinsing. *Warning:* Do not apply oven cleaner to colored porcelain tubs; it could cause fading. And be careful not to get the oven cleaner on your shower curtain; it can ruin both plastic and fabric.

Clean grimy tile grout lines Ready for an all-out attack on grout grunge? First, make sure you have plenty of ventilation—it's a good idea to use your exhaust fan to suck air out of a small bathroom. Put on your rubber gloves and spray oven cleaner into the grout lines. Wipe the cleaner off with a sponge within five seconds. Rinse thoroughly with water to reveal sparkling grout lines.

> **TAKE CARE** Most oven cleaners contain highly caustic lye, which can burn the skin and damage the eyes. Always wear long rubber gloves and protective eyewear when using oven cleaner. The mist from oven cleaner spray can irritate nasal membranes. Ingestion can cause corrosive burns to the mouth, throat, and stomach that require immediate medical attention. Store oven cleaner well out of children's reach.

Clean ovenproof glass cookware You've tried everything to scrub those baked-on stains off your Pyrex or CorningWare cookware. Now try this: Put on rubber gloves and cover the cookware with oven cleaner. Then place the cookware in a heavy-duty garbage bag, close it tightly with twist ties, and leave overnight. Open the bag outdoors, keeping your face away from the dangerous fumes. Use rubber gloves to remove and wash the cookware.

Clean a cast-iron pot If you need to clean and re-season that encrusted secondhand cast-iron skillet you found at a yard sale, start by giving it a good spraying with oven cleaner and placing it in a sealed plastic bag overnight. (This keeps the cleaner working by preventing it from drying.) The next day, remove the pot and scrub it with a stiff wire brush. Then, wash it thoroughly with soap and water, rinse well, and immediately dry it with a couple of clean, dry cloths. *Note:* This technique eliminates built-up gunk and grease, but not rust. For that, you'll need to use vinegar. Don't leave it on too long, though. Prolonged exposure to vinegar can damage your cast-iron utensil.

Remove stains from concrete Get those unsightly grease, oil, and transmission fluid stains off your concrete driveway or garage floor. Spray them with oven cleaner. Let it settle for 5-10 minutes, then scrub with a stiff brush and rinse it off with your garden hose at its highest pressure. Severe stains may require a second application.

Strip paint or varnish For an easy way to remove paint or varnish from wooden or metal furniture, try using a can of oven cleaner; it costs less than commercial paint strippers and is easier to apply (that is, if you spray rather than brush it on). After applying, scrub off the old paint with a wire brush. Neutralize the stripped surface by coating it with vinegar, and then wash it off with clean water. Allow the wood or metal to thoroughly dry before repainting. Don't use oven cleaner to strip antiques or expensive furnishings; it can darken the wood or discolor the metal.

✳ Oven Mitts

Use as beverage cozy or egg warmer Keep that mug of java or tea from getting cold when you're called away by placing an oven mitt over it. The glove's insulation will keep it warm until you get back. You can also use an oven mitt to keep boiled eggs warm for up to half an hour. Conversely, an oven mitt will help keep a cold drink colder longer.

Use for dusting and polishing Although oven mitts are typically confined to kitchen duty, they're actually great for dusting and polishing around your house. Use one side of the mitt to apply wax or polish to your furniture, and the other side to buff it up. It's a great way to use old mitts or all those extra ones you've collected.

When pruning thorny plants Although oven mitts may be a bit too awkward to use for weeding or planting seedlings in your garden, they can come in awfully handy when it comes time to prune trees, hedges, and bushes—particularly those thorny devils such as holly, firethorn, and rosebushes.

Remove hot engine parts Keeping an oven mitt in your car's glove compartment or trunk can make life a lot easier when you need to handle hot radiator caps and the like during an on-the-road emergency.

Change a hot lightbulb Did the lightbulb on your reading lamp just blow out? Don't scorch your fingers when replacing it. Once you've removed the lampshade, put on an oven mitt, remove the dead bulb from the socket, and toss it into the garbage. That way, you won't still be blowing on your fingertips when screwing in the new bulb.

✳ Paintbrushes

Use for delicate dusting A feather duster or dust rag is fine for cleaning shelves and such, but neither one is much good when you need to get into the tiny cracks and crevices of chandeliers, wicker furniture or baskets, and all sorts of knick-knacks. That's when a small natural-bristle paintbrush can be indispensable. The soft bristles are perfect for cleaning out areas that are otherwise impossible to reach. It's also excellent for dusting delicate items such as porcelain or carved-wood figurines.

Brush off beach chairs Keep a clean, dry paintbrush in your car specifically for those return trips from the beach. Use it to remove sand from beach chairs, towels, toys, the kids, and even yourself before you open the car door or trunk. You'll wind up with a lot less to vacuum the next time you clean your vehicle.

Brush on the sauce A small synthetic-bristle paintbrush can be invaluable in the kitchen. You can use it to brush on pie glaze, marinades, and sauces while baking or roasting. You can also use it to paint on the barbecue sauce when grilling burgers and steaks in the great outdoors. To top it all off, a paintbrush is easier to clean than most conventional pastry brushes.

Apply stain remover to clothes Let's face it: Pouring detergent or stain remover onto a soiled garment is often a hit-or-miss proposition—and when you miss, it usually involves grabbing the paper towels to soak up a spill. Make life easier for yourself. Use a small paintbrush to apply liquid stain remover to dirty shirt collars and such. It's neater and a lot more accurate.

Clean your window screens Are your window screens screaming out for a good cleaning? Use a large, clean paintbrush to give them a good dusting. Then shake off the brush, dip it into a small dish of kerosene, and "paint" both sides of your screens. Dry off the mesh with a clean cloth.

Cover up seeds when sowing Sow your seeds with a little TLC. When planting seeds in rows, use a large paintbrush to gently brush them over with soil. This lets you distribute the exact amount of soil needed and prevents overpacking.

Natural-bristle brushes work best with alkyd/oil-based paint. But use a synthetic-bristle brush with latex paint because the water in the paint can ruin natural bristles. Before cleaning any brush, wipe excess paint onto newspaper. Clean a brush used with alkyd paint in mineral spirits until you get out all the paint, then shake out. To clean out latex paint, wash the brush thoroughly with soapy water, rinse clean, and shake out. Many latex paints contain acrylics that won't wash out completely with soap and water. In this case, finish up with mineral spirits.

super item
✳**33** *uses!* **Pantyhose**

✳ PANTYHOSE **AROUND THE HOUSE**

Find lost small objects Have you ever spent hours on your hands and knees searching through a carpet for a lost gemstone, contact lens, or some other tiny, precious item? If not, count yourself among the lucky few. Should you ever be faced with this situation, try this: Cut a leg off an old pair of pantyhose, make sure the toe section is intact, and pull it up over the nozzle of your vacuum cleaner hose. (If you want additional security, you can even cut off the other leg and slip that over as well.) Secure the stocking in place with a tightly wound rubber band. Turn on the vacuum, *carefully* move the nozzle over the carpet, and you'll soon find your lost valuable attached to the pantyhose filter.

Vacuum your fish tank If you have a wet-dry shop vacuum, you can change the water in your fish tank without disturbing the gravel and tank accessories. (You'll still have to relocate the fish, of course.) Just pull the foot of an old nylon stocking over the end of the vacuum's nozzle, secure it with a rubber band, and you are ready to suck out the water.

Buff your shoes Bring out the shine in your freshly polished shoes by buffing them with a medium-length strip of pantyhose. It works so well, you may retire that chamois cloth for good.

Keep your hairbrush clean If you dread the prospect of cleaning out your hairbrush, here's a way to make the job much easier. Cut a 2-inch (5-centimeter) strip from the leg section of a pair of pantyhose, and stretch it over and around the bristles of your new (or newly cleaned) hairbrush. If necessary, use a bobby pin or a comb to push the hose down over the bristles. The next time your brush needs cleaning, simply lift up and remove the pantyhose layer—along with all the dead hair, lint, etc. on top—and replace it with a fresh strip.

Wrap up wrapping paper Keep your used rolls of wrapping paper from tearing and unraveling by storing them in tubes made by cutting the leg sections off old pairs of pantyhose. (Don't forget to leave the foot section intact.) Or, if you have a bunch of used rolls, you can simply put one in each leg of a pair of pantyhose and hang them over a hanger in your closet.

Remove nail polish Can't find the cotton balls? Moisten strips of recycled pantyhose with nail polish remover to take off your old nail polish. Cut the material into 3-inch (7.5-centimeter) squares, and store a stack of them in an old bandage container or makeup case.

Keep spray bottles clog-free If you recycle your spray bottles to use with homemade cleaners or furniture polishes, you can prevent any potential clogs by covering the open end of the tube—the part that goes inside the bottle—with a small, square-cut piece of pantyhose held in place with a small rubber band. This works especially well for filtering garden sprays that are mixed from concentrates.

Substitute for stuffing Is your kid's teddy bear or doll losing its stuffing? Get out a needle and thread and prepare the patient for an emergency "stuffing transplant." Replace the lost filler with narrow strips of clean, worn-out pantyhose (ball them up, if possible). Stitch the hole up well, and a complete recovery is guaranteed. This works well with throw pillows and seat cushions too.

Organize your suitcase As any seasoned traveler knows, you can squeeze more of your belongings into any piece of luggage by rolling up your clothes. To keep your bulkier rolls from unwrapping, cover them in flexible nylon tubes. Simply cut the legs off a pair of old pantyhose, snip off the foot sections, and stretch the stockings over your rolled-up garments. Happy travels!

Take a citrus bath Make your own scented bath oil by drying and grinding up orange and/or lemon peels and then pouring them into the foot section of a recycled pantyhose. Put a knot about 1 inch (2.5 centimeters) above the peels, and leave another 6 inches (15 centimeters) or so of hose above that before cutting off

DID *You* KNOW?

Nylon, the world's first synthetic fiber, was invented at E. I. DuPont de Nemours, Inc., and unveiled on October 28, 1938. Instead of calling a press conference, company vice president Charles Stine chose to make the landmark announcement to 3,000 women's club members at the New York World's Fair, introducing it with live models wearing nylon stockings. Stine's instincts were right on the money: By the end of 1940, DuPont had sold 64 million pairs of stockings. Nylon actually made its big-screen debut a year earlier, when it was used to create the tornado that lifted Dorothy out of Kansas in *The Wizard of Oz*.

PANTYHOSE*

the remainder. Tie the stocking to the bathtub faucet with the peels suspended below the running water. In addition to giving your bath a fresh citrus fragrance, you can use the stocking to exfoliate your skin.

Hold mothballs or potpourri Looking for an easy way to store mothballs in your closet or to make sachets of potpourri to keep in your dresser drawers? Pour either ingredient into the toe section of your recycled nylons. Knot off the contents, then cut off the remaining hose. If you plan to hang up the mothballs, leave several inches of material before cutting.

Make a ponytail scrunchy Why buy a scrunchy for your ponytail when you can easily make one for nothing? Just cut a horizontal strip about 3-inches (7.5 centimeters) wide across a pantyhose leg, wrap it a few times around your ponytail, and you're done.

Use to hang-dry sweaters Avoid getting clothespin marks on your newly washed sweaters by putting an old pair of pantyhose through the neck of the sweater and running the legs out through the arms. Then hang the sweater to dry on your clothesline by clipping the clothespins onto the pantyhose instead of the wool.

Bundle blankets for storage For an effortless and foolproof way to keep blankets and quilts securely bundled before they go into temporary storage, wrap them up in large "rubber bands" made from the waistbands from your used pantyhose. You can reuse the bands year after year if needed.

Tie up boxes, newspapers, magazines If you run out of twine (or need something stronger—say, for a large stack of glossy magazines), tie up your bundles of boxes, newspapers, and other types of recyclable paper goods using an old pair of pantyhose. Cut off the legs and waistband, and you'll be able to get everything curbside without any snags.

❋ PANTYHOSE **IN THE KITCHEN**

Store onions in cutoff bundles Get the maximum shelf life out of your onions by hanging them in nylon holders that provide the good air circulation needed to keep them fresh. Place the onions one at a time into the leg of a clean pair of pantyhose. Work the first one down to the foot section. Tie a knot above it and add the next one—repeat until done. Cut off the 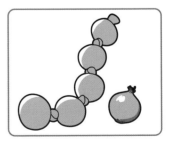 remaining hose, and then hang the stocking in a cool, dry area of your kitchen. You can easily remove your onions when needed by snipping off each knot, starting from the bottom.

Make a pot or dish scrubber Clean those stains off your nonstick cookware by making a do-it-yourself scrub pad. Crumple up a pair of clean old pantyhose, moisten it with a bit of warm water, add a couple of drops of liquid dishwashing detergent, and you're good to go. You can also make terrific scrubbers for dishes—as well as walls and other nonporous surfaces—by cutting off the foot or toe section, fitting it over a sponge, and knotting off the end.

Make a flour duster Looking for a simple way to dust baking pans and surfaces with exactly the right amount of flour? Just cut the foot section off a clean old pantyhose leg, fill it with flour, tie a knot in it, and keep it in your flour jar. Give your new flour dispenser a few gentle shakes whenever you need to dust flour onto a baking pan or prepare a surface for rolling out dough for breads or pastries.

Keep a rolling pin from sticking Getting pie dough to the perfect consistency is an art form in itself. Although you can always add water to dough that's too dry, it often results in a gluey consistency that winds up sticking to your rolling pin. Avoid the hassle of scraping clean your rolling pin by covering it with a piece of pantyhose. It will hold enough flour to keep even the wettest pie dough from sticking to the pin.

Secure trash bags How many times have you opened your kitchen trash can only to discover that the liner has slipped down (and that someone in your house has covered it over with fresh garbage anyway)? You can prevent such "accidents" by firmly securing the garbage bag or liner to your trash can with the elastic waistband from a recycled pair of pantyhose; tie a knot in the band to keep it tight. You can also use this method to keep garbage bags from slipping off the edge of your outdoor garbage bins.

Dust under the fridge Having trouble catching those dust bunnies residing underneath and alongside your refrigerator? Round them up by balling up a pair of old pantyhose and attaching it with a rubber band to a coat hanger or yardstick. The dust and dirt will cling to the nylon, which can easily be washed off before being called back for dusting duty.

 DID *You* KNOW?

You have probably heard that you can temporarily replace a broken fan belt with pantyhose in an emergency. Well, don't believe it—it won't work! Jim Kerr, automotive technician instructor at the Saskatchewan Institute of Applied Arts and Sciences and "Tech Talk" columnist for CanadianDriver.com, says, "Pulleys in most vehicles require flat belts, not the rounded shape pantyhose would present. Even on a V-belt pulley, they fly off as soon as the engine starts. We know; we've tried it." A much better idea is to replace the belts before they get in bad condition.

Stake delicate plants Give your young plants and trees the support they need. Use strips of pantyhose to attach them to your garden stakes. The nylon's flexibility will stretch as your seedlings or saplings fill out and mature—unlike string or twine, which can actually damage plant stalks if you tie it too tightly.

Store flower bulbs in winter Pantyhose legs make terrific sacks for storing your flower bulbs over winter, since they let air freely circulate around the bulbs to prevent mold and rot. Simply cut a leg off a pair of pantyhose and place your bulbs inside, knot off the end, and place ID tags on each sack using a strip of masking tape. Hang them up in a cool, dry space, and they'll be ready for planting in the spring.

Prevent soil erosion in houseplants When moving a houseplant to a larger or better accommodation, put a piece of pantyhose at the bottom of the new pot. It will act as a liner that lets the excess water flow out without draining the soil along with it.

Support melons Keep small melons such as cantaloupe and muskmelons off the ground—and free of pests and disease—by making protective sleeves for them from your old pantyhose. Cut the legs off the pantyhose. As your young melons start to develop, slide each one into the foot section, and tie the leg to a stake to suspend the melon above the ground. The nylon holders will stretch as the melons mature, while keeping them from touching the damp soil, where they would be susceptible to rot or invasion by hungry insects and other garden pests.

Keep deer out of your garden If you've been catching Bambi and her friends nibbling on your crops, put up a "No Trespassing" sign they will easily understand. Simply fill the foot sections of some old pantyhose with human hair clippings collected from hairbrushes or your local barbershop—or, even better, use Rover's fur after a good brushing. Tie up the ends, and hang up the nylon satchels where the deer tend to snack. They won't be back for seconds. The hair or fur will lose its scent after a while, so replace every four or five days as needed.

Clean up after gardening Here are two recycling tips in one: Save up your leftover slivers of soap, and place them in the foot section of an old nylon stocking. Knot it off, and hang it next to your outdoor faucet. Use the soap-filled stocking to quickly wash off your hands after gardening and other outdoor work without worrying about getting dirt on door handles or bathroom fixtures inside your house.

Cover a kids' bug jar What child doesn't like to catch fireflies—and hopefully release them—on a warm summer night? When making a bug jar for your youngster, don't bother using a hammer and nail to punch holes in the jar's metal lid (in fact, save the lids for other projects). It's much easier to just cut a 5- or 6-inch (15-centimeter) square from an old pair of pantyhose and affix it to the jar with a rubber band. The nylon cover lets plenty of air enter the jar, and makes it easier to get the bugs in and out.

Apply stain to wood crevices Getting wood stain or varnish into the tight corners and crevices of that unfinished bookcase or table that you just bought can be a maddening task. Your brush just won't fit into them and give them an even coating. But there's really nothing to it once you know the secret. Just cut a strip from an old pair of pantyhose, fold it over a few times, and use a rubber band to affix it to the tip of a wooden Popsicle stick. Dip your homemade applicator into the stain or varnish, and you'll have no trouble getting it into those hard-to-reach spots.

Test a sanded surface for snags Think you did a pretty good job sanding down that woodworking project? Put it to the pantyhose test. Wrap a long piece of pantyhose around the palm of your hand and rub it over the wood. If the pantyhose snags onto any spots, sand them until you're able to freely move the nylon over the surface without any catches.

Patch a hole in a screen Don't invite the bugs in for a bite; use a small square of pantyhose to temporarily patch that hole in your window screen. You can secure the

DID *You* KNOW?

According to the Toy Industry Association, legendary doll maker Madame Alexander came up with the concept for pantyhose in the early 1950s, when she started sewing tiny pairs of silk stockings onto her dolls' underpants to keep them from slipping down. But Allen Gant, Sr., of Burlington, North Carolina, invented pantyhose as we know them, and they were first produced in 1959 by Glen Raven Mills, his family's textile business. Another pantyhose pioneer is Hollywood actress Julie Newmar, best known as the original Catwoman on the old *Batman* TV series in the late 1960s, who holds a patent for "ultra-sheer, ultra-snug" pantyhose.

patch by simply applying some rubber cement around the hole before pressing the patch in place. When you're ready to fix the hole with a piece of screening, peel off the nylon and the glue. If you want the patch to last a bit longer, sew it onto the screen with thread.

Clean your pool Want a more effective way to skim the debris off the surface of your pool water? Cut a leg off a pair of pantyhose and fit it over your pool's skimmer basket. It will catch a lot of tiny dirt particles and hairs that would otherwise make their way into—and possibly clog—your pool's filter unit.

Make a paint strainer Strain your paint like the pros: Use a pantyhose filter to remove the lumps of paint from an old can of paint. First, cut a leg off a pair of old pantyhose, clip the foot off the leg, and make a cut along the leg's length so that you have a flat piece of nylon. Then cut the leg into 12- to 14-inch (30- to 32-centimeter) sections to make the filters. Stretch the nylon over a clean bucket or other receptacle and hold it in place with a rubber band or perhaps even the waistband from that pair of pantyhose. Now slowly pour the paint into the bucket.

super item ***25*** *uses!* # Paper Bags

* PAPER BAGS **AROUND THE HOUSE**

Dust off your mops Dust mops make it a breeze to get up the dust balls and pet hair around your home, but how do you get the stuff off your mop? Place a large paper bag over the mop head; use a piece of string or a rubber band to keep it from slipping off. Now give it several good shakes (a few gentle bumps wouldn't hurt either). Lay the mop on its side for a few minutes to let the dust in the bag settle. Then carefully remove the bag for easy disposal of your dusty dirt.

Clean artificial flowers Authentic silk flowers are actually pretty rare these days; most are now made of nylon or some other man-made material. But regardless of whether they're silk or something else, you can easily freshen them up by placing them in a paper bag with 1/4 cup salt. Give the bag a few gentle shakes, and your flowers will emerge as clean as the day you purchased them.

Carry your laundry If your laundry basket is already overflowing, or (gasp!) the plastic handle suddenly gives out, you can always use a sturdy shopping bag to pick up the slack. A bag with handles will probably make the job easier, but any large bag will do in a pinch. Just be sure your laundry is completely dry before using the bag on the return trip. Otherwise, your freshly cleaned clothes could wind up under your feet.

Cover your kids' textbooks Helping your children make book covers for their textbooks isn't only fun, it's also a subtle way to teach kids to respect public property. And few materials rival a paper bag when it comes to making a rugged book cover. First, cut the bag along its seams to make it a flat, wide rectangle, then place the book in the center. Fold in the top and bottom edges so the bag is only slightly wider than the book's height. Next, fold over the sides to form sleeves over the book covers. Cut off the excess, leaving a couple of inches on either side to slide over the front and back covers. Put a piece of masking tape on the top and bottom of each sleeve (over the paper, not the book) to keep it on tight, and you're done. Lastly, let your child put his or her personal design on each cover.

Create a table decoration Use a small designer shopping bag with handles to make an attractive centerpiece for your dining room table or living room mantel. Fill a small cup with some water and place it in the middle of the bag. Place a few fresh-cut flowers in the glass, and presto! All done.

Make your own wrapping paper Need to wrap a present in a hurry? You don't have to rush out to buy wrapping paper. Just cut a large paper bag along the seams until it's a flat rectangle. Position it so that any printing is facing up at you, put your gift on top and fold, cut, and tape the paper around your gift. If you wish, personalize your homemade wrapping paper by decorating it with markers, paint, or stickers.

DID *You* KNOW?

Are paper shopping bags better for the environment than their plastic counterparts? Not really, according to the U.S. Environmental Protection Agency. Paper bags generate 70 percent more air pollutants and 50 times more water pollutants than plastic bags. What's more, it takes four times as much energy to make a paper bag as it does to manufacture a plastic bag, and 91 percent more energy to recycle paper than plastic. On the other hand, paper bags come from a renewable resource (trees), while most plastic bags are made from nonrenewable resources (polyethylene, a combination of crude oil and natural gas). So what's the answer? Bring your own cloth shopping bags with you to the market!

Reuse as gift bags What to do with those small gift bags with handles favored by most boutiques? Why not use them to package your own gifts? They're ideal for holding items such as bath supplies, jewelry, perfume, and even most books. Simply add some shredded crepe paper, a personalized card, and you're all set.

Recycle as towel or tissue dispensers Add a simple but elegant touch to your guest bathrooms by using small "boutique bags" as paper towel or tissue dispensers. You can even embellish them with your own personal touches, such as ribbons or stickers that match your decor.

Reshape knits after washing Put the shape back into your wool sweater or mittens by tracing the contours of the item on a paper bag before you wash it. Then use your outline to stretch the item back to its original shape after washing it.

Store linen sets Have you ever emptied the contents of your linen closet looking for the flat sheet to match the fitted one you just pulled out? You can easily spare yourself some grief by using medium-sized paper bags to store your complete linen sets. Not only will your shelves be better organized, but you can also keep your linens smelling fresh by placing a used fabric softener sheet in each bag.

Use as a pressing cloth If your ironing board's cover appears to have seen its last steam iron, don't sweat it. You can easily make a temporary pressing cloth by splitting open one or two paper bags. Dampen the bags and lay them over your ironing board to get those last few shirts or skirts pressed for the workweek.

Pack your bags Getting ready to leave on a family vacation? Don't forget to pack a few large shopping bags—the kind with handles—in your luggage. They're guaranteed to come in handy to bring home the souvenirs you pick up, or perhaps your soiled laundry or beach towels.

Bag your recycled newspapers Double up on your recycling efforts by using large paper bags to hold your newspapers for collection. It not only spares you the time and effort needed to tie up your bundles with string, but it also makes it easier to sort out your magazines, newsprint, and glossy pages.

✳ PAPER BAGS **IN THE KITCHEN**

Make cleanups easier Cut open one or two paper bags and spread them out over your countertop when peeling vegetables, husking corn, shelling peas, or any other messy task. When you're done, simply fold up the paper, and toss it into the trash for a fast and easy cleanup.

Keep bread fresh If you live in a high-humidity area, your bread will stay fresher when stored inside a paper bag rather than a plastic one. The paper's ability to "breathe" will keep the bread's crust crisp while allowing the center of the loaf to stay soft and moist.

Use to ripen fruit Many fruits—including avocados, bananas, pears, peaches, and tomatoes—will ripen better when placed in a paper bag. To hasten the ripening process of any fruit, place an already ripe apple or banana peel in the same bag and store it at room temperature. To ripen green bananas, wrap them in a damp dishtowel before placing them in the bag. Once your fruits have adequately ripened, you can halt the process by putting them in the refrigerator.

Store mushrooms Remove your store-bought mushrooms from their mesh packaging and place them in a paper bag inside your refrigerator to keep them fresh for up to five days.

✱ PAPER BAGS **IN THE GARDEN**

Store geraniums in winter Although they're considered to be annuals, geraniums are easy to overwinter. First, remove the plants from their pots or carefully dig them up from your garden bed, shake off as much soil as possible, and place each plant in its own paper bag. Cover each bag with a second paper bag turned upside down and store them in a cool, dry place. When spring arrives, cut off all but 1 inch (2.5 centimeters) of stem and repot. Place them in a sunny spot, water regularly, and watch your plants "spring" back to life.

Feed your plants Bonemeal is an excellent source of nutrients for all the plants in your garden. You can easily make your own by first drying your leftover chicken bones in a microwave oven (depending on the quantity, cook them for 1-4 minutes on High). Then place the dried bones in a sturdy paper bag and grind them up using a mallet, hammer, or rolling pin. When done, distribute the powder around your plants and watch them thrive.

Add to compost Brown paper bags are a great addition to any garden compost heap. Not only do they contain less ink and pigment than newsprint, but they will also attract more earthworms to your pile (in fact, the only thing the worms like better than paper bags is cardboard). It's best to shred and wet the bags before adding to your pile. Also, be sure to mix them in well to prevent them from blowing away after they dry.

Dry your herbs To dry fresh herbs, first wash each plant under cold water and dry thoroughly with paper towels. Make sure the plants are completely dry before you proceed to reduce the risk of mold. Take five or six plants, remove the lower leaves, and place them upside down inside a large paper bag. Gather the end of the bag around the stems and tie it up. Punch a few holes in the bag for ventilation, then store it in a warm, dry area for at least two weeks. Once the plants have dried, inspect them carefully for any signs of mold. If you find any, toss out the whole bunch. You can grind them up, once you've removed the stems, with a rolling pin or a full soda bottle, or keep them whole to retain the flavor longer. Store your dried herbs in airtight containers and away from sunlight.

Kids' Stuff Make a **life-size body poster** of your child. Start by cutting up 4-6 **paper bags** so they lie completely flat (any print should be facing down). Arrange them into one big square on the floor and **tape** the undersides together. Then have your child lie down in the middle, and use a **crayon** to trace the outline of his or her entire body. Give him or her **crayons or watercolor paints** to fill in the face, clothing, and other details. When your kid is finished, hang it up in his or her room as a terrific **wall decoration**.

✳ PAPER BAGS **FOR THE DO-IT-YOURSELFER**

Move snow off your windshield If you're tired of having to constantly scrape ice and snow off your car's windshield during the winter months, keep some paper bags on hand. When there's snow in the forecast, go out to your car and turn on the wipers. Then, shut off the engine with the wipers positioned near the middle of your windshield. Now, split open a couple of paper bags and use your car's wipers to hold them in place. After the last snowflake falls, pull off the paper to instantly clear your windshield. *Note:* To prevent damaging your car's wipers, *do not* turn on the ignition until you've removed the snow and paper from the windshield.

Make a fire starter Looking for an easy way to get a fire going in your fireplace? Simply fill a paper bag with some balled-up newspaper and perhaps some bits of candle wax. Stick the bag under your logs, light it, then sit back and enjoy your roaring fire.

Spray-paint small items You don't have to make a mess every time you need to spray-paint a small item. Just place the object to be painted inside a large shopping bag and spray away; the bag will contain the excess spray. Once the item has dried, simply remove it and toss away the bag.

Build a bag kite Make a simple bag kite for your children to play with by folding over the top of a paper bag to keep it open. Glue on pieces of party streamers under the fold. Reinforce the kite by gluing in some strips of balsa wood or a few thin twigs along the length of the bag. Poke a couple of holes above the opened end, and attach two pieces of string or yarn (put a piece of masking or transparent tape over the holes to prevent them from tearing) and tie the ends onto a roll of kite string. It should take off when the kids start running.

✱ Paper Clips

Open shrink-wrapped CDs Opening shrink-wrap, especially on CDs, can be a test of skill and patience! Save your fingernails and teeth from destruction. Twist out the end of a paper clip and slice the wrap. To prevent scratches, slip the clip under the folded section of wrap and lift up.

Use as hooks for hanging Paper clips make great impromptu hooks. Making a hanging ceramic plaque? Insert a large, sturdy paper clip on the back before the clay hardens.

Use as zipper pull Don't throw away your jacket or pocketbook just because the zipper pull broke. Untwist a small paper clip enough to slip it through the hole. Twist it closed and zip! For a more decorative look, thread beads over the paper clip or glue on sequins before closing.

Hold the end of transparent tape Got a roll of transparent tape without a dispenser? Don't drive yourself nuts trying to locate and lift the end of the tape. Stick a paper clip under the end the next time you use the roll.

Make a bookmark Paper clips make great bookmarks because they don't fall out. A piece of ribbon or colorful string attached to the clip will make it even easier to use and find.

Pit cherries Need a seedless cherry for a recipe? Don't like to pit the cherry while you're eating it? Clip it to pit it! Over a bowl or sink, unfold a clean paper clip at the

---

SCIENCE FAIR

Want to amaze your friends? Challenge them to make a **paper clip float on water**. Give them a cup of water and a paper clip. When they fail, you show them how to do it. Tear off a piece of **paper towel**—larger than the clip—and place it on top of the water. Put the **paper clip** on top of the paper towel and wait a few seconds. The towel will sink, leaving the clip floating. It's magic! Actually, it's the surface tension of the water that allows the clip to float. As the paper towel sinks, it lowers the paper clip onto the water without breaking the surface tension.

center and, depending on cherry size, insert either the clip's large or small end through the top. Loosen pit and pull. To de-pit cherries but leave stems intact, insert the clip in the bottom. Cherry juice stains, so watch your clothing.

Extend a ceiling fan chain Put away the step stool and put an end to your ballet routine while trying to reach a broken or too-short ceiling fan chain. To extend the chain, just fasten a chain of paper clips to its end.

✳ Paper Plates

Make index cards It's inevitable—at the eleventh hour your child will say, "I need index cards for school tomorrow." If you don't have any, use paper plates and a ruler. Measure out a 3 x 5 or 4 x 6 (A7 or A6) card on the plate and cut. Use the first card as a template for the rest.

Protect stored dishes Prevent stored dishes from clattering and breaking, especially when you are moving, by inserting a paper plate between each dish when packing.

Paint can drip catcher Painters scrape the paintbrush on the side of the can to remove excess paint. To prevent drips from falling on the floor, place a paper plate under the can.

Make Frisbee flash cards Drilling your kids with flash cards can be a drag, but here's a way to make it fun. Write the numbers, letters, words or shapes you are teaching on paper plates and let the kids toss them like Frisbees across the room when they get a correct answer.

Make a snowman decoration When the cold wind blows and cabin fever peaks, paper plates can provide an inexpensive, creative outlet for kids. They can use them to make masks, mobiles, and seasonal decorations. To create a cute winter snowman, use two paper plates. Cut the rim off one plate to make it smaller. Staple the smaller plate to the larger plate, creating a head and body. Make boots and hat out of black construction paper and mittens out of red paper and glue on. Decorate the face with googly eyes, buttons, pipe cleaners, or draw on features with crayon or marker.

✳ Paper Towels

Mess-free bacon zapping Here's a sure-fire way to cook bacon in your microwave oven. Layer two paper towels on the bottom of your microwave. Lay slices of bacon side by side, on the paper towels. Cover with two more paper towels. Run your microwave on High at 1-minute intervals, checking for crispness. It should take 3-4 minutes to cook. There's no pan to clean, and the towels absorb the grease. Toss them for easy cleanup.

Clean silk from fresh corn If you hate picking the silk off a freshly husked ear of corn, a paper towel can help. Dampen one and run it across the ear. The towel picks up the silk, and the corn is ready for the boiling pot or the grill.

Strain grease from broth That pot of chicken broth has been bubbling for hours, and you don't want to skim off the fat. Instead, use a paper towel to absorb the fat. Place another pot in the sink. Put a colander (or a sieve) in the new pot and put a paper towel in the colander. Now pour the broth through the towel into the waiting pot. You'll find that the fat stays in the towel, while the cleaner broth streams through. Of course, be sure to wear cooking mitts or use potholders to avoid burning your hands with the boiling-hot liquid.

Keep produce fresh longer Don't you hate it when you open the vegetable bin in the refrigerator and find last week's moldy carrots mixed with the now-yellow lettuce? Make your produce last long enough so you can eat it. Line your vegetable bins with paper towels. They absorb the moisture that causes your fruits and vegetables to rot. Makes cleaning up the bin easier too.

Keep frozen bread from getting soggy If you like to buy bread in bulk from the discount store, this tip will help you freeze and thaw your bread better. Place a paper towel in each bag of bread to be frozen. When you're ready to eat that frozen loaf, the paper towel absorbs the moisture as the bread thaws.

Clean a can opener Have you ever noticed that strange gunk that collects on the cutting wheel of your can opener? You don't want that in your food. Clean your can opener by "opening" a paper towel. Close the wheel on the edge of a paper towel, close the handles, and turn the crank. The paper towel will clean off the gunk as the wheel cuts through it.

SCIENCE FAIR

Learn how all other colors are actually mixes of the **primary colors** of red, blue, and yellow. Cut a **paper towel** into strips. With a **marker**, draw a rectangle or large circle on one end of each strip. Try interesting shades of **orange, green, purple, or brown**. Black is good too. Place the other end of the strip into a **glass jar** filled with **water**, leaving the colored end dry and draped over the side of the jar. As the water from the jar slowly (about 20 minutes) moves down the towel and into the color blot, you'll see the **colors separate**. This also demonstrates **capillary attraction**— the force that allows the porous paper to soak up the water and carry it over the side of the jar.

Keep cast-iron pots rust-free Stop rust from invading your prized collection of cast-iron pots. After they're clean, place a paper towel in each to absorb any moisture. Store lids separately from the pots, separated by a lining of paper towels. No more ugly surprises when you reach for the pot again.

Make a place mat for kids Your darling grandchildren are coming for an extended visit, and though they are adorable, they're a disaster at mealtime. Paper towels can help you weather the storm. Use a paper towel as a place mat. It will catch spills and crumbs during the meal and makes cleaning up easy.

Test viability of old seeds You've just found a packet of watermelon seeds dated from two springs back. Should you bother to plant them or has their shelf life expired and they're best planted in the garbage can? To find out for sure, dampen two paper towels and lay down a few seeds. Cover with two more dampened paper towels. Over the next two weeks, keep the towels damp and keep checking on the seeds. If most of the seeds sprout, then plant the rest of the batch in the garden.

Clean a sewing machine Your sewing machine is good as new after its recent tune-up, but you're worried about getting grease from the machine onto the fabric for that new vest you're sewing. Thread the sewing machine and stitch several lines up a paper towel first. That should take care of any residual grease so you'll be ready to resume your sewing projects.

Make a beautiful kids' butterfly Use colored markers to draw a bold design on a paper towel. Then lightly spray water on the towel. It should be damp so that the colors start to run, but do not soak. When the towel is dry, fold it in half, open it up, and then gather it together using the fold line as your guide. Loop a pipe cleaner around the center to make the body of the butterfly and twist it closed. To make antennae, fold another pipe cleaner into a **V** shape and slip it under the first pipe cleaner at the top of the butterfly.

✳ Peanut Butter

Get chewing gum out of hair There it is. The piece of chewing gum you gave to your child not ten minutes ago is now a wadded mess in his hair. Apply some peanut butter and rub the gum until it comes out. Your child's hair may smell like peanut butter until you shampoo it, but it's better than cutting the gum out.

Remove price-tag adhesive You've removed the price tag from that new vase you've just purchased but you're left with that pesky gummy glue on the glass. Remove it easily by rubbing peanut butter on it.

Bait a mouse trap You know the mice are out there, scurrying around your kitchen at night. It's time to get tough. Lay traps, but bait them with peanut butter. They can't resist, and it's nearly impossible for them to swipe without tripping the trap. You'll be rid of the critters in no time.

Eliminate stinky fish smell If you're trying to eat more fish for health reasons, but hate the smell that hangs in your house after you've cooked it, try this trick. Put a dollop of peanut butter in the pan with the frying fish. The peanut butter absorbs the odor instead of your furnishings.

Plug an ice-cream cone Ice-cream cones are fun to eat but a bit messy too. Here's a delectable solution: Plug up the bottom of an ice-cream cone with a bit of peanut butter. Now, when munching through that scoop of double chocolate fudge, you'll be protected from leaks. And there's a pea-nutty surprise at the end of the treat.

✳ Pencils

Ease a new key into a lock You just had a new house key made, but you can't seem to fit it into your front door lock. Rub a pencil over the teeth of the key. The graphite powder should help the key open the door.

Use as hair accessory Take a pencil to school to help with your … hair. A pencil can help give lift to curly hair if you don't have a pick. Two pencils crossed in an **X** also can stabilize and decorate a hair bun, plus provide you a new writing tool if you lose yours during the day.

Decorate a picture frame Dress up the frame for this year's class picture with pencils. Glue two sharpened pencils lengthwise to the frame. Sharpen down two other pencils to fit the width of the frame.

SCIENCE FAIR

Are your eyes deceiving you? Cut a small **piece of paper**, about 2 inches (5 centimeters) square. Turn the square so it's a diamond. On one side, draw an animal or a person. On the other side, draw a setting for the animal, or a hat and hair for the person. Examples are a cheetah and grasslands or a boy with a hat. Next **tape** the bottom point of the diamond onto the point of a **pencil**. Then, holding the pencil so the picture is upright, **twirl** the pencil rapidly between your hands. You should see **both images** from the two sides of the paper **at the same time**.

Repel moths with pencil shavings If you're tired of finding your winter sweaters filled with moth holes after you've stored them for the season, this may help. Empty your electric pencil sharpener into little cloth sacks and use as sachets and in your closet. The cedar shavings will signal the moths to skedaddle.

Stake a small plant Got a small plant that needs some support? Don't know if it needs watering? A pencil can help with both problems. It's the perfect-sized stake for a small plant, tied with piece of old pantyhose or a cloth strip. Or stick a pencil in the pot of that house-plant to see if the soil needs watering yet.

Lubricate a sticky zipper Your zipper is refusing to budge, no matter how hard you tug and pull. Pick up a pencil and end your frustration. Run the pencil lead along the teeth of the zipper to unstick it. In no time you'll be zipping out the door with your jacket safely zipped up.

✳ Pencil Erasers

Shine your coins If you've just inherited a rather grimy coin collection from your uncle, but you'd like to see it with more luster, try an eraser to shine up the coins. But don't do this to rare and valuable coins—you can erase their value along with their surface patina.

Store pins or drill bits A box is not the most handy place to keep sewing pins. What if the box spills? What if you have a hard time grabbing just one when you're laying out pattern pieces? Here's the solution: Stick pins in an eraser. They won't fall out, and it's easy to grab the ones you need. This is also a good tip if you're storing several small drill bits.

Clean off crayon marks Your toddler has gone wild with the crayons, but he drew on the walls and not on paper. You've tried everything to get it off, but not this: an eraser. Try "erasing" the crayon marks to get the wall back to a clean slate.

Remove scuff marks on vinyl floors Those new shoes of your husband's have left black streak marks all over the kitchen floor. An eraser will take them off in no time. Give him the eraser and have him do it.

Clean your piano keys Whether it's a baby grand piano that fills the corner of the living room, a more conventional upright, or just a fold-away electronic keyboard, cleaning the keys can be a nightmare project of dust and finger marks. And when you clean it, it's hard to reach some spots to remove dirt. The sides of the black keys are especially difficult to clean. Find an eraser that fits between the ivories and the black keys and you'll have 86'ed the dirt on the 88s. This works well whether you have a piano with real ivory keys or the more common plastic ones.

Cushion picture frames Don't you hate it when that heavy mirror or picture frame gets slightly crooked? Tired of worrying about the black marks and scrapes the frame is making on the wall? Glue erasers to the bottom corners of the frame. The pictures will now hang straighter and not leave their mark.

Remove residue from stick-on labels That gray gummy substance on the new picture frame you just purchased is a sight to behold and not coming off with plain soap and water. Rub the residue with an eraser and watch the stuff just peel away.

✳ Pepper

Stop a car radiator leak A heat wave has hit your town, and your aging, leaking car radiator isn't too happy about it. If it's overheating because of a small leak, pepper can help. Before you bring your car to a mechanic for a more thorough repair, pour a handful of pepper into your radiator. It will temporarily plug the leaks until you can get some help.

Use as a decongestant Is your nose stopped up? Are your ears plugged? Do you have a cold? Forget the over-the-counter medications. Nothing gets things flowing again faster than some cayenne pepper. Sprinkle it on your food and grab some tissues.

Keep colors bright That new cherry-red shirt you just purchased is fantastic, but just think how faded the color will look after the shirt has been washed a few times. Add a teaspoon of pepper to the wash load. Pepper keeps bright colors bright and prevents them from running too.

Get bugs off plants There's nothing more frustrating than a swarm of bugs nibbling at your fledgling garden. Just when things are starting to pop up, the bugs are there, chowing down. Mix black pepper with flour. Sprinkle around your plants. Bugs take a hike.

 DID *You* KNOW?

The black pepper on your table actually starts out as a red berry on a bush. When the pea-size berry is placed in boiling water for ten minutes, it shrinks and turns black, becoming the familiar peppercorn that we fill our pepper grinders with. Of course, some of us skip that step and buy pepper already ground. Either way, black pepper is an ancient spice and the most common one in the world.

Deter deer from your garden Your freshly budding garden seems as if it's ringing the dinner bell for the neighborhood deer. They'll find another place to dine if you spray your bushes with a cayenne and water mixture.

Keep ants out of the kitchen Two or three of your annual summer visitors have invaded your kitchen. Those ants are looking for sugar. Give them some pepper instead. Cayenne pepper sprinkled in spots where the ants are looking, such as along the backs of your countertops or on your baseboards, will tell them that no sugar is ahead.

Kill an ant colony If you find the ants' home colony a little too close to yours and it is causing them to relocate to your kitchen, cayenne pepper can help get rid of it. Pour the pepper down the ant hole and say so long to ants.

super item *31 uses! Petroleum Jelly

*PETROLEUM JELLY **FOR PERSONAL GROOMING**

Moisturize your lips and more If you don't want to pay a lot for expensive lip balm, makeup remover, or even facial moisturizer, then your answer is a tube of petroleum jelly. It can soothe lips, take off foundation, eye shadow, mascara, and more. It will even act as a moisturizer on your face.

Make emergency makeup Oh no! You've run out of your favorite shade of eye shadow. What do you do now? It's easy—make your own. Add a bit of food coloring to petroleum jelly and apply as usual. This is a quick way to make stopgap blush, lipstick, or eye shadow.

Lengthen the life of perfume You've picked out a great scent to wear on your night out, but it's got to last. Worry not. Dab a bit of petroleum jelly on your pulse points. Then spray on the perfume. Now you can dance the night away and not worry about your perfume turning in early.

Remove a stuck ring Is your wedding ring stuck? Trying to get it off can take a lot of tug and pull. Apply some petroleum jelly and it will glide right off.

Soften chapped hands If you're constantly applying hand lotion to your tired, chapped hands, but then taking it off again so you can get more work done, try this tip. Apply a liberal amount of petroleum jelly to your hands just before you go to bed. By morning, they'll be soft and smooth.

No more messy manicures During home manicures, it's hard to keep the nail polish from running over on your cuticles. Petroleum jelly can help your manicures look more professional. Dab some along the base of your nails and the sides. If polish seeps off the nail during the manicure, all you do is wipe off the petroleum jelly and the sloppy nail polish is gone.

Smooth wild eyebrow hairs If you have runaway eyebrows—the ones where the hairs won't lie flat but curl up instead, control the wildness with some petroleum jelly. Rub a dab into your brows. They'll calm down and behave.

Stop hair dye runs There's nothing more embarrassing than a home hair color job gone awry. Imagine finishing applying that new auburn shade to your tresses when you notice that you've dyed your hairline and part of your forehead too. Next time, run a bit of petroleum jelly across your hairline. If dye seeps off your hair, the petroleum jelly will catch it.

Heal windburned skin You've just had a glorious hike through the countryside in autumn. And as much as you enjoyed the changing colors of the season, the hike has left you with an unpleasant souvenir: windburn. Grab a jar of petroleum jelly and apply it liberally to your face or wherever you've been chapped. The jelly helps relieve the pain.

Help prevent diaper rash It's so heartbreaking to hear a baby experiencing the pain of diaper rash. Help is just a few moments away. Petroleum jelly sets up a protective coat on the skin so the rash can heal. No more pain.

No more shampoo tears Thinking of buying special no-tears shampoo for your child? Forget about it. If you have some petroleum jelly, you have the solution. Rub a fair amount into your baby's eyebrows. It acts as a protective shield against shampoo running down into his eyes.

✽ PETROLEUM JELLY **AROUND THE HOUSE**

Smoother closing shower curtains Stop the water from squirting out onto the bathroom floor. Get that shower curtain into place quickly. Lubricate the curtain rod with petroleum jelly and you'll whip that curtain across the shower in no time.

Take out lipstick stains You set the table at that lovely dinner party with your favorite cloth napkins, but your girlfriends left their mark all over them. Now dotted with lipstick stains, those napkins may be headed for the trash. But try this first. Before you wash them, blot petroleum jelly on the stain. Launder as usual and hopefully you will kiss the stains good-bye.

Eject wax from candlesticks The long red tapers you used at last night's candlelit dinner were a beautiful sight until you saw the candle wax drippings left in the candleholders. Next time apply petroleum jelly to the insides of the holders before you put the candles in. The wax will pop out for easy cleaning.

Remove chewing gum from wood Did you discover bubble gum stuck under the dining room table or behind the headboard of Junior's bed? Trouble yourself about it no further. Squeeze some petroleum jelly on the offending wad, rub it in until the gum starts to disintegrate, then remove.

Make vacuum parts fit together smoothly It's nice that your vacuum cleaner comes with so many accessories and extensions. But it's frustrating when the parts get stuck together and you have to yank them apart. Apply a bit of petroleum jelly to the rims of the tubes and the parts will easily slide together and apart.

Shine patent-leather shoes You've got a great pair of patent-leather shoes and a dynamite bag to match. The luster stays longer if you polish the items with petroleum jelly.

Restore leather jackets You don't need fancy leather moisturizer to take care of your favorite leather jacket. Petroleum jelly does the job just as well. Apply, rub it in, wipe off the excess, and you're ready to go.

Keep ants away from pet food bowls Poor Fido's food bowl has been invaded by ants. Since she prefers her food without them, help her out with this idea. Ring her food bowl with petroleum jelly. The ants will no longer be tempted by the kibble if they have to cross that mountain of petroleum jelly.

Grease a baseball mitt Got a new baseball mitt, but it's as stiff as a dugout bench? Soften it up with petroleum jelly. Apply liberal amounts. Work it into the glove, then tie it up with a baseball inside. Do this in the winter, and by the spring you'll be ready to take the field.

Keep a bottle lid from sticking If you're having a hard time unscrewing that bottle of glue or nail polish, remember this tip for when you finally do get it open. Rub a little petroleum jelly along the rim of the bottle. Next time, the top won't stick.

Soothe sore pet paws Sometimes your cat's or dog's paw pads can get cracked and dry. Give a little tender loving care to your best friend. Squirt a little petroleum jelly on the pads to stop pain. They'll love you for it.

 DID *You* KNOW?

Although there are many generic versions of petroleum jelly, the only real major brand is Vaseline. Because of this, the online American Package Museum has included a jar of Vaseline petroleum jelly in its collection of classic packaging designs—a collection that also includes Alka-Seltzer and Bayer Aspirin. Why did the site include Vaseline? "Vaseline is a well-established brand with a 145-year-old history," says Ian House, who created the site. "It also seems to enjoy popularity as a cultural icon for humorous reasons. Nobody knows quite what to do with it ... but nobody can seem to live without it!"

Mask doorknobs when painting You're about to undertake painting the family room. But do you really want to fiddle with removing all the metal fixtures, including doorknobs? Petroleum jelly rubbed on the metal will prevent paint from sticking. When you're done painting, just wipe off the jelly and the unwanted paint is gone.

Stop battery terminal corrosion It's no coincidence that your car battery always dies on the coldest winter day. Low temperatures increase electrical resistance and thicken engine oil, making the battery work harder. Corrosion on the battery terminals also increases resistance and might just be the last straw that makes the battery give up. Before winter starts, disconnect the terminals and clean them with a wire brush. Reconnect, then smear with petroleum jelly. The jelly will prevent corrosion and help keep the battery cranking all winter long.

Protect stored chrome If you're getting ready to store the kids' bikes for the winter, or stow that stroller until your next baby comes along, stop a moment before you stash. Take some petroleum jelly and apply it to the chrome parts of the equipment. When it's time to take the items out of storage, they'll be rust-free. The same method works for machinery stored in your garage

Keep an outdoor lightbulb from sticking Have you ever unscrewed a lightbulb and found yourself holding the glass while the metal base remains in the socket? It won't happen again if you remember to apply petroleum jelly to the base of the bulb before screwing it into the fixture. This is an especially good idea for lightbulbs used outdoors.

Seal a plumber's plunger Before you reach for that plunger to unclog the bathroom toilet, find some petroleum jelly. Apply it along the rim of the plunger and it will help create a tighter seal. Whoosh, clog's gone.

Lubricate cabinets and windows Can't stand to hear your medicine cabinet door creak along its runners? Or how about that window that you have to force open every time you want a breeze in the house? With a small paintbrush, apply petroleum jelly to the window sash channel and cabinet door runners. Let the sliding begin.

Stop squeaking door hinges It's so annoying when a squeaky door makes an ill-timed noise when you're trying to keep quiet. Put petroleum jelly on the hinge pins of the door. No more squeaks.

Remove watermarks on wood Your most recent party left lots of watermark rings on your wood furniture. To make them disappear, apply petroleum jelly and let it sit overnight. In the morning, wipe the watermark away with the jelly.

Keep squirrels away from bird feeder Feed the birds, not the squirrels. Keep the varmints off the pole of your bird feeder by greasing it with petroleum jelly. Squirrels slide right off, leaving the birds to eat in peace.

Pillowcases

Dust ceiling fan blades Have you ever seen dust bunnies careening off your ceiling fan when you turn it on for the first time in weeks? Grab an old pillowcase and place it over one of the ceiling fan blades. Slowly pull off the pillowcase. The blades get dusted and the dust bunnies stay in the pillowcase, instead of parachuting to the floor.

Clear out cobwebs There's a cobweb way up high in the corner of your dining room. Before you take a broom to it, cover the broom with an old pillowcase. Now you can wipe away the cobweb without scratching the wall paint. It's also easier to remove the cobweb from the pillow than to pull it out of the broom bristles.

Cover a baby's changing table Have you priced those expensive changing-table covers lately? Forget about it! Pick up a few of the cheapest white pillowcases you can find and use those to cover the changing table pad. When one is soiled, just slip it off and replace with a clean one.

Make a set of linen napkins Who needs formal linen napkins that need to be pressed every time you use them? Pillowcases are available in a wide array of colors and designs. Pick a color or design you like, and start cutting. If you're really ambitious, sew a 1/2-inch (1.25-centimeter) hem on each edge. You'll have a new set of colorful napkins for a fraction of the cost of regular cloth napkins.

Prepare travel pillows Road trips can be a lot of fun, but a little dirty too. Your youngsters may want to bring their own pillows along, but they'll stain them with candy, food, and markers. Take their favorite pillows and layer several pillowcases on each. When the outside one gets dirty, remove it for a fresh start.

Use for wrapping paper Trying to wrap a basketball or an odd-shaped piece of art? Is your wrapping paper not doing the trick? Place the gift in a pillowcase and tie closed with a ribbon.

Store your sweaters Stored in plastic, winter sweaters can get musty. But stored just in a closet, they're prey to moths. The solution can be found among your linens. Put the sweaters in a pillowcase for seasonal storage. They will stay free from dust but the pillowcase fabric will allow them to breathe.

Protect clothing hanging in a closet You've just laundered a favorite dress shirt or skirt and you know you won't be wearing it again for a while. To protect the garment, cut a hole in the top of an old pillowcase and slip it over the hanger and clothing.

Stash your leather accessories You reach up to pull a leather purse or suede shoes down from a shelf. Of course, the item is dusty and now you have to clean it. Save yourself the time and hassle next time by storing infrequently used items in a pillowcase. They'll be clean and ready to use when the occasion arises.

Keep matching sheets together Solve this host nightmare. Your recently arrived overnight guests want to go to bed, but it's not made. You run to the linen closet, but you can't find a matched set of sheets. Next time, file away your linens. Place newly laundered and folded sheets in their matching pillowcase before putting them in the closet.

Machine-wash your delicates Sweaters and pantyhose can get pulled out of shape when they twist around in the washer. To protect these garments during washing, toss them into a pillowcase and close with string or rubber band. Set the machine on the delicate setting, add the soap, and worry not about knots.

Machine-wash stuffed animals Your child's Beanie Babies collection is cute but mighty dusty. Time for a bath. Place them in a pillowcase and put them in the washer. The pillowcase will ensure they get a gentle but thorough wash. If any parts fall off the stuffed animals, they'll be caught in the pillowcase so you can reattach them after their washing machine bath.

Kids' Stuff Kids love to personalize their bedrooms. You can help kids as young as 4 or 5 do just that by making a **pillowcase into a wall hanging**. Let the youngster choose a pillowcase color, and then slit a hole about 1 inch long in each side seam. Use **fabric paints** to create a design or scene or let him **rubber-stamp** a picture on the pillowcase. Stick a **dowel** through the seam openings. Cut a length of **yarn** about 30 inches (75 centimeters) long. Tie one end of the yarn to each end of the dowel. Hang on the wall and let the little one collect the compliments.

Use as a traveling laundry bag When you travel, you always want to keep your dirty laundry separate from your clean clothes. Stick a pillowcase in your suitcase and toss in the dirty laundry as it accumulates. When you get home, just empty the pillowcase into the washer and throw in the pillowcase as well.

Wash a lot of lettuce in washing machine Expecting a large crowd for an outdoor salad luncheon? Do you have 20 heads of lettuce to wash? Here's your solution: Place one pillowcase inside another. Pull apart the lettuce heads and fill the inside case with lettuce leaves. Close both pillowcases with string or rubber band, and throw the whole package in the washing machine with another large item, such as a towel, to balance it. Now run the spin cycle a few times. Your leaves come out rinsed and dried. It's better than a salad spinner.

✳ Pipe Cleaners

Decorate a ponytail Need a fresh look for your hair? Tired of using plain old ribbons? Once you have your hair in a ponytail, twist a pipe cleaner around the hair band. Twist a couple together for an even brighter effect.

Use as an emergency shoelace Your shoelace broke and you're about to go out on the court to play that grudge match in basketball. A pipe cleaner is a good stopgap tie-up. Just thread in your shoe as you would a shoelace and twist it up at the top.

Safety pin holder Safety pins come in so many sizes, it's hard to keep them together and organized. Thread safety pins onto a pipe cleaner, through the bottom loop of each pin, for easy access.

Clean gas burners Have you noticed that your stovetop burners are not firing on all their jets? Do you see an interrupted circle of blue when you turn a burner on? Poke a pipe cleaner through the little vents. This cleans the burner and allows it to work more efficiently. This works for pressure cooker safety valves, or pressure cookers' too.

Make napkin rings Colorful pipe cleaners are an easy and fast resource for making napkin rings. Just twist around the napkin and place on the table. If you want to get adventurous, use two, one for the napkin ring, attach the other pipe cleaner to it, shaped into a heart, shamrock, flower, curlicue, or something else.

Use as twist tie You're ready to close up that smelly bag of kitchen garbage when you discover you are out of twist ties. Grab a pipe cleaner instead.

?? DID You KNOW?

According to reliable sources, pipe cleaners were invented in the late 19th century in Rochester, New York, by J. Harry Stedman, who also came up with the idea of issuing transfers between local streetcars. Although pipe smoking has declined dramatically since then, pipe cleaners have flourished, having been co-opted by the arts-and-crafts community. Technically, the pipe cleaners used in classrooms, summer camps, Scout troops, and so on are called chenille stems. These stems come in various colors and widths and are fuzzier than the real pipe cleaners smokers use.

Use as a travel toy If you're worried about having a bored, wiggly child on your hands during your next long car or plane ride, throw a bunch of pipe cleaners into your bag. Whip them out when the "Are we there yet?" questions start coming your way. Colorful pipe cleaners can be bent and shaped into fun figures, animals, flowers, or whatever. They even make cool temporary bracelets and necklaces.

Use as a mini-scrubber Pipe cleaners are great for cleaning in tight spaces. Use one to remove dirt from the wheel of a can opener or to clean the bobbin area of a sewing machine.

Decorate a gift To give a special touch to a birthday or holiday present, shape a pipe cleaner into a bow or a heart. Poke one end through a hole in the card, and affix it to the package with a dab of glue.

super item *44 uses!* Plastic Bags

Line a cracked flower vase Grandmother's beautiful flower vase is a sight to behold when it's filled with posies. The problem is the vase leaks from a large crack that runs its length. Line the vase with a plastic bag before you fill it with water and add the bouquet, giving fresh life to a treasured heirloom.

Bulk up curtain valances You've picked out snazzy new curtain balloon valances for your bedroom. The problem is the manufacturer has only sent you enough stuffing to make the valances look a bit better than limp. Recycle some plastic bags by stuffing them in the valances for a resilient pouf.

Stuff crafts or pillows There are a number of ways to stuff a craft project: with beans, rice, fabric filler, plastic beads, pantyhose, and so on. But have you ever tried stuffing a craft item or throw pillow with plastic bags? There are plenty on hand, so you don't have to worry about running out, and you're recycling.

Make party decorations Here is an easy way to create streamers for a party using plastic bags. Cut each bag into strips starting from the open end and stopping short of the bottom. Then attach the bag bottom to the ceiling with tape.

Drain bath toys Don't let Rubber Ducky and all of the rest of your child's bath toys get moldy and create a potential hazard in the tub. Instead, after the bath is done, gather them up in a plastic bag that has been punctured a few times. Hang the bag by its handles on one of the faucets to let the water drain out. Toys are collected in one place, ready for the next time.

Keep kids' mattresses dry There's no need to buy an expensive mattress guard if bed-wetting is a problem. Instead, line the mattress with plastic garbage bags. Big bags are also useful to protect toilet-training toddlers' car seats or car uphol-stery for kids coming home from the swimming pool.

Make a laundry pocket pickin's bag You may think that the laundry's all done, until you open the dryer to find a tissue paper left in someone's pocket has shredded and now is plastered all over the dryer drum. Hang a plastic bag near where you sort laundry. Before you start the wash, go through the pockets and dump any contents in the bag for later sorting.

Treat chapped hands If your hands are cracked and scaly, try this solution. Rub a thick layer of petroleum jelly on your hands. Place them in a plastic bag. The jelly and your body's warmth will help make your hands supple in about 15 minutes.

✳ PLASTIC BAGS **FOR STORING STUFF**

Store extra baby wipes Shopping at the warehouse grocer, you picked up a jumbo box of baby wipes at a great price. You've got enough wipes to last for several months, as long as they don't dry out before you can use them. To protect your good investment, keep the opened carton of wipes in a plastic bag sealed with a twist tie.

Collect clothes for thrift shop If you're constantly setting aside clothes to give to charity, but then find them back in your closet or drawers, try this solution: Hang a large garbage bag in your closet. That way, the next time you find something you want to give, you just toss it in the bag. Once it's full, you can take it to the local donation center. Don't forget to hang a new bag in the closet.

Cover clothes for storage You'd like to protect that seersucker suit for next season. Grab a large, unused garbage bag. Slit a hole in the top and push the hanger through for an instant dustcover.

Store your skirts If you find you have an overstuffed closet but plenty of room to spare in your dresser, conduct a clothes transfer. Roll up your skirts and place them

DID *You* KNOW?

"Paper or plastic?" You hear the question every time you check out at the super-market. Though plastic bags have been around for nearly fifty years, they didn't start getting wide use at super-markets until 1977. Within two decades, plastic had replaced paper bags as the most common grocery bag. Today four out of five bags used at the grocer's are plastic. Thankfully, supermar-kets have implemented recycling programs for the proliferating bags.

each in a plastic bag. That will help them stay wrinkle-free until you're ready to wear one.

Keep purses in shape Ever notice that if you've changed purses and leave an empty one in your closet, it deflates and loses its shape? Fill your purse with plastic bags to retain its original shape.

Tip **Storing Plastic Bags**

> All those shopping bags are spilling out of the utility drawer in your kitchen. Here are some better ways to store them:
> • Stuff them inside an empty tissue box for easy retrieval.
> • Poke a bunch down a cardboard tube, such as a paper towel or mailing tube or even a section of a carpet tube.
> • Fill a clean, empty gallon (4-liter) plastic jug. Cut a 4-inch (10-centimeter) hole in the bottom. Stuff with bags and hang by its handle on a hook. Pull the bags out of the spout.
> • Make a bag "sock." Fold a kitchen towel lengthwise with the wrong side facing out. Stitch the long edges together. Sew 1/2-inch (1.25-centimeter) casings around the top and bottom openings and thread elastic through them, securing the ends. Turn the sock right side out, sew a loop of ribbon or string on the back to hang it up, stuff bags into the top opening, and pull them out from the bottom one.

✳PLASTIC BAGS **KEEPING THINGS CLEAN**

Protect hand when cleaning toilet When cleaning your toilets with a long-handled brush or a shorter tool, first wrap your hand in a used plastic bag. You'll be able to do the appropriate scrubbing without your hand getting dirty in the process.

Prevent steel wool from rusting A few days ago you got a new steel wool pad to clean a dirty pot. Now that steel pad is sitting useless in its own pool of rust. Next time, when you're not using the pad, toss it into a plastic bag where it won't rust and you'll be able to use it again.

Make bibs for kids The grandkids just popped in, and they're hungry. But you don't have any bibs to protect their clothes while they eat. Make some by tying a plastic bag loosely around the kids' necks so their clothes stay free of stains. You can make quick aprons this way too.

Create a high-chair drop cloth Baby stores are quite happy to sell you an expensive drop cloth to place under your child's high chair. Why spend the money on a sheet of plastic when you have all those large garbage bags that can do the job? Split the seams of a bag and place it under the high chair to catch all the drips and dribbles. When it gets filthy, take it outside and shake, or just toss it.

Line the litter box Nobody likes to change the cat's litter box. Make the job quick and easy by lining the box with an open plastic bag before pouring in the litter. Use two bags if you think one is flimsy. When it's time to change the litter, just remove the bags, tie, and throw into the trash.

Needle-free Christmas tree removal O Christmas tree, how lovely are thy branches! Until those needles start dropping. When it's time to take down your tree, place a large garbage bag over the top and pull down. If it doesn't fit in one bag, use another from the bottom and pull up. You can quickly remove the tree without needles trailing behind you.

Keep polish off your hand You want to polish up your scruffy white sandals. The problem is, you're going to get more polish on your hands than your shoes. Before you polish, wrap your hand in a plastic bag before inserting it into the sandal. Then when polish runs off the sandal straps, your hand is protected. Leave the bag in the sandal until the polish is dry.

✳PLASTIC BAGS IN THE KITCHEN

Cover a cookbook You're trying a new recipe from a borrowed cookbook that you don't want to get splattered during your creation. Cover the book with a clear plastic bag. You'll be able to read the directions, while the book stays clean.

Bag the phone Picture this: You're in the middle of making your famous snickerdoodle cookies. You're up to your elbows in dough. The phone rings. Now what? Wrap your hands in a plastic bag and answer the phone. You won't miss a call or have to clean the phone when you're done.

Scrape dishes Your extended family of 25 has just finished their Sunday dinner. Time to clean the dishes. Here's an easy way to get rid of the table scraps: Line a bowl with a plastic bag and scrape scraps into it. Once it's full, just gather up the

SCIENCE FAIR

It is said that a plastic bag can carry about 20 pounds (9 kilograms) of groceries before you need to double-bag. Find out **how much a bag can hold** without its handles breaking. For this experiment, you will need a **kitchen scale**, a **plastic**

bag, and a **bunch of rocks**. Place the bag on the scale. Fill it with rocks until the scale reads 10 pounds (4.5 kilograms). Lift the bag. Does it hold? Add more rocks in 2-pound (.9-kilogram) increments, testing the bag's strength after each addition. When the handles start to tear, you'll know the bag's actual strength.

handles and toss. Place the bowl in a prominent place in your kitchen so everyone can scrape their own dishes when bringing them to the sink.

Crush graham crackers Don't spend hard-earned grocery dollars on a box of pre-crushed graham crackers or a ready-to-fill graham cracker crust. It's much cheaper and a real snap to crush graham crackers yourself. Just crumble several graham crackers into a plastic bag. Lay the bag on the kitchen counter and go over it several times with a rolling pin. In no time, you'll have as many graham cracker crumbs as you need, plus the remainder of a box of crackers to snack on as well.

Replace a mixing bowl If you're cooking for a crowd and are short on mixing bowls, try using a plastic bag instead. Place all the dry ingredients to be mixed in the bag, gather it up and gently shake. If the ingredients are wet, use your hands to mix.

Spin dry salad greens The kids will enjoy helping you with this one. Wash lettuce and shake out as much water as you can in the sink. Then place the greens in a plastic grocery bag that has been lined with a paper towel. Grab the handles and spin the bag in large circles in the air. After several whirls, you'll have dry lettuce.

Ripen fruit Some of the fruit from that bushel of peaches you just bought at the local farm stand are hard as rocks. Place the fruit with a few already ripe pieces or some ripe bananas in a plastic bag. The ripe fruit will help soften the others through the release of their natural gas. But don't leave them for more than a day or two or you'll have purple, moldy peaches.

✱PLASTIC BAGS **IN THE YARD**

Protect plants from frost When frost threatens your small plants, grab a bunch of plastic bags to protect them. Here's how: Cut a hole in the bottom of each bag. Slip one over each plant and anchor it inside using small rocks. Then pull the bags over the plants, roll them closed, and secure them with clothespins or paper clips. You can open the bags up again if the weather turns warm.

Start poinsettia buds for Xmas You want that Christmas poinsettia to look gorgeous by the time the holidays arrive. You can speed up Mother Nature by placing the poinsettia in a large, dark garbage bag for several weeks to wake up the plant's buds.

Protect fruit on the tree Are there some apples in your orchard you want to protect or some plums that need a little more time on the tree? Slip the fruit into clear plastic bags while still on the trees. You'll keep out critters while the fruit continues to ripen.

Protect your shoes from mud It rained hard last night, and you need to get out in the garden to do your regular weeding. But you're worried about getting mud all over your shoes. Cover them in plastic bags. The mud gets on the bag, not on the shoes, and your feet stay dry so you can stay out longer in the garden.

Clean a grill easily That neighborhood barbecue was a blast, but your grill is a sorry mess now. Take the racks off and place them in a garbage bag. Spray oven cleaner on the grill and close up the bag. The next day, open the bag, making sure to keep your face away from the fumes. All that burned-on gunk should wipe right off.

Cover garage-sale signs If you've gone to the trouble of advertising your upcoming garage sale with yard signs but worry that rain may hurt your publicity campaign before even the early birds show up, protect the signs by covering them with pieces cut from clear plastic bags. Passersby can still see the lettering, which will be protected from smearing by the rain.

Store outdoor equipment manuals Your weed-whacker spindle just gave out and you have to replace it. But how? Stash all your outdoor equipment's warranties and owner's manuals in a plastic bag and hang it in your garage. You'll know exactly where to look for help.

Protect your car mirrors A big snowstorm is due tonight, and you've got a doctor's appointment in the morning. Get a step ahead by covering your car's side mirrors with plastic bags before the storm starts. When you're cleaning off the car the next morning, just remove the bag. No ice to scrape off.

Make a jump rope "I'm bored!" cries your child as you're trying to finish your yard work. Here's a simple solution: Make a jump rope by twisting up several plastic bags and tying them together end to end. Talk about cheap fun.

✳PLASTIC BAGS ON THE GO

Pack your shoes Your next cruise requires shoes for all types of occasions, but you worry that packing them in the suitcase will get everything else dirty. Wrap each pair in its own plastic bag. It will keep the dirt off the clothes, and you can rest assured you've packed complete pairs.

DID *You* KNOW?

Protect your hands when pumping gas You've stopped at the gas station for a fill-up while on your way to meet friends for lunch. The last thing you want is to greet them with hands that smell of gasoline. Grab one of those plastic bags you keep in your car and cover your hands with it while you pump.

Stash your wet umbrella When you're out in the rain and running to your next appointment, who wants to deal with a soggy umbrella dripping all over your clothes and car? One of those plastic bags that newspapers are delivered in is the perfect size to cover your umbrella the next time it rains. Just fold the umbrella up and slip it into the bag.

Make an instant poncho Leave a large garbage bag in your car. The next time it rains unexpectedly, cut some arm slits and one for your head. Slip on your impromptu poncho and keep dry.

Scoot in the snow Your neighborhood just got 6 inches (15 centimeters) of snow and the kids are hoping to take advantage of it right now. Grab some garbage bags, tie one around one each of their waists, and let them fanny-slide down the hills.

✱PLASTIC BAGS **FOR THE DO-IT-YOURSELFER**

Cover ceiling fans You're painting the sun porch ceiling, and you don't want to remove the ceiling fans for the process. Cover the blades with plastic bags to protect them from paint splatters. Use masking tape to keep the bags shut.

Store paintbrushes You're halfway through painting the living room, and it's time to break for lunch. No need to clean the paintbrush. Just stick it in a plastic bag and it will remain wet and ready to use when you return. Going to finish next weekend, you say? Stick the bag-covered brush in the freezer. Defrost next Saturday and you are ready to go.

Contain paint overspray If you've got a few small items to spray-paint, use a plastic bag to control the overspray. Just place one item at a time in the bag, spray-paint, and remove to a spread-out newspaper to dry. When you're done, toss the bag for a easy cleanup.

✱ Plastic Containers

Trap plant-eating slugs Sock it to those slugs eating your newly planted vegetable plants. Dig a hole the size of a plastic container near the plant. Place the container, flush with the ground, in the hole. Fill the container with beer or salted water and place cut potatoes around the rim to attract the slugs. Slugs crawl in, but they don't crawl out.

Wipe out dangerous wasps Those wasps have been getting a little too close for comfort, threatening to bring your child's outing to the park to a screeching halt. Take a plastic container and fill it with water sweetened with sugar. Cut a hole in the lid. Wasps will be attracted to the water and crawl inside, trapped.

Keep ants away from picnic table You watch helplessly as the ants march up the picnic table leg, onto the tabletop, and into the picnic meal. Here's a foolproof way to stop them in their tracks: Place a plastic container on the bottom of each picnic table leg. Fill with water. The ants won't be able to crawl past.

Use as a portable dog dish The next time you go out for a hike with your dog, pack a portion of its food in a plastic container. Of course, you can pack another container with a snack for yourself. An empty container also makes a great water bowl on the go.

Organize your sewing area You're sitting down at your sewing area to start on your Christmas craft projects. But instead of sewing, you're hunting for that extra bobbin or the right-color thread. Plastic containers can help you bring order to your sewing area. Fill several with thread spools, others with implements such as seam rippers and measuring tapes. Yet another can be filled with pins.

✱ Plastic Lids

Stop a sink or tub If your drain stopper has disappeared, but you need to stop the water in the sink or bathtub, here's a stopgap solution: Place a plastic lid over the drain. The vacuum created keeps the water from slip-sliding away.

Keep the fridge clean Drippy bottles and containers with leaks can create a big mess on your refrigerator shelves. Create coasters from plastic lids to keep things clean. Place the lids under food containers to stop any potential leaks. If they get dirty, throw them in the dishwasher, while your fridge shelves stay free of a sticky mess.

Use as kids' coasters Entertaining a crowd of kids and want to make sure your tabletops survive? (Or at least give them a fighting chance!) Give kids plastic lids to use as coasters. Write their names on the coasters so they won't get their drinks mixed up.

Use as coasters for plants Plastic lids are the perfect water catcher for small houseplants. One under each plant will help keep watermarks off your furniture.

Scrape nonstick pans We all know that stuff often sticks to so-called nonstick pans. And, of course, using steel wool to get it off is a no-no. Try scraping off the gunk with a plastic lid.

Separate frozen hamburgers The neighborhood block party is next week, but you have the hamburger meat now. Season the meat as desired and shape it into patties. Place each patty on a plastic lid. Then stack them up, place in a plastic bag, and freeze. When the grill is fired up, you'll have no trouble separating your pre-formed hamburgers.

Prevent paintbrush drips Worried about getting messy paint drips all over yourself while you're touching up a repair job on the ceiling? Try this trick. Cut a slot in the middle of a plastic lid. The kind of plastic lid that comes on coffee cans is the perfect size for most paintbrushes. Insert the handle of your paintbrush through the lid so that the lid is on the narrow part of the handle just above your hand. The lid will catch any paint drips. Even with this shield, always be careful not to put too much paint on your brush when you are painting overhead.

Close a bag Out of twist ties? Need to get that smelly garbage bag out of the house? Grab a plastic lid, cut a slit in it, gather the top of the bag, and thread it through. The bag's now completely sealed and ready for disposal.

✳ Plastic Tablecloths

Make a shower curtain A colorful tablecloth can make a great-looking shower curtain to match your bathroom decor. Punch holes about 6 inches (15 centimeters) apart and 1/2 inch (1.25 centimeters) from one edge of a hemmed tablecloth. Insert shower curtain rings or loop strings through the holes and loosely tie to the curtain rod.

Make a high-chair drop cloth Bombs away! It's par for the course for a baby to get more food on the floor than in his or her mouth. Catch the debris and protect your floor by spreading a plastic tablecloth under the high chair.

Collect leaves Save all that bending at leaf-raking time. Don't pick the leaves up to put them in a wheelbarrow to transport them to the curb or leaf pile. Just rake the leaves onto an old plastic tablecloth, gather up the four corners, and drag the tablecloth to the curb or pile.

❋ Plastic Wrap

Treat a hangnail Get rid of a hangnail overnight while you sleep. Before going to bed, apply hand cream to the affected area, wrap the fingertip with plastic wrap, and secure in place with transparent tape. The plastic wrap will confine the moisture and soften the cuticle.

Treat psoriasis Here is a method often recommended by dermatologists to treat individual psoriasis lesions. After you apply a topical steroid cream, cover the area with a small piece of plastic wrap and use adhesive tape to affix the wrap to your skin. The wrap will enhance the effect of the steroid, seal in moisture, and inhibit proliferation of the rash.

Enhance liniment effect For pain in your knee or other sore spots, rub in some liniment and wrap the area with plastic wrap. The wrap will increase the heating effect of the liniment. Make sure to test on a small area first to make sure your skin does not burn.

Keep ice cream smooth Ever notice how ice crystals form on ice cream in the freezer once the container has been opened? The ice cream will stay smooth and free of those annoying, yucky crystals if you rewrap the container completely in plastic wrap before you return it to the freezer.

Keep fridge top forever clean Make the next time you clean the top of your refrigerator the last time. After you've gotten it all clean and shiny, cover the top with over-

DID *You* KNOW?

Saran (polyvinylidene chloride) was accidentally discovered in 1933 by Ralph Wiley, a Dow Chemical Company lab worker. One day Ralph came across a vial coated with a smelly, clear green film he couldn't scrub off. He called it eonite, after an indestructible material featured in the "Little Orphan Annie" comic strip. Dow researchers analyzed the substance and dubbed the greasy film Saran. Soon the armed forces were using it to spray fighter planes, and carmakers used it to protect upholstery. Dow later got rid of the green color and unpleasant odor and transformed it into a solid material, which was approved for food packaging after World War II and as a contact food wrap in 1956.

lapping sheets of plastic wrap. Next time it's due for a cleaning, all you need do is remove the old sheets, toss them in the trash, and replace with new layers of wrap.

Protect computer keyboard Hooray! You are off on vacation and won't be tapping that computer keyboard for a couple of weeks. Cover your computer keyboard with plastic wrap during long periods of inactivity to keep out dust and grime.

Repair a kite Flying kites with the kids is a lot of fun, but it can also be frustrating when the kite gets torn by a tree branch or fence. For a temporary fix that will keep the kite airborne for a while, cover the tear with plastic wrap and affix it to the kite with transparent tape.

Keep stored paint fresh Your leftover paint will stay fresh longer if you stretch a sheet of premium plastic wrap over the top of the can before tightly replacing the lid.

> **TAKE CARE** When microwaving foods covered with plastic wrap, always turn back a corner of the wrap or cut a slit in it to let steam escape. Never use plastic wrap when microwaving foods with a high sugar content; they can become extremely hot and melt the wrap.

✳ Plungers

Remove car dents Before forking over big bucks to have an auto body repair shop pull a dent out of your car, try this: Wet a plumber's plunger, push it over the dent, and then pull it out sharply.

Catch chips when drilling ceiling Before you use a star drill to make an overhead hole, remove the handle from a plunger and place the cup over the shank of the drill. The cup will catch falling chunks of plaster, cement, or brick.

Use as an outdoor candleholder Looking for a place to put one of those bug-deterring citronella candles? Plant a plunger handle in the ground and put the candle in the rubber cup.

✳ Popsicle Sticks

Emergency splint for a finger You've got a kid with an apparent broken finger and you're on the way to the emergency room. Use a Popsicle stick as a temporary splint for the finger. Tape it on with adhesive tape to help stabilize the finger until it can be set.

Teach letters to future artists and writers Popsicle sticks are just the thing for spreading finger paint. Or, for a fun way to help youngsters practice their letters, let them use Popsicle sticks to write letters in a pile of shaving cream, whipped cream, or pudding.

Skewer kids' food It's more fun to eat food if you get to play with it first, as the parents of many picky eaters know. Popsicle sticks are good to have in your bag of tricks at mealtime. Skewer bites of hot dog, pineapple, melon, and more. Or give kids a stick and have them spread their own peanut butter and jelly.

Label your plantings Is that parsley, sage, rosemary, or thyme popping up from your garden? Remember what you planted by using Popsicle sticks as plant labels. Just write the type of seeds you planted on the stick with indelible marker.

Keep track of paint colors You're out in the garage searching through the cans of leftover paint. Did you paint the living room with a paint called Whipped Cream or Sand? Don't get mixed up again. After you've painted a room, dip a Popsicle stick in the can. Let it dry. Write the name of the paint and the room where it was used on the stick. Now you'll know what color to use when it's time to paint again. These guides can also help a home decorator pick out fabrics and decorative items.

> *Kids' Stuff* Here's a great little gift to encourage young readers. All you need is a **Popsicle stick**, **paint**, **craft foam**, **glue**, and a **marker**. Paint the Popsicle stick in a bright color, such as red. When it's dry, write on one side a reading slogan such as "I love to read" or "I'll hold the page." Then cut a shape out of the craft foam, such as a heart, flower, a cat, or a dog. Glue the shape to the top of the Popsicle stick, and you have a **homemade bookmark**.

✳ Pots and Pans

Catch draining engine oil No need to run out and buy an oil-collecting pan. When it is time to change the oil in your car engine, just stick an old 5-quart (4.75-liter) or larger pot beneath the drain plug.

Create an instant birdbath You can quickly provide feathered visitors to your backyard with a place to refresh themselves. Just set an old pan atop a flowerpot and keep it filled with water.

Use as a large scoop Leave those 50-pound (20-kilogram) sacks of fertilizer and grass seed in the garden shed and use a pot to carry what you need to the place you're tending. A small pot with a handle also makes a terrific boat bailer or dog-food scoop.

Make an extra grill You've got a big barbecue planned, and your grill is not big enough to handle all those burgers and dogs. Improvise an auxiliary grill by building a fire in an old, large pot. Cook on a cake rack placed over the pot. After you are finished, put the pot's cover on to choke out the fire and save the charcoal for another cookout.

✳ Potatoes

Make a decorative stamp Forget those expensive rubber stamps that go for up to $10 or more apiece. A potato can provide the right medium for making your own stamp for decorating holiday cards and envelopes. Cut a potato in half widthwise. Carve a design on one half. Then start stamping as you would with a wooden version.

Remove stains on hands Your family's favorite carrot soup is simmering on the stove, and you've got the orange hands to show for it. Otherwise hard-to-remove stains on hands from peeling carrots or handling pumpkin come right off if you rub your hands with a potato.

Extract salt for soup Hm, did you go a bit overboard when salting the soup? No problem. Just cut a few potatoes into large chunks. Toss them into the soup pot still on the stove. When they start to soften, in about 10 minutes, remove them and the excess salt they have absorbed. Save them for another use, such as potato salad.

Remove a broken lightbulb You're changing a lightbulb in the nightstand lamp, and it breaks off in your hand. So now the glass is off, but the stem's still inside. Unplug the lamp. Cut a potato widthwise and place it over the broken bulb. Twist, and the rest of the lightbulb should come out easily.

Remove tarnish on silverware High tea is being served at your house later today, and you're out of silver polish. Grab a bunch of potatoes and boil them up. Remove them from the water and save them for another use. Place your silverware in the remaining water and let it sit for an hour. Then remove the silverware and wash. The tarnish should be gone.

Keep ski goggles clear You can't keep a good lookout for trees and other skiers through snow goggles that fog up during your downhill descent. Rub raw potato over the goggles before you get on the ski lift, and the ride down should be crystal clear.

End puffy morning eyes We all hate waking up in the morning and looking at our mug in the mirror. What are those puffy spots on your face? Oh yeah, those are your eyes. A little morning TLC is what you need. Apply slices of raw, cold potatoes to your peepers to make the puffiness go away.

Lure worms in houseplants The worms crawl in and the worms crawl out of the roots of your favorite houseplant. The roots are suffering. What to do? Slice raw potato around the base of the plant to act as a lure for the worms. They'll crawl up to eat, and you can grab them and toss them out.

Feed new geraniums A raw potato can give a fledgling geranium all the nutrients it could desire. Carve a small hole in a potato. Slip a geranium stem into the hole. Plant the whole thing, potato and all.

Hold a floral arrangement in place If you have a small arrangement of flowers that you'd like to stabilize but have none of that green floral foam on hand to stick the flower stems in, try a large baking potato. Cut it in half lengthwise and place it cut side down. Poke holes where you want the flowers and then insert the stems.

Restore old, beat-up shoes Try as you might, your old shoes are just too scuffed to take a shine anymore. They don't have holes, and they are so nice and comfy that you hate to throw them away. Before you give them the brush-off, cut a potato in half and rub those old shoes with the raw potato. After that, polish them; they should come out nice and shiny.

Make a hot or cold compress Potatoes retain heat and cold well. The next time you need a hot compress, boil a potato, wrap it in a towel, and apply to the area. Refrigerate the boiled potato if you need a cold compress.

SCIENCE FAIR

Here's a way to demonstrate the **power of air pressure**. Grasp a **plastic straw** in the middle and try to **plunge it into a potato**. It crumples and bends, unable to penetrate the potato. Now grasp another straw in the middle, but

this time, put your **finger** over the top. The straw will plunge right into the tuber. When the air is trapped inside the straw, it presses against the straw's sides, stiffening the straw enough to plunge into the potato. In fact, the deeper the straw plunges, the less space there is for the air and the stiffer the straw gets.

* Return Address Labels

Tag your bags Address labels aren't only for sticking on envelopes. They can be an effective, inexpensive way of making sure your lost items stand a chance of finding their way home. Place an address label—covered with a small piece of transparent or clear packing tape to prevent wear—inside your laptop PC bag, designer eyewear case, gym bag, knapsack, and all pieces of luggage—whether they are tagged or not.

Label your stuff Few folks bother to take out insurance on their collection of personal electronics equipment, but replacing a high-end PDA, camera, camcorder, or MP3 player can run into some serious money. Still, a tape-covered address label conspicuously placed on your gear just may facilitate its safe return. Of course, there are no guarantees in these matters, but at least the policy is cheap enough.

Hang on to your umbrella A well-made umbrella can last for years, but that won't help if it's left behind on a bus or train. Minimize the risk of your loss becoming someone else's gain by sticking an address label on the umbrella handle and wrapping it once around with clear packing tape. This protects the label from the elements—and makes it considerably more difficult to remove.

Secure school supplies It's one of the universal truths of parenthood: Kids' pencil cases, folders, markers, and other school supplies are forever disappearing. You may be able to lessen the losses, however, by affixing address labels with a piece of transparent tape to the contents of your child's desk and backpack.

Identify items for repair Do you suffer separation anxiety when you bring your beloved stereo equipment or another precious item into the repair shop? You may feel better if you place an address label on the base or some other unobtrusive, undamaged area. *Note:* This practice is not recommended for all personal treasures—you probably wouldn't want to label paper documents, paintings, photos, and such.

Rubber Bands

Stop sliding spoons Plop! The spoon slipped into the mixing bowl again, and now you have to fish it out of the messy batter. This time, after you rinse off the spoon, wrap a rubber band around the top of the handle to catch the spoon and avoid the mess.

Secure your casserole lids Don't spill it! That's what you say when you hand somebody your lovingly prepared casserole dish to carry in the car on the way to that potluck dinner. You won't have to worry if you secure the top to the base with a couple of wide rubber bands.

Anchor your cutting board Do you find yourself chasing your cutting board around the counter when you're chopping up veggies? Give the board some traction by putting a rubber band around each end.

Get a grip on twist-off tops Ouch! The tops on most beer bottles these days are supposed to be twist-off, but for some reason they still have those sharp little crimps from the bottle-opener days. And those little crimps can really dig into your hand. Wrap the top in a rubber band to save the pain. The same trick works great for smooth, tough-to-grip soda bottle tops too.

Get a grip on drinking glasses Does arthritis make it tough for you to grasp a drinking glass securely, especially when it is wet with condensation? Wrap a couple of rubber bands around the glass to make it easier to grip. Works great for kids, too, whose small hands sometimes have a hard time holding a glass.

Reshape your broom No need to toss out that broom because the bristles have become splayed with use. Wrap a rubber band around the broom a few inches from the bottom. Leave it for a day or so to get the bristles back in line.

DID *You* KNOW?

The first rubber band was patented in 1845 by Stephen Perry, who owned a manufacturing company in London.

A key ingredient in making rubber bands is sulfur. When it is added to the rubber and heated—a process known as vulcanization—it makes the rubber strong and stretchy and prevents it from rotting. The process of making rubber bands is surprisingly similar to making a loaf of bread. First the dry ingredients are mixed with natural rubber. The resulting friction and chemical reaction heats and partially vulcanizes the rubber. The rubber is cooled, then rolled out like bread dough. It's extruded into a long tube, and the tube is heated to finish the vulcanization. Then it's rinsed, cooled, and sliced into bands.

Childproof kitchen and bath cabinets The grandkids are coming! Time to get out the rubber bands and temporarily childproof the bathroom and kitchen cabinets you don't want them to get into. Just wrap the bands tightly around pairs of handles.

Keep thread from tangling Tired of tangled thread in your sewing box? Just wrap a rubber band around the spools to keep the thread from unraveling.

Make a holder for your car visor Snap a couple of rubber bands around the sun visors of your car. Now you have a handy spot to slip toll receipts, directions, maybe even your favorite CD.

Thumb through papers with ease Stop licking your finger. Just wrap a rubber band around your index finger a few times the next time you need to shuffle papers. Not too tight, though! You don't want to cut off circulation to your fingertip.

Extend a button Having trouble breathing? Maybe that top shirt button is a tad too tight. Stick a small rubber band through the buttonhole, then loop the ends over the button. Put on your tie and breathe easy.

Use as a bookmark Paper bookmarks work fine, until they slip out of the book. Instead, wrap a rubber band from top to bottom around the part of the book you've already read. You won't lose your place, even if you drop the book.

Cushion your remote control To protect your fine furniture from scratches and nicks, wrap a wide rubber band around both ends of the television remote control. You'll be protecting the remote too—it will be less likely to slide off a table and be damaged.

Secure bed slats Do the slats under your mattress sometimes slip out? Wrap rubber bands around their ends to make them stay in place.

Tighten furniture casters Furniture leg casters can become loose with wear. To tighten up a caster, wrap a rubber band around the stem and reinsert.

Gauge your liquids Hm, just how much finish is left in that can up on the shelf anyway? Snap a band around the liquid containers in your workshop to indicate how much is left and you'll always know at a glance.

Wipe your paintbrush Every time you dip your paintbrush, you wipe the excess against the side of the can. Before you know it, paint is dripping off the side of the can and the little groove around the rim is so full of paint that it splatters everywhere when you go to hammer the lid back on. Avoiding all this mess is easy. Just wrap a rubber band around the can from top to bottom, going across the middle of the can opening. Now, when you fill your brush, you can just tap it against the rubber band and the excess paint will fall back into the can.

✳ Rubber Jar Rings

Keep rug from slipping If you have a throw rug that tends to skate across the floor, keep it in place by sewing a rubber jar ring or two on the underside in each corner.

Play indoor quoits What else can you do to keep antsy pre-schoolers happily occupied on a rainy day? Turn a stool or small table upside down and let them try to toss rubber jar rings over the legs.

Protect tabletops Protect your tabletops from scratches and watermarks by placing a rubber jar ring under vases and lamps.

✳ Rubbing Alcohol

Clean bathroom fixtures Just reach into the medicine cabinet the next time you need to clean chrome bathroom fixtures. Pour some rubbing alcohol straight from the bottle onto a soft, absorbent cloth and the fixtures. No need to rinse—the alcohol just evaporates. It does a great job of making chrome sparkle, plus it will kill any germs in its path.

Remove hair spray from mirrors When you are spritzing your head with hair spray, some of it inevitably winds up on the mirror. A quick wipe with rubbing alcohol will whisk away that sticky residue and leave your mirror sparkling clean.

Clean venetian blinds Rubbing alcohol does a terrific job of cleaning the slats of venetian blinds. To make quick work of the job, wrap a flat tool—a spatula or maybe a 6-inch (15-centimeter) drywall knife—in cloth and secure with a rubber band. Dip in alcohol and go to work.

Keep windows sparkling and frost-free Do your windows frost up in the wintertime? Wash them with a solution of 1/2 cup rubbing alcohol to 1 quart (1 liter) water to prevent the frost. Polish the windows with newspaper after you wash them to make them shine.

Dissolve windshield frost Wouldn't you rather be inside savoring your morning coffee a little longer instead of scrape, scrape, scraping frost off your car windows? Fill a spray bottle with rubbing alcohol and spritz the car glass. You'll be able to wipe the frost right off. Ah, good to the last drop!

Prevent ring around the collar To prevent your neck from staining your shirt collar, wipe your neck with rubbing alcohol each morning before you dress. Feels good too.

TAKE CARE Don't confuse denatured alcohol with rubbing alcohol. Denatured alcohol is ethanol (drinking alcohol) to which poisonous and foul-tasting chemicals have been added to render it unfit for drinking. Often, the chemicals used in denatured alcohol are not ones you should put on your skin. Rubbing alcohol is made of chemicals that are safe for skin contact—most often it's 70 percent isopropyl alcohol and 30 percent water.

Clean your phone Is your phone getting a bit grubby? Wipe it down with rubbing alcohol. It'll remove the grime and disinfect the phone at the same time.

Remove ink stains Did you get ink on your favorite shirt or dress? Try soaking the spot in rubbing alcohol for a few minutes before putting the garment in the wash.

Erase permanent markers. Did Junior decide to decorate your countertop with a permanent marker? Don't worry, most countertops are made of a nonpermeable material such as plastic laminate or marble. Rubbing alcohol will dissolve the marker back to a liquid state so you can wipe it right off.

Remove dog ticks Ticks hate the taste of rubbing alcohol as much as they love the taste of your dog. Before you pull a tick off Fido, dab the critter with rubbing alcohol to make it loosen its grip. Then grab the tick as close to the dog's skin as you can and pull it straight out. Dab again with alcohol to disinfect the wound. This works on people too.

Get rid of fruit flies The next time you see fruit flies hovering in the kitchen, get out a fine-misting spray bottle and fill it with rubbing alcohol. Spraying the little flies knocks them out and makes them fall to the floor, where you can sweep them up. The alcohol is less effective than insecticide, but it's a lot safer than spraying poison around your kitchen.

Make a shapeable ice pack The problem with ice packs is they won't conform to the shape of the injured body part. Make a slushy, conformable pack by mixing 1 part rubbing alcohol with 3 parts water in a self-closing plastic bag. The next time that sore knee acts up, wrap the bag of slush in a cloth and apply it to the area. Ahhh!

Stretch tight-fitting new shoes This doesn't always work, but it sure is worth a try: If your new leather shoes are pinching your feet, try swabbing the tight spot with a cotton ball soaked in rubbing alcohol. Walk around in the shoes for a few minutes to see if they stretch enough to be comfortable. If not, the next step is to take them back to the shoe store.

S

super item *65 uses! **Salt**

Clear flower residue in a vase Once your beautiful bouquet is gone, the souvenir it leaves behind is not the kind of reminder you want: deposits of minerals on the vase interior. Reach inside the vase, rub the offending ring of deposits with salt, then wash with soapy water. If your hand won't fit inside, fill the vase with a strong solution of salt and water, shake it or brush gently with a bottle brush, then wash. This should clear away the residue.

Clean artificial flowers You can quickly freshen up artificial flowers—whether they are authentic silk ones or the more common nylon variety—by placing them in a paper bag with 1/4 cup salt. Give the bag a few gentle shakes, and your flowers will emerge as clean as the day you bought them.

Hold artificial flowers in place Salt is a great medium for keeping artificial flowers in the arrangement you want. Fill a vase or other container with salt, add a little cold water, and arrange your artificial flowers. The salt will solidify, and the flowers will stay put.

Keep wicker looking new Wicker furniture can yellow with age and exposure to the sun and elements. To keep your wicker natural-looking, scrub it with a stiff brush dipped in warm salt water. Let the piece dry in the sun. Repeat this process every year or every other year.

Give brooms a long life A new straw broom will last longer if you soak its bristles in a bucket of hot, salty water. After about 20 minutes, remove the broom and let it dry.

Ease fireplace cleanup When you're ready to turn in for the night but the fire is still glowing in the hearth, douse the flames with salt. The fire will burn out more quickly, so you'll wind up with less soot than if you let it smolder. Cleanup is easier, too, because the salt helps the ashes and residue gather into easy sweepings.

Make your own brass and copper polish When exposure to the elements dulls brass or copper items, there's no need to buy expensive cleaning products. To shine your candlesticks or remove green tarnish from copper pots, make a paste by mixing equal parts salt, flour, and vinegar. Use a soft cloth to rub this over the item, then rinse with warm, soapy water and buff back to its original shine.

Remove wine from carpet Argggh! Red wine spilled on a white carpet is the worst. But there's hope. First, while the red wine is still wet, pour some white wine on it to dilute the color. Then clean the spot with a sponge and cold water. Sprinkle the area with salt and wait about 10 minutes. Now vacuum up the whole mess.

Clean grease stains from rugs Did that football-watching couch potato knock his greasy nachos onto your nice white carpet? Before you kill him, mix up 1 part salt to 4 parts rubbing alcohol and rub it hard on the grease stain, being careful to rub in the direction of the rug's natural nap. Or better yet, have him do it. Then you can kill him.

Remove watermarks from wood Watermarks left from glasses or bottles on a wood table really stand out. Make them disappear by mixing 1 teaspoon salt with a few drops of water to form a paste. Gently rub the paste onto the ring with a soft cloth or sponge and work it over the spot until it's gone. Restore the luster of your wood with furniture polish.

DID *You* KNOW?

Salt may be the key to life on Mars. Thanks to Mars missions, scientists have confirmed two things about the Red Planet: There's plenty of ice and plenty of salt. Of course, life as we know it requires water. And while temperatures on Mars are either too high or too low for fresh water, the presence of salt makes it possible that there is life-sustaining salt water below the planet's surface.

Restore a sponge Hand sponges and mop sponges usually get grungy beyond use long before they are really worn out. To restore sponges to a pristine state, soak them overnight in a solution of about 1/4 cup salt per quart (liter) of water.

Relieve stings, bites, and poison ivy Salt works well to lessen the pain of bee stings, bug bites, and poison ivy:

- Stung by a bee? Immediately wet the sting and cover with salt. It will lessen the pain and reduce the swelling. Of course, if you are allergic to bee stings, you should get immediate medical attention.

- For relief from the itching of mosquito and chigger bites, soak the area in salt water, then apply a coating of lard or vegetable oil.

● When poison ivy erupts, relieve the itching by soaking in hot salt water. If the case is very unfortunate, you might want to immerse yourself in a tub full of salt water.

S

Keep windows and windshields frost-free As you probably know, salt greatly decreases the temperature at which ice freezes. You can use this fact to keep the windows in your home frost-free by wiping them with a sponge dipped in salt water, then letting them dry. In the winter, keep a small cloth bag of salt in your car. When the windshield and other windows are wet, rub them with the bag. The next time you go out to your car, the windows won't be covered with ice or snow.

Deodorize your sneakers Sneakers and other canvas shoes can get pretty smelly, especially if you wear them without socks in the summertime. Knock down the odor and soak up the moisture by occasionally sprinkling a little salt in your canvas shoes.

Make a scented air freshener Buying fragranced air fresheners can get expensive. Here is a wonderful way to make your room smell like a rose any time of the year: Layer rose petals and salt in a pretty jar with a tight-fitting lid. Remove the lid to freshen the room.

Give goldfish a parasite-killing bath The next time you take your goldfish out of its tank to change the water, put Goldie in an invigorating saltwater bath for 15 minutes while you clean the tank. Make the bath by mixing 1 teaspoon plain (noniodized) salt into 1 quart (1 liter) freshwater. (Just like the tank water, you should let tap water sit overnight first to let the chlorine evaporate.) The salt water kills parasites on the fish's scales and helps the fish absorb electrolytes. Don't add salt to the fish's tank, though. Goldfish are freshwater fish and can't spend a lot of time in salt water.

Clean your fish tank To remove mineral deposits from hard water in your fish tank, rub the inside of the tank with salt, then rinse the tank well before reinstalling the fish. Use only plain, not iodized, salt.

 DID *You* KNOW?

The United States is the world leader in salt production. In 2002 the U.S. produced 43.9 million metric tons of salt, according to the Salt Institute. China was second, with 35 million metric tons. Among other nations producing significant amounts of salt were Germany, with 15.7 million metric tons; India, with 14.8 million metric tons; and Canada, with 13 million metric tons.

Repel fleas in pet habitats If Fido enjoys his doghouse, chances are fleas do too. Keep fleas from infesting your pet's home by washing down the interior walls and floor every few weeks with a solution of salt water.

End the ant parade If ants are beating a path to your home, intercept them by sprinkling salt across the door frame or directly on their paths. Ants will be discouraged from crossing this barrier.

✳ SALT **IN THE KITCHEN**

Freshen your garbage disposal Is an unpleasant odor wafting from your garbage disposal? Freshen it up with salt. Just dump in 1/2 cup salt, run the cold water, and start the disposal. The salt will dislodge stuck waste and neutralize odors.

Remove baked-on food Yes, you can remove food that has been baked onto cooking pans or serving plates. In fact, it's easy. Baked-on food can be "lifted" with a pre-treatment of salt. Before washing, sprinkle the stuck-on food with salt. Dampen the area, let it sit until the salt lifts the baked-on food, then wash it away with soapy water.

Soak stains off enamel pans You can run out of elbow grease trying to scrub burned-on stains off enamel pans. Skip the sweat. Soak the pan overnight in salt water. Then boil salt water in the pan the next day. The stains should lift right off.

Keep oven spills from hardening The next time food bubbles over in your oven, don't give it a chance to bake on and cool. Toss some salt on the stuff while it is still liquid. When the oven cools, you'll be able to wipe up the spill with a cloth. The same technique works for spills on the stovetop. The salt will remove odors too, and if you'd like to add a pleasant scent, mix a little cinnamon in with the salt.

Scrub off burned milk Burned milk is one of the toughest stains to remove, but salt makes it a lot easier. Wet the burned pan and sprinkle it with salt. Wait about 10 minutes, then scrub the pan. The salt absorbs that burned-milk odor too.

Clean greasy iron pans Grease can be tough to remove from iron pans, because it is not water-soluble. Shortcut the problem by sprinkling salt in the pan before you wash it. The pan will absorb most of the grease. Wipe the pan out and then wash as usual.

Clean discolored glass Did your dishwasher fail to remove those stubborn stains from your glassware? Hand-scrubbing failed too? Try this: Mix a handful of salt in a quart of vinegar and soak the glassware overnight. The stains should wipe off in the morning.

S

Clean your cast-iron wok No matter how thoroughly you dry them, cast-iron woks tend to rust when you wash them in water. Instead, when you're done cooking, but while your wok is still hot, pour in about 1/4 cup salt and scrub it with a stiff wire brush. Wipe it clean, then apply a light coating of sesame or vegetable oil before stowing it. Don't clean a wok with a nonstick coating this way, because it will scratch the coating.

Remove lipstick marks from glassware Lipstick smudges on glassware can be hard to remove, even in the dishwasher. That's because the emollients designed to help lipstick stay on your lips do a good job sticking to glassware too. Before washing your stemware, rocks glasses, or water tumblers, rub the edges with salt to erase lipstick stains.

Brighten up your cutting boards After you wash cutting boards and breadboards with soap and water, rub them with a damp cloth dipped in salt. The boards will be lighter and brighter in color.

Clean the refrigerator We all have to do it sometime, and today it's your turn. You've removed all the food and the racks from the fridge. Now mix up a handful of salt in 1 gallon (3.7 liters) or so of warm water and use it with a sponge to clean the inside of the refrigerator. The mixture isn't abrasive, so it won't scratch surfaces. And you won't be introducing chemical fumes or odors.

Speed cleanup of messy dough Here's a way to make short work of cleanup after you've rolled out dough or kneaded breads. Sprinkle your floury countertop with salt. Now you can neatly wipe away everything with a sponge. No more sticky lumps.

Erase tea and coffee stains Tea and coffee leave stains on cups and in pots. You can easily scrub away these unattractive rings by sprinkling salt onto a sponge and rubbing in little circles across the ring. If the stain persists, mix white vinegar with salt in equal proportions and rub with the sponge.

Shine your teapot spout Teapots with seriously stained spouts can be cleaned with salt. Stuff the spout with salt and let it sit overnight or at least several hours. Then run boiling water through the pot, washing away the salt and revealing the old sparkle. If the stain persists, treat the rim with a cotton swab dipped in salt.

DID You KNOW?

Salt was surely the first food seasoning. Prehistoric people got all the salt they needed from the meat that made up a large portion of their diet. When humans began turning to agriculture as a more reliable food source, they discovered that salt—most likely from the sea—gave vegetables that salty taste they craved. As the millennia passed, salt gradually made life more comfortable and certain as people learned to use it to preserve food, cure hides, and heal wounds.

Clean your coffee percolator If your percolated coffee tastes a bit bitter these days, try this: Fill the percolator with water and add 4 tablespoons salt. Then percolate as usual. Rinse the percolator and all of its parts well and the next pot you make should have that delicious flavor we all love.

Revive overcooked coffee You made a pot of coffee and then got distracted for an hour. Meanwhile, the coffee continued to cook in the pot and now it's bitter. Before you throw out the brew, try adding a pinch of salt to a cup.

> *Kids' Stuff* Here's a **craft dough** easily fashioned into detailed **ornaments, miniature foods,** and **dolls.** In a bowl, slowly stir 1 cup **salt** into 1 cup boiling water. After the salt dissolves, stir in 2 cups **white all-purpose flour.** Turn the dough out onto a work surface and knead until smooth. If the dough sticks, add flour by the tablespoon until it is pliant. It should be easy to shape into balls, tubes, wreaths, and other shapes. Air-dry your creations or bake them in a 200°F (95°C) oven for up to two hours; time depends on thickness. Or microwave on High 1-2 minutes. Apply **paint;** protect and shine with **clear nail polish** or varnish.

Prevent grease splatters How many times have you been burned by splattering grease while cooking bacon when all you wanted was a hearty breakfast? Next time, add a few dashes of salt to the pan before beginning to fry foods that can splatter. You'll cook without pain and you won't have to clean grease off your cooktop.

Speed up cooking time In a hurry? Add a pinch or two of salt to the water you are boiling food in. This makes the water boil at a higher temperature so the food you are cooking will require less time on the stovetop. Keep in mind: Salt does not make the water boil faster.

Shell hard-boiled eggs with ease Ever wonder whether there's a secret to peeling hard-boiled eggs without breaking the shell into a million tiny pieces? There is, and now it's out of the box! Add a teaspoon of salt to your water before placing the eggs in it to boil.

Make perfect poached eggs You *know* it's possible to keep the whites intact when you poach eggs—you've had them in a restaurant. But no matter how careful you are, the whites always diffuse into the water when you poach eggs at home. Here's the secret the restaurant chefs know: Sprinkle about 1/2 teaspoon salt into the water just before you put in your eggs. This helps to "set" the whites in a neat package. A dash of vinegar also helps, and improves the taste of the eggs too.

Test an egg's freshness In doubt about whether your eggs are fresh? Add 2 teaspoons salt to 1 cup water and gently place the egg in the cup. A fresh egg will sink. An old one floats.

Shell pecans easier Pecans can be tough nuts to crack. And once you do crack them, it can be tough to dig out the meat. Soak the nuts in salt water for several hours before shelling, and the meat will come cleanly away from the shells.

Wash spinach more easily Fresh spinach leaves are lovely to look at, but their curving, bumpy surface makes it difficult to wash away all the dirt that collects in the crevices. Try this trick: Wash spinach leaves in salted water. Dirt is driven out along with salt in the rinse water, and you can cut the rinses down to just one.

Keep salad crisp Do you need to prepare leafy salad in advance of a dinner party? Lightly salt the salad immediately after you prepare it, and it will remain crisp for several hours.

Revive wrinkled apples Do your apples need a face-lift? Soak them in mildly salted water to make the skin smooth again.

Stop cut fruit from browning You're working ahead, making fruit salad for a party and you want to make sure your fresh-cut fruit looks appetizing when you serve the dish. To ensure that cut apples and pears retain their color, soak them briefly in a bowl of lightly salted water.

Use to whip cream and beat eggs The next time you whip cream or beat eggs, add a pinch of salt first. The cream will whip up lighter. The eggs will beat faster and higher, and they'll firm up better when you cook them.

Keep your milk fresh Add a pinch of salt to a carton of milk to make it stay fresh longer. Works for cream too.

Prevent mold on cheese Cheese is much too expensive to throw away because it has become moldy. Prevent the mold by wrapping the cheese in a napkin soaked in salt water before storing it in the refrigerator.

Extinguish grease fires Store your box of salt next to the stove. Then, should a grease fire erupt, toss the salt on it to extinguish the flames. *Never* pour water on a grease fire—it will cause the grease to splatter and spread the fire. Salt is also the solution when the barbecue flames from meat drippings get too high. Sprinkling salt on the coals will quell the flames without causing a lot of smoke and cooling the coals as water does.

DID *You* KNOW?

The concentration of salt in your body is nearly one-third of the concentration found in seawater. This is why blood, sweat, and tears are so salty. Many scientists believe that humans, as well as all animals, need salt because all life evolved from the oceans. When the first land dwellers crawled out of the sea, they carried the need for salt—and a bit of the supply—with them and passed it on to their descendants.

Pick up spilled eggs If you've ever dropped an uncooked egg, you know what a mess it is to clean up. Cover the spill with salt. It will draw the egg together and you can easily wipe it up with a sponge or paper towel.

✳SALT **IN THE LAUNDRY**

Clean your iron's metal soleplate It seems to happen on a regular basis. No matter how careful you are while ironing, something melts onto the iron, forming a rough surface that is difficult to remove. Salt crystals are the answer. Turn your iron onto high. Sprinkle table salt onto a section of newspaper on your ironing board. Run the hot iron over the salt, and you'll iron away the bumps.

Make a quick pre-treatment You're out to a restaurant dining with friends and notice that a little salad dressing has spotted your slacks. You know it can't be checked with water, but here's an idea that will stop the stain from ruining your clothing. Drown the spot in salt to absorb the grease. When you get home, wash as usual.

Remove perspiration stains Salt's the secret to getting rid of those stubborn yellow perspiration stains on shirts. Dissolve 4 tablespoons salt in 1 quart (1 liter) hot water. Just sponge the garment with the solution until the stain disappears.

DID *You* KNOW?

One of the several words salt has added to our language is *salary.* It comes from the Latin word *salarium,* which means "salt money" and refers to that part of a Roman soldier's pay that was made in salt or used to buy salt—a life-preserving commodity. This is also the origin of the phrase "worth one's salt."

Set the color in new towels The first two or three times you wash new colored towels, add 1 cup salt to the wash. The salt will set the colors so your towels will remain bright much longer.

✳SALT **IN THE GARDEN**

Stop weeds in their tracks Those weeds that pop up in the cracks of your walkways can be tough to eradicate. But salt can do the job. Bring a solution of about 1 cup salt in 2 cups water to a boil. Pour directly on the weeds to kill them. Another equally effective method is to spread salt directly onto the weeds or unwanted grass that come up between patio bricks or blocks. Sprinkle with water or just wait until rain does the job for you.

Rid your garden of snails and slugs These little critters are not good for your plants. But there's a simple solution. Take a container of salt into the garden and douse the offenders. They won't survive long.

Clean flowerpots without water Need to clean out a flowerpot so that you can reuse it? Instead of making a muddy mess by washing the pot in water, just sprinkle in a little salt and scrub off the dry dirt with a stiff brush. This method is especially handy if your potting bench is not near a water source.

✳ SALT **IN THE BATH**

A pre-shampoo dandruff treatment The abrasiveness of ordinary table salt works great for scrubbing out dandruff before you shampoo. Grab a saltshaker and shake some salt onto your dry scalp. Then work it through your hair, giving your scalp a massage. You'll find you've worked out the dry, flaky skin and are ready for a shampoo.

Condition your skin You've heard of bath salts, of course. Usually this conjures images of scented crystals that bubble up in your tub and may contain coloring and other stuff that leave a dreaded bathtub ring. Now strip that picture to its core, and you've got salt. Dissolve 1 cup table salt in your tub and soak as usual. Your skin will be noticeably softer. Buy sea salt for a real treat. It comes in larger chunks and can be found in health food stores or the gourmet section of a grocery store.

Give yourself a salt rubdown. Try this trick to remove dead skin particles and boost your circulation. Either while still in the tub, or just after stepping out of the tub—while your skin is still damp—give yourself a massage with dry salt. Ordinary salt works well; the larger sea salt crystals also do the job.

Freshen your breath the old-fashioned way Store-bought mouthwash can contain food coloring, alcohol, and sweeteners. Not to mention the cost! Use the recipe Grandma used and your breath will be just as sweet. Mix 1 teaspoon salt and 1 teaspoon baking soda into 1/2 cup water. Rinse and gargle.

Open hair-clogged drains It's tough to keep hair and shampoo residues from collecting in the bathtub drain and clogging it. Dissolve the mess with 1 cup salt, 1 cup baking soda, and 1/2 cup white vinegar. Pour the mixture down the drain. After 10 minutes, follow up with a 1/2 gallon (2 liters) boiling water. Run your hot-water tap until the drain flows freely.

Remove spots on tub enamel Yellow spots on your enamel bathtub or sinks can be lessened by mixing up a solution of salt and turpentine in equal parts. Using rubber gloves, rub away the discoloration and then rinse thoroughly. Don't forget to ventilate the bathroom while performing this cleaning task.

✳ Saltshakers

Cut back on sugar You can cut back on sugar but still keep your sweet tooth happy if you fill a saltshaker with sugar. For sugar-restricted diets, use your sugar shaker as an alternative to dipping into the sugar bowl, and sprinkle lightly over food.

Use as a cinnamon/sugar dispenser Cinnamon toast is a great comfort food, and everyone likes it made a certain way. Mix sugar and cinnamon to your taste in a saltshaker. Once you've found the proportions you like, you can make it easily and consistently every time. Your cinnamon/sugar shaker is also perfect for sprinkling a little flavor on cereal.

Use for flour-dusting Baking is sometimes a messy job, so make at least one part of it tidier by putting flour into a large saltshaker. It's perfect for dusting your cake pans or muffin cups. Keep it neat and keep it handy in the cupboard, especially if you have an aggressively helpful junior chef!

 Colored Salt

> Want to bring a little unexpected fun to your dinner table? Try colored salt! Put a few tablespoons of salt into a plastic sandwich bag and add a few drops of food coloring. Work it gently with your fingers to mix, and let dry in the open bag for about a day. Just cut a hole in the corner of the bag to pour the festive salt into your shaker. As a bonus, your colored table or kosher salt is wonderful homemade glitter!

Use to apply dry fertilizer If you use dry fertilizer, try putting it in a saltshaker to use when fertilizing seedlings. It gives you lots of application control so you can prevent fertilizer burn on your tender babies.

✳ Sand

Protect and store garden tools Your gardening tools are meant to last longer than your perennials, so keep them clean and protected from the elements. Fill a 5-gallon (19-liter) bucket with builder's sand (available at masonry supply and home centers) and pour in about 1 quart (1 liter) of clean motor oil. Plunge shovels and other tools into the sand a few times to clean and lubricate them. To prevent rust, you can leave the tool blades in the bucket of sand for storage. A coffee can filled with sand and a little motor oil will give the same protection to your pruners and hand trowels.

Clean a narrow-neck vase You've held on to your bouquet as long as possible, but it's finally time to toss it along with the water it was sitting in. Now the vase needs cleaning, but the opening is too narrow for your hand. Put a little sand and warm, sudsy water in the vase, and swish gently. The sand will do the work of cleaning the residue inside for you!

Hold items while gluing Repairing small items, such as broken china, with glue would be easy if you had three hands—one for each piece along with one to apply the glue. Since you only have two hands, try this: Stick the biggest part of the item in a small container of sand to hold it steady. Position the large piece so that when you set the broken piece in place, the piece will balance. Apply glue to both edges and stick on the broken piece. Leave the mended piece there, and the sand will hold it steady until the glue dries.

Carry in trunk for traction A bag of sand in the trunk of your car is good insurance in icy weather against getting stuck or spinning out from a parking spot. Throw in a clean margarine tub as well, to use as a scoop. For those with rear-wheel-drive vehicles, a bag or two of sand will also give you some extra traction.

✳ Sandpaper

Sharpen sewing needles Think twice before throwing out a used piece of fine-grit sandpaper; the unused edges or corners are perfect for tucking into your sewing box. Poking your sewing needles through sandpaper a few times, or twisting them inside a folded piece of sandpaper, will make them sharper than ever.

Sharpen your scissors Are your scissor cuts less than crisp? Try cutting through a sheet of fine-grit sandpaper to finish off the edge and keep your cuts clean.

Remove fuzzy pills on sweaters If you're fighting a losing battle with the fuzz balls on your sweaters, a little sandpaper will handle them. Use any grit, and rub lightly in one direction.

Remove scorches on wool Take some medium-grit sandpaper to any small scorch spots on your woolen clothing. The mark left by a careless spark will be less noticeable with some light sanding around the edges.

Hold pleats while ironing If you're a pleat perfectionist, keep some fine- or medium-grit sandpaper handy with your iron. Put the sandpaper under the pleat to hold it in place while you iron a nice sharp fold.

Kids' Stuff You or your little Leonardo can make a beautiful **one-of-a-kind T-shirt**. Have the youngster use **crayons** to draw a bold design on the rough side of a sheet of **sandpaper.** Lay the T-shirt on your **ironing board** and slip a sheet of **aluminum foil** inside, between the front and back of the shirt. Place the sandpaper onto the T-shirt, design side down. Using an **iron** on the warm setting, press the back of the sandpaper in one spot for about ten seconds and then move on to the next spot until the entire design has been pressed. Let the shirt cool to set the design, launder on a cool setting, then hang to dry.

Roughen slippery leather soles New shoes with slippery soles can send you flying, so take a little sandpaper and a little time to sand across the width of the soles and roughen up the slick surface. It's thriftier and easier than taking your new shoes to a repair shop to have new rubber soles put on.

Remove ink stains and scuff marks from suede A little fine-grit sandpaper and a gentle touch is great for removing or at least minimizing an ink stain or small scuff mark on suede clothing or shoes. Afterward, bring up the nap with a toothbrush or nailbrush. You might avoid an expensive trip to the dry cleaner!

Use to deter slugs Slugs are truly the unwelcome guests that will never leave, but you can stop them from getting into your potted plants in the first place. Put those used sanding disks to work under the bases of your pots, making sure the sandpaper is wider than the pot base.

Remove stubborn grout stains Sometimes your bathroom abrasive cleaner is just not abrasive enough. Get tough on grout stains with fine-grit sandpaper. Fold the sandpaper and use the folded edge to sand in the grout seam. Be careful not to sand the tile and scratch the finish.

Open a stuck jar Having a tough time opening a jar? Grab a piece of sandpaper and place it grit side down on the lid. The sandpaper should improve your **grip** enough to do the job.

Make an emery board If you don't have an emery board handy the next time you need to smooth your nails, just raid the sandpaper stash in the garage workshop. Look for a piece marked 120 grit or 150 grit on the back.

Sandwich and Freezer Bags

S

Protect your pictures You just picked up a batch of beautiful photos of your newest grandchild. Before you pass them around your bridge party, encase each in a small, clear sandwich bag. Then you can hear the oohs and aahs without smudges on your pictures.

Freeze a washcloth for a cold pack It's hard to predict when someone in your household will next suffer a burn, teething pain, or another bump or scrape. Be ready. Freeze a wet washcloth in a sandwich or freezer bag. Pull it out of the freezer the next time someone needs some cold care.

Protect your padlocks When the weather is cold enough to freeze your padlocks on the outdoor shed or garage, remember that a sandwich bag can help. Slip one over the lock and you'll avoid frozen tumblers.

Make a fabric-softener dispenser Who can ever remember to add the fabric softener to the wash at the right time? You won't have to again. Punch some pinholes in a sealable plastic bag and, holding it over the washer basin, fill it with fabric softener. Seal the bag and toss into the laundry. The softener dispenses slowly through the pinholes during the wash and you won't have to remember that extra step.

Display baby teeth Your daughter has lost her first tooth and wants to show it off. You don't want to lose that precious memento of this important rite of passage. Place it in a sealable plastic bag. She can easily display it, and you won't worry about the tooth getting lost.

Make baby wipes for pennies You could buy the outrageously expensive baby wipes at the store or purchase some in bulk and hope they don't dry out before you use them up. Or you can just take the thrifty parent's way out: Make your own baby wipes by placing soft paper towels in a sealable bag with a mixture of 1 tablespoon gentle antibacterial soap, 1 teaspoon baby oil, and 1/3 cup water. Use enough of the mixture just to get the wipes damp, not drenched.

SANDWICH AND FREEZER BAGS

DID *You* KNOW?

Of course, we haven't always carried our ham-and-cheese sandwiches to work in plastic bags. Sandwich-size plastic bags were first introduced in 1957. Seven years later, Mobil Corp. introduced sandwich bags with tuck-in flaps, also known as Baggies. Just in case you are too young to remember, before plastic bags, we wrapped our sandwiches in paper or wax paper, like they still do in most delis.

Mold soap scraps into a new bar The thrifty among us hate to throw out a sliver of soap. Yet they're impossible to use when they get small. Instead, start collecting them all in a sealable plastic bag. When you have several, place the bag in a pan of warm, not boiling, water. Watch the soap pieces melt. When the mixture cools, you have a new bar of soap.

Starch craft items You've just completed that handmade Christmas stocking for your grandchild. But the last fabric ornaments to attach need to be starched. Throw them in a sealable plastic bag that contains a bit of starch. Shake until covered, remove, and let dry. Save the starch in the bag for your next craft project.

Feed the birds Be kind to the birds in your yard during the lean winter months. Mix some birdseed with peanut butter in a sealable plastic bag. Seal the bag and mix the ingredients by kneading the outside of the bag. Then place the glob in a small net bag or spread on a pinecone. Attach to a tree and await the grateful flock.

❊ SANDWICH AND FREEZER BAGS **IN THE KITCHEN**

Store grated cheese Pasta or pizza is always better with a dash of freshly grated Parmesan cheese. But who wants to bother with getting the grater out every time you want that taste? Instead, take a wedge of Parmesan cheese, grate the whole thing at once, and then double bag it in two self-closing bags to protect the freshness. Or stick the grater in the bag with the cheese wedge and pull it out for a short grate when the pesto gets to the table. That way you won't have to clean the grater after each use.

Make a pastry bag Pastry bags can be cumbersome, expensive, and hard to clean. Stop scrounging around the kitchen drawer for the pastry bag tip. Place the food to be piped, be it deviled-egg mix or decorating frosting, into a sealable bag. Squish out the air and close the top. Snip off a corner of the bag to the size you want—start conservatively—and you are ready to begin squeezing.

Dispose of cooking oil Unless you want the plumber for a best friend, don't clog your kitchen drain with used cooking oil. Instead, wait for it to cool, then dump it in a sealable plastic bag. Toss the bag into the trash.

Color cookie dough without stained hands Experienced bakers know what a mess your hands can be after coloring cookie dough. Here's a clean idea: Place your prepared dough in a bag, add the drops of food coloring, and squish around until the color is uniform. You can use the dough now or stick it in the freezer ready to roll out when the next occasion arises.

Stop ice crystals on ice cream It's truly annoying to open up that container of mint chocolate chip ice cream from the freezer to find unappetizing crystals forming on the frozen dessert. Place your half-full ice-cream container in a sealable bag and no crystals will form.

Store extra ice cubes It's a common experience. You open the freezer to grab some ice cubes from the ice cube maker and they're all stuck together, sometimes clogging the ice cube dispenser on the front of the fridge. When your tray fills up, toss the cubes in a sealable freezer bag. They won't stick together and you'll have easy access to the ice.

Soften hard marshmallows You're about to pull out that bag of marshmallows from your kitchen cabinet to make s'mores around the dying grill when you notice that the once-fluffy puffs have turned hard as rocks. Warm some water in a pan. Place the marshmallows in a sealable plastic bag, seal, and place in the pan. The warmth will soften them up in no time.

Melt chocolate without a mess Melting chocolate in a microwave or double boiler leaves you with a messy bowl or pot to wash. Here's a mess-free method: Warm some water in a pan (do not boil). Place the chocolate you want to melt in a sealable freezer bag. Seal and place the bag in the pan. In a few moments, you have melted chocolate, ready to bake or decorate with. You can even leave the bag sealed and snip off a bottom corner of the bag to pipe the chocolate onto a cake. When you are done, just toss the bag.

Keep soda from going flat You have to run out for a few errands and you don't want to take that soda with you. Leave the opened bottle or can at home zipped up in a large self-closing bag. That should help keep the fizz in until you get back.

Grease your pans If you're never quite sure how to handle shortening and butter when greasing a cake pan or cookie sheet, here's a tip: Place a sandwich bag over your hand, scoop up a small amount of shortening or butter from the tub, and start greasing. You can leave the bag in the canister of shortening for next time.

> ***Kids' Stuff*** **Dyed dry pasta** in different shapes and sizes is great for getting kids' creative juices flowing. They can use it to make string jewelry on yarn, or to decorate a picture frame or pencil canister, for example. To dye the pasta, put a handful of **pasta** in a **sealable plastic bag**. Add several drops of **food coloring**. Next squirt in a few drops of **rubbing alcohol**. Seal the bag. Shake it up so the coloring dyes the pasta. Spread the pasta out on foil and let dry.

Use as kids' gloves There's nothing more welcome than helping hands in the kitchen. But when they're little hands that tend to get dirty and leave prints all over the place, then something must be done. Before they start "helping" you make those chocolate chip cookies, place small sandwich bags over their hands. These instant gloves are disposable for easy cleanup.

Make a funnel That handiest of kitchen tools, the funnel, can be replicated easily with a small sandwich bag. Fill the bag with the contents you need funneled. Snip off the end and transfer into the needed container. Then just toss the bag when the funneling is done.

✳ SANDWICH AND FREEZER BAGS **FOR STORING THINGS**

Protect your fragile breakables There's a precious family heirloom, a statue, a vase, or a trinket that needs some extra padding when storing. Here's what to do: Place it gently in a self-closing bag, close the bag most of the way, blow it up with air, then seal it. The air forms a protective cushion around the memento.

Save your sweaters You're about to put away that pile of winter sweaters for the season. Don't just throw them in a box without protection. Place each sweater in a sealable plastic bag and seal. They'll be clean and moth-free when the cold weather rolls around again. Save the bags for next spring when the sweaters need to be stored again.

Create a sachet If your drawers are starting to smell musty, a sealable bag can be your dresser's best friend. Fill the bag with potpourri—for example, flower petals along with a few crushed fragrant leaves and a couple of drops of aromatic oil. Punch a bunch of small holes in the bag. Then place in the drawer. Your drawers will smell fresh again soon.

Add cedar to your closet Cedar closets smell great, and, more important, they repel moths. If you aren't lucky enough to have a cedar closet, you can easily create the next best thing. Fill a sealable bag with cedar chips—the kind you buy at a pet store for the hamster cage. Zip it closed, then punch several small holes in it. Hang the bag in your closet (a pants hanger is handy for this) and let the cedar smell do its work.

Make a pencil bag Do the kids have trouble keeping track of their school pencils, pens, and rulers? Puncture three holes along the bottom edge of a sealable freezer bag so it will fit in a three-ring binder. Now the young scholars can zip their supplies in and out of the bag.

?? DID *You* KNOW?

The self-sealing plastic bag became a part of our lives in 1969, when Dow Chemical introduced the Ziploc bag. A wide variety of sealable bags has been developed since then, including snack, sand- wich, quart (liter), gallon (3.7 liter), and 2-gallon (7.4 liter) sizes, and double- strength freezer bags. There are even ones with flat bot- toms to make them easy to pour into. The vegetable bag, with holes in it to help keep veggies fresh, was short- lived, however. You can even get sealable bags in small pouches of 10 and 8 bags, so you can take a bagful of bags with you.

SANDWICH AND FREEZER BAGS*

De-clutter the bathroom Here's a quick cleanup solution: Guests are coming over and the bathroom is strewn with Hubby's razor, shave cream, and more. Quickly gather up all the supplies in one clear sealable bag. That way, he will know where his shaving supplies are and you don't have to deal with them. Now, if we could just do something about the whiskers in the sink!

Make a bath pillow Ready for a nice hot bath? Want to luxuriate in the warm water with bubbles and champagne? Well, here's the perfect, and cheap, thing to make your bath experience complete: Blow up a gallon-size (3.7-liter) sealable plastic bag and you'll have a comfortable pillow during your soak.

Clean your dentures No more dentures in a cup by your bedside. Toss your teeth in with their cleaner in a sealable plastic bag. They'll be clean and ready to go in the morning.

Organize your makeup Many of us have scads of makeup. Pats of ill-advised eye shadow and samples of powder and blush from department stores fill our makeup cases. Problem is, there are only a few cosmetics we really use every single day. Stash those favorites in a sealable plastic bag so you don't have to hunt around for them every morning.

Stash dirty clothes Chocolate ice cream is careering down your child's white Sunday-best shirt. If you can keep the stain from drying, it will be a lot easier to get out. Change your child's shirt and spray the stained shirt with stain remover if you have a small bottle handy or just soak in water if you don't. Then seal the shirt in a sealable plastic bag, and it will be ready for the wash when you get home.

Hold spare clothes Toilet training a child? Need to be ready for meal mishaps? Put a change of clothes for your son or daughter in a sealable plastic bag, and keep it in the trunk of your car. You won't have to think twice the next time you have an "accident."

Carry detergent for washing If you're planning a trip to a friend's beach house and think you'll be doing a few loads of laundry while you're there, premeasure some detergent in a bag that you can pour out when the time comes. Beats lugging a big box of detergent down to the shore.

Carry wet washcloth for cooling off Going for a long trip on a hot and sticky day? Use a sealable bag to take along a wet washcloth that has been soaked in water and lemon juice so that everyone can get a refreshing wipe-off. This is a good trick for fast on-the-road face and hand cleanups anytime.

Keep your valuables dry and afloat Whoops! You tipped the canoe and got dunked. No biggie, until that sinking feeling hits—your car keys and cell phone are at the bottom of the lake. Avoid this disaster by putting your valuables in a sealable bag. Blow air into it before you seal the bag so it will float. A sealable bag is perfect for keeping valuables dry at the water park or beach too.

> *Kids' Stuff* This is a great and **yummy activity** if you're outdoors. Pour a small box of instant **pudding mix** in a **sealable plastic bag** and add the amount of **milk** called for on the box. Seal it up and then seal that bag in **another sealable bag**. Now you're ready to **play football**. Toss the bag of pudding around with your friends until it mixes and the pudding forms. Open the first bag and remove the second bag. Pour the pudding into flat-bottomed **ice-cream cones** and chow down.

Create a beach hand cleaner You're sitting on the beach and it's time for lunch. But before you reach into your cooler, you want to get the grit off your hands. Baby powder in a sealable plastic bag is the key. Place your hands in the bag, then remove them and rub them together. The sand is gone.

Apply bug spray to your face It's difficult to cleanly apply bug spray to your face without squirting yourself in the eyes or getting it on your hands. Instead, throw some cotton balls into a plastic bag, squirt in the bug spray, seal, and shake. Now use the cotton balls to apply the bug spray.

Cure car sickness The last thing you need in your car is a child throwing up. Make your child feel better and head off the mess and stench. Place a few cotton balls in a sealable plastic bag. Squirt in 2 drops lavender oil. If motion sickness strikes, the child can open the bag and take a few whiffs of the oil.

Use as a portable water dish Your furry best friend has happily hiked alongside you during your trek in the great outdoors. You take a break, and he gives you one of those longing looks as you draw on your canteen. No problem. You pull a sealable plastic bag full of water from your pack and hold it open while Buddy laps his fill.

✳ Screening

Store pierced earrings Keep your pierced and hook earrings organized and ready at-a-glance with a spare piece of window screen. Cut a square of screen with metal shears or utility scissors and cover the edges of the square with duct or cloth tape. Then push the earrings through the holes in the screen. If you like, you can hang the screen square on the wall by attaching string or floral wire to the top corners.

Get rid of paint lumps You want to do a touch-up paint job, but your used can of paint has some lumps in it. Instead of going through the bother of straining the paint into another container, try this: Cut a circle of screening sized to fit inside the can (use the lid as a guide). Place the screen circle on top of the paint and push it gently down to the bottom with your stir stick. The lumps will now be trapped at the bottom of the can. Stir up the paint and get to work.

Protect newly planted seeds Who knows what is walking around your garden at night, so protect newly planted seeds by covering them with a sheet of screen material. It also might deter the neighborhood felines from using your nice, fluffy soil as a cat box. When the seedlings emerge, you can bend the screening to make cages.

✳ Shampoo

Revitalize leather shoes and purses You don't need expensive mink oil to bring life back to your leather shoes and purses. A little shampoo and a clean rag will do the job. Rub shampoo into worn areas in circles to clean and bring back the color of your accessories. It will protect your shoes from salt stains as well.

Lubricate a zipper If your zipper gets stuck, don't yank on it until it breaks. Put a drop of shampoo on a cotton swab and dab it onto the zipper. The shampoo will help the zipper to slide free, and any residue will come out in the next wash.

Resize a shrunken sweater Oh no, you've shrunk your favorite sweater! Don't panic, you can bring it back to full size again with baby shampoo and warm water. Fill a basin with warm water, squirt in some baby shampoo, and swish once with your hand. Lay the sweater on top of the water and let it sink on its own and soak for 15 minutes. Gently take your sweater out without wringing it and put it in a container, then fill the sink again with clean water. Lay the sweater on top and let it sink again to rinse. Take the sweater out, place it on a

DID *You* KNOW?

One of the longest-running advertising campaigns in history, "the Breck Girl," was the brainchild of Edward Breck, a member of the family that started Breck Shampoo Co. The ads, featuring wholesome, beautiful girls with gorgeous hair, began in 1936, during the Great Depression, although they didn't go national until 1947. Only two artists were used during the 40-year campaign. The best known was Ralph William Williams, who took over the job in 1957. Among the models for Williams's Breck girls were Cybill Shepherd, Kim Basinger, and Brooke Shields—all unknowns at the time. The campaign ceased soon after Williams's death in 1976.

towel, and roll the towel to take out most of the moisture. Lay the sweater on a dry towel on a flat surface and gently start to reshape it. Come back to the sweater while it's drying to reshape a little more each time. Your patience will be rewarded!

Wash houseplant leaves Houseplants get dusty too, but unlike furniture they need to breathe. Make a soapy solution with a few drops of shampoo in a pot of water, dunk in a cloth and wring it out, and wipe those dusty leaves clean.

DID **You** KNOW?

In the early 1900s, Martha Matilda Harper invented the reclining chair used when shampooing hair at beauty salons—unfortunately, she never patented it. But Harper was still a success. She emigrated from Canada to the United States as a young girl, bringing her own recipe for a hair "tonic" (shampoo). Eventually she went from making her tonic in a shed to opening her own shop, where she offered the Harper Method. She enticed wealthy women to leave their homes for a health-conscious salon experience where they would be shampooed and pampered by professionals. She was her own best advertisement, with hair that reached down past her feet.

Clean your car The grease-cutting power of shampoo works on the family grease monkey's baby as well. Use about 1/4 cup shampoo to a bucket of water and sponge up the car as usual. Use a dab of shampoo directly on a rag or sponge for hard-to-remove tar spots.

Remove sticky gunk from pet fur Did Rex or Fluffy step on tar or roll in what you hope is gum? Rub a tiny amount of shampoo on the spot and gently draw out the sticky stuff toward the end of the fur. Rinse with a wet cloth.

Lubricate stubborn nuts and bolts Got a nut and bolt that won't come apart? If your spot lubricant isn't handy or you've run out, try a drop of shampoo. Let it seep into the threads and the bolt will be much more cooperative.

Remove bandages painlessly Now you don't have to say "Ready?" when removing a bandage. Rub just a drop of shampoo on and around the bandage to let it seep through the air holes. It will come off with no muss and definitely no fuss.

Revitalize your feet Give your feet a pick-me-up while you sleep. Rub a little shampoo all over your feet and put on a light pair of cotton socks. When you wake up, your feet will feel smooth and silky.

Remove your eye makeup You can't beat no-tears baby shampoo for a thrifty eye makeup remover. Put a drop on a damp cotton pad to gently remove the makeup, then rinse clear. No frills, no tears!

Give yourself a bubble bath Shampoo makes a nice and sudsy bubble bath. It's especially relaxing if you love the scent of your favorite shampoo, and the tub will rinse cleaner.

Substitute for shaving cream You're on the road and discover you forgot to bring your shaving cream. Don't use soap to lather up. With its softening agents, shampoo is a much better alternative.

Clean grimy hands In place of soap, some straight shampoo works wonders for cleaning stubborn or sticky grime from your hands. It even works well to remove water-based paint.

Remove hair spray from walls If you've been using hair spray to kill flies, or you've just noticed hair spray buildup on your bathroom walls, reach for the shampoo. Put some on a wet sponge to clean, and wipe off suds with a clean, wet sponge. Shampoo is tailor-made to handle hair product buildup.

Clean the tub and faucets Need to do a quick tub cleanup before guests arrive? Grab the handiest item—your shampoo! It does a great job on soap scum because it rinses clean. You can use it to buff a shine into your chrome faucets as well.

Use to wash delicates Shampoo makes a great cleanser for your delicates. It suds up well with just a drop, and you get two cleaning products for the price of one!

Clean brushes and combs Skin oils can build up on your combs and brushes faster than you realize. And if you're tucking them into your purse or pocket, they're accumulating dust and dirt as well. Give them a fresh start in a shampoo bath. First comb any loose hair out of the brush, then rub a little shampoo around the bristles or along the teeth of the comb. Put a small squirt of shampoo in a tall glass of water, let the comb and brush sit for a few minutes, swish, and rinse clean.

DID *You* KNOW?

SHAMPOO*

300

Shaving Cream

Use to clean hands The next time your hands get dirty on a camping trip, save that hard-lugged water for cooking and drinking. Squirt a little shaving cream in your hands and rub as you would liquid soap. Then wipe your hands off with a towel.

Prevent bathroom mirror fog-up Before you shower, wipe some shaving cream onto your bathroom mirror. It will keep it from fogging up so you don't have to wait to get to work with your toiletries or shaving after you get out of the shower.

DID You KNOW?

From the late 1920s through the early 1960s, one of the best things about a long, tedious car ride were the signs every hundred yards or so advertising Burma-Shave, a brushless shaving cream. Here are some of the more memorable ones:

Shaving Brushes …
You'll Soon See 'Em …
On The Shelf …
In Some Museum …
Burma-Shave.

Are Your Whiskers …
When You Wake …
Tougher Than …
A Two-Bit Steak? …
Try … Burma-Shave.

Within This Vale …
Of Toil … And Sin …
Your Head Grows Bald …
But Not Your Chin—Use …
Burma-Shave.

Golfers!
If Fewer Strokes …
Are What You Crave …
You're Out Of The Rough …
With … Burma-Shave.

Remove stains from carpeting Junior is very sorry for spilling a little juice on the carpet, so make it "all better" with some shaving cream on the spot. Blot the stain, pat it with a wet sponge, squirt some shaving cream on it, and then wipe clean with a damp sponge. Use the same technique on your clothes for small stains; shaving cream can remove that spot of breakfast you discovered you're wearing during your once-over in the bathroom.

Silence a squeaky door hinge A squeaky door hinge can ruin a peaceful naptime. With its ability to seep into nooks and crannies, a little shaving cream on the hinge will let you check on the baby undetected.

* Sheets

Make a beanbag bull's-eye Are the kids rained out of their ball game? Here's one way to ease their disappointment and let them give their pitching arms a workout anyway. Draw a large bull's-eye on a sheet. Tape the sheet to a wall and let the kids pitch beanbags at it.

Use as a tablecloth It is your turn to host the whole clan for Thanksgiving. You're using every table in the house, but you don't have enough tablecloths. A patterned sheet makes an attractive festive table covering.

Repel deer from your yard Circle the garden with a cord about 3 feet (1 meter) above the ground, then tie strips of white sheets to it every 2 feet (60 centimeters); a tail-height flash of white is a danger sign to a deer.

Scoop up all those fall leaves No reason to strain your back by constantly lifting piles of leaves into a wheelbarrow or bag. Just rake the leaves onto a sheet laid on the ground. Then gather the four corners and drag the leaves to the curb or leaf pile.

Wrap up the old Christmas tree After removing holiday decorations, wrap an old sheet around the tree so that you can carry or pull it out of the house without leaving a trail of pine needles.

✳ Shoe Bags

Organize your utility closet A hanging shoe bag is a great organizer in the utility closet. Use its pockets to store sponges, scrub brushes, and other cleaning utensils—and even some bottles of cleaning products. It's also good for separating your clean, lemon-oil, and lint-free rags so you'll always have the right one for the job.

Organize your office area Free up some valuable drawer space in your office with an over-the-door shoe holder. Its pockets can store lots of supplies that you need to keep handy, like scissors, staples, and markers. You can use the pockets to organize bills and other "to do" items as well.

Organize your bathroom A shoe bag can keep lots of everyday bathroom items handy and neat. Brushes, shampoo, hand towels, hair spray—almost everything can be stored at your fingertips instead of cluttering the shower or counter.

Organize your child's room A shoe bag hung over their bedroom door is a great way to help your kids organize their small toys. Whether your child likes dolls, dinosaurs, or different-colored blocks, a shoe bag puts the toys on display and kids can keep them sorted themselves.

Organize car-trip toys and games Cut a shoe bag to fit the back of your car seat, and let your children make their own choices for back seat entertainment.

Organize your bedroom Instead of lifting a hanger to get a belt, or rummaging through your drawer for a scarf, try organizing your clothing accessories with an over-the-door shoe bag. The pockets can be used in the bedroom for keeping socks, gloves, and much more than shoes handy.

✳ Shoe Boxes

Make a gift ribbon dispenser You will thank yourself each time you look for ribbon to wrap a present, if you use a shoe box to make this handy ribbon dispenser. Take a used broom handle or piece of a bamboo garden stake— anything you can use as a small dowel—and cut it a little longer than the length of the shoe box. Cut two holes for the dowel, one in each short

end of the box, at a height where a spool of ribbon slipped onto the dowel would spin freely. Slip your ribbon spools onto the dowel as you poke it from one end of the shoe box through to the other. Once the dowel is in place, you can duct tape it at either short end to keep it from slipping out. You could also cut holes along one long side of the shoe box for each spool of ribbon, and pull a little bit of each ribbon through the hole. Now you're ready to wrap!

Use for play bricks Kids can get creative using a collection of shoe boxes as building bricks. Tape the lids on for them. You can even let the little ones color the "bricks" with poster paint.

Get your stuff organized There are lots of ways shoe boxes can help you get organized besides collecting old photos and receipts. Label the boxes and use them to store keepsakes, canceled checks, bills to be paid, and other items you want to keep track of. For a neater appearance, cover the boxes with contact paper or any other decorative self-adhesive paper.

Pack yummy gifts Shoe boxes are the perfect size for loaves of homemade bread, but of course, you can also pack cookies in them.

Use as a whelping box Puppies or kittens on the way! To reduce the risk of the mother rolling onto a newborn and smothering it, place one or several puppies or kittens in a towel-lined shoe box while the others are being born.

✳ Shortening

Clean ink stains Next time a leaky pen leaves your hands full of ink, reach for a can of shortening. To remove ink stains from your hands and also from vinyl surfaces, rub on a dollop of shortening and wipe the stains away with a rag or paper towel.

Remove sticky adhesives Don't wear down your fingernails trying to scratch off resistant sticky labels and price tags. Instead use shortening to remove them (and their dried glue and gum residue) from glass, metals, and most plastics. Simply coat the area with shortening, wait 10 minutes, and scrub clean with a gentle scrub-sponge.

Polish galoshes To make dirty galoshes shine like new again, rub on some shortening and wipe with a clean rag or cloth.

Tip **Using Shortening**

> ● Keep shortening away from sunlight to keep it from turning rancid.
> ● Never leave shortening unattended while frying.
> ● The most efficient temperature for frying with shortening is 325°F-350°F (165°C-180°C). Do not overheat shortening or it will burn. If shortening starts to smoke, turn off the heat and let it cool.
> ● If shortening catches fire, cover the pan with its lid, turn off the heat, and let it cool. Never put water on burning or hot shortening: It may splatter and burn you.

Soothe and prevent diaper rash Next time the baby is fussing from a painful case of diaper rash, rub some shortening on his bottom for fast relief. It will soothe and moisturize his sensitive skin.

Remove tar from fabric Tar stains on clothing are icky and tough to remove, but you can make the job easier with a little help from some shortening. After scraping off as much of the tar as you can, put a small glob of shortening over the remaining spot. Wait 3 hours, and then launder as usual.

Keep snow from sticking to shovel Before you dig out the car or shovel the driveway after a snowstorm, coat the blade of your snow shovel with shortening or liquid vegetable oil. It will not only keep snow from sticking but also make shoveling less tiring and more efficient.

Remove makeup All out of your regular makeup remover? Don't fret: Just use a dab of shortening instead. Your face won't know the difference.

Moisturize dry skin Why pay for fancy creams and lotions to moisturize your skin when ordinary shortening can do the trick at a fraction of the cost? Some hospitals even use shortening to keep skin soft and moist, and you can too. Next time your hands are feeling dry and scaly, just rub in a little shortening. It's natural and fragrance-free.

Repel squirrels Keep pesky squirrels from getting at a bird feeder. Just grease the pole with a liberal amount of shortening and the rodents won't be able to get a claw hold to climb up.

✳ Shower Curtains

Line cabinet shelves Don't discard your old vinyl shower curtains or tablecloths. Turn them into easy-to-clean shelf liners instead. Simply cut to shelf size and set in

SHORTENING*

304

place, using some rubber cement to hold them if you prefer. When it's time for cleaning, just wipe with a damp sponge.

Make a protective apron For those extra messy jobs around the house, wear a home-made apron made from an old shower curtain. Make a cobbler's style apron, with a vest as well as a skirt. Use pinking shears to cut the vinyl to size. Poke two holes at the top of the vest for cords or ribbons to tie around your neck, and make two more holes in the sides for tying it around your waist.

Durable painting drop cloth Save an old shower curtain liner and use it as a drop cloth the next time you paint a room. The material is heavier and more durable than that used in commercially sold plastic drop cloths!

Protect floor under high chair Even the best-behaved and cutest babies leave a mess on the floor when they eat. Protect your floor or carpet and make cleanup a breeze. Cut a 36- to 48-inch (about 1-meter) square from an old shower curtain and place it under the baby's high chair. You can use the leftover scraps to make bibs too.

Cover picnic tables and benches Don't let a yucky table or sticky benches spoil your next picnic. Use an old shower curtain as a makeshift tablecloth (or as a table-cloth liner). Bring an extra shower curtain and fold it over a sticky or dirty picnic bench before you sit down to eat.

DID *You* KNOW?

In the early 1920s, Waldo Semon, a rubber scientist, was none too thrilled when he first discovered polyvinyl chloride, commonly known as vinyl. He was trying to develop a new adhesive, and this stuff just didn't stick at all! But Waldo was quick to recognize the material's potential and began experimenting with it, even making golf balls and shoe heels out of it. Soon vinyl products like raincoats and shower curtains reached the consumer. Today vinyl is the second-largest selling plastic in the world, and the vinyl industry employs more than 100,000 people in the United States alone.

Protect table when cutting fabric Next time you're cutting a pattern on your dining room table, put a shower curtain or plastic tablecloth under it before you cut. The scissors will glide more easily across the surface and you'll protect the tabletop from an accidental nick.

Block weeds in mulched beds Those old shower curtains will also come in handy next time you do any landscaping with gravel or bark chips. Just place the shower curtain under the mulching material to prevent annoying weeds from poking through.

✳ Skateboards

Use as a laundry cart If your home has a laundry chute, keep a basket atop a skateboard directly below the chute. When you're ready to do the laundry, simply roll the load over to the washer.

Make a shelf Is your kid an avid skateboarder? When he or she is ready for a new skateboard, turn the old one into a shelf for his or her room. Support it on a couple of metal shelf brackets. You can remove the wheels or leave them on.

Use as a painter's scooter. Crawling along the floor to paint a baseboard can get real old real fast. Borrow your kid's skateboard and save your knees. Sit cross-legged on the skateboard and roll along with your paintbrush and can.

✳ Soap

Loosen stuck zippers Zipper stuck? Rub it loose with a bar of soap along the zipper's teeth. The soap's lubrication will get it moving.

Unstick furniture drawers If your cabinet or dresser drawers are sticking, rub the bottom of the drawer and the supports they rest on with a bar of soap.

Lubricate screws and saw blades A little lube with soap makes metal move through wood much more easily. Twist a screw into a bar of soap before driving it and rub some on your handsaw blade.

Remove a broken lightbulb If a bulb breaks while still screwed in, don't chance nicks and cuts trying to remove it. First, turn off the power. Insert the corner of a large, dry bar of soap into the socket. Give it a few turns and that base will unscrew.

Say farewell to fleas Fed up with those doggone fleas? Put a few drops of dish soap and some water on a plate. Place the plate on the floor next to a lamp. Fleas love light—they will jump on the plate and drown.

DID *You* KNOW?

Contrary to popular belief, hanging a perfumed bar of soap won't necessarily keep deer off your property. Stephen Vantassel, who runs Wildlife Damage Control in Springfield, Massachusetts, says that how long or how well soap works depends on a number of factors, including the type of plant you are protecting and the location of the soap. However, studies have shown that soap, especially tallow-based soap, will stop deer from making lunch out of your shrubbery. Local gardening centers can advise you about commercial spray repellents.

Deodorize your car Want your car to smell nice, but tired of those tree-shaped pine deodorizers? Place a little piece of your favorite-smelling soap in a mesh bag and hang it from your rearview mirror.

Mark a hem Forget store-bought marking chalk. A thin sliver of soap, like the ones left when a bar is just about finished, works just as well when you are marking a hem, and the markings wash right out.

Make a pin holder Here's an easy-to-make alternative to a pincushion. Wrap a bar of soap in fabric and tie the fabric in place with a ribbon. Stick in your pins. As a bonus, the soap lubricates the pins, making them easier to insert.

Prevent cast-iron marks Nip cookout cleanup blues in the bud. Rub the bottom of your cast-iron pot with a bar of soap before cooking with it over a sooty open flame. Look, Ma! No black marks!

 Homemade Soap

> Handcrafted soap makes a great gift and is easy to make. You need a solid bar of glycerin (from a drugstore); soap molds (from a crafts store); a clean, dry can; a double boiler; food coloring; and essential oil. Place the glycerin in the can and put the can in a double boiler, which has water in the top as well as the bottom, and heat until the glycerin melts. For color, mix in food coloring. Spray a mold with nonstick cooking spray and fill it halfway with melted glycerin. Add a few drops of essential oil and fill the rest with glycerin. Let it harden.

Keep stored clothes fresh Pack a bar of your favorite scented soap when you store clothes or luggage. It will keep your clothes smelling fresh till next season and prevent musty odor in your luggage.

Save those soap slivers When your soap slivers get too tiny to handle, don't throw them away. Just make a small slit in a sponge and put the slivers inside. The soap will last for several more washings. Or make a washcloth that's easy for little hands to hold by putting the soap slivers in a sock.

* Socks

Protect stored breakables Want to protect Grandma's precious vase or your bobble head collection? Wrap it up! Slip the item into a sock to help protect it from breaking or chipping.

Cover kids' shoes when packing Does Junior insist on bringing along his favorite old sneakers? Before you toss them into the suitcase, cover each one with an adult-size sock to protect the rest of the clothing.

Polish your car A big old soft sock makes a perfect hand mitt for buffing the wax on your car.

Keep hands clean changing tire If you ever get a flat tire on your way to a fancy party or job interview, you'll thank yourself for having the foresight to throw a pair of socks in the trunk. Slip the socks on your hands while handling the tire, and they'll be clean when you arrive.

Protect floor surfaces The next time you need to move a heavy table or sofa across a smooth floor, put socks over the legs and just slide the piece.

Store your work goggles Shop goggles won't fit in an eyeglass case, so just slip them into a sock to protect them from getting scratched. You can even nail or screw the sock to the wall or bench so you will always know where the goggles are.

Wash bag for dainty lingerie Protect your precious delicates in the washing machine. Slip them into a sock and tie the ends.

Use as cleaning mitts Save those old or solo socks to use as cleaning mitts. Slip them on, and they are great for cleaning in tight corners and crevices.

Clean shutter and blind slats Forget wasting money on those expensive gadgets and gizmos for cleaning venetian blind slats. Just slip a sock over your hand and gently rub the dust off. You can use some dusting spray on the sock, if you like.

Clean rough plaster walls Use nylon or Ban-Lon socks, instead of a sponge or cloth, to clean rough plaster walls. No small pieces of material will be left behind.

Wash small stuffed animals Does your child's favorite stuffed fuzzy need a bath? Slip small stuffed animals into a sock and tie the end to prevent buttons, eyes, and other decorative items from coming loose.

Protect a wall from ladder marks To prevent marks on the wall when you're leaning your ladder on it, slip socks over the ladder top ends. For safety reasons, however, make sure someone is holding the ladder.

✳ Soda Pop

Clean car battery terminals Yes, it's true, the acidic properties of soda pop will help to eliminate corrosion from your car battery. Nearly all carbonated soft drinks contain carbonic acid, which helps to remove stains and dissolve rust deposits. Pour some soda pop over the battery terminals and let it sit. Remove the sticky residue with a wet sponge.

Loosen rusted-on nuts and bolts Stop struggling with rusted-on nuts and bolts. Soda pop can help to loosen any rusted-on nuts and bolts. Soak a rag in the soda pop and wrap it around the bolt for several minutes.

Remove rust spots from chrome Are you babying an older car—you know, one of those babies that has real chrome on the outside? If the chrome is developing small rust spots, you can remove them by rubbing the area with a crumpled piece of aluminum foil dipped in cola.

Make cut flowers last longer Don't throw away those last drops of soda pop. Pour about 1/4 cup into the water in a vase full of cut flowers. The sugar in the soda will make the blossoms last longer. *Note:* If you have a clear vase and want the water to remain clear, use a clear soda pop, such as Sprite or 7-Up.

Clean your toilet Eliminate dirt and odor with a simple can of soda. Pour into the toilet, let sit for an hour, then scrub and flush.

 DID *You* KNOW?

Ginger has long been a traditional remedy for nausea, and recent scientific research has shown that ginger ale does work better than a placebo. Ginger ale was first marketed about 100 years ago by a Toronto pharmacist named John McLaughlin. McLaughlin kept trying new formulas until he patented what is now known throughout the world as Canada Dry Ginger Ale. Soda pops—carbonated beverages—originally were served only to customers at drugstore soda fountains. McLaughlin was one of the pioneers of the technology of mass bottling, which allowed customers to take soda pop home in bottles.

Keep drains from clogging Slow drain and no drain cleaner in the house? Pour a 2-liter bottle of cola down the drain to help remove the clog.

Get gum out of hair It's inevitable—kids get gum in their hair. Put the gummy hair section in a bowl with some cola. Let soak for a few minutes and rinse.

Make a roast ham moist Want to make your ham juicier? Pour a can of cola over your traditional ham recipe and follow regular baking instructions. Yum!

Clean your coins Who wants dirty money? If coin collecting is your hobby, use cola to clean your stash. Place the coins in a small dish and soak in cola for a shimmering shine. Of course, you don't want to do this with very rare and valuable coins.

Remove oil stains from concrete Here's how to remove oil stains from concrete driveways and garage floors: Gather up a small bag of cat litter, a few cans of cola, a stiff bristle broom, bucket, laundry detergent, bleach, eye protection, and rubber gloves. Cover the stain with a thin layer of cat litter and brush it in. Sweep up the litter and pour cola to cover the area. Work the cola in with a bristle broom, and leave the cola for about twenty minutes. Mix 1/4 cup laundry detergent with 1/4 cup bleach in 1 gallon (3.7 liters) warm water and use it to mop up the mess.

* Spices

Make a hair tonic You can spice up your hair care regimen with a homemade tonic that will enhance your natural color and impart shine. For dark hair, use 1 tablespoon crumbled sage or 1 sprig chopped fresh rosemary or a mixture of 1 teaspoon allspice, 1 teaspoon ground cinnamon, and 1/2 teaspoon ground cloves. For blond hair, use 1 tablespoon chamomile. Pour 1 cup boiling water over the herb or spice mix, let it steep for 30 minutes, strain it through a coffee filter, and let it cool. Pour it repeatedly over your hair (use a dishpan to catch the runoff) as a final rinse after shampooing.

Treat minor cuts If you nick your finger while chopping vegetables for dinner, you may not even need to leave the kitchen for first aid. Alum, the old-fashioned pickling salt at the back of your spice cupboard, is an astringent. In a pinch, sprinkle some on a minor cut to stanch the flow of blood.

Keep feet smelling sweet If you use sage only to stuff turkeys, then you've been missing out. Sage is great for preventing foot odor because it kills the odor-causing bacteria that grow on your feet in the warm, moist environment inside your shoes. Just crumble a leaf or two into your shoes before you put them on. At the end of the day, just shake the remains into the trash.

Deodorize bottles for reuse You'd like to reuse those wonderful wide-mouthed pickle jars, but simply washing them with soap and water doesn't get rid of the pickle smell. What to do? Add 1 teaspoon dry mustard to 1 quart (1 liter) water, fill the jar, and let it soak overnight. It'll smell fresh by morning. This solution banishes the odor of tomatoes, garlic, and other foods with strong scents.

Keep your thermos fresh You just uncapped the thermos bottle you haven't used for six months, and the inside smells musty. To keep it from happening the next time, place a whole clove inside the thermos before capping it. A teaspoon of salt works too. Be sure to empty and rinse the thermos before using it.

Scent your home What could be more welcoming than the smell of something good cooking? Instead of using commercial air fresheners, simply toss a handful of

DID *You* KNOW?

What's the difference between a spice and an herb? The basic guideline is this: If it's made from a plant's leaf, it's an herb; if it's made from the bark, fruit, seed, stem, or root, it's a spice. Parsley and basil are typical herbs because we eat their leaves. Cinnamon (the bark of a tree) and pepper (the fruit of a vine) are considered spices. Then what to call salt, perhaps the most essential food enhancer of all but not a plant product at all? *Seasoning* is the word that describes anything used to flavor foods, regardless of its origin.

whole cloves or a cinnamon stick in a pot of water and keep it simmering on the stove for half an hour. Or place a teaspoon or two of the ground spices on a cookie sheet and place it in a 200°F (93°C) oven with the door ajar for 30 minutes. Either way, your house will naturally smell spicy good.

Keep woolens whole Woolen clothing can last a lifetime—if you keep moths away. If you don't have a cedar-lined chest or closet, preserve your cold-weather clothing using clove sachets. Purchase some small drawstring muslin bags at a tea shop or health food store, and fill each one with a handful of whole cloves. To prevent any transfer of oils or color to clothes and to contain any spills, put the sachet in a small plastic bag, but don't seal it. Attach it to a hanger in your closet or tuck one in your sweater chest for woolens without holes.

Keep ants at bay Flour, sugar, and paprika can all fall prey to ants. Keep these cooking essentials safe by slipping a bay leaf inside your storage containers. If you're concerned about the flour or sugar picking up a bay leaf flavor, tape the leaf to the inside of the canister lid. This trick works inside cabinets, too, where sachets of sage, bay, stick cinnamon, or whole cloves will smell pleasant while discouraging ants.

Stamp out silverfish These pesky critters frequent places with lots of moisture, such as kitchens, baths, and laundry rooms. Hang an aromatic sachet containing apple pie spices, sage, or bay leaves on a hook in your bathroom vanity and behind the washer, or keep a few in decorative baskets along baseboards.

Control insects in the garden You don't have to use harsh pesticides to control small-insect infestation outdoors. If ants are swarming on your garden path, add 1 tablespoon ground black pepper (or another strong-smelling ground spice, such as ground cloves or dry mustard) to 1 cup sifted white flour and sprinkle the mixture on and around the pests. They'll vanish within the hour. Sweep the dry mix into the garden or yard instead of trying to hose it off; water will just make it gooey.

Deter plant-eating animals Everyone knows that hot peppers make your mouth burn. So if rodents are attacking your ornamental plants, the solution may be to make them too "hot" for the critters. In fact, hot peppers are the basis for many commercial rodent repellents. Chop up the hottest pepper you can find (habañero is best) and combine it with 1 tablespoon ground cayenne pepper and 1/2 gallon (2 liters) water. Boil the mix for 15-20 minutes, then let it cool. Strain it through cheesecloth, add 1 tablespoon dishwashing liquid, and pour it into a spray bottle. Spray vulnerable plants liberally every five days or so. The spray works best for rabbits, chipmunks, and woodchucks, but may also deter deer, especially if used in combination with commercial products.

Shield your vegetable garden For centuries, gardeners have used companion planting to repel insect pests. Aromatic plants such as basil, tansy, marigolds, and sage are all reputed to send a signal to bugs to go elsewhere, so try planting some near your prized vegetables. Mint, thyme, dill, and sage are old-time favorites near cabbage family plants (cabbage, broccoli, cauliflower, and brussels sprouts) for their supposed ability to fend off cabbage moths. Best of all, you can eat the savory herbs!

Tip **Toothache and Oil of Cloves**

> If you have a toothache, get to a dentist as soon as possible. Meanwhile, oil of cloves may provide temporary relief. Place a drop directly into the aching tooth or apply it with a cotton swab. But don't put it directly on the gums. An active ingredient in the spice oil, eugenol, is a natural pain reliever.

✳ Sponges

Make flowerpots hold water longer If your potted houseplants dry out too quickly after watering, when you repot them, try this simple trick for keeping the soil moist longer. Tuck a damp sponge in the bottom of the pot before filling it with soil. It'll act as a water reservoir. And it will also help prevent a gusher if you accidentally overwater.

An unwelcome mat for garden Anyone who's ever cleaned a floor with ammonia knows that the smell of this strong, everyday household cleaner is overpowering. Throw browsing animals "off the scent" of ripening vegetables in your garden by soaking old sponges in your floor-cleaning solution and distributing them wherever you expect the next garden raid.

Keep your veggies fresh Moisture that collects at the bottom of your refrigerator bins hastens the demise of healthful vegetables. Extend their life by lining bins with dry sponges. When you notice that they're wet, wring them out and let them dry before putting them back in the fridge. Every now and then, between uses, let them soak in some warm water with a splash of bleach to discourage the growth of mold.

Sop up umbrella overrun It's raining, and the family has been tramping in and out with umbrellas all day. Your umbrella stand has only a shallow receptacle to catch drips. Suddenly there's a waterfall coming out of it! Protect your flooring from umbrella stand overflow with a strategically placed sponge in its base. If you forget to squeeze it out, it'll dry on its own as soon as the weather clears.

Stretch the life of soap A shower is so refreshing in the morning—until you reach for the soap and are treated to the slimy sensation of a bar that's been left to marinate in its own suds. You'll enjoy bathing more and your soap will last longer if you park a sponge on the soap dish. It'll absorb moisture so soap can dry out.

> *Kids' Stuff* Making seeds grow seems magical to young children. For an easy and renewable **play garden** with a minimum of mess, all you need is an **old soap dish**, a **sponge**, and **seeds** of a plant such as lobelia, flax, or chia (yes, the same "chia" as in Chia Pet; look for the seed at health food stores). Cut the sponge to fit the dish, add water until it's moist but not sopping, and sprinkle the seed liberally over the top. Prop an **inverted glass bowl** over it until the seeds begin to grow. A bright window and a daily watering will keep it going for weeks.

Protect fragile items If you're shipping or storing small, fragile valuables that won't be harmed by a little contact with water, sponges are a clever way to cushion them. Dampen a sponge, wrap it around the delicate item, and use a rubber band to secure it. As it dries, the sponge will conform to the contours of your crystal ashtray or porcelain figurine. To unpack it, just dip the item in water again. You'll even get your sponge back!

Lift lint from fabric To quickly remove lint and pet fur from clothes and upholstery, give the fabric a quick wipe with a dampened and wrung-out sponge. Just run your fingers over the sponge and the unwanted fuzz will come off in a ball for easy disposal.

✳ Spray Bottles

Mist your houseplants Keep your houseplants healthy and happy by using an empty trigger-type spray bottle as a plant mister. Clean the bottle by filling it with equal parts water and vinegar—don't use liquid soap, as you may not be able to get it all out—let the solution sit for an hour, and rinse it out thoroughly with cold water. Repeat if necessary. Then, fill the bottle with lukewarm warm water, and use it to frequently give your plants a soothing, misty shower.

Help with the laundry An empty spray bottle can always be put to good use around your laundry room. Use clean, recycled bottles to spray water on your clothes as you're ironing. Or fill a spray bottle with stain remover solution so that you can apply it to your garments without having to blot up drips.

Cool off in summer Whether you're jogging around the park, taking a breather between volleyball matches, or just sitting out in the sun, a recycled spray bottle filled with water can make a great summer companion. Use it to cool off during and after your workouts, or while simmering on the beach (or in beach traffic).

Keep car windows clean Be sure to include a recycled spray bottle filled with windshield cleaner in the trunk of your car as part of your roadside emergency kit. Use it to clean off your car's headlights, mirrors, and of course, windows whenever needed. During winter months, mix in 1/2 teaspoon antifreeze, and you can spray it on to melt the ice on your windshield or mirrors.

Spray away garden pests Keep a few recycled spray bottles on hand to use around the yard. Here are two immediate uses:

● Fill one with undiluted white vinegar to get rid of the weeds and grass poking out of the cracks in your concrete, as well as ants and other insects— but be careful not to spray it on your plants; the high acidity could kill them.

● For an effective homemade insecticide recipe that works on most soft-bodied pests, but won't harm your plants, mix several cloves crushed garlic, 1/4 cup canola oil, 3 tablespoons hot pepper sauce, and 1/2 teaspoon mild liquid soap in 1 gallon (3.7 liters) water. Pour some into your spray bottle, and shake well before using.

✳ Squirt Bottles

Stop cooking oil drips Tired of cleaning up the oil spills around your kitchen? Fill a cleaned, recycled squirt bottle with olive oil or another favorite cooking oil. It's a lot easier to handle than a jar or bottle, and you can pour precisely the right amount of oil over your salads or into your frying pan without having to worry about drips or spills.

Substitute for a baster If you can't find your kitchen baster, or one that's in working condition, a cleaned squeeze bottle makes a dandy substitute. Simply squeeze out some air first, and use it to suck up the fat from your roasts and soups. You can even effectively use it to distribute marinades and drippings over meat.

Put the squeeze on condiments Recycled squirt bottles are great for storing condiments and other foodstuffs that are typically sold in jars—such as mayonnaise, salad dressing, jelly and jams, or honey. In addition to having fewer sticky or messy jars in your refrigerator, you'll also be lightening the load in your dishwasher by eliminating the need for knives or spoons. Make sure you give the bottles a thorough cleaning before using.

Clean out crevices A clean, empty squeeze bottle may be just the cleaning tool you need to get the dust out of the corners of your picture frames and other tight spaces. Use it to give a good blast of air to blow out the dirt you can't otherwise reach.

Let the children play Fill up a few clean squeeze bottles with water, then give them to your kids to squirt each other with in the yard on those hot summer days. It will keep them cool while they burn off some energy.

✳ Steel Wool

Turn nasty sneakers nice If your sneakers are looking so bad that the only thing you'd do in them is, well, *sneak* around, some steel wool may keep them from the trash can. Moisten a steel wool soap pad and gently scrub away at stains and stuck-on goo. Wipe them clean with a damp sponge or send them through the washer, and you may be able to enjoy many more months of wear.

Crayons begone Your toddler just created a work of crayon art on paper. Unfortunately, it's on the *wall*paper. Use a bit of steel wool soap pad to just skim the surface, making strokes in one direction instead of scrubbing in a circle, and your wall will be a fresh "canvas" in no time.

"Shoo" heel marks away Those black marks that rubber soles leave behind just don't come off with a mop, no matter how long you try. To rid a vinyl floor of unsightly smudges, gently rub the surface with a moistened steel wool soap pad. When the heel mark is gone, wipe the floor clean with a damp sponge.

Tip **No Steel Wool on Stainless Steel**

> An oft-repeated advice is to clean stainless steel with steel wool. Yet stainless steel manufacturers caution against using any abrasive on stainless steel. Steel wool may make stainless steel look better, but it scratches the surface and ultimately hastens rusting. The safest way to care for stainless steel is to wash with a sponge and mild soap and water.

Sharpen your scissors Sometimes you just want a small piece of a steel wool soap pad for a minor job. Cutting it in half with a pair of scissors will help keep the scissors sharp while giving you the pint-size pad you need for your project.

Rebuff rodents Mice, squirrels, and bats are experts at finding every conceivable entry into a house. When you discover one of their entry points, stuff it full of steel wool. Steel wool is much more effective than foam or newspaper because even dedicated gnawers are unlikely to try to chew through such a sharp blockade.

Keep garden tools in good shape Nothing will extend the life of your gardening tools like a good cleaning at the end of each growing season. Grab a wad of fine steel wool from your woodshop (000, or "three aught," would be a good choice), saturate it with the same ordinary household oil you use on squeaky door hinges, and rub rust off your shears, loppers, shovels, and anything else with metal parts. Wipe them clean with a dry rag, sharpen any blades, and reapply a bit of oil before storing them for the winter.

S * Straws

Keep jewelry chains unknotted You're dressing for dinner out, and you reach into your jewelry box for your best gold chain only to find that it's tangled and kinked. Next time, run it through a straw cut to the proper length and close the clasp before putting it away. It'll always be ready to wear.

Give flowers needed height Your flower arrangement would be just perfect, except a few of the flowers aren't tall enough. You can improve on nature by sticking each of the too-short stems into plastic straws, trimming the straw to get the desired height, and inserting them into the vase.

Get slow ketchup flowing Anticipation is great, but ketchup that comes out of the bottle while your burger and fries are still hot is even better. If your ketchup is recalcitrant, insert a straw all the way into the bottle and stir it around a little to get the flow started.

Improvise some foamy fun To make enough cheap and easy toys for even a large group of children, cut the ends of some plastic straws at a sharp angle and set out a shallow pan of liquid dish soap diluted with a little bit of water. Dip a straw in the soap and blow through the other end. Little kids love the piles of bubbles that result.

Make a pull-toy protector Pull toys are perennial favorites of young children, but you can spend all day untying the knots that a toddler will inevitably put in the pull string. By running the string through a plastic straw (or a series of them), you can keep it untangled.

 DID *You* KNOW?

The quest for a perfectly cold mint julep led to the invention of the drinking straw. Mint juleps are served chilled, and their flavor diminishes as they warm up. Holding a glass heats the contents, so the custom was to drink mint juleps through natural straws made from a section of hollow grass stem, usually rye. But the rye imparted an undesirable "grassy" flavor. In 1888 Marvin Stone, a Washington, D.C., manufacturer of paper cigarette holders, fashioned a paper tube through which to sip his favorite libation. When other mint julep aficionados began clamoring for paper straws, he realized he had a hot new product on his hands.

Have seasonings, will travel Maybe you're on a low-sodium diet and need potassium
salt that most restaurants don't keep on the table, or perhaps you want salt
and pepper to season your brown-bag lunch just before you eat it. Straws provide an easy way to take along small amounts of dry seasonings. Fold one end
over and tape it shut, fill it, and fold and tape the other end. If moisture is a
concern, use a plastic straw.

Fix loose veneer The veneer from a favorite piece of furniture has lost its grip near the edge of the piece.
A bit of yellow carpenter's glue is the obvious
solution for re-adhering the veneer, but how do
you get the glue under there? Veneer can be very
brittle, and you don't want to break off a piece
by lifting it up. The solution: Cut a length of
plastic drinking straw and press it to flatten it

somewhat. Fold it in half and fill one half with glue, slowly dripping the glue
in from the top. Slip the filled half under the veneer and gently blow in the
glue. Wipe off any excess, cover the area with wax paper and a wood block, and
clamp overnight.

✳ String

Polish silverware more easily Remember Dad or Grandpa taking a photograph of the
dining room table beautifully set for holiday meals? The rich shine of polished
silverware was part of what made it so beautiful. To get your silverware looking
that good, run a length of string through some silver polish and use it to get at
those hard-to-reach spots between fork tines.

Make wicks for watering plants Keeping plants watered
while you're on a short trip is easier than you
think. Fill a large container with water and
place it next to your potted plants. Cut pieces of
string so they're long enough to hang down to
the bottom of the container at one end and be
buried a few inches in the soil of the pots at the
other. Soak the strings until they're thoroughly

wet and put them in position. As the soil begins to dry, capillary action will
draw water from the reservoir to the pots through the strings.

Stop the sound of a dripping faucet If a leaky faucet going "plop ... plop ... plop" is
keeping you awake at night, there's a way to silence it until the plumber
arrives. Tie a piece of string to the fixture with one end right where the water
is oozing out and the other end hanging down to the bottom of the sink
basin. Water droplets will travel down the string silently instead of driving
you to distraction.

Use as a straight-line guide Trimming a long hedge straight is a near-impossible feat unless you use a visual guide. Drive two stakes into the ground, one at each end of the hedge. Measure the height you want for the trimmed hedge, then run the string between the two stakes, tying it to each one at that exact height. As you clip away, cut down to the string line but no farther; the top of your hedge will be straight as an arrow.

Make a quick package opener Next time you're preparing a box for mailing, take a second to make it easier for the recipient to open. Place a piece of string along the center and side seams before you tape, allowing a tiny bit to hang free at one end. That way, the recipient just needs to pull the strings to sever the tape without resorting to sharp blades that might damage delicate contents. Do the same for packing boxes when you move.

Outline garden features When you're making a new garden, lay common bright white string on the ground to outline paths and beds. From an upstairs window or other high vantage point, you'll be able to tell at a glance if borders are straight and whether the layout is pleasing.

Measure irregular objects A cloth tape measure is the ideal tool for measuring odd-shaped objects, but you may not have one if you don't sew. Wrap a plain piece of string around the item instead, then hold it up to a ruler to get the measurement you need.

Plant perfectly straight rows It's harder than it looks to make straight garden rows freehand. Use string two ways to keep plants in line:

- For planting heavy seeds such as beans, put sticks in the ground at each end of a row and run a piece of string between to guide you as you plant.

- To plant dozens of lightweight seeds in a snap, cut string to the length of a row, wet it thoroughly, then sprinkle the seed directly on it. The moisture will make seeds stick long enough to lay the string in a prepared furrow. Just cover the string with soil and you're done!

Stop slamming doors Is a slamming door getting on your nerves? Here are two ideas for using string to control the way a door closes:

- A piece of light twine tied to both sides of a knob and running around the door edge provides just enough friction to slow it down and prevent a loud slam when it shuts.

- Use thicker rope the same way to temporarily prop open a door that automatically locks when it closes or to make sure pets don't get trapped in one room of the house.

✳ Styrofoam

Keep nail polish nice When applying nail polish, a foam pellet or a small chunk cut from a block of foam packaging placed between each finger or toe will help spread them apart and keep the polish unblemished until it can dry.

Make your own shipping pellets You'd like to use foam to ship some fragile things, but all you've got is sheets or blocks of foam, not pellets. No problem. Just break up what you have into pieces small enough to fit in a blender and pulse it on and off to shred the foam into perfect packing material.

Hold treats for freezing and serving To prepare a quantity of snow cones or ice-cream cones in advance, cut a foam block to size so it will fit flat in your freezer. Cut holes just large enough and close enough to hold cones so they won't touch, fall over, or poke through the bottom. Fill the cones and slip them into the waiting holes. Then pop the whole thing into the freezer ready for serving at a moment's notice.

❓ DID *You* KNOW?

Ask anyone what kind of material those coffee cups, packing material, picnic coolers, and other white foam products are made from, and they'll reply Styrofoam. But strictly speaking, Styrofoam, a trademark of the Dow Chemical Company, refers only to durable extruded polystyrene, like that used in the blue insulation boards familiar to anyone who's been around a construction site. Those other more commonplace white foam items that you can easily tear or crumble are made of cheaper expanded polystyrene and are better referred to as foam plastic or styrene foam.

Make a buoyant tray for the pool Styrofoam is nearly unsinkable. Use the scraps from a construction project to make a drink holder or tray that will float in your pool:

- To make a soda-can holder, cut two pieces to the size you want the finished holder to be, then cut holes the same size as a soda can in one piece. Glue the piece with holes on top of the other piece, using a glue gun with hot-melt glue.

- To make a tray with a rim, just glue small strips of foam that are at least 1 inch (2.5 centimeters) high around the edge of a larger tray-size section of the material.

Make a kickboard A sharp kitchen knife is all you need to cut a scrap of Styrofoam insulation into a kickboard for your swimming pool.

Help shrubs withstand winter Sometimes shrubs need a
little help to survive winter's ravages. Leftover
sheets of extruded tongue-and-groove
Styrofoam insulation are perfect for the job.
They're rigid, waterproof, and block wind and
road salt. Here are two ways to use the material:

- To give moderate protection, cut two
  Styrofoam sheets and lash them together to
  form a pup tent over the plant. To hold the pieces in place, drive bamboo
  garden stakes through the bottom of each piece into the ground.

- For something more substantial, fit pieces together to box in the plants on
  four sides. Put a stake inside each corner and join the pieces with duct or
  packing tape.

Plants in containers that overwinter outdoors are more likely to survive with
Styrofoam protection too.

Tip **Recycling Foam Pellets**

Even with lots of creative reuse, sometimes foam packing pellets just
come in faster than they go out again. If you've got more than you can
handle, remember that packing and shipping businesses often accept
clean pellets for reuse. Just call to confirm before you bring them in.

✳ Sugar

Keep cut flowers fresh Make your own preservative to keep cut flowers fresh longer.
Dissolve 3 tablespoons sugar and 2 tablespoons white vinegar per quart (liter)
of warm water. When you fill the vase, make sure the cut stems are covered by
3-4 inches (7-10 centimeters) of the prepared water. The sugar nourishes the
plants, while the vinegar inhibits bacterial growth. You'll be surprised how long
the arrangement stays fresh!

Nix nematode worms in garden If your outdoor plants look unhealthy, with ugly
knots at the roots, chances are they've been victims of an attack of the nematodes! The nematode worm, nemesis of many an otherwise healthy garden, is
a microscopic parasite that pierces the roots of plants and causes knots. You
can prevent nematode attacks by using sugar to create an inhospitable environment for the tiny worms. Apply 5 pounds (2 kilograms) sugar for every
250 square feet (25 square meters) of garden. Microorganisms feeding on the
sugar will increase the organic matter in the soil, thereby eliminating those
nasty little nematodes.

Kids' Stuff Here's an easy way to make **old-fashioned rock candy** with the kids, with no strings, paper clips, sticks, or thermometers needed: Make syrup by stirring 2 1/2 cups **sugar** into 1 cup **hot water.** Pour the syrup into several **open dishes** and set aside. Add a grain of sugar to act as a seed crystal in each container. Within days or weeks you should be able to collect glittering crystals of rock candy. Use a spoon to scoop it out, then rinse and dry the candy before you eat it.

Clean greasy, grimy hands Your work is done for the day, but your hands are still covered with grease, grime, or paint. To clean filthy hands easily and thoroughly, pour equal amounts of olive oil and sugar into the cupped palm of one hand, and then gently rub your hands together for several minutes. Rinse thoroughly and dry. The grit of the sugar acts as an abrasive to help the oil remove grease, paint, and grime. Your hands will look and feel clean, soft, and moisturized.

Make a nontoxic fly trap Keep your kitchen free of flies with a homemade fly trap that uses no toxic chemicals. In a small saucepan, simmer 2 cups milk, 1/4 pound (113 grams) raw sugar, and 2 ounces (56 grams) ground pepper for about 10 minutes, stirring occasionally. Pour into shallow dishes or bowls and set them around the kitchen, patio, or anywhere the flies are a problem. The pesty bugs will flock to the bowls and drown!

Exterminate roaches If you hate smelly, noxious pesticides as much as you loathe cockroaches, don't call an exterminator. Instead, when you have a roach infestation, scatter a mixture of equal parts sugar and baking powder over the infested area. The sugar will attract the roaches, and the baking powder will kill them. Replace it frequently with a fresh mixture to prevent future infestations.

Soothe a burned tongue That slice of piping-hot pizza sure looked great, but ouch! You burned your tongue when you bit into it. To relieve a tongue burned by hot pizza, coffee, tea, or soup, reach for the sugar bowl and sprinkle a pinch or two of sugar over the affected area. The pain will begin to subside immediately.

Keep desserts fresh You used sugar to sweeten the cake batter; now use it to keep the finished cake fresh and moist. Store the cake in an airtight container with a couple of sugar cubes, and it will stay fresh for days longer. Store a few lumps of sugar with cheese the same way to prevent the cheese from molding.

✳ Talcum Powder

Keep ants away For an effective organic ant repellent, scatter talcum powder liberally around house foundations and known points of entry, such as doors and windows. Other effective organic repellents include cream of tartar, borax, powdered sulfur, and oil of cloves. You can also try planting mint around the house foundations.

Fix a squeaky floor Don't let squeaky floorboards drive you crazy. For a quick fix, sprinkle talcum powder or powdered graphite between the boards that squeak. If that doesn't do the trick, squirt in some liquid wax.

Remove bloodstains from fabric To remove fresh bloodstains from clothing or furniture, make a paste of water and talcum powder and apply it to the spot. When it dries, brush away the stain. Substitute cornstarch or cornmeal if you are out of talcum powder.

Get rid of greasy carpet stain A greasy stain can spoil the look of the most luxurious carpeting. You can remove greasy stains from a carpet with a combination of talcum powder and patience. Just cover the affected area with talcum powder and wait at least 6 hours for the talcum to absorb the grease. Then vacuum the stain away. Baking soda, cornmeal, or cornstarch may be substituted for the talcum powder.

> **TAKE CARE** Health care experts warn that scented talcum powder may cause skin allergies and worsen body odors. They recommend only unscented powder, used on dry skin. Women are advised not to use talcum powder in the vaginal or anal areas, where excessive powdering has been linked to an increased risk of ovarian cancer.

Degrease polyester stains Your favorite polyester shirt or blouse may come back in style someday, but you'll have to get rid of that ugly grease stain before you wear it. To get rid of grease stains on polyester, sprinkle some talcum powder directly onto the spot and rub it in with your fingers. Wait 24 hours, and gently brush. Repeat as necessary until the stain is completely gone.

Loosen tangles and knots Don't break a fingernail trying to untie that knot in your shoelace. Sprinkle some talcum powder on shoelaces (or any knotted cords) and the knots will pull apart more easily. Use talcum powder to help untangle chain necklaces too.

super item *30 uses! Tape

✳TAPE **IN THE KITCHEN AND DINING ROOM**

Safely pick up glass shards Why risk cutting yourself picking up bits of broken glass from the kitchen floor? Just hold a long piece of transparent tape tightly at each end and use it to blot up all the shards.

Create a no-fly zone Make your own fly and pest strips that are free of polluting toxic chemicals and poisons. Cover empty paper towel or toilet paper rolls with transparent tape, sticky side out, and hang them in the kitchen or wherever else you need them.

Mark start of plastic-wrap roll If you've ever had trouble finding the beginning of a roll of plastic food wrap, you'll appreciate this time-saving trick: Put a piece of transparent tape on your finger, sticky side out, and dab your finger on the roll until you find the edge. Use a short piece of tape to lift the edge and pull gently.

Prevent salt and pepper spills Many salt and pepper shakers, especially ceramic ones, have to be filled through a hole in the bottom. Before you refill one of these shakers, tape over the holes on top. That way you won't have any wasteful spills when you turn the shaker upside down to fill it. Also, remember to tape the tops when moving to a new home, or even when you're just transporting the shakers to and from a picnic.

Keep hands free at grocery Next time you go food shopping, bring some tape with you and use it to affix your shopping list to the handle of your grocery cart. This will free both your hands and you won't keep misplacing or dropping your list.

Make candles fit snugly Don't let loose candles spoil the romantic mood or cause a fire at your next candlelight dinner. If the candles don't fit snugly into the holder, wrap layers of tape around their bottom edges until they fit just right.

✳TAPE **AROUND THE HOUSE**

Keep spare batteries handy You won't be behind the times for long if you remember to tape extra batteries to the back of your wall clock! When the clock stops and it's time to replace the batteries, they'll be readily at hand.

Code your keys Are you always groping around to find the right key when you get home in the dark? Just wrap some tape around the top of your house key, and you'll be able to feel for the right key when it is too dark to see. Or if you have several similar-looking keys that you can't tell apart, color-code them with different-colored tape.

Prevent jewelry tangles To keep fine chains from tangling when you travel, cover both sides of each chain with transparent tape. You can also use tape to keep a pair of earrings from separating.

Mark a phone number for quick reference Use transparent tape to highlight numbers in the phone book that you often look up. The tape will make the page easier to find and you will also be able to find the number easily without having to search the whole page.

Contain grease stains on paper You may never be able to get rid of grease spots on books or important papers, but you can keep them from spreading with a little help from some transparent tape. Affix tape over both sides of the spot to keep the grease from seeping through to other pages or papers.

Keep papers from blowing in the wind If you have to make a speech or accept an award at an outdoor event, bring a roll of transparent tape with you. When it's your turn to talk, place some tape on the lectern, sticky side out, to prevent your papers from blowing away.

Find your favorite photo negative Before framing a favorite photograph, tape the negative to the back of the picture. If you ever want to make copies of the photo, you won't have to go searching through piles of old negatives to find the right one.

Deter cat from scratching Stop naughty cats and kittens from scratching your fine furniture! Sprinkle ground red pepper on a strip of tape and attach it to the areas you don't want them to scratch. They hate the smell, and they'll quickly get the message.

Keep flowers upright in vase To keep cut flowers from sagging in their vase, crisscross several pieces of transparent tape across the mouth of the vase, leaving spaces where you can insert the flowers. The flowers will look perky and fresh for a few extra days.

DID You KNOW?

Scotch tape got its name from an insult hurled at Richard Drew, the 3M company engineer who invented it. In 1925, five years before he invented the world's first and best-known transparent cellophane tape, Drew invented masking tape. He was field-testing his first masking-tape samples to find the right amount of adhesive when a frustrated body-shop painter exclaimed, "Take this tape back to those Scotch bosses of yours and tell them to put more adhesive on it!"

Make sewing easier Let transparent tape simplify your sewing: Use it to hold a zipper in place when you're making a garment. (You can sew through the tape and remove it when you're done.) Keep badges, patches, or name tags in place when sewing them onto shirts, uniforms, or caps. Tape hooks, eyes, and snaps to garments when sewing so they won't slip. Just pull the tape off when you're done. Tape a pattern to the material; when you cut the pattern, you'll have a reinforced edge.

End loose ends on thread spools Put an end to time-wasting frustrating searches for loose ends of thread. Just tape the ends to the top or bottom of the spool when you're done sewing and they'll be at your fingertips and ready to use next time you sew.

Remove lipstick from silk Why pay an expensive dry-cleaning bill to remove a lipstick spot from a silk scarf or dress when you can do it yourself for free? Just place a piece of transparent tape (or masking tape) over the spot and yank it off. If you can still see some of the lipstick color, sprinkle on some talcum powder or chalk and dab until the powder and the remaining lipstick disappear.

DID **You** KNOW?

Transparent tape is made from an acetate film derived from wood pulp or cotton fibers. It is formed into paper-thin sheets and wound onto giant rolls before being coated with adhesive. Twenty-nine raw materials go into the adhesive used in transparent tape. Even after the film and adhesive have been produced, 10 separate steps remain to be done before a roll of tape is manufactured.

Clean your nail file Clean a nail file easily and effectively. Simply place a piece of transparent tape over it, press, and pull off. The tape will pick up all the dirt embedded in the surface of the file.

✳TAPE **FOR THE DO-IT-YOURSELFER**

Keep picture nails from damaging wall Before driving a nail into the wall, put a piece of tape on the wall at the site. This will prevent the paint from peeling off if you have to remove the nail, and it will prevent wallboards from cracking too.

Keep screws handy When doing household repairs, place loose screws, nuts, and bolts directly on a piece of transparent tape so they won't roll around and get lost.

Stick some double-sided tape on your workbench and use it to hold screws and such in place while you're working on a project.

Mend a broken plant stem Use transparent tape to add support to a broken plant stem. Just wrap the stem in tape at the damaged area and leave the tape on until it mends. The taped plant will keep growing as long as moisture can continue to travel up the stem.

Make a seed strip Make your own seed strip to create perfectly straight rows in your garden with almost no effort. Sprinkle some seeds on a piece of wax paper and use your fingers to arrange and align them. After removing the excess, take a strip of transparent tape and place it over the seeds. Then just bury the tape in the garden and you will soon have perfect rows.

Catch cricket invaders If noisy crickets have invaded your basement or garage, try trapping them with packaging tape. Take a strip of the tape and place on the floor, sticky side up. Later, just release your catch into the wild or feed them to a cricket-eating pet.

✱TAPE **FOR SAFETY'S SAKE**

Make safety markers for a car emergency You'll be a lot safer when your car breaks down at night if you have safety markers on hand to warn oncoming drivers. You can make your own safety markers easily at home. Just put strips of brightly colored reflector tape on some old coffee cans. Keep them in the trunk of your car for use in an emergency.

Mark dark stairways Stop stumbling on those poorly lit cellar or outdoor stairways or worrying about guests tripping and falling. Simply apply reflector tape along the edges of the steps and you and your guests will be able to see exactly where you're stepping.

Make pets visible at night Don't let your beloved family pet get hit by a car during the night. Put reflector tape on Rover's collar so drivers will be able to see him immediately in the dark.

✱TAPE **FOR THE KIDS**

Secure baby's bib Stop bits of food from getting under a child's bib by taping the edges of the bib to her clothes.

Makeshift childproofing If you bring a baby or small child with you when visiting a home that isn't childproofed, bring a roll of transparent tape along too. Use it to cover electrical outlets as a temporary safety measure. Although it will not confer a lot of protection, it could give you the extra time you need to remove a child from a potentially hazardous situation.

Make multicolored designs Tape a few different-colored markers or pencils together and give them to the kids to draw multicolored designs. Be careful not to use too many, so the children can maintain control of the drawings.

super item 23 uses! Tea

✳ TEA **FOR HEALTH AND BEAUTY**

Cool sunburned skin What can you do when you forget to use sunscreen and have to pay the price with a painful burn? A few wet tea bags applied to the affected skin will take out the sting. This works well for other types of minor burns (i.e., from a teapot or steam iron) too. If the sunburn is too widespread to treat this way, put some tea bags in your bathwater and soak your whole body in the tub.

Relieve your tired eyes Revitalize tired, achy, or puffy eyes. Soak two tea bags in warm water and place them over your closed eyes for 20 minutes. The tannins in the tea act to reduce puffiness and soothe tired eyes.

Reduce razor burn Ouch! Why didn't you remember to replace that razor blade *before* you started to shave? To soothe razor burn and relieve painful nicks and cuts,

 DID **You** KNOW?

Legend has it that tea originated some 5,000 years ago with the Chinese emperor Shen Nung. A wise ruler and creative scientist, the emperor insisted that all drinking water be boiled as a health precaution. One summer day, during a rest stop in a distant region, servants began to boil water for the royal entourage to drink when some dried leaves from a nearby bush fell into the pot. As the water boiled, it turned brown. The emperor's scientific curiosity was aroused, and he insisted on tasting the liquid. It was just his cup of tea.

apply a wet tea bag to the affected area. And don't forget to replace the blade before your next shave.

Get the gray out Turn gray hair dark again without an expensive trip to the salon or the use of chemical hair dyes. Make your own natural dye using brewed tea and herbs: Steep 3 tea bags in 1 cup boiling water. Add 1 tablespoon each of rosemary and sage (either fresh or dried) and let it stand overnight before straining. To use, shampoo as usual, and then pour or spray the mixture on your hair, making sure to saturate it thoroughly. Take care not to stain clothes. Blot with a towel and do not rinse. It may take several treatments to achieve desired results.

Condition dry hair To give a natural shine to dry hair, use a quart (liter) of warm, unsweetened tea (freshly brewed or instant) as a final rinse after your regular shampoo.

Tan your skin with tea Give pale skin a healthy tan appearance without exposure to dangerous ultraviolet rays. Brew 2 cups strong black tea, let it cool, and pour into a plastic spray bottle. Make sure your skin is clean and dry. Then spray the tea directly onto your skin and let it air-dry. Repeat as desired for a healthy-looking glowing tan. This will also work to give a man's face a more natural look after shaving off a beard.

Drain a boil Drain a boil with a boiled tea bag! Cover a boil with a wet tea bag overnight and the boil should drain without pain by the time you wake up next morning.

Soothe nipples sore from nursing When breast-feeding the baby leaves your nipples sore, treat them to an ice-cold bag of tea. Just brew a cup of tea, remove the bag, and place it in a cup of ice for about a minute. Then place the wet tea bag on the sore nipple and cover it with a nursing pad under your bra for several minutes while you enjoy a cup of tea. The tannic acid in the wet tea leaves will soothe and help heal the sore nipple.

Soothe those bleeding gums The child may be all smiles later when the tooth fairy arrives, but right now those bleeding gums are no fun whatsoever. To stop the bleeding and soothe the pain from a lost or recently pulled tooth, wet a tea bag with cool water and press it directly onto the site.

Relieve baby's pain from injection Is the baby *still* crying from that recent inoculation shot? Try wetting a tea bag and placing it over the site of the injection. Hold it gently in place until the crying stops. The tannic acid in the tea will soothe the soreness. You might try it on yourself the next time an injection leaves your arm sore.

Dry poison ivy rash Dry a weepy poison ivy rash with strongly brewed tea. Simply dip a cotton ball into the tea, dab it on the affected area, and let it air-dry. Repeat as needed.

Stop foot odor Put an end to smelly feet by giving them a daily tea bath. Just soak your tootsies in strongly brewed tea for 20 minutes a day and say good-bye to offensive odors.

Make soothing mouthwash To ease toothache or other mouth pain, rinse your mouth with a cup of hot peppermint tea mixed with a pinch or two of salt. Peppermint is an antiseptic and contains menthol, which alleviates pain on contact with skin surfaces. To make peppermint tea, boil 1 tablespoon fresh peppermint leaves in 1 cup water and steep for several minutes.

✳TEA AROUND THE HOUSE

Tenderize tough meat Even the toughest cuts of meat will melt in your mouth after you marinate them in regular black tea. Here's how: Place 4 tablespoons black tea leaves in a pot of warm (not boiling) water and steep for 5 minutes. Strain to remove the leaves and stir in 1/2 cup brown sugar until it dissolves. Set aside. Season up to 3 pounds (1.5 kilograms) meat with salt, pepper, onion, and garlic powder, and place it in a Dutch oven. Pour the liquid over the seasoned meat and cook in a preheated 325°F (165°C) oven until the meat is fork tender, about 90 minutes.

Clean wood furniture and floors Freshly brewed tea is great for cleaning wood furniture and floors. Just boil a couple of tea bags in a quart (liter) of water and let it cool. Dip a soft cloth in the tea, wring out the excess, and use it to wipe away dirt and grime. Buff dry with a clean, soft cloth.

Create "antique" fashions Soak white lace or garments in a tea bath to create an antique beige, ecru, or ivory look. Use 3 tea bags for every 2 cups of boiling water and steep for 20 minutes. Let it cool for a few minutes before soaking the material for 10 minutes or more. The longer you let it soak, the darker the shade you will get.

Tip **Dyeing with Herbal Teas**

> Using regular tea to dye fabrics has been around for a long time and was first used to hide stains on linens. But you can also use herbal teas to dye fabric different colors and subtle hues. Try using hibiscus to achieve red tones and darker herbal teas like licorice for soft brown tints. Always experiment using fabric scraps until you obtain the desired results.

Shine your mirrors To make mirrors sparkle and shine, brew a pot of strong tea, let it cool, and then use it to clean the mirrors. Dampen a soft cloth in the tea and wipe it all over the surface of the mirrors. Then buff with a soft, dry cloth for a sparkly, streak-free shine.

TEA✳

329

Control dust from fireplace ash Keep dust from rising from the ashes when you clean out your fireplace. Before you begin cleaning, sprinkle wet tea leaves over the area. The tea will keep the ashes from spreading all over as you lift them out.

Perfume a sachet Next time you make a sachet, try perfuming it with the fragrant aroma of your favorite herbal tea. Just open a few used herbal tea bags and spread the wet tea on some old newspaper to dry. Then use the dry tea as stuffing for the sachet.

✳TEA IN THE GARDEN

Give roses a boost Sprinkle new or used tea leaves (loose or in tea bags) around your rosebushes and cover with mulch to give them a midsummer boost. When you water the plants, the nutrients from the tea will be released into the soil, spurring growth. Roses love the tannic acid that occurs naturally in tea.

Feed your ferns Schedule an occasional teatime for your ferns and other acid-loving houseplants. Substitute brewed tea when watering the plants. Or work wet tea leaves into the soil around the plants to give them a lush, luxuriant look.

Prepare planter for potting For healthier potted plants, place a few used tea bags on top of the drainage layer at the bottom of the planter before potting. The tea bags will retain water and leach nutrients to the soil.

Enhance your compost pile To speed up the decomposition process and enrich your compost, pour a few cups of strongly brewed tea into the heap. The liquid tea will hasten decomposition and draw acid-producing bacteria, creating desirable acid-rich compost.

✳ Tennis Balls

Fluff down-filled clothes and comforters Down-filled items like jackets, vests, comforters, and pillows get flat and soggy when you wash them. You can fluff them up again by tossing a couple of tennis balls into the dryer when you put them in.

Sand curves in furniture Wrap a tennis ball in sandpaper and use it to sand curves when you're refinishing furniture. The tennis ball is just the right size and shape to fit comfortably in your hand.

Cover your trailer hitch To protect chrome trailer hitches from scratches and rust, cut a tennis ball and slip it over your hitching ball. The tennis ball will keep moisture out and rust away.

Massage your back Give yourself a relaxing and therapeutic back massage. Simply fill a long tube sock with a few tennis balls, tie the end, and stretch your homemade massager around your back just as you would a towel after a shower or bath.

Keep swimming pool oil-free Float a couple of tennis balls in your swimming pool to absorb body oils from swimmers. Replace the balls every couple of weeks during high-use periods.

Make bike kickstand for soft soil To prevent a bicycle kickstand from sinking into soft grass, sand, or mud, cut a slit in a tennis ball and put it on the end of the kickstand.

Store your valuables at gym Here's a neat way to hide and store valuables when you're working out at the gym. Make a 2-inch (5-centimeter) slit along one seam of a tennis ball and insert the valuables inside. Keep the ball in your gym bag among other sporting gear. Just remember not to use the doctored ball next time you're out on the tennis court!

Park right every time Make parking your car in the garage easier. Hang a tennis ball on a string from the garage ceiling so it will hit the windshield at the spot where you should stop the car. You'll always know exactly where to park.

SCIENCE FAIR

Teach kids about **gravity**. Stand on a chair holding **two tennis balls**, one in each hand, and extend your arms so they're at the same distance from the floor. Ask the kids to observe as you release both balls at once. Did they hit the floor at the same time? Now repeat using a **tennis ball** and a much lighter **Ping-Pong ball**. Again ask which will land first. Most will guess the heavier tennis ball, but they'll **land at the same time** because gravity exerts the same force on all objects regardless of their weight. Of course, if you try this with a ball and a feather, the kids will also learn that less dense objects fall slower due to air resistance.

Massage your sore feet For a simple but amazingly enjoyable and therapeutic foot massage, take your shoes off, place a tennis ball on the floor, and roll it around under your feet.

Get a better grip on bottle caps If your hands are weakened by arthritis or other ailments, you probably have a difficult time removing twist-off bottle caps. An old tennis ball may help. Simply cut a ball in half and use one of the halves to enhance your grip.

✳ Tires

Protect your vegetables Plant your tomatoes, potatoes, eggplants, peppers, or other vegetables inside tires laid on the ground. The tires will protect the plants from harsh winds, and the dark rubber will absorb heat from the sun and warm the surrounding soil.

Make a wading pool for kids To make an impromptu wading pool for toddlers, drape a shower curtain over the center of a large truck tire and fill it with water.

Make a classic tire swing A swing made from an old tire is a timeless source of pleasure for children of all ages. To make one in your backyard, drill a few drainage holes in the bottom of the tire. Drill two holes for bolts in the top, bolt two chains to the tire, and suspend it by the chains from a healthy branch of a hardwood tree. Use 3/16-inch (18-millimeter) playground chain. Put some wood chips or other soft material under and around the swing to cushion falls.

𝒯ip Tire Checkup

> Spending five minutes a month to check your tires can protect against avoidable breakdowns and crashes, improve vehicle handling, increase gas mileage, and extend the life of your tires. Here are some guidelines:
> ● Check tire air pressure at least once a month and before going on a long trip. Don't forget the spare.
> ● Inspect for uneven wear on tire treads, cracks, foreign objects, or other signs of wear or trauma. Remove bits of glass and other objects wedged in the tread.
> ● Make sure your tire valves have caps.
> ● Do not overload your vehicle.

Store plumbing snakes An old bicycle tire is just the right size to store metal snakes used to clean plumbing lines or "fish wires" used to run electrical cables inside walls. Just lay the snake or fish wire inside the tire, where it will expand to the shape of the tire and become encased within it. Then you can hang the tire conveniently on a hook in your workshop, garage, basement, or shed.

✳ Tomato Juice

Deodorize plastic containers To remove foul odors from a plastic container, pour a little tomato juice onto a sponge and wipe it around the inside of the container. Then wash the container and lid in warm, soapy water, dry well, and store them separated in the freezer for a couple of days. The container will be stench-free and ready to use again.

Remove skunk stink from dog Is there a dog alive that hasn't been
sprayed by a skunk at least once? If your dog gets skunked,
douse the affected area thoroughly with undiluted
tomato juice. Make sure to sponge some of the juice
over the pet's face, too, avoiding its eyes. Wait a few
minutes for the acids from the tomatoes to neutralize
the skunk smell and then give the dog a shampoo or
scrub with soap and water. Repeat as necessary over several
days until the smell is completely gone.

Rid fridge of odors Did a power failure cause the food to spoil and become malodorous
in your fridge? Get rid of spoiled-food smells in your refrigerator and freezer
with the help of some tomato juice. After disposing of the bad food that caused
the smell, thoroughly wipe the insides of the fridge and freezer with a sponge
or washcloth doused in undiluted tomato juice. Rinse with warm, soapy water
and wipe dry. If traces of the smell remain, repeat the procedure or substitute
vinegar for the tomato juice.

Restore blond hair color If you're a blonde who has ever gone swimming in a chlorine-
treated pool, you know it can sometimes give your hair an unappealing green
tint. To restore the blond color to your hair, saturate it with undiluted tomato
juice, cover it with a shower cap, and wait 10-15 minutes. Then rinse thoroughly, shampoo, and soon you'll be ready to have more fun.

Relieve a sore throat For temporary relief of sore throat symptoms, gargle with a mixture of 1/2 cup tomato juice and 1/2 cup hot water, plus about 10 drops hot
pepper sauce.

✱ Toothbrushes

Use as all-purpose cleaners Don't throw out your old toothbrushes. Instead, use them
to clean a host of diverse items and small or hard-to-reach areas and crevices.
Use a toothbrush to clean artificial flowers and plants, costume jewelry, combs,
shower tracks, crevices between tiles, and around faucets. Also clean computer
keyboards, can-opener blades, and around stove burners. And don't forget the
seams on shoes where the leather meets the sole.

Brush your cheese grater Give the teeth of a cheese grater a good brushing with an old
toothbrush before you wash the grater or put it in the dishwasher. This will
make it easier to wash and will prevent clogs in your dishwasher drain by getting rid of bits of cheese or any other item you may have grated.

Remove tough stains Removing a stain can be a pain, especially one that has soaked
deep down into soft fibers. To remove those deep stains, try using a soft-bristled nylon toothbrush, dabbing it gently to work in the stain-removing agent
(bleach or vinegar, for example) until the stain is gone.

Clean silk from ears of corn Before cooking shucked corn, take an old toothbrush and gently rub down the ear to brush away the remaining clingy strands of silk. Then you won't have to brush them out from between your teeth after you eat the corn!

Clean and oil your waffle iron A clean, soft toothbrush is just the right utensil to clean crumbs and burned batter from the nooks and crannies of a waffle iron. Use it to spread oil evenly on the waffle iron surface before the next use too.

Apply hair dye Dyeing your hair at home? Use an old toothbrush as an applicator. It's the perfect size.

Clean gunk from appliances Dip an old toothbrush in soapy water and use it to clean between appliance knobs and buttons, and raised-letter nameplates.

DID *You* KNOW?

The ancient Chinese were apparently the first to use toothbrushes, which they made with bristles from the necks of cold-climate pigs. The first toothbrushes in America were manufactured in the late 19th century, but toothbrushing did not become a two- or three-times-a-day habit for many common folks until after World War II, when returning GIs brought home their army-enforced habits. By then DuPont had invented the nylon bristle, which, unlike the natural bristles used earlier, dried completely between brushings and was resistant to the growth of bacteria. Nylon bristles are still used in most toothbrushes made today.

* Toothpaste

Remove scuffs from shoes A little toothpaste does an amazing job of removing scuffs from leather shoes. Just squirt a dab on the scuffed area and rub with a soft cloth. Wipe clean with a damp cloth. The leather will look like new.

Clean your piano keys Has tickling the ivories left them a bit dingy? Clean them up with toothpaste and a toothbrush, then wipe them down with a damp cloth. Makes sense, since ivory is essentially elephant teeth. However, toothpaste will work just as well on modern pianos that usually have keys covered with plastic rather than real ivory.

Spiff up your sneakers Want to clean and whiten the rubber part of your sneakers? Get out the non-gel toothpaste and an old toothbrush. After scrubbing, clean off the toothpaste with a damp cloth.

Clean your clothes iron The mild abrasive in non-gel toothpaste is just the ticket for scrubbing the gunk off the bottom plate of your clothes iron. Apply the toothpaste to the cool iron, scrub with a rag, then rinse clean.

Polish a diamond ring Put a little toothpaste on an old toothbrush and use it to make your diamond ring sparkle instead of your teeth. Clean off the residue with a damp cloth.

Deodorize baby bottles Baby bottles inevitably pick up a sour-milk smell. Toothpaste will remove the odor in a jiffy. Just put some on your bottle brush and scrub away. Be sure to rinse thoroughly.

Prevent fogged goggles Whether you are doing woodworking or going skiing or scuba diving, nothing is more frustrating (and sometimes dangerous) than fogged goggles. Prevent the problem by coating the goggles with toothpaste and then wiping them off.

Prevent bathroom mirrors from fogging Ouch! You cut yourself shaving and it's no wonder—you can't see your face clearly in that fogged-up bathroom mirror. Next time, coat the mirror with non-gel toothpaste and wipe it off before you get in the shower. When you get out, the mirror won't be fogged.

Shine bathroom and kitchen chrome They make commercial cleaners with a very fine abrasive designed to shine up chrome, but if you don't have any handy, the fine abrasive in non-gel toothpaste works just as well. Just smear on the toothpaste and polish with a soft, dry cloth.

Clean the bathroom sink Non-gel toothpaste works as well as anything else to clean the bathroom sink. The tube's sitting right there, so just squirt some in, scrub with a sponge, and rinse it out. Bonus: The toothpaste will kill any odors emanating from the drain trap.

Remove crayon from walls Did crayon-toting kids get creative on your wall? Roll up your sleeves and grab a tube of non-gel toothpaste and a rag or—better yet—a scrub brush. Squirt the toothpaste on the wall and start scrubbing. The fine

 DID *You* KNOW?

Ancient Egyptians used a mixture of ox-hoof ashes, burned eggshells, myrrh, pumice, and water to clean their teeth. And for most of history, tooth-cleaning concoctions were used mostly by the wealthy. That began to change in 1850, when Dr. Washington Sheffield of New London, Connecticut, developed a formula we would recognize as toothpaste. He called it Dr. Sheffield's Creme Dentifrice. It was his son, Dr. Lucius Tracy Sheffield, who observed collapsible metal tubes of paint and thought, Why not toothpaste? To this day, Sheffield Laboratories, the company Dr. Washington Sheffield founded in 1850, continues to make toothpaste and put it in tubes.

abrasive in the toothpaste will rub away the crayon every time. Rinse the wall with water.

Remove ink or lipstick stains from fabric Oh no, a pen opened up in the pocket of your favorite shirt! This may or may not work, depending on the fabric and the ink, but it is certainly worth a try before consigning the shirt to the scrap bin. Put non-gel toothpaste on the stain and rub the fabric vigorously together. Rinse with water. Did some of the ink come out? Great! Repeat the process a few more times until you get rid of all the ink. The same process works for lipstick.

Remove watermarks from furniture You leave coasters around. But some people just won't use them. To get rid of those telltale watermark rings left by sweating beverages, gently rub some non-gel toothpaste on the wood with a soft cloth. Then wipe it off with a damp cloth and let it dry before applying furniture polish.

Remove beach tar Getting that black beach tar on your feet can put a small crimp in your vacation, but it is easy enough to remove. Just rub it with some non-gel toothpaste and rinse.

Clear up pimples Your teenager is bemoaning a prominent pimple, and the day before the dance too! Tonight, have her or him dab a bit of non-gel, nonwhitening toothpaste on the offending spot, and it should be dried up by morning. The toothpaste dehydrates the pimple and absorbs the oil. This remedy works best on pimples that have come to a head. Caution: This remedy may be irritating to sensitive skin.

> **TAKE CARE** All toothpaste, including gels, contains abrasives. The amount varies, but too much can damage your tooth enamel. People with sensitive teeth in particular should use a low-abrasive toothpaste. Ask your dentist which is the best toothpaste for you.

Clean smells from hands The ingredients in toothpaste that deodorize your mouth will work on your hands as well. If you've gotten into something stinky, wash your hands with toothpaste, and they'll smell great.

✳ Toothpicks

Mark rare, medium, and well done Your guests want their steaks done differently at the family cookout, but how do you keep track of who gets what? Easy. Just use different-colored toothpicks to mark them as rare, medium, and well done and get ready for the accolades.

Stick through garlic clove for marinade If you marinate foods with garlic cloves, stick a toothpick through the clove so you can remove it easily when you are ready to serve the food.

Keep pots from boiling over Oh darn! It seems like all you have to do is turn around for one minute and the pot is boiling over, making a mess on the stovetop. Next time, just stick a toothpick, laid flat, between the lid and pot. The little space will allow enough steam to escape to prevent the pot from boiling over. This also works with a casserole dish that's cooking in the oven.

Microwave potatoes faster The next time you microwave a potato, stick four toothpick "legs" in one side. The suspended potato will cook much faster because the microwaves will reach the bottom as well as the top and sides.

 DID *You* KNOW?

- Buddhist monks used toothpicks as far back as the 700s, and researchers have even found toothpick grooves in the teeth of prehistoric humans.

- Toothpicks were first used in the United States at the Union Oyster House, the oldest restaurant in Boston, which opened in 1826.
- In 1872 Silas Noble and J. P. Cooley patented the first toothpick-manufacturing machine.

- One cord of white birch wood, (also known as the toothpick tree) can make 7.5 million toothpicks.

Control your use of salad dressing Restrict your intake of carbs and calories from salad dressing. Instead of removing the foil seal when you open the bottle, take a toothpick and punch several holes in the foil. This will help prevent overuse of the dressing and make it last longer.

Keep sausages from rolling around When cooking sausages, insert toothpicks between pairs to make turning them over easy and keep them from rolling around in the pan. They'll cook more evenly and only need to be turned over once.

Mark start of tape roll Instead of wasting time trying to find the beginning of a tape roll, just wrap it around a toothpick whenever you are done using the tape, and the start of the roll will always be easy to find. No more frustration, and you can use the time you just saved to attack something else on your to-do list.

Use to light candles When a candle has burned down and the wick is hard to reach, don't burn your fingers trying to use a small match to light it. Light a wooden toothpick instead and use it to light the wick.

Clean cracks and crevices To get rid of dirt, grime, and cobwebs in hard-to-reach cracks or crevices, dip an ordinary toothpick in some alcohol and run it through the affected area. Also try this to clean around the buttons of your phone.

Apply glue to sequins If you're working on a project that calls for gluing on sequins or buttons, squirt a little glue on a piece of paper and dip in a toothpick to apply small dabs of glue. You won't make a mess, and you won't waste glue.

Make sewing easier Make sewing projects easier and complete them faster. Just use a round toothpick to push fabrics, lace, or gatherings under the pressure foot as you sew.

Touch up furniture crevices The secret to a good paint touch-up job is to use as little paint as possible, because even if you do have the right paint, the stuff in the can may not exactly match the sun-faded or dirty paint on the furniture. The solution: Dip the end of a toothpick in the paint and use it to touch up just the crevice. Unlike a brush, the toothpick won't apply more paint than you need, and you won't have a brush to clean.

Repair small holes in wood Did you drive a finish nail or brad into the wrong spot in your pine project? Don't panic. Dip the tip of a toothpick into white or yellow glue. Stick the toothpick in the hole and break it off. Sand the toothpick flush to the surface and you will never notice the repair.

Repair a loose hinge screw You took the door off and removed the hinges before you painted it. Now as you reattach the hinges, a screw just keeps turning without tightening—the hole is stripped. The fix is easy: Put some glue on the end of a toothpick and stick it in the hole. Break it off. Add one or two more toothpicks with glue until the hole is tightly filled, breaking each one off as you go. Re-drill the hole and you're ready to screw the hinge in place.

Repair a bent plant stem If the stem of your favorite plant has folded over, it by no means dooms the plant. Straighten the stem and support it by placing a toothpick against the stem and wrapping the toothpick on with tape. Water the plant. Keep your eye on the plant—depending on how fast it grows, the stem will regain its strength and you'll need to remove the splint so you don't strangle the stem.

TAKE CARE Overuse of toothpicks can damage tooth enamel and lacerate gums. If you have bonding or veneers, be extra careful to avoid breakage. Toothpicks can also cause wear to tooth roots, especially in the elderly whose gums have pulled away, exposing the roots.

Repair a leaky garden hose If your garden hose springs a leak, don't go out and buy another one; just find the hole and insert a toothpick in it. Cut off the excess part of the toothpick. The water will make the wood swell, plugging up the leak every time.

Foil those cutworms Cutworms kill seedlings by encircling the stem and severing it. To protect your seedlings, stick a toothpick in the soil about 1/4 inch (60 millimeters) from each stem. This prevents a cutworm from encircling it.

✳ Twist Ties

Organize electrical cords Does the top of your computer desk look like wild vines have overtaken it? Is there a thicket of wires behind your entertainment center? Tame the jungle of electrical wires by rolling each one up neatly and securing the extra length with a twist tie.

Make a trellis All you need are some twist ties and some of those plastic rings from soda six-packs to make a terrific trellis for climbing annual vines such as peas or morning glories. Just use the twist ties to join together as many of the six-pack rings as you want. Attach the trellis between two stakes, also using twist ties. You can even add sections to the trellis as the plant grows so that it looks like the plant is climbing on its own. At the end of the season, just roll the trellis up for storage and you can use it again next year.

Tie up plant stems Twist ties are handy for securing a drooping plant stem to a stake or holding vines to a trellis. Don't twist the ties too tight, because you might injure the stem and restrict its growth.

Temporarily repair eyeglasses Whoops! Your specs slip off because that tiny screw that holds the earpiece fell out. Secure the earpiece temporarily with a twist tie. Trim the edges off the tie so that you just have the center wire. After you insert and tie it off, snip the excess with scissors.

Use for emergency shoelace Don't have a replacement shoelace handy? Try some twist ties. Use one tie across each opposing pair of eyelets.

Code your keys Got several similar-looking keys on your chain? Quickly identify them with twist ties of different colors secured through the holes in the keys.

Hang Christmas tree ornaments Some of those Christmas tree ornaments have been in the family for generations. As extra insurance against breakage, secure them to the tree with twist ties.

Make an emergency cuff link Oh, brother, you are in trouble! You packed a nice shirt with French cuffs to wear to the wedding, but you forgot your cuff links. Well, it's not so bad. Secure the cuffs with twist ties. Pull the ties through so the twist is discreetly hidden inside the cuff.

Bind loose-leaf paper Hold sheets of loose-leaf paper together by inserting twist ties in the holes.

U

✱ Umbrellas

Use as a drying rack An old umbrella makes a handy drying rack. Just strip off the fabric and hang the frame upside down from your shower bar. Attach wet clothing with clothespins. Plus, your new drying rack easily folds up for storage.

Clean a chandelier The next time you climb up there to clean the chandelier or ceiling fan, bring an old umbrella with you. Open the umbrella and hook its handle on the fixture so that it hangs upside down to catch any drips or dust.

Cover your picnic food To keep flies from feasting on your picnic before you do, open an old umbrella and cut off the handle. Place the umbrella over the dishes. It will shield your repast from the sun too.

Signal in a crowd The next time you and your sweetie go to a crowded event, carry a couple of identical bright-colored umbrellas. If you get separated, you can hold the umbrellas over your head and open them up to find each other in a flash.

Block plant overspray Houseplants love to be misted with water, but your walls don't love to get soaked with overspray. Stick an open umbrella between the plants and the wall and give your plants a shower.

Make plant stakes The wind caught your umbrella, turned it inside out, and ripped the fabric. Before you toss it into the trash, remove the umbrella's ribs. They make excellent supports for top-heavy garden plants, such as peonies.

Make an instant trellis Remove the fabric from an old umbrella and insert the handle into the ground to support climbing vines such as morning glories. The umbrella's shape, covered with flowers, will look terrific in the garden.

Shield your seedlings You thought you waited long enough before planting your seedlings outside, but now they're predicting a killer frost tonight. Sacrifice an old umbrella to save the seedlings. Open the umbrella, then cut off the handle. Place the umbrella over the seedlings to keep the frost them.

Vanilla Extract

Freshen up the fridge Having trouble getting rid of that bad odor in your refrigerator, even after scrubbing it out? Wipe down the inside of the fridge with vanilla extract. To prolong the fresh vanilla scent, soak a cotton ball or a piece of sponge with vanilla extract and leave it in the refrigerator.

Deodorize your microwave Is the odor of fish, or some other strong smell, lingering in your microwave? Pour a little vanilla extract in a bowl and microwave on High for one minute. Now, that's better.

Neutralize the smell of fresh paint If you would rather not have the unpleasant smell of fresh paint in your house, mix 1 tablespoon vanilla extract into the paint can when you open it. The house will smell delicious!

Sweeten the smell of your home It's an old Realtor's trick. Put a drop or two of vanilla extract on a lightbulb, turn on the light, and your house will be filled with the appealing scent of baked goods in the oven.

Use as perfume Try it! Just put a dab of vanilla extract on each wrist. You'll smell delicious, and many people find the scent of vanilla to be very relaxing.

Repel bugs Everybody likes the smell of vanilla. Everybody but bugs, that is. Dilute 1 tablespoon vanilla extract with 1 cup water and wipe the mixture on your exposed skin to discourage mosquitoes, blackflies, and ticks.

Relieve minor burns Yee-oow! You accidentally grabbed a hot pot or got splattered with grease in the kitchen. Grab the vanilla extract for quick pain relief. The evaporation of the alcohol in the vanilla extract cools the burn.

Vegetable Oil

Help remove a splinter That stubborn splinter just won't come out. Take a break from poking at your finger for a few minutes and soak it in vegetable oil. The oil will soften up your skin, perhaps just enough to ease that splinter out with your tweezers.

Remove labels and stickers Used jars—both plastic and glass—are always handy to have around. But removing the old labels always leaves a stubborn sticky residue. Soak the label with vegetable oil and the label will slide right off. Works great for sticky price tags too.

Separate stuck glasses When stacked drinking glasses get stuck together, it seems like nothing you can do will separate them. But the solution is simple: Just pour a little vegetable oil around the rim of the bottom glass and the glasses will pull apart with ease.

Tip Oiling Cutting Boards

> To restore and preserve dried-out wooden kitchen items such as cutting boards and salad bowls and tongs, use salad bowl oil—a food-safe oil that won't get rancid and is designed to protect wood that will come into contact with food. Don't use regular vegetable oil. Vegetable oil will soak into dried-out wood and make it look much better, but it never really dries and can get rancid after soaking into the wood.

Smooth your feet Rub your feet with vegetable oil before you go to bed and put on a pair of socks. When you awaken, your tootsies will be silky-smooth and soft.

Prevent clippings from sticking to your mower The next time you turn over your lawn mower to remove the stuck-on grass clippings, rub some vegetable oil under the housing and on the blade. It will take a lot longer for the clippings to build up next time.

Control mosquitoes in the birdbath It's so satisfying to watch birds enjoying the garden bath you provide. But unfortunately, that still water is a perfect breeding ground for mosquitoes. Floating a few tablespoons of vegetable oil on the surface of the water will help keep mosquitoes from using the water, and it won't bother the birds. But it's still important to change the water twice a week so any larvae don't have time to hatch.

Season cast-iron cookware After washing and thoroughly drying a cast-iron skillet or wok, use a paper towel to wipe it down with vegetable oil. Just leave a very thin layer of oil. It will prevent the pan from rusting and season it for the next time you use it.

✳ Vegetable Peelers

Slice slivers of cheese or chocolate When you need cheese slivers that are thinner than you can cut with a knife, or you want to decorate a cake with fine curlicues of chocolate, reach for the vegetable peeler.

Sharpen your pencils No pencil sharpener handy? A vegetable peeler will do a fine job of bringing your pencil to a point.

Soften hard butter fast You're ready to add the butter to your cake mix when you discover that the only sticks you have are as hard as a rock. When you need to soften cold, hard butter in a hurry, shave off what you need with a vegetable peeler. You'll have soft butter in moments.

Renew scented soaps Ornamental scented soaps are a great addition to the powder room because they make the room smell great as well as adding a decorative touch. But after a while, the surface of exposed ornamental soaps dries out, causing the scent to fade. To renew the scent, use a vegetable peeler to skim off a thin layer, revealing a new moist and fragrant surface.

super item *175 uses! Vinegar

✳ VINEGAR **AROUND THE HOUSE**

Clear dirt off PCs and peripherals Your computer, printer, fax machine, and other home office gear will work better if you keep them clean and dust-free. Before you start cleaning, make sure that all your equipment is shut off. Now mix equal parts white vinegar and water in a bucket. Dampen a clean cloth in the solution—never use a spray bottle; you don't want to get liquid on the circuits inside—then squeeze it out as hard as you can, and start wiping. Keep a few cotton swabs on hand for getting to the buildups in tight spaces (like around the keys of your PC keyboard).

Clean your computer mouse If you have a mouse with a removable tracking ball, use a 50/50 vinegar-water solution to clean it. First, remove the ball from underneath the mouse by twisting off the cover over it. Use a cloth, dampened with the solution and wrung out, to wipe the ball clean and to remove fingerprints and dirt from the mouse itself. Then use a moistened cotton swab to clean out the gunk and debris from inside the ball chamber (let it dry a couple of hours before reinserting the ball).

Tip **Buying Vinegar**

> Vinegar comes in a surprising number of varieties—including herbal organic blends, Champagne, rice, and wine—not to mention bottle sizes. For household chores, however, plain distilled white vinegar is the best and least expensive choice, and you can buy it by the gallon (3.7 liters) to save even more money. Apple cider vinegar runs a close second in practicality and is also widely used in cooking and home remedies. All other types of vinegar are strictly for ingestion and can be pretty pricey as well.

Clean your window blinds You can make the job of cleaning mini-blinds or venetians considerably less torturous by giving them "the white glove treatment." Just put on a white cotton glove—the kind sold for gardening is perfect—and moisten the fingers in a solution made of equal parts white vinegar and hot tap water. Now simply slide your fingers across both sides of each slat and prepare to be amazed. Use a container of clean water to periodically wash off the glove.

Unclog and deodorize drains The combination of vinegar and baking soda is one of the most effective ways to unclog and deodorize drains. It's also far gentler on your pipes (and your wallet) than commercial drain cleaners.

- To clear clogs in sink and tub drains, use a funnel to pour in 1/2 cup baking soda followed by 1 cup vinegar. When the foaming subsides, flush with hot tap water. Wait five minutes, and then flush again with cold water. Besides clearing blockages, this technique also washes away odor-causing bacteria.

- To speed up a slow drain, pour in 1/2 cup salt followed by 2 cups boiling vinegar, then flush with hot and cold tap water.

Get rid of smoke odor If you've recently burned a steak—or if your chain-smoking aunt recently paid you a surprise visit—remove the lingering smoky odor by placing a shallow bowl about three-quarters full of white or cider vinegar in the room where the scent is strongest. Use several bowls if the smell permeates your entire home. The odor should be gone in less than a day. You can also quickly dispense of the smell of fresh cigarette smoke inside a room by moistening a cloth with vinegar and waving it around a bit.

Wipe away mildew When you want to remove mildew stains, reach for white vinegar first. It can be safely used without additional ventilation and can be applied to almost any surface—bathroom fixtures and tile, clothing, furniture, painted surfaces, plastic curtains, and more. To eliminate heavy mildew accumulations, use it full strength. For light stains, dilute it with an equal amount of water. You can also prevent mildew from forming on the bottoms of rugs and carpeting by misting the backs with full-strength white vinegar from a spray bottle.

Clean chrome and stainless steel To clean chrome and stainless steel fixtures around your home, apply a light misting of undiluted white vinegar from a recycled spray bottle. Buff with a soft cloth to bring out the brightness.

Shine your silver Make your silverware—as well as your pure silver bracelets, rings, and other jewelry—shine like new by soaking them in a mixture of 1/2 cup white vinegar and 2 tablespoons baking soda for two to three hours. Rinse them under cold water and dry thoroughly with a soft cloth.

Polish brass and copper items Put the shimmer back in your brass, bronze, and copper objects by making a paste of equal parts white vinegar and salt, or vinegar and baking soda (wait for the fizzing to stop before using). Use a clean, soft cloth or paper towel to rub the paste into the item until the tarnish is gone. Then rinse with cool water and polish with a soft towel until dry.

TAKE CARE
● Do not apply vinegar to jewelry containing pearls or gemstones because it can damage their finish or, in the case of pearls, actually disintegrate them.
● Do not attempt to remove tarnish from antiques, because it could diminish their value.

Erase ballpoint-pen marks Has the budding young artist in your home just decorated a painted wall in your home with a ballpoint original? Don't lose your cool. Rather, dab some full-strength white vinegar on the "masterpiece" using a cloth or a sponge. Repeat until the marks are gone. Then go out and buy your child a nice big sketch pad.

Unglue stickers, decals, and price tags To remove a sticker or decal affixed to painted furniture or a painted wall, simply saturate the corners and sides of the sticker with full-strength white vinegar and carefully scrape it off (using an expired credit card or a plastic phone card). Remove any sticky remains by pouring on a bit more vinegar. Let it sit for a minute or two, and then wipe with a clean cloth. This approach is equally effective for removing price tags and other stickers from glass, plastic, and other glossy surfaces.

Burnish your scissors When your scissor blades get sticky or grimy, don't use water to wash them off; you're far more likely to rust the fastener that holds the blades together—or the blades themselves—than get them clean. Instead, wipe down the blades with a cloth dipped in full-strength white vinegar, and then dry it off with a rag or dish towel.

Get the salt off your shoes As if a winter's worth of ice, slush, and snow wasn't rough enough on your shoes and boots, the worst thing, by far, is all the rock salt that's used to melt it. In addition to leaving unsightly white stains, salt can actually cause your footwear to crack and even disintegrate if it's left on indefinitely. To remove it and prevent long-term damage, wipe fresh stains with a cloth dipped in undiluted white vinegar.

Clean your piano keys Here's an easy and efficient way to get those grimy fingerprints and stains off your piano keys. Dip a soft cloth into a solution of 1/2 cup white vinegar mixed in 2 cups water, squeeze it out until there are no drips, then gently wipe off each key. Use a second cloth to dry off the keys as you move along, then leave the keyboard uncovered for 24 hours.

Deodorize lunch boxes, footlockers, and car trunks Does your old footlocker smell like, well, an old footlocker? Or perhaps your child's lunch box has taken on the bouquet of week-old tuna? What about that musty old car trunk? Quit holding your breath every time you open it. Instead, soak a slice of white bread in white vinegar and leave it in the malodorous space overnight. The smell should be gone by morning.

Freshen a musty closet Got a closet that doesn't smell as fresh as you'd like? First, remove the contents, then wash down the walls, ceiling, and floor with a cloth dampened in a solution of 1 cup each of vinegar and ammonia and 1/4 cup baking soda in 1 gallon (3.7 liters) water. Keep the closet door open and let the interior dry before replacing your clothes and other stuff. If the smell persists, place a small pan of cat litter inside. Replenish every few days until the odor is gone.

Brighten up brickwork How's this for an effortless way to clean your brick floors without breaking out the polish? Just go over them with a damp mop dipped in 1 cup white vinegar mixed with 1 gallon (3.7 liters) warm water. Your floors will look so good you'll never think about cleaning them with anything else. You can also use this same solution to brighten up the bricks around your fireplace.

Revitalize wood paneling Does the wood paneling in your den look dull and dreary? Liven it up with this simple homemade remedy: Mix 1 pint warm water, 4 tablespoons white or apple cider vinegar, and 2 tablespoons olive oil in a container, give it a couple of shakes, and apply with a clean cloth. Let the mixture soak into the wood for several minutes, then polish with a dry cloth.

Restore your rugs If your rugs or carpets are looking worn and dingy from too much foot traffic or an excess of kids' building blocks, toy trucks, and such, bring them back to life by brushing them with a clean push broom dipped in a solution of 1 cup white vinegar in 1 gallon (3.7 liters) water. Your faded threads will perk up, and you don't even need to rinse off the solution.

Remove carpet stains You can lift out many stains from your carpet with vinegar:

- Rub light carpet stains with a mixture of 2 tablespoons salt dissolved in 1/2 cup white vinegar. Let the solution dry, then vacuum.

- For larger or darker stains, add 2 tablespoons borax to the mixture and use in the same way.

- For tough, ground-in dirt and other stains, make a paste of 1 tablespoon vinegar with 1 tablespoon cornstarch, and rub it into the stain using a dry cloth. Let it set for two days, then vacuum.

- To make spray-on spot and stain remover, fill a spray bottle with 5 parts water and 1 part vinegar. Fill a second spray bottle with 1 part nonsudsy ammonia and 5 parts water. Saturate a stain with the vinegar solution. Let it settle for a few minutes, then blot thoroughly with a clean, dry cloth. Then spray and blot using the ammonia solution. Repeat until the stain is gone.

Tip **Vinegar and Floor Cleaning**

> Damp-mopping with a mild vinegar solution is widely recommended as a way to clean wood and no-wax vinyl or laminate flooring. But, if possible, check with your flooring manufacturer first. Even when diluted, vinegar's acidity can ruin some floor finishes, and too much water will damage most wooden floors. If you want to try vinegar on your floors, use 1/2 cup white vinegar mixed in 1 gallon (3.7 liters) warm water. Start with a trial application in an inconspicuous area. Before applying the solution, squeeze out the mop thoroughly (or just use a spray bottle to moisten the mop head).

✻ VINEGAR **IN THE GARAGE**

Remove bumper stickers If those tattered old bumper stickers on your car make you feel more nauseated than nostalgic, it's time to break out the vinegar. Saturate the top and sides of the sticker with undiluted distilled vinegar and wait 10-15 minutes for the vinegar to soak through. Then use an expired credit card (or one of those promotional plastic cards that come in the mail) to scrape it off. Use more full-strength vinegar to get rid of any remaining gluey residue. Use the same technique to detach those cute decals your youngster used to decorate the back windshield.

Clean windshield wiper blades When your windshield actually gets blurrier after you turn on your wipers during a rainstorm, it usually means that your wiper blades are dirty. To make them as good as new, dampen a cloth or rag with some full-strength white vinegar and run it down the full length of each blade once or twice.

Keep car windows frost-free If you park your car outdoors during the cold winter months, a smart and simple way to keep frost from forming on your windows is by wiping (or, better yet, spraying) the outsides of the windows with a solution of 3 parts white vinegar to 1 part water. Each coating may last up to several weeks—although, unfortunately, it won't do much in the way of warding off a heavy snowfall.

Care for your car's carpets A good vacuuming will get up the sand and other loose debris from your car's carpeting, but it won't do diddly for stains or ground-in dirt. For that, mix up a solution of equal parts water and white vinegar and sponge it into the carpet. Give the mixture a couple of minutes to settle in; then blot it up with a cloth or paper towel. This technique will also eliminate salt residues left on car carpets during the winter months.

Remove candle wax Candles are great for creating a romantic mood, but the mood can quickly sour if you wind up getting melted candle wax on your fine wood furniture. To remove it, first soften the wax using a blow-dryer on its hottest setting and blot up as much as you can with paper towels. Then remove what's left by rubbing with a cloth soaked in a solution made of equal parts white vinegar and water. Wipe clean with a soft, absorbent cloth.

Give grease stains the slip Eliminate grease stains from your kitchen table or counter by wiping them down with a cloth dampened in a solution of equal parts white vinegar and water. In addition to removing the grease, the vinegar will neutralize any odors on the surface (once its own aroma evaporates, that is).

Conceal scratches in wood furniture Got a scratch on a wooden tabletop that grabs your attention every time you look at it? To make it much less noticeable, mix some distilled or cider vinegar and iodine in a small jar and paint over the scratch with a small artist's brush. Use more iodine for darker woods; more vinegar for lighter shades.

> **TAKE CARE** Don't use vinegar—or alcohol or lemon juice—on marble tabletops, countertops, or floors. Vinegar's acidity can dull or even pit the protective coating—and possibly damage the stone itself. Also, avoid using vinegar on travertine and limestone; the acid eats through the calcium in the stonework.

Get rid of water rings on furniture To remove white rings left by wet glasses on wood furniture, mix equal parts vinegar and olive oil and apply it with a soft cloth while moving with the wood grain. Use another clean, soft cloth to shine it up. To get white water rings off leather furniture, dab them with a sponge soaked in full-strength white vinegar.

Wipe off wax or polish buildup When furniture polish or wax builds up on wood furniture or leather tabletops, get rid of it with diluted white vinegar. To get built-up polish off a piece of wood furniture, dip a cloth in equal parts vinegar and water and squeeze it out well. Then, moving with the grain, clean away the polish. Wipe dry with a soft towel or cloth. Most leather tabletops will come clean simply by wiping them down with a soft cloth dipped in 1/4 cup vinegar and 1/2 cup water. Use a clean towel to dry off any remaining liquid.

Revitalize leather furniture Has your leather sofa or easy chair lost its luster? To restore it to its former glory, mix equal parts white vinegar and boiled linseed oil in a recycled spray bottle, shake it up well, and spray it on. Spread it evenly over your furniture using a soft cloth, give it a couple of minutes to settle in, then rub it off with a clean cloth.

Refresh your refrigerator Did you know that vinegar might be an even more effective safe cleanser for your refrigerator than baking soda? Use equal parts white vinegar and water to wash both the interior and exterior of your fridge, including the door gasket and the fronts of the vegetable and fruit bins. To prevent mildew growth, wash the inside walls and bin interiors with some full-strength vinegar on a cloth. Also use undiluted vinegar to wipe off accumulated dust and grime on top of your refrigerator. Of course, you'll still want to put that box of baking soda inside your refrigerator to keep it smelling clean when you're done.

Steam-clean your microwave To clean your microwave, place a glass bowl filled with a solution of 1/4 cup vinegar in 1 cup water inside, and zap the mixture for five minutes on the highest setting. Once the bowl cools, dip a cloth or sponge into the liquid and use it to wipe away stains and splatters on the interior.

DID *You* KNOW?

Taken literally, vinegar is nothing more than wine that's gone bad; the word derives from the French *vin* (wine) and *aigre* (sour). But, in fact, anything used to make alcohol can be turned into vinegar, including apples, honey, malted barley, molasses, rice, sugarcane, and even coconuts. Vinegar's acidic, solvent properties were well known even in ancient times. According to one popular legend, Cleopatra is said to have wagered she could dispose of a fortune in the course of a single meal. She won the bet by dissolving a handful of pearls in a cup of vinegar ... and then consuming it.

Disinfect cutting boards To disinfect and clean your wood cutting boards or butcher block countertop, wipe them with full-strength white vinegar after each use. The acetic acid in the vinegar is a good disinfectant, effective against such harmful bugs as *E. coli*, *Salmonella,* and *Staphylococcus.* Never use water and dishwashing detergent, because it can weaken surface wood fibers. When your wooden cutting surface needs deodorizing as well as disinfecting, spread some baking soda over it and then spray on undiluted white vinegar. Let it foam and bubble for five to ten minutes, then rinse with a cloth dipped in clean cold water.

Deodorize your garbage disposal Here's an incredibly easy way to keep your garbage disposal unit sanitized and smelling clean: Mix equal parts water and vinegar in a bowl, pour the solution into an ice cube tray, and freeze it. Then simply drop a couple of "vinegar cubes" down your disposal every week or so, followed by a cold-water rinse.

Wash out your dishwasher To keep your dishwasher operating at peak performance and remove built-up soap film, pour 1 cup undiluted white vinegar into the bottom of the unit—or in a bowl on the top rack. Then run the machine through a full cycle without any dishes or detergent. Do this once a month, especially if you have hard water. *Note:* If there's no mention of vinegar in your dishwasher owner's manual, check with the manufacturer first.

Clean china, crystal, and glassware Put the sparkle back in your glassware by adding vinegar to your rinse water or dishwater.

- To keep your everyday glassware gleaming, add 1/4 cup vinegar to your dishwasher's rinse cycle.

- To rid drinking glasses of cloudiness or spots caused by hard water, heat up a pot of equal parts white vinegar and water (use full-strength vinegar if your glasses are very cloudy), and let them soak in it for 15-30 minutes. Give them a good scrubbing with a bottle brush, then rinse clean.

- Add 2 tablespoons vinegar to your dishwater when cleaning your good crystal glasses. Then rinse them in a solution of 3 parts warm water to 1 part vinegar and allow them to air-dry. You can also wash delicate crystal and fine china by adding 1 cup vinegar to a basin of warm water. Gently dunk the glasses in the solution and let dry.

- To get coffee stains and other discolorations off china dishes and teacups, try scrubbing them with equal parts vinegar and salt, followed by rinsing them under warm water.

Clean a coffeemaker If your coffee consistently comes out weak or bitter, odds are, your coffeemaker needs cleaning. Fill the decanter with 2 cups white vinegar and 1 cup water. Place a filter in the machine, and pour the solution into the coffeemaker's water chamber. Turn on the coffeemaker and let it run through a full brew cycle. Remove the filter and replace it with a fresh one. Then run clean water through the machine for two full cycles, replacing the filter again for the second brew. If you have soft water, clean your coffeemaker after 80 brew cycles—after 40 cycles if you have hard water.

Clean a teakettle To eliminate lime and mineral deposits in a teakettle, bring 3 cups full-strength white vinegar to a full boil for five minutes and leave the vinegar in the kettle overnight. Rinse out with cold water the next day.

Cut the grease Every professional cook knows that distilled vinegar is one of the best grease cutters around. It even works on seriously greasy surfaces such as the fry vats used in many food outlets. But you don't need to have a deep fryer to find plenty of ways to put vinegar to good use:

● When you're finished frying, clean up grease splatters from your stovetop, walls, range hood, and surrounding countertop by washing them with a sponge dipped in undiluted white vinegar. Use another sponge soaked in cold tap water to rinse, then wipe dry with a soft cloth.

● Pour 3-4 tablespoons white vinegar into your favorite brand (especially bargain brands) of liquid dishwashing detergent and give it a few shakes. The added vinegar will not only increase the detergent's grease-fighting capabilities, but also provide you with more dishwashing liquid for the money, because you'll need less soap to clean your dishes.

● Boiling 2 cups vinegar in your frying pan for 10 minutes will help keep food from sticking to it for several months at a time.

● Remove burned-on grease and food stains from your stainless steel cookware by mixing 1 cup distilled vinegar in enough water to cover the stains (if they're near the top of a large pot, you may need to increase the vinegar). Let it boil for five minutes. The stains should come off with some mild scrubbing when you wash the utensil.

● Get that blackened, cooked-on grease off your broiler pan by softening it up with a solution of 1 cup apple cider vinegar and 2 tablespoons sugar. Apply the mixture while the pan is still hot, and let it sit for an hour or so. Then watch in amazement as the grime slides off with a light scrubbing.

● Got a hot plate that looks more like a grease pan? Whip it back into shape by washing it with a sponge dipped in full-strength white vinegar.

● Fight grease buildups in your oven by wiping down the inside with a rag or sponge soaked in full-strength white vinegar once a week. The same treatment gets grease off the grates on gas stoves.

Tip **Homemade Wine Vinegar**

> Contrary to popular belief, old wine rarely turns into vinegar; usually a half-empty bottle just spoils due to oxidation. To create vinegar, you need the presence of *Acetobacter,* a specific type of bacteria. You can make your own wine vinegar, though, by mixing one part leftover red, white, or rosé wine with 2 parts cider vinegar. Pour the mixture into a clean, recycled wine bottle and store it in a dark cabinet. It just might taste as good, if not better, on your salads than some of those fancy wine vinegars sold at upscale food shops.

Brush-clean can opener blades Does that dirty wheel blade of your electric can opener look like it's seen at least one can too many? To clean and sanitize it, dip an old toothbrush in white vinegar, and then position the bristles of the brush around the side and edge of the wheel. Turn on the appliance, and let the blade scrub itself clean.

Remove stains from pots, pans, and ovenware Nothing will do a better job than vinegar when it comes to removing stubborn stains on your cookware. Here's how to put the power of vinegar to use:

- Give those dark stains on your aluminum cookware (caused by cooking acidic foods) the heave-ho by mixing in 1 teaspoon white vinegar for every cup of water needed to cover the stains. Let it boil for a couple of minutes, then rinse with cold water.

- To remove stains from your stainless steel pots and pans, soak them in 2 cups white vinegar for 30 minutes, then rinse them with hot, soapy water followed by a cold-water rinse.

- To get cooked-on food stains off your glass ovenware, fill them with 1 part vinegar and 4 parts water, heat the mixture to a slow boil, and let it boil at a low level for five minutes. The stains should come off with some mild scrubbing once the mixture cools.

- They call it nonstick, but no cookware is stainproof. For mineral stains on your nonstick cookware, rub the utensil with a cloth dipped in undiluted distilled vinegar. To loosen up stubborn stains, mix 2 tablespoons baking soda, 1/2 cup vinegar, and 1 cup water and let it boil for 10 minutes.

Clear the air in your kitchen If the smell of yesterday's cooked cabbage or fish stew is hanging around your kitchen longer than you'd like, mix a pot of 1/2 cup white vinegar in 1 cup water. Let it boil until the liquid is almost gone. You'll be breathing easier in no time.

Refresh your ice trays If your plastic ice trays are covered with hard-water stains—or if it's been a while since you've cleaned them—a few cups of white vinegar can help you in either case. To remove the spots or disinfect your trays, let them soak in undiluted vinegar for four to five hours, then rinse well under cold water and let dry.

Make all-purpose cleaners For fast cleanups around the kitchen, keep two recycled spray bottles filled with these vinegar-based solutions:

- For glass, stainless steel, and plastic laminate surfaces, fill your spray bottle with 2 parts water, 1 part distilled white vinegar, and a couple of drops of dishwashing liquid.

- For cleaning walls and other painted surfaces, mix up 1/2 cup white vinegar, 1 cup ammonia, and 1/4 cup baking soda in 1 gallon (3.7 liters) water and pour some into a spray bottle. Spritz it on spots and stains whenever needed and wipe off with a clean towel.

Make an all-purpose scrub for pots and pans How would you like an effective scouring mix that costs a few pennies, and can be safely used on all of your metal cookware—including expensive copper pots and pans? Want even better news? You probably already have this "miracle mix" in your kitchen. Simply combine equal parts salt and flour and add just enough vinegar to make a paste. Work the paste around the cooking surface and the outside of the utensil, then rinse off with warm water and dry thoroughly with a soft dish towel.

Sanitize jars, containers, and vases Do you cringe at the thought of cleaning out a mayonnaise, peanut butter, or mustard jar to reuse it? Or worse, getting the residue out of a slimy vase, decanter, or container? There is an easy way to handle these jobs. Fill the item with equal parts vinegar and warm, soapy water and let it stand for 10-15 minutes. If you're cleaning a bottle or jar, close it up and give it a few good shakes; otherwise use a bottle brush to scrape off the remains before thoroughly rinsing.

Clean a dirty thermos To get a thermos bottle clean, fill it with warm water and 1/4 cup white vinegar. If you see any residue, add some uncooked rice, which will act as an abrasive to scrape it off. Close and shake well. Then rinse and let it air-dry.

Purge bugs from your pantry Do you have moths or other insects in your cupboard or pantry? Fill a small bowl with 1 1/2 cups apple cider vinegar and add a couple of drops of liquid dish detergent. Leave it in there for a week; it will attract the bugs, which will fall into the bowl and drown. Then empty the shelves, and give the interior a thorough washing with dishwashing detergent or 2 cups baking soda in 1 quart (1 liter) water. Discard all wheat products (breads, pasta, flour, and such), and clean off canned goods before putting them back.

Trap fruit flies Did you bring home fruit flies from the market? You can make traps for them that can be used anywhere around your house by filling an old jar about halfway with apple cider. Punch a few holes in the lid, screw it back on, and you're good to go.

✳ VINEGAR **FOR THE COOK**

Tenderize and purify meats and seafood Soaking a lean or inexpensive cut of red meat in a couple of cups of vinegar breaks down tough fibers to make it more tender—and in addition, kills off any potentially harmful bacteria. You can also use vinegar to tenderize seafood steaks. Let the meat or fish soak in full-strength vinegar overnight. Experiment with different vinegar varieties for added flavor, or simply use apple cider or distilled vinegar if you intend to rinse it off before cooking.

Keep corned beef from shrinking Ever notice how the corned beef that comes out of the pot is always smaller than the one that went in? Stop your meat from shrinking by adding a couple of tablespoons of apple cider vinegar to the water when boiling your beef.

Make better boiled or poached eggs Vinegar does marvelous things for eggs. Here are the two most useful "egg-samples":

● When you are making hard-boiled eggs, adding 2 tablespoons distilled vinegar for every quart (liter) of water will keep the eggs from cracking and make them easier to shell.

● When you are poaching eggs, adding a couple of tablespoons of vinegar to the water will keep your eggs in tight shape by preventing the egg whites from spreading.

Wash store-bought produce You can't be too careful these days when it comes to handling the foods you eat. Before serving your fruits and vegetables, a great way to eliminate the hidden dirt, pesticides, and even insects, is to rinse them in 4 tablespoons apple cider vinegar dissolved in 1 gallon (3.7 liters) cold water.

DID You KNOW?

Authentic balsamic vinegar comes solely from Modena, Italy, and is made from Trebbiano grapes, a particularly sweet white variety grown in the surrounding hills. Italian law mandates that the vinegar be aged in wooden barrels made of chestnut, juniper, mulberry, or oak. There are only two grades of true balsamic vinegar—which typically sells for $100-$200 for a 100-milliliter bottle: *tradizionale vecchio*, vinegar that is at least 12 years old, and *tradizionale extra vecchio*, vinegar that's aged for at least 25 years (some balsamic vinegars are known to have been aged for more than 100 years).

Remove odors from your hands It's often difficult to get strong onion, garlic, or fish odors off your hands after preparing a meal. But you'll find these scents are a lot easier to wash off if you rub some distilled vinegar on your hands before and after you slice your vegetables or clean your fish.

Get rid of berry stains You can use undiluted white vinegar on your hands to remove stains from berries and other fruits.

Control your dandruff To give your dandruff the brush-off, follow up each shampoo with a rinse of 2 cups apple cider vinegar mixed with 2 cups cold water. You can also fight dandruff by applying 3 tablespoons vinegar onto your hair and massaging into your scalp before you shampoo. Wait a few minutes, then rinse it out and wash as usual.

Condition your hair Want to put the life back into your limp or damaged hair? You can whip up a terrific hair conditioner by combining 1 teaspoon apple cider vinegar with 2 tablespoons olive oil and 3 egg whites. Rub the mixture into your hair, then keep it covered for 30 minutes using plastic wrap or a shower cap. When time's up, shampoo and rinse as usual.

Protect blond hair from chlorine Keep your golden locks from turning green in a chlorinated pool by rubbing 1/4 cup cider vinegar into your hair and letting it set for 15 minutes before diving in.

Apply as antiperspirant Why not put the deodorizing power of vinegar to use where it matters most? That's right, you don't need a roll-on or spray to keep your underarms smelling fresh. Instead, splash a little white vinegar under each arm in the morning, and let it dry. In addition to combating perspiration odor, this method also does away with those deodorant stains on your garments.

Soak away aching muscles Got a sore back, a strained tendon in your shoulder or calf, or maybe you're just feeling generally rundown? Adding 2 cups apple cider vinegar to your bathwater is a great way to soothe away your aches and pains, or to simply to take the edge off a stressful day. Adding a few drops of peppermint oil to your bath can lend an able assist as well.

Freshen your breath After you consume a fair portion of garlic or onions, a quick and easy way to sweeten your breath is to rinse your mouth with a solution made by dissolving 2 tablespoons apple cider vinegar and 1 teaspoon salt in a glass of warm water.

Ease sunburn and itching You can cool a bad sunburn by gently dabbing the area with a cotton ball or soft cloth saturated with white or cider vinegar. (This treatment is especially effective if it's applied before the burn starts to sting.) The same technique works to instantly stop the itch of mosquito and other insect bites, as well as the rashes caused by exposure to poison ivy or poison oak.

Banish bruises If you or someone you care about has a nasty fall, you can speed healing and prevent black-and-blue marks by soaking a piece of cotton gauze in white or apple cider vinegar and leaving it on the injured area for one hour.

Soothe a sore throat Here are three ways that you can make a sore throat feel better:

● If your throat is left raw by a bad cough, or even a speaking or singing engagement, you'll find fast relief by gargling with 1 tablespoon apple cider vinegar and 1 teaspoon salt dissolved in a glass of warm water; use several times a day if needed.

- For sore throats associated with a cold or flu, combine 1/4 cup cider vinegar and 1/4 cup honey and take 1 tablespoon every four hours.

- To soothe both a cough and a sore throat, mix 1/2 cup vinegar, 1/2 cup water, 4 teaspoons honey, and 1 teaspoon hot sauce. Swallow 1 tablespoon four or five times daily, including one before bedtime. *Warning:* Children under one year old should never be given honey.

Breathe easier Adding 1/4 cup white vinegar to the water in your hot-steam vaporizer can help ease congestion caused by a chest cold or sinus infection. It can also be good for your vaporizer: The vinegar will clear away any mineral deposits in the water tubes resulting from the use of hard water. *Note:* Check with the manufacturer before adding vinegar to a cool-mist vaporizer.

Treat an active cold sore The only thing worse than a bad cold is a bad cold sore. Fortunately, you can usually dry up a cold sore in short order by dabbing it with a cotton ball saturated in white vinegar three times a day. The vinegar will quickly soothe the pain and swelling.

Make a poultice for corns and calluses Here's an old-fash-ioned, time-proven method to treat corns and calluses: Saturate a piece of white or stale bread with 1/4 cup white vinegar. Let the bread soak in the vinegar for 30 minutes, then break off a piece big enough to completely cover the corn. Keep the poultice in place with gauze or adhesive tape, and leave it on overnight. The next morning, the hard, callused skin will be dissolved, and the corn should be easy to remove. Older, thicker calluses may require several treatments.

Get the jump on athlete's foot A bad case of athlete's foot can drive you hopping mad. But you can often quell the infection, and quickly ease the itching, by rinsing your feet three or four times a day for a few days with undiluted apple cider vinegar. As an added precaution, soak your socks or stockings in a mixture of 1 part vinegar and 4 parts water for 30 minutes before laundering them.

Pamper your skin Using vinegar as a skin toner dates back to the time of Helen of Troy. And it's just as effective today. After you wash your face, mix 1 tablespoon apple cider vinegar with 2 cups water as a finishing rinse to cleanse and tighten your skin. You can also make your own facial treatment by mixing 1/4 cup cider vinegar with 1/4 cup water. Gently apply the solution to your face and let it dry.

Say good-bye to age or sun spots Before you take any drastic measures to remove or cover up those brown spots on your skin caused by overexposure to the sun or hormonal changes, give vinegar a try. Simply pour some full-strength apple cider vinegar onto a cotton ball and apply it to the spots for 10 minutes at least twice a day. The spots should fade or disappear within a few weeks.

Soften your cuticles You can soften the cuticles on your fingers and toes before manicuring them by soaking your digits in a bowl of undiluted white vinegar for five minutes.

Make nail polish last longer Your nail polish will have a longer life expectancy if you first dampen your nails with some vinegar on a cotton ball and let it dry before applying your favorite polish.

Clean your eyeglasses When it's more difficult to see with your glasses on than it is with them off, it's a clear indication that they're in need of a good cleaning. Applying a few drops of white vinegar to your glass lenses and wiping them with a soft cloth will easily remove dirt, sweat, and fingerprints, and leave them spotless. Don't use vinegar on plastic lenses, however.

Treat a jellyfish or bee sting A jellyfish can pack a nasty sting. If you have an encounter with one, pouring some undiluted vinegar on the sting will take away the pain in no time, and let you scrape out the stinger with a plastic credit card. The same treatment can also be used to treat bee stings. But using vinegar on stings inflicted by the jellyfish's cousin the Portuguese man-of-war is now discouraged because vinegar may actually increase the amount of toxin released under the skin. *Warning:* If you have difficulty breathing or the sting area becomes inflamed and swollen, get medical attention at once; you could be having an allergic reaction.

✻ VINEGAR **IN THE BATHROOM**

Wash mildew from shower curtains Clean those ugly mildew stains off your plastic shower curtain by putting it and a couple of soiled towels in your washing machine. Add 1/2 cup laundry detergent and 1/2 cup baking soda to the load,

DID *You* KNOW?

The world's only museum dedicated to vinegar, the International Vinegar Museum, is located in Roslyn, South Dakota. Housed in a building that was the former town hall, the museum is operated by Dr. Lawrence J. Diggs, an international vinegar consultant also known as the Vinegar Man (visit him online at www.vinegarman.com). The museum showcases vinegars from around the world, has displays on the various methods used to make vinegar, and even lets visitors sample different types of vinegars. It's also among the world's least expensive museums: Admission for adults is $2; for those under 18, $1; and "instant scholarships for those too poor to pay."

and wash it in warm water on your machine's regular cycle. Add 1 cup white vinegar to the first rinse. Before the machine goes into the spin cycle, remove the curtain and let it hang-dry.

Shine ceramic tiles If soap scum or water spots have dulled the ceramic tiles around your sink or bath, bring back the brightness by scrubbing them with 1/2 cup white vinegar, 1/2 cup ammonia, and 1/4 cup borax mixed in 1 gallon (3.7 liters) warm water. Rinse well with cool water and let air-dry.

Whiten your grout Has the grout between the tiles of your shower or bathtub enclosure become stained or discolored? Restore it to its original shade of white by using a toothbrush dipped in undiluted white vinegar to scrub away the dinginess.

Clean sinks and bathtubs Put the shine back in your porcelain sinks and bathtubs by giving them a good scrubbing with full-strength white vinegar, followed by a rinse of clean cold water. To remove hard-water stains from your tub, pour in 3 cups white vinegar under running hot tap water. Let the tub fill up over the stains and allow it to soak for four hours. When the water drains out, you should be able to easily scrub off the stains.

Shine up your shower doors To leave your glass shower doors sparkling clean—and to remove all of those annoying water spots—wipe them down with a cloth dipped in a solution of 1/2 cup white vinegar, 1 cup ammonia, and 1/4 cup baking soda mixed in 1 gallon (3.7 liters) warm water.

Disinfect shower door tracks Use vinegar to remove accumulated dirt and grime from the tracks of your shower doors. Fill the tracks with about 2 cups full-strength white vinegar and let it sit for three to five hours. (If the tracks are really dirty, heat the vinegar in a glass container for 30 seconds in your microwave first.) Then pour some hot water over the track to flush away the gunk. You may need to use a small scrub brush, or even a recycled toothbrush, to get up tough stains.

DID *You* KNOW?

Some researchers believe vinegar will ultimately be adopted as a simple and inexpensive way to diagnose cervical cancer in women—especially those living in impoverished nations. In tests conducted over a two-year period, midwives in Zimbabwe used a vinegar solution to detect more than 75 percent of potential cancers in 10,000 women (the solution turns tissue containing precancerous cells white). Although the test is not as accurate as a Pap smear, doctors believe it will soon be an important screening tool in developing countries, where only 5 percent of women are currently tested for this often fatal disease.

Remove mineral deposits from showerheads Wash away blockages and mineral deposits from removable showerheads by placing them in 1 quart (1 liter) boiling water with 1/2 cup distilled vinegar for 10 minutes (use hot, not boiling, liquid for plastic showerheads). When you remove it from the solution, the obstructions should be gone. If you have a nonremovable showerhead, fill a small plastic bag half full with vinegar and tape it over the fixture. Let it sit for about 1 hour, then remove the bag and wipe off any remaining vinegar from the showerhead.

Wipe down bathroom fixtures Don't stop at the shower when you're cleaning with vinegar! Pour a bit of undiluted white vinegar onto a soft cloth and use it to wipe your chrome faucets, towel racks, bathroom mirrors, doorknobs, and such. It'll leave them gleaming.

> **TAKE CARE** Combining vinegar with bleach—or any other product containing chlorine, such as chlorinated lime (sold as bleaching powder)—may produce chlorine gas. In low concentrations, this toxic, acrid-smelling gas can cause damage to your eyes, skin, or respiratory system. High concentrations are often fatal.

Fight mold and mildew To remove and inhibit bathroom mold and mildew, pour a solution of 3 tablespoons white vinegar, 1 teaspoon borax, and 2 cups hot water into a clean, recycled spray bottle and give it a few good shakes. Then spray the mixture on painted surfaces, tiles, windows, or wherever you see mold or mildew spots. Use a soft scrub brush to work the solution into the stains or just let it soak in.

Disinfect toilet bowls Want an easy way to keep your toilet looking and smelling clean? Pour 2 cups white vinegar into the bowl and let the solution soak overnight before flushing. Including this vinegar soak in your weekly cleaning regimen will also help keep away those ugly water rings that typically appear just above the water level.

Clean your toothbrush holder Get the grime, bacteria, and caked-on toothpaste drippings out of the grooves of your bathroom toothbrush holder by cleaning the openings with cotton swabs moistened with white vinegar.

Wash out your rinse cup If several people in your home use the same rinse cup after brushing their teeth, give it a weekly cleaning by filling it with equal parts water and white vinegar, or just full-strength vinegar, and let it sit overnight. Rinse thoroughly with cold water before using.

✳ VINEGAR **IN THE LAUNDRY**

Soften fabrics, kill bacteria, eliminate static, and more There are so many benefits to be reaped by adding 1 cup white vinegar to your washer's rinse cycle that it's surprising that you don't find it prominently mentioned inside the owner's manual of every washing machine sold. Here are the main ones:

- A single cup of vinegar will kill off any bacteria that may be present in your wash load, especially if it includes cloth diapers and the like.

- A cup of vinegar will keep your clothes coming out of the wash soft and smelling fresh—so you can kiss your fabric-softening liquids and sheets good-bye (unless, of course, you happen to like your clothes smelling of heavy perfumes).

- A cup of vinegar will brighten small loads of white clothes.

- Added to the last rinse, a cup of vinegar will keep your clothes lint- and static-free.

- Adding a cupful of vinegar to the last rinse will set the color of your newly dyed fabrics.

Clean your washing machine An easy way to periodically clean out soap scum and disinfect your clothes washer is to pour in 2 cups vinegar, then run the machine through a full cycle without any clothes or detergent. If your washer is particularly dirty, fill it with very hot water, add 2 gallons (7.5 liters) vinegar, and let the agitator run for 8-10 minutes. Turn off the washer and let the solution stand overnight. In the morning, empty the basin and run your washer through a complete cycle.

Stop reds from running Unless you have a fondness for pink-tinted clothing, take one simple precaution to prevent red—or other brightly dyed—washable clothes from ruining your wash loads. Soak your new garments in a few cups of undiluted white vinegar for 10-15 minutes before their first washing. You'll never have to worry about running colors again!

Brighten your loads Why waste money on that costly all-color bleach when you can get the same results using vinegar? Just add 1/2 cup white vinegar to your machine's wash cycle to brighten up the colors in each load.

Make new clothes ready to wear Get the chemicals, dust, odor, and whatever else out of your brand-new or secondhand clothes by pouring 1 cup white vinegar into the wash cycle the first time you wash them.

Whiten your dingy crew socks If it's getting increasingly difficult to identify the white socks in your sock drawer, here's a simple way to make them so bright you can't miss them. Start by adding 1 cup vinegar to 1 1/2 quarts (1.5 liters) tap water in a large pot. Bring the solution to a boil, then pour it into a bucket and drop in your dingy socks. Let them soak overnight. The next day, wash them as you normally would.

Get the yellow out of clothing To restore yellowed clothing, let the garments soak overnight in a solution of 12 parts warm water to 1 part vinegar. Wash them the following morning.

Soften up your blankets Add 2 cups white vinegar to your washer's rinse water (or a washtub filled with water) to remove soap residue from both cotton and wool blankets before drying. This will also leave them feeling fresh and soft as new.

Spray away wrinkles In a perfect world, laundry would emerge from the dryer freshly pressed. Until that day, you can often get the wrinkles out of clothes after drying by misting them with a solution of 1 part vinegar to 3 parts water. Once you're sure you didn't miss a spot, hang it up and let it air-dry. You may find this approach works better for some clothes than ironing; it's certainly a lot gentler on the material.

Flush your iron's interior To eliminate mineral deposits and prevent corrosion on your steam iron, give it an occasional cleaning by filling the reservoir with undiluted white vinegar. Place the iron in an upright position, switch on the steam setting, and let the vinegar steam through it for 5-10 minutes. Then refill the chamber with clean water and repeat. Finally, give the water chamber a good rinsing with cold, clean water.

Clean your iron's soleplate To remove scorch marks from the soleplate of your iron, scrub it with a paste made by heating up equal parts vinegar and salt in a small pan. Use a rag dipped in clean water to wipe away the remaining residue.

Sharpen your creases You'll find the creases in your freshly ironed clothes coming out a lot neater if you lightly spray them with equal parts water and vinegar before ironing them. For truly sharp creases in slacks and dress shirts, first dampen the garment using a cloth moistened in a solution of 1 part white vinegar and 2 parts water. Then place a brown paper bag over the crease and start ironing.

> **TAKE CARE** Keep cider vinegar out of the laundry. Using it to pretreat clothes or adding it to wash or rinse water may actually create stains rather than remove them. Use only distilled white vinegar for laundering.

Make old hemlines disappear Want to make those needle marks from an old hemline disappear for good? Just moisten the area with a cloth dipped in equal parts vinegar and water, then place it under the garment before you start ironing.

Erase scorch marks Did your iron get too hot under the collar—or perhaps on a sleeve or pant leg? You can often eliminate slight scorch marks by rubbing the spot with a cloth dampened with white vinegar, then blotting it with a clean towel. Repeat if necessary.

Dull the shine in your seat Want to get rid of that shiny seat on your dark pants or skirt? Just brush the area lightly with a soft recycled toothbrush dipped in equal parts white vinegar and water, then pat dry with a soft towel.

Remove cigarette smell from suits If you find yourself in a situation where you wind up heading home with the lingering smell of cigarette smoke on your good suit or dress, you can remove the odor without having to take your clothes to the dry cleaner. Just add 1 cup vinegar to a bathtub filled with the hottest water your tap can muster. Close the door and hang your garments above the steam. The smell should be gone after several hours.

Reshape your woolens Shrunken woolen sweaters and other items can usually be stretched back to their former size or shape after boiling them in a solution of 1 part vinegar to 2 parts water for 25 minutes. Let the garment air-dry after you've finished stretching it.

✳ VINEGAR **FOR REMOVING STAINS**

Brush off suede stains To eliminate a fresh grease spot on a suede jacket or skirt, gently brush it with a soft toothbrush dipped in white vinegar. Let the spot air-dry, then brush with a suede brush. Repeat if necessary. You can also generally tone up suede items by lightly wiping them with a sponge dipped in vinegar.

Pat away water-soluble stains You can lift out many water-soluble stains—including beer, orange and other fruit juices, black coffee or tea, and vomit—from your cotton-blend clothing by patting the spot with a cloth or towel moistened with undiluted white vinegar just before placing it in the wash. For large stains, you may want to soak the garment overnight in a solution of 3 parts vinegar to 1 part cold water before washing.

Unset old stains Older, set-in stains will often come out in the wash after being pretreated with a solution of 3 tablespoons white vinegar and 2 tablespoons liquid detergent in 1 quart (1 liter) warm water. Rub the solution into the stain, then blot it dry before washing.

Sponge out serious stains Cola, hair dye, ketchup, and wine stains on washable cotton blends should be treated as soon as possible (that is, within 24 hours). Sponge the area with undiluted vinegar and launder immediately afterward. For severe stains, add 1-2 cups vinegar to the wash cycle as well.

Get the rust out To remove a rust stain from your cotton work clothes, moisten the spot with some full-strength vinegar and then rub in a bit of salt. If it's warm outdoors, let it dry in the sunlight (otherwise a sunny window will do), then toss it in the wash.

Clear away crayon stains Somehow or other, kids often manage to get crayon marks on their clothing. You can easily get these stains off by rubbing them with a recycled toothbrush soaked in undiluted vinegar before washing them.

Remove rings from collars and cuffs Are you tired of seeing those old sweat rings around your shirt collars? What about the annoying discoloration along the edges of your cuffs? Give them the boot by scrubbing the material with a paste made from 2 parts white vinegar to 3 parts baking soda. Let the paste set for half an hour before washing. This approach also works to remove light mildew stains from clothing.

Pretreat perspiration stains Want to see those sweat marks disappear from shirts and other garments? Just pour a bit of vinegar directly onto the stain, and rub it into the fabric before placing the item in the wash. You can also remove deodorant stains from your washable shirts and blouses by gently rubbing the spot with undiluted vinegar before laundering.

Make pen ink disappear Did someone in your house come home with a leaky pen in his pocket? Treat the stain by first wetting it with some white vinegar, then rub in a paste of 2 parts vinegar to 3 parts cornstarch. Let the paste thoroughly dry before washing the item.

> *Kids' Stuff* Making **tie-dyed clothing** is tons of fun for kids of all ages. Start with a few **white T-shirts**, then use as many colors as allowed by your local supermarket's selection of unsweetened Kool-Aid powder mixes. Dissolve each package of **Kool-Aid** into 1 ounce **vinegar** in its own bowl or container. Use **rubber bands** to twist your shirts into unusual shapes, then dip them into the bowls (snap on a pair of rubber gloves beforehand). After drying, set your colors by placing a pillowcase or thin dish towel over each shirt and ironing it with a **medium-hot iron**. Wait at least 24 hours, then wash each shirt separately.

Soak out bloodstains Whether you nick yourself while shaving, or receive an unexpected scratch, it's important to treat the stains on your clothing as soon as possible; bloodstains are relatively easy to remove before they set but can be nearly impossible to wash out after 24 hours. If you can get to the stain before it sets, treat it by pouring full-strength white vinegar on the spot. Let it soak in for 5-10 minutes, then blot well with a cloth or towel. Repeat if necessary, then wash immediately.

✳ VINEGAR **IN THE GREAT OUTDOORS**

Use as insect repellent Planning a camping trip? Here's an old army trick to keep away the ticks and mosquitoes: Approximately three days before you leave, start taking 1 tablespoon apple cider vinegar three times a day. Continue using the vinegar throughout your trek, and you just might return home without a bite. Another time-honored approach to keep gnats and mosquitoes at bay is to moisten a cloth or cotton ball with white vinegar and rub it over your exposed skin.

Maintain fresh water when hiking Keep your water supply fresh and clean tasting when hiking or camping by adding a few drops of apple cider vinegar to your canteen or water bottle. It's also a good idea to use a half-vinegar, half-water rinse to clean out your water container at the end of each trip to kill bacteria and remove residue.

Clean outdoor furniture and decks If you live in a hot, humid climate, you're probably no stranger to seeing mildew on your wooden decks and patio furniture. But before you reach for the bleach, try these milder vinegar-based solutions:

- Keep some full-strength white vinegar in a recycled spray bottle and use it wherever you see any mildew growth. The stain will wipe right off most surfaces, and the vinegar will keep it from coming back for a while.

- Remove mildew from wood decks and wood patio furniture by sponging them off with a solution of 1 cup ammonia, 1/2 cup white vinegar, and 1/4 cup baking soda mixed in 1 gallon (3.7 liters) water. Keep an old toothbrush on hand to work the solution into corners and other tight spaces.

- To deodorize and inhibit mildew growth on outdoor plastic mesh furniture and patio umbrellas, mix 2 cups white vinegar and 2 tablespoons liquid dish soap in a bucket of hot water. Use a soft brush to work it into the grooves of the plastic as well as for scrubbing seat pads and umbrella fabric. Rinse with cold water; then dry in the sun.

Make a trap to lure flying insects Who wants to play host to a bunch of gnats, flies mosquitoes, or other six-legged pests when you're trying to have a cookout in your yard? Keep the flying gate-crashers at bay by giving them their own VIP section. Place a bowl filled with apple cider vinegar near some food, but away from you and guests. By the evening's end, most of your uninvited guests will be floating inside the bowl.

Give ants the boot Serve the ants on your premises with an eviction notice. Pour equal parts water and white vinegar into a spray bottle. Then spray it on anthills and around areas where you see the insects. Ants hate the smell of vinegar. It won't take long for them to move on to better-smelling quarters. Also keep the spray bottle handy for outdoor trips or to keep ants away from picnic or children's play areas. If you have lots of anthills around your property, try pouring full-strength vinegar over them to hasten the bugs' departure.

Clean off bird droppings Have the birds been using your patio or driveway for target practice again? Make those messy droppings disappear in no time by spraying them with full-strength apple cider vinegar. Or pour the vinegar onto a rag and wipe them off.

✴ VINEGAR **IN THE GARDEN**

Test soil acidity or alkalinity To do a quick test for excess alkalinity in the soil in your yard, place a handful of earth in a container and then pour in 1/2 cup white vinegar. If the soil fizzes or bubbles, it's definitely alkaline. Similarly, to see if your soil has a high acidity, mix the earth with 1/2 cup water and 1/2 cup baking soda. This time, fizzing would indicate acid in the soil. To find the exact pH level of your soil, have it tested or pick up a simple, do-it-yourself kit or meter.

Clean a hummingbird feeder Hummingbirds are innately discriminating creatures, so don't expect to see them flocking around a dirty, sticky, or crusted-over sugar-water feeder. Regularly clean your feeders by thoroughly washing them in equal parts apple cider vinegar and hot water. Rinse well with cold water after washing, and air-dry them outdoors in full sunlight before refilling them with food.

Speed germination of flower seeds You can get woody seeds, such as moonflower, passionflower, morning glory, and gourds, off to a healthier start by scarifying them—that is, lightly rubbing them between a couple of sheets of fine sandpaper—and soaking them overnight in a solution of 1/2 cup apple cider vinegar and 1 pint (half liter) warm water. Next morning, remove the seeds from the solution, rinse them off, and plant them. You can also use the solution (minus the sandpaper treatment) to start many herb and vegetable seeds.

Keep cut flowers fresh Everyone likes to keep cut flowers around as long as possible, and there are several good methods. One way is to mix 2 tablespoons apple cider vinegar and 2 tablespoons sugar with the vase water before adding the flowers. Be sure to change the water (with more vinegar and sugar, of course) every few days to enhance your flowers' longevity.

Tip **A Myth About Vinegar**

> It's a rural legend that you can substantially lower your soil's pH (which is the same as raising its acidity), by simply pouring a vinegar-water solution around your yard. In fact, it takes a lot of hard work to lower the pH of high-alkaline soil. You can, however, use vinegar around the garden to help existing plants (see the tips below for treating plant diseases and encouraging blooms on azaleas and gardenias). But even that takes diligence—and repeated applications. Also, vinegar loses most of its potency after a rainfall. So you'll need to reapply any treatments after those surprise downpours.

Wipe away mealybugs They're among the most insidious and common pests on both houseplants and in the garden. But you can nip a mealybug invasion in the bud by dabbing the insects with a cotton swab dipped in full-strength white vinegar. You may need to use a handful of swabs, but the vinegar will kill the fluffy monsters and any eggs left behind. Be vigilant for missed targets, and break out more vinegar-soaked swabs if you spot bugs.

Eliminate insects around the garden If the bugs are feasting on the fruits and vegetables in your garden, give them the boot with this simple, nonpoisonous trap. Fill a 2-liter soda bottle with 1 cup apple cider vinegar and 1 cup sugar. Next, slice up a banana peel into small pieces, put them in the bottle, add 1 cup cold water, and shake it up. Tie a piece of string around the neck of the bottle and hang it from a low tree branch, or place it on the ground, to trap and kill the six-legged freeloaders. Replace used traps with new ones as needed.

Encourage blooms on azaleas and gardenias A little bit of acid goes a long way toward bringing out the blooms on your azalea and gardenia bushes—especially if you have hard water. Both bushes do best in acidic soils (with pH levels between 4 and 5.5). To keep them healthy and to produce more flowers, water them every week or so with 3 tablespoons white vinegar mixed in 1 gallon (3.7 liters) water. Don't apply the solution while the bush is in bloom, however; it may shorten the life of the flowers or harm the plant.

Stop yellow leaves on plants The sudden appearance of yellow leaves on plants accustomed to acidic soils—such as azaleas, hydrangeas, and gardenias—could signal a drop in the plant's iron intake or a shift in the ground's pH above a comfortable 5.0 level. Either problem can be resolved by watering the soil around the afflicted plants once a week for three weeks with 1 cup of a solution made by mixing 2 tablespoons apple cider vinegar in 1 quart (1 liter) water.

Treat rust and other plant diseases You can use vinegar to treat a host of plant diseases, including rust, black spot, and powdery mildew. Mix 2 tablespoons apple cider vinegar in 2 quarts (2 liters) water, and pour some into a recycled spray bottle. Spray the solution on your affected plants in the morning or early

DID *You* KNOW?

Looking for a nontoxic alternative to commercial weed killers? Vinegar is the way to go. In field and greenhouse studies, researchers at the Agricultural Research Service in Beltsville, Maryland, proved vinegar effective at killing five common weeds—including the all-too-common Canada thistle—within their first two weeks aboveground. The vinegar was hand-sprayed in concentrations varying between 5 and 10 percent. But that's old news to seasoned gardeners who've been using undiluted apple cider vinegar for ages to kill everything from poison ivy to crabgrass (and, regrettably, the occasional ornamental plant that grew too close to the target).

evening (when temperatures are relatively cool and there's no direct light on the plant) until the condition is cured.

Clean your lawn mower blades Grass, especially when it's damp, has a tendency to accumulate on your lawn mower blades after you cut the lawn—sometimes with grubs or other insects hiding inside. Before you park your mower back in the garage or toolshed, wipe down the blades with a cloth dampened with undiluted white vinegar. It will clean off leftover grass on the blades, as well as any pests that may have been planning to hang out awhile.

Keep out four-legged creatures Some animals—including cats, deer, dogs, rabbits, and raccoons—can't stand the scent of vinegar even after it has dried. You can keep these unauthorized visitors out of your garden by soaking several recycled rags in white vinegar, and placing them on stakes around your veggies. Resoak the rags about every 7-10 days.

SCIENCE FAIR

Mix 1/2 cup **vinegar** and 1/4 teaspoon **salt** in a **glass jar**. Add 25 **copper pennies** to the solution, and let them sit for five minutes. While you're waiting, take a large **iron nail** and clean it off with some baking soda applied to a damp sponge. Rinse off the nail, and place it into the solution. After 15 minutes, the **nail will be coated with copper**, while the pennies will shine like new. This is a result of the acetic acid in the vinegar combining with the copper on the pennies to form copper acetate, which then accumulates on the nail.

Exterminate dandelions and unwanted grass Are dandelions sprouting up in the cracks of your driveway or along the fringes of your patio? Make them disappear for good by spraying them with full-strength white or apple cider vinegar. Early in the season, give each plant a single spritz of vinegar in its midsection, or in the middle of the flower before the plants go to seed. Aim another shot near the stem at ground level so the vinegar can soak down to the roots. Keep an eye on the weather, though; if it rains the next day, you'll need to give the weeds another spraying.

✳ VINEGAR **PET CARE**

Keep the kitties away If you want to keep Snowball and Fluffy out of the kids' playroom, or discourage them from using your favorite easy chair as a scratching post, sprinkle some full-strength distilled white vinegar around the area or onto the object itself. Cats don't like the smell of vinegar and will avoid it.

Unmark your pet's spots When housebreaking a puppy or kitten, it'll often wet previously soiled spots. After cleaning up the mess, it's essential to remove the scent from your floor, carpeting, or sofa. And nothing does that better than vinegar:

- On a floor, blot up as much of the stain as possible. Then mop with equal parts white vinegar and warm water. (On a wood or vinyl floor, test a few drops of vinegar in an inconspicuous area to make sure it won't harm the finish.) Dry with a cloth or paper towel.

- For carpets, rugs, and upholstery, thoroughly blot the area with a towel or some rags. Then pour a bit of undiluted vinegar over the spot. Blot it up with a towel, then reapply the vinegar—let it air-dry. Once the vinegar dries, the spot should be completely deodorized

Add to pet's drinking water Adding a teaspoon of apple cider vinegar to your dog or cat's drinking water provides needed nutrients to its diet, gives it a shinier, healthier-looking coat, and acts as a natural deterrent to fleas and ticks.

Directly protect against fleas and ticks To give your dog effective flea and tick protection, fill a spray bottle with equal parts water and vinegar and apply it directly to the dog's coat and rub it in well. You may have more trouble doing this with cats, because they really hate the smell of the stuff.

Clean your pet's ears If you've noticed that Rover has been scratching around his ears a lot more than usual lately, a bit of vinegar could bring him some big relief. Swabbing your pet's ears with a cotton ball or soft cloth dabbed in solution of 2 parts vinegar and 1 part water will keep them clean and help deter ear mites and bacteria. It also soothes minor itches from mosquito bites and such. *Warning*: Do not apply vinegar to open lacerations. If you see a cut in your pet's ears, seek veterinary treatment.

Remove skunk odor If Fido has an unpleasant encounter with an ornery skunk, here are some ways to help him get rid of the smell:

- Bathe your pet in a mixture of 1/2 cup white vinegar, 1/4 cup baking soda, and 1 teaspoon liquid soap in 1 quart (1 liter) 3% hydrogen peroxide. Work the solution deep into his coat, give it a few minutes to soak in, then rinse him thoroughly with clean water.

- Bathe your pet in equal parts water and vinegar (preferably outdoors in a large washtub). Then repeat the procedure using 1 part vinegar to 2 parts water, followed by a good rinsing.

- If you happen to have an unscheduled meeting with skunk, use undiluted vinegar to get the smell out your own clothes. Let the affected clothing soak in the vinegar overnight.

✳ VINEGAR **FOR THE DO-IT-YOURSELFER**

Wash concrete off your skin Even though you wear rubber gloves when working with concrete, some of the stuff inevitably splashes on your skin. Prolonged contact with wet concrete can cause your skin to crack, and may even lead to eczema. Use undiluted white vinegar to wash dried concrete or mortar off your skin, then wash with warm, soapy water.

Remove paint fumes Place a couple of shallow dishes filled with undiluted white vinegar around a freshly painted room to quickly get rid of the strong paint smell.

Degrease grates, fans, and air-conditioner grilles Even in the cleanest of homes, air-conditioner grilles, heating grates, and fan blades eventually develop a layer of dust and grease. To clean them, wipe them with full-strength white vinegar. Use an old toothbrush to work the vinegar into the tight spaces on air-conditioner grilles and exhaust fans.

Disinfect air-conditioner and humidifier filters An air-conditioner or humidifier filter can quickly become inundated with dust, soot, pet dander, and even potentially harmful bacteria. Every 10 days or so, clean your filter in equal parts white vinegar and warm water. Let the filter soak in the solution for an hour, then simply squeeze it dry before using. If your filters are particularly dirty, let them soak overnight.

Keep the paint on your cement floors Painted cement floors have a tendency to peel after a while. But you can keep the paint stuck to the cement longer by giving the floor an initial coat of white vinegar before you paint it. Wait until the

DID **You** KNOW?

You just came across an old, unopened bottle of vinegar, and you wonder: Is it still any good? The answer is an unqualified yes. In fact, vinegar has a practically limitless shelf life. Its acid content makes it self-preserving and even negates the need for refrigeration (although many people mistakenly believe in refrigerating their open bottles). You won't see any changes in white vinegar over time, but some other types may change slightly in color or develop a hazy appearance or a bit of sediment. However, these are strictly cosmetic changes; the vinegar itself will be virtually unchanged.

VINEGAR*

369

vinegar has dried, then begin painting. This same technique will also help keep paint affixed to galvanized metal._

Get rid of rust If you want to clean up those rusted old tools you recently unearthed in your basement or picked up at a tag sale, soak them in full-strength white vinegar for several days. The same treatment is equally effective at removing the rust from corroded nuts and bolts. And you can pour vinegar on rusted hinges and screws to loosen them up for removal.

Peel off wallpaper Removing old wallpaper can be messy, but you can make it peel off easily by soaking it with a vinegar solution. Spray equal parts white vinegar and water on the wallpaper until it is saturated and wait a few minutes. Then zip the stuff off the wall with a wallpaper scraper. If it is stubborn, try carefully scoring the wallpaper with the scraper before you spritz.

Slow hardening of plaster Want to keep your plaster pliable a bit longer to get it all smoothed out? Just add a couple of tablespoons of white vinegar to your plaster mix. It will slow down the hardening process to give you the extra time you need.

Revive your paintbrushes To remove dried-on paint from a synthetic-bristle paintbrush, soak it in full-strength white vinegar until the paint dissolves and the bristles are soft and pliable, then wash in hot, soapy water. Does a paintbrush seem beyond hope? Before you toss it, try boiling it in 1-2 cups vinegar for 10 minutes, followed by a thorough washing in soapy water.

✳ Vodka

Make your own vanilla extract Here's an unusual homemade treat you can use to spice up a gift basket, and it takes only minutes to make. Get one real dried vanilla bean (available at specialty food stores) and slice it open from top to bottom. Place it in a glass jar and cover it with 3/4 cup vodka. Seal the jar, and let it rest

DID *You* KNOW?

Essential to James Bond's martini—and so intrinsic to Russian culture that its name derives from the Russian word for water *(voda)*—vodka was first made in the 1400s as an antiseptic and painkiller before it was drunk as a bev- erage. But what exactly is it? Classically, vodka starts as a soupy mixture of ground wheat or rye that's fermented (sugars in the grain are con- verted into alcohol by yeast), then distilled (heated until the alcohol evaporates and then condenses). Flavorings such as citrus were originally added to mask the taste of impurities, but are used today for enhancement and brand identification.

in a kitchen cabinet for 4-6 months, shaking it occasionally. Filter your home-made vanilla extract through an unbleached coffee filter or cheesecloth into a decorative bottle and watch the face of your favorite cook light up with pleasure!

Clean glass and jewelry In a pinch, a few drops of vodka will clean any kind of glass or jewelry with crystalline gemstones. So although people might look at you askance, you could dip a napkin into your vodka on the rocks to wipe away the grime on your eyeglasses or dunk your diamond ring for a few minutes to get it sparkling again. But don't try this with contact lenses! Also avoid getting alcohol on any gemstone that's not a crystal. Only diamonds, emeralds, and the like will benefit from a vodka bath.

Use as a hygienic soak Vodka is an alcohol, and like any alcohol, it kills germs. If you don't have ordinary rubbing alcohol on hand, use vodka instead. You can use it to soak razor blades you plan to reuse, as well as to clean hairbrushes, tooth-brushes, and pet brushes, or on anything else that might spread germs from person to person or animal to animal.

Keep cut flowers fresh The secret to keeping cut flowers looking good as long as pos-sible is to minimize the growth of bacteria in the water and to provide nourishment to replace what the flower would have gotten had it not been cut. Add a few drops of vodka (or any clear spirit) to the vase water for antibacterial action along with 1 teaspoon sugar. Change the water every other day, refreshing the vodka and sugar each time.

Kill weeds in the yard For a quick and easy weed killer, mix 1 ounce (30 milliliters) vodka, a few drops liquid dish soap, and 2 cups water in a spray bottle. Spray it on the weed leaves until the mixture runs off. Apply it at midday on a sunny day to weeds growing in direct sunlight, because the alcohol breaks down the waxy cuticle covering on leaves, leaving them susceptible to dehydration in sunlight. It won't work in shade.

W

✴ Wallpaper

Line your drawers Wallpaper remnants can be a great substitute for shelf liner paper when used to line dresser drawers or closet shelves—especially designs with raised patterns or fabrics, which may add a bit of friction to prevent things from moving around. Cut the wallpaper into strips sized in both length and width to accommodate the space.

Restore a folding screen If you have an old folding screen that's become torn or stained over the years, give it a new, younger look by covering it with leftover wallpaper. Use masking tape to hold the strips at top and bottom if you don't want to glue it on top of the original material.

Protect schoolbooks If your child goes through book covers on textbooks on a semi-regular basis, get your hands on some old rolls of wallpaper. Book covers made of wallpaper are typically more rugged than even the traditional brown paper bag sleeves; they can hold their own against pens and pencils, and are much better at handling the elements, especially rain and snow.

Make a jigsaw puzzle What to do with your leftover wallpaper? Why not use a piece to make a jigsaw puzzle? Simply cut off a medium-sized rectangular piece and glue it onto a piece of thin cardboard. Once it's dried, cut it up into a bunch of curvy and angular shapes. It'll give you, or the kids, something to do on a rainy or snowbound day.

✴ Wax Paper

Fail-safe cake decorating You made a special birthday cake, and now comes the moment of truth: Can you pipe out the lettering in frosting on the first try? Not many of us can, so try this trick to make it easier. Cut a piece of wax paper the same size as your cake, using the cake pan as a guide. Then pipe the name and the message onto the paper and freeze it. After just half an hour it should be easy to handle. Loosen the frosting and slide it off onto the cake using a spatula. Everyone will think you're a cake-decorating professional!

Funnel spices into jars Filling narrow-mouthed spice jars can make a big mess on your kitchen counter. Roll a piece of wax paper into a funnel shape and pour spices into your jars without spilling a single mustard seed. In a pinch, you can even funnel liquids by using a couple of layers of wax paper offset so the seams in the layers don't line up.

Speed kitchen cleanup Wax paper can help keep all kinds of kitchen surfaces clean.

- Line vegetable and meat bins with a layer of wax paper. When it needs replacement, just wad it up and throw it in the trash or, if it's not stained with meat juices, the compost pile.

- If your kitchen cabinets don't extend to the ceiling, a layer of wax paper on top will catch dust and grease particles. Every month or two, just fold it up, discard it, and put a fresh layer down.

- If you're worried about meat juices getting into the pores of your cutting board, cover it with three layers of wax paper before slicing raw meat and throw the paper out immediately. It beats scrubbing the cutting board with bleach!

Tame the waffle-eating waffle iron Having trouble extricating waffles from your waffle iron? Nonstick surfaces don't last forever. You can't fix the problem permanently, but if you just want to get it to work today, put a layer of wax paper in between the plates of your waffle iron for a few minutes while it heats up. The wax will be transferred to the plates, temporarily helping waffles pop out again.

Uncork bottles with ease If you keep a bottle of cooking wine in your kitchen, you probably uncork it and recork it many times before using it up. Instead of struggling with the cork each time, wrap some wax paper around the cork before reinserting it. It'll be easier to remove the next time, and the paper helps keep little bits of cork from getting into the wine.

 DID *You* KNOW?

Wax paper is an example of how important packaging can be to a product's success. Before 1927, wax paper was sold in pre-cut sheets in envelopes, but housewives and deli owners alike were frustrated by the tendency of the sheets to stick together on warm summer days. Then an enterprising inventor, Nicholas Marcalus, put wax paper on a roll in a box with a built-in cutter, and the product as we know it today came to be. In fact, Reynolds wax paper is called Cut-Rite after this packaging innovation, which was awarded a patent and is used for a multitude of products today.

WAXPAPER

373

Keep cast iron rust-free Cast iron devotees agree that this superior cooking material is well worth a little extra effort to keep it in tip-top shape. To prevent rust from forming on cast iron between uses, rub a sheet of wax paper over your skillet or Dutch oven after washing, while it's still warm. Then place the sheet between the pot and the lid to store.

Keep candles from staining table linens Candles in colors that coordinate with your dining room linens make a lovely finishing touch to table settings—and it's helpful to store them all together—but if you store the candles with table linens, the candle color can rub off on the linens. To avoid this, wrap colorful candles in plain wax paper before storage. Avoid paper with holiday patterns, which can also stain linens.

Store delicate fabrics Treasured lace doilies and other linens handed down in your family can decay quickly if not stored with care. A sheet of wax paper between each fabric piece will help block extraneous light and prevent transfer of dyes without trapping moisture.

Stop water spotting Company's coming, and you want every room of the house to look its best. To keep bathroom fixtures temporarily spotless, rub them with a sheet of wax paper after cleaning them. The wax that transfers will deflect water droplets like magic—at least until the next cleaning.

Give your car antenna a smooth ride If you have a newer vehicle, your car antenna probably retracts each time you turn off the ignition, carrying grime with it that can eventually bring your antenna (and your reception) to a grinding halt. Every now and then, rub the antenna with a piece of wax paper to coat the shaft and help it repel dirt.

Make a snow slide go faster Everyone knows, the more slippery the slide, the more fun it is! Keep tots swooshing on their tushes by balling up a large piece of wax paper and rubbing it all over the slide surface.

Kids' Stuff What kid wouldn't like **homemade "stained glass"** art that takes only minutes to make? First, make **crayon shavings** using a **vegetable peeler**. Keep each color separate. Put a paper towel or bag on your counter. Place a sheet of **wax paper** on top, sprinkle it with crayon shavings, and cover with another layer of wax paper and paper towel. Press it for a few minutes using a **warm iron** and remove the paper towel layers. Cut your new see-through art into **sun-catching medallions** or **colorful bookmarks** using craft scissors to create a decorative edge.

Protect surfaces from glue Woodworkers know that there's enough glue in a wood joint if some squeezes out when they clamp the joint. They also know that excess glue will be a real pain to remove if it drips on the workbench or, worse, bonds the clamping blocks to the project. To prevent this, cover the bench with strips of wax paper and put pieces of wax paper between the clamping blocks and the project. The glue won't adhere to, or soak through, the wax.

Make educational place mats One way to make learning fun is with personalized place mats featuring math facts or other lessons your child is trying to memorize. Take several flash cards and sandwich them between layers of wax paper cut to place-mat size. Sandwich that between two layers of paper towels and press it all with a warm iron to "laminate" the flash cards in place. Remove the paper towels before use.

super item *62 uses!* WD-40

Treat your shoes Spray WD-40 on new leather shoes before you start wearing them regularly. It will help prevent blisters by softening the leather and making the shoes more comfortable. Keep the shoes waterproof and shiny by spraying them periodically with WD-40 and buffing gently with a soft cloth. To give the old "soft shoo" to squeaky shoes, spray some WD-40 at the spot where the sole and heel join and the squeaks will cease.

Separate stuck glassware What can you do when you reach for a drinking glass and get two locked together, one stuck tightly inside the other? You don't want to risk breaking one or both by trying to pull them apart. Stuck glasses will separate with ease if you squirt some WD-40 on them, wait a few seconds for it to work its way between the glasses, and then gently pull the glasses apart. Remember to wash the glasses thoroughly before you use them.

Free stuck Lego blocks When Junior's construction project hits a snag because some of the plastic blocks are stuck together, let WD-40 help get them unstuck. Spray a little on the blocks where they are locked together, then wiggle them gently and pull them apart. The lubricant in WD-40 will penetrate into the fine seam where the blocks are joined.

Tone down polyurethane shine A new coat of polyurethane can sometimes make a wood floor look a little *too* shiny. To tone down the shine and cut the glare, spray some WD-40 onto a soft cloth and wipe up the floor with it.

Remove strong glue You didn't wear protective gloves when using that super-strong glue and now some of it is super-stuck to your fingers! Don't panic. Just reach for the WD-40, spray some directly on the sticky fingers, and rub your hands together until your fingers are no longer sticky. Use WD-40 to remove the glue from other unwanted surfaces as well.

TAKE CARE

● Do not spray WD-40 near an open flame or other heat source, or near electrical currents or battery terminals. Always disconnect appliances before spraying.

● Do not place a WD-40 can in direct sunlight or on hot surfaces. Never store it in temperatures above 120°F (50°C) or puncture the pressurized can.

● Use WD-40 in well-ventilated areas. Never swallow or inhale it (if swallowed, call a physician immediately).

Get off that stuck ring When pulling and tugging can't get that ring off your finger, reach for the WD-40. A short burst of WD-40 will get the ring to slide right off. Remember to wash your hands after spraying them with WD-40.

Free stuck fingers Use WD-40 to free Junior's finger when he gets it stuck in a bottle. Just spray it on the finger, let it seep in, and pull the finger out. Be sure to wash Junior's hand and the bottle afterward.

Loosen zippers Stubborn zippers on jackets, pants, backpacks, and sleeping bags will become compliant again after you spray them with WD-40. Just spray it on and pull the zipper up and down a few times to distribute the lubricant evenly over all the teeth. If you want to avoid getting the WD-40 on the fabric, spray it on a plastic lid; then pick it up and apply it with an artist's brush.

Exterminate roaches and repel insects Don't let cockroaches, insects, or spiders get the upper hand in your home.

● Keep a can of WD-40 handy, and when you see a roach, spray a small amount directly on it for an instant kill.

● To keep insects and spiders out of your home, spray WD-40 on windowsills and frames, screens, and door frames. Be careful not to inhale the fumes when you spray and do not do this at all if you have babies or small children at home.

Keep puppies from chewing Your new puppy is adorable, but will he *ever* stop chewing up the house? To keep puppies from chewing on telephone and television-cable lines, spray WD-40 on the lines. The pups hate the smell.

Clean and lubricate guitar strings To clean, lubricate, and prevent corrosion on guitar strings, apply a small amount of WD-40 after each playing. Spray the

WD-40 on a rag and wipe the rag over the strings rather than spraying directly on the strings—you don't want WD-40 to build up on the guitar neck or body.

Keep wooden tool handles splinter-free No tools can last forever, but you can prolong the life of your wood-handled tools by preventing splintering. To keep wooden handles from splintering, rub a generous amount of WD-40 into the wood. It will shield the wood from moisture and other corrosive elements and keep it smooth and splinter-free for the life of the tool.

Unstick wobbly shopping-cart wheels Attention supermarket shoppers: Keep a can of WD-40 handy whenever you go food shopping. Then when you get stuck with a sticky, wobbly-wheeled shopping cart, you can spray the wheels to reduce friction and wobbling. Less wobbling means faster shopping.

Remove chewing gum from hair It's one of an adult's worst nightmares: chewing gum tangled in a child's hair. You don't have to panic or run for the scissors. Simply spray the gummed-up hair with WD-40, and the gum will comb out with ease. Make sure you are in a well-ventilated area when you spray and take care to avoid contact with the child's eyes.

 DID *You* KNOW?

- In 1953 Norm Larsen founded the Rocket Chemical Company in San Diego and, with two employees, set out to develop a rust-preventing solvent and degreaser for the aerospace industry. On the fortieth try, they succeeded in creating a "water displacement" compound. The name WD-40 stands for "Water Displacement—40th Try."
- In 1958, a few years after WD-40's first industrial use, the company put it in aerosol cans and sold it for home use—inspired by employees who snuck cans out of the plant to use at home.
- In 1962, when U.S. astronaut John Glenn circled the Earth in *Friendship VII*, the space capsule was coated with WD-40 and so was the Atlas missile used to boost it into space.
- In 1969 Rocket Chemical renamed itself the WD-40 Company after the product.

Break in a new baseball glove Use WD-40 instead of neat's-foot oil to break in a new baseball glove. Spray the glove with WD-40, put a baseball in the palm, and fold it sideways. Take a rubber band or belt and tie it around the folded glove. The WD-40 will help soften the leather and help it form around the baseball. Keep the glove tied up overnight, and then wear it for a while so it will begin to fit the shape of your hand.

✽ WD-40 **FOR CLEANING THINGS**

Remove tough scuff marks Those tough black scuff marks on your kitchen floor won't be so tough anymore if you spray them with WD-40. Use WD-40 to help remove tar and scuff marks on all your hard-surfaced floors. It won't harm the surface, and you won't have to scrub nearly as much. Remember to open the windows if you are cleaning a lot of marks.

Clean dried glue Clean dried glue from virtually any hard surface with ease: Simply spray WD-40 onto the spot, wait at least 30 seconds, and wipe clean with a damp cloth.

Degrease your hands When you're done working on the car and your hands are greasy and blackened with grime, use WD-40 to help get them clean. Spray a small amount of WD-40 into your hands and rub them together for a few seconds, then wipe with a paper towel and wash with soap and water. The grease and grime will wash right off.

Remove decals You don't need a chisel or even a razor blade to remove old decals, bumper stickers, or cellophane tape. Just spray them with WD-40, wait about 30 seconds, and wipe them away.

Remove stickers from glass What were the manufacturers thinking when they put that sticker on the glass? Don't they know how hard it is to get off? When soap and water doesn't work and you don't want to ruin a fingernail or risk scratching delicate glass with a blade, try a little WD-40. Spray it on the sticker and glass, wait a few minutes, and then use a no-scratch spatula or acrylic scraper to scrape the sticker off. The solvents in WD-40 cause the adhesive to lose its stickiness.

Wipe away tea stains To remove tea stains from countertops, spray a little WD-40 on a sponge or damp cloth and wipe the stain away.

Clean carpet stains Don't let ink or other stains ruin your fine carpet. Spray the stain with WD-40, wait a minute or two, and then use your regular carpet cleaner or gently cleanse with a sponge and warm, soapy water. Continue until the stain is completely gone.

Get tomato stains off clothes That homegrown tomato looked so inviting you couldn't resist. Now your shirt or blouse has a big, hard-to-remove tomato stain! To

WD-40*

remove stains from fresh tomatoes or tomato sauce, spray some WD-40 directly on the spot, wait a couple of minutes, and wash as usual.

Clean toilet bowls You don't need a bald genie or a specialized product to clean ugly gunk and lime stains from your toilet bowl. Use WD-40 instead: Spray it into the bowl for a couple of seconds and swish with a nylon toilet brush. The solvents in the WD-40 will help dissolve the gunk and lime.

Clean your fridge When soap and water can't get rid of old bits of food stuck in and around your refrigerator, it's time to reach for the WD-40. After clearing all foodstuffs from the areas to be treated, spray a small amount of WD-40 on each resistant spot. Then wipe them away with a rag or sponge. Make sure you wash off all the WD-40 before returning food to the fridge.

Condition leather furniture Keep your favorite leather recliner and other leather furniture in tip-top shape by softening and preserving it with WD-40. Just spray it on and buff with a soft cloth. The combination of ingredients in WD-40 will clean, penetrate, lubricate, and protect the leather.

Pretreat blood and other stains Oh no! Your kid fell down and cut himself while playing, and there's blood all over his brand-new shirt. After you tend to the wound, give some first aid to the shirt too. Pretreat the bloodstains with WD-40. Spray some directly on the stains, wait a couple of minutes, and then launder as usual. The WD-40 will help lift the stain so that it will come out easily in the wash. Try to get to the stain while it is still fresh, because once it sets, it will be harder to get rid of. Use WD-40 to pretreat other stubborn stains on clothing, such as lipstick, dirt, grease, and ink stains.

Clean chalkboards When it comes to cleaning and restoring a chalkboard, WD-40 is the teacher's pet. Just spray it on and wipe with a clean cloth. The chalkboard will look as clean and fresh as it did on the first day of school.

Remove marker and crayon marks Did the kids use your wall as if it was a big coloring book? Not to worry! Simply spray some WD-40 onto the marks and wipe with a clean rag. WD-40 will not damage the paint or most wallpaper (test fabric or other fancy wall coverings first). It will also remove marker and crayon marks from furniture and appliances.

Rejuvenate the barbecue grill To make a worn old barbecue grill look like new again, spray it liberally with WD-40, wait a few seconds, and scrub with a wire brush. Remember to use WD-40 only on a grill that is not in use and has cooled off.

Renew faded plastic furniture Bring color and shine back to faded plastic patio furniture. Simply spray WD-40 directly on the surface and wipe with a clean, dry cloth. You'll be surprised at the results.

Prevent snow buildup on windows Does the weather forecast predict a big winter snowstorm? You can't stop the snow from falling, but you can prevent it from building up on your house's windows. Just spray WD-40 over the outside of your windows before the snow starts and the snow won't stick.

Keep shovel or chute snow-free Here is a simple tip to make shoveling snow quicker and less strenuous by keeping the snow from sticking to your shovel and weighing it down. Spray a thin layer of WD-40 on the shovel blade, and the snow will slide right off. If you have a snow thrower, spray WD-40 on the inside of the chute so snow won't stick and clog the chute.

Protect a bird feeder To keep squirrels from taking over a bird feeder, spray a generous amount of WD-40 on top of the feeder. The pesky squirrels will slide right off.

Remove cat's paw marks Your cat may seem like a member of the family most of the time, but that isn't what you are thinking about when you have to clean a slew of paw marks off patio furniture or the hood of your car. To remove the paw marks, spray some WD-40 on them and wipe with a clean rag.

Keep animals from flowerbeds Animals just love to play in your garden, digging up your favorite plants you worked so hard to grow. What animals *don't* love is the smell of WD-40. To keep the animals out and your flowers looking beautiful all season, spray WD-40 evenly over the flowerbeds one or more times over the course of the season.

Tip **The Little Red Straw**

"I lost the red straw!" has been a common cry among countless users of WD-40 over the years. In response, the company introduced a notched cap, designed to hold the straw in place across the top of the can when not in use. Because the straw exceeds the width of the can by a substantial margin, the notch may be of little use to those with limited storage space. To save space, store the straw by bending it inside the lip of the can or simply tape it to the side as it was when first purchased. A snug rubber band will also work well.

Repel pigeons Are the pigeons using your balcony more than you are? If pigeons and their feathers and droppings are keeping you from enjoying the view from your balcony, spray the entire area, including railings and furniture, with WD-40. The pigeons can't stand the smell and they'll fly the coop.

Keep wasps from building nests Don't let yellow jackets and other wasps ruin your spring and summer fun. Their favorite place to build nests is under eaves. So next spring mist some WD-40 under all the eaves of your house. It will block the wasps from building their nests there.

Remove doggie-doo Uh-oh, now you've stepped in it! Few things in life are more unpleasant than cleaning doggie-doo from the bottom of a sneaker, but the task will be a lot easier if you have a can of WD-40 handy. Spray some on the affected sole and use an old toothbrush to clean the crevices. Rinse with cold water and the sneakers will be ready to hit the pavement again. Now, don't forget to watch where you step!

Kill thistle plants Don't let pesky prickly weeds like bull and Russian thistle ruin your yard or garden. Just spray some WD-40 on them and they'll wither and die.

✱ WD-40 IN THE GREAT OUTDOORS

Winterproof boots and shoes Waterproof your winter boots and shoes by giving them a coat of WD-40. It'll act as a barrier so water can't penetrate the material. Also use WD-40 to remove ugly salt stains from boots and shoes during the winter months. Just spray WD-40 onto the stains and wipe with a clean rag. Your boots and shoes will look almost as good as new.

Remove old wax from skis and snowboards To remove old wax and dirt from skis and snowboards, spray the base sparingly with WD-40 before scraping with an acrylic scraper. Use a brass brush to further clean the base and remove any oxidized base material.

Protect your boat from corrosion To protect your boat's outer finish from salt water and corrosion, spray WD-40 on the stern immediately after each use. The short time it takes will save you from having to replace parts, and it will keep your boat looking like it did on the day you bought it for a long time to come.

Remove barnacles on boats Removing barnacles from the bottom of a boat is a difficult and odious task but you can make it easier and less unpleasant with the help of some WD-40. Spray the area generously with WD-40, wait a few seconds, and then use a putty knife to scrape off the barnacles. Spray any remnants with WD-40 and scrape again. If necessary, use sandpaper to get rid of all of the remnants and corrosive glue still left by the barnacles.

Spray on fishing lures Salmon fishermen in the Pacific Northwest spray their lures with WD-40 because it attracts fish and disguises the human odor that can scare them off and keep them from biting. You can increase the catch on your next fishing trip by bringing a can of WD-40 along with you and spraying it on *your* lures or live bait before you cast. But first check local regulations to make sure the use of chemical-laced lures and bait is legal in your state.

WD-40*

381

> When you need to apply tiny amounts of WD-40 to a specific area, such as the electrical contacts on an electric guitar, an aerosol spray is overkill. Instead, store some WD-40 in a clean nail-varnish bottle (with cap brush) and brush on as needed.

Untangle fishing lines To loosen a tangled fishing line, spray it with WD-40 and use a pin to undo any small knots. Also use WD-40 to extend the life of curled (but not too old) fishing lines. Just take out the first 10 to 20 feet of line and spray it with WD-40 the night before each trip.

Clean and protect golf clubs Whether you're a duffer or a pro, you can protect and clean your clubs by spraying them with WD-40 after each use. Also use WD-40 to help loosen stuck-on spikes.

Remove burrs To remove burrs from a horse's mane or tail without tearing its hair out (or having to cut any of its hair off!) just spray on some WD-40. You'll be able to slide the burrs right out. This will work for dogs and cats, too.

Protect horses' hooves Winter horseback riding can be fun if you are warmly dressed but it can be downright painful to your horse if ice forms on the horseshoes. To keep ice from forming on horseshoes during cold winter rides, spray the bottom of the horse's hooves with WD-40 before you set out.

Keep flies off cows If flies are tormenting your cows, just spray some WD-40 on the cows. Flies hate the smell and they'll stay clear. Take care not to spray any WD-40 in the cows' eyes.

DID *You* KNOW?

WD-40 is one of the few products with its own fan club. The official WD-40 Fan Club has more than 63,000-members and is growing. Over the years members have contributed thousands of unique and sometimes strange uses for the product. But according to Gary Ridge, president and CEO of the WD-40 Company, the strangest use of all occurred in China. "In Hong Kong some time ago there was a python caught in the suspension of a public bus," he said. "They used WD-40 to get that little slippery guy out of there!"

Clean your hearing aid To give your hearing aid a good cleaning, use a cotton swab dipped in WD-40. Do not use WD-40 to try to loosen up the volume control (it will loosen it too much).

Relieve bee-sting pain For fast relief of pain from a bee, wasp, or hornet sting, reach for the WD-40 can and spray it directly on the bite site. It will take the "ouch" right out.

Remove stuck prostheses If you wear a prosthetic device, you know how difficult it can be to remove at times, especially when no one is around to help. Next time you get stuck with a stuck prosthesis, spray some WD-40 at the junction where it attaches. The chemical solvents and lubricants in WD-40 will help make it easier to remove.

✳ WD-40 **IN THE GARAGE**

Keep dead bugs off car grille It's bad enough that your car grille and hood have to get splattered with bugs every time you drive down the interstate, but do they have to be so darn tough to scrape off? The answer is no. Just spray some WD-40 on the grille and hood before going for a drive and most of the critters will slide right off. The few bugs that are left will be easy to wipe off later without damaging your car's finish.

Clean and restore license plate To help restore a license plate that is beginning to rust, spray it with WD-40 and wipe with a clean rag. This will remove light surface rust and will also help prevent more rust from forming. It's an easy way to clean up lightly rusted plates and it won't leave a greasy feel.

Remove stuck spark plugs To save time replacing spark plugs, do it the NASCAR way. NASCAR mechanics spray WD-40 on stuck plugs so they can remove them quickly and easily. Perhaps that's one reason why WD-40 has been designated as NASCAR's "official multi-purpose problem-solver."

Coat a truck bed For easy removal of a truck-bed liner, spray the truck bed with WD-40 before you install the liner. When it comes time to remove it, the liner will slide right out.

Remove "paint rub" from another car You return to your parked car to find that while you were gone, another vehicle got a bit too close for comfort. Luckily there's no dent, but now your car has a blotch of "paint rub" from the other car on it. To remove paint-rub stains on your car and restore its original finish, spray the affected area with WD-40, wait a few seconds, and wipe with a clean rag.

Revive spark plugs Can't get your car to start on a rainy or humid day? To get your engine purring, just spray some WD-40 on the spark-plug wires before you try starting it up again. WD-40 displaces water and keeps moisture away from the plugs.

WD-40*

Clean oil spots from driveway Did a leaky oil pan leave a big ugly spot in the middle of your concrete driveway? To get rid of an unsightly oil spot, just spray it with a generous amount of WD-40 and then hose it down with water.

* Weather Stripping

Keep appliances in place Affixing small pieces of weather stripping to the bottom of telephones, electric can openers, PC speakers, and similar items will help keep them from sliding off counters or desktops.

Add traction to boots Some rubber boots may be great at keeping out moisture, but don't prevent you from slipping on ice-, snow-, or slush-covered surfaces. But you can usually improve the traction of your waterproof footwear by gluing a few strips of flat weather stripping onto the toe, middle, and heel sections.

Get a grip on tools Wrapping the handles of tools such as hammers, axes, and wrenches with flat weather stripping will not only give you a better and more comfortable grip on them, but it might even prevent wooden handles from getting damaged. Spiral the weather stripping around the handle, overlapping it half a width.

Fix leaky car windows Use small slivers of household weather stripping to patch up the dented weather stripping around car windows to prevent wind and water from getting inside your car. You can also use it to firm up sagging rubber gaskets around your car's trunk or doors.

* Window Cleaner

Reduce swelling from bee stings Spritzing some window cleaner on a bee sting is a quick way to reduce the swelling and pain. But first be sure to remove any stinger. Flick it sideways to get it out—don't tweeze it—then spray. Use only spray-on window cleaner that contains ammonia and never use a concentrated product. It is the small amount of ammonia that does the work, and beekeepers have known for years that a very dilute solution of ammonia helps relieve stings.

Get off that stuck ring That ring felt a little tight going on, and now … oops!… it's stuck. Spray a little window cleaner on your finger for lubrication and ease the ring off.

Clean your jewelry Use window cleaner to spruce up jewelry that is all metal or has crystalline gemstones, such as diamonds or rubies. Spray on the cleaner, then use an old toothbrush for cleaning. But don't do this if the piece has opaque stones such as opal or turquoise or organic gems such as coral or pearl. The ammonia and detergents in the cleaner can discolor these porous lovelies.

Remove stubborn laundry stains If laundering with detergent isn't enough to get tough stains such as blood, grass, or tomato sauce out of a fabric, try a clear ammonia-based spray-on window cleaner instead. (It's the ammonia in the window cleaner that does the trick, and you want uncolored cleaner to avoid staining the fabric.) Spray the stain with the window cleaner and let it sit for up to 15 minutes. Blot with a clean rag, rinse with cool water, and launder again. A few tips:

- Do a test on a seam or other inconspicuous part of the garment to see if the color runs.

- Use cool water and don't put the garment in the dryer until the stain is completely gone.

- Don't use this on silk, wool, or their blends.

- If the fabric color seems changed after using window cleaner on it, moisten the fabric with white vinegar and rinse it with water. Acidic vinegar will neutralize alkaline ammonia.

DID *You* KNOW?

Will spraying window cleaner on a pimple really help make it go away? Although the formula varies by brand, window cleaners generally contain ammonia, detergents, solvents, and alcohol. This combination will clean, disinfect, and dry out skin. So as long as you keep it out of your eyes and have no allergies to the ingredients, it probably will help suppress pimples.

✳ Yogurt

Make moss "paint" for the garden Wouldn't it be nice to simply paint some moss between the cracks of your stone walkway, on the sides of flowerpots, or anywhere else you want it to grow? Well, you can. Just dump a cup of plain active-culture yogurt into your blender along with a handful of common lawn moss and about a cup of water. Blend for about 30 seconds. Use a paintbrush to spread the mixture wherever you want moss to grow—as long as the spot is cool and shady. Mist the moss occasionally until it gets established.

Make a facial mask You don't have to go to a spa to give your face a quick assist:

- To cleanse your skin and tighten the pores, slather some plain yogurt on your face and let it sit for about 20 minutes.

- For a revitalizing facial mask, mix 1 teaspoon plain yogurt with the juice from 1/4 slice of orange, some of the orange pulp, and 1 teaspoon aloe. Leave the mixture on your face for at least five minutes before rinsing it off.

Relieve sunburn For quick, temporary relief of mild sunburn, apply cold plain yogurt. The yogurt adds much needed moisture and, at the same time, its coldness soothes. Rinse with cool water.

Make play finger paint Ready for some messy rainy-day fun? Mix food coloring with yogurt to make finger paints and let the little ones go wild. You can even turn it into a lesson about primary and secondary colors. For example, have the kids put a few drops of yellow food coloring and a few drops of blue in the yogurt to make green finger paint. Or mix red and blue to produce purple.

Cure dog or cat flatulence If Bowser has been a bit odoriferous lately, the problem may be a lack of the friendly digestive bacteria that prevent gas and diarrhea. The active culture in plain yogurt can help restore the helpful bacteria. Add 2 teaspoons yogurt to the food for cats or small dogs weighing up to 14 pounds (6 kilograms). Add 1 tablespoon for medium-sized dogs weighing 15-34 pounds (7-15 kilograms). Add 2 tablespoons for large dogs weighing 35-84 pounds (16-38 kilograms). Add 3 tablespoons for dogs larger than that.

Zippers

Secure your valuables Nothing ruins a vacation like reaching into your pocket and discovering it has been picked. To keep your wallet, passport, and other valuables safe, sew a zipper into the inside pocket of your jacket to keep items safely zipped inside.

Make a sock puppet Create a happy sock puppet that will keep kids amused for hours. Just sew on buttons for the nose and eyes and some yarn for hair, and use a small smiling upturned zipper for the mouth.

Create convertible pants Here's a great idea for hikers and bikers who like to travel light. Cut the legs off a pair of jeans or other comfortable pants above the knee. Then reattach the legs with zippers. Zip off the legs when it gets warm, zip them back on for cool mornings and evenings. Besides lightening your load, you won't need to search for a place to change.

Zucchini

Use as a rolling pin A large zucchini works great for rolling out dough for biscuits or piecrust. The zucchini has just the right shape and weight, and the dough won't stick to its smooth skin.

Use as exercise weights Zucchini come in a large range of sizes, so you'll have no trouble finding a couple that are just the right weight for your arm exercises.

Use as Mr. Zucchini Head Got some bored kids on your hands? Dust off that old Mr. Potato Head set and hand the youngsters a couple of large zucchini. The new vegetable is sure to renew their interest in the old toy.

Juggle 'em! Okay, okay, we're impressed. You can juggle three balls. Now let's see how you do with three zucchini!

Index

Note: **Boldface** entries and page numbers refer to main A-Z headings in text.

✳ Indicates a Super Item.

SCIENCE FAIR FEATURES

These simple experiments for kids demonstrate basic science using everyday items.

MORE...
extraordinary
uses for
ordinary things

1,715 ALL-NEW Uses for Everyday Items

Reader's Digest

The Reader's Digest Association, Inc.
New York, NY | Montreal

Simple!

Clever!

Creative!

Fresh!

contents

Introduction
The Joy of Old-Fashioned Smarts 8

Smart!

Easy!

Ingenious!

Fast!

Introduction

The Joy of Old-Fashioned Smarts

Plastic CD cases make great **photo frames!**

It's amazing just how clever television commercials have become. There they are—happy, pretty people cleaning their homes, cooking their dinner, grooming their gardens, and using the most *ingenious* new contraptions and solutions, all specially available to you now at this one-time, amazing low price.

"*Hmmm*," you can't help but think, "maybe if I bought *that* thing, then cleaning my kitchen floor might be easier!"

We've coined a word for this phenomenon: Contraptionism. You name the task—from planting a plant to chopping vegetables to cleaning a shower—and you can find a clever contraption created to get it done faster and easier. And why not? Entrepreneurs make great livings selling clever gizmos meant to make our lives better.

But there are problems with contraptionism. These gadgets usually just accomplish one task. They're either too expensive (crush garlic easier for just $40!), or too cheap (flimsy plastic that bends with the wind). They accumulate in our closets and drawers, often going unused. And they often have a short life—either you need to buy refills, or they break. Sure, on occasion, you come across that one gadget that really does deliver on its promise. But mostly, contraptionism has a not-so-happy ending.

So let us tell you about some of *our* favorite contraptions. An old pair of panty hose. A banana peel (without the banana). A strand of uncooked spaghetti. A roll of duct tape.

These tried-and-true devices for easy living are options that are wiser, smarter, more frugal, a tiny bit old-fashioned, and nearly always a lot more fun to use. Because if you could wash your windows, clean your floors, shine your kitchen tiles, tenderize your meat, poach your eggs, remove old wallpaper and unclog a drain all with the same bottle of inexpensive vinegar, you'd do it … wouldn't you?

And this is what *More Extraordinary Uses for Ordinary Things* is all about: finding the fun in the ordinary and the ingenious in the everyday. And by doing so, saving yourself incredible amounts of time and money.

How We Put This Book Together

We sent our intrepid team of researchers and writers out to talk with chefs, landscapers, grandmothers, herbalists, pet-store owners, carpenters, decorators, and so many more everyday experts. Their task: Find their very best tips and tricks for getting things done quicker, easier, cheaper—and by only using items already available around the house.

What they came back with was thousands of ingenious hints and tips on most every subject imaginable. We honed the list down to 1,715 of the best, and they fill the pages ahead. Now, we've covered similar terrain in other Reader's Digest books, so we worked extra hard to make sure that everything in *More Extraordinary Uses for Ordinary Things* is new and different. And we most assuredly succeeded!

These tips will take you on a wide-ranging tour through your everyday life. We'll visit your kitchen, den, closets, and bedroom; we'll tour your garden and yard; we'll even be with you in your car and on vacation. We'll also be there with you as you take on the tasks of everyday living: cooking, cleaning, mending, sorting the mail, remedying a cut or a cold, rejuvenating those droopy geraniums.

We've asked for help from people you'll recognize, like that great-aunt or uncle who may be getting older, but who still knows how to remove a splinter with an onion, de-gunk a skillet with baking soda and borax, or use an ordinary plastic bag to clean a shower head. Pet owners share their tricks for getting their finicky dogs to eat; homemakers show us how to organize a drawer with an egg carton; creative parents teach us how to remove crayon from a wall with shaving cream.

While ingenuity is priceless, it's also got other benefits: It's usually accomplished without chemicals (and is therefore healthier for you, your family, your home, and the environment). It's parsimonious (who needs contraptionism when you can buy just one thing, like baking soda, to accomplish a multitude of tasks?), and, well, it's just a lot more fun.

Great Advice Ahead!

The thirteen chapters in *More Extraordinary Uses for Ordinary Things* each focus on an integral part of everyday life:

For the cooks of the house, we've gathered hundreds of ingenious cooking tips and tricks using everyday ingredients. What's the one secret ingredient that will turn a supermarket tomato from marginal to magnificent? How can you extend the shelf life of vegetables and other perishables? What's the most tried and true method for baking bread, that goes back thousands of years but is as close as your own garden shed?

For the housekeepers of the house, we've given you more ideas for faster, easier cleaning than you can shake a broomstick at.

What two ingredients can you blend together in seconds to make a wonderful cleaner for a wooden floor? What everyday lunch treat can you use to get something sticky out of a carpet?

For the groggy person standing in front of the bathroom mirror at 7 a.m., we tell you surprising ways to look and feel refreshed. What early morning drink is a great soother of puffy eyes? What everyday breakfast food is a natural lipstick stain-remover?

For the handyman (or woman) of the house, we show you incredibly fast and easy fix-its for many common problems. What does virtually every woman have in her medicine cabinet that does double duty removing scratches and dents in wood? What's the easiest way to remove ancient wallpaper?

For the neat freak in every home, we show you the very best ways to conquer clutter without big investments in fancy boxes and shelves. Don't toss those old egg cartons and milk jugs! Use them instead of buying prefabricated, pricey store-bought clutter contraptions!

As they searched out clever ideas for better everyday living, the writers and researchers of *More Extraordinary Uses for Ordinary Things* often discovered that necessity was the mother of invention. One expert for the home repairs chap-

Let us tell you about some of our favorite contraptions: an old pair of panty hose, a **banana peel** (without the banana), a strand of uncooked spaghetti, a roll of duct tape.

ter replaced the old, wood-frame windows in his house only to discover the new ones drafty enough to chill his family to the bone in winter. His solution? Thick strips of folded paper towel held in place by masking tape.

More exciting was another expert's serendipitous discovery. Trying to revive his dog's interest in dry food, this fast-fixes maven decided to mash a banana and stir a bit of it into his dog's bowl. The pooch ate it like there was no tomorrow and finickiness is now a thing of the past.

The author of the cooking chapter struck gold when she asked family and friends about unusual ways of accomplishing common tasks. She quickly learned about buttering the lip of a pitcher to help stop dribbles, and using a garlic press to crush sugar cubes. One expert revealed that instead of buying a pricey electric sandwich press, he uses a heavy cast-iron skillet for even better results. This clever approach to everyday living is what 21st century "folk wisdom" is all about.

More Extraordinary Uses for Ordinary Things also provides a goldmine's worth of special features that inform, instruct, and entertain: **What's the Story?** brings you the surprising histories of household items new and old.

Make Your Own offers up simple, natural recipes for everything from dog biscuits to nasal spray to natural insecticides for your plants.

Household Superstars! details some of the many uses for the most useful and popular home ingredients, like baking soda, duct tape, petroleum jelly, plastic bags, salt, vinegar, and WD-40.

Curiosity Corner lets you dip into a veritable grab bag of curiosities of all stripes, from how many ingredients it took to build the world's

largest sandwich, to how to estimate air temperature by the frequency of a cricket's chirp, and to understand why a candle can be used to unstick a stuck drawer.

So whether you thrill at the possibility of discovering new ways to use everyday things, or simply want ways to save a few dollars and do things better, this anticontraption bible is for you. Dip into it and dip out, peruse the chapters with a fine tooth comb, or read it from beginning to end … no matter how you use it, this will become the busiest book in the house (and the garage, the garden shed, the lavatory, the playroom, and pretty much everywhere else). And remember, the busier this book is, the more money and time you will save!

—*The Editors*

Chapter One

Cooking and Serving Shortcuts

Are the microwave and a fridge full of frozen meals the best dinner companions you've ever had? Or do you find yourself standing over a hot stove for a few precious hours each night after a long day at work to make a meal for your family?

Whether you love to cook or you find it just another chore, there are easier, faster, and simply smarter ways to kitchen happiness that will not only save you time, but will make daily dinner drudgery delicious!

Not every hint in this magician's bag of cooking tricks will save you time, though. But money-saving, creative solutions to kitchen problems are shortcuts to worry-free cooking, and that's what this chapter is all about!

If your soup is too salty, add a drop of sugar. If your curry is too spicy, applesauce will cool it down. Run out of oil to grease a pan? Use the cut-side of a potato. The hints that follow give you dozens of great ideas and in many cases get you out of a pretty pickle. So let's get cooking!

Fruits, breads, and vegetables make terrific *edible bowls!*

Fast Fixes

Counteract salt with sugar
Did you oversalt Grandma Kate's famous beef stew as it burbled away on your stove? Save it with a teaspoon of granulated sugar, which will absorb excess salt and help balance the taste. No sugar handy? Stir in a teaspoon of honey.

Degrease gravy with baking soda
Sometimes the cooking juices you've used in your gravy are so greasy that they look like an oil slick. Counteract the problem with a pinch or two of baking soda, stirred into the juices just enough to absorb the grease. (Be careful, though: If you overdo it, you'll taint the flavor, and it'll taste metallic.)

Curry sauce too spicy?
Tone it down with applesauce. Add ⅓ cup applesauce for each cup of curry sauce, then taste. If necessary, continue stirring in a bit of applesauce until the curry is acceptable.

Two more for dinner (surprise!)
You cooked the perfect-sized roast for a small get-together, and guess what? Meat shrinks when cooked, so you've got a third smaller entree than you started out with, and *then* the doorbell rings.

What to do? Carve the entire roast into thin strips, toss that large salad you were planning on, top with the beef, and you'll have just ratcheted up the size of your main course.

Rescue a cracked egg
You're boiling an egg and the shell cracks. No reason to throw it out if you have white vinegar in the cupboard. Simply add 1 teaspoon vinegar to the cooking water to coagulate the egg white and stop it from seeping out.

Salsa too hot?
Stir in a drop or two of vanilla extract. Whether it's the vanillin, sugars, or amino acids in vanilla that takes the heat down a notch or two, vanilla extract is the coolest condiment for the job.

Soup too garlicky?
Pack a mesh pouch, gauze bag, or metal tea ball with dried parsley flakes or fresh parsley sprigs and drop it into the pot. After 5 minutes or so, the flakes will absorb some of the taste of the offending ingredient. Once the garlic taste has been adequately toned down, remove the parsley and discard it.

ADD SWEET FLAVOR TO OUT-OF-SEASON SUPERMARKET TOMATOES
Those commercially grown pink tennis balls that pass for tomatoes do have flavor hiding deep inside: Just drizzle tomato slices with a little **rice vinegar** (on supermarket shelves everywhere). You'll be amazed at the difference it makes!

Fat Catchers!

Do you skim the fat off your simmering stew, soup, or sauce with a teaspoon? Stop!
Here are three easy and effective ways to reduce artery-clogging fat in the pot:

1
Float a large lettuce leaf on the surface and it will draw the fat right in. Repeat the process with fresh leaves as necessary.

2
Float two or three ice cubes on the surface and you'll soon see fat globules clinging to them. Scoop the cubes out (before they melt!) and continue cooking your now-healthful dish.

3
Slip an uncooked egg white onto the simmering soup or stew or sauce. Left alone for a few minutes, it will absorb the fat as it cooks; simply scoop out the solidified egg white with a slotted spoon, and discard it.

Poultry Prescriptions

Simple skinning

Want to make skinning a piece of poultry or even a whole bird a snap? Put it in the freezer until it partially freezes (generally 1½–2 hours). You'll be able to pull the skin off with no trouble.

Chicken money-saver

Buy whole birds and cut them up with poultry shears. Freeze the pieces in portion-size freezer bags. If chicken is your family's favorite dish, you'll make up the cost of the shears (under $20) in a few weeks!

Butter(milk) up chicken cutlets

To tenderize chicken cutlets and pack them with flavor, rinse the breasts, pat dry, and marinate them in buttermilk for 2–3 hours, in the fridge, before cooking.

Stuffing stopper

Want to make sure stuffing doesn't fall out when you roast a bird? When cooking a stuffed bird of any size, just plug a raw potato into the cavity and the stuffing will stay put.

Tea-riffic flavor

To give chicken or turkey breasts or thighs a light, smoky flavor and help them retain moisture as they cook, brew 2 strong cups of your favorite spice-flavored tea blend. Once the tea cools, add seasonings of choice—black pepper, salt, paprika, and garlic—to taste, pour into a large self-sealing plastic bag, and add the chicken or turkey pieces. Put in a shallow dish and marinate in the fridge for at least 2 hours before cooking.

Carrot and celery rack

Forget hard-to-clean, traditional roasting racks! Instead, crisscross whole carrots and celery stalks on the bottom of the roasting pan, and top with your chicken or turkey. Once it's done, your bird will emerge from the pan without a hitch, and the pan gravy will be enhanced by the vegetables!

Simple roux starters for gravy

Combine excess pan fat with enough all-purpose flour until you can roll it into small balls about half the size of a walnut, and freeze on a cookie sheet covered with a paper towel. When frozen, transfer the balls to a plastic bag and store in the freezer for future use. The next time you need to make gravy, pluck out a roux starter ball from the bag and melt it in the saucepan before stirring in the other ingredients. Is your already-cooked gravy too thin? Drop in a roux starter, whisk well, season to taste, and serve.

GLAZE WITH VERMOUTH

About 15 minutes before you're ready to take your chicken or turkey out of the oven, brush the skin with **white vermouth.** It will take on a rich brown color, thanks to the sugars in the fortified wine.

Double-Duty Kitchen Tools

Some of the most ordinary kitchen gadgets and tools come in handy in ways you never imagined, in some cases making them worth a lot more than you paid.

Vegetable peeler
Run a peeler along the corners of a block of cheese or chocolate to create hearty ribbons to use as a garnish.

Colander
Use as a steamer for vegetables. Fill a stockpot with 2–3 inches of water, bring to a boil, put a heatproof or metal vegetable-filled colander inside, and cover.

Garlic press
Turn sugar cubes into granular sugar by placing one cube at a time into a garlic press and squeezing it shut. One cube equals 1 teaspoon of sugar.

Melon baller
Use smaller ballers to core apples and pears and scoop cookie dough onto a baking sheet. Use larger ones to scoop ice cream into a bowl.

Ice cream scoop
Lightly coat an ice cream scoop with cooking spray and use it to spoon even amounts of batter into cupcake or muffin tin liners. The sweeping release arm will help clean all batter from the scoop, and you won't waste a drop.

Pizza cutter
The sharp wheel on a pizza cutter makes cutting through all kinds of other foods a breeze. Use the cutter to separate waffle segments and to neatly slice a grilled cheese sandwich.

Tongs
Sturdy metal tongs measuring about 16 inches long are like having an extra set of heatproof hands. Use them to turn chops frying in a skillet, to toss salads, to mix pasta with sauce, and to rotate cake and pie pans in the oven.

Empty wine bottle
Don't have a rolling pin or a meat pounder handy? Use an empty wine bottle as a stand-in rolling pin (flour it first) or as a meat pounder to flatten chicken or veal cutlets for more even cooking.

Go Fish

Something's fishy

Before preparing fresh fish, halve a lemon and rub both hands with the cut ends to help keep your hands from absorbing the fishy odor. (If you didn't know you had a tiny scratch or cut on your hand, you will now!) If frying is your cooking method of choice, wash the pan you used and pour in ½ inch white vinegar; the acetic acid should banish any lingering fish smell.

Ease scaling with vinegar

To make scaling a fish less of a chore, rub white vinegar on the scales and let sit for about 10 minutes. The scales will come off so easily that they may make more of a mess than usual, so put the fish in a plastic bag before you do this. Just scale the fish in the bag with one hand while holding the fish by the tail with your other hand.

Keep poached fish firm

When poaching fish, squeeze fresh lemon juice into the poaching liquid to help the fish cook evenly. For each pound of fish, use the juice of half a lemon.

Foil moisture loss when baking

Low-fat fish like bass, flounder, grouper, halibut, and red snapper can easily dry out as they bake. To seal in the moisture, simply wrap each fillet or whole fish in aluminum foil before putting it into the oven.

Freezing fresh-caught fish

When you bring more fish home from the lake than you can eat, here's the smartest way to freeze them. Take an empty milk carton large enough to hold the fish, place the fish inside, and fill the carton with water. Seal the opening with tape and place the carton in the freezer. When you thaw the fish, you won't have to worry about scraping off ice crystals or pulling off some of the flesh with the wrapping.

Cool down shrimp

To ensure tender, well-textured meat, place shrimp in the freezer for 10–15 minutes before you cook them. Just be sure not to overcook them because you think they need time to warm up in the boiling water. (They don't.)

Make oyster-shucking easier
Soaking oysters in club soda for 5–10 minutes will make it easier for you to open the shells.

Stop lobster squirts
When cracking and twisting the legs and claws off a whole lobster, guard against the occasional squirt by putting a napkin between the crustacean and your hand. Any squirts will hit the napkin, not your silk blouse sleeve or starched white cuff (or dinner companion's sweater).

Improve canned seafood
If you detect a slight metallic taste in canned seafood, soak it as directed below, drain, and pat the seafood dry with paper towels.

- **Water-packed tuna** Soak in a mixture of cold water and lemon juice for 15 minutes (2 parts water, 1 part juice).

- **Canned crab** Soak the crabmeat in ice water for 5–10 minutes.

- **Canned shrimp** Soak the shrimp in a mixture of 2 tablespoons vinegar and 1 teaspoon dry sherry for 15 minutes.

Cut the salt in anchovies
If you like the taste of anchovies but wish they weren't quite so salty, soak them in ice water for 10–15 minutes, and then drain them well before tossing them in a Caesar salad or arranging them on top of a pizza.

make your own
Salt Substitute

Here's a delicious, all-purpose, low-sodium seasoning that will enhance fish, meat, and poultry dishes. Make it in large batches to always have it on hand.

Who-Needs-Salt Mix
Sour salt, arrowroot, and powdered orange peel in this recipe may sound unusual, but they can usually be found in supermarkets.

> 1 tablespoon celery seeds
> 1 tablespoon onion powder
> 1 tablespoon freshly ground black pepper
> 2¼ teaspoons cream of tartar
> 1½ teaspoons garlic powder
> 1½ teaspoons sugar
> 1½ teaspoons arrowroot
> 1½ teaspoons powdered orange peel
> ¾ sour salt (citric acid powder)
> ½ teaspoon white pepper
> ½ teaspoon dried dill
> ½ teaspoon dried thyme, crumbled
> ⅓ teaspoon powdered lemon peel
> ¼ teaspoon cayenne

1. Place all ingredients in a blender or food processor. Grind for 8–10 seconds or until the mixture is fine.

2. Use a funnel to fill a glass salt shaker with the mixture.

3. Put the rest of the mixture in an airtight jar and store in a cool, dark place.

From Reader's Digest Great Recipes for Good Health

Red Meat? Read On!

Hamburgers with a difference

To flavor and moisten hamburger patties, add ¼ cup finely minced onion and 2 tablespoons barbecue sauce. Blend the ingredients into the ground beef or turkey with your hands (which you've washed with antibacterial soap, of course!), taking care not to overwork the mixture.

Variations of the ingredients are endless— you can add everything from minced garlic or celery or other crisp vegetables paired with chili sauce, ketchup, Worcestershire sauce, or steak sauce. You could also mix a teaspoon of chili powder or cumin (or ½ teaspoon of both) into the meat to give the patties a hint of Tex-Mex flavor, or even a drop of curry powder to add some Indian spice.

Speed defrosting with salt

Defrost frozen meats quickly and safely by soaking them in cold salt water for several hours. Mix ¼ to ½ cup kosher salt or any other coarse-grain salt with 2 quarts water, then submerge the meat and refrigerate it. Once the meat has thawed, just discard the salt water and get cooking!

Making better burgers

Your last backyard barbecue was a big success, and your hamburgers certainly passed muster. But you can notch up a burger's wow quotient with a few easy tricks.

- **Keep 'em juicy** For a juicer grilled burger, add ½ cup cold water to the ground meat, and shape patties as you normally would. Prepare the patties shortly before you grill them.

- **Flash freeze** Keep hamburger patties from breaking during grilling by freezing them for 5 minutes just before they go on the grill.

- **Poke dents** Use your forefinger to make two or three dents in the center of a patty before placing it on the grill. This speeds even distribution of heat so the burger will cook faster.

- **Toast herbs** You can easily flavor and scent grilled burgers by giving your hot coals an herbal treatment. Place leafy fresh herbs like basil, savory, and rosemary directly on the coals.

BASTE WITH A PAINTBRUSH

A clean paintbrush dipped in vegetable or canola oil is perfect for making your grill nonstick before slapping on burgers or any other meat. Season your steak, chicken, or fish with the same brush, now dipped not in oil but in grilling sauce.

Bake your bacon for a streak o' lean that's crispier, meatier, and less greasy.

Bathe flank steak in ginger ale

Lend flank steak an Asian touch by marinating it in ¾ cup of ginger ale mixed with 3 minced garlic cloves, ¾ cup orange juice, ¼ cup soy sauce, and ½ teaspoon sesame oil. Cover and keep in the refrigerator for 4–8 hours. This recipe makes enough marinade for 1½ pounds flank steak.

Wake up brisket with coffee

Barbara's Brisket (Barbara being an innovative home cook who resides in New Jersey) uses coffee and chili sauce to give brisket a new twist. To enjoy this twice-cooked dish for yourself, combine 2 cups brewed coffee with 1½ cups store-bought chili sauce in a mixing bowl. Stir in 1 chopped onion, 2 tablespoons brown sugar, and salt and freshly ground black pepper to taste.

Place a 5-pound brisket in a roasting pan, then pour the bowl of sauce over the meat. Cover tightly with a lid or foil and bake for 2 hours in a preheated 325°F oven. Remove the pan from the oven and transfer the meat to a platter to cool. Now slice the meat, lay slices in the sauce in the pan, and cover again. Bake at 325°F for another 2 hours or until the brisket is fork-tender.

Meatloaf in a bag

Put all the ingredients for a meatloaf into a large self-sealing plastic bag and squish it with both hands to evenly distribute the seasonings throughout the meat. Turn the bag inside out into a prepared loaf pan, gently press it into shape, and bake. No messy hand, no bowl to wash!

Keep meatloaf moist

Spritzing the top of the loaf with water will keep it from cracking and drying out as it cooks. Open the oven door and brush tomato sauce or ketchup over the top of the loaf about 15 minutes before it has finished cooking.

Easy slices without tearing

To slice thin steaks or stew cubes from a roast prior to cooking, wrap the meat in heavy-duty plastic wrap and freeze for 10 minutes. This

Household Superstar!
10 Kitchen Uses for Salt

1 Sprinkle on a whole chicken 24 hours prior to roasting, for the most flavorful and juicy clucker you've ever eaten.

2 Release juices in meats by seasoning them with salt an hour before cooking.

3 Prevent pancakes from sticking to the griddle by wiping the griddle between batches with coarse salt wrapped in cheesecloth.

4 Prevent cheese mold by wrapping the cheese in a paper towel dampened with salt water.

5 Clean dirt and grit from leafy greens by soaking them in cold salt water for up to 15 minutes, then rinsing the greens thoroughly under cold running water.

6 Keep apples, pears, and potatoes from browning as you slice them by dropping each new slice into a bowl of lightly salted cold water.

7 Keep hardboiled eggs intact and make them easier to peel by adding a pinch of salt to the cooking water.

8 Make milk last almost twice as long in the refrigerator by adding a pinch of salt each time you open a new carton.

9 Neutralize bitter coffee that's been sitting on the warmer too long by adding a dash of salt to your cup.

10 Enhance the flavor of cocoa drinks and desserts with a pinch of salt.

method works for every cut, from London Broil to inexpensive chuck roast.

Quick 'n' easy pork glaze

If you have apricot jelly, soy sauce, and powdered ginger in your pantry, you've got the makings of a simple but delicious glaze. Just whisk together ¼ cup apricot jelly, 2 tablespoons soy sauce, and ¾ teaspoon ginger and brush it onto a pork tenderloin or rolled pork roast before cooking. If you're pan-cooking pork chops on top of the stove, glaze the browned top of the chops after you've flipped them over once.

Ham too salty?

Give ham bought as "fully cooked" a taste test before warming the slices. If the ham's on the salty side, place the slices in a dish of low-fat milk for 20 minutes before heating them. (Once you remove the slices from the milk, rinse them under cold running water and pat dry with paper towels.) The ham won't pick up the taste of milk but will lose some of its saltiness. Soak whole precooked hams in milk for an hour before heating (just remember to drain, rinse, and pat the meat dry).

Baking bacon!

Laying bacon over a wire rack set on a rimmed baking sheet and baking it at 375°F has two advantages: 1) It makes the slices less greasy because the fat drips onto the sheet, and 2) the bacon stays flat and tastes meatier. If you prefer your bacon fried, prevent it from curling and splattering grease by dipping the slices in cold water before you fry them.

Cup o' joe for lamb

To give lamb stew a beautiful dark color and great flavor, add 1 cup black coffee to the stew pot about halfway through the cooking process.

Perfect Pasta, Right-on Rice

The ideal meal stretcher

You invited six friends over for a buffet dinner, and one couple shows up with two out-of-town friends, another with their strapping teenage son. Help! Make a beeline for the cupboard and pull out a box of pasta—your best bet as a filling meal stretcher. Dig around your pantry and look for a can of tomatoes or condensed soup. Boil the pasta while your friends mingle and snack, heating up the soup (undiluted) or tomatoes at the same time. Drain the cooked pasta, dump it into a large bowl, and toss it with the soup or tomatoes and plenty of grated hard cheese, preferably Parmesan or Romano. (If you have no soup or tomatoes, toss the pasta with a little olive oil and grated hard cheese—a surprisingly delicious combo.) Add the steaming bowl of pasta to the buffet table, and your guests—with the possible exception of Tyler, high school football team center—will have their fill.

Stop spaghetti showers

You're rummaging through a kitchen cabinet for a can of beans and accidentally knock over the half-used box of spaghetti—and the dried strands rain down on the floor. How to keep it from happening again? Save an empty potato chip can (tall and cylindrical and lidded) and recycle it as a dry pasta canister.

Carrot ribbon pasta

Carrots add more nutrients and some vibrant color to a simple pasta dish. Clean and peel the carrots, then use your peeler to shave wide carrot ribbons. Sauté the ribbons in butter and seasonings, such as ginger, black pepper, and salt, then add to cooked and drained pasta. Forgo the red sauce and toss with Parmesan cheese.

Keep pasta pots from boiling over

Before adding water to your pasta pot, coat the interior lightly with nonstick cooking spray. The water won't boil over, even when you add the pasta. If you have no spray on hand, add a teaspoon of olive oil to the water as it cooks. This trick works for boiled rice as well.

Toss leftover pasta...

But don't throw it out! Toss it in a stickproof, ovenproof pan with a teaspoon of olive oil, pour two beaten eggs over it, sprinkle with cheese, and bake until golden brown. Slice the frittata into wedges and have it for another dinner with a small green salad! Money saving, simple, and delish!

Jazz up rice

Instead of boiling your rice in plain water, use chicken or beef stock, tomato juice, or even equal parts orange juice and water. Or just sprinkle dried oregano, cumin, turmeric, and any other herb or spice into the water before adding the rice. You could also add minced onion, garlic, or lemon or orange zest to turn rice from the same-old, same-old into a brand new dish each time it's set on the table.

Fluff it up!

It's easy to keep rice grains from sticking together as they cook. Try one of these methods to ensure you'll spoon out the fluffiest of servings.

- Soak the rice in a bowl of cold water for 30–60 minutes before cooking. Soaking will also make the rice cook faster. Drain and rinse before cooking.

- Put the rice in a colander and rinse it under cold running water several times to remove the surface starch that makes the grains stick together.

- Add the juice of half a lemon to the cooking water. Grating the lemon rind and adding the zest will give rice another taste note and a bit of visual interest.

Fun with chow fun!

Before being cooked, rice noodles need to soak in room-temperature water for several hours (1 hour at least). If you can't cook the noodles immediately, keep them moist by sandwiching them between damp paper towels.

Curiosity Corner
The Great Spaghetti Tree Hoax!

What's said to be the world's greatest April Fools' joke was pulled on the banger-and-mash loving, fish-and-chips munching British public on April 1, 1957. The BBC news show *Panorama* reported on a bumper spaghetti crop in southern Switzerland, the result of an unusually mild winter.

"The spaghetti harvest here in Switzerland is not, of course, carried out on anything like the tremendous scale of the Italian industry," the respected anchorman Richard Dimbleby intoned, as a rural Swiss family was shown harvesting spaghetti from tree limbs and tucking it into baskets. "Many of you, I'm sure," Dimbleby continued, "will have seen pictures of the vast spaghetti plantations in the Po Valley. For the Swiss, however, it tends to be more of a family affair."

Dimbleby also explained the mystery of tree-grown pasta coming in uniform lengths, calling it "the result of many years of patient endeavor by past [plant] breeders who succeeded in producing the perfect spaghetti."

At the time, spaghetti was rarely eaten in Great Britain, which in those days was slow to embrace foreign food. How many of the audience fell for the joke and how many recognized it instantly for what is was is unknown. What *is* known is that hundreds of viewers called the BBC to inquire about the segment, many of them asking how they could grow and cultivate their own spaghetti trees. Staying in character (and impeccably so), BBC customer service representatives replied, "Place a sprig of spaghetti in a tin of tomato sauce and hope for the best."

Eggs and Cheese

Enrich omelets and scrambled eggs

Hot sauce and salsa, shove over: make your scrambled eggs and omelets silken and sinfully rich by whisking in 1 tablespoon of prepared mayonnaise of any type for each egg.

No more cracks

Keep the shells of hardboiled eggs intact by rubbing them with a lemon before cooking. The shells won't crack and will be much easier to peel once they're cool. Achieve the same result by adding 1 teaspoon lemon juice or a small wedge of lemon to the cooking water.

Devilishly easy

When preparing deviled eggs, take these two steps toward perfect alignment: Keep yolks centered as the eggs boil by stirring the water nonstop. Cut a thin slice off opposite sides of the hardboiled eggs to make the halves stuffed with filling sit up perfectly straight on the serving platter.

Perfect slices

Make hardboiled egg slices neat and clean by lightly wiping or spraying the knife blade with vegetable oil or cooking spray. No oil or spray on hand? Run the knife under cold running water just before slicing.

Spray before grating

A cheese grater is no fun to wash clean, but you can make the job easier by taking action in advance. Just spray the grater with cooking spray or use a clean rag to rub it with vegetable oil.

What's the Story?
The Real Word on Cheese Mold

Some cheeses, like Roquefort, Danish Blue, and Stilton, are moldy by design. But that block of Cheddar in the back of your fridge is moldy because fungus spores have invaded it. The good news is that you can save it. Just cut the moldy area plus at least 1 inch of mold-free cheese off and discard it. If you spot mold on Brie, goat cheese, or another soft cheese, it can't be rescued—so throw it out or you'll risk getting violently ill.

You may have heard that you can "treat" mold on cheese by rubbing a vinegar-soaked rag over the mold. Not true. Nor is the advice to put moldy cheese in a plastic bag with a few sugar cubes, mistakenly said to draw out mold. That's the word from the HomeWise Web site from the University of Idaho. The Web site quotes Dr. Sandra McCurdy, University of Idaho Extension food safety specialist. "By the time you see mold spots in cheese," she reports, "the mold has already begun to put down its invisible 'roots.'" That's the reason deep cuts are necessary to remove mold from hard cheese.

Dr. McCurdy says that cheese mold "just happens" in the home refrigerator. So play it safe. Don't leave cheese out of the fridge for more than two hours, and always keep your eye peeled for even the tiniest spot of mold.

Vegetables and Fruits

Rescue wilted veggies

Revive wilted vegetables by soaking them for an hour in 2 cups water mixed with 1 tablespoon apple cider vinegar. Pat dry and prepare as usual. Alternatively, plunge limp veggies into hot water, remove, and then plunge them into a bowl of ice water mixed with a little cider vinegar.

Easy-cheesy creamed spinach

If you like creamed spinach, you'll go for this recipe. Sauté 1 clove finely minced garlic in 1 tablespoons butter for 30–40 seconds. Add about 20 ounces prewashed spinach leaves and toss until just wilted. Stir in ¼ cup ricotta cheese and salt and freshly ground black pepper to taste, then enjoy a rich and flavorful twist on a favorite side dish. For a low-fat version, use reduced-fat ricotta.

Liven up green beans

Flavor steamed green beans and give them a little kick to boot by tossing them in this mixture: 2 tablespoons melted butter, ½ teaspoon chili powder, and a dash or two of garlic powder.

Got milk?

Adding milk to the cooking water can enhance certain vegetables. Two examples:

- The whiteness of cauliflower becomes all the whiter when you add ⅓ cup milk to the cooking water.
- Sweet corn-on-the-cob gets even sweeter when milk is added to the water.

"Almost the real thing" vegetable lasagna

Here's a recipe that may fool even the most die-hard carnivore. Replace the meat in a lasagna recipe with a mixture of diced zucchini, lentils, and ground walnuts—a combination that closely resembles ground beef. Then just follow the recipe and enjoy a high-protein lasagna that tastes much like the classic meat version.

Quick-bake potatoes

Cut baking time in half (without microwave help!) by choosing smaller potatoes and standing them up in the cups of a muffin tin before putting them in the oven. To reduce baking time for a full-size spud by 15 minutes, insert a long nail into the flesh. This will distribute the heat through the potato more speedily.

Muffin tin hint redux

Stuffed green peppers sometimes lean to one side while cooking in the oven. Give them firm

COFFEE CAN LID AS FRUIT KEEPER

Instead of wasting plastic wrap, try this method of storing a half grapefruit or cantaloupe in the fridge. Simply set the fruit cut-side down on a clean plastic **coffee can lid.**

Store your lemons in water to make them **jucier!**

footing by setting each pepper in the cup of a muffin tin sprayed with a little nonstick cooking spray to ensure easy removal.

Cola-caramelized onions

To ease the work of caramelizing onions, you need only three ingredients: 2–3 sweet Vidalia onions, steak sauce, and cola. Slice the onions about ¾ inches thick and set in a microwavable 9-by-13-inch dish. Pour cola over the onions to cover. Stir in 2 teaspoons steak sauce and microwave at 50 percent power for 30 minutes. No trouble, great taste!

Save those veggie tops!

Beet greens? Fennel fronds? Carrot tops? Don't throw them out! Cut them away from their respective vegetables, wash and dry them well, chop them, and sauté them in a bit of olive oil with garlic to taste for a healthy side dish. Or mince them fine and mix them together with scrambled eggs, salad greens, or leftover pasta.

Toothbrush as veggie cleaner

Use a soft-bristled toothbrush to clean mushrooms and other sensitive vegetables before cooking. A medium- or hard-bristled brush is more suitable for potatoes.

How to slice dried fruit

Have you ever tried to cut dried fruit into small bits only to have your knife stick on the fruit? Simply squeeze a lemon section over the fruit you're about to cut or sprinkle the fruit with a few drops from your pre-squeezed lemon juice. Your knife will slice through with ease.

Juicier lemons

Store your lemons in a sealed jar of water, and when it's time to squeeze them, you'll get twice as much juice. Another trick is to prick the skin once or twice with a sharp knife and then microwave it on medium power for 15 seconds before slicing and squeezing.

Soups and Salads

Quick fix for bland soup

Does your soup lack something ... like, say, *taste*? Kick up the flavor by dissolving a beef or chicken bouillon cube in hot water and whisking it into the soup.

Soup stretchers

If you're heating up leftover soup for two or more people and it looks a little skimpy, stir in some cooked rice or pasta. Pearl barley is also a good soup stretcher, and instant or quick-cooking barley will cook in the simmering broth in less than 15 minutes.

In the bag

As you cut salad ingredients, put them in a small plastic garbage bag (fresh from the box, of course). When you've finished, hold the bag closed with your hand and shake. The ingredients will be thoroughly tossed, and you can refrigerate them in the bag until serving time.

Hold the tomatoes

When making green salads ahead of time, add sliced tomatoes only after the salad is on the plate. The greens in your salad bowl will stay crisper in the fridge sans tomatoes, which contribute to lettuce wilt.

"Fast Italian" Broccoli Salad

It's sexy, all right, and easy. Toss room-temperature steamed broccoli florets in a dressing made with ½ cup plain marinara spaghetti sauce, 2 tablespoons olive oil, 1 tablespoon red wine vinegar, 1 tablespoon chopped Italian parsley, and salt and freshly ground black pepper to taste. Buon appetito!

Straight-to-the-Pot Soup Thickeners

To thicken a soup, add ...

Frozen spinach While your soup is cooking, put clumps of frozen spinach into the pot. If you prefer, defrost the spinach in the microwave and drain off excess liquid.

Sweet potato Prick a few holes in a small sweet potato and microwave it on high for a few minutes until it's partially cooked. Slice into quarters, mash with a fork, and then add the lumpy pulp to the pot. As the soup cooks, use a fork to mash the pulp further, if necessary.

Bread As the soup cooks, remove the crust from a slice or two of bread and dice the bread into small cubes. A hearty multigrain will work like a charm, and rich white bread will do the job, too.

Mashed potatoes or instant potato flakes Don't want to change the flavor of your soup? Then add either of these two forms of potatoes.

Oatmeal Toss a small amount of uncooked plain, quick-cooking oatmeal or even leftover cooked oatmeal into the pot. Because it's bland, oatmeal shouldn't affect your soup's flavor—but to counteract the blandness you may need to add more seasoning.

Keep it fresh

A chef's trick to saving lettuce for up to two weeks is a snap! Pull the leaves off the core, dry them well, fill a sink with cold water and submerge them for 20 minutes. Remove, dry thoroughly, wrap in paper towels, and store in your lettuce keeper.

Clean Hands, Dry Eyes

Any cook knows how hard it can be to get food stains and smells off hands and to chop eye-stinging onions. Fight back with these helpful hints.

Stain-Free Hands

Rub with lemon juice. Berries and beets are notorious stainers. Remove stains by rubbing them with 1–2 teaspoons fresh lemon juice and then washing your hands with soap and water.

Rub with a potato. Even chopped carrots, red bell peppers, and pumpkin can leave their marks. Rub a raw potato on your fingers to help remove the stains.

Odor-Free Hands (onions, garlic, fish)

Rub on stainless steel surface. This strange-but-true chef's trick works: rub garlicky hands repeatedly on a flat stainless steel surface, and they'll be fresh as a daisy.

Rub with rosemary. Rub your hands with sprigs of fresh rosemary to rid them of garlic and onion smells.

Rub with vinegar. Use a little white vinegar as a hand balm. To avoid oniony hands to begin with, rub vinegar over your hands *before* peeling onions.

Rub with salt. Sprinkle table salt into your palm and rub your hands together to remove smells of garlic and onions. Rinse and dry.

Scrub with sugar. Pour 1 tablespoon sugar in your palm, wet it with 1 teaspoon liquid soap, and rub your hands and fingers together as when washing them. Rinse and dry.

Scrub with toothpaste. Handling fish can leave your hands with an odor that just won't quit. Squeeze toothpaste on a washcloth wetted with cold water, then scrub to remove the smell.

Rub with lemon. Cut a lemon, squeeze a good bit of its juice over your hands, and rub hands and fingers together as when washing them. Rinse under running water.

Tear-Free Eyes

"Bread" your knife. Cut a small piece of bread and insert your chopping knife partway down to the hilt. As you slice the onions, the bread will absorb some of the fumes.

Toss onions in the freezer. Freeze onions for 10–15 minutes before slicing them. The cold helps minimize the fumes that cause tears.

Chop near a stove burner. If you can safely position your cutting board on a gas range stovetop, chop onions with one or two of the burners turned on low. The heat attracts onion fumes and neutralizes them.

Light a candle. Burn a candle near your work area to burn off some of the fumes emanating from sliced onions.

Run the faucet Bring your cutting board over near the sink, and run the faucet on cold while you slice your onion; the chemicals released are actually drawn to dampness (hence their ability to make your eyes tear), and will choose a running stream of water instead of your peepers.

Boons for Bakers

Flour taste test

Can't remember whether flour in your canister is all-purpose or self-rising? Taste it. If it's salty, it's self-rising flour, so called because it contains baking powder and salt to make it rise.

Is your baking powder fresh?

You're not sure how long that can of baking powder has been in your pantry, but you can easily learn whether it's still viable. Scoop ½ teaspoon of the powder into a teacup and pour in ¼ cup hot water. If it bubbles up a storm, it's okay to use; if it fizzes only barely, it's time to buy a new can.

Speed dough's rise

Heat makes dough rise more quickly. Still, if it rises too quickly the flavor will suffer—something that cooks who've tried microwaving dough for a few minutes on low power could probably tell you. Instead, position the bowl or pan over the pilot light of a gas stove or on a heating pad set on medium heat.

Keep hands clean

When working with dough, don't flour your hands to prevent dough from sticking to your skin. Instead, pour a few drops of olive oil into your palm and work it into your hands as you would hand lotion.

Easy greasing

Save the waxy wrappers of margarine and butter and put their buttery residue to good use. Store them in a plastic bag in the refrigerator. When a recipe calls for greasing the pan, press one or two of the wrappers into service.

Muffin release

Muffins or cupcakes stuck to the bottom of the metal muffin tin? While the pan is still hot, set it on a wet towel. The condensation in the bottom of the tin will make the treats easier to remove.

Ice in the oven?

Yes, if you're baking bread and want a better loaf. When you put the bread in the oven, put a second pan holding 6–8 ice cubes on one of the oven racks. The resulting steam will help the bread bake more evenly and give it a crispier crust.

Lighten up quick breads

If your favorite special banana-nut bread, cinnamon coffee cake, or carrot-zucchini muffins are super-tasty but heavy, substitute buttermilk for the milk in the recipes; it will lighten the texture of any quick bread you bake. Experiment to find what gives you the best results: all buttermilk, equal parts buttermilk and milk, and so on.

Butter replacement

If a baking recipe calls for so much butter that you feel your arteries clogging just reading it, substitute a 50/50 mixture of unsweetened applesauce and buttermilk. Best used in light-colored or spiced baked goods, this substitute imparts a slightly chewier texture—the reason you'll want to replace all-purpose flour with pastry flour or cake flour.

A honey of a cookie

Honey will help home-baked cookies stay softer and fresher longer. Replace sugar with honey cup for cup, but decrease other liquids in the recipe by ¼ cup per 1 cup honey.

Flowerpot Cookery

Clay pot cookery is a kitchen tradition that goes back thousands of years. Even a simple, unglazed terra cotta flowerpot will work perfectly! Simply wash your unglazed, unpainted, pot in hot soapy water and air-dry. Oil the pot's interior and lip with vegetable oil until the clay will absorb no more. Place the pot on a baking sheet topped with aluminum foil, and place in a cold oven. Heat to 400°F and turn off immediately. Repeat oiling and heating one more time, and your pot is ready to use.

Baking the bread:

1
Lightly grease the interior of a 6-inch flowerpot with vegetable oil or cooking spray.

2
Prepare your favorite bread recipe as usual and roll 12 ounces of dough into a ball. Place in flowerpot and let rise according to the recipe.

3
Bake at 350°F for 25–30 minutes or until the top is golden brown. Let the bread cool on a wire rack and then gently thwack the bottom of the pot to remove it.

How Sweet It Is

Easy creaming
This important step in many a cake recipe—creaming the butter and sugar—can be a tedious and lengthy task. If the butter is cold, you can speed up the creaming process by warming the sugar a bit on the stovetop or in the microwave.

One-egg replacement
If you're baking a cake that calls for one more egg than you have on hand, you can substitute 1 teaspoon of cornstarch.

Or go fruity
Replace one egg in a cake or sweetbread recipe with one small mashed banana or a half-cup of applesauce. For chocolate cakes, try substituting mashed prunes.

Spaghetti cake tester
If you don't have a wire cake tester, use an uncooked strand of spaghetti. Gently push the spaghetti into the center of the cake and pull it out. If your spaghetti comes out clean, the cake is done.

Improvised cake decorator
Use a clean plastic mustard or ketchup squirt bottle as a cake decorator. Fill it with icing and then pipe scallops, flowers, and other designs onto cakes with ease. Or use it to make squiggles of pesto or sour cream on top of soups or chocolate on desserts.

Pie bubbling over?
If a pie starts bubbling over as it bakes, cover any spills with salt. You'll prevent the spill from burning and avoid that terrible scorched smell.

Lick a Yogurtpop!
Lollipops and Popsicles may be fat-free, but they're also mostly sugar. A custard-style frozen yogurtpop, on the other hand, is full of healthful stuff—and to most palates, a lot tastier.

Making a yogurtpop couldn't be simpler. Just spray unflavored cooking spray into a small paper cup (the kind dispensed at water fountains), spoon in your favorite yogurt, and freeze. In about a half hour, insert a sturdy plastic spoon in the middle, bowl side first.

Depending on the temperature of your freezer, the pops should be ready in about an hour. For a pop that will remind you of the old Creamsicle of your youth, blend vanilla yogurt with softened frozen orange juice concentrate and freeze as directed above.

Best of all, the treated overflow will bake into a dry, light crust that you can wipe off easily when the oven has cooled.

Make piecrust flakier
Flaky piecrusts are the talented baker's hallmark. You can improve flakiness by replacing 1 tablespoon ice water in your crust recipe with 1 tablespoon chilled lemon juice or white vinegar.

Fruit piecrusts too soggy?
To keep the juice in fruit from seeping into the crust of a baking pie, crumble up something to absorb it. A layer of plain, crisp flatbread will absorb the juice and introduce a savory note to the pie, while biscotti or amaretti cookies will keep it tasting sweet.

Slice meringue with ease

Your knife will glide through a meringue-topped pie if you butter it on both sides before slicing. A 10-second solution, if that!

Thrifty chocolates

If you're a chocoholic, have extra freezer space, and are always looking for ways to pinch pennies, this hint may be tailor-made for you. Buy chocolate Easter bunnies and Santas after the holidays when prices are slashed. Store them in the freezer, and then melt them or shave off chocolate curls for use when cooking. Or, if you prefer, just thaw Old Saint Nick and gobble him up whenever you need a chocolate fix.

Turn coffee into granita

Use a yogurt cup to make this refreshing icy dessert, similar to Italian ice. Pour freshly brewed coffee into several clean yogurt cups or similar small-size containers to freeze. Remove and then plop the frozen coffee into the food processor. Process on the frappe setting until crystals form. Spoon the crystals into the cups and freeze for about a half hour before serving.

Homemade granita options: Add milk and sugar (or sugar substitute) to your coffee before freezing or just go with black. Good toppings for granita include whipped cream and a sprinkling of cinnamon.

No cake tester? Use a strand of *raw spaghetti* instead!

Smart Solutions, Easy Improvements

Marinate in plastic bags

You can eliminate washing bowls, spoons, and even pots by marinating meats and poultry in large self-sealing plastic bags. Open the bag and pour in the liquids and seasonings—soy sauce, ketchup, ground ginger, black pepper, crushed garlic, herbs, and so on. Zip the bag shut and shake it to blend. Now add the meat, zip the bag, and shake. Refrigerate 6–8 hours or overnight. Occasionally take the bag out of the fridge and shake it to redistribute the marinade.

Butter stops the dribbles

Dab a bit of butter onto the spout of your creamer or milk pitcher and you'll put an end to the drips and dribbles.

Oil your measuring cup

Sticky liquids like honey and syrup are tough to measure and pour, and a little always remains behind. Oiling the measuring cup will make it harder for viscous liquids to stick and will give you a more accurate serving.

Keep salt on popcorn

Want salt to stick better to hot-air popcorn? Give it something to cling to by lightly coating just-popped corn with vegetable-based cooking spray. Avoid olive oil cooking spray because the flavor can overpower popcorn's taste.

Add tang to sauce with ginger ale

Ginger ale will perk up tomato sauces, but be careful not to overdo it. A third of a cup of ginger ale added to a medium-size saucepan of marinara or a tomato juice–based beef stew will subtly enhance the flavor.

Brighten the taste of OJ

For fresher flavor in orange juice, add the juice of 1 lemon per half gallon. By the glass, squeeze in the juice of a quarter lemon, then set the rind on the rim for a bit of flair.

Flavor plain chips

Bet you didn't know how easy it is to make your own garlic-flavored potato chips. Just place a peeled garlic clove in a bag of plain chips, fasten the bag shut with a clamp or clothespin, and let sit for 6–8 hours; shake the bag occasionally to even out the flavor. Open the bag, discard the clove, and crunch away.

Dress up pancake syrup

Adding chopped strawberries and a little lemon zest to syrup will make it a lot more interesting. Combine ½ cup pancake syrup, ½ cup strawberries, and ½ teaspoon grated orange rind in a microwavable bowl and heat on high power for 30–60 seconds. Top pancakes, waffles, or French toast with the syrup and dig into what's now a tastier and more healthful dish. (Strawberries are packed with vitamin C and manganese.)

Savvy Substitutions

No lemon?

When a recipe calls for lemon juice and the one you thought was in the fruit bowl has flown the coop, a lime is obviously your best bet should you have one on hand. If not, use the same amount of white wine.

Salt mimic

A chef's trick for reducing the amount of salt in a recipe is to replace it with half as much lemon juice. If a recipe calls for ½ teaspoon of salt, substitute ¼ teaspoon lemon juice and shelve the sodium.

Vanilla imitators

If you run out of vanilla just as the batter recipe calls for it, substitute an equal amount of maple syrup or a liqueur such as Frangelico or Baileys Irish Cream.

Powder for powder

Cake recipes often call for baking powder, but if you're without it, try this: For each teaspoon called for, substitute a mix of ½ teaspoon cream of tartar and ¼ teaspoon baking soda. The mixture won't store well, so make it fresh should you ever need it again.

Ersatz bread crumbs

Making a meatloaf or meatballs, but you're running short of bread crumbs? Substitute oatmeal, crushed unsweetened cereal, crumbled crackers, or instant mashed potato flakes.

A surprising pan prepper

You've got the vegetables chopped, the meat ready, and you're about to fire up your skillet when you discover that you're out of oil. Rub the skillet with half of a potato, and your food won't stick.

Caught Without Cookware?

You loaned your cake pans to a neighbor, she's on vacation, and you want to bake a cake. Or you're the one who's on vacation, and the supposedly fully equipped cabin in the woods you've rented can't even cough up a loaf pan for the carrot-zucchini bread you crave during your back-to-basics stay. Here are great solutions when you don't have the pot or pan or small appliance you need:

Ceramic bowls Use an ovenproof ceramic bowl in place of a cake pan, or try ovenproof cereal bowls for individual cakes. Just be sure to place them on a baking tray before putting them in the oven; bowls can be too hot to handle even with hot pads or a dishtowel.

Coffee can A quick bread will bake just fine in a coffee can. Be sure to spray the interior with nonstick cooking spray and dust with flour.

Dutch oven If you don't have a slow cooker, a Dutch oven will do the job just as well. Combine the ingredients for your stew or braised dish in the pot, cover, and cook in a slow oven (250–350°F) for 3–4 hours or until any meat in the dish is fork-tender.

Sour cream stand-in

To make a substitute for 1 cup sour cream, blend 1 cup cottage cheese, ⅓ cup buttermilk, and 1 tablespoon lemon juice until smooth. The lemon juice will sour its creamy partners.

Practical Advice

Stop the drip

Wrap a terry-cloth sweatband, headband, or bandana around a bottle of olive oil to prevent drips. When your wrap becomes too oily, just toss it in the washing machine.

Elbow grease aid

Trouble twisting off the lid of a new jar of spaghetti sauce, applesauce, or such? Turn the jar upside down and give it a thwack with the heel of your hand; you should hear a popping sound, signaling the release of air. Now turn the jar over, and you may be able to twist off the lid with ease.

Separate packaged bacon

Before opening a package of bacon, curl the package up with your hands a few times, turning it over each time. When you open the package, you'll find it easier to peel away individual slices.

Keep wooden tools in good shape

Sprinkle your wooden salad bowls and cutting boards with salt and then rub them with a lemon to freshen them. The salt-and-lemon treatment will help your salad bowl to impart freshness, not smells, to the ingredients. And when you chop, slice, and dice, your knife won't lift any dried wood bits from the board.

"Micropeel" garlic

Here's a tip to make working with garlic a snap. Microwave garlic cloves for 15 seconds and the skins will slip right off, allowing you to slice, mince, and chop without delay. Bonus hint: As you chop garlic, juices released make the tiny

Flatten That Cookbook!

You're following a recipe in your favorite cookbook—a big book chock-full of pages. But every time you turn your back to add a new ingredient or stir the batter, the pages flip and you lose your place. It's enough to make your blood boil like a bubbling stockpot! To call a truce in the book battle, you could buy a Plexiglas cookbook holder or you could use something you already have: a clear glass baking dish. Just turn to the page where your recipe is printed and flatten the book with the dish. It will not only keep your cookbook open but also will give you a crystal-clear view of the type.

pieces stick to your knife. Sprinkling a bit of salt on both the cutting board and the garlic will go a long way toward solving the problem.

Super lid opener

Too-tight lids on jars can make you feel like a weakling when they just won't budge. A simple way to get them open? Don a pair of rubber dishwashing gloves. With your grip secured, the lid will twist off with minimal effort.

Don't forget the ice cube tray!

Whether you're preparing baby food, storing leftover sauces, or making perfect-sized portions of no-cook fudge, the flexible plastic ice cube tray is your invaluable multitasker. It's a versatile kitchen aid you don't want to forget.

Who'da Thunk It Helpers

Hair dryer as salad green dryer

You've rinsed and spun your salad, but those green leaves are still wet. Don't waste paper towels to dry each one; instead, set your hair dryer on low/cool and gently wave it over the greens.

Teaspoon as a ginger peeler

Finding it impossible to peel ginger without losing some of its precious flesh? Here's a chef's secret: If you're a righty, hold the ginger in your left hand, and using a teaspoon, firmly scrape the edge of the spoon along the knob with your right. The papery skin will peel right off.

Dental floss as slicer

Held taut, floss slices layer cakes, tender quick breads, soft cheeses, butter, and plenty of other soft foods even better than a sharp knife.

Plastic soda bottle as funnel

Cut off the top third of the bottle and turn it upside down. Now you can easily funnel leftover sauces, gravies, kidney beans, or even grease into containers for storage or trash.

Handsaw as rib separator

A sharp (and rust-free) handsaw works wonders when you're serving those juicy racks of ribs at your annual summertime gathering. Slip the blade between the bones, give it one or two good saws, and the result will be perfectly separated ribs.

Coffee filter as gravy strainer

Beef and poultry drippings from a roast make the most delicious, flavorful gravy base but are often small grease bombs. Save the flavor and kill the fat by straining the cooking juices through a paper coffee filter.

Scissors as herb chopper

Use clean household scissors to snip fresh herbs and green onions into salads or mixing bowls. Scissors are also perfect for cutting steam vents in the top crust of a pie about to be put in the oven.

Flowerpots as kitchen tool caddie

Store serving spoons, whisks, tongs, and other kitchen tools in flowerpots set at the back of a countertop. To make the pots more decorative, paint each one in a different pastel color.

Wood rasp as lemon zester

A clean, fine metal rasp from your toolbox or workshop is the perfect zester for lemons, limes, oranges, and virtually any other citrus fruit. Its tiny raised nubs scrape the fruit's skin and leave zest of a perfect granularity that would please the fussiest chef.

SHOEHORN AS CORN KERNEL REMOVER

A clean **shoehorn** has at least two uses in the kitchen. Scrape the wide end along a corn cob to remove the kernels, and use the narrow end to gently release baked muffins from their tin.

Storing Fresh Food

A surplus of spuds?

If you find you've peeled too many potatoes for a potato salad or casserole, don't toss the uncooked extras. Put them in a bowl, cover with cold water, and add a few drops of vinegar. Now they will keep in the fridge for 3–4 days.

Brown-bag your lettuce

Lettuce will keep longer if you transfer it from a plastic bag to a roomier paper bag before storing it in the refrigerator. Lettuce likes a little air, but don't think that calls for removing the limp and discolored outermost leaves; they may not be pretty, but these leaves help keep the inner leaves crisper.

TLC for contents of crispers

Line the crisper drawer of your refrigerator with paper towels, which will absorb the excess moisture that does no favors for the veggies inside. Replace the towels as they become damp. Another way to dehumidify the drawer is to tuck two or three brand new clean kitchen sponges among the vegetables, squeezing moisture out over the sink as needed.

Toast freshens lettuce

Keep lettuce crisp in your refrigerator by storing it in a sealed plastic bag with a slice of almost-burned toast. The toast will absorb some of the excess moisture that would otherwise wilt the lettuce. As long as you replace the toast when it gets soggy, the lettuce should stay crisp for up to two weeks.

Keep greens fork fresh

Keep kale, collards, mustard greens, and other greens fresh longer by storing them in the refrigerator with a stainless steel fork or knife. Just open the storage bag, slip in the utensil, and reclose.

Celery Care 101

Celery is all about crispness, so when it starts to go soft, you may as well throw it out. Right? Not necessarily. Try this first: Put limp stalks in a bowl of cold water with a few slices of raw potato. After an hour or so in this starchy bath, the stalks may deliver the crunch you expect.

What's the Story?
Deciphering Dates on Food Packages

The packages of most perishable foods are marked with a date indicating how long you may consume the product. But guess what? Except for infant formula and some baby foods, there are no federal regulations governing product dating in regard to safety. The best you can do is understand the three types of dating that food manufacturers stamp on their products.

The sell-by date tells a store how long to keep a product on the shelves, but the period for safe use of the product is longer. Exactly how much longer, however, is uncertain.

The best-if-used-by date is the last date the product will be at its peak quality or flavor and has nothing to do with food safety.

The use-by date gives the last day the manufacturer recommends you should use the product, and therefore may be the most helpful.

keep your eggs fresh for weeks
by coating them
with oil

Even crisp celery may turn brown, but you can stop browning before it starts. Before storing the stalks in the fridge, soak them for 30 minutes in 1 quart cold water mixed with 1 teaspoon lemon juice—a trick that will also crisp celery just before it's served.

Get the most out of a lemon

When a recipe calls for a few drops of lemon, don't slice the lemon and squeeze. Simply puncture the rind with a toothpick and gently squeeze out the small amount of juice you need. Then cover the hole with a piece of tape and store the lemon in the fridge for later use. Waste not, want not!

Oiled eggs

Prolong the life of fresh eggs by dipping a paper towel into vegetable oil and rubbing the shells before storing the eggs in the fridge. The oil will keep the eggs fresh for an additional 3–4 weeks!

Vinegar and cheese

To keep cheese fresh, wrap it in a piece of soft cloth dampened with vinegar. It should come as no surprise that cheesecloth is ideal for the purpose.

Store potatoes with ginger

Unused potatoes will last longer if you add a piece of fresh gingerroot to their storage bin. It's said that one root vegetable helps keep another root vegetable fresh—and a potato tuber is a root of sorts.

Longer-lasting milk

If you buy more milk than you can use before the expiration date, extend its life with couple of pinches of baking soda. Baking soda reduces milk's acidity, thus staving off spoilage.

Storing Baked Goods

Cookies on tissue

Keep crisp cookies crisp by crumpling tissue paper (the kind popular as gift-wrap) and placing it in the bottom of the cookie jar. It will help absorb any moisture that seeps in.

The birthday cake's in the bag

If you want to bake a cake for a special occasion down the road—like your daughter's 21st birthday or your parent's golden wedding anniversary party—you can actually bake it several months ahead of time and freeze it. The trick is to triple-wrap the layers. Here's how:

1. After taking three layer pans out of the oven, let the layers cool completely.

2. Wrap each layer separately in plastic wrap and then in aluminum foil, making each package as airtight as possible.

3. Pop all three layers into a large freezer bag and seal it, squeezing out the air as you do.

When the big day arrives, defrost the layers before removing the wrap. Then assemble the cake and frost it, secure in the knowledge that your creation will taste as fresh as if it were baked yesterday.

Instant cake dome

If you don't have a fancy cake plate with a glass dome, keep your cake fresh and the frosting intact by covering it with a large bowl turned upside down.

Well-bread cake

Once you cut into a scrumptious three-layer cake, the exposed part of what's left gets stale quickly. Here's a way to slow drying. Place a slice of bread over the cut surface of the cake and hold it in place with a couple of toothpicks. As the bread dries out, the cake will stay moist for later enjoyment.

A trick for store-bought pies

You've eaten two slices of a luscious peach pie and start to wrap it with plastic wrap. Not so fast! If you cover the pie first with an upside down paper plate or aluminum foil pie plate and then wrap it in plastic, the pie will have a little breathing room and stay fresh for a week or more.

Storing a meringue-topped pie

When storing the remains of a meringue pie in the fridge, how do you cover it without ruining the meringue? Rub a large piece of plastic wrap with a stick of butter, making sure it's greased completely. Fit it over the pie plate butter-side down. The next time you want a slice of pie, the wrap will peel off without sticking.

A crisp bread freshener

To keep sliced bread fresh longer, just stick a small, fresh stalk of celery in the bag with the bread. Celery has a high water content but stays dry on the outside, so what better moisturizer could you find?

An apple every two days

The moisture from an apple will keep soft cookies soft. Just place the cookies in an airtight tin and put an apple slice (skin side down) on top before closing it. Replace the apple slice every two days if any resident cookie monsters haven't already polished off the contents.

Freeze Breeze!

That big icy compartment above (or below) your refrigerator can do far more than just store meats and instant waffles. Here's how to use it to make everyday items (including ice cubes!) go the distance:

"Instant" tea

When you brew a full pot of tea and have a lot left over, pour the tea into ice cube trays and freeze it. Later, you can use the tea cubes to chill a fresh batch of iced tea without diluting it, or melt the cubes in the microwave instead of brewing a fresh pot. You can freeze surplus coffee in the same way.

Freeze eggs?

Yes, but only raw yolks and whites. Just break eggs into an air-tight plastic container and add 1 teaspoon of salt or honey for each cup of eggs. (About five whole eggs make a cup.) Cover the container and mark it with the additive you chose so you'll know whether to use the thawed eggs in a sweet or savory recipe.

Brown-bag ice cubes

Keep ice cubes from sticking together by storing them in your freezer inside a paper bag. (It'll keep you from cursing as you wield an ice pick or hammer.)

Crystal-free ice cream

When you serve only part of a package of ice cream and return the rest to the freezer, ice crystals tend to form on the surface. You can prevent crystals from forming by tucking a layer of plastic wrap onto the surface of the ice cream before closing the carton and putting it back in the freezer.

Breathe Life into Leftovers

Surplus grilled tuna or salmon

If you grilled too much salmon or tuna for that dinner party, you have the base for a tasty salad. In a large bowl, combine 1½ cups cooked tuna or salmon, a 15-ounce can of white beans, 3 thinly sliced green onions, 2 tablespoons Italian parsley, 1 minced garlic clove, and ⅓ cup of your favorite Italian dressing. Toss and enjoy!

Long life for veggies

Save all leftover veggies for up to a week. Dice them; lightly sauté your mixture in olive oil with savory seasonings such as oregano, basil, and black pepper. Add leftover rice or other grains. Use as filling for a quiche or to fortify a meatloaf.

Get a head start on gravy

Whirl almost any kind of leftover soup that has no bones in a blender or food processor to make a quick sauce or gravy for vegetables or meat.

Jazz up salsa

Add leftover corn kernels to your jarred salsa. Stirring in corn will not only make for a more colorful presentation but will also tone down a salsa you find too hot for your taste.

Oatmeal muffins

Don't toss out the unserved cooked cereal left in the pot when breakfast is done. Instead, use it in batter when making muffins. Add the baking powder, eggs, and other ingredients as the recipe directs, and you may find you like the result.

Beware of the Great Thaw

If there's a power outage in your home while you're on vacation, it's essential for you to know about it before you return home and go foraging in your freezer. If your electric power was off for a long time and the food in the freezer thawed and refroze, the entire household could come down with food poisoning.

How to know whether the power goes out when you travel? Before you leave, place a plastic bag full of ice cubes in your freezer, and check it when you return. If the cubes have become a solid block, a power outage of some duration occurred. If the ice cubes are as you left them, all is well.

Overripe fruit = great smoothies

Don't relegate overripe fruit to the compost or trash. Freeze it and call on your frozen bananas, strawberries, and peaches to make a delicious smoothie with yogurt or your liquid of choice. Your smoothies may even taste better, thanks to the concentrated sugars in overripe fruit.

Leftover wine makes great salad dressings

Don't pour that leftover red or white down the drain! Put it in an airtight jar and store it in the fridge. When it's time to make a vinaigrette, you can combine the wine even-steven with vinegar for a dressing with extra punch.

Freeze leftover wine

If a few inches of pinot grigio or zinfandel remain in the bottle at the end of a party or meal, don't let it go to waste. Pour it into an ice cube tray, and the next time you're making a sauce, a casserole, soups, or stews that call for a splash of white or red, you'll have it handy. The cube will melt quickly, so no defrosting will be required.

Red wine as meat tenderizer

If you have some leftover red wine, put it to work as a meat tenderizer and marinade. Simply put the meat in a self-sealing bag or lidded container and pour the leftover wine over it. Whether cooked on the grill or under the broiler, the meat on the plate will have a juicy, tender texture.

Remember the croquette

How much leftover chicken do you have on hand? Make too much ham for the holidays? Talking too much turkey? Never fear..the croquette is here! Mince the offending leftover very finely to make 2 cups, add a tablespoon or two of prepared white sauce and a beaten egg, shape into tightly packed, small logs, and refrigerate for an hour. Remove the croquettes from the fridge, roll in fine breadcrumbs, heat up a few tablespoons of vegetable oil in a stickproof frying pan, and lightly fry until golden brown. The best news? If you don't finish these leftovers, they'll freeze perfectly ... for up to six months! Talk about going the distance!

Leftover sauce from pot roast?

Turn it into a homemade ragu so good that your family will think that a real chef is in the kitchen! Chop up small pieces of leftover pot roast, return it to its sauce, add 2 cups of red wine and 2 cans of crushed tomatoes. Blend well, bring to a simmer, cover, and continue to cook for 30 minutes.

Household Superstar!

10 Cool Uses for Resealable Kitchen Storage Bags

1 Speed the ripening of fruit by sealing it in a bag.

2 Crush graham crackers for piecrust by putting them in a bag and running a rolling pin over it.

3 Crush nuts by placing them in a plastic bag and pounding them with a hammer.

4 Put the ingredients for meatloaf in a plastic bag, seal it, and gently massage the bag.

5 Seal frozen poultry in a plastic bag and submerge it in cold water for several hours for the safest way to thaw chicken, turkey, and game birds.

6 Marinate meat and poultry in a large plastic bag placed in a shallow bowl in the refrigerator.

7 Knead dough in a large plastic bag to keep your hands from getting sticky.

8 Turn a plastic bag into a pastry bag by snipping off a small corner.

9 Protect the recipe card you're using from splatters by enclosing it in a plastic bag.

10 Use a plastic bag as a glove when the phone rings and your hands are oily or covered in flour.

Setting the Perfect Table

Mini bouquets

When your garden is in bloom, cut small bouquets and arrange them in empty jam jars, glass water bottles, or clean mustard pots. If you have a long table, line them up in the center for a centerpiece your guests will remember.

Color coordinate your vases

Add another dimension to the floral arrangements you use as a centerpiece. A few drops of food coloring in the water of a clear glass vase will make a pretty setting prettier.

Can it

Some products, including Italian plum tomatoes and espresso, come in especially artful cans. Once you've consumed the contents, use the cans to create a centerpiece. Set small leafy green plants of different heights in three cans and arrange the colorful planters in the center of the table.

The sit-down test

Before your guests arrive, make sure that your centerpiece isn't so tall that it will block their line of vision: place your centerpiece in the middle of the table, pull out a chair, and take a seat. If the tallest flowers or other decorative items are taller than face height, shorten them so that guests can make eye contact.

You've been framed!

Use small picture frames (matched or unmatched) as place cards holders. If you're

a practiced calligrapher, write each guest's name on a piece of good-quality paper cut to fit the frame, or simply choose a nice computer font and print out your guests' names. Slide each "card" into its frame.

Mix and (mis)match?

When good friends are coming over for a dinner party, make things more interesting and unexpected by varying the place settings—a brightly colored Fiesta Dinnerware plate here, a rose-patterned fine china plate there. The result is not only eclectic, but also a great conversation starter.

Use Grandma's silver

Gone are the days when silver was hauled out only on special occasions; use it for everyday casual dinner parties as a reminder of that great woman. Don't worry if it's tarnished … it'll lend the table a bit of retro character!

Ready to Serve

No time to dust?

Let low mood lighting help out! Make a beeline for all the candles you own and place them (carefully, and not near drapes) around the living room and dining room—votive candles on windowsills, candelabras on the mantelpiece, pillar and jar candles here and there. If the lights in both rooms have dimmers, set the light to barely there and bask in the complexion-enhancing, dirt-hiding glow.

No-stick napkins

How to keep napkins from sticking to the bottom of your drinking glasses? Press the bottom of each glass in a plateful of salt, then shake off excess salt. However scant, the salt should break the bond and keep napkin and glass separated.

Chill wine in a hurry

Here's a foolproof way to quick-chill champagne and other white wines. Place the bottle in an ice bucket or other tall plastic container, and add just enough ice cubes to make a 2-inch layer on the bottom. Sprinkle the ice with a few tablespoons of salt and continue to layer ice and salt up to the neck of the bottle. Now add cold water until it reaches the top of the ice. After only 15 minutes (about half the time it would take in a freezer), you'll be able to uncork the bottle and pour properly chilled bubbly for your guests.

Wine bottle cork won't budge?

Run hot water over a towel and wrap the towel around the neck of a stubborn wine bottle. This easy treatment will help the glass neck of the bottle expand just enough to make the cork easier to pull out.

Serve Food in Food

Fruits, breads, and vegetables all make terrific edible receptacles and pretty presentations.

Hard rolls Slice the top off a sourdough roll or other hard roll and remove bread from the interior. Then fill with individual portions of tuna or chicken salad for each guest at your table.

Bell peppers Hollow out red, yellow, or green bell peppers, slice a bit off the bottom so they'll stand straight, and use as condiment "dishes" on your buffet or picnic table.

Pineapple After you carve the fruit out of a pineapple, the shell makes a lovely serving platter—especially for a tiki party! Halve the rind lengthwise and be sure to leave the leaves on.

Melons Hollow out a cantaloupe or honeydew melon half, and serve honeydew chunks in the cantaloupe shell and vice versa. Clever!

Martini-style salads

Dress up the simplest of salads by lining martini glasses with lettuce leaves and add a scoop of chicken, tuna, or egg salad. Pierce an olive with a toothpick and set it in the salad at an angle, à la the classic martini.

Dine alfresco

Why stay inside on a nice evening? Move dinner outside! Cover your patio table with a simple bedsheet (fancy or not), bring your chairs outside, light some candles, and create an instant moveable feast!

Chapter Two

Canny Kitchen Cleanups

The kitchen is the heart of the home, but let's face it: It can also be the messiest room in the house. The unwashed dishes, the overstuffed cabinets and cupboards, the splattered stove top—if you have little time on your hands or a large family, you might think that a dirty kitchen is just a fact of life. Guess again!

The good news is that to keep a kitchen clean, you don't have to spend money on those overpriced or supercheap miracle cleansers and gizmos advertised on TV. To keep your kitchen organized, you don't need a bachelor's degree in organizational management, either. All it takes is a bit of resolve and a good browse of the following pages packed with timesaving, money-saving hints and tips on how to make your kitchen a clean, calm oasis.

Wipe away
pencil marks with
rye bread!

Wash Up, Wipe Down

Add vinegar to your mop water

Add a few drops of white vinegar to your mopping bucket to remove soap traces. If the floor is linoleum or vinyl tile, add a little baby oil to the mop water to bring a soft gleam to the surface—a mere 1 or 2 capfuls at most, or you'll turn the floor into a skating rink.

Bleach painted walls

Mix a solution of 1 gallon water and ½ cup chlorine bleach to give your kitchen walls a brightening sponge-down after frying or sautéing.

Erase pencil marks with rye bread

Remove your young Picasso's kitchen wall pencil sketches with a slice of fresh rye bread (seeded or not). An art-gum eraser can also erase the marks, without the thrill.

Wash away wallpaper grime

If your kitchen walls are covered with waterproof wallpaper, remove excess dirt with a vacuum cleaner, then wash the walls with a solution of ½ cup lemon juice, ½ cup dishwashing liquid, and 1 quart water. Before starting, wash a tiny section in an out-of-sight place to make sure the paper will tolerate the mixture.

Keep stainless steel stainless

Stainless steel kitchen sinks aren't quite as immune to ugly marks as their name suggests. Here are some solutions to various problems:

- **Rust marks** Rub the area with a drop of lighter fluid, and then clean it with non-abrasive scouring powder and water.

Red Alert

It's easy to accidentally turn on the switch that activates the garbage disposal when you really meant to flip a light switch. The resulting racket and grinding action can be startling—and even dangerous. To stay on the safe side, paint the disposal switch with some bright red nail polish so there's no mistaking which switch is which.

- **Water marks** Rub with a cloth dampened with rubbing alcohol.
- **Other marks** Rub marks with white vinegar or club soda, both of which are excellent polishers.

Lemon stain lifter

Getting that tomato sauce stain off your countertop or cabinet is easier than you think. Simply wet the stain with lemon juice, let sit for 30 minutes or so, and then sprinkle baking soda on the abrasive side of an all-purpose kitchen sponge and scrub the discolored area. Most stains will vanish, and your kitchen will smell fresher.

Sterilize your sink

Germs can hang around in your sink on microscopic food particles. To kill them off, fill a spray bottle with full-strength rubbing alcohol. After you finish washing dishes, spray the sink with alcohol and then rub it down with a clean dishtowel or paper towel.

Tea thyme for porcelain

Charming though they are, porcelain sinks are hard to clean because abrasive cleaners dull (and often scratch) porcelain surfaces. Take the gentle route and clean your sink with fresh lemon thyme tea. Place 4–5 bunches of fresh lemon thyme in a 3-gallon metal bucket and fill it with boiling water. Steep for 5–6 hours and strain. Stop up your sink, pour in the tea, and let it sit overnight. When you drain it the next morning, you'll find a gleaming white sink that smells fresh as, well, a sprig of lemon thyme.

Almost-free all-purpose cleaner

Why buy an antibacterial spray cleaner if you can make one in less than five minutes? Combine 1 cup rubbing alcohol, 1 cup water, and 1 tablespoon white vinegar in a spray bottle. Spritz on kitchen surfaces including tile and chrome, wipe off, and watch how quickly the germ-killing polish evaporates.

Dynamic grease-busting duo

The chemistry between baking soda and vinegar is so powerful that this combo can flush grease out of kitchen drains. Just pour ½ cup baking soda into a clogged drain and follow it with ½ cup white vinegar. Cover the drain for a few minutes as the chemical reaction dissolves the grease—then flush the drain with warm water. A caveat: Never use this method after trying a commercial drain cleaner; the cleaner could react with vinegar to create dangerous fumes.

Ice-cold disposal degreaser

Degrease your garbage disposal by occasionally grinding five or six ice cubes along with ½ cup baking soda. The ice congeals the grease, priming it for attack by the fast-acting sodium bicarbonate and sending it down the drain. To flush out any residue, fill the stoppered sink with 2–3 inches hot water and run the water through the disposal.

Household Superstar!
10 Nonbaking Uses for Baking Soda

1 Remove stains from plastic utensils and rubber spatulas with a baking soda paste rubbed on with a sponge or scouring pad.

2 Protect stained enamel cookware, which can be scratched by abrasive cleaners, by coating the stain with a baking soda paste—then wipe it off after an hour.

3 Add 2 tablespoons of baking soda to your dishwashing liquid to clean greasy dishes.

4 Deodorize your dishwasher by pouring in half a box of baking soda and running the empty washer through the rinse cycle.

5 Dip a damp cloth in baking soda and rub it on china to remove coffee stains.

6 Shine stainless steel by sprinkling it with baking soda and rubbing with a damp cloth.

7 Moisten grease stains on your stovetop with water, cover them with baking soda, and wipe clean with a damp cloth.

8 Clean your coffeemaker by brewing 1 quart of water mixed with ¼ cup baking soda.

9 Loosen burned-on food from cast iron skillets by adding 2 tablespoons baking soda to 1 quart water and boiling the solution for 5 minutes.

10 Remove residue from a thermos by putting in ¼ cup baking soda and 1 quart water and letting it soak overnight.

Kitchen Odor Chasers

Borax in the bin
Garbage cans are great incubators for odor-causing mold and bacteria. To fend off accumulations of these microscopic marauders, sprinkle ½ cup borax in the bottom of your garbage can and renew it with every emptying.

Cabbage as culprit
Boiled cabbage is one of the most healthful foods around, but the odor it gives off as it cooks is a major turn-off. To sweeten the air (and perk up cabbage's flavor at the same time), add half a lemon to the cooking water.

Bake a batch of brownies
There's no better natural kitchen deodorizer than a batch of baking brownies. Doesn't matter if they're homemade or out of a box, and your family will thank you for it.

Bake an air freshener
Don't buy an air freshener when you can get rid of kitchen odors at a fraction of the cost with baked lemon. Simply slice 2 lemons, put them on a foil-lined cookie sheet, and bake them in a preheated oven at 225°F for 60–90 minutes. To prolong the cleansing effect once the heat's turned off, open the oven door and leave the lemons on the rack for a few hours.

Odor-killing drain cleaner
Using salt and baking soda to unclog a drain will put an end to bad drain odors at the same time. Pour 1 cup salt into the drain followed by 1 cup baking soda. Pour a kettle full of boiling water down the drain and let all that hard-working sodium get busy.

Disposal deodorizers
Wherever food gets ground up every day, odor-causing bacteria follow, thriving in the cracks and crevices deep inside a garbage disposal. To keep unpleasant smells from wafting out of your disposal, try grinding any of these odor busters:

- Citrus peels—lemon, lime, orange, or grapefruit

- Two or three bunches of fresh mint

SPICE IN THE AIR

When kitchen air gets stale, liven it up by simmering a handful of whole cloves, 3–4 whole nutmegs, 4–5 **cinnamon sticks**, and perhaps a few **orange** or lemon **peels** in a large pot of water for an hour. But don't just pour this bubbling deodorizer down the drain! Instead, strain the cooled liquid into spray bottles and use it in the kitchen and elsewhere whenever the air could use a little freshening.

Debugging the Kitchen

Store flour and rice with bay leaves

Tiny sawtooth grain weevils, rice weevils, and other bugs can enter paper or cardboard containers of flour, rice, oatmeal, and breakfast cereal through the tiniest of cracks. Keep them at bay (so to speak) by putting a few dried bay (also known as laurel) leaves in the containers.

Freeze the buggers

Some bug eggs are in the containers before you bring your groceries home and have yet to hatch. Kill off any eggs by keeping your products in the freezer for the first day or two.

Two other bug chasers

One or two whole nutmegs buried in a sack of flour or box of rice or such will help keep weevils and other tiny invaders out. Some people claim to have successfully repelled bugs by placing sticks of spearmint gum (unwrapped) at different points on the floor of the cabinet where susceptible foodstuffs are stored.

Pop goes the weevil

If your dried beans or peas are under attack by hungry weevils, add a bit of dried hot pepper to the storage container. They'll hotfoot it out of the box or bag in a flash.

Ants hate grits

It's not that ants don't like to eat this dried-corn breakfast food; they just don't like crawling over powdery or grainy substances. When you see a line of ants on the march in your kitchen, spoon a long thin line of grits in their path and watch them beat a retreat.

make your own
Flypaper

Houseflies gravitate to the kitchen because—you got it—that's where the food is. Take a cue from housekeepers of old and trap flies with flypaper, which you can easily make all by yourself.

Sticky-Icky Flypaper

Hang these sticky strips underneath top cabinets, in doorways, and from window frames. No hooks needed—just secure the string hangers with masking tape or duct tape.

> 1 brown paper grocery bag
> String
> Tape
> ⅔ cup sugar
> ⅔ cup light corn syrup
> ⅔ cup water

1. Cut the bag into strips 1½ inches wide and 1–3 feet long. Cut 5-to-6-inch pieces of string and secure them to the top of the strips with transparent tape.

2. Combine sugar, corn syrup, and water in a heavy 2-quart saucepan and bring the mixture to a boil over high heat.

3. Reduce the heat to medium and cook until the liquid thickens.

4. Use a pastry brush to coat the strips with the liquid, and then hang them wherever flies congregate.

Keep bugs out of your grains with **bay leaves!**

Spicy ant repellents

If you know where ants are entering your kitchen from the outside, sprinkle a good bit of cayenne pepper or ground cinnamon outside their door as an unmistakable "not welcome" mat. Ants have an aversion to both the powdery texture and powerful smell of these spices.

Fend off fruit flies

No need to keep the fruit bowl empty on the kitchen countertop just because these unwanted guests tend to help themselves. Send them packing with one of the following:

- **Mint or basil leaves** Scatter a few mint or basil sprigs near fresh fruit when you set it out; fruit flies hate the smell and will stay clear.
- **Rubbing alcohol** Rub a little alcohol on a counter next to a bunch of bananas or a ripening melon, tomato, or avocado.
- **Apple cider** Pour cider into a jar or bowl, and fruit flies will be drawn to the sweet-smelling liquid, only to drown.

Build nonpoisonous roach motels

Wrap the outside of an empty jelly jar with masking tape, and rub the inside of the jar with petroleum jelly. Pour in an inch of beer and top it with a few small pieces of ripe fruit and 4–5 drops of almond extract. Place the unlidded jar under the sink or anywhere else cockroaches lurk. Roaches will be drawn to the appetizing aroma, climb into the jar (the tape gives them traction), and drop inside to feast—but thanks to the slippery walls, they'll be unable to escape. To dispose of the tipsy roaches, fill the jar with hot water and flush the contents down the toilet.

Borax on high shelves

Cockroaches like to roam any high spots they can reach, so fetch a stepladder and sprinkle borax on the top of your kitchen cabinets. (Side benefit: The borax will be out of reach of children and pets.) Roaches poisoned by the borax will take it back to the nest, where their fellow roaches will start dropping like flies.

Caring for Your Fridge

Keep it clean

The surface of white refrigerators and freezers gets dirty more quickly than you'd like, especially around the handles. Even the hardware shows fingerprints and spotting. Make your fridge or freezer gleam in one of these ways:

- Scrub it with equal parts ammonia and water.

- Rub it down with club soda, which cleans and polishes at the same time.

- For a glossier finish, wash and rinse the surface, then apply car paste wax and buff it to a shine with a clean soft cloth.

- Polish any chrome trim with a cloth dipped in rubbing alcohol.

Keep a tight seal

The flexible rubber or plastic gasket framing the inside edge of your refrigerator door seals cold air in and warm air out. When cleaning your refrigerator, don't neglect it! Wipe grime off with a soft cloth dampened with rubbing alcohol and finish by rubbing the gasket with a little mineral oil to prevent cracking.

Scrub with salt

You're cramming today's groceries on a high shelf of the fridge and a small bowl of leftover sauce in the back gets wedged in at an angle and begins to leak. To get rid of the gummy mass, sprinkle it with salt. Then dip a plastic scrubber or abrasive sponge in hot water and rub the stain vigorously. Repeat until it's gone, each time wiping the area with a wet paper towel.

Litter box lesson

If cat litter can absorb the really pungent odors in Fluffy's litter box, it can certainly soak up the lesser odors that so easily arise in your fridge. Keeping a small, uncovered bowl of natural clay cat litter on a shelf of the refrigerator will block odors before they take hold.

Deodorize with a spud

A food that will absorb food odors? Indeed! To diminish refrigerator smells, peel a raw potato,

---

CHARCOAL BRIQUETTE ODOR EATERS

Store three or four **charcoal briquettes** in your refrigerator. Simply put them in a small mesh bag (the kind that holds supermarket onions) and stick them on a fridge shelf. After a month, refresh the briquettes by dumping them into a heavy stainless steel pot and warming them; ventilate the kitchen well while doing this. Once the briquettes are cool, put them back in the bag and return them to the fridge.

cut it in half, and place each half on a small saucer. Now place the potato halves on different shelves in the fridge. When the cut surface of a potato turns black, trim the black part away and return the potato to the fridge with its absorbent powers restored.

Lemon-fresh fridge

Mold and mildew can grab on to your refrigerator and not let go—and banishing the odors takes drastic action. Squeeze a lemon into a cup of water and throw the peel in with the mixture. Unplug the fridge and empty it (we said it was drastic!), nestling ice cream and other meltable items in a tub, sink, or ice chest filled with ice. Then, microwave the lemon water to almost boiling and place it inside the empty refrigerator.

Close the door and let the deodorizer sit for half an hour. The citrus fumes will freshen the smell and soften any food accumulations.

Remove the bowl, wash the fridge's interior, and restock it with your food and beverages.

Two ways to speed defrosting

If you have a freezer that isn't self-defrosting, you can speed defrosting to keep frozen foods from spoiling or going soft. Hasten the process by aiming a stream of hot air at the ice with a hair dryer. Another trick is to boil water in a couple of saucepans, place them in the freezer (on trivets if the floor is plastic), and close the freezer door to trap the steam. In no time at all you'll be able to pry off large slabs of ice with a dinner knife (carefully, of course).

Use your oven when defrosting

If you have a self-cleaning oven, you can use it to store frozen foods as you defrost the freezer. These ovens are so well insulated that they'll keep foods frozen for hours. Just don't turn it on!

Curiosity Corner
Salted Superstitions

In ancient times, salt was so coveted as a preservative and medicine and flavoring that it hastened the advance from nomadic to agricultural life, spurred the opening of new trade routes, and influenced religious rites and rituals in almost every culture. In the Roman Empire, salt was considered so essential that Roman soldiers were given a salarium (salt allowance) as part of their pay.

(*Salarium* is the origin of the word *salary*.)

Not surprisingly, all kinds of superstitions swirled around this precious commodity. A vial of salt worn around the neck was thought to keep evil spirits away, though vampires were repelled only by direct assaults with salt. According to Irish folklore, a bag of salt tied onto children's nightgowns kept them from being stolen by fairies in their sleep.

The best known (and still current) salt superstition is found in cultures around the world: "Spilling salt brings bad luck." And its second page: "Toss a pinch of spilled salt over the left shoulder to keep the bad luck at bay." Spirits who brought misfortune were thought to stand behind a person to the left, and a pelt of salt in the eyes would make them flee.

Hot Tips for Stove Cleaning

Keeping your stove's sides tidy

If you have crumbs, spills, and stains sticking to the sides of your stove, pick up inexpensive T-shaped plastic gaskets from a home-improvement store. Slipping them between your freestanding stove and the adjacent countertops will keep goo and gunk from sticking to the stove's sides. When gaskets get soiled (and boy, will they get soiled), simply remove them, wash them, and reinstall them.

Baked-on grates

If your stovetop grates are cast iron, and something has baked onto them, wipe them with nontoxic oven cleaner, and place them in your oven the next time you self-clean it. Remove and wipe clean.

Salt a grease spill while cooking

If grease spills over in your oven while you're roasting meat, sprinkle salt over the grease before it has a chance to bake on. Close the oven door and let the cooking continue. By cleanup time, the spill will have transformed itself into an easily removed pile of ash.

A poultice for broiler pans

Broiler pans with burned-on food are a major pain in the neck to clean. To make the job less of a chore, heat the pan and sprinkle laundry detergent over the affected area. Now cover the detergent with wet paper towels, wait 15 minutes, remove the towels, and you'll see how much easier it is to scrape and scrub the gunk off.

In-the-bag rack cleaning

A typical way to wash a dirty oven rack is to submerge it in soapy water in the bathtub to loosen the grime—but who wants to clean a greasy tub afterward? Instead, put the rack in a large, heavy-duty plastic trash bag and add ⅓ cup dishwashing liquid, 1 cup white vinegar, and enough hot water to almost fill the bag. Seal the bag and place it in a bathtub full of warm water for an hour. Then remove the rack from the bag and scrub, rinse, and air-dry.

CLEAN A GAS RANGE WITH AN ICE SCRAPER

If you can't budge baked-on food on your stove, turn off all the burners and pilot lights, spray the area with WD-40, and let it sink in. After a few minutes, scrape the mess off the stove using a **plastic ice scraper**. Then wash the burner in hot soapy water and wipe it dry with a dish towel.

Ease a rack's slide

When you clean your oven racks, don't forget to clean the oven wall ridges they slide in and out on. Scrub with soap-filled steel wool pads, rinse off the soap and dry the ridges, then wipe them with vegetable oil to keep the racks gliding smoothly.

A scrub for exhaust filters

Once a month, take the filter off the hood above your stove and spray it all over with WD-40. After an hour, scrub with a toothbrush and then put it in the dishwasher for a final cleaning.

Microwave cleanup shortcut

The quickest way to clean a microwave oven is to throw a handful of wet paper towels inside and run it on High for 3–5 minutes. You don't need a science lesson to know that the steam from the towels will soften the grime. Once the towels cool down, use them to wipe the oven's interior.

Carpet a dirty microwave floor with baking soda

To remove cooked-on spills from the floor or turntable of a microwave, make a paste of 2 parts baking soda to 1 part water and apply it to the hardened goop. After 5–6 minutes, wipe up the baking soda with a wet sponge or cloth and remove any residue with a paper towel.

Make a mini steam bath

The easiest way to melt the nasty gunk that accumulates on the walls of your microwave (and ours) is to fill a heatproof glass bowl with water, nuke on High for 2 minutes, don't open the door for another 2 minutes, and then wipe with a soft rag. The steam will have reconstituted the icky, caked-on muck, making it a cinch to wipe off.

What's the Story?
The Invention of the Microwave Oven

Like a number of other machines, medicines, and modern necessities, microwave ovens were invented by accident. In 1945, a self-educated Raytheon company engineer named Percy Spencer was visiting the lab where magnetrons were being tested (magnetrons are the power tubes of radar sets). As he stood next to one of the machines, he suddenly felt the chocolate peanut bar in his pocket begin to melt.

His curiosity piqued, Spencer sent an assistant out for a bottle of popcorn kernels—and when he held the kernels near a magnetron, popcorn kernels exploded all over the lab. The next morning, Spencer brought in a kettle, cut a hole in the side, and put in an uncooked egg. He then moved a magnetron next to the kettle and switched it on. A skeptical engineer peeked into the hole just in time to catch a face full of egg; the egg burst because the yolk cooked faster than the egg white.

Spencer had discovered that food can be cooked with high-frequency radio waves, and in 1946 he patented the Radar Range, an oven the size of a refrigerator and costing $3,000 (almost $35,000 in today's money). In the years that followed, the concept was refined, and rare is the modern home, office, or restaurant that isn't equipped with the machine that revolutionized the way we cook.

Dishwashers (Hands, Too!)

Wash your dishwasher

After washing load after load of greasy dishes, your dishwasher gets dirty, and its interior gets coated with grease that will show up as film on plates and glassware. Assuming you do NOT have a septic tank, you can keep your dishes film-free by taking the two simple steps below. (You may have to repeat the process once or twice to make sure the washer's innards have been cleansed of all grease.)

- Pour 1 cup liquid bleach in a bowl and place on the bottom rack of the dishwasher. Then run the machine on the wash setting only.
- With the first washing complete, open the washer and pour a cup of vinegar into the same bowl and run the machine through a full cycle.

Clip dishwasher spray-arm debris

If your dishwasher seems to have fallen down on the job lately, the spray arms could be clogged with mineral deposits or other debris. Open the washer and take a peek at the top of the three-pronged spray arms to see if the holes look clogged (in most washers, one three-pronged spray arm sits under the top rack and the second arm sits on the dishwasher floor). Test for clogging by sticking a wooden toothpick into one of the holes; if it shows signs of dirt when pulled out, the holes need cleaning.

Unfasten the clips or screws holding the spray arms in place and put the arms in the kitchen sink. Then unbend a paper clip and insert the long end into each spray hole, moving it around to dislodge the blockage. Finish the job by rinsing the spray arms under the faucet and fastening them back in their proper places. Dishwasher back up to speed!

A cleansing (and colorful) drink

After washing grease and miniscule food remains off plates and pots and pans over and over again, a dishwasher can begin to take on an unpleasant odor. To freshen it up, put some powdered orange or lemon drink mix into the detergent dispenser (same amount as your dishwasher detergent) and run the washer through a full cycle. This wacky-but-wise cleaning trick will not only degrease the dishwasher but also help remove rust stains.

Get a jump on odors

A way to keep odors out of your dishwasher in the first place? Just add ½ cup lemon juice to the detergent receptacle each time you use the machine.

Give it the old-fashioned scrub

Save a few bucks on your electric bill and get super-clean dishes in the process. Fill up your sink with warm water, add a few squirts of natural dish soap, pull on your rubber gloves, and have at it. If your dishes are really a mess, let them soak for 10 minutes in lemon juice-infused hot water; if they're still sticky, sprinkle them with kosher salt and dish soap, before rinsing them until they're squeaky clean.

Washing Dishes by Hand

Who says washing dishes in the sink is drudgery? Only people who don't appreciate the simple satisfaction of doing things the old-fashioned way, if only occasionally. Some people see standing over the sink washing dishes as much-welcome "quiet time," ideal for thinking or perhaps listening to music or talk radio. And there's something to be said for watching that beautiful china plate sparkle like new as you move it from the sink to the dish rack.

There's surely no need to tell you how to wash dishes, but we're happy to offer three hints that may be new to you:

Sanitize with a short soak.
If you're so germ-shy that even antibacterial dishwashing liquid isn't enough to put your mind at ease, soak washed dishes in a sink in a solution of 1 tablespoon household bleach to 1 gallon water. After 5 minutes, rinse well with fresh water and air-dry.

Keep rubber-gloved hands odor free.
Unlined rubber gloves may leave an odor reminiscent of auto tires on your hands. How to prevent it? Rub lotion on your hands before slipping on the gloves. No rubbery smell and a hand moisturizing treatment as you wash!

Clear up cloudy glass.
Ovenproof casserole dishes of clear glass may be marred with large cloudy spots even though they're clean as a whistle. Eggs, milk, cheese, and other proteins are the culprits, and none can stand up to white vinegar. All removal takes is rubbing the spots with a vinegar-soaked sponge or cleaning cloth.

About Those Small Appliances

De-bitter your coffee grinder with rice

When you grind your own coffee beans, it's almost impossible to brush all of the residue out of the grinder when you're done—and accumulated residue can make coffee taste bitter. To get rid of the residue, run a cup of raw white rice through the grinder once every month. The rice will clean the grinder and sharpen the blades at the same time.

Hold the spices

If you ever use your coffee grinder to grind spices, be sure to clean all of the remnants out of the grinder before switching back to coffee beans. How to go about it? By grinding two or three slices of cut-up, plain white bread in the machine.

Grind bread, clean meat grinder

Before cleaning a meat grinder, run a piece of bread through it to clean fatty meat particles out of the feed screw. A regular washup of the parts is rarely enough to get the feed screw truly clean.

Purge coffee stains from a carafe

Over time, caffeine will discolor the glass carafe of your automatic coffeemaker, but you can easily make it look like new. Here's how:

1. Fill a quarter of the carafe with water.
2. Cut a lemon into 4 wedges, squeeze the juice of 2 of them into the water, and drop all 4 lemon wedges into the carafe.
3. Add 2 tablespoons salt and swirl the carafe around for 2–3 minutes.
4. Empty the carafe and scrub the inside with soapy water. Rinse and dry and return the crystal-clear carafe to its base.

Clean your toaster with a toothbrush

If your toaster is clogged with hard-to-reach crumbs, unplug it and loosen the crumbs with a small paintbrush or soft toothbrush. Avoid damaging the machine's heating elements by brushing very lightly. Once you've broken the stubborn crumbs apart, turn the toaster upside down, hold it over the kitchen sink, and gently shake out the debris.

Clean your toaster oven window

If the window of your toaster oven gets so caked with grime that you can barely see inside, try one of following fixes:

- Open the oven door and the spray the glass with a solution of 2 parts hydrogen peroxide, 2 parts white vinegar, and 1 part dishwashing liquid. Let stand for half an hour.
- Wipe the window with household ammonia and let stand for 20–30 minutes.

Wipe off either substance with paper towels. If any residue remains, scrape it off with a plastic (not metal) windshield scraper. Finally, clean the oven window with a spray of vinegar or commercial glass cleaner.

Give uncooked **rice** a whirl in your coffee grinder to clean it!

Melted plastic on your toaster?

If you inadvertently leave a plastic bag or plastic wrap so close to a toaster that it touches the metal surface, the plastic will melt onto it when you toast bread—and it won't come off with normal washing. To get rid of it, let the toaster cool and try one of these removal methods.

- Rub the melted plastic vigorously with a damp sponge coated with baking soda.

- Coat the blob with petroleum jelly and then toast a slice of bread. The heated jelly will soften the plastic and make it easier to wipe off with a soft cloth. When the toaster cools, scrub away residue with baking soda and a damp sponge.

- Spray the plastic with WD-40 and let it soak in for a few minutes. Then wipe the goop off with a damp cloth.

Easy blender cleaning

Sure, you always flush out the blender jar under the kitchen sink faucet, and sometimes you even give it a proper washing. But that's hardly enough to keep it hygienically correct. Pour 1 cup water and ¼ cup vinegar into the jar and add a squirt of dishwashing liquid. Put on the jar top and blend the mixture for 1 minute. Now rinse the jar and wipe it dry, and your blender will be ready to whir germ-free.

Hose out stuck food

If food gets lodged in your food processor or blender and trying to remove it is driving you nuts, take the machine's bowl or jar outside—no, not to smash it with a sledgehammer, but to direct a strong stream of water from your garden hose to the gummed-up works. Take a newspaper with you and set the machine on it so it won't get soiled.

Keep appliances dust-free

Sometimes it seems that dust gathers more quickly on countertop appliances than anywhere. If this happens to you, cover the appliances with dish towels or—if you're always looking for still one more way to use panty hose—a stocking leg cut to size.

Brush away espresso

If you're a fan of espresso, you're also familiar with how finely ground Italy's favorite coffee is. To keep it from clogging up the filter screen on your espresso maker, scrub the screen gently after each use with a soft toothbrush. If any bits remain, remove them with a straight pin.

Rack it up to prevent toaster oven fires

One of the leading causes of toaster oven fires is the greasy, grimy rack (and you know you have one, same as us). Think about it: the baked cheese dripped cheddar, which burned. The cinnamon bun dripped sugar, which also burned. Maybe the glob dripped onto the heating element and set off a spark. What to do? The next time you clean your (real) oven, wipe the toaster oven racks down with non-toxic oven cleaner and simply place them inside your oven to be cleaned.

De-pulp your juicer

It's easy to forget that electric juicers are traps for all manner of fruit (and therefore, food) particles. Keep it clean as a whistle to prevent bacteria buildup (and illness!) by cleaning it thoroughly: disassemble it, wipe out the pulp and discard it, and fill your kitchen sink with hot, soapy water. Soak everything but the motor casing for 10 minutes, remove the pieces from the sink, and scrub with a soft toothbrush. Dry well, reassemble, and juice for all you're worth!

Household Superstar!
9 Practical Kitchen Uses for Vinegar

1 To clean your refrigerator, wipe it inside and out with a 50/50 mixture of white vinegar and water (and don't forget the door gasket).

2 Prevent mildew in the fridge's vegetable bins by washing them with full-strength vinegar.

3 Steam clean your microwave oven's interior by putting a bowl with ¼ cup vinegar and 1 cup water inside and microwaving it on High for 5 minutes.

4 Disinfect a wooden cutting board by wiping it with full-strength white vinegar after each use.

5 Sanitize and deodorize your garbage disposal by grinding ice cubes made with half vinegar, half water.

6 To make drinking glasses gleam, add 2 tablespoons vinegar to your dishwasher as the rinse cycle begins.

7 Remove coffee stains from china cups by scrubbing them with equal parts vinegar and salt.

8 Clean a coffeemaker by running 2 cups vinegar and 1 cup water through a brewing cycle (hold the coffee!).

9 Eliminate mineral deposits in a teakettle by boiling 3 cups full-strength white vinegar in it for 5 minutes, then letting it sit overnight.

Cleaning Cookware

Choice cast iron cleaners

Both coarse salt and borax (sodium borate) are more cast iron–friendly than dishwashing detergents, so use either to get burned food off a treasured pan that may have been passed down from your grandmother. Just sprinkle the crystals into the pan and scrub with a wet sponge or paper towel. Then rinse with fresh cold water and dry immediately (cast iron is quick to rust).

A cast iron DO

Rub vegetable oil on the inside of a cast iron skillet to keep it seasoned—and do it after each wash and any other time you please.

A cast iron DON'T

Soaking a cast iron skillet in soapy water can deplete the fat that seeps into the porous surface and seasons the skillet—and an unseasoned skillet is a recipe for frustration. You'll be contending with food that sticks and burns and seems almost impossible to clean off.

Scrub away scorched milk

Yikes! You left the milk you were heating on the burner too long, and it began to simmer and fill the air with a scorching smell. How to get rid of it? Wet the bottom of the pan and sprinkle it with salt. Let the salt sit for about 10 minutes and then wash the pan as you usually do. Cleaned pot, vanished odor.

Boil burned-on food

If burned food won't come off a pot, fill the pot with water and add a squirt of dishwashing liquid and 1 tablespoon salt. Bring the water to a boil and then turn off the heat. After about 15 minutes, discard the mixture and use a plastic scraper or scrubber to remove the loosened gunk.

Two aluminum restorers

When aluminum pots and pans become discolored after extended use, revive the luster with either cream of tartar or vinegar and then wash and dry as usual.

- **Cream of tartar** Fill the pan with hot water and add cream of tartar (2 tablespoons powder to 1 quart water). Bring to a boil, then reduce heat and let the mixture simmer for 10 minutes.
- **Vinegar** Combine equal parts white vinegar and water in the pan and simmer for 10–12 minutes.

Note: Avoid using alkaline cleaners like baking soda and bleach on aluminum, which may discolor it even more.

Rub out rust with a potato

With regular use, metal pie pans can rust. To get rid of rust, cut a potato in half, dip the exposed flesh into scouring powder, and rub the rust with your spud "sponge."

Toothpaste for stainless cookware

Fingerprints all over your nice, sparkling new stainless cookware? No problem? Dampen it with lukewarm water, apply an inch of low-abrasion toothpaste, and brush away those unsightly marks. Rinse, dry, and ogle your new shiny cookware again.

Four Ways to Clean Copper Pots

Copper cookware is beautiful—and it darn well should be, considering what it costs. To keep it looking like all it's worth, try these out-of-the-ordinary cleansers.

1
Salt and vinegar

Fill a spray bottle with vinegar and 3 tablespoons salt, shake until the salt dissolves, and give the copper a good spray. Let the pots sit for 10–12 minutes and then scrub them clean.

2
Lemon juice and cream of tartar

Mix these into a paste that's thin enough to spread but thick enough to cling. Apply to copperware with a clean cloth, and let it stand for 5 minutes before washing with warm water.

3
Worcestershire sauce

Yep, you heard right. Soak a sponge with the sauce and rub it over the surface of copper pots and pans. Let it sit 1–2 minutes and then wipe clean. Rinse well and dry.

4
Half a lemon and salt

If you find stubborn stains on your copperware, dip lemon halves in salt and rub the stains away.

Cleaning China, Glassware, and Utensils

No-spots glassware

To prevent spotting on glass pitchers, candle-sticks, drinking glasses, and any other everyday or special occasion glassware, soak a piece for 3–4 minutes in a bath of 2 gallons water and ½ cup white vinegar. Shake off any water droplets and then dry and polish the piece with a clean soft cloth.

Protect a teapot

When you store your treasured china teapot at the back of a cabinet for a long time, chances are it will be banged by the dishes up front at some point. To protect the spout, slip a toilet paper tube over it and secure the tube with masking tape. Or sheathe the spout with the thumb from an old leather glove or thick mitten. You'll also want to use one of these sheathes when you're packing the teapot for a move.

Remove invisible film

Though drinking glasses, mugs, and everyday plates and bowls might look clean after a washing, they could still be covered with a thin film of grease, invisible to the naked eye. See for yourself by making a thin paste of baking soda and water, dipping a sponge into it, and rubbing the glass or china surface well. Rinse, dry with a soft cloth, and your dishes may sparkle as never before and even feel different to the touch.

Tea for crystal

If residue dries inside a crystal pitcher that won't tolerate hard scrubbing without being scratched, fill it with a mixture of 2 parts strong black tea and 1 part white vinegar. After it sits overnight, discard the solution and wash the pitcher with a soft cloth dipped in soapy water.

Cleaning etched crystal

If you have deeply etched crystal, use an old-fashioned shaving brush or large make-up brush to work soapy water into the ridges and crevices at cleaning time. These brushes are rigid enough to root out dirt without scratching the crystal. To rinse, hold the piece under running water.

Smooth out nicks and scratches

If you notice a small nick on the edge of a drinking glass, use an emery board to smooth it out. To eliminate a scratch on a glass, rub it out with non-gel white toothpaste on a soft cloth, then rinse. The mildly abrasive toothpaste will smooth the glass just enough to make the scratch invisible.

Despotting stainless

If you think that vinegar and a paper towel are all you need to rub spots off stainless steel knives, forks, and spoons, guess again! The spots will come clean only if you dip the vinegar-soaked paper towel into a saucer of baking soda. After rubbing off the spots, wash the utensils as you usually do and dry them thoroughly right away.

Whiten bone handles

In time, bone-handled knives begin to yellow. Unless you love the antiqued look, wrap a yellowed handle in a piece of flannel moistened with hydrogen peroxide. Let it sit for a day or so, then unwrap. Rinse and dry a knife, and the handle will be good as new.

Easy waxing for wood

To keep your wooden spoons and salad sets looking like new, wash and dry them and then rub them down with wax paper. The thin coating of wax will help keep wood from drying out.

Scrub that butcher block

Putting your wooden cutting board in the dishwasher is a no-no, as is letting it soak in your sink. That said, keep it clean and you'll avoid bacterial mishaps and the not-so-pleasant

Oil Stein, Drink Brew

So you bought a colorful beer stein on your trip to Germany or to one of the faux German villages so often found in alpine areas here and there. You even occasionally drink from it instead of just letting it gather dust on the mantelpiece. But there's trouble in Löwenbräu City: The stein's lid will barely budge when you exert thumb pressure. What a pickle!

Never fear. Simply spray the lid hinge with WD-40 and let it sit for 12–15 minutes. Then wipe off the oil with a soft cloth and give the stein a good washing. Now get out the bratwurst and Muenster cheese and toast your quick fix with an easy-to-down cool one.

illnesses that are related to them. To clean your wooden cutting board, scrub it well with a lightly-abrasive cleansing powder and a nylon scrubbing pad, and wipe it down with hot, soapy water. Rinse, dry it well, and be safe.

Wrap silver in plastic

When putting away silverware, wrap each utensil in two layers of plastic wrap to shut out air. Exposure to air causes the oxidation that tarnishes silver.

NO SMOKING (STAINS) ALLOWED

When you throw a party and you're tolerant enough to let smoking guests puff away on the patio, you may find cigarette stains on a piece of china as you collect all of the post-party dishes. To make short work of the stains, dip the **cork from a wine bottle** into salt and use it to scour away the tobacco tar.

Odds 'n' Ends

Shake it freely
Salt and pepper shakers tend to clog up in humid whether. To keep the moisture out of your salt, add a few grains of raw rice or some crumbled saltine crackers to the shaker. To keep ground black pepper from clogging, add a few black or white peppercorns.

Keep brown sugar from hardening
Prevent brown sugar from turning into a brick by putting either a few dried prunes or a 1-by-3-inch strip of orange peel in the box. Then tape the box closed and store it in a sealed plastic bag—preferably in the freezer.

Keep olive oil fresh
Unless you use olive oil in large quantities, try this trick to make your supply last: add a drop of sugar to the bottle and it will stay fresher longer. And keep it away from your stove, where the heat will turn it rancid.

Storing things within things
If your kitchen storage space is sparse, store items in containers you rarely use. One neglected container is the picnic cooler that sees use only in the warm months. Likewise, that stockpot in the back of the cabinet could hold napkins and other items bought in quantity at your local warehouse store.

Number your containers
If you have lots of plastic containers, you know how frustrating it can be to match them to their lids. A simple solution? Label both container and lid with a number. It's much easier to match a 2 with a 2 or a 5 with a 5 than repeatedly trying lids on for size.

Tame your stray grocery bags with a **pants hanger!**

Hang paper bags

If you're a natural-born hoarder but have no place to store all those brown paper bags you've brought home from the supermarket, clamp them together with an old pants hanger and hang them from a hook on the pantry or mudroom door.

Clean that can opener

To loosen the grime on an electric or manual can opener, spray the blade and gears with WD-40 and let it sit for 6–8 minutes. Then brush away the grime with an old hard-bristle toothbrush. You could also tackle the blade and gears with a toothbrush dipped in hot soapy water—the soap of choice being antibacterial dishwashing liquid.

Storing a thermos

Empty thermoses tucked away in cabinets tend to take on a sour smell, but you can guard against odors after washing and drying a just-used thermos:

- Drop a few denture cleaning tablets into the thermos and fill it with water. Let it sit for an hour or so, then wash, rinse, and dry.

- Put a teaspoon of sugar in the thermos and screw the lid on tightly. The sugar will absorb unwanted odors.

Keep your board from sliding

To keep your cutting board from slip-sliding away while you're trying to chop on it, try this simple trick: dampen a small piece of paper towel and place it between the bottom of the board and the countertop. Press down, and your board won't budge.

Cleaning cutting boards

Freshen both the look and smell or a stained or greasy cutting board by sprinkling it with salt

Sanitizing Kitchen Sponges

When a sponge starts to smell like a dead animal, it's time to throw it away. What's not so obvious is that even slightly odoriferous sponges have seen their day. These innocent-looking germ hotbeds can quickly become one of the filthiest things in your kitchen—the reason you should sanitize seemingly okay sponges every three or four days at the very least. Two courses of action:

- Soak a sponge overnight in a mixture of 1 cup hot water, ½ cup white vinegar, and 3 tablespoons salt. The next day, rinse and squeeze the sponge several times to rid it of all of the cleaning liquid.

- Put a wet sponge (emphasis on wet) in the microwave and heat it on High for 2 minutes. Stay there until the microwave beeps because there's a chance (though an extremely slight one) that the sponge could burst into flames.

and rubbing the board with the cut side of half a lemon. If a wooden cutting board won't come clean, try sanding the entire surface with very fine-grit sandpaper (160–240), pressing lightly. When the board is smooth, coat it with mineral oil or olive oil to keep the wood from drying and to give the board a nice sheen.

Keeping garlic fresher longer

The papery peel from fresh garlic does a lot more than cover it; left in the canister in which you store your garlic (on your countertop, not your fridge please), it releases enzymes which help keep your garlic fresher for longer. So after you peel a clove, put the skin back in the storage container with the rest of the bulb. Amazing!

Chapter Three

Creative Housekeeping

The miraculous housecleaning products found on store shelves today—everything from labor-saving devices like self-propelling vacuum cleaners to flashy washing machines—are astonishing in their breadth.

But, some of our favorite twenty-first century housecleaning methods were tried and true hundreds of years ago: salt, tea, vinegar, lemon, and any number of other all-natural items cut through grime just as well now as they did in days long past.

Lifting grease off wallpaper with a slice of bread, polishing bronze with a wedge of lemon, scattering tea leaves on the floor before sweeping—such simple techniques are timeless. This isn't to say, of course, that modern science hasn't advanced housekeeping in ways that make it infinitely easier. Still, supplementing commercial products with the no-nonsense cleaning and laundering methods found in the coming pages is more than worthwhile. As you try them, you'll discover the pleasures of self-sufficiency and spare your pocketbook in the bargain.

Polish your silver with *banana peels!*

Cleaning Floors and Walls

Wipe scuffs off hardwood floors

Head into the bathroom to arm yourself with the tools to remove scuff marks. First, try squeezing a little toothpaste (the non-gel, non-whitening kind) onto an old toothbrush, scrub the marks gently, and wipe up the paste with a damp cloth. If that doesn't do the job, dab some baby oil or petroleum jelly onto a dry cloth and rub the mark, then remove any residue with a rag or paper towel.

Protect floors when rearranging furniture

Need to move heavy furniture out of the way to clean? Rearranging the living room for a big party? Protect your precious hardwood floors—and save yourself the trouble of dealing with scratches later—by pulling heavy socks over furniture legs and securing them with masking tape. This trick will also make it easier to push heavy furniture around. For everyday floor protection, consider putting adhesive bandages or moleskin patches on the bottom of furniture legs. If you have a rocking chair, affix a long strip of masking tape to the bottom of each rocker to help keep hardwood floors unmarred.

Take down waxy buildup

If you wax a vinyl or linoleum floor, you know all too well how wax builds up over time. Here are two easy ways to remove it:

- **Club soda for vinyl** Working in sections, pour a little club soda onto a vinyl floor and scrub it with the abrasive side of a kitchen sponge. Let the soda sit for

The Dirt on Garage (and Basement) Floors

They're often the least thought-of floors in (and out) of the house, but garage and unfinished basement floors take a lot of hard knocks, on a daily basis. Never mind your car: if you store your lawn mower, leaf blower, or string trimmer in this space, you're bound to experience all manner of oil and grease spills here. And if your floor is made from porous, unsealed cement—and it probably is—the surface will absorb odors like a brand-new sponge. The simplest way to remove odors is to head to the nearest pet supply shop, and pick up a large pail of non-clumping kitty litter.

1. Blot any oil or grease from the surface with newspaper; the floor should be fairly dry.

2. Spread a healthy amount of kitty litter on the stain, and using a broom, sweep it over the area until it's covered.

3. Let stand for 24 hours, and sweep or vacuum up the litter. Magic!

5 minutes, then wipe up the loosened wax with a wad of cheesecloth or panty hose.

- **Rubbing alcohol for linoleum** Mop a linoleum floor with a solution of 3 cups water to 1 cup rubbing alcohol. Use a sponge mop to scrub it in well, then rinse it thoroughly.

Buff that scuff with **toothpaste!**

Liquidate heel marks on vinyl

Vinyl floors are highly susceptible to heel marks, especially from rubber heels. An easy way to wipe the marks off? Just spray them with WD-40, let sit for 5–6 minutes, and then rub the marks with a soft cloth.

Vinegar for tile and linoleum

These materials are practical choices for flooring in kitchens, bathrooms, and mudrooms—all of which receive some of the most punishing wear in the house. Keep your frequent cleanups of these areas simple by mopping with a solution of ½ cup white vinegar to 1 gallon warm water.

A clean sweep with tea

Rural Japanese housekeepers traditionally strewed still-damp tea leaves over the floor before sweeping—and some no doubt still do. Dust and dirt cling to leaves and are easier to push into a dust pan. You can then throw the contents into a garden bed or compost pile.

MORE VINEGAR FOR STONE AND BRICK

These tough flooring materials can stand a larger dose of **acidic vinegar**, so scrub stone or brick floors with a solution of 1 cup vinegar in 1 gallon water. The operative word is "scrub," since the most effective way to clean is to get down on your hands and knees and work with a stiff scrub brush.

(Talk about an eco-friendly cleanser!) Just don't use tea leaves on unbleached wood or carpeting, since tea may stain.

Erasing crayon marks from walls

Junior may be a real Rembrandt, but even so, you probably don't want him defacing your walls with crayons. Try these techniques to clean up surprise murals.

- Lightly rub the area with a clean, dry fabric softener sheet.

- Rub vigorously with a clean art-gum eraser—or ask your young artist do it.

- Squirt shaving cream on the markings and scrub with a toothbrush or a scrub brush.

- Soften the markings with a hair dryer and wipe them off with a cloth moistened with a little baby oil.

Cleaning wood-paneled walls

Most wood paneling needs only a good dusting every once in a while, but you can give it a more thorough cleaning with a simple homemade solution—one best applied with panty hose, whose texture is perfect for abrasive yet gentle scrubbings. Combine 2 cups water, 1 cup white vinegar, and ¼ cup lemon juice in a pail and mix well. Dip a handful of wadded panty hose in the solution and wipe the paneling, working from the bottom of the wall upward so you won't have to deal with drips.

Wallpaper washups

How can you restore luster to dingy washable wallpaper? First fill a pail with 1 quart water and mix in ½ teaspoon dishwashing liquid. Then dip a soft cloth in the liquid and wring it out until no excess water remains. Gently rub the wallpaper with the cloth and blot it dry with a lint-free towel.

make your own
Floor Cleaner

Clean a hardwood floor with herbal tea? You bet, as long as it's combined with a few other ingredients. The tannic acid in some herbs—in this case, peppermint—attack dirt without damaging the floor finish. As with any mopping, wring the mop several times as you clean; letting the floor get too wet could warp the floorboards.

Pep-It-Up Floor Wash

To make the peppermint tea good and strong, use 6 tea bags to 1 quart water and let the tea steep for at least 2–3 hours.

   1 quart water
   6 peppermint tea bags
   1 quart white vinegar
   2 tablespoons baby oil
   1 teaspoon dishwashing liquid

1. In a large saucepan, boil 1 quart water, remove from heat, and add 6 peppermint tea bags. Let steep 2 hours.

2. Pour tea in a mop pail and add vinegar, baby oil, and dishwashing liquid. Stir with a large kitchen spoon to mix.

3. Dip a clean mop into the solution, wring or squeeze it out, and mop away.

If wallpaper is soiled with a greasy stain, try one of these remedies:

- Brush talcum powder onto the stain, let sit for at least half an hour, and then brush it off; repeat as necessary.

- Fold a brown paper bag and hold it over the stain. Press a warm iron to the spot so that the grease is drawn into the paper. Repeat as necessary until the spot is gone, repositioning the bag each time.

Caring for Carpets

Baby your carpet

Cooking fumes, cigarette and cigar smoke, and other odors can cling to carpeting and make your house smell musty. When a little freshening is in order, spread a liberal coating of baby powder over the carpet using a flour sifter. Leave the powder in place for a few hours or overnight, then vacuum it up. Baking soda will do the job, too, though you may want to throw in a bit of ground cinnamon or nutmeg to sweeten its smell (if you have a darker carpet).

Steam away furniture footprints

When you move a piece of furniture in a carpeted room, its footprints stay behind. The tools to raise the crushed fibers? Your iron and a fork. Put the iron on the steam setting and hold it about ¼ inch above the carpet, then fluff out the steamed fibers with the fork tines.

Inexpensive homemade carpet cleaner

Before spending money on commercial carpet-cleaning solutions, mix 1 part white vinegar to 10 parts hot water, or if you choose, ½ cup household ammonia in 2 cups hot water. Use either in a carpet-cleaning machine or apply with a scrub brush and elbow grease. Rinse the cleaned carpet with a damp cloth. To help dissipate any lingering odors, open your windows and, if necessary, place an oscillating fan in the room.

It's all in the alum

Alum, or potassium aluminum sulfate, does a great job cleaning carpet when combined with water and vinegar. (You can find alum in pharmacies and some supermarkets.) To make your own cleaner, pour 2 gallons hot water into a

Choose Your Rug Wisely

It happens all the time: that stunning rug calls out to you at the store, and you plunk down a pretty penny for it, imagining that those luscious golds and reds and creams will lighten up your living room or den (and they probably will). You bring it home, put it down, and you were right: it's *gorgeous*! Unfortunately, Fluffy and Fido are *just* as drawn to it as you are, and like a big vomit magnet, it seems to attract your furry friends at the precise moment that they need to hack up a hairball or barf up a biscuit. (Sound familiar? It's remarkable!) Remember this the next time you go rug or carpet shopping, and plan accordingly. You'll still have to clean it, but your stain woes will be much less serious if you don't buy that light-colored rug of your dreams!

large pail and add 2 cups alum, 1 cup white vinegar, and ¾ cup cinnamon tea (for scent). Now dip a sponge mop into the solution, squeeze out the excess, and mop one section of

Peanut Butter to the Rescue

Peanut butter as a carpet cleaner? It's a nutty idea, but nutty in a *good* way. Peanut butter helps remove chewing gum from a carpet.

First, heat the area with a hair dryer to loosen the gum. Press the area gently with a plastic bag, which should lift at least some of the gum; you could also try scraping it up with a plastic spatula. Some gum will remain in the carpet, which is where the peanut butter comes in: Its natural oils help the carpet fibers detach from the gum.

Rub a small dollop of peanut butter into the spot, let it sit for 5 minutes, and then wipe it up with a damp cloth. Now dab the spot with warm water mixed with 1 teaspoon dishwashing liquid. The final step? Have a little "chat" with the family member whom you suspect put you to so much trouble.

carpet at a time. Be sure to rinse the mop in fresh water after each cleaning as you work your way around the room.

Clean up paint spills with vinegar

Don't waste time crying over spilt paint on your carpet. Instead, spring into action before it sets: mix 1½ teaspoons vinegar and 1½ teaspoons laundry detergent into 2 cups warm water. Now sponge away the paint (a task that takes time and a lot of elbow grease), and rinse with cold water. If you're lucky, what might have been an unwelcome (and permanent) decorating touch will be gone.

Beat a rug

Dust and dander collect daily on (and in) area rugs, so shake 'em out the old-fashioned way: Hang the rug over a rail or taut clothesline and beat it. Your beater? A tennis racquet.

Flip the pricey ones

Did Fido relieve himself on your priceless Peshawar that you inherited from Aunt Mabel? No need to cry! Scoop up the mess, turn the rug over, place a bucket under the offending spot, and pour water—repeatedly—through the underside of the stain and into the bucket until the spot is gone. This will clean the delicate fibers without the need for scrubbing.

Baby it!

Yet another great use for mild baby wipes is as a simple carpet stain cleaner. Blot up a spill with a damp (but not soaking wet) baby wipe. This will lift out the stain before it sets.

Shaving cream to the rescue

To clean a stain that hasn't yet set, squirt non-gel shaving cream directly onto the stain and wipe clean with a damp rag or sponge.

Club soda with a twist

Every waitress and bartender knows how reliable a stain remover club soda is. To use it on a stained carpet, pour it onto the stain, leave it for 3 minutes, and dab it up with a paper towel or sponge.

Ammonia reliever

To clean tougher stains, mix 1 cup household ammonia in ½ gallon warm water, sponge it onto the stain, and dab it until the stain disappears.

Clobbering Common Carpet Stains

Below are treatments for five common carpet stains—treatments that work on upholstery as well. Your follow-up after removing as much of the stain as you can is to rinse the wet spot with warm water, then lay a heavy cloth towel or several layers of paper towels on top. Weigh this blotter down with heavy books or pots and pans and leave it in place until the treated spot dries.

Red wine

Liberally pour salt onto the stain and dab with a cloth dipped in club soda. Or blot the spill with a paper towel, pour a little white wine onto the stain, and scrub with a damp cloth. If neither method works, mix 1 teaspoon dishwashing liquid with 1 cup warm water and pour a little onto the stain; then blot the stain with a paper towel and repeat with a solution of ⅓ cup white vinegar and ⅔ cup water.

Fruit and fruit juice

Pick up any solid pieces of fruit, then stir 1 tablespoon laundry detergent and 1½ tablespoons white vinegar into 2 cups water. Work the solution into the stain and blot.

Grease or oil

Accidentally drop that family-size bucket of takeout fried chicken on the den carpet? Sprinkle the grease spots liberally with cornmeal or cornstarch, let sit for several hours, and vacuum it up. Or work shaving cream into the stains, let it dry, and rub it off with a damp soft cloth.

Coffee and tea

Choose one of these three methods and act fast. Pour club soda liberally onto the stain and blot, repeating as necessary. Or blot with a solution of equal parts white vinegar and water. Or beat an egg yolk, rub it into the stain, and blot it.

Ketchup

Jump right on this one because once a ketchup stain sets, it won't come out (ever). Grab the salt and sprinkle it over the spill, let sit for a few minutes, and vacuum. Sponge up any residue and continue salting and vacuuming until the stain is completely gone.

Sprucing Up Furniture

Double-duty dusting formula

Here's a duster that's also good for moisturizing dry wood. In a teacup, mix ¼ cup linseed oil with 1 teaspoon lemon balm tea. Dip your dusting cloth into the mixture (soaking up only a small amount at a time) and rub it vigorously into the wooden surface to be cleaned. Use a soft clean cloth to wipe away any residue.

Removing stuck-on candle wax

If your candlelight dinner party ended with hot wax dripped onto your nice mahogany table, here's how to remove it without scratching the wood. Put a few ice cubes in a plastic bag and rest the bag on the wax until it becomes brittle. Then gently lift the wax with the edge of a spatula or credit card. Gently rub a soft cloth dampened with a solution of 1 part apple cider vinegar to 10 parts warm water to take care of any residue.

Three wood surface fixes

You don't have to look any farther than the kitchen or bathroom when you need to take care of these three problems.

- **Stuck paper** To remove paper stuck to a wood surface (say, because the kids were busy doing crafts projects), pour a few drops of olive oil over the paper, wait about 20 minutes as the oil softens it, and then use a clean dry cloth to remove the paper and oil. (Not only is olive oil harmless to wood, but it may do it some good.)

- **Burn mark** If a wood surface suffers a slight burn from a mislaid cigarette or a lit match, rub a little mayonnaise into the burn, let it sit for a few minutes, and wipe

Blast from the Past

Stripped pine furniture may be thought of by interior decorators as "so seventies," but what's wrong with lending a touch of hippie chic to a room? A stripped hutch or table or armoire can look like a million dollars to the right eyes.

Stripped wood furniture may be fashionably retro, but it's also quick to dry out. Besides regular dusting and the occasional wipe-down with soapy water, it needs a little oil—and here's how to make a moisturizer and apply it:

Stir ½ teaspoon lemon oil into 1 cup mineral oil (not to be confused with mineral spirits, a paint thinner). Put only a drop or two of the mixture on a soft cloth and rub it onto a small area of the wood with a circular motion, repeating until all surfaces are oiled.

Now step back and admire your spruced-up sideboard or hutch—so handsome that you may decide it's just the place to display your mood ring and Led Zeppelin LPs.

it off with a clean damp cloth. Mayo also removes crayon marks from wood.

- **Tape** If adhesive tape is stuck to a wood floor or piece of furniture, don't just yank it off or you may remove some of the finish. Apply a little rubbing alcohol to the tape, then rub the area with a cloth dipped in a solution of 1 teaspoon dishwashing liquid and 2 cups warm water.

Get rid of water rings and spots

It's bound to happen: A party guest doesn't use a coaster, and her glass leaves a white ring or spots on a wood table. The unsightly marks will disappear like magic if you dampen a cloth, apply a dab of toothpaste, and rub the area gently. For a stubborn spot, add a little baking soda to the toothpaste. Dry the area and then polish the surface as usual; if you're lucky, all traces of the damage will vanish.

Homemade furniture polish

A simple polish made from two kitchen staples will leave wooden furniture with a nice shine and pleasant smell. Combine 2½ cups vegetable oil with 1½ cups lemon juice, mix well, and pour the solution into a 16-ounce spray bottle. Spray on finished wooden surfaces and polish with a soft cloth.

Because the polish contains lemon juice, you'll have to store it in the fridge, where it will keep for up to six months. Non-hydrogenated oil won't congeal, so the polish will never need "thawing."

Caring for vinyl upholstery

Though vinyl upholstery is durable, it has a weakness—body and hair oil can cause it to harden and even crack. To keep vinyl-covered furniture in good shape, clean it regularly, especially when it gets a lot of use. Dampen a cloth in water, dip it in white vinegar, and gently wipe the vinyl surfaces to cut through oils. Now add a few drops of mild dishwashing liquid to a bucket of water, stir well, and wash the vinyl with a soft cloth dipped into the soapy water. Rinse with a damp cloth and dry.

Foam away dirt

For spot cleaning dirty sofa cushion corners, upholstered chair arms, and the like, whip up some foam. First, make sure the fabric can be safely cleaned with water-based agents (check the cleaning instructions tag). If it can, vacuum the soiled fabric thoroughly to remove loose dirt. Mix 1 part mild laundry detergent with

Give melted-on **candle** **wax** the freeze!

4 parts distilled water in a bowl. (Distilled water doesn't leave watermarks on fabric.) Using a hand mixer, beat the solution until a good head of foam builds. Carefully apply foam to the upholstery, working in small sections and using a clean sponge or cloth. Let dry, then wipe it off with a cloth dampened with white vinegar diluted with distilled water (1 part vinegar to 6 parts water).

Removing stains from vinyl furniture

To remove stubborn marks from vinyl furniture (tablecloths, too), try rubbing the stain with a cloth dipped in milk. (Whether the milk is 1 percent, 2 percent, or whole doesn't matter.) Then wash with soapy water as directed above and dry.

Scorch mark on upholstery

Whether someone was smoking on the sly or accidentally dropped a match on your fancy jacquard chair is irrelevant: you've now got an expensive repair to deal with. Don't despair! You may be able to blot out the char with paper towels. Wet a paper towel with distilled water and dab it on the mark (don't rub). Now blot it with a dry paper towel. If that doesn't work, put a drop of mild liquid laundry detergent on a wet paper towel and treat the spot. After a minute or two, blot up the detergent with a wet paper towel and then blot the area one last time with a dry one.

Touching up leather

Though leather is hard to stain, it can easily sustain watermarks. Just wipe these away with white vinegar—but only after testing on an out-of-sight area of the upholstery. To get rid of scuff marks, rub them with a pencil eraser.

Take a lesson from Flicka or Willie Mays

If you're lucky enough to own a sofa or club chair made of heavier, saddle leather, take care of it not with expensive and fancy leather cleaners, but with old fashioned saddle soap or baseball mitt softener. Treat once or twice a year, depending on how dry or humid your home is.

Make Glass and Metals Shine

Keep glass tabletops sparkling

If you have a glass table, you're used to cleaning it often to remove smudge marks. To add a nice shine every time, squeeze the juice of a halved lemon onto the surface and rub it with a clean cloth. Remove any excess juice, then buff the tabletop with a wad of newspaper.

Cut the mess when cleaning a chandelier

To clean all the pendants and bangles and bits on a crystal chandelier, do you have to go to the trouble of taking it apart? Not if you use this relatively easy method and don't mind standing on a ladder. First, make sure the ladder is secure and that your shoes have good, gripping soles. Second, flip out the tray at the top of the ladder and set a small bowl of diluted rubbing alcohol on top (1 part alcohol to 3 parts water). Slip an old cotton glove over your hand, dip your fingers into the alcohol, and wipe the glass clean with your forefinger and thumb. Then soak a second cotton glove in fresh water and go over the same areas. Dry all of the parts of the chandelier with a clean, soft cotton cloth.

Cleanups for drippy candlesticks

You might have more than romantic memories to remind you of your candlelight dinner: a table full of wax-encrusted candlesticks. Gather up the candlesticks and head to the kitchen, where you have several cleaning options.

- Hold the candlesticks under running hot water and rub the wax off with a soft cloth. Wash them in hot soapy water until any wax residue is gone.

- If the candlesticks are glass, lay them in the microwave on a paper towel and run the oven at its lowest setting for 3 minutes. When you open the door, you'll find the wax on the towel, not the candlesticks.

- Pop candlesticks of any material into the freezer for a couple of hours. When you take them out you'll probably be able to lift the wax right off.

PEWTER TO BE PROUD OF

Pewter bowls and candlesticks are not only attractive but also easy to clean—you can usually restore the gentle sheen by simply wiping pewter pieces with a damp cloth. If smudges and smears remain, head for the fridge or fireplace. A rubdown with **cabbage leaves** or moistened wood ashes will make pewter look like new.

Household Superstar!
10 Ways to Clean with Lemons

1 Shine chrome with the inside of a lemon rind.

2 Remove beverage stains from marble by rubbing it with lemon juice.

3 Remove water spots from the metal parts of shower doors.

4 Mix lemon juice with borax to clean a toilet bowl.

5 Deodorize a smelly humidifier by pouring 3–4 teaspoons of lemon juice into the water.

6 Sweeten the smells coming from the fireplace by throwing a few lemon peels on the burning logs.

7 To keep ants, fleas, and cockroaches away, add the juice of 1 lemon to 1 gallon of mop water.

8 Rid garments of mildew by rubbing a paste of lemon juice and salt on the affected area.

9 To make white socks look really white again, throw them into a pot of boiling water with 2 lemon halves.

10 Soak delicate fabrics in lemon juice instead of bleach.

Clean fireplace doors

Fireplace doors covered with soot and carbon can spoil the cozy effect of a fire. But it's not hard to clean the glass. If the dirty side of the glass is easy to reach, leave the doors attached when cleaning. If you need to remove the doors, lay them on a soft towel to clean. (Most doors have spring-loaded clips at the top for easy removal.) Start by scraping away any built-up deposits with a razor blade. Then fill a gallon bucket with water, add 1 cup white vinegar and ½ teaspoon dishwashing liquid, and scrub with newspaper crumpled into a ball. Rinse well with a clean sponge or towel, dry the doors, and stand back and admire the view.

Mirror, mirror …

Your mirrors will show nary a streak if you wash them with equal parts water and white vinegar. But it's your technique that matters: Spray-cleaning a mirror can end with moisture seeping behind the glass and turning the silvering black. Instead, dip a clean sponge or wadded-up newspaper (sans colored ink) into the solution and clean the mirror. Wipe dry with a soft cloth, a paper towel, or more newspaper.

Cleaning monitors and TV screens

Less is more when cleaning a computer monitor or TV screen: Turn off the monitor, and then simply dust with a clean cloth, preferably an antistatic wipe. Wipe the screen with a clean cloth barely dampened with water, from top to bottom; if fingerprints and other marks remain, add a small amount of white vinegar to the cloth and wipe again. Liquid crystal display (LCD) laptop screens should be wiped very lightly, and only with a clean cloth (paper towels can scratch the sensitive surface). *Never* clean an LCD screen with commercial glass cleaners, which contain ammonia, acetone, ethyl alcohol, or other substances that can do serious damage.

Reduce tarnish with charcoal or rice

Although sooner or later you'll need to polish your silver pieces, you can make the task easier by keeping tarnish to a minimum. Protect you silver from tarnish-causing moisture by placing a few charcoal briquettes or a small bowl of rice in the cabinet where you keep silver; both are super absorbent. Place a briquette inside a silver teapot or coffee pot to prevent moisture from building up.

Shine silver with banana peels

Is your grandmother's cherished silver tea set tarnished? Polish it with banana peels or toothpaste. Whichever you use, rinse the pieces well after wiping them clean and then buff them dry with a soft cloth.

- **Banana peels** Remove the banana (and cat it—it's packed with heart-healthy potassium), and gripping it, massage your silver with the inside of the peel. For tougher tarnishes, puree the peel in a blender, and massage in the paste. Remove with a soft cloth.

- **Toothpaste** Rub non-gel white toothpaste onto the tarnished pieces and work it in with a damp soft cloth.

Keep brass looking golden

For a tarnish-free shine, clean any brass item in one of these two ways: Sprinkle a slice of lemon with baking soda and rub it onto the brass. Or sprinkle salt onto a soft cloth dipped in white vinegar and rub the surface. Rinse the brass with a cloth dipped in warm water and then buff it dry. For some extra shine, rub just-cleaned brass with a little olive oil.

Ketchup makes brass shine

A good way to clean knickknacks, drawer pulls, and other pieces made of brass is to boil them in ketchup or hot sauce! Just put the items in a saucepan, cover with ketchup (more practical and economical than using Tabasco), and place the pan over high heat. Bring to a boil, then lower the heat and simmer until the brass shines like new. Rinse with warm water and dry with a soft cloth.

Chores Around the House

Use a ruler to clean your louvers

The slats in louvered doors and shutters attract dust in a flash, but cleaning them can be a real chore. Speed the task with fabric softener and a ruler. Wrap a fabric softener sheet (or a cloth sprayed with fabric softener) around a ruler and clean the louvers by running the makeshift tool over each slat. A bonus: Fabric softening agents repel dust, so you won't need to dust quite so often.

Baking soda freshens artificial flowers

While artificial blooms may last forever, they attract lots of dust. You can't use water on silk or crepe, so give the flowers a baking soda bath instead. Put at least a cup of baking soda in a large plastic bag, insert the flower heads, and close the top of the bag around the stems. Grasp the top of the bag tightly and shake it vigorously so the soda can absorb all the dust and grime. Remove the flowers, shake off the soda, and dust residue off the petals with a soft toothbrush or artist's paintbrush.

Stained marble tabletop?

Marble makes a beautiful countertop or tabletop, but this porous stone is a real stain magnet. To remove a beverage stain, rub a paste of baking soda and equal parts water and lemon juice into the area, rinse with water, and wipe dry.

To remove other kinds of marble stains (including scuff marks on a marble floor), shake a good amount of salt over the area. Wet the salt with sour milk for as long as two days, checking periodically to see whether the salt–sour milk combo has done its job. When it has, mop up the salty little puddle with a sponge.

Scrub away soot

It's hard to keep a fireplace spotless, but these easy cleanups will make it look miles better.

- Clean the tiles or bricks around the fireplace with a scrub brush moistened with white vinegar.

- Rub soot marks off the hearth and surrounding tiles or bricks with an art-gum eraser.

- After removing ashes from the fireplace, set a plate of baking soda inside for a day to get rid of the sooty odor.

Vinegar for vases

It's hard to clean dirty, long-necked vases and bottles. Make the task easier by filling the vessel

FRESHENING A MATTRESS

To rid a mattress of urine or any other odors, sprinkle it liberally with **baking soda**, let sit for a day or two, and then vacuum well.

The Home Library

Who but the super-rich has a library in the house? Pretty much everyone. It doesn't have to be a wood-paneled room lined floor to ceiling with oak shelves; a library is merely a collection of books. And whether books are shelved in a room fit for a king or stacked haphazardly in a single pine bookcase, they must be cleaned. Keep your favorite hardcover tomes in best-selling shape and you'll have them forever. Here's how:

To dry a damp book, fan out the pages and sprinkle on cornstarch or talcum powder to soak up the moisture. Let sit for 5–6 hours and then brush off the white stuff.

To get rid of insects that reside in books, place an infested book in a plastic bag and pop it into the freezer for a day or two. No more bugs or larvae.

To freshen up a musty-smelling volume, pour some clean cat litter into a paper bag and keep the book in the bag for a week or so. Then remove the book and brush off any litter.

Mildewed pages? Wipe away the mold with a cloth barely moistened with a solution of 1 part white vinegar to 8 parts water. To dry, open the book to the affected pages and place it in the sun; let it sunbathe for no more than half an hour or the paper will fade and yellow.

Use a clean, soft paintbrush to dust one book at a time, brushing the covers and the outer edges of the pages. Do not dust a shelf of books with a feather duster, which will only redistribute most of the dust on the volumes.

Household Superstar!
13 Reasons to Take Salt Seriously

1 Extend a straw broom's life by soaking the bristles in hot salt water.

2 Toss salt onto a log fire to prevent soot from building up in the chimney.

3 Keep windows frost-free by wiping with a sponge dipped in salt water.

4 Remove watermarks from wood tables with a paste of salt and water.

5 Spiff up wicker furniture by scrubbing with a stiff brush dipped in salt water.

6 Clean copper, bronze, brass, and pewter with a paste of salt and white vinegar.

7 Scrub away rust stains with salt mixed with turpentine.

8 Brighten cutting boards by rubbing with a damp cloth dipped in salt.

9 Refresh kitchen sponges by soaking them in salt water.

10 Pour salt into a washing machine overflowing with suds.

11 Add salt to the washing machine's rinse cycle to sharpen colors.

12 Make clothespins last longer by boiling them in salted water.

13 Sprinkle salt on an ironing board to clean an iron.

with warm water and an equal amount of vinegar. Add up to ¾ cup of uncooked rice and shake vigorously. (If cleaning a vase or a bottle without a lid, put a sheet of aluminum foil on the top, mold it to the sides, and grip the top tightly as you shake.) The rice acts as an abrasive that scrapes the glass clean.

Whiten piano keys

If you wonder how your piano keys got so yellow, don't despair: You can restore their whiteness a few simple ways. Use a soft cloth to rub the keys with lemon juice and salt or with a 50/50 mix of rubbing alcohol and water; or apply mayonnaise and gently scrub with a soft cloth or soft toothbrush.

Whichever method you choose, prevent seepage by holding a piece of cardboard between the keys as you work your way down the keyboard. Wipe off each key with a slightly damp cloth before moving on to the next one. Let the keys air-dry—and then sit down and take it away, maestro!

Shine up your ivory

Bring ivory pieces back to their former luster by rubbing them with a lemon wedge dipped in salt. Let the juice dry, then wipe the piece with a clean cloth. Finally, buff with a second cloth.

Dusting a ceiling fan

All you need for a dust-free ceiling fan cleanup is a ladder, an old cotton sock, and a bucket of soapy water. Stir 1 teaspoon dishwashing liquid into 1 gallon water. Dip the sock into the water and wring it out. Slip the sock over your hand, climb the ladder, and rub your stockinged hand over each blade. Take care to clean the blades on both sides—the heaviest dust layer is on the top. The dust will be transferred directly to the damp sock, not to the air. A breeze, no?

In the Bathroom

Keep showerheads unclogged

If you live in an area with hard water, you've probably noticed how mineral deposits can clog showerheads. No need to buy a new one—just use denture tablets or vinegar to unclog it.

- If you're able to remove the shower-head, dissolve 4–5 denture tablets in a bowl of water and put the head in to soak. Or let it soak overnight in white vinegar. (For extra cleaning action, heat the vinegar in the microwave first.)

- If the showerhead isn't removable, pour the denture tablet solution or vinegar into a plastic bag, tape or tie the bag to the fixture so the showerhead is completely immersed, and leave the bag in place for 1–2 hours.

To make sure the showerhead is fully unclogged, clean out the holes with a needle, piece of wire, or toothpick. Then wipe the head with a cloth dipped in vinegar.

Good-bye to grime and soap scum

Forget about those store-bought "miracle" products. Instead, stir 3 tablespoons baking soda and ½ cup household ammonia into 2 cups

Septic Systems and Bleach

While bleach is a must-have cleaner that can do everything from whiten laundry to kill off pesky mold, it has to be used carefully in homes with septic systems. To make sure that no bleach gets into your groundwater or septic tank when you're scrubbing your tile or sink, use a toothbrush, and be sure to wipe any excess off the surface material with a water-dampened cloth.

warm water. Once you've wiped the solution on and rinsed it off with a sponge or rag, bathroom surfaces will gleam!

Make glass shower doors sparkle

Glass shower doors are a convenient addition to any bathroom but can quickly cloud up with soap scum. For some heavy-duty cleaning, try:

- **Shaving cream** Squirt the foam on and wipe clean with a dry rag; the foam will leave a film that keeps the door from fogging and makes it harder for scum to stick.

KEEP CHROME SHINY

Chrome faucets and other bathroom fixtures get spotted in seconds, but you can shine them just as fast with **fabric softener sheets**. Keep some on hand in the bathroom and wipe off fixtures as needed. Rubbing alcohol, white vinegar, and the inside of a lemon rind will do a good job, too.

Unclog your showerhead with denture tablets!

- **White vinegar** Keep a spray bottle filled with vinegar and a sponge by (or in) the shower so you can make washing down the surfaces part of your post-shower routine.

- **Baking soda-plus** Make a solution of ¼ cup dishwashing liquid, ¼ cup hydrogen peroxide, and ¼ cup baking soda. Then scrub it on the doors with a sponge—and, if you have time, all of the other shower surfaces as well.

- **Vegetable oil** Simply pour a little vegetable oil on a sponge or paper towel and scrub the doors, adding more oil as you go.

- **Furniture polish** Use a cloth to rub polish directly on doors, then wipe it off with a clean cloth. The polish will not only clean but will also leave a protective coating against soap scum buildup.

Mildew-free shower curtains

The moist environment of a bathroom is just made for mildew, so don't be surprised when it pops up on your shower curtain. You can keep it at bay for a while, at least, by soaking curtains and liners in salt water before hanging them. Once they're up and any mildew appears just …

- Add ½ cup borax and ½ cup vinegar to 2 cups water, pour onto the affected areas and let sit for 8–10 minutes. Then scrub with a sponge or cloth.

- Mix 2 tablespoons dishwashing liquid with 1 pint household bleach and spray the solution on the curtain.

- Make a paste of vinegar and salt and spread it on the mildewed area. Let dry for 1–2 hours and then clean it off with a damp cloth.

Lemony toilet cleaner

Make a paste of 2–3 parts borax and 1 part lemon juice (stir the juice in gradually until you have the right consistency) and apply it to a stained toilet bowl, rim included. Let sit for 1½–2 hours, and then scrub it off with a toilet brush. This treatment is especially effective for getting rid of the bowl ring that often appears at water level.

Clean that ceiling

You're probably so busy cleaning the fixtures and tiles in your bathroom that you don't even think about the ceiling. Look up, but prepare yourself what you might see—mildew, spotting, built-up grime. For an easy cleanup, fill a mop bucket with equal parts water and white vinegar. Then don goggles or other protective eyewear. Dip a long-handled sponge mop into the vinegar, squeeze it out, and reach up to clean one section of ceiling at a time. One more spic-and-span surface, one spiffier-looking bathroom.

Good riddance to grout grime

The grouting between bathroom tiles is a magnet for dirt and germs, and it's easy to miss these hard-to-reach crevices during regular cleaning. Every so often:

- Make a paste of 1 part borax, 2 parts baking soda, and 1–2 parts water and scrub it onto the grout with a toothbrush.

- Rub away grime with a new pencil eraser, well suited to reaching these narrow spaces.

- Scrub with a mouthwash containing a tooth-whitening agent.

- Soak a cotton ball in household bleach and set it on a spot of badly stained countertop grouting for a few hours; for walls, attach the cotton ball with duct tape.

Solutions for stubborn scum and water spots

Non-porcelain surfaces in the bathroom—including ceramic tiles around sinks and tubs and fiberglass and acrylic shower stalls—can become dulled by water spots and built-up scum just as easily as tubs and sinks. Tackle these heavily soiled surfaces with vigor and …

Toilet Cleaning Made Easy

Cleaning a toilet ranks somewhere around zero on the Pleasant Cleaning Tasks scale, but you have no choice but to tackle it. Here are a few ways to make the job easier and pocket the cost of specialty cleansers.

Chalky tablets Drop 2 antacid tablets or 1 denture tablet containing sodium bicarbonate into the bowl, let them dissolve for about 20 minutes, then scrub the bowl with a toilet brush. A vitamin C tablet will do the trick as well.

Mouthwash Grab a bottle of mouthwash from the medicine cabinet and pour ¼ cup into the bowl. After about half an hour, scrub the bowl with a toilet brush and flush.

Cola Empty a can of cola into the bowl and let sit for 30–60 minutes before scrubbing and flushing.

- 2 cups salt dissolved in 1 gallon hot water.

- ½ cup vinegar, 1 cup ammonia, and ¼ cup baking soda added to 1 gallon warm water.

Apply one of the solutions, let sit for about 15 minutes, then scrub off and rinse.

Brush away rust stains

To get rid of hard-water rust stains on commodes, tubs, and sinks, just squeeze a little toothpaste onto an old toothbrush and scrub away. Or scrub the stain with a paste of borax and lemon juice or a solution of equal parts turpentine and salt. Whichever method you choose, attack rust stains right away. The sooner you deal with them, the easier they are to remove.

Window Treatments

Gelatin for window curtains

Machine washable cotton drapes may emerge from the washer fresh as a daisy, but more often than not, they come out so wrinkled that you're in for a tough time at the ironing board. How to keep wrinkling to a minimum when washing cotton curtains? Dissolve 1 tablespoon plain gelatin in 1 cup boiling water and add to the final rinse cycle. The same trick restores shine to polished cotton curtains.

Use a blackboard eraser

You've washed your windows, and when you step back to admire your handiwork you spot those dreaded streaks. What's worse, you can't tell if they're on the inside or the outside of the pane. You'll have to reclean the panes on both sides, but with what? One of the best tools is a clean blackboard eraser, rubbed in a circular motion. To keep from guessing about which side of a window is streaked, try this trick next time: Use an up-and-down motion when cleaning and drying one side of the window and a back-and-forth motion on the other side. You'll now know which side to "erase."

Two old window-washing standbys

People have probably argued about the best ways to clean windows since glass was invented. Two formulations that never disappoint are 1) half a cup of ammonia in 2 gallons warm water or 2) a cup of white vinegar in 1 quart water. To remove isolated smudges and execute other quick cleanups, wipe windowpanes with a soft cloth dipped in white vinegar.

Dust window screens with a roller

It's nice to open a window to get a breath of fresh air, but the effect isn't nearly as pleasant when the screen is full of dust, pollen, and other airborne debris. For a quick cleanup, dig a brush-type hair roller out of the bathroom drawer and run it lightly over the screen. If the

STREAKING: READ ALL ABOUT IT!

One of the biggest window-washing challenges is to prevent streaking. For starters, wash your windows on a cloudy day, when they'll dry more slowly and leave fewer streaks. You'll also ward off streaking by using the right equipment, which needn't be costly or even commercial. Crumpled up, no-colored-ink **newspaper** is ideal for streak-free cleaning and drying. So is the packing paper used by professional movers—merely newsprint without ink.

last time you used a hair roller was around 1989 and you haven't happened upon a stray one under the sofa, dust the screen with a lint remover used for clothing.

Effervescent washer

One of the simplest and most effective glass window cleaners around is club soda, which dries without streaking. Just pour it into a spray bottle and spritz the windows, then dry with a cloth.

Solve the dirty windowsill problem

If you like fresh air and keep your windows open, even a window screen won't be able to keep out all the dust and soot that soils indoor sills. Outdoor sills fare even worse, of course, since theirs surfaces tend to trap dirt in pits and cracks. To make cleaning windowsills a breeze, wash them thoroughly, let dry, and spray the sills lightly with clear floor wax. Smooooooth …

Awesome awnings

A good spray with the garden hose every once in a while will help keep window awnings clean and free of debris, but they also need a thorough cleaning every few months. Scrub awnings made of canvas and most other materials with a brush dipped in warm water and mild detergent. If you're faced with stubborn stains or mildew, sprinkle baking soda onto a stain and let it sit for about 5 minutes before rinsing it off with the garden hose. Treat mildew with a solution of 1 part colorfast bleach and 3 parts water; just let it soak into the material for 3–4 minutes and then rinse.

Don't wash windows on a hot day!

It might be tempting to do your window washing on a warm day, but you'll wind up worse off than you were when you started. Why? Your window washing solution will dry on contact, leaving your windows streaky.

Buck Up and Clean the Blinds

Of all household chores, cleaning slatted blinds (vertical or horizontal) may be the most tedious—the reason it's so often neglected. Help is at hand. With these two techniques, you'll get rid of all that dust and dirt on your blinds with no trouble.

Clean with a glove All you need to wash blinds is a clean thick cotton glove (a gardening glove is ideal) and a small bowl of fabric softener. Pull on the glove, dip your fingers into the bowl, and simply slide your forefinger and middle finger along both sides of each slat. Fabric softener not only cleans hard surfaces but also slows dust buildup.

Clean with a kitchen spatula Wrap a cotton cloth around a spatula and secure it with a rubber band. Dip the spatula in either a 50/50 vinegar-water solution or rubbing alcohol and run your makeshift cleaning tool along the slats. Of course, you could also apply vinegar water or alcohol to the blinds with the gloved-hand technique. No more hidden blinds, no more self-reproach.

Always-new curtain rods for the green-conscious

Hate to clean and dust your curtain rods? So do we, so, we don't. Instead, for smaller windows, we head outside and find an appropriate length and width of fallen tree branch (that's key: it has to be on the ground when you find it)—generally 5 feet long and 3 inches in circumference for a 4-foot-wide window—and run it through the tops of our curtains or through curtain rings. If it starts to get dingy or dusty, simply look for another to replace it, remove the first one, and use it as kindling.

Routing Household Pests

Lure ants with sugar

Give ants what they want: sugar. Make a trap by adding 23 teaspoons sugar to 1 cup water, moisten a few paper towels or old kitchen sponges in the solution, and set them in spots where ants are seen. Leave the traps overnight and check them in the morning. If they're crawling with ants (almost a certainty), sweep the traps into an empty dustpan and dump a pot of hot water over them. Repeat the process until no ants are left to lure.

Repel ants with vinegar

If ants love sugar, it only makes sense that they hate vinegar. To get rid of these unwelcome pests, mix equal parts white vinegar and water in a spray bottle and squirt it on counters, windowsills, baseboards, and anywhere else ants show up.

Spiced-out silverfish

These wingless insects enjoy munching on, among other things, paper, glue, and starch. What they *don't* like? Herbs. Leave sachets or tea bags of dried lavender, mint, sage, or bay leaves in bathroom and kitchen cabinets, where silverfish typically congregate. Wiping down surfaces with lavender oil or a similarly potent herbal solution should also encourage silverfish to make tracks.

Lethal treat for cockroaches

Ingesting baking soda will kill roaches, but you'll need to make it palatable. Bait the pests by mixing baking soda with equal parts confectioners' sugar and sprinkling the mixture inside cabinets and other cockroach hidey-holes.

Minty mouse repellent

Whip up a quart of peppermint tea—not for your morning pleasure but to repel those mice you've heard scurrying about at night. Boil 2 cups water, turn off the heat and add 4–6 peppermint tea bags, and let the tea steep for 6–8 hours. Now stir in 2 teaspoons dishwashing liquid to make the super-strong solution stick to surfaces longer. Fill a spray bottle with the tea and coat baseboards and any areas where you suspect mice are entering.

Ground those flying insects

As much as you may enjoy the aromas of basil, oranges, and cloves, houseflies and other flying insects are repelled by them—one whiff and they'll wing their way elsewhere. So chase them off while treating yourself to some nice scents.

- Put dried basil in organza and muslin sachets (sold at craft and kitchenware stores). Hang the bags in the kitchen and anywhere else flies and other winged pests like to buzz around, and they'll quickly stop dropping by.

- Make a pomander—a whole orange stuck with cloves. Hang it from a light fixture or hook, and you'll enjoy pest-free air and a nice scent as well.

Trap mice with melted cheese

Mice are crafty at stealing a piece of cheese from a mousetrap. The trick is to make sure the trap will trip while mice are nibbling the treat. How to do it? Just set the cheese in the trap and heat it with a lit match so the cheese melts. Unable to spirit it away, mice will sample the melted cheese long enough for the trap to spring shut.

Everyday Laundry Tips

Outfox the sock bandit

Face it: The invisible sock bandit who hangs around washing machines and snatches one sock from a pair will never be apprehended, but here's a way to thwart him: Give each family member a mesh produce bag for stashing soiled socks. Then, on washday, tie the bags closed and toss them into the washer and dryer. The sneaky thief will leave empty-handed, and you'll have to replace socks only when they wear out.

Freshen a laundry hamper

Hampers are handy for keeping dirty laundry in one place, but they can get a little ripe when packed with soiled clothes. Two ways to prevent hamper smells:

- Cut the foot off a pair of old panty hose, fill it with baking soda, knot it, and toss this makeshift odor eater into the hamper. Replace the baking soda every month or so.

- Keep a box of baking soda next to the hamper and sprinkle some on soiled clothes as you throw them in the washer, where the soda will freshen and soften the load.

Whiter whites

Do your white T-shirts tend toward gray? White socks look dirty no matter how many times they're washed? Try one of these tried and true methods for making whites stay white.

- Soak in a solution of 1 gallon water and 1 cup baking soda.

- Soak in hot water in which you've dissolved 5 aspirin tablets (325 milligrams each).

---

make your own
Fabric Softener

There's no need to spend money on commercial fabric softeners when you probably have all the ingredients you need to make your own. See for yourself with this simple recipe.

Lickety-Split Fabric Softener

You can also use this solution to make a fabric softener sheet to toss in the dryer. Just dilute with water, dip in a washcloth and wring it out, and add the washcloth to your load of wet clothes.

2 cups white vinegar
2 cups baking soda
4 cups water

1. Combine ingredients in a gallon-size pail or pot and stir to dissolve the baking soda.

2. Pour the solution into a plastic bottle with a lid. (An old liquid detergent bottle is ideal.)

3. To use, add ¼ cup softener to the washer's final rinse cycle.

- Add 1 cup of white vinegar to the washing machine's rinse cycle.

Blacker blacks, darker darks

While faded and distressed-looking garments are the rage for some age groups, you may prefer not to look as if the last time you went clothes-shopping was 1998. Herewith, some tips for keeping black and dark-colored wardrobe items looking like new.

Add **coffee** to your rinse cycles to keep dark clothes dark!

- For blacks, add 2 cups brewed coffee or tea to the rinse cycle.
- For dark colors like navy blue or plum, add 1 cup table salt to the rinse cycle.
- For denim that will be slow to fade, soak jeans in salt water or a 50/50 solution of water and white vinegar before the first wash. Turn the jeans inside out before putting them in the machine and turn the temperature setting to cold.

Two starch substitutes

No need to run out to the store to buy starch to stiffen your shirt collars or restore body to shapeless clothing. Make your own by pouring 2 cups water into a jar and adding 2 tablespoons cornstarch. Screw the jar lid on tightly and shake well. Now pour the solution into a spray bottle for use when ironing.

If your permanent press items are looking a bit shapeless, don't use starch when ironing.

Instead, add a cup of powdered milk to the final rinse cycle of the wash. Got milk? Got shape.

Boil yellowed cottons

With time, white cotton and linen tend to turn yellow—hardly the fresh, crisp look for which cotton is famous. Let sodium come to the rescue by mixing ¼ cup salt and ¼ cup baking soda with 1 gallon water in a large cooking pot. Add the yellowed items and boil for 1 hour.

Brightening rugs and curtains

If cotton rugs or cotton curtains have faded, simply add ⅓ cup salt to your laundry detergent to brighten the colors. If a rug is too large for the machine washing, scrub it well with a clean rag dipped in salt water.

Banish odors

Know that "new" smell of dye or chemicals that comes with just-bought sheets or shirts? Have a teenager who thinks nothing of leaving sweaty clothes in a locker or gym bag for weeks on end? Worse, ever have a run-in with a skunk? Grab two old deodorizer standbys. First, add ½ cup baking soda to 1 gallon water and presoak any smelly washable items for about 2 hours. Then, as you machine-wash them, add ½ cup white vinegar to the rinse cycle.

An improv drying rack

Running a dryer bumps up your electric bill, so if you're thrifty, you'll want to air-dry any items you can. But don't think you need a sunny day or even a clothesline or store-bought drying rack. Just suspend an old (clean) refrigerator shelf or oven rack from a beam in your garage or basement and hook wet clothes on coat hangers onto the rack. Smart move!

Listerine in your washing machine

Add half a cup of mouthwash to your empty washing machine and run it through a cycle to disinfect it simply with a household product that virtually everyone has in their bathroom.

Dry sweaters with panty hose

Don't pin sweaters directly to your drying line; instead, run an old pair of panty hose through one sleeve, through the neck, and out the other sleeve, and clothes pin the hose to the line.

Keeping Your Iron Clean

You're pressing your nicest 100 percent cotton white blouse or shirt in preparation for dinner with your boss when—oh no!—the iron leaves a black streak on the collar. Sound familiar? You can say good-bye to marred garments by cleaning your iron regularly. Try one of these methods to rid the soleplate of burned starch and other debris:

- Lay several sheets of wax paper on the ironing board, turn the iron on low and the steam off, and run the iron back and forth over the wax paper several times.

- Fill the iron with white vinegar, turn the heat on high, switch on the steam, and let the iron spew for about 5 minutes. Empty the iron and refill it with cool water. Shake the iron gently, drain it, and wipe the soleplate with a clean cloth.

- Unclog steam vents by poking them with a cotton swab dipped in a solution of equal parts water and white vinegar. A toothpick will unclog smaller vents.

Clean your dryer vent ... from the outside

Stuffed-up dryer vents can, in worst case scenarios, cause fires, but most of us never think of examining the vent from the outside, on a regular basis. To do so, carefully lift up the vent flap and clean it out ... assuming that it's not inhabited by any of the following creatures: pigeons, skunks, fox kits, snakes (yuck), field mice, or racoons (this is a favorite passageway into a warm house).

If you do have visitors, call your local animal control.

The Science of Removing Stains

When you attack stains with ordinary household staples, you transform yourself into a domestic mad scientist (no lab coat required). With the right formula you can remove almost any kind of stain from clothing, and there's no reason not to experiment with ingredients that "do no harm"—in alphabetical order, baking soda, cornstarch, flour, lemon juice, liquid detergent, a raw potato, shampoo, and white vinegar. Follow stain treatments with a regular wash. (To treat garments without machine washing, see "Saving Stained Clothing," pages 197-98.)

Blood	As quickly as possible, soak a bloodstained item of clothing in a pot of cold salt water. After 3–4 hours, rub the stain with liquid detergent and launder.
Coffee	Presoak the stain in a solution of 1 quart water, 1 tablespoon white vinegar, and 1 teaspoon laundry detergent.
Grass	Either soak grass stains in full-strength white vinegar or brush non-gel, non-whitening toothpaste directly on the stain.
Gravy	Cover the stain with baking soda, cornstarch, flour, or salt, all of which soak up grease. After brushing the substance off, pour liquid laundry detergent and hot water directly onto the stain.
Ink	Pour salt on an ink stain that's still wet, gently dab with a wet paper towel, and then brush off the salt; repeat as necessary.
Mud	Rub the stain with a peeled slice of raw potato, and then soak the garment in cold water for at least 15 minutes.
Mustard	Stir 1 tablespoon white vinegar and ½ teaspoon liquid laundry detergent into 1 quart warm water. Sponge the solution on the stain and let air-dry. Before washing the garment, apply liquid detergent directly to the spot.
Ring around the collar	Rub shampoo directly onto the stain with your finger or a toothbrush. Let sit for 25–30 minutes before washing the shirt. (Make sure the shampoo you use contains ammonium lauryl sulfate, an ingredient that cuts through oil.)

Special Care for Special Items

Fluff fluffy stuff with a sneaker

When drying a feather-filled item—whether a pillow, duvet, or parka—toss a sneaker into the dryer, too (the less smelly, the better). The soft-soled shoe will make a bit of a racket, but it will fluff up the item nicely as it bounces around.

Speed-dry a wet blanket

Make a soggy blanket fresh from the washing machine look warm and welcoming again in no time. First, put two large towels in the dryer and let them heat for 20 minutes. Now throw in the blanket and let the towels soak up the moisture. Take the blanket out when it's still damp and drape it over the backs of two chairs (ideally, lawn chairs out in the sun) or two parallel clotheslines to air-dry.

Prevent panty hose runs

Runs in a pair of panty hose can ruin the look of the sharpest outfit, so take preventive action when you bring them home from the store. Wash new panty hose, let them dry, and then soak for 3 hours in a solution of 1 gallon water and 2 cups salt.

Salt your new jeans

Nothing's more comfortable than a pair of jeans, but it can take a little time before the stiffness wears off. Hasten the process by throwing a new pair of jeans into the washing machine with ½ cup salt. They'll feel softer the first time you pull them on.

New life for soiled whites

It's a sad day when a favorite white shirt or blouse just can't be seen in public anymore—yellow stains, a dreary cast, and seemingly permanent ring around the collar. But all is not lost. Perk up the garment (and yourself) by working a paste of vinegar and baking soda directly onto stained and soiled areas, then hang the garment outside in the sun for a couple of hours. If the collar remains soiled, pour a capful of 3 percent hydrogen peroxide along the ring. Now wash in hot water as you normally would and make room in the closet for your old friend.

Kettle-clean your felt hat

To deep clean your wool felt hat, fill a teakettle with water, place it on the stove, and bring it to a boil. Carefully hold the hat above the steam, rotating it as necessary. Brush with a dry toothbrush, and let dry.

Wash silk in hair shampoo

Use a protein-based hair shampoo and cool water to hand-wash silk; the protein will feed the protein in the silk, giving it body, and making it last longer.

Chapter Four

Winning the War on Clutter

Some people keep their living quarters so orderly that it's almost scary. Others seem congenitally incapable of controlling clutter, and their houses look as if Hurricane Bruno just blew through.

From all appearances, a talent for organizing is like music or athletics or math: You've either got it, or you don't, and if you're reading this, you know who you are!

Many of the simple solutions in this chapter may work so well that keeping your house orderly will not only be easy, but fun, too. Clutter-controlling hints also give you creative ways to use things you already have, like cardboard boxes, shoe boxes, and plastic containers. Other hints call for common items that aren't normally used for storage, but which work perfectly, like a suitcase, a stockpot, and even a pair of panty hose. It's a well-known fact that orderly surroundings have a positive psychological effect on the psyche. So applying the advice found in this chapter might not only help you dig out from under the mess, but boost your spirits, too!

Corral your shoes in a
laundry basket!

Smart Storage Strategies

How to clean out a drawer

Thought you knew how? Guess again! To organize a drawer in the most efficient manner, have a plastic trash bag and three shoe boxes or similarly sized containers at the ready. Dump the contents of the drawer onto the bed or floor and start sorting the bits and pieces, distributing them like this:

- Put anything you *want to throw away* in the trash bag.

- Place anything you *want to store* elsewhere in the first box.

- Stash anything *worth giving to charity* in the second box.

- Save any *candidates for a garage sale* in the third box.

Now stash everything that's left over back in the drawer. Plan your trip to the dump, the storage facility, your favorite charity, and your upcoming garage sale.

No cheese, please

The next time you order pizza to go at the pizza parlor, chat up the cashier and ask if you could have an extra box. Pizza boxes make excellent containers for everything from road maps to souvenir newspapers to children's artwork.

CD storage

Your CD rack is filled, and you've taken to stacking new CDs beside it on the floor. Time to put that empty shoe box to good use! Sort your CDs and put the ones you rarely listen to in the box; label each box according to genre of music and return it to its former place (probably on a closet shelf). Stack other shoe boxes on top as your CD collection grows.

Special storage for special stuff

Turn shoe or hat boxes into a keepsake box for each member of the family. Covering the boxes in different-colored contact paper will distinguish them from one another and make them more durable as well. You could also let your child use tempera paint to paint his or her box. The boxes will ensure that all medals, ribbons, special greeting cards, and any other paraphernalia worth keeping doesn't get lost in the shuffle.

THE HOME ORGANIZER'S DREAM BOX

Wine and liquor boxes have 12 compartments, each about a foot tall and just begging to hold rolled-up posters, holiday decorations sorted by type, and whatever other flotsam and jetsam you want to keep in order. The boxes are always easy to come by, since wine and liquor store personnel are more than happy for you take a few off their hands.

The Small Container Hall of Fame

Some common items found in the average home have achieved such status among organized homemakers that we hereby induct them into the Small Container Hall of Fame. Buy an indelible marker and a roll of first aid tape, and label, label, label! When the contents change, relabel.

Cigar box
Hard to find, but when you do, they're worth their weight in gold. Look for them at tag and rummage sales.

Berry basket
This small, ventilated plastic basket from the supermarket is good for storing anything that needs a little air, like kitchen sponges and soap pads.

Coffee can
It's roomy and has a lid. Who could ask for more? Just keep the contents dry.

Film canister Soon to be extinct, but not yet. Hoard film canisters and use them to hold rings and earrings, small change for tolls, fishing flies, and garden seeds.

Hanging shoe bag
Perhaps the best all-purpose holder known to man and woman. Hang it on a closet door, in a bathroom, in a home office, or in a child's room and start stuffing the roomy pockets.

Baby wipes container
Sturdy and stackable, this rectangular plastic receptacle is ideal for small office supplies, sewing paraphernalia, small tools, and cookie cutters.

Ice cube tray
The plastic ice cube tray has two more compartments than the egg carton but no lid—which make it the perfect drawer divider for itsy-bitsy odds and ends. Fill it with small office necessities or rings and earrings, put it away, and you're good to go.

Egg carton
Twelve small compartments and an attached lid make this lightweight container the choice for buttons, washers, tacks, paper-clips, pushpins, and more.

make your own

Newspaper Clipping Preservative

The acidic nature of newsprint means that newspaper clippings will not only yellow but will also eventually disintegrate. To save articles reporting your golf trophy, your grandson's acceptance to Harvard, or your wife's distinguished service award, give the clippings a Milk of Magnesia bath. Though "milk of magnesia" is a common term for magnesium hydroxide, $Mg(OH)_2$, it is trademarked as an over-the-counter antacid and laxative.

$Mg(OH)_2$ Clipping Saver

Before soaking a clipping, make sure the ink won't run by adding a drop to a tiny area of print, preferably outside the margins of the article you want to preserve.

   1 Milk of Magnesia Tablet
   1 liter club soda
   1 large nonaluminum bowl
   Shallow glass pan

1. Combine the tablet and club soda in a bowl and let sit overnight.

2. Pour a ¼-inch layer of the soda mix into the pan and submerge the clipping for 60–90 seconds.

3. Lay the clipping on a double layer of paper towels, and then cover with another double layer and press gently to absorb the water.

4. Remove towels and air-dry the clipping on a wire rack or screen.

Storing gift-wrapping paper

Save long, cardboard mailing tubes and use them to store leftover wrapping paper. The tubes will make use of the air space in the corner of a storage closet. You could also attach a plastic bag filled with gift cards and spools of ribbon to a tube with a metal binder clamp or a clothespin. Tape the tubes together with masking tape, and group by occasion or holiday.

Jot it down

You reorganized your drawers and closets last spring, and you can't remember where you stashed the measuring tape or the heating pad. Prevent wasting time hunting things down by recording their new locations in a notebook labeled "Where It's At" (or, if you're a stickler for grammar, "Where It Is"). Better still, use your computer and save the list on your hard drive so you won't have to hunt down your notebook!

Curtail junk mail

A combo of three things in your household will slow the flow of junk mail that adds to clutter: 1) a pen or computer; 2) paper; and 3) a postal stamp. Write and ask the American Direct Marketing Association (DMA) to remove your name and address from their mailing lists. *Their* address? Direct Marketing Association, Mail Preference Service, P. O. Box 643, Carmel, NY 10512 (www.the-dma.org). Don't expect a quick fix, however; it takes a few months for the DMA to dam the flood of mail. Or if you live in Canada, contact the Canadian Direct Marketing Association at Concorde Gate, Suite 607, Don Mills, ON M3C 3N6 (www.the-cma.org).

Organized Entryways and Living Areas

Here's your hat (and your keys)

A hat rack in the foyer is the handiest place to park jackets, scarves, dog leashes, keys, and—oh yes!—hats. If you're a woodworker with an artistic bent, you could turn the right fallen tree limb into a sculptural rack that works equally well as a functional item and decorative feature.

A hanger rack from scratch

Turn a straightened coat hanger and clothespins into a hanger rack on the back of an entryway closet door. Do the same on the back of a kitchen cupboard door to hold extra dish towels.

1. Measure the door and cut a piece of wire that will leave 2–3 inches of space at each end.

2. Mount a screw eye in the center, then another at each end. Run the hanger wire through the screw eyes and bend both ends around the outer eyes with pliers.

3. Now clip clothespins to the wire and use them to hold mittens, caps, and any other small items of clothing.

Shoe catcher

Devote a plastic laundry basket not to your wash, but to wet shoes. Place it just inside the mudroom door as a catchall for sneakers, galoshes, and anything muddy. (A large, shallow basket is more eye pleasing, but plastic is the utilitarian choice because it's so much easier to clean.) To speed the drying of wet shoes, use two items that normally belong in the kitchen: a cookie sheet and a cooler rack. Place the cookie sheet near the mudroom door, set the rack on top, and you have a wet shoe catcher that allows for better air circulation.

Clear the way

If access to your garage is through the laundry room, you don't want to dodge clutter each time you pass through, especially if the space is tight. One way to keep the coast clear is to mount two plastic milk crates side-by-side on the wall above the washer. Use them to hold your detergent and other laundry supplies, and they'll not only stay out of the way but will be right at hand when you need them.

Impromptu umbrella holder

If you have a tall cylindrical garbage bin that's seen its day, think twice about retiring it. A coat of paint or a layer of contact paper will turn it into an umbrella stand for your entryway. The real article can cost a pretty penny, but your recycled stand will do just as well. Note: If the can is metal,

Household Superstar!
27 Things to Store in Panty Hose

Only 27 things? What *can't* you store in panty hose? (Basically, liquids, grains, flour, and anything that won't fit.) Among the items to stash in a panty hose leg or foot are these, listed in orderly fashion—i.e., alphabetically.

1 Apples

2 Badminton shuttlecocks

3 Colored pencils

4 Curling irons

5 Dog toys

6 Eagle Scout merit badge sash

7 Flower seed packets

8 Golf balls

9 GPS trackers

10 Hair clips

11 Instant oatmeal

12 Jellybeans

13 Kazoos

14 Lightbulbs

15 Mothballs

16 Narcissus bulbs

17 Oreos

18 Ping-pong balls

19 Q-tips

20 Ribbons

21 Take-out menus

22 Undies

23 Vampire teeth

24 Walkie-talkies

25 X-ray eyeglasses

26 Yo-yos

27 Zip discs

spray the interior with clear lacquer to prevent rust.

Feng shui this!

According to the principles of the ancient Chinese art of feng shui (pronounced *fung schway*), placing furniture and objects to align with magnetic north optimizes energy flow, or chi, and brings the home environment into harmony (or something like that). If you want to give feng shui a whirl, rearrange your furniture accordingly to see if it makes a difference in your sense of orderliness and well-being. Stranger things have happened.

That mountain of magazines

It just keeps mounting, doesn't it? To reduce clutter without giving up the articles, invest in a craft knife to slice out the pages you want and then save them in a "To Read" file. A craft knife will not only give you a cleaner cut but also will do the job three times faster than scissors.

Storing tablecloths

A tablecloth folded like a sheet is a tablecloth that will have to be ironed. Keep tablecloths crease-free by hanging them over a towel rod mounted on the inside of a storage closet door. If the rod isn't round, slice paper towel tubes lengthwise and fit them over the rod to minimize wrinkling.

Take care with collectibles

The best storage compartments for tender antiques are polyethylene plastic containers, acid-free cardboard boxes, and enameled metal storage cabinets. But if a lack of space demands that you store collectibles in a wooden cabinet or drawers, take these measures to keep stamps, dolls, textiles, and metals (including coins) from being damaged by the sulfuric and acidic vapors given off by both unfinished and painted wood.

• Keep items out of contact with the wood by wrapping them in acid-free tis-

Store questro om blankets or pillows in an *antique suitcase!*

sue paper or prewashed, unbleached cotton muslin.

- Seal wood box interiors with at least two coats of polyurethane varnish.
- Whether you collect comics or stamps, give them the right conditions: no excessive light, heat, moisture, or dust.

Double-duty furniture

Your great-great-grandfather's footlocker in the attic can do more than just gather dust. Topped with a runner, it makes a coffee table that's a conversation piece as well as a storage unit. Pack it with extra blankets or sheets or use it for board games, playing cards, and any sports equipment small enough to fit in.

A bookkeeper

A device to keep books from falling off open-ended shelves, that is. To secure the books, cut two wooden dowels to size and stain them to match the shelves. Screw two teacup hooks on each shelf end, pinching the hooks on the bottom shelf closed so they'll hold the dowels in place. Slide the dowels through the hooks, and you have two bars that will keep books in place on your airy but precarious shelves.

Mount a CD cabinet in an entryway

Get rid of that painting you never liked and replace it with this organizing marvel. Basically a bookcase divided into individual squares meant to hold 10 or so compact discs each, it's also a perfect way for family members to keep their keys and cell phones instantly "grab-able" first thing in the morning.

Kitty litter tubs for storage

Perfect for organizing everything from toys to infrequently-used linens, these uber-storage containers have more uses than we have room here! Wash them thoroughly, label them, and use them to store dishes, tools, small kitchen appliances, boxes of photos, cassette tapes, and much more.

In the Bedroom

Between the sheets

There's no room for the set of flannel sheets you were given for your birthday, so where can you keep them? Hide the two halves of the set side by side between the mattress and the box springs at the foot of the bed.

Three square feet of extra space

Doesn't sound like much, but it's enough to hold the towels or shoes that won't fit into your bulging linen closet or even your stack of weekly magazines that you insist you'll get around to reading some day. What is it? A suitcase. Going on a trip? Dump the contents in a cardboard box you store in a corner of the bedroom with a sheet thrown over it. Whether you're home or away, your stuff is still all in one place and out of sight. Be careful, however: Don't store things in a suitcase that smells of mold or mildew, which will do whatever you've stashed away no favors. Also be sure to wrap any glass or ceramic objects in bubble wrap to protect them when the suitcase is moved.

Two-level clothes rod

If the clothes rod in your bedroom closet is high up, suspend a second rod below it. Cut a second rod to the desired length, and then do the same with two vertical lengths of light but sturdy chain. Attach steel rings to both ends of the chains and hang the lower rod from the original.

Under-the-bed dresser drawer

Have an old dresser up in the attic? If you're smart, you're storing what you don't need in its drawers. But you can also bring one of its drawers right into your bedroom and keep it out of sight. Just attach casters to the bottom four corners for a rolling chest that's kept under the bed.

Homemade sock organizer

You may not be able to keep a sock from losing its mate, but you *can* bring order to the pairs you keep in a dresser drawer. To avoid rummaging through a big pile of socks to find what you want, cut shoe boxes in half and then position them so the open ends fit snugly against the front of the drawer. (Or, if you're handy with a bow saw or coping saw, cut two or three fiberboard dividers to the drawer depth.) Sort dress socks, casual socks, and athletic socks into the appropriate compartments, and you'll be able to zero in on what you're looking for in a jiff.

Door stops = hangers

When screwed into the back of a closet door, door stops with rubber tips make excellent hangers for shoes. Group the stops in pairs, setting them a few inches apart. Shoes hung, floor space cleared!

Swinging from the ceiling

A length of brightly colored plastic chain will keep the stuffed animals in a child's bedroom off the floor and out of the way. Hang the chain in a corner at the appropriate height, affixing the ends to both walls. To make it possible for your little one to hang up the toys, stitch a loop of hem binding to each one and use S-hooks to suspend the stuffed animals from the chain.

"The baseball corner"

That's what you'll call the corner shelf you make in Mikey's bedroom so he can keep all of

Hold the Gold *(and Silver and ...)*

Keeping jewelry neat and accessible can be a challenge even for the most organized person. For every perfectly organized jewelry box, there are at least 10 that amount to a jumbled mess of necklaces, bracelets, rings, pins (ouch!), and mismatched earrings. Try these no-extra-cost storage ideas—gems in themselves!

Silverware box

If your grandmother's wooden silverware box is sitting empty in the attic, odds are the velvet-lined interior is in good enough shape to hold your jewelry. The velvet will slow silver jewelry from tarnishing, while the compartments will keep it in order, particularly necklaces, which can be held in place by the utensil dividers. Polish the exterior wood to a nice sheen, and keep it on your bureau as a showpiece.

Needlepoint canvas

Tiny squares of leftover needlepoint canvas are perfect for storing pierced earrings. Make them more secure by slipping the mesh into a plastic bag before storing them in your jewelry drawer.

Prescription pill containers

Don't throw these out when empty; the tinted brown plastic is just transparent enough to show the jewelry.

Egg cartons and ice cube trays

The compartments of egg cartons and ice cube trays are just the right size for keeping jewelry separated, organized, and visible. Especially great for keeping pairs of earrings together! Line cartons or trays side by side in a drawer.

Pierced earring holder

Clip a skirt hanger onto the waistband of an old pair of panty hose and you have an instant pierced earring holder. Just push the studs through the nylon and attach the backs. Hang from a closet rod. You'll be able to see your collection all at once, keep pairs of earrings from being separated, and have immediate access.

Herb or spice jars

Repurpose well-washed 1-ounce plastic or glass spice jars as jewelry holders. They're small, see-through, and perfect for keeping pairs of earrings together and storing rings, pins, and chain-link bracelets. Keep in your jewelry drawer or stash in a suitcase when traveling.

his baseball equipment in one place. Here's how to put it together.

1. Cut a 12-by-12-by-17-inch triangle from ¾-inch plywood.

2. Bore 1½-inch diameter holes for the baseballs.

3. Cut bat slots with a coping saw.

4. Nail the shelf to ½-by-2-inch cleats fastened to wall studs.

Now watch Mikey take pride in keeping everything together on his own special shelf.

Storing loose change

Instead of keeping loose change in a dish on your dresser, let resealable plastic kitchen bags be your organizers. Sort the change into separate plastic bags, putting a few coin rollers in with the appropriate coins. Then stack the bags in the corner of a drawer until you're ready to cash the coins in for bills. If you live in an area where coin-sorting machines are available, by all means use them (if you don't mind paying a small fee). Still, don't think you're a Luddite if you prefer to roll your own coins, which to some people is as meditative an exercise as washing dishes.

A pared-down "wallet"

When leaving for your morning walk or run, you usually take a few dollar bills along in case you decide to stop for a sports drink or newspaper on the way home. The easiest and most lightweight alternative to a wallet? A metal binder clip, which will firmly secure the bills (and your ID, if you like) to the waistband of your running shorts or sweats.

Jewelry within reach

Draping necklaces and bracelets from the hooks on a coat rack mounted on the wall next to your dressing table is a smart idea. For one thing, your baubles are right at hand. For another, they add a nice decorative touch to an expanse of bare wall.

Kitchen Storage Tips

Compartmentalize your cabinets

To keep your kitchen cabinets from becoming a jumble of boxes and bags and cans, gather some flat-bottomed rectangular baskets or small wooden or cardboard boxes—shoe boxes are usually ideal. Line up the containers on the shelves and reserve each for a different kind of food—one for sugar, syrup, and other sweet stuff, one for baking-related items like flour and baking soda, and so on. If you use boxes, you can paint them to blend with your kitchen's color scheme. Whether you spiff them up or not, label the containers with their contents so you don't confuse the sugar with the salt (yuck).

Organize spices by style of cuisine

Is your spice rack a mess? Can't find the cumin when you need it? Arrange them in a low-sided, unlidded box (old cigar boxes work great) by type of cuisine, and whenever you're cooking Italian food (or Mexican, German, French, Asian, Indian, Middle Eastern, or good old American), the appropriate spices will be together in one place. Cumin, oregano, cilantro, and red pepper? Sounds like Mexican. Tarragon, parsley, sorrel, bay? French. Label each box according to its nationality, and whenever you're in the mood for that style of cuisine, your spice hunting will be kept to a minimum.

New rack = less racket

Tired of having to take the pots and pans out of a cabinet to get to the cookie sheets on the bottom? (Bang, bang, bang!) Transfer a metal desk file organizer to the kitchen. This compartmentalized metal rack will allow you to store cookie sheets, jelly-roll pans, and thin wooden or acrylic cutting boards vertically. The upshot?

Label, Label, Label

Labeling devices should come with a warning: *Use with caution.* Some people are so enamored of hand-held label printers at first that they go on a labeling binge, labeling every shelf in the pantry and linen closet and toying with the idea of labeling the pets so nobody will confuse Fluffy with Fido.

Actually, compact label printers are a godsend for anyone whose constant refrain is, "If I only knew which box I put it that in.…" It's amazing how many boxes go unlabeled when people move. Then they have to sift through a stack of boxes to find the can opener—or go out and buy a new one. And it's not just boxes you should label, moving or not. Marking home videos, file folders, and any other objects that don't immediately reveal their contents will make your life much easier and also remind family members where to put things.

Sure, you can use your computer to print out sheets bearing the words Baby Books, Old CDs, San Francisco Souvenirs, and the like, and tape them to boxes. But it's faster to key in the letters on you labeler and then print out the self-sticking tag.

You'll be able to pluck flat items out of a crowded cabinet with ease.

Newspaper buffers for nonstick cookware

When you nest nonstick saucepans and pots one inside another, you're almost sure to scratch the delicate coating. To keep nonstick cookware scratch-free, simply tuck a newspaper sheet into each pot and nest them without worrying.

Protect your knives (and yourself) with a **paper towel tube!**

Rack 'em up

There's the pot, but where's the darned lid? Rummaging through a cluttered cabinet full of pots and pans can be an exercise in frustration. A solution to the problem is as near as your toolbox. Just mount an ordinary towel rack or two on the back of the cabinet door and slide the lids between rack and door. The knobs on the lids will keep them from falling through.

Keep your storage lids on

Ever find yourself faced with the perfect storage container for that batch of tomato sauce you made, but the container lid has made its way to who knows where? Keep all the lids organized—and together—by storing them inside the largest empty kitchen storage bin you have.

Protect fine china

When stacking fine china in the cabinet, keep dinner plates scratch free by alternating them with paper plates. For salad plates and saucers, use coffee filters for the same purpose. China teacups are best stored right-side up. If your cabinet won't accommodate all the cups, create an extra tier of cabinet space by setting a coated wire rack inside. Or, you ask, why not hang the cups from hooks attached to the bottom of the shelf above? Hooks are fine for everyday china, but hanging antique teacups means they'll be bearing their own weight—a bad idea if you want to give these heirlooms all of the tender loving care they deserve.

Let it slide

In some wooden kitchen cabinets, the drawers sit on wooden slides on the bottom rather than lubricated metal slides at the sides. Dirt easily accumulates on the slides and makes opening and closing drawers anything but smooth. To rectify the problem, clean wooden glides with soap and water. Then, when the slides are dry, rub candle wax on all wood-to-wood contact points. Friction-worn wooden slides can also be fixed right up with the insertion of one or two smooth-headed thumbtacks or upholstery tacks. Smooth sailing from here on out.

Multipurpose furniture

Have an old china cabinet lurking in the attic? Put it to use in the kitchen, if you have the room: instead of storing grandma's plates in it, turn it into storage for spices, measuring cups, and baking tools, or anything that otherwise clogs your cabinets.

Hats off to plates

Whether you keep inheriting piles of plates from well-meaning relatives, or you just can't resist them at tag sales and antique fairs, don't let them overrun your cupboards. Empty out those old hatboxes you have, and use them to store plates on top of each other, separated by pieces of soft cardboard or paper plates. Label the boxes and stow them in the attic or on a basement shelf.

Sheathe your kitchen knives

The razor-sharp knives you use for cooking can be dangerous, so never keep them loose in a drawer with other kitchen tools. If you don't have the countertop space for a butcher-block knife holder, fashion protective sheaths for your knives from empty paper towel tubes. To make a sheath, just flatten a tube, fold over one end and staple or tape it closed, then slide a knife in the other end. For small knives, use toilet paper tubes.

Keep small appliances in clear plastic containers

Kitchen counters a mess? Can't find the coffee grinder behind the electric pepper mill? Large, clear plastic storage containers are a great way to keep small tools used infrequently out of the way, but still in sight, on a garage, basement, or walk-in pantry shelf.

What's the Story?
The Arrival of Plastic

When did man-made plastic first appear? It made its debut at the 1862 Great International Exhibition in London, the work of British chemist Alexander Parkes, who named his cellulose-derived creation Parkesine—the first organic material able to retain its shape after being heated and molded. Six years later, an enterprising Albany, New York, printer named John Wesley Hyatt discovered that the solvent action of camphor on cellulose nitrate under heat and pressure created a clear and durable material—celluloid, which transformed photography and, in the early 20th century, movie film.

The first mass-marketed plastic, Bakelite, was introduced in 1907. The phenol-formaldehyde resin—perfected in Yonkers, New York, by Belgian-born Leo Hendrik Baekeland—was used to manufacture everything from telephone handsets to kitchenware to engine parts. Teflon made its first appearance in 1937, and nylon one year later. The arrival of polyester in 1942 would transform the manufacture of clothing, as anyone who donned a leisure suit or pink polyester pantsuit in the 1970s could attest.

Today's liquid crystal polymers and other new plastics in no way resemble Mr. Parkes's rudimentary invention. Little could he have dreamed that a century and a half later, flying machines would be as ubiquitous as horse-drawn carriages, and that one of those machine's bodies would be plastic: the Boeing 787 Dreamliner, made from the same reinforced plastic used for golf club shafts.

Repackage dried food in plastic

If your cabinet space is cramped (and whose isn't?) repackage dried food products. Food manufacturers seem to delight in filling containers only two-thirds (or even half) full—and as the food diminishes, the size of the box doesn't. Gain precious room by transferring most of your dry food to see-through plastic containers (and then label and date them!). Flat rectangular containers work best, since they're stackable and ideal for storing tea bags, dried beans, rice, pasta, and cereal.

Ready-made picnic totes

A six-pack container (the kind used for beer or cola) is ideal for carrying picnic supplies from the kitchen to the car to the blanket spread out in the meadow or park. Bind plastic utensils with a rubber band and put them in one compartment, then fill the other compartments with picnic paraphernalia such as rolled up napkins, salt and pepper shakers, squeeze bottles of ketchup or mustard or mayo, and a can of insect spray.

Smart idea for storing leftovers

If you have a label-making machine, here's an idea that may not have occurred to you. Store all of your leftovers on the same rack, and label the shelf so no one forgets where to put them. No machine? Cut a piece of paper to size, write "Leftovers" in indelible ink, and tape the label onto the rim of the rack with transparent tape. Designating a leftovers shelf and labeling it will make it much less likely the remains of the steamed broccoli you enjoyed in April won't be covered in mold in June.

A movable candy bin

When organizing your kitchen cabinets with the aid of baskets or boxes, keep a special one for candy. Either place the goodies bin on a low shelf that the kids can reach or on a high shelf where it's out of reach.

Three-ring recipes

A box will keep your recipe cards all in one place, but a three-ring binder will go it one better. Slip the cards into pocketed plastic photo holders made for ring binders. Arrange recipes by type and then tape a colored plastic file tab on the first page of each category: soups, chicken dishes, and so forth. Using a binder will make it easier to browse through your cards and choose the perfect recipe for the occasion.

Scan your recipes

If you're computer savvy, clear your clutter by scanning all of those yellowing recipes into computer files. Organize them into style of food, entree, desserts, holiday favorites, salads—the possibilities are endless. This will enable you to search for recipes with a couple of keystrokes!

DECANT BIG BAGS OF FLOUR
If large bags of flour, sugar, cereal, or pasta are on sale, don't worry about keeping them on your cabinet shelves; empty the bags into individual, supersize clear plastic **storage containers**, label them, and stack them on an out-of-the-way shelf in the basement.

The Clutter-Free Bathroom

Downsize your essentials

If the total of family members in your household equals three, do you really need 18 bath towels, 12 hand towels, and 10 washcloths? And how many bottles and tubes of cosmetics and ointments and painkillers crowd medicine cabinet shelves and vanity drawers? The first task for the clutter fighter is to get rid of what you don't need; the second is to look for ways to save space—and here are ways to do both.

- To free up shelf space, attach three or four towel rods on the back of the door and hang a week's supply of towels from the rods.

- Make two bathroom toolkits, and store one in a ready-to-go ziplock bag for quick packing. Include tweezers, nail clippers, scissors, Q-tips, and cotton balls.

Search out shelf space

If you have a window, a shelf supported by brackets of the same material will hold towels and supplies.

A 2-foot expanse of wall is room enough for two- or three-tiered shelving, good for holding supplies of any kind. Get more mileage out of it by attaching a board to the bottom and installing hooks for hanging wet towels.

Racks to the rescue

Wish you had more towel racks in your bathroom? Forgo time-consuming installation and simply stand a coat rack in the corner—ideal for hanging towels and bathrobes.

Lunch Box to First-Aid Kit

Your son Henry outgrew his superhero lunch box a long time ago and consigned it to the attic, but there's life in the colorful aluminum carrying case yet. It's just the right size to hold bandages, gauze, scissors, and tape on one side and a bottle of isopropyl alcohol and an antiseptic spray or ointment—plus the cotton balls used to apply them—on the other.

Keep the kit in a bathroom cabinet, and you'll be able to grab everything at once whenever you have to run out to the yard and treat little Henry Jr.'s cuts and scrapes.

When it comes to *storing* towels, a wine rack meant for countertops fits the bill. You'll want to put the rack, which will accommodate from five to 10 rolled-up towels, depending on the design—wherever it seems most practical—the floor, perhaps, or atop a cabinet. A bonus: Besides saving space, the rack brings an attractive architectural note to the bathroom.

Hang tiered baskets

Those tiered wire baskets made for decluttering the kitchen will come in handy in the bathroom as well—and the less room you have, the more you need to make use of the bathroom's air space. Hang a set of tiered baskets from the ceiling and then stash rolled hand towels in the largest basket and toiletries or what-have-you in the smaller ones.

An unused lunch box makes a perfect *first-aid kit!*

Toiletries to go

Here's a clever space-saving idea for large families with too few bathrooms: Turn small wicker baskets into toiletry caddies and keep one in each family member's bedroom. Everyone can then carry his or her toiletries to the bathroom as needed.

Paint each basket a different color and fill it with customized supplies—for Dad, his preferred toothpaste, shaving cream and razor, and other grooming supplies; for Mom, cosmetics, hair care products, and the like. Whatever you load into the baskets will help keep bathroom countertops clutter-free.

Move meds out

Removing your prescription and over-the-counter pharmaceuticals from a bathroom cabinet to the kitchen or bedroom will do more than save space in one of the home's smallest rooms. The warmth and humidity in bathrooms can degrade the stability and potency of some drugs, so put them in a lidded plastic container or shoebox and store them in a cool, dry place. You'll want to make sure the medicines are out of the reach of children, of course.

Mount a magnet

A magnetic knife holder mounted on the bathroom wall makes an ideal holder for small metal necessities like nail clippers, tweezers, and toenail scissors. No more searching for small stuff in a messy drawer or cabinet!

A hair fashions box

Present your favorite little girl with a compact, compartmentalized box with a clasp (a flat fishing tackle box is ideal), and then ask her to sort her hair accessories into the compartments by type. If she is so young she has difficulty opening the box, ask her to bring it to you whenever she likes. As she observes you taking items from the box and returning them to their proper places, she'll learn to keep her hair accessories and other belongings in order on her own.

In the Workshop and Garage

The magic of magnets

Given a magnet's powerful hold over metal, it's no wonder that so many home-repair folks feel a strong attraction to magnets. They come in handy for a multitude of tasks around the workshop—everything from organizing your workbench to cleaning up spills. Here are a half-dozen fantastic ways to put them to work for you.

- Fix a large round magnet to the wall next to your workspace (or suspend it from the ceiling, if necessary) to keep small metal parts and tools from getting lost in the middle of repair work.

- Before using steel wool, wrap a small bar magnet inside the pad to catch any loose steel strands or particles and keep them from messing up your work area.

- Place small round magnets inside jars or boxes of screws and brads to prevent or contain spillage if they're accidentally knocked over.

Neat Ways to Store Lumber

Keeping loose lumber around your workshop can be dangerous for you and damaging to the wood. But an old wooden ladder can straighten things out. Secure the ladder rail to a wall with wood brackets, and then use the spaces between the rungs to sort different lengths of lumber. You could also stand several pieces of lumber in an old golf bag or keep them bound together inside a pants leg cut from an old pair of jeans.

- Put a bar magnet inside a plastic sandwich bag to pick up spilled nails, nuts, or washers—or even to clean up metal filings. The objects will stick to the outside of the bag, which you can then turn inside out to contain them.

- Magnetize the head of a screwdriver by rubbing it several times with a small horseshoe magnet.

- Hot-glue several magnet strips inside your toolbox or workbench drawer to keep your favorite flat tools at the ready.

Childproof your
power cords with a
key ring!

Pull the plug on power tools

If you're unable to lock up your power tools or place them out of the reach of young children, you can still prevent curious youngsters from plugging them in. Simply slip an ordinary key ring through the hole on the power prongs.

Hang a power cord

Loose power cords can be hazardous around the workbench. Besides posing a danger underfoot, they take up precious space in your work area and can be a real pain to untangle. Keep them neat and out of the way by screwing a few large bicycle hooks into the ceiling joists above your workbench and threading the cords through the open loops. Finally, a way to keep that jungle of wires off the floor and out of your workspace!

Cords for clamps

Don't toss out those old bungee cords; wrapped around furniture, appliances, and other household items, they make excellent band clamps when you tackle repairs. Although the cords aren't adjustable, they can be combined to create almost any desired length or, in the case of long cords, shortened by multiple wrappings.

Keep supplies in the gutter

Who says gutters have to be outside? Not the savvy do-it-yourselfer. Mount a couple of vinyl rain gutters around your work area for an inexpensive yet sturdy way to store lengths of molding, lumber, PVC pipe, and dowels. Simply screw the mounting brackets into the wall studs and snap in the gutters. You could also use the bare gutter brackets to hold wire coils, extension cords, and hoses.

Make the cut

Here's a sharp idea: Remove the serrated cutting strip from a box of aluminum foil or plastic wrap, cut it in half with a metal cutter or shears, and tack or nail one of the sections to the least-used side of your workbench. Make sure the teeth are positioned slightly above the top of the surface. You'll never have to search again for a knife or scissors to cut a piece of tape, rope, or sandpaper.

A place for parts

Make your own parts bins out of recycled plastic milk jugs. Leave the caps on the jugs (seal them with epoxy, if needed), and cut off about ⅓ of the side panel with a utility knife or scissors. Fill the jugs with nails, screws, nuts, and other small parts, then place them on a small bookshelf or cabinet. You can also stand the jugs upright, of course, and the handles make for easy transport.

Prevent rust on tools

If your garage is damp and you store tools there, prevent rusting by lightly coating them with petroleum jelly or car wax. If you're storing tools you don't use often, spray them with a silicone lubricant and wrap them in aluminum foil. The next time you use the tools, just wipe them with a soft cloth.

Hammock in the garage?

Yes, but not for lazing about. Make use of the space above your car by stringing a hammock from screw eyes fastened to the garage walls' exposed joists. Presto! A sling for light but bulky items such rolled-up small rugs, basketballs, hockey and lacrosse sticks, and exercise mats.

Repurposing Has Its Rewards

A quick look through your home recycling bin can usually turn up a bunch of items that can significantly reduce the clutter around your workshop. Here are a few suggestions to get you started.

- Use empty prescription pill bottles, film canisters, glass jars, coffee cans, and the see-through plastic tops from CD spindles to hold nails, screws, and other fasteners.

- Turn an old ice cube tray or a muffin pan into an organizer for washers, tacks, brads, nuts, and bolts.

- Number the 12 compartments in an egg carton and use each cup to hold disassembled parts in the order they're removed.

- Use cardboard tubes from paper towels, gift-wrapping paper, and toilet paper rolls to neatly hold extension cords, ropes, and dowels.

- Mount a large block of recycled Styrofoam near your workbench to use as a "pincushion" for drill bits, screwdrivers, pens, punches, wrenches, and other tools.

- Glue a piece of cardboard onto the bottom of a building brick (the type with holes in it) and use the brick to hold files, drill bits, brushes, craft knives, and the like.

Your Home Office

The No. 1 home office storage space

Forget about fancy desk dividers or those costly built-in shelves; the most important home office storage space under your roof is the hard drive of your computer. Your Rolodex, appointment book, desk calendar, and business card holder (not to mention pictures of your children) that seem to travel about on your worktable will be immediately available in the most uncluttered way possible, if you digitize them.

Filing cabinet as conference table base

Well, a round conference table that can seat two or three. The space between the tabletop and the floor won't go to waste if you use a metal filing cabinet or an old bedside chest as a support. Use ¾-inch plywood for the top and bolt it to the top of the cabinet. Then cover with a tablecloth that almost reaches the floor. Store rarely-used files in the cabinets below, and you'll be crawling under the table only once in a blue moon.

A secret filing cabinet

No intrigue here—just a filing cabinet that looks like anything but. What is it? A straw rectangular basket with a lid, something more often found in a living area than a home office. A basket with dimensions of roughly 20-by-20-by-10 inches should accommodate around 30 files of average size or up to a dozen well-stuffed file folders. Placed under or beside your worktable, the basket is decorative as well as functional.

Invest in a small safe

Store deeds, birth certificates, insurance information, and passports in a fireproof safe that can be stowed on the top shelf of a closet. Out of sight, but not out of mind.

Door-top bookshelf

When you run out of space for books, put a shelf in the space above the door and below the ceiling. If you have a piece of lumber in the garage or storeroom, you have yourself a shelf whose only cost is the support brackets you buy at the home store. A coat of paint on a sawn-to-size board will keep it from looking like a makeshift shelf in a college dorm room.

Tips for Packing, Mailing, and Shipping

Some of those things you're trying to keep in order are mailed to you (hello, catalog shopping) and others are things you want to send—say a care package to you son at summer camp. Herewith a few tips for making things run smoothly when you pack and ship or prepare a letter for mailing.

Rustle up free packing material

Wadded-up newspaper is probably the first thing you reach for when packing something in a box, but you can also use several other items you most likely have on hand—like these:

- Plastic grocery bags
- Paper grocery bags
- Dry cleaning bags
- Paper strips from your shredder
- T-shirts bound for the dustbin

Store such stuff in paper bags in the basement or garage so they won't steal space in your closets or cabinets.

Pop some popcorn

Unbuttered air-popped popcorn makes excellent packing material because it's soft and light as a feather. It's also green—not because popcorn is now coming in colors (it isn't), but because its biodegradability makes it environmentally correct.

Towel fragile items

You've collected everything you need for your college-age daughter's care package, and it's time to pack up all the items you need. Instead of filling the box with packing peanuts, why not use something she can keep? That would be bath towels and, if she has kitchen facilities, dish towels. Wrapped several times around fragile items, towels provide protection and make a nice gift.

No-stick hands

Those infernal polystyrene packing peanuts cling to your hands when you unpack a shipment. To keep the peanuts from sticking, simply rub your hands with a fabric softener sheet.

Keep paper-shredder blades sharp

Cutting aluminum foil will sharpen your scissors, and the shiny stuff will do the same for the blades in your paper shredder. Lay a sheet of 8½-by-11-inch paper on two sheets of heavy-duty aluminum foil as a cutting guide, then snip away. Feed the sheets of foil through the shredder one at a time, and the blades with sharpen right up.

A good-looking bulletin board

A jungle of Post-it notes and envelopes and papers stuck to a bulletin board isn't the prettiest sight to behold. So make your easy-to-reach "filing system" more attractive by covering the board with felt and attaching ribbons to hold your stuff. Start by choosing felt in the color of your choice. Then cut it 4–5 inches larger than the board on all four sides, pull it taut over the board, and staple the overage to the back. Use upholstery tacks to secure ribbons to the board, pulling them as taught as possible so that paper slipped behind the ribbons won't fall through. You could crisscross the ribbons to create a diamond pattern over the whole board, or position them to look like latticework—as long as it works, the design is up to you.

A real vertical file

"Vertical file" is business slang for "wastebasket." But an actual vertical file borrowed from your child's toy box will keep mail, tickets, and papers of similar size from cluttering up your workspace. What is it? A Slinky. Set it on your worktable and slide stray papers in between the wires.

A business card album

A small photo album is ideal for keeping business cards in order. Simply slip a card or two in the protective plastic sleeves made for ring binders. With a ring binder to leaf through, your days of shuffling through a stack of cards for the one you seek are gone.

Office-in-a-closet

Tight on space but long on office need? Turn a spare coat closet into your workspace at home; if you're lucky enough to have a double closet, even better. Remove the doors, attach a thick plank of plywood from one inside wall to the other; use upper shelves to store less frequently used items such as a dictionary, extra stationery, your laptop. Slip a filing cabinet under the "desk," add a lamp, and you'll be good to go.

Keep documents in a scrapbook

Scrapbooks outfitted with plastic sleeves or pockets are ideal for keeping business contracts and other documents in order.

MISPLACED YOUR PENCIL SHARPENER?

In a pinch, sharpen a pencil with a **vegetable peeler**. This kitchen instrument beats a pocketknife when you have to rely on something other than your usual tool.

Storing Holiday Decorations

Tangle-free twinklers

What are the holidays without strings of lights, whether they illuminate trees, mantels, or yard displays? And what are fresh-out-of-storage cords of lights if not tangled? All you need to keep them orderly is an empty coffee can and its lid.

First, slice the plastic lid of the can with a sharp knife and insert one end of the light cord. Then wrap the cord of lights around the can, taping the end to the can to keep everything in place. Before putting on the lid, fill the can with extra bulbs and an extension cord. No tangles, no misplaced accessories!

Give fragile items top billing

Tree and mantel ornaments range from wooden toy drummers to delicate winged doves made of crystal—the latter and their ilk needing special care. If you pack fragile items with other ornaments, first wrap them in tissue and put them in a self-sealing plastic bag. When putting them in the storage box, be sure to place them on top of the other ornaments so they won't be damaged as you dig into the box next year.

Storing big stuff

The Santa on your lawn, complete with sleigh and reindeer, isn't inflatable. Rather, the components of the merry tableau are made of molded plastic that can't be squashed flat—and unless you have room to spare, they present a storage problem bigger than Santa's toy bag. Your first step toward smart storage is to save zippered garment bags, which should be large enough to hold one or two or the pieces—or more,

depending on their size. Then hang the bags from rafters in the attic or basement. You could also consider hanging a hammock between two rafters and heaving the bagged pieces into it.

Make bows easy to spot

Have an extra glass canister that you haven't found a use for?

If it's tall and has a lid, store self-sticking bows in the canister so that, come gift-wrapping time, you'll see what your choices are at a glance.

How to store candles

If stored in a hot place, candles tend to warp and curve—and a curving candle is good only for the person who enjoys candle making and melts down candles. Prevent the problem by choosing a storage spot that stays below 75°F for the year, even if that means the cellar or a closet. Wrap individual candles in tissue paper and lay them flat in a plastic container or a cardboard box— or, in the spirit of repurposing, paper-towel tubes or cylindrical potato chip cans.

New life for wrapping paper

Don't throw away wrapping paper and tissue that piles up as your family opens gifts. Instead, use it to keep the holiday ornaments you'll soon be storing from getting scratched or chipped, or donate it to a pet care center. Choose one or all of these three options:

- Wrap each ornament in leftover paper when placing in the storage box. If desired, store ornaments by type and Christmas tree balls by color. However you choose to store, label each box with the contents.

- Feed the wrapping paper into a shredder. Then use the paper ribbons as packing material to keep your ornaments in good shape.

- Donate shredded wrapping paper to a veterinary clinic. Many veterinarians use shredded paper as bedding for the animals in their care. Just call first to make sure the paper is wanted and needed.

Holiday spirit in a black plastic bag

Look at old clothing, furniture, appliances, electronic equipment, and odds and ends of any sort not as "just something to get rid of" but as items that would be welcomed by the less fortunate. Organizations or charitable groups will accept virtually anything that is still in good condition. Clothing can be donated to the clothes closet of a local house of worship or a charitable consignment store.

A cardboard box filled with gently worn shoes or a black plastic trash bag filled with towels and sheets that no longer match your color scheme becomes a vessel of hope, not of refuse bound for the city dump. Either deliver your goods to the charity in person or schedule a pickup. Your reward is less the tax deduction you can take for donated goods than the knowledge that someone in need will benefit from a "new" shirt, pair of shoes, sofa, or even the connection to the world at large, a computer.

GREETING CARD ART

If you enjoy tackling crafts projects with your kids or on your own, look at the **holiday cards** you receive as a wealth of raw material. Snipping images from the cards and using them to create collages or abstract compositions gives you artworks suitable for framing. Even better, it consolidates the wishes of friends and family into a memento that's both aesthetically pleasing and meaningful.

Garlanding Made Easy

The artificial garlands you draped on the staircase drew raves from friends and family last Christmas, but this year you're not sure which lengths of garland went where. There they sit in a large plastic box, and you foresee wasting your time by laying and re-laying them alongside the second-floor railing until they all come together as they should.

How to eliminate the guesswork? Take these three simple steps before putting the garlands away for storage.

1

Tag the lengths with their location, numbering them in order from the top railing to the newel post at the bottom.

2

Use twist-ties to mark the spots where the lengths were tied to the banister to make swags.

3

Label the storage box clearly ("Staircase Garland") so it won't be confused with any other garlands you might have used.

This 'n' That

Elevated basement storage

Storing furniture and other large items in the basement is risky because of the humid conditions. If you have no choice but to keep Grandma Lila's old cherrywood sideboard there for a while, safeguard it or any other vulnerable item from moisture by placing it on a wooden pallet and covering it with a large tarp.

If you're wondering where to find a free pallet, check with the nearest grocery store. An alternative platform is a 1-inch slab of plywood supported by cinder blocks.

Attic air-freshener

Your attic contains everything from hanging bags of clothes to old hats and gloves and scarves. So wouldn't it be nice if it didn't smell like an attic? Banish mustiness with the lava rocks used for barbecue grills. Just scoop rocks into four or five mesh bags and hang the bags from the attic's beams. Every few months, refresh the rocks by setting them outside in the sun for 4–6 hours. Lava rocks left out in the sun should absorb musty odors for years on end.

The wandering shower caddy

It doesn't take an Einstein to realize that a shower caddy needn't be confined to the bathroom. Use it anywhere inside the house to stock items of all sorts—laundry room supplies, gardening products and small tools, and so on. Just hang the caddy from a doorknob or from a sturdy hook or nail on the wall of the garage, basement, workshop, or garden shed.

TLC for anything framed

You should not only store framed photographs and artworks properly to extend their life but also label them as clearly as possible—the latter accomplished by taping a photograph of the framed piece to its wrapper (use a Polaroid or the printout of a digital shot). Wrapping paintings, framed prints, lithographs, and photographs takes some time, but pays off in the end. Wrap each piece in acid-free tissue paper and sandwich it between two layers of ¼-inch foam board cut a bit larger than the frame. Tape the corners and middle of the board, then wrap the package in brown paper. After taping the paper at every seam, attach the photograph of the piece within.

Bonus hint 1: Never wrap artwork of any kind in plastic, which can trap moisture and cause warping or the growth of mold.

Bonus hint 2: Wear cotton gloves when handling an oil painting. Touching the surface (back or front) will leave oils and salts from your hands—substances that can eventually crack or otherwise damage dried oil paint.

Two ways to hang twine

Say that you need to keep three balls of twine or string fairly handy—jute twine for bundling newspapers and flattened cardboard for recycling; nylon garden twine for tying plants to stakes; and colored string for gift-wrapping. How would you go about saving yourself from fishing for them in drawers or tool bin? Try these two tricks:

- Install three hooks on a wall or on the back of a door, spacing them 6–8 inches apart. Now slide a cord or ribbon (or a length of twine from the ball itself, for that matter) through each spool and knot it. Hang a ball of twine from each hook, and your twine is easily accessible.

- Use funnels instead of hooks. Choose funnels large enough to hold a ball of twine and nail the top rim of each to the wall. Put a ball of twine in each funnel and run the ends out of the spouts—and presto! A twine dispenser that works like a charm.

Bank on this one

Bank statements seem to accumulate faster than you can say "prime interest rate," especially when you're so busy you can't find the time to check them. A quick fix: Each time a statement arrives in the mail, scan it and save it as a file in your computer. The result? All the info you need, and no paper to take up space.

Free labels for your stuff

Some charities that send out promotional mailings include a small batch of personalized address labels in the packet. If they've gotten your name and address right, you can use the unsolicited gift to label personal items as well as envelopes. Paste the labels inside books, on the underside of staplers and other small pieces of office equipment, and on the back of your cell phone. With the aid of tape, you could even affix one of the labels to your umbrella or the inner cuffs of mittens or gloves.

What's the Story?
Science's Take on Tangling

When you put away last year's Christmas tree lights, you carefully looped the strings so they wouldn't get tangled. And here they are—one big mess. It's enough to tie a neatnik in knots.

Relax: Physics, not you, is to blame. In October 2007, experiments conducted at the University of California, San Diego, showed that strings basically tie themselves when agitated. Physics Professor Douglas Smith and research assistant Dorian Raymer wrote in the prestigious journal *Proceedings of the National Academy of Sciences* that they had developed a mathematical formula explaining why strings and cords knot so easily.

Their method? Shaking strings placed in boxes. The result? Roughly half of the shaken strings came out of the box knotted.

We'll spare you the particulars of knot theory (a mathematical branch of topology) and let a scientist encapsulate why strings of lights tangle themselves. During an interview aired on National Public Radio (NPR) in December 2007, Stanford University Professor Keith Devlin— known on NPR as The Math Guy—laid it out:

"[Smith and Raymer's] program gave them tremendous insight into how Christmas tree lights or iPod earphone cords ... get tangled up. What we know now is that roughly half of the times a knot forms, it begins to form within the first two or three seconds of shaking. So even if you've only taken that Christmas tree box up the stairs into the attic, the chances are high that you're going to tangle it."

See there? The tangling of strings of lights isn't always caused by haphazard storage habits but rather by forces beyond your control.

Chapter Five

Making Your Home *Sweet* Home

Okay, you're no Martha Stewart or Christopher Lowell. But honestly, who is (except, of course, for Martha or Christopher)? And for that matter, do we really need to be them?

When it comes to decorating, our list of helpful household items and intuitive but surprising tips includes almost everything in the house and will make you feel like you could easily teach Martha herself a thing or two. This chapter is about using what you already have to make the place you call home look, feel, and function to meet your needs, your style, and your budget. You'll find loads of practical ways to create fresh looks by reusing, refurbishing, and repurposing.

Ever thought of whitewashing or glazing wallpaper to give it a brighter feel or using a beat-up old ladder as a design feature? Ever throw away a piece of fabric or an old glass bottle just because you're not sure what to do with it? You're about to discover how easy it is to update all sorts of furnishings and accessories by using what you have on hand. So get inspired, get to work, and get ready to delight in being your own decorator.

Turn your living space
into a photo gallery with
a clothesline!

Changes Around the House

Looking for the best free decorator?

No problem! Just look in a mirror. This two-step trick will turn you into an interior decorator without costing a penny.

1. "Edit" a room by putting everything that *isn't* furniture out of sight. Remove personal items, linens (leave the curtains if it's a pain to take them down), pillows, throw rugs, lamps, artwork, electronics, books, and magazines.

2. Look at what's left. By getting down to the bones of a room, you'll gain a better perspective on what you have and whether it works for you.

Most likely, you'll decide to reposition or eliminate some furniture. Perhaps a fresh coat of paint or adapting your existing window treatments is all you need. Or it may have been all that "stuff" that was making an attractive room look dowdy or overcrowded. With the room stripped down to basics, you can envision the space and its contents anew, see fresh possibilities, and improve the room—and at no cost whatsoever.

Laundry basket as pillow nest

What can you do when all those fancy throw pillows get in the way? Convert an old wicker laundry basket into a pillow holder. If you have a plastic laundry basket, cover it with a sheet by setting the basket on it and folding the sides and corners into the basket itself (like you were wrapping a gift). Fill with pillows and no one will know that you didn't buy it at that fancy design shop.

New furniture from spare chairs

Nobody ever seems to have enough small tables, but many of us have too many chairs. If so, think about converting those extra chairs into something more useful. In most cases, straight-backed armless chairs with hard, flat seats are easiest to work with.

- Paint two chairs of different designs in the same color to make an attractive pair of bedside "tables."

- Refinish or paint a straight-backed chair that has arms and set it in the mudroom as a catchall for hats, bags, and umbrellas.

PUT TOGETHER A NO-FRILLS DESIGN KIT

Use the tried and true design-planning method that's easy, cheap, fun, and free of any sales pressure—a do-it-yourself design kit made with a **ruler,** a **pencil,** graph paper, a pencil, construction paper, and a tape measure.

That old woven basket will make a great place to **store pillows!**

• Make a coffee table substitute with two or three wooden chairs; they needn't match so long as the seats are approximately the same height. Saw off the back of each one at seat level and sand well; you may also need to trim off any corner protuberances that rise a bit above seat level. To guard against stains, paint the chairs with water-resistant enamel. When the paint dries, line up the little tables as a unique and practical coffee table.

Lay that sledgehammer down!

Renovating a kitchen brings out the beast in the homeowner, but don't destroy those cabinets yet. Instead, consider how you might reuse them in another part of the house. You could …

• Hang wall cabinets in the workroom or garden shed, removing the doors for open shelving.

• Put two single or one double wall cabinet (standard depth approximately 12 inches) in a kid's closet to hold toys and clothes or in a hall closet for storing seasonal gear.

• Add casters to a base cabinet to make a rolling cart for the laundry room.

• Make a study desk or worktable with a couple of base cabinets topped with a plain, smooth-surfaced old door.

• Stack two single or double top cabinets to make a nifty storage unit for sewing and craft supplies.

Create a strong focal point in any room

The focal point of a room is the first visual element to which the eye is immediately drawn. Rooms without an obvious focal point tend to look bland, disorganized, or incomplete, regardless of the quality of the furnishings. To add flair to a blah, unfocused room, the quick and inexpensive fix is to use items you already have. Decide on the logical focus of attention, and then go through your storage closets and attic for things you've tucked away or forgotten.

- Bright throw pillows or a quilt will add impact to a plain-Jane bed.

- Frame that beautiful silk scarf or lace shawl you haven't worn in years and hang it on the wall behind the bed.

- If your fireplace and mantel don't grab the eye, use leftover paint to set them off with a floor-to-ceiling background panel of a different color. Hang a large mirror or a display of eye-catching pottery plates above the mantel.

- Get rid of clutter to bring the eye to a focal point: Remember that less is more, so rotate collectibles instead of displaying all of your treasures all the time.

Shelving from odds and ends

Instead of spending big bucks on shelving, look around you: What about those wooden trays you never use? A shallow drawer from an old dresser or desk? Or the sturdy in-out boxes someone at the office was about to give the heave-ho? Maybe the decorated drawer fronts from a baby's old chest would make fun shelves for a growing youngster. The size and weight of a makeshift shelf will determine the kind of brackets and hardware you need when attaching it to a wall, so take your "shelf" to a good hardware store and ask for advice. If you

A Tiny Touch of Originality

Remember what refrigerators used to look like? Today they're likely to be covered with more magnets than a millipede has legs. While the fridge as magnetic bulletin board filled with notes, photos, take-out food menus, and you-name-it is a boon to busy folks, it will benefit greatly from the occasional decluttering. And why not use magnets that reflect *you,* not the taste of some anonymous designer? Make your own simply by hot gluing small magnets, sold at craft stores, to tiny souvenirs and found objects like small seashells; clip-on earrings (clips removed); lapel pins from museums; smooth, flat river rocks; or unusual buttons.

plan to load anything heavy on the shelf, like books, attach it to a wall stud or studs.

New uses for louvered shutters

Don't throw out those old louvered shutters until you've considered the possibilities. Hinge three or more shutters together so they'll fold accordion-style, to create handsome, practical screens for indoors and out. Long shutters make an attractive screen to separate sleeping and dressing areas in a bedroom or to shade a sunny area on a porch or patio. Secure a panel of hinged shutters to the wall behind a plain bed for a knockout headboard. Have a weird corner space calling out for something? Stand up a tall louvered screen to soften the angle.

Bonus idea: Metal or vinyl louvered shutters, laid flat over two sawhorses, make a great outdoor potting table for gardeners. Water and air go through the slats, making it easy to wash and dry pots and garden tools, water and drain houseplants, and hose away dirt and debris.

Color Your World

Save those leftover paints

Whenever the decorating bug bites, you'll be very glad you didn't toss out your half-empty paint cans. Hang on to them to create small "patch" tests during those redecorating binges. Better still, use them for:

- Patching nicks and scratches in existing wall paint
- Priming for new paint
- Redoing or touching up old furniture and accessories
- Painting a closet or pantry
- Painting the inside of a small cupboard
- Tinting other paints to create color washes
- Creating multicolor faux finishes
- Doing decorative stenciling
- Painting trim work on everything from furniture to picture frames

Transfer small amounts of leftover paints to wide-mouthed plastic storage containers, like clean mayonnaise or peanut butter jars. Label by color, type of paint, and manufacturer. Air and moisture are the enemies of stored paint, so be sure tops and lids seal tightly. Alkyd and oil-based paint will form their own protective skins in the containers. For latex (water-based) paint, lay a layer of plastic wrap atop the paint before putting the lid on. And always store leftover paints in a cool, dry place, away from direct sunlight.

Make that bookcase pop!

One of the simplest ways to add depth to a room is to paint or wallpaper the inside backs of built-in bookcases and display shelving—a great way to use leftover decorating materials. If you paint, keep in mind that darker colors appear to recede, fooling the eye into seeing a deeper recess—hence

What's the Story?

The Famous Novelist Who "Invented" Interior Design

Modern interior design owes its origins to one of America's greatest fiction writers. Edith Wharton (1862-1937), born Edith Newbold Jones to a socially prominent New York family, went on to skewer her own class in *The House of Mirth*, her Pulitzer Prize–winning *The Age of Innocence*, and other widely read novels and story collections. But it was her first book, *The Decoration of Houses* (1897) that punctured the pretensions of upper-class Victorian decorating and set out many principles that guide interior design to this day.

Collaborating with architect Ogden Codman Jr., the well-traveled Mrs. Wharton brought her knowledge of French and Italian home decor to the mix, comparing European lightness, elegance, and comfort to the "exquisite discomfort" of the dreary, cold, overstuffed drawing rooms of New York's upper crust. Her book is credited with elevating interior decoration from lady's hobby to profession. Not the bestseller she hoped for, *The Decoration of Houses* did earn her first royalty check, sold steadily for many years, and is still studied today.

Age Furniture with Candles

Do you like the worn, "shabby chic" look that's all the rage but don't want to spend the (large) amounts of money that these pieces cost? Use a common household candle to reproduce the look on any wooden piece of furniture (new or old) that you plan to paint.

1

First, prime the piece with an under-color primer (as though the furniture had been painted this color previously) and allow the prime coat to dry thoroughly.

2

Rub a white candle along edges and corners, around knobs and pulls, randomly over chair arms—wherever the furniture finish would be worn away by frequent use. Be generous with the wax but brush away any flaky bits.

3

Now paint the piece with a coat of the main color, which won't adhere to the wax. If you need another coat of the top color—a possibility if you're painting a light color over a darker one—rub a little more wax over the exposed places.

4

When the piece is completely dry, just rub away the wax with a soft cotton cloth dipped in warm water.

a larger room. A solid or discreetly patterned wallpaper will achieve the same effect.

Spruce up trim with color

Before starting a large-scale "freshening" project, look up at your wall moldings and trim, and check your supply of leftover paints. In general, a single trim color is carried throughout the home to unify the spaces from room to room. But you could add color to, say, a child's room, family room, or game room by painting the trim in an accent color. (To maintain the visual flow with the rest of the house, keep doors and window frames in the overall trim color.)

Don't strip that wallpaper; glaze it!

If your wallpaper has fallen out of style but you dread the hideous job of stripping it, apply a glaze to soften colors and tone down patterns. Far less mess, much less time—and with luck, you already have the key ingredients: white latex interior paint, latex glazing liquid, water, and a small amount of colored latex for tinting the wash. This is a great two-person project—the application requires coordination but goes very quickly.

1. Mix 1 part white latex to 1 part white glaze Add water to thin. As you add the water, test the mix on a paper remnant or a small, out-of-the-way patch of wall. If the wash is too strong, add more water and test again. (Water can account for up to half of the finished product).

2. Once you're happy with the look, wash the mix over the paper with a lint-free cloth, using a swirling motion as if you were cleaning the wall. Work in sections and work fast, because glaze dries rapidly.

3. Use a brush to apply the glaze wash at corners and edges, tamping with a cloth to remove brush strokes. Then, step back and pat yourself on the back for having chosen such a clever and attractive solution.

Take an old ladder and …

Give it a new lease on life. It may be too wobbly to stand on, but an aged wooden ladder—with its many nicks, paint splatters, and worn-down rungs—has *character*.

- Prop it against an outside wall and use the rungs to display plants.

- Add some heavy-duty hooks and hang the ladder horizontally on a mudroom or porch wall to make a handy catchall for coats, hats, gloves, wet swimsuits and towels, and whatever else your family usually dumps on the floor.

- Suspend an old but still-sturdy ladder from the kitchen ceiling and equip it with metal S-hooks for a unique, cost-free pot rack. Point is, that ladder may not be ready for retirement yet—just a change of career.

Rainbow colors for outdoor furniture

Outside, you have five lawn chairs that have seen better days. Inside, you have five cans of leftover paint. Here's your chance to make good use of those paints you've been saving and to go a little crazy with color to boot. There's no rule that all outdoor furniture has to look the same, so be adventurous and go for the bold. As long as you prepare surfaces well by sanding and cleaning and follow manufacturers' instructions, you can use leftover interior paints on outdoor pieces and protect them with a polyurethane finish. Rusty metal furniture should be scraped as needed and primed with a rust-resistant undercoat. Thanks to modern technology, you can also spray paint faded plastic yard furniture.

Bright Ideas for Lamps and Lighting

Use a light-diffusing slipcover for a shade

Lamplight owes its beauty more to the lampshade than the bulb. To soften harsh light from a fabric or paper shade, try this gathered slipcover—especially easy for a round shade. Check your flame-retardant remnants and linen closet for a lightweight fabric in a pale-to-medium color or pattern, and rustle up some narrow ribbon to make the fabric gather.

1. Cut the material about twice as wide as the smaller circumference of the shade (longer for a shade with one very wide end) and about 2 inches longer than the top-to-bottom measurement. Piece the fabric if needed, perhaps alternating solid and patterned panels.

2. Seam together the short sides of the fabric. Fold over and stitch the top and bottom edges to make ½-inch pockets, leaving a small opening in each. Now take the ribbon and cut lengths twice as long as the shade's top and bottom circumferences and wrap one end of each length tightly with tape, like a shoelace tip.

3. Thread ribbon through the pockets, playing with the fabric so the gathers are evenly distributed. Tie off excess ribbon as little bows. To secure the cover, tack down top and bottom edges with thread or double-sided fabric tape. The finished shade's look will be as soft and pretty as the lamplight.

Caution: Halogen lights get very hot, so stick with heat-appropriate shades for those lamps.

Perk up your lampshades

Did you know you can spray paint a fabric shade for a snappier look? And you won't have to buy paint if you have some craft paint or leftover latex on hand.

- Using a ratio of 1 part paint to 10 parts water, mix enough to fill a regular-size plastic spray bottle. Be sure the lampshade is clean and free of dust. Protect the inside of the shade with paper secured by masking tape. Begin by spraying a light, even coat; let dry. Spray on more paint, drying between coats, until you have the intensity of color you want.

- Add design by using painter's tape to make vertical or diagonal stripes. Or cut shapes from a coated paper, attaching them to the unpainted shade with spray adhesive (follow instructions for a temporary bond). After spray painting, remove the cutouts once the paint is dry. For a soft, mottled effect, use the same paint formula and dab paint, a little at a time, directly onto the shade with a natural sea sponge. The fabric will diffuse the color, creating a light and airy look.

Silhouettes on the shade

Give extra interest to a plain paper or fabric lampshade with dark or black construction paper cutouts—also a fun way to decorate for special occasions. (Think leaf patterns for Thanksgiving, snowflake silhouettes for a winter holiday, hearts for Valentine's, jack-o-lanterns for Halloween, footballs for a Super Bowl party.) A medium-weight card stock works, too. Translucent white, cream, gold, beige, and pastel shades give the best effect. When cutting out the shapes, size them to the shade—not too large and not too small. Affix the shapes to the inside of the shade with double-sided tape, taking special care that paper doesn't touch, or lie too close to, the lightbulb. Now turn on the lamp and see how the silhouettes appear almost "embedded" in the light. Paper cutouts will begin to curl over time, but they're easy to remove and replace.

Sky's-the-limit lamp bases

Picture your beautiful ceramic flowerpot illuminating your living room. It's relatively simple to convert just about any non-fragile container, large or small, into a one-of-a-kind lamp base. Most containers need a hole drilled in the bottom or side for the cord. You can cannibalize an old lamp for no-cost parts, but if you lack experience with electrical wiring you should take your object of choice to a home store or electrical supplier for help. You might have to spend some money (store-bought lamp kits have almost everything you need)—but compared to a new lamp, you'll be shocked (no pun intended!) by how much you'll save when you create your own. Great lamp bases can be repurposed out of old:

Decorate a drab lampshade with a *paper silhouette.*

- Inexpensive vases
- Tag-sale pitchers
- Large coffee mugs
- Overturned ceramic mixing bowls
- Loving cup-style trophies
- Books that have been placed atop each other and glued together
- Antique wooden boxes
- Flower pots

Paint an old lamp base

Spark up an old or inexpensive wooden, metal, plastic, or even glass lamp base with a coat of paint. Use paint you already have, but check the info on the can to be sure the paint is suitable for the lamp base material. If you must buy paint, one spray can or one small can of enamel should be plenty for a pair of medium-sized lamps. (Glass requires special paint, available from craft suppliers, for a permanent finish.) Color and design are up to you. Anything goes, from an antique finish to a thoroughly modern industrial look.

Before painting, use flexible painter's tape to mask off the fittings and any areas that you want to keep paint-free, such as a metal base or trim. Also tape over the top of the socket to avoid getting paint on the contact points.

Bedazzle an ordinary chandelier

A plain chandelier can become a dazzler when hung with artful strands of crystals and beads. Go through what you have already—leftover glass beads and faux pearls from other craft and sewing projects, crystal baubles from an unused chandelier, beads from broken or no longer fashionable costume jewelry. Look for beads with sparkle. Though stringing with pliable wire will allow you to form shapes, dental floss and

The Stunning Side of Seam Binding

If you sew, you know that inexpensive rayon seam binding has a lovely, silky look and comes in many colors. But did you know it can also substitute for expensive ribbon in some decorating projects? For instance, rejuvenating an old lampshade by wrapping it entirely in silk satin or grosgrain ribbon can cost a small fortune. By using seam binding instead, you'll get the same elegant look. Generally available in ½-inch widths for about 40 cents per yard (less through discounters), seam binding will also work in woven ribbon projects, ribbon flowerets, and even some ribbon needlework. Give it a try. Here's a notion: Rummage through your sewing supplies for all unused bindings and fabric tapes and visualize them not as ho-hum sewing notions but as colorful trims, bows, piping, appliques … whatever strikes your inner decorator's fancy.

beading thread are just as strong as wire. String baubles and beads in interesting combinations, and then loop and swag them on your light fixture (turned off at the switch) until you have a look you like. Then turn on the light and appraise the dazzling results.

Paint a simple ceiling medallion

Plain, flush ceiling light fixtures are the Cinderellas of room lighting; they work so very hard, yet no one pays them any attention. But with a little leftover latex paint, some string, and a ladder, you can dress up an underwhelming ceiling light for the palace ball. The idea is to mimic a circular plaster medallion. On paper, work out an attractive design, such as concentric circles in different colors and shades.

Remember that you'll be painting upside down, so keep the design simple.

Tie a pencil to one end of the string, tape the other end to the center of the fixture, and mark off your outside circle. Use the string compass to mark other circles and semi-circles and a straightedge for lines. Evaluate your design from ground level before painting. If you're not confident of your painting abilities, use flexible painter's tape to outline sections of your medallion as you proceed. Wipe away any mistakes with a wet cloth. With some advance practice, you might add shading and highlighting to give your faux medallion a 3-D look.

Make dinner more intimate

Soft lamplight adds intimacy, and you can duplicate that romantic experience in your dining room, using a lamp and a table runner you already have, plus some masking or painter's tape. Lay the runner on your dining table and position the lamp. If the runner has a cutwork pattern, you may be able to slip the lamp cord through. Otherwise, cut a slit in the runner, just wide enough for the plug, at the point where the cord exits the lamp base. (You can also do this with a tablecloth you don't mind cutting.) Run the cord under the fabric and tape it to the table. Now tape the cord to the inside of a table leg and run it to nearest electrical outlet. To keep anyone from tripping, tape loose cord unobtrusively to the floor. Dim the room lights to get the full effect.

Beautiful botanical candles

Turn plain candles into boutique-worthy, botanical beauties, using the bounty of your garden and nonflammable household glue. Choose small, flat-faced flowers like violets, pansies, or nasturtiums, and press them for a few hours in a telephone book. Flatten ordinary lawn grass (unmowed), fern stems, plant leaves, and flower petals in the same way. Glue the natural material to the lower half of candles. Tip: If you're not going to use the candles immediately, dip them in paraffin melted in a double boiler. A thin coat of paraffin will protect the botanicals and preserve their colors.

ABRACADABRA!

Beeswax candles can cost a pretty penny. If you've got ordinary candles you haven't used, you can get the unique appearance of beeswax by wrapping your candles in **a sheet of beeswax**. Crafts suppliers sell very affordable sheets of beeswax (approximately 8-by-11 inches) in honeycombed or plain textures. With a sharp kitchen or craft knife, cut a rectangle equal to the circumference and height of your candle. Use a hairdryer to soften the beeswax just enough to make it pliable. Wrap the candle and press the beeswax edges together to close the seam.

Ordinary Things Worth Saving

Let's face it: you can't hang on to everything, no matter how devoted a problem solver you are. But there are some basic decorating tools and materials that are worth saving for new projects. Paints, fabric, and wallpaper remnants are obvious. After all, you chose the colors and patterns, so you'll probably like them in new applications. Here are some more prosaic leftovers that won't need to be bought again. Plus, they all have everyday household uses, so saving them means you can find them when you need them.

Special purpose glues and adhesive tapes

Paint solvents

Metal hooks and brackets of any size

Picture hangers

Grommet dies and hole punching tools

Metal hinges

Specialty cutting tools and scrapers

Cleaned paint brushes, rollers, and wooden stirrers

Drop cloths

Regular and heavy-duty metal staples

Upholstery tacks

Curtain rods, hooks, and rings

Metal hooks and brackets of any size

Sandpaper and steel wool

Measuring cups and spoons no longer used for cooking

Tea lights in a sandy bed

Want an economical way to transform any fairly large, shallow, flameproof container into an unexpected light show? Simple! From a treasured silver or wooden tray to a serving platter with gently sloped sides to a simple sheet pan—you're sure to have a suitable container around the house. Even the lid of a large popcorn tin will do. Line the container bottom with aluminum foil and add a smooth layer of clean sandbox or aquarium sand. No sand? Try table or rock salt or small dried legumes such as green and yellow split peas or black beans. Embed tea lights to the top of their sides. Use a small paint or makeup brush to sweep away any material on the candle itself.

Sparkling votive holders

A little glitter and clear-drying household glue will turn a humble votive candleholder into the shimmering, sparkling star of any candle display. Check first that both glitter and glue are not flammable. Brush the votive holder with glue and roll it in glitter. A really thorough coat of glue will produce a nearly opaque glitter covering; less glue, applied randomly, will give the look of a dusting of glitter. If you don't have any glitter, lightly brush on glue and roll the holder in granulated sugar, table salt, or kosher salt. You can't wash these votive holders, but when stored in plastic wrap they will keep their sparkle for quite some time.

Glassware candleholders

Got tons of candles but not enough candle holders? Look through your good, better, and best glassware, and even mundane items like jelly jars, canning jars, tumblers, and imprinted drinking glasses. A mix of pretty glasses with candles—different sizes, shapes, and colors—will make an intriguing arrangement on a table and mantel. Two or three stemmed crystal wine or water goblets can be sublime candleholders on a formal dining table. Float tea candles in cocktail glasses, filled about two-thirds with water. Pillar candles will rest easy inside flat-bottomed water glasses. For glassware with concave or convex bases, adhere pillars or tapers to the inside base with removable putty and pour in enough salt to support the candle. (Salt will catch drips and is easily disposed of.) For a really spectacular look, use a dripless candle and substitute metallic glitter or glass seed beads for the salt.

Light Up That Mantel

During the holiday season, illuminated nativity scenes and menorahs and all kinds other religious or merely decorative lights take pride of place on fireplace mantels the world over. But why not light up a mantel at other times as well? Just forgo packing away your string of lights this year, and hang onto extra bulbs. Here are five ideas to get your imagination going—but first, some cautions: Be very careful that lights are never near water or flammable materials, and unplug lights whenever there's no responsible adult in the room, when you leave the house, or when you turn in for the evening. Use lights that don't heat up, and always check wiring for breaks and wear before using.

- Hide lights in an arrangement of silk flowers or a leafy artificial topiary.
- Feed a strand of lights loosely into a large colored glass bottle or jar.
- Arrange lights in polished silver or brass bowls and cups lined up across the mantel.
- Encircle the frame of a mantel mirror with lights taped just behind the frame edge.
- Fill a long, narrow metal tray with marbles or flat, Asian-style river rocks, and embed twinkle lights among them.

Decorating for a Party

Garden-fresh flower arrangements

Instead of spending money at the florist for your table arrangements, pick flowers and greenery from your own garden. No garden? Shop the floral section in your grocery for bargains on bunches of flowers that are several days old but still fresh looking. If you're lucky and live near a well-stocked farmers' market, go there first. Another idea: Fill in fresh floral arrangements with your own artificial flowers. In the tangle of blossoms and leaves, it's hard the see the difference between real and faux.

A pumpkin vase for autumn flowers

Move over, Martha! Remove the top of a medium-sized pumpkin and scrape out seeds and pulp, as you would for a jack-o-lantern. In the bottom, cut a hole slightly larger than an ordinary glass kitchen or canning jar that will fit comfortably inside the pumpkin. Fill the jar with water, and add your flowers. You can cut the pumpkin a day or two in advance if you have a cool, shaded place to store it (outside, if the weather is cooperative). Wrap the pumpkin inside and out with several layers of wet paper towels, rewetting the towels as needed.

Protect your holiday decorations from Fido

Are you worried about pulling out Grandma's priceless collection of Christmas vases from the attic, only to have your new puppy, kitten, or grandchild knock them over? Worry no more. Attach a drop of plumber's putty to the bottom surface of your treasures, display them as planned, and they'll stay *put* until the holiday is over.

Don't hide Grandma's silver!

Silver used to be just for special occasions, but there is no better way to add a splash of sparkle to any room than to stand up silver utensils in tall, clear glassware; for a rustic look, place that fancy ware in green antique mason jars (lid off, please), and arrange together on the mantle or wherever a bright light might shine down on Grandma's collection.

DRESS TABLES WITH NATURE'S BOUNTY

An autumn centerpiece of **leaves** at the height of their color is cost-free and beautiful. Add some of nature's dried bounty, like thistle and wild grasses, and light the table with earth-toned candles—exquisite. You can also use leaves as place cards; write names in metallic permanent marker. If you have clear glass charger plates, slip a perfect fall leaf under each charger when you set the table.

Fall arrangement from the wild

To make an eye-pleasing dried arrangement for a fall mantle, coffee table, or sideboard, fill a plain, tall glass vase or deep glass bowl with brown rice, dried beans, or bird seed—simple staples that will not only support your arrangement but also look surprisingly elegant. Or go on a hike and collect dried grasses, cattails, thistle, milkweed, and other long-stemmed flora.

Create a cost-free lightscape with glasses

Forget costly flowers! Instead, gather an interesting selection of drinking glasses, glass bottles, and decorative glass vases and bowls. Include cut glass pieces if you have any. Arrange glass items almost randomly on your dining table or buffet, and add ordinary white candles to some of the containers. Clear glass and crystal will create a wintry look; a mix of clear and colored glass will yield a jewel-like effect.

A hearts-and-flowers centerpiece

How to add heart to a Valentine's dining table without a lot of cost or effort? You'll need a handful of common household items, one of those little plastic sharpeners children keep in their pencil boxes, and thin bamboo skewers.

1. Cut two lengths of waxed paper 18–24 inches long. Place a larger piece of newspaper on your ironing board and then lay one sheet of waxed paper on top.

2. With a pencil sharpener, shave pink and red crayons and the scatter the shavings randomly over the surface of the waxed paper, making sure there aren't any clumps or hard pieces.

3. Lay the second sheet of waxed paper over the shavings-covered sheet, then place another piece of newspaper on top. Run an iron on a low-medium setting (no steam, please) over the newspaper until the crayon shavings are melted and the waxed paper sheets stick together completely.

4. After the paper has cooled, use a template to trace hearts in several sizes. Cut them out and attach a bamboo skewer to each heart with a couple drops of glue.

Add the hearts to your floral arrangement so that they appear to be sprouting upward. The hearts will be translucent in the light—candlelight, of course, for an intimate Valentine's dinner.

A creepy Halloween door wreath

Add some ghoulish fun to the mix when trick-or-treaters come to the door. Some of the essentials, including a magazine and spent flowers, are probably right at hand in your house or yard.

1. Tear pages from a magazine and crumple the paper to make something resembling a chrysanthemum bloom. The resemblance doesn't have to be close; you're going for an effect, not realism.

2. Using a glue gun, glue the "flowers" to cover the wreath form, then spray the wreath and flowers with black paint. So you won't saturate the paper, apply the paint in several layers, letting it dry between coats.

3. If you have some dead and dry garden leftovers, such as purple coneflowers, zinnias, or magnolia leaves, glue them into the wreath. To finish, tie 3 feet or more of wide red ribbon diagonally around the wreath and let the ends trail. Or tie a bow if you have extra ribbon.

4. Hang the wreath on your front door and wait for the arrival of small goblins armed with vampire teeth and paper bags.

Create a Seasonal Centerpiece
with Found Objects

One of the most expensive decorating items you can buy are seasonally correct, holiday-specific centerpieces sold at most florists, but there's no reason to spend the money if you have access to a mirror, a few wide-bottom candles, putty, and extra greenery from your garden. To make a stunning dining table centerpiece that you'll use year after year, holiday after holiday, you'll need these materials, some of which you probably already have:

An inexpensive, beveled mirror, 2–3 feet long and 1 foot wide

Platter "feet"

2–3 wide-bottom candles, depending on the length of the mirror

Plumber's putty

Holiday greenery and flowers

If your dining table is long enough, avail yourself of a mirror that's 3 feet long and 1 foot wide; the narrow size will enable guests to see each other and chat over dinner. Plumber's putty and feet can be purchased inexpensively at any hardware or home repair center.

1. Turn the mirror over, and glue the small, round platter feet at each corner. This will keep your centerpiece from sitting flush to the table.

2. Turn the mirror back over, and stand each candle on its surface, at equal distances from each other. If you're using a 3-foot long mirror, attach three candles, equidistance, starting with the middle candle.

3. Apply plumber's putty to the bottom of each candle, and secure it to the mirror by pressing firmly but carefully. Repeat with each candle.

4. Cover the mirror with seasonal decorations such as pine trimmings, roping, holiday decorations, and poinsettias. For Easter, nestle colored eggs among the trimmings.

5. At the end of the holiday, dispose of any fresh trimmings, carefully remove the candles, wipe the mirror with a solution of 50 percent water and 50 percent white vinegar, dry, and store safely until the next holiday.

Clever Cover-ups

Slipcover a headboard

Remember how Grandma would fold her best quilt or comforter over the foot of the bed so it wouldn't get mussed during the day? That's the inspiration for quick, cost-free, and very modern bedstead slipcovers—one at each end. Use fabric or a bed sheet you already have; only a few yards will bring a whole new look to a plain vanilla bed. Take the vertical and horizontal (between the end posts) measurements for the head and footboards, then double the vertical measurement of each board. (If the horizontal measurement is wider than your fabric, you'll have to seam two lengths together.) If you use a sheet, cut it down to size. Hem the edges and add fabric ties to both sides. This look can be as nostalgic as Grandma's bed or as sleek as a New York loft. Slipcovering is also a smart way to protect the finish on an antique or much-treasured bed and continue to use it as intended.

Window drapery to doorway curtain

Curtaining doorways is a very old way to keep heat in or out of interior spaces (think tent flaps). So if you have a set of long win-dow drapes you're not using, you've got ready-to-go door curtains. For a standard door, mount a curtain rod at or slightly above the door frame. Extend the rod six or more inches beyond the frame, making room to slide the curtain to one side so you can easily close and open the door. Then hang one drapery panel that's long enough to reach to the floor. (Standard door frames are approximately 7 feet tall, but measure yours just in case.) Metal or plastic curtain rings or clips make it easier to move the curtain along the rod. To prevent billowing on windy days you can sew weights such as metal hardware washers inside the hems.

Tile an old tabletop

A battered and bruised wooden coffee table or small side table can become a canvas for tiles, even for beginners. You'll need tiles (saved from a renovation project) or purchased from a tile or

Household Superstar!

10 Reasons to Grab the Tape When the Going Gets Tough

Here are 10 around-the-house decorating dilemmas that an adhesive tape can resolve in no time.

1 Fabric tape to mend broken seams in slip covers

2 Painter's tape to make even stripes while painting, without measuring

3 Painter's tape to mask edges of baseboards and door and window frames when painting

4 Brightly colored, waterproof electrician's tape to decorate and identify children's plastic toys and adult tools

5 Double-sided tape to secure throw rugs to the floor and seat cushions to chairs

6 Clear shipping tape and a permanent marker to label paint and solvent cans

7 Masking tape to wrap the metal portion of paint brush handles to catch drips

8 Nonslip tape to mend worn spots on the underside of rubber-backed bath mats

9 Double-sided acid-free scrapbooking tape to mount and frame precious art on paper

10 Adhesive-backed Velcro tape as a temporary closure on a cabinet door with a broken latch

home store (look for sales). Measure the tabletop to determine how many you need. If you're careful with your measurements and buy tiles of the right size, you can probably cover the entire top without making any tile cuts. Keep in mind that you must leave approximately ⅛ to ¼ inch of space between tiles for grouting.

- Sand the tabletop and clean off the dust. (If you want to refinish or paint your table, do so before sanding.) Then lay out the tiles on the tabletop in your pattern of choice and make any changes and adjustments. Affix the tiles with tiling adhesive or white glue. (If using glue, be sure it's dry before grouting.)

- Grout the tiles with commercial grout, which is available in many colors. As you work, wipe off excess grout with a damp sponge. To remove any remaining grout film, wash again with water after the grout has dried. And there you have it—a table that may as well be brand new.

A quick change for dining chairs

If the upholstered seats of your dining room chairs are removable—some lift out and others are attached only by screws underneath—you're in luck! You can make a quick, temporary change with some fabric and strong masking tape. Use what you have on hand: fabric remnants, a tablecloth or bed coverlet, large scarves, sheets or pillowcases. Mix and match colors and patterns if you like. Choose a medium-weight material, since heavy or highly textured fabrics won't always give a smooth, finished appearance. Remove the chair seat and use it as a template to cut a piece of material extending 3–4 inches beyond the edges. Then center the seat, top down, on the wrong side of the fabric. Drape the fabric over one side of the chair bottom and secure it with a piece of tape. Do the same on the other side, pulling the fabric taut. Repeat on the other two sides, and then tape all four folds all the way to the corners. Fold the fabric over each corner for a neat finish. Secure the cover with an extra layer of tape, replace the seat, and voila!

Rug on rug

You know the problem: wall-to-wall carpeting that's flattened, matted, and stained in a heavily trafficked area but otherwise in good condition. The solution? Scout your home for the perfect area rug to cover the trouble spot—a rug that could be in the next room or stashed away in the attic. If you have a carpet remnant that would look great but is too large, ask a local carpet dealer to cut it to size and bind the edges.

Covering the nicks

Did your beloved Aunt Betty accidentally ram into your treasured coffee table with her walker? Did your grandson motor his tricycle through the house and into the legs of that antique rolltop desk? Don't weep, and don't call a pro: If the nick is shallow, color it with a similar-hued indelible marker. If the nick is deep (but still superficial), soften a small amount of white candle wax and using a small butter spreader, massage it into the gash. Wait for it to harden, and then color it with the right-colored marker. Any deeper than that? Call for help.

Wallpapered storage boxes

Cardboard boxes—free from the grocery or liquor store or purchased from a business supply store—have to be America's favorite storage units. They're also ugly and not always easy to stash out of sight. So pretty them up with leftover wallpaper, preferably vinyl coated. Prepasted wallpaper can be cut to size,

Leaf It to You

Leaves make beautiful printing stamps for decorating fabric—and hey—they fall *free* from the trees! Even if you live in the most urban of cities, you can find leaves in parks, public gardens, and on your own potted plants sitting on your windowsill. Look for fresh, well-shaped leaves with prominent spines and veins.

- Flatten the leaves by pressing them for a day or two in a phone book weighted with something heavy, like more books.
- To use a leaf to stamp fabric, brush fabric paint evenly on its top side. Test the leaf stamp first on a fabric scrap, laying the leaf on the material and pushing—not rubbing—it down with your fingers.

Practice until you get the look you like, and then stamp fabric for a tea towel, a throw pillow, or whatever your heart desires. Leaf stamps won't last very long, but you can always gather more as they fall.

dampened, and pasted on in a relative blink. Unpasted paper can be stuck down with wallpaper paste, craft glue, or rubber cement. Arrayed on open shelves or neatly stacked under a desk or along a wall, revamped boxes look attractive, and their wallpaper covers are durable enough to take a good deal of wear.

Add Dash with Fabrics

Sewing box embellishment for pillows

To jazz up throw pillows and pillowcases, look through your sewing and craft supplies for interesting and unusual embellishments. Ribbons, lace, rickrack, buttons, beads, tassels, bits of fabric for appliqués, yarn, netting, old handkerchiefs and antimacassars, stencils, and decorative stamps for fabric painting—practically anything that won't break and will wash can perk up a plain throw pillow or pillowcase. Here are four simple, quick, and cost-free ideas:

- Tie on a satin or grosgrain ribbon. Two yards or less will wrap around a 12-by-12-inch pillow and let you tie a pretty bow. Tack under the bow and on the back of the pillow.

- Sew a band of lace or decorative trim around the hem of a pillowcase. Seam the trim to cover the seam line at the pillowcase opening.

- Sew a row of mismatched buttons in any direction—vertical, horizontal, or diagonal—on one side of a tailored throw pillow for an unexpectedly wry look.

- Sew pretty tassels to the corners of a throw pillow, or sew or glue tasseled fabric trim around the pillow edges.

Make a duvet cover with sheets

Sleeping under a down-filled duvet is blissful, but washing or dry cleaning it frequently is less than heavenly to your pocketbook. Instead of buying a pricey duvet cover, hunt up a couple of flat bed sheets that will fully cover your duvet. Pin the sheets together, right sides facing, and sew bottoms and sides together with a straight seam.

Turn the cover right side out and slip it over your duvet. The simplest closures are sewn-on ribbon or fabric tape ties, Velcro, or snaps.

Now you have a cost-free duvet cover that can be washed as often as you like; under normal conditions, your duvet will need washing or cleaning just once or twice a year.

Save a too-short curtain

Don't toss your old house curtains if they're too short for your new windows; just add a bottom panel. Search your fabrics and be ingenious. For one panel, measure the width of your curtain and add seam allowances. Now determine how much you need for the length you want; include seam and hem allowances. If your fabric is large enough, you're practically home. Remove stitching from the curtain hems and trim. Cut the extra fabric to your measurements. Seam, hem, and hang your "new" old curtain.

A plush bath towel shower curtain

If you enjoy the luxury of terry-cloth bath sheets, this is an idea for you. Two terry-cloth bath sheets are nearly the same size as a standard shower curtain (70–72 inches wide by 70–74 inches long). Use bath sheets you already have: white bath sheets will create a spa feeling; bright colors can add "pow" to a plain bathroom. Don't seam the towels; simply overlap the edges and sew together, stitching down the selvage. Add grommets near the top (grommet kits are available at fabric stores). The standard number of holes is 12. To determine spacing, measure the full width of the sewn curtain and subtract 4 inches to leave 2 inches free at each side. Now divide the remainder by 12.

Picture This...

Cheap art

Think outside the box and frame an interesting magazine cover, a child's painting, a piece of needlework, a collection of men's silk ties, coins, exotic stamps, a photo collage, a map, or post-cards from your favorite vacation spot. An example: Save seed packets when you plant in the spring; open packets at the back to preserve the graphic fronts. You may already have some small frames; if not, you can purchase inexpensive 3-by-5 or 5-by-7-inch photo frames at discount stores. Cover the cardboard backing that comes with the frames in leftover wrapping paper or fabric, then attach the seed packets with double-sided tape. Now find just the right place to hang your new "botanical prints"—quick, easy, cost-free, and a pleasing memento of your summer garden.

Old frames in new colors

Use leftover paints to refurbish old picture frames for a cost-free way to highlight artwork and add splashes of color to your decor. Remove everything from the frame and clean it well; if the frame is ornate, use damp cotton swabs to

Cleaning Pictures under Glass

Picture frames and glass don't usually get filthy dirty, but they do collect dust, residue from heat sources, and fingerprints. Regular dusting and an occasional cleaning will keep them in good shape. To wash glass, dampen a cloth in a mild vinegar and water solution, wring almost dry, and wipe the glass. Don't spray liquid directly on the glass; it can easily seep under the frame and damage the mat or, worse, the artwork. Polish glass with a coffee filter or used dryer sheet; they're lint-free.

get into the nooks and crannies. Dry thoroughly, sand lightly if the frame is wood, and simply brush or spray with your color choice. You can give your frame an antique finish by sanding the dry paint back to the original finish and rubbing the whole frame with brown shoe polish, buffing well. Create a contemporary frame by painting it with high-gloss auto paint.

SHOE POLISH FOR AN ANTIQUE FINISH

Sand a new frame and rub on and buff off a thin coating of brown or reddish-brown **shoe polish** for an antique frame finish.

For added nostalgia in your home frame some *vintage seed*

Individualizing picture mats

Aside from paintings on canvas, most graphic art is framed under a mat—a cardboard border with a quality paper veneer—that prevents the image from touching (and sticking to) the glass. Cutting mats the meticulous professional way isn't easy, but even a rank amateur can make attractive mats with glue and materials found around the house. Start with the cardboard mat that came with the frame; if the commercial border is just paper, use it as a template to cut a piece of cardboard. Choose something attractive to cover the cardboard. Consider the frame and the photo or artwork, and pick something that will complement both. It won't take much of any of the following to create an individualized mat:

- Remnant wallpaper
- Curtain or upholstery fabric
- Any leftover medium-weight fabric
- Fake leather, suede, or fur
- Wrapping paper or foil
- Parchment paper
- Résumé paper or card stock
- Origami paper
- Shelf or drawer lining paper
- Wide ribbon or lace
- Magazine or old book pages

Cut a piece of material slightly larger than the dimensions of the mat. Thinly coat the cardboard with glue and affix the material, smoothing to eliminate air pockets and wrinkles. When dry, cut away the material from the outside edges. Now turn the mat face down and cut excess material diagonally from each top corner to opposite bottom corner, taking care not to cut into the cardboard. Fold the flaps over, trim away all but about ½ inch, and glue the edges.

Whitewashing a gilt frame

When a new gold gilt or painted frame looks *too* new, tone it down with a wash of white. Dilute a small amount of leftover white interior paint—latex with water, alkyd or oil-based with turpentine or mineral spirits—to make a thin wash. Be sure the frame is clean of dust and grease. Use a clean cotton cloth to apply the wash, wiping away excess paint as you go. Let dry. One or two coats should be enough—you want to calm the flashiness of new gilt, not cover it up.

A CD case photo gallery

Here's a great decorating project for teenagers, who tend to take lots of photos and have tons of empty CD cases. Twelve or more clear transparent CD cases, adhered to the wall with poster putty or low-tack, double-sided tape, make a totally awesome gallery. Standard cases measure 5½ by 5 inches—just right for 3-by-5 photo prints and other featherweight items. Pictures can be changed whenever the mood strikes, just by opening the case. Rad? You bet.

"Clothesline" photo displays

Create a modern photo display by using these everyday office supplies. Scrounge desk drawers for clear 8½-by-11-inch acrylic document sleeves and some metal binder clips. Mount your photos in the sleeves and nail both ends of a length of wire or rope to the wall, clothesline fashion, leaving a little slack. (If you have some thin computer cable you're not using, use it to give the display a high tech look.) Now clip the photo sleeves to the hanging line. Because it's so easy to change photos whenever you want, your display will never get old.

make your own
Air Freshener

Never buy a commercial air freshener again; make your own! Many people swear by homemade fresheners made with baking soda or vinegar, which act as deodorizers as well as adding a gentle scent.

Double Treat Room Spray

Both lemon and baking soda are traditional odor eaters, and this recipe couldn't be simpler.

   1 teaspoon baking soda
   1 tablespoon lemon juice
   2 cups water

1. Combine the ingredients in a bowl and let the mixture fizz.

2. When fizzing subsides, stir well.

3. Pour the mixture into a spritzer (a spray bottle that produces a fine mist). Spray rooms that need freshening two or three times a day.

The Glue Gun:
Every Home Decorator's Best Friend

Whether you're new to repurposing items found around your home or you're a seasoned pro who sews your own drapes, you'll want to make sure you have an inexpensive glue gun in your home design arsenal. Available for around $10, a basic model will enable you to add your own personal touches to virtually every room in your house, from the bedroom to the bathroom and beyond.

Have some great linens or textiles kicking around that you don't want to get rid of? You don't have to. Use them, along with your glue gun, to add appliqués to drapes, wallpaper, shower curtains, bed coverings, headboards, and more. Be creative: Appliqués can mean far more than just cut pieces of cloth or textile. Poke around your sewing kit and dig up some older-looking buttons to create a fabulous design treatment.

Too many Christmas ornaments for your tree? Make a reusable holiday wreath by glue-gunning extra ornaments to a twig wreath form (available at craft shops); at the end of the holiday, simply store it for next year.

Create one-of-a-kind gift boxes with everything from plain cardboard shipping containers to dilapidated shoeboxes: cover with fabric, glue-gun in place, and dress up with buttons, bows, and trim. What does it cost? Virtually nothing.

Love that bargain lamp but hate the boring shade? Get to a trimming store, pick up some inexpensive fringe or seam edging, and glue gun it to the edging of the shade.

Happy Holidays Decor

Spotlight the tree

Forget those gnarly miles of tree lights and use a spotlight instead. If you have track lighting, position your tree so the track fixtures can bathe it in light. Or use the portable indoor uplight that's now highlighting a big house-plant. A gooseneck or swivel desk lamp will also work; locate it so the light strikes the tree but not people's eyes. Basically any light you can direct will bring out the beauty of your holiday tree, without all the fuss and bother.

Fragrant holiday window box

Use your winter garden as the palette from which to fill a detachable window box with aromatic pine and pinecones; spruce and cedar clippings; sprigs of boxwood, holly, or mistletoe; and clusters of red or white berries. Place it on an inside window ledge, mantle, or fireplace shelf, or even your holiday table—a picturesque way to bring the colors and fragrances of winter indoors for the holidays.

First, remove any soil and wash the box with baking soda or vinegar and water. Most fresh-cut winter greenery will last for a week or more if you mist it daily. If you plan to add water to the box, plug drain holes with clay or putty. Protect paint finishes and furniture from drips and condensation by cutting a disposable diaper

to the size of the bottom of the box and laying it, plastic side down, under the box. (Just as for babies, check and change diapers as often as needed.)

Offbeat homemade gift-wrapping

Instead of buying expensive wrapping paper, look around the house for creative and eco-smart substitutes. Newspaper, paper bags, crepe paper, painter's masking paper, parchment paper, paper place mats, fabric napkins you don't use, comic book pages, the kids' construction and drawing paper, bubble wrap—the possibilities are endless. Use stamps, stencils, and stickers to embellish your wrap, and substitute brightly colored yarns, workshop twines and cords, fabric trims and bindings, torn strips of fabric, or an old fabric measuring tape, for store-bought bows.

Dried citrus ornaments

Those extra oranges and lemons in your fridge that may be past their prime can be transformed into warmly translucent tree ornaments. Cut fruit into ¼-inch slices, lay the slices flat on a stick-proof cookie sheet, and place in the oven on the lowest setting for several hours. Test for dryness by lightly touching the pulp; if it feels sticky, leave the slices in the oven a short while

Dyeing Easter Eggs
(with Mother Nature's Help)

In this chart, quantities are based on 1 quart of liquid. Amounts of dyeing ingredients are approximate; more dyestuff and longer dye baths produce the deepest colors. All boiled eggs should be stored in the refrigerator, and any that have soaked in hot or warm water for several hours should not be eaten.

Dye Source	Quantity	Color
Beet juice	half strength or more of the vinegar water	deep pink
Cranberry juice	full-strength	light pink
Paprika	3 tablespoons or more	brick red
Yellow onion skins	up to 4 packed cups	sienna
Turmeric	3 or more tablespoons	yellow-green
Brewed coffee	1 quart strong coffee plus water to cover	brown
Blueberries	up to 4 cups	lavender
Purple grape juice	half or more of the liquid	blue-gray
Red cabbage	4 or more cups, chopped (boil and then soak overnight)	robin's egg blue
Spinach or grass	up to 4 cups	green
Red wine	full strength or diluted with water only	deep purple

longer; it's important to remove the fruit before it begins to brown. Cool on a wire rack. Thread the dried fruit slices with ribbon or yarn and hang them where they'll catch the tree lights. Preserve dried fruit slices by a spraying them with a clear acrylic finish.

Easter eggs, naturally

Budding young chemists and kids with curiosity will really enjoy helping to make naturally colored Easter eggs with ingredients straight from the cupboard and fridge. This family project costs nothing, but the delight in learning is priceless.

1. Gently wash eggs with soapy water and dry.

2. Place a single layer of eggs in a non-metal pot with the dye source (see chart at left).

3. Add 2 tablespoons vinegar to 1 quart water. Bring to a boil, reduce to a simmer for 15–20 minutes, and remove pot from burner. If you like the color as it is, dab off excess dye with a paper towel and set the eggs on a rack to dry. To deepen the color, leave eggs in the pot until cool. To get even richer shades, put cool eggs in a bowl, strain the dye water, and pour it over the eggs. Store the submerged eggs in the fridge for a few hours or overnight.

Snow globes from empty jars

Make your own old-fashioned snow globe at home with clean, plain, glass kitchen jars and whatever small holiday items you have—dig out those little plastic Santas and reindeer and ceramic elves and angels that have taken up permanent residence in the bottom of your decorations box. (Don't use wood or metal items.) Any size glass jar will work, so long as the objects will fit inside and the lid fits tightly. Small and medium olive, pimiento, and baby

Divine Twine

Those beautiful filigreed balls sold in high-priced decorator boutiques can be yours for nothing when you make them yourself. All you need is a spool of household twine, white glue, water, and a balloon.

- For each ball, soak several feet of twine in a mixture of 1 part white glue to 1 part water. Then blow up and tie a small round balloon.

- Wrap the balloon with the saturated twine, wrapping randomly. When it suits your eye, clip the twine and set the balloon on top of a drinking glass. Allow the twine to dry for at least a day, or until the balloon begins to deflate.

- Time to pop the balloon and remove it. Spray the ball with gold, silver, or copper metallic paint. Dust with glitter for a holiday look, if you like. Then pile the finished balls in a shallow bowl and set it in a place of honor. Divine!

food jars are ideal for small globes. You may have to buy several items—waterproof epoxy glue, distilled water, white glitter, and glycerin (available from pharmacies)—but you'll need only small amounts.

1. Roughen the inside surface of the jar lid with sandpaper or steel wool and then glue on your object or objects with epoxy; let dry. Fill the jar almost to the top with distilled water and add a drop of glycerin.

2. Glycerin thickens the water so glitter will swirl; for larger jars, add a couple of drops. Now add a pinch or two of glitter.

3. Screw the jar lid on tightly, being careful not to dislodge glued-on object. Finally, turn the jar over and enjoy the snowstorm.

Chapter Six

Nature's Home Remedies

These days, we can't get enough of all things health-related, be they the tried and true traditional remedies for what ails you (think aspirin and Alka-Seltzer) or the stuff that your grandmother swore by: the witch hazel and Epsom salt, the chamomile tea and the castor oil, the hydrogen peroxide and the mustard plaster.

And while many of these health-giving remedies are valid, there is also wisdom in the proverb, "Moderation in all things."

That said, it really does pay to stock your medicine cabinet with home remedies. Homemade witch hazel is, for example, more effective than its commercial equivalent because it isn't distilled. The herb feverfew staves off migraines more effectively when you chew the fresh leaves instead of swallowing a capsule. A hair dryer may help stunt a cold better than a pill (really!). And oh, the uses our distant forebears found for salt and stinging nettle, cloves, and castor oil! Leafing through the pages that follow may encourage you to emulate those hardy souls. (But remember to consult your doctor before using all but the most benign remedies.)

Have arthritis?
Reach for the
turmeric!

Fighting Colds and Flu

Kick the chicken soup up a notch

When science proved that Grandma's chicken soup really does help fight colds, the luscious favorite secured its place in the pantheon of healing foods. Chicken soup works not only because steam rising from the bowl helps clear congestion, but also because anti-inflammatory compounds in the broth slow the movement of neutrophils, white blood cells that spur the formation of mucus in the lungs and nose. To punch up chicken soup's cold-fighting abilities even more, add two peeled and minced garlic cloves to the simmering soup. Garlic contains antiviral sulfur compounds, and it's also said to boost the immune system.

Fire up the hair dryer

Inhaling heated air can stunt a cold's severity when you feel one coming on. Studies show that warm air kills rhinoviruses working their way up the nose. In one test conducted in England, subjects who breathed warm air had half the symptoms of those who inhaled air at room temperature, so set your hair dryer to warm (not hot), hold it at least 18 inches from your face, and inhale the warm air for as long as you can—preferably 20 minutes or so but 2 or 3 minutes at the very least.

Sip (and gargle) echinacea tea

Echinacea purpurea, or purple coneflower, can indeed help prevent colds and relieve the symptoms of colds and influenza alike. It works by boosting levels of the body chemical properdin, which strengthens defense mechanisms against infections. Drinking 3 cups of echinacea tea a

Rudolph Syndrome

You'd think the reddening (and soreness) of the nostril rims that results from constant nose blowing would have a name. Up until now, it hasn't, so let's call it Rudolph Syndrome (RS), after Santa's red-snooted reindeer. How to remedy this unsightly, uncomfortable redness? Simply rub a little petroleum jelly or Chapstick on the rim of the nostrils, replenishing it as necessary. Ah, sweet relief.

day will guard against colds, but limit consumption to 7- to 8-week periods so as not to risk nausea, fevers, and other side effects. (Resume sipping after a couple of weeks, and hope a rhinovirus doesn't target you when echinacea is taking "time off.") You can also gargle echinacea tea up to three times a day to soothe a sore throat.

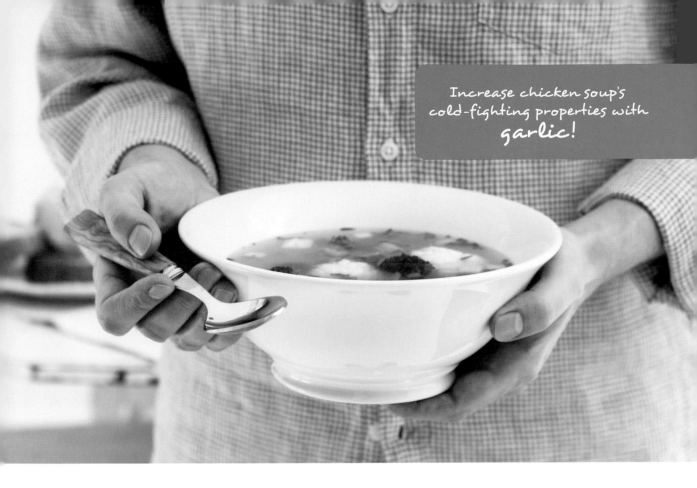

Cool that fever

In a cold's first stages, you can help your body bring down fever by giving yourself a sponge bath every hour or so. Dip a natural sponge in tepid water, lightly wring it out, and use it to bathe your face, shoulders, chest, and extremities. If the fever persists, drink 1–2 cups ginger tea every few hours; the ginger will promote sweating, which is the body's way of cooling itself.

Fight coughs with thyme

Thyme is a natural expectorant, so brew a pot of thyme tea to fight that nagging cough. Just steep 2 tablespoons dried thyme leaves in 6 cups hot water for 10 minutes. Strain the liquid into a teacup, sweeten with honey if desired, and sip a cupful two or three times a day.

Three simple sore throat gargles

Invade the kitchen cabinet rather than the medicine cabinet to cure your sore throat. Here's how:

- **Honey** Honey coats the throat and has mild antibacterial properties. Stir 1–3 teaspoons into 1 cup warm water and gargle two or three times a day.

- **Salt** Salt water has been used as a gargle for centuries because it works so well: It draws moisture from the mucous membranes (thereby diluting mucus) and helps cleanse the throat of phlegm. Dissolve ½ teaspoon salt in 1 cup warm water and gargle three or four times daily.

- **Peppermint** The menthol in peppermint helps open the nasal passages, especially when you gargle strong peppermint tea. Pour 1 cup boiling water over 3 peppermint tea bags and let steep for 4–5 minutes. Gargle with the cooled solution two or three times a day.

A fiery gulp

For a practical way to rid yourself of throat congestion, whisk 1 teaspoon honey into 8 ounces warm water. Now whisk in ½ teaspoon hot red pepper (or Tabasco) sauce. (If this is too spicy for you, experiment by adding a few drops at a time.) Drink the concoction slowly; follow it with a small ginger ale chaser, which will cool the burn.

Pass the peas to relieve a stuffy nose

Use a frozen bag of peas as a flexible, bendable, cold pack to set on the bridge of your nose or on your cheekbones to reduce swelling. Put them back in cold storage to refreeze, and repeat as necessary.

Swat the flu bug with elderberry

If you feel you've been bitten by the flu bug, drink 3–4 cups of elderberry tea daily or take 20–30 drops of elderberry tincture in a glass of water. In Europe, elderberry (*Sambucus nigra*) has a long history as an antiviral herb, and research bears it out. In one study, 9 out of 10 test group subjects who consumed elderberry saw flu symptoms subside in two days, while symptoms in the group that consumed no elderberry continued for six days.

Curiosity Corner
Red Magic

Over a century ago, one of the most common cold cures was bought by the yard: red flannel, which was associated with warmth and healing. Why red? Because of the superstition that the color red kept evil spirits at bay. Less metaphysically, flannel was said to "draw out" a cold when worn next to the skin.

Flannel came on the scene in the late nineteenth century, when a napped cotton called flannelette appeared in dry goods stores. While considered inferior to wool, this new fabric didn't itch the skin. Mothers tied red flannel scarves around their children's necks to relieve sore throats (in addition to keeping away the evil eye). Many men wore red flannel union suits under their clothing to protect themselves not only from colds and the flu but to prevent attacks of gout and rheumatism. For back pain, flannelette bands were worn around the waist. In time, the fabric that sealed in heat without itching came to be known simply as flannel. Had it not come along, many a lumberjack, alternative band member, and flannel pajama-wearer would, in a manner of speaking, be left out in the cold.

Easing Asthma, Bronchitis, and Allergies

Inhale eucalyptus vapors

If you're lucky enough to have access to dried *Eucalyptus globulus,* just boil crumbled leaves and let them steep for 4–5 hours; strain out the leaf pieces before heating the liquid for inhalation. (Alternatively, add 5–10 drops commercial eucalyptus oil to the steaming water.) Place the bowl at the edge of a table, sit down, bend your head over the bowl, and put the towel over your head to form a tent. Breathe the vapors for about 10 minutes, taking care not to get too close to the steam. Lungs all better, plus a refreshing facial!

Bronchitis double dose

The head-clearing pungency of freshly grated horseradish paired with the acidic aroma of lemon helps dissolve mucus in the sinuses and bronchial tubes. To make a piquant cough medicine, grate a peeled horseradish root into a bowl (or cheat and use prepared horseradish) and transfer 1 cup grated horseradish to a small bowl. Add ⅓ cup lemon juice and stir well.

Dose yourself with ½ teaspoon of the mixture at a time, taking it two or three times a day. The expectorant action should set you coughing after each dose, ridding your lungs of mucus.

Loosen mucus with mullein

Mullein (*Verbascum thapsus*), a longtime folk remedy for respiratory ailments, contains saponins that loosen phlegm and promote expectoration. It also contains gelatinous mucilage that tones and soothes the mucous membranes. To make mullein tea, steep 2 teaspoons dried mullein leaves in just-boiled water for 10 minutes. Herbalists advise drinking the tea up to three times a day to ease bronchial distress.

Elecampane the expectorant

Buy elecampane tea or liquid extract, sweeten the tea with honey, and drink 1–2 cups a day to stimulate the lungs' natural "housecleaning" mechanism. The active principle in elecampane (*Inula helenium*) is alantolactone, a proven

FIGHT ASTHMA WITH FISH

Omega 3, the fatty acids found in **sardines**, tuna, salmon, mackerel, sardines, and other oily fish, works much like a class of drugs called leukotriene inhibitors, which disable bodily compounds that contribute to inflammation of the airways.

expectorant with roots back to New World settlers, who used elecampane to treat the symptoms of asthma, whooping cough, pneumonia, and tuberculosis.

Chamomile's two faces

For an allergy-fighting tea, pour 1 cup boiling water over 2–3 teaspoons minced flower heads of German chamomile, steep for 10 minutes, strain, and drink three to four times daily. A caveat: while chamomile is a traditional hay fever fighter, it actually aggravates symptoms in anyone allergic to ragweed, a chamomile cousin. For everyone else, the azulene content in chamomile has antiallergenic properties that have led doctors worldwide to prescribe chamomile preparations for respiratory tract infections and allergies.

Use bleach to quell sniffles

If you have a sudden case of the sniffles that won't go away and you don't have allergies (or a cold), you may (unbenownst to you!) be living with mold. If you spot it in your bathroom, kill it instantly with a 50/50 mixture of household bleach and water. Spray it directly onto the offensive spots and let it sit. The mold will be stopped in its tracks within minutes, along with (hopefully) your runny nose!

Nettle and hay fever

If you have access to fresh stinging nettle (it's a common garden weed), wear gloves when harvesting and washing the leaves (the plant's not called stinging nettle for nothing). Add 4 ounces of the leaf to 6 cups of boiling water. Lower

make your own
Nasal Spray

Here's a homemade spray that will flush allergens from nasal passages. The isosmotic solution parallels the concentration of salt found in the body, making the spray mild but effective.

Salt Water Sniffle-Stopper

This spray works best at room temperature. Discard any unused solution after two days or it may become contaminated.

> 1 quart water
> 1 tablespoon chamomile tea
> 2 teaspoons salt

1. Place water in a medium saucepan, add tea and salt, and bring to a low simmer.

2. Stir until salt is dissolved, then let cool to room temperature.

3. Pour solution into an empty nose spray bottle. Spray twice in each nostril as needed, holding the other nostril closed each time.

heat and simmer until the water turns green, then strain through a fine sieve into a large teapot. During hay fever season, drink a cup of nettle tea in the morning and one in the evening, sweetening it with honey if you like. Studies have yet to definitively confirm the efficacy of stinging nettle (*Urtica dioica*) for treating hay fever, but legions of people swear by nettle's powers to ease runny noses and watery eyes.

What Does That Mean?

You probably already know the meaning of many of the words in this list, not all of which apply only to herbal remedies. But when it comes to self-treatment, having a fuller grasp of the terminology becomes all the more important. Here's a great place to start:

Active principle A plant chemical proven to have a medical effect.

Antiseptic A substance that prevents or stops the growth of microorganisms that cause infection.

Astringent A substance that draws together the soft tissues, such as skin or mucous membranes.

Decoction A drink or liquid extract made by boiling plant bark, roots, berries, or seeds in water.

Diuretic A substance that increases the flow of urine.

Emollient A substance that softens and soothes the skin and mucous membranes.

Essential oil A plant oil that vaporizes readily and is often obtained by steam distillation; used interchangeably with *volatile oil*.

Expectorant A substance that loosens and helps to expel phlegm.

Infusion A preparation in which flowers, leaves, or stems are steeped in water that is not boiling.

Liquid extract Concentrated infusion made by soaking an herb in distilled water, grain alcohol, or glycerin for a long period.

Mucous membrane Lining of a body passage, such as the throat, that protects itself with secretions of mucus.

Photosensitivity Sensitivity to sunlight, resulting in rash or burning sensation, brought on by ingestion or application of certain substances.

Plaster Gauze or cloth in which medicine has been wrapped. A plaster is applied to the skin.

Poultice An herbal preparation that is usually applied directly to the affected area to relieve pain or swelling.

Purgative A very strong laxative.

Tannins Astringent and bitter compounds found in the seeds and skins of grapes, which slow oxidation and aging.

Tincture An herbal liquid extract that generally involves macerating the herb in alcohol.

Volatile oil A plant oil that vaporizes readily and is often obtained by steam distillation; used interchangeably with *essential oil*.

Wash A liquid herbal medicine preparation for external use.

No-Drugs Headache Relief

Running hot and cold

To cure a tension headache (caused by contractions in the head and neck, and brought on by—among other things—stress, anxiety, and lack of sleep) without painkilling drugs, dip a washcloth in hot water, wring it out, and fold it into compress. Now place it on your forehead or the back of your neck to relax tight muscles. To ease a vascular headache (including migraine and cluster headaches, and stemming from the contraction and expansion of blood vessels in a particular area of the head), follow the same procedure, but using cold water, which constricts the blood vessels and reduces blood flow, taking the pressure off a hurting head.

A cup o' Joe makes the headache go

A clinical trial in Illinois found that caffeine, which reduces the swelling of blood vessels, can reduce both the intensity and frequency of headaches. Subjects in one group were given caffeine alone, and 58 percent reported complete relief. Subjects in the other group were given caffeine in combination with ibuprofen, and 70 percent saw symptoms disappear.

Sinus headache self-massage

Use your middle fingers to massage the points of the face just opposite your nostrils—that is, at the level of the tip of your nose. Massage with clockwise circles for 2 or 3 minutes.

> To soothe a throbbing headache, soak your feet—in water and **mustard!**

Head-to-toe headache remedy

Blood drawn to the lower body will reduce pressure in the blood vessels of the head, and what's lower than your feet? To help soothe a throbbing vascular headache, soak your feet in a small tub filled with hot water mixed with mustard powder. After a half hour or so, hotfoot it to the nearest towel, dry your feet, and feel better!

Sip ginger tea

When it comes to treating headaches, ginger works especially well for migraines. Make a tea by pouring 3 cups water over 2 tablespoons freshly grated ginger. Let steep 4–5 minutes, then strain through a small sieve into a teacup. Ginger tea bags are also available, but the tea lacks the punch of fresh gingerroot tea.

WEAR A HEADBAND

Tie a **scarf, necktie, or bandana** tightly around your forehead to reduce the flow of blood to your scalp, and in turn, to throbbing, swollen blood vessels.

Eyes, Ears, and Mouth

Eye can see clearly now

Carrots, celery, kale, and parsley: Taken together, all contribute to the trouble-free operation of the optic system. Either juice the veggies for an eye-friendly beverage or puree to make a cold soup. The ideal proportions? Two parts carrots, 2 parts kale, 1 part celery, 1 part parsley. For best results, consume 2 cups of juice or soup a day. Vary the mix by incorporating spinach, endive, collards, tomatoes, and melons. Bon appétit!

Tea for two

Two puffy eyes, that is. Take two wet tea bags, place them on tired or swollen eyes, and lie down for 15–20 minutes as the tea soothes and refreshes. Green tea is ideal for these mini-compresses, but black tea and herbal teas work well, too. An added benefit: some herbalists claim that tea-bag compresses speed the healing of a black eye.

Let's 'ear it for mullein and garlic!

Paired with garlic, mullein (*Verbascum thapsus*) makes soothing earache drops you can keep on hand in the refrigerator. In a sterilized jar, combine 1 crushed clove garlic with 2 tablespoons dried or fresh mullein flower (minced if fresh), and ½ cup olive oil. Screw the lid on tightly and shake to blend. Store in a cool, dark place, shaking the jar daily. After two weeks, strain the oil into another jar and store it in the fridge. To treat an earache, bring the oil to room temperature or hold the jar under warm running water. With a sterile eyedropper, add 2–3 drops to the ear, then gently massage the ear to help the oil move through the ear canal.

Bubble away ear trouble

Dropping 3 percent hydrogen peroxide into the ear makes earwax easier to extract and will hasten the healing of an earache. Fill a sterile eyedropper with peroxide, lie on your side, and squeeze the liquid into the affected ear until it feels full. Let the peroxide bubble away for 3–5 minutes, then press a washcloth or folded paper towel against the ear and turn over to let it drain. Rinse the ear by repeating the process with water. Dry, then work softened earwax out of the ear with a cotton swab. Do not use hydrogen peroxide in your ear if you suspect that you have a perforated eardrum.

Homemade breath freshener

The makings for a super-duper, anti-bad–breath mouthwash is living right there in your spice rack. To make a mouthwash, pour 2 cups water into a saucepan and add 1 tablespoon cardamom seeds and 1 tablespoon whole cloves. If you like, add a few mint leaves and a little sugar to improve the taste (mint is a proven halitosis fighter). Bring to a boil, remove from heat, and let steep for 3–4 hours. Strain the solution into a bottle and gargle as needed. Cardamom is jam-packed with antiseptic qualities that kill the bacteria responsible for bad breath. Cloves, which have a long history as a breath freshener, are also antibacterial.

Brown stains on teeth?

If your teeth advertise your fondness for coffee, tea, or cigarettes, supplement your whitening toothpaste with a folk treatment: Add a dash of baking soda to your favorite whitening toothpaste and brush away.

Saltwater rinse for toothaches

Swishing warm salt water in the mouth can relieve toothache pain for the short term. Salt draws out some of the fluids from swollen gums as it soothes. How strong a solution to use? Two to 3 teaspoons salt in 8 ounces warm water.

Lips chapped?

Can't find that tube of lip balm you just bought? Try a benign oil of any sort instead. Soothe cracked, dry lips with a drop of olive, corn, safflower, or canola oil. Vegetable shortening and the trusty multitasker known as petroleum jelly also work well.

Ears ringing?

You may be suffering from tinnitus. Taking 120 milligrams of gingko extract (like Ginkgold and Ginkai) a day may reduce your symptoms, because it dilates your blood vessels. (But don't take it if you're also taking prescription anticoagulants, like Coumadin, or about to undergo surgery. And, as always, get your doctor's approval.)

Don't dry those baby blues

Dry eyes is so common that over-the-counter remedies for this ailment abound. What are the causes? Everything from pollution and smoke to age. The cure? Leave the packaged remedies at the drugstore, and eat a banana instead. Bananas are rich in potassium, which helps to control the balance of sodium and the release of fluid in your cells.

Clove Oil to the Rescue!

It's Saturday, the dentist's office is closed, and your sore tooth has gotten so bad you're entertaining thoughts of fishing your wrench out of the toolbox and pulling the offender out on the spot. But wait! You can ease the pain temporarily and save your sanity. The secret? Oil of clove, which you can either purchase or make at home. (Couldn't-be-easier recipe: Pour 1 cup vegetable oil over ¼ cup whole cloves and let sit overnight).

Put a few drops of clove oil on a cotton ball, place the ball on your sore tooth, and bite down. Keep your jaw shut tight for 3–4 minutes as the oil numbs the pain and kills bacteria. Now remove the cotton ball and make a mouthwash from 6 ounces water, ¼ teaspoon salt, and 6–8 drops clove oil. Swish the solution around in your mouth for about 30 seconds to kill still more bacteria, and rinse. Bear in mind that undiluted clove oil inside the mouth can cause burning, tissue or nerve damage, and pain. In large doses, clove oil taken orally can cause vomiting, sore throat, seizure, difficulty breathing, kidney failure, or liver damage. Clove oil shouldn't be applied to broken skin. Children, pregnant or nursing women, and people with diabetes, kidney, or liver disease or bleeding disorders should avoid taking clove oil.

Help lower blood pressure with bananas

Slice a 'naner into your breakfast cereal in the morning for Mother Nature's potassium-laden gift to those of us with high blood pressure. Check with your doctor first, as always.

Soothe Back, Joint, and Muscle Pain

Tin can massage

A cold, unopened 12-ounce beverage can makes a great back massager, whether it's filled with cola or club soda or beer. To loosen muscle tissue and spur blood flow to the area, stand against the wall with the can on its side wedged between your back and the wall. Then move from side to side to make the can roll. This impromptu massager does an especially good job of relaxing the rhomboids next to the shoulder blades and the lats lower down the back.

A back support for drivers

To make a lower back support to use in the car when you drive, fold a medium-size bath towel lengthwise, then roll it up; the roll should be about 1 foot long. Now cut the leg of an old pair of panty hose to size and slip the towel inside. In the car, tuck the makeshift cushion between the small of your back and the car seat, and you'll ride in comfort and with back-friendly posture.

Plast from the past

To give this favorite old pain remedy a shot, combine powdered mustard seed and all-purpose flour in a bowl (1 part mustard seed to 2 parts flour) and slowly stir in water to make a paste. Spread the mixture on one side of a 12-by-12-inch square of cheesecloth and fold. Now place the plaster on the ache, securing it with a bandage or slipping it under a tight T-shirt. Leave the plaster in place for no more than 20–30 minutes at a time. If any skin irritation occurs, remove it immediately.

More curry = less arthritis pain

Turmeric, one of the principal spices in curry powder, is as medicinal as it is culinary. The compound in turmeric called curcumin has been shown in clinical trials to reduce swelling associated with arthritis. If you find curries too spicy, use powdered turmeric as a seasoning, sprinkling it over meats, eggs, and dark green leafy vegetables like spinach.

Eat and drink ginger

Incorporating ginger into your diet will bring at least some relief from rheumatoid arthritis and osteoarthritis pains. For best results, take ½ teaspoon of powdered ginger or 6 teaspoons of fresh ginger once a day, whether in food or tea.

Painful leg cramp relievers

Standing barefoot on a cold floor decreases blood flow and could help relax tightened leg muscles, so if you're hit with these painful leg cramps in the middle of night, get out of bed and stand on a cold floor.

Quinine for cramping

To prevent cramps, make tonic water part of those 8 ounces of water we're told to drink eight times a day. (Just leave out the gin!) Quinine, from the bark of the South American cinchona tree, is the only drug actually proved effective for leg cramps, but serious side effects, including irregular heartbeat, put quinine on the prescription only list. What you *can* buy, and in any grocery store, is tonic water—called so because it's flavored with beneficial quinine.

Calming Gastrointestinal Distress

Stomach soothers

Got indigestion? Nausea? An ordinary tummy ache? Certain herb leaves, flowers, and seeds have traditionally been used to remedy gastrointestinal problems. Among them, in alphabetical order, are angelica, anise, caraway seed, chamomile, cinnamon, fennel seed, ginger, marjoram, oregano, and peppermint. And all can be used to make an herbal infusion or herbal tea.

Tummy taming turmeric

To alleviate stomach cramps, add a teaspoon of this very mild, flavorless, bright red powdered herb to an 8-ounce glass of water, or simply sprinkle it over whatever you're eating. Turmeric is an ancient Indian and Middle Eastern remedy for treating colicky babies and is a recognized antispasmodic.

Juniper as a gastrointestinal tract calmative

To make an infusion of this traditional digestive aid, stir 2 tablespoons oil of juniper into 2 cups boiling water. Once it's cool, drink small portions over the course of 24 hours.

Live in the Windy City?

To help keep flatulence under control, try one of these herbal teas or infusions.

- **Caraway seed** Pour 1 cup boiling water over 1–2 teaspoons freshly crushed caraway seeds. Steep 10–15 minutes, then strain. Drink a cupful two to four times a day between meals.

- **Fennel seed** Follow the directions for caraway seed tea, substituting fennel, then drink before or after meals.

- **Dried peppermint leaf** Pour 1 cup just-boiled water over 1 tablespoon dried peppermint, infuse for 10–15 minutes, and strain. Drink a warm cup of tea three or four times a day.

- **Dill seed** For a mild dill seed infusion, pour 1 cup just-boiled water over 1 teaspoon ground dill seeds and let sit for 10–15 minutes. Strain, then drink before or after meals.

- **Anise seed** Follow the directions for infusing dill seed, substituting anise for dill seed. (Caution: Some people may be allergic to anise.)

Go for the ginger

Sip a cup of virtually miraculous ginger tea after meals to help keep your digestive system in good working order. Gingerroot, which could be called the queen of digestive herbs, has been used for thousands of years to treat indigestion and diarrhea. Research over the past quarter century has shown that two compounds in ginger—gingerols and shogaols—also work on the inner ear and central nervous system as well as the gastrointestinal tract, helping to reduce nausea and dizziness.

What's the Story?
Castor Oil: Our Ancestors' Cure-All

Well into the twentieth century, a bottle of castor oil could be found in virtually every doctor's office, hospital, and home. It was used primarily as a laxative and stomachache cure but also to treat colds and skin problems.

Children in particular were subjected to the foul-tasting oil, which was given at the first hint of a sniffle, cough, or cramp. Many adults took it once a week as a purgative believed to "clean out the system." The oil was also used to induce labor and help a mother recover after childbirth.

Castor oil is extracted from the seeds of the castor bean plant (*Ricinus communis*)—the source of ricin, a deadly poison. But do not fear! The oil is denatured and made safe to use when it is extracted through cold compression and undergoes steam treatment. The venerable product is still on the market, so why not literally hold your nose and give it a try?

Sip cider vinegar

Stir 2 teaspoons cider vinegar into 8 ounces water and enjoy your "vinegar cocktail" up to three times a day for improved digestion and to fend off an impending stomachache. Apple cider vinegar, unlike white vinegar, contains malic acid, which helps to adjust the stomach's pH (the balance of alkalinity and acidity).

Treat diarrhea with berries

Simmer 1–2 tablespoons astringent blackberries, bilberries, or blueberries or their dried leaves in 1½ cups water for 10 minutes, then strain, for diarrhea relief. Drink 1 cup of this diarrhea-fighting tonic several times a day, preparing it fresh each time. Some herbalists recommend drinking 1 shot glass (2 tablespoons) every 4 hours.

Old-timey constipation cure

Your grandmother loved it for a reason: One of the primary uses for castor oil is as a laxative; taking 1–2 teaspoons on an empty stomach will give results in about 8 hours. Castor oil works because a component in the oil breaks down into a substance that stimulates the large and small intestines. Note: This is not recommended for repeated use, as it impairs absorption of nutrients.

Grease the skids with blackstrap molasses

This most refined molasses also contains lots of calcium, magnesium, potassium, and iron, in addition to easing constipation. Of course, it's essentially concentrated cane sugar so you'll want to brush your teeth after swallowing so you don't make your dentist rich. How much to take? One tablespoon before going to bed.

Grow a Physic Garden

Physic (or *physick)* was the name given to gardens of healing plants grown by physicians and monks in ancient times and by home gardeners well into the nineteenth century. Why not plant your own with some of the herbs shown here? By investing a little sweat and the cost of seeds, you'll have the makings of infusions, teas, and balms. Just choose a sunny spot with rich soil for your garden. Perennial plants will grow from season to season, while annuals must be reseeded or transplanted.

Basil

Annual. Harvest the young leaves of what's called "the king of herbs" as needed. Uses: Flatulence, lack of appetite, cuts, and scrapes.

Chamomile, German

Annual. Use the flower heads for infusions and salves. Uses: Indigestion, anxiety, skin inflammations.

Feverfew

Perennial. Use leaves and flowers for teas; chew leaves to ease headache pain. Uses: Headaches (including migraines), arthritis, skin conditions.

Lemon balm

Perennial. A relative of mint, lemon balm is a versatile medicinal herb. Uses: Anxiety, insomnia, wounds, herpes, insect bites, flatulence, upset stomach.

Parsley, Italian

Biennial. Like its curly cousin *P. crispum,* this herb is loaded with nutrients. Uses: Flatulence, bad breath.

Sage

Perennial. Sage's genus name, *Salvia,* means "to heal," reflecting its early use as a medicinal, not culinary, herb. Uses: Mouth and throat inflammations.

St. John's wort

Perennial. The glossy leaves and yellow flowers are this herb's active parts. Uses: Mild to moderate depression. (Talk to your doctor first.)

Thyme

Perennial. The active principle in thyme, thymol, is a strong antiseptic. Uses: Coughs, congestion, indigestion, gas.

Plumbing Problems?

The little red infection fighter

To prevent urinary tract infections (UTIs), drink 12 ounces to 4½ cups of no-sugar-added cranberry juice each day. Capsules of dried cranberry powder are also available—but in some brands, six capsules are the equivalent of only 2½ ounces of juice. Medical researchers learned as early as the 1840s that the hippuric acid in cranberries inhibits the growth of *E. coli* bacteria, the most common cause of UTI. The acid also keeps *E. coli* from adhering to the urinary tract walls and from spreading from the bladder to the kidneys.

Eat your parsley to ease your pain

Mince parsley leaves (Italian or curly), add 1 teaspoon to 1 cup boiling water and let steep 3–5 minutes. Strain, then drink up to 3 cups of tea a day. Because a volatile oil in the leaves and roots of parsley has diuretic properties, parsley tea is useful for treating mild bladder problems, reducing urinary tract inflammation, and even facilitating the passage of small kidney stones. Caution: Anyone with chronic kidney disease should consult a doctor before using parsley, and excessive ingestion of the herb can cause the skin to be photosensitive.

A cup o' corn silk

To make tea, place this natural diuretic in a teapot and add boiling water (¼ cup washed corn silk to 1 cup water). Let steep for 5–6 minutes, then strain into a teacup and drink up to 3 cups a day. Corn silk tea bags are also available. This natural remedy has been shown in tests to have anti-inflammatory properties that fight UTIs; it's also a traditional folk remedy for cystitis, urethritis, and prostatitis.

What's the Story?

Does "Natural" Mean "Safe"?

Not always. Even plain water can be lethal if you drink too much of it. (A water overdose actually dilutes the salt in the body and leads to a condition called hyponatremia.)

Take heed of the age-old advice to practice "moderation in all things" and follow these general guidelines:

- Always ask your physician or pharmacist about any possible interactions with prescription medications, and only use natural or herbal remedies under the advice and supervision of a physician.
- Never use herbal remedies when pregnant or nursing.
- If you aren't growing your own herbs, buy only from reputable sources, preferably at a store with reliable sales staff.
- Never exceed the recommended dosage.
- Discontinue use if you notice any negative side effects.
- Store products in a cool, dry place out of the reach of children.
- Do not use commercial products after one year from date of purchase.

Gotta love lovage

To ease the discomfort associated with a mild inflammation of the urinary tract, make lovage tea by pour 1 cup boiling water over 1 teaspoon minced dried lovage root, which is a member of the carrot family but tastes more like celery. Steep 10 minutes, then strain and drink. A note of caution: It should be avoided by anyone with chronic kidney problems.

Drink to kidney health!

(But do it with fruit juice, please, not booze.) Making sure you drink one or two 8-ounce glasses of fruit juice (especially cranberry juice, lemonade, or orange juice) a day will contribute to overall kidney health. That's because the ascorbic and citric acids in fruit juices acidify the urine and have an antiseptic effect on the kidneys. Just don't overdo it—a good rule to follow in any case, but especially when ingesting anything acidic.

Praise the weed and pass the teapot!

The dandelion isn't just any old weed: it has a long history as a medicinal, and its benefits are related to the kidneys in at least two ways. First, dandelion reduces fluid retention resulting from kidney disorders. Second, dandelion may be able to speed the passing of a small kidney stone. If you feel the pain that signals movement of a stone, drink as much dandelion tea as you can. A strong diuretic, dandelion stimulates blood circulation through the kidneys, increasing urine output and helping to flush out the stone. Dandelion tea bags are easily available, but you can also make your own. Wash dandelion leaves and root thoroughly and then chop finely. Add 3 tablespoons to 2 cups water, boil for 3 minutes, and let sit for 10–12 minutes before straining.

Dandelion tea may hasten the passing of kidney stones!

Foot Care

Beat athlete's foot

To put athlete's foot on the run, make a foot-bath with 1 tablespoon salt dissolved in 6 quarts warm water. Soak the affected foot for 10 minutes to help kill the fungus. To make the solution still more antifungal, add 1–2 table-spoons tea tree oil.

Fight toenail fungus

If you think you can't control a fungus without prescription drugs, think again—for the short term, at least. Mix equal parts warm water, vinegar (white or cider), and mouth-wash, with a tablespoon of powdered cinnamon. Soak, dry feet, and then sprinkle with cornstarch. There's no guarantee the fungus won't return, but at least you can keep it in check without expensive drugs.

Got stinky feet?

Strong black tea will not only kill odor-causing bacteria but will close pores and help keep your feet less sweaty. Simmer 3 black tea bags in 2 cups water for 15 minutes, then dilute the tea with 2 quarts water. Once it's nice and cool, pour tea into a plastic tub (hold the milk and sugar), and soak those ripe dogs for 30 minutes. No more stinky feet.

Salty dogs

While Epsom salt—named for the English town where it was first mined commercially—has long been used to soothe dry, sore feet, ordinary table salt will do in a pinch. Pour 2 gallons warm water into a plastic tub, add 1 cup table salt, and stir with your hand to dissolve. Soak your feet in the solution for at least 20 minutes,

Kitchen-Cupboard Odor Eater

Take shoes (warm and airless), sweat (secreted by the eccrine glands on the soles of your feet), and poor hygiene (neglecting to scrub your feet when you shower) and you have a recipe for funky feet. Whether your stocking feet are only mildly odoriferous or smelly enough to fell a crowd at 40 paces, turn to the kitchen cupboard to help control the odor.

What to take off the shelf? Baking soda and cornstarch. Mix the powders 50/50 and sprinkle the mixture on your feet before you put on your socks. Baking soda helps neutralize the skin acids that harbor odor-causing bacteria, while cornstarch absorbs sweat. Sprinkling some of the powder into your shoes will also help to neutralize odors.

then rub them vigorously with a towel to slough off dead skin cells.

Terrific tired tootsie trick

If your feet are tired and aching, scatter a few pencils on the floor and pick them up…with your toes. This little workout rejuvenates and invigorates your dogs as much as a quick foot massage.

Cool that hot foot with peppermint

Give hot feet the chill-down by soaking them in iced peppermint tea for 10 minutes. All pepped up, they'll be ready to take you on a three-mile jog or an hourlong power walk.

Healing Cuts, Bruises, and Other Skin Problems

Treat a cut with garlic

To treat a cut or abrasion, gently wash the wound with soapy, warm water and pat it dry with a clean, soft cloth. Then bruise a peeled clove of garlic and press it against the cut for 5–10 minutes, securing it with a bandage if you like. Garlic contains allicin, which has been shown to inhibit the growth of several kinds of bacteria and protect against infection. (Fresh garlic is an irritant, so never leave garlic in any form—infused, minced, or whole—on the skin for more than 20 minutes at a time. Remove it immediately if it irritates the skin.)

Black pepper stops bleeding

Shaking a good amount of black pepper onto a bleeding cut will stop the blood flow pronto. Why? Because the pepper constricts the blood vessels. Many people who've tried this remedy claim that a wound treated with black pepper heals with less scarring.

Lessen bruising with an onion

Immediately press the cut end of a raw onion on a superficial bruise and keep it in place for 15 minutes. Why? Because the allicin in onions (the compound that makes your eyes water) stimulates the lymphatic flow in the body, helping to flush away excess blood in the just-injured tissue that creates the discoloration we call a bruise.

Aloe Straight from the Leaf

Commercial aloe vera lotions and creams are a dime a dozen, but an aloe treatment is yours for free if you have access to an aloe vera plant. Better still, fresh gel is generally more effective than store-bought lotions, which often contain more non-aloe emollients than aloe.

To get the real stuff, go straight to the leaf itself. Plants will keep well indoors, in a cool, sunny spot.

1. Cut off a 3-inch section of fleshy aloe leaf, slice open the inner portion, and scrape out the mucilaginous gel with a spoon, stopping short of the rind.
2. Apply the gel to the skin two or three times a day, washing the skin between applications to make it more receptive to glucomannan and aloe's other anti-inflammatory substances.

Be careful not to get aloe gel on your clothes, since it can leave a yellow stain.

Soothe sunburn with green tea

Just add 3 green tea bags to 1 quart just-boiled water, remove the pan from the heat, and let steep for 2–3 hours. Use a cotton ball or very soft cloth to dab the sunburned area with the cooled tea, and let the cooling tannins do their work.

Conquer the (creeping) cooties with alder bark

To get rid of lice, simmer 2 tablespoons chipped alder bark in 2 quarts white vinegar, then let cool before straining into a container with a lid. Using a cotton ball, apply to the scalp or other affected areas four times daily. Do *not* ingest the mixture, and be aware that alder bark may temporarily color the skin.

Chamomile salve

Melt ½ cup petroleum jelly in a double boiler and stir in 1 tablespoon chamomile flowers. Heat for 2 hours or until the flowers are crisp. Tightly fit a jelly bag atop a glass jar and squeeze the hot mixture through. Once the salve cools, apply to a mild skin rash up to four times a day. Choose the more efficacious German chamomile *(Matricaria recutita)* over Roman, or English, chamomile *(Chamaemelum nobile)*.

Double-duty paste for bee stings

A baking soda–vinegar paste applied to a bee sting immediately after removing the stinger will get some alkaline and acidic action going (use 2 parts baking soda to 1 part vinegar). When the paste dries, wipe it off with a clean, damp cloth.

Papaya milk for stings

Forget about milking a papaya after that painful bee or wasp sting. Instead, use commercial meat tenderizer, which contains papain. Moisten a teaspoonful of tenderizer with a little water and rub it onto the sting as quickly as possible; papain's protein-digesting properties help break down the venom.

Oatmeal and panty hose to cure hives

Cut a panty-hose leg off at the knee and put these four ingredients into the foot: ½ cup rolled oats; ½ cup dry powdered milk; and ¼ cup each dried chamomile flowers and lavender. Knot the nylon bag closed and hold it under warm (not hot) running water as you fill your bathtub. Submerge the bag and let the water cool. (Hot water makes hives worse, not better). Soak for half an hour, and every 5 minutes or so, hold the bag over the rash and squeeze to release the soothing stuff inside.

Douse skin rashes with witch hazel

The bark and leaves of the witch hazel plant contain high proportions of naturally astringent tannins and an aromatic oil—the perfect recipe for soothing itchy skin rashes.

Pimple pastes

Applied to pimples, quick 'n' easy homemade pastes will make pimples disappear quickly. Try these three.

- **Baking soda** Moisten ¼ teaspoon baking soda with a few drops of water and dab it onto pimples. Leave it for 5 minutes, then wipe it off with a washcloth dipped in cool water.

- **Oatmeal** Use some of your morning oatmeal as a pimple-fighter. Dab the cooked, cooled oatmeal onto broken-out skin, cover with a warm-water washcloth compress, and let sit for 15 minutes. Repeat daily until the pimples are gone.

- **Cornstarch and lemon juice** Make a paste with 1 teaspoon cornstarch and 1 teaspoon lemon juice. Apply to pimples and let sit for 4–5 minutes before gently washing your face with cool water.

Witch Hazel from Your Garden

If you have a witch hazel bush (*Hamamelis virginiana*) in your yard and it's at least 3 feet tall, you can prepare your own witch hazel astringent for treating skin irritations, cuts, and scrapes. Going the homemade route has two advantages: It puts you in touch with a time when self-sufficiency was a way of life, and your homemade astringent is more effective than witch hazel products that have undergone steam distillation and lost most of their tannins.

Because the leaves have to dry, it takes about a week to make witch hazel. Snip leaves at the stem base and rinse them well. To harvest bark, lop off a branch and scrape off the bark. Place the leaves and bark on paper towel–lined trays and store them in a dark place at 70–90°F for seven days.

While witch hazel can be prepared in a number of ways, the easiest is to use a blender. Blend the dried plant matter for 1–2 minutes, then combine it with water (1 tablespoon plant matter to 1 cup water). Pour into a saucepan, bring to a boil, and simmer for 20 minutes. Remove from heat and let steep for 2 hours. Strain through cheesecloth or a fine sieve into sterilized jars and use as needed. Good job!

Lifeguards never had zits!

The white zinc oxide cream slathered over the noses of lifeguards as a sunscreen is also an effective acne fighter. Dab a little zinc oxide cream or ointment before bed and it will not only help dry up pimples but is also said to prevent scarring.

Wards off vampires, too!

Rubbing a freshly cut clove of raw garlic on a pimple will help dry it up and make it disappear.

Just treat pimples right before going to bed, since garlic doesn't have to be on your breath to make those around you wrinkle their noses.

Kitchen-cupboard eczema salve

A white creamy substance good for soothing eczema comes not from the medicine cabinet but the kitchen cupboard: vegetable shortening. Coat the affected area with shortening, cover with plastic wrap, and secure the wrap with surgical tape. Leave it on for 2–4 hours at a time, if possible, repeating daily until the rash calms down.

Two ways to stop shingles from itching

Shingles, or *herpes zoster*, is caused by the varicella-zoster virus—the same virus that causes chicken pox. (It isn't as contagious as chicken pox but can be passed on to anyone who's susceptible.) The rash consists of small, crusting blisters that itch like the dickens, and both of these home remedies can bring relief:

- **Aloe gel** Apply gel to affected area to calm the itch

- **Nail polish remover and aspirin** Pour 3 tablespoons nail polish remover into a small cup, add two crushed aspirin, and stir until the aspirin dissolves. Use a

cotton ball to apply the solution to shingles blisters, and let it air-dry for hours-long relief.

Cure warts with a "garlic press"

Slice a fresh peeled garlic clove, place it on the wart, and bind it with a gauze bandage. Leave the garlic in place as long you're able to, and repeat the process morning and night. Because of its general antiviral activity, garlic has been said to cure warts even when other methods have failed.

Rosewater for chapped skin

To make a lotion for chapped skin (and a fragrant one, at that) mix ½ cup rosewater with ¼ cup glycerin and rub it into the skin as needed. This essential cupboard companion is as popular as ever in Asia and the Middle East, where it is used both to flavor food and in rituals. Find it in pharmacies and health food stores.

T(r)opical wart remover

Make several shallow cuts in an unripe green papaya, and collect the sap that it releases. When it congeals, mix it with water to make a thin paste. Before applying the paste, protect the skin surrounding the wart by swabbing on

ALOE FOR BLISTERS

Speed blister healing by rubbing it with gel from an **aloe vera** leaf. Slice open a leaf and use a spoon to scrape out the gel (see "Aloe Straight from the Leaf," page 171). Dab it on the blister, cover with a bandage, then reapply and rebandage once a day.

a thin layer of petroleum jelly (papain, the enzyme in papaya, is an irritant so powerful that it's an ingredient in meat tenderizers). Using a cotton swab, carefully apply the paste to a wart morning and night until it breaks down and disappears. Papain breaks down proteins in dead tissue, making it a wart remover of long standing.

Turmeric treats ringworm

If you have a bottle of the Indian spice turmeric in your kitchen cabinet, you have an antiviral powder that has been used in Asia as a ringworm remedy for centuries. In a small bowl, mix enough of the powdered root to make a paste. Apply the paste to the affected area with a cotton swab, cover it with a bandage, and leave it on for 20–60 minutes. Repeat three or four times a day. Note: Turmeric may irritate sensitive skin, so test it first on clear skin; if redness develops, try another treatment.

Seal in moisture with vegetable shortening

Dry skin and rashes alike benefit from a soak with a wet washcloth for several minutes, then a gentle rubdown with vegetable shortening. Cover the affected area and leave it on for 1–2 hours. Wipe the shortening off with a clean soft cloth and repeat the treatment as needed.

Relieve swimmer's itch

Protect yourself from swimmer's itch in freshwater lakes by spreading petroleum jelly on skin not covered by a swimsuit.

1,001 Ways to Remove Warts

We're not promising to run down all of the folk remedies tried over the ages to remove warts, since that would be one those lists that supposedly stretches all the way around the equator. Suffice to say that untold numbers of methods have been recorded. People washed warts in rainwater pooled in tree stumps. They pressed raw potatoes, banana peels, and any number of saps and oils on warts. They also believed in the Theory of Transference—the notion that an ailment could be transferred from the patient to a tree, animal, or object. Blood was drawn from a wart, placed on a grain of corn, and fed to a chicken. Warts could be "sold" to a folk healer called a wart charmer.

Surprising as it is, many of the most far-fetched wart remedies have been documented as successful. Some medical researchers now believe the body may be able to rid itself of warts through the power of hypnotic suggestion. Case in point: One physician who had no success in treating a man with multiple warts put the patient in an X-ray room and told him he was going to zap him with radiation. In fact, the doctor ran the X-ray machine without delivering any rays—and the man's warts fell off the next day.

Aiding Sleeplessness and Anxiety

A tryptophan snack before bed

Serotonin is a brain chemical that helps you sleep, and tryptophan is an amino acid the body uses to make serotonin. Two tryptophan-rich foods are turkey and bananas, your tickets to drowsy dreamland.

Drink passionflower tea

Despite its name, passionflower won't make your honeymoon all the more memorable. In fact, it will put you to sleep. Infuse 3 passionflower tea bags in 3 cups just-boiled water for 30–60 minutes and sip a cup half an hour before going to bed. Sweet dreams! (FYI, the "passion" in the name refers to the Crucifixion of Christ, not lust.) Alkaloids in the flower can help allay both insomnia and anxiety, conditions that often go hand in hand.

Calming Epsom salt bath

To calm yourself, pour 2 cups Epsom salt into a tub full of warm water, and soak to your heart's content. Epsom salt (magnesium sulfate) not only cleans and tones the skin but also may lower blood pressure—just what you need after a day so awful that your anxiety level is sky high.

Make a hops pillow

Hops pillows were popular sleep aids in days of yore, and it's easy to make a modern version. Take a zippered throw pillow or chair cushion cover and stuff it full of dried hops (available at natural product stores, online, and perhaps at the nearest brewery). If you like, throw in a handful of dried lavender, also a sedative herb, to sweeten the smell. When you retire for the night, put the pillow near enough to you head that you'll be able to breathe in the aroma. To keep the hops active, you'll need to dampen them with grain alcohol every three or four weeks.

Try St. John's Wort

A cup of St. John's wort tea can safely be drunk up to three times a day to allay mild depression, nervousness, and insomnia; capsules and liquid extracts are also available. Be aware, though, that some people using the herb have experienced delayed photosensitivity—an abnormal reaction to sunlight that usually results in a skin rash. This best-selling herb is Germany's leading antidepressant, outselling even Prozac. Studies show that hypericin and other compounds in St. John's wort act in tandem to prevent the enzyme monoamine oxidase (MAO) from breaking down serotonin, dopamine, and other amines that elevate mood and emotions. Check with your doctor before use.

Tomato paste snore stopper

If your bed mate's snoring is cutting into your sleep time, help is in the pantry. Put a small can (4–5 ounces) of tomato paste in the pocket of a cotton T-shirt and secure it closed with a safety pin. Have the snorer put the shirt on backward before going to sleep, and it will keep him (or her) from rolling over into prime snoring position: on the back.

Give yourself a soak

There's a reason why in-the-know parents give their babies warm baths before bedtime or nap-time: warm water is a natural relaxant. So fill the tub, turn the lights down low, soak for a few minutes, and crawl into a freshly made bed for no-lose snooze.

Pre-sleep sip

Chamomile, which is known to have sedating qualities, is an ideal sleep inducer. If you can get good quality tea bags, they'll do perfectly; if you can grow fresh chamomile in a small pot on a windowsill, all the better. Snip them about an inch below the flower, tie a few of them together with kitchen string, and steep them in a mug of hot water. Delicious!

White noise as sleep therapy

Studies have long proven that white noise—defined as noise that combines sounds of all different frequences so that they virtually cancel each other out—is an effective, completely non-narcotic, safe, and peaceful sleep aid. Where to get it? You can buy white noise machines, or even less expensively, CDs and tapes. Load them into your bedroom CD player, turn the lights down, climb into bed, and remember to set the alarm!

Keep your cool!

The term "warm and cozy" doesn't always translate to the right conditions for falling asleep; resist the urge to keep the heat up, and instead, lower your bedroom's thermostat to 65–70°F, and if possible, open the window a crack for good ventilation. Sleep experts maintain that cooler bedroom temperatures result in a sounder, better snooze.

Household Superstar!
8 Ways Petroleum Jelly Is Kind to Your Body

While petroleum jelly is usually thought of as a moisturizer, it was developed as a salve to heal and protect cuts and abrasions—and it's more versatile than you might think. Here are eight ways to use it:

1. Prevent chafing of back skin subjected to a backpack's straps and upper thighs clothed in denim by rubbing petroleum jelly on the vulnerable areas.

2. Rub petroleum jelly on dry, scaly patches of psoriasis to lubricate them and lessen itching.

3. To keep a crusted cold sore from bleeding, coat it with petroleum jelly applied with a cotton swab, not your fingers.

4. Spread a thick layer of petroleum jelly on an infested scalp, and when you wipe it off, the lice should go with it.

5. Dab a hemorrhoid with petroleum jelly, which is contained in many over-the-counter hemorrhoid treatments.

6. A layer of petroleum jelly on a small wound keeps moisture in and bacteria out.

7. Dab petroleum jelly under your nose to trap some of the pollen spores making their way toward your nostrils.

8. Rub petroleum jelly on the insides of your nostrils to moisten the mucous membranes and make nosebleeds less likely.

Caring for Baby

Diaper rash soothers

The exposure of a baby's skin to urine and poop cause diaper rash, especially when diaper changes are delayed. Soap can irritate the skin even more if it contains alcohol—and though most commercial baby wipes are alcohol-free, so are three cost-free diaper rash soothers in your cabinets:

- **"Toasted" cornstarch** Although moisture-absorbing cornstarch can be used straight from the box, it works better when dried in the oven. Just spread it on a cookie sheet and dry it in a 150°F oven for 10 minutes. Let cool before using.

- **Honey** The sugar in honey absorbs water, denying infection-causing bacteria the moisture they need to survive. Ask your doctor before using honey on children under 12 months of age; if ingested, honey can cause botulism.

- **Petroleum jelly** Wiping petroleum jelly on the rash gives Baby's skin a protective coating so the rash can heal.

A spicy baby powder substitute

The spice fenugreek has been shown to soothe diaper rash. Either apply it directly to the skin, like baby powder, or mix it with a little water to form a paste to apply sparingly to irritated areas.

Prevent diaper rash with salt and zinc

Stir 1 tablespoon salt into 4 cups boiling water and let the solution cool to room temperature. Wipe it onto your baby's bottom, then gently dab it dry. Now apply a zinc oxide lotion to create a barrier against wetness.

Easiest rash preventive of all?

Air! The less time a baby's bottom is covered by a diaper, the less she risks suffering diaper rash. At nap time, just place an unfastened diaper under your child or put the baby on towels placed over a waterproof sheet.

A rash remedy from the garden

Calendula, a marigold cousin, has long been used to treat skin rashes, so keep a homemade wash in the nursery to soothe Baby's skin.

Cut the flower heads from a calendula plant and let them dry. Pick the petals off over a bowl and put 1 heaping tablespoon petals into a bowl. Pour 3 cups just-boiled water over the petals, let steep for 1 hour, then strain into a bottle. Apply to the baby's bottom or other red or itchy areas up to four times a day.

Chamomile for congestion?

If your baby is 6 months or older and is stuffy, try easing her congestion with weak chamomile tea—weak meaning 1 chamomile tea bag steeped in 2 cups hot water for no more than 3 minutes. Put the lukewarm tea in her baby bottle and let her sip on it two or three times a day. Check with your pediatrician first; chamomile can trigger allergic reactions in some people.

Soothe heat rash with a baking soda bath

Heat rash can make babies miserable, and here's a way to help "take the red out": Add baking soda to Baby's lukewarm bathwater—2 teaspoons to each gallon of water. Then let Baby air-dry instead of wiping him with a towel. You can also gently press the rash with a cool, wet washcloth several times a day.

Two herbal teas for colic

Much to Baby's distress, the periodic intestinal spasms known as colic start at about 3–4 weeks of age and usually don't end until two or three months later. One colic fighter is the volatile oil in fennel seed, shown to expel gas and relieve cramps and flatulence in the process. Another is peppermint leaf, which calms the intestinal tract and stimulates the bile flow that aids digestion.

To make a fennel tea, pour 1 cup boiling water over 1 teaspoon crushed fennel seeds. For peppermint tea, pour 1 cup boiling water over 1 tablespoon crushed leaves. Let either tea steep for 5 minutes, then strain. Cool tea before giving to Baby.

A caution: Give peppermint tea to babies with care. The menthol in peppermint can cause a choking sensation, so start with a single sip and discontinue use if the child chokes or seems to find the tea disagreeable.

Stopping Baby's nosebleed

Your fingers, a facial tissue or soft washcloth, and patience are all the equipment you need to stop a small child's nosebleed. Seat the baby on your lap and lean him slightly forward. Now, with the tissue or washcloth in hand, gently pinch his nostrils shut. Apply constant (though gentle) pressure for 10 minutes, making sure you don't release pressure to check and see whether the bleeding has ceased.

How to keep Baby still all this time? Watch a favorite video or, if you can handle it, leaf through a picture book to hold his attention.

Sore throat for Snookums?

If your baby's old enough to be eating solids, warm beverages like tea or broth can be soothing. (No honey in the tea, please, since honey may contain spores that could grow in the baby's immature digestive tract.) Cool apple juice is another sore throat soother for the little one.

Dr. McFolk's Medicine Bag

Homemade hydration aid

Sports drinks are full of electrolytes—the salts that need replenishing after the body sweats—and are almost essential for keeping athletes and runners hydrated. You can make your own for next to nothing. Dissolve 1 teaspoon salt and 4 teaspoons sugar in 1 quart water, and you have a drink that isn't colored or adorned with a fancy label but that will nonetheless maintain your electrolyte balance and keep you hydrated.

Milk thistle for liver health

Our forebears used the weed milk thistle to "clean the liver," and they were on to something. Silymarin, a substance contained in the seeds, prevents toxins from penetrating the liver and stimulates the regeneration of liver cells—the reason milk thistle has been used in the treatment of hepatitis, cirrhosis, and jaundice.

If you think you can just harvest milk thistle weed and use the seeds to make a therapeutic tea, think again. Teas are ineffective because the active principles in milk thistle seeds aren't water-soluble. Instead, try milk thistle capsules and liquid extracts, making sure they contain 200–400 milligrams of silymarin.

Peanut butter for hiccups

Believe it or not, peanut butter may take care of those annoying hiccups. It's not the peanut butter per se that works but what it takes to swallow it. Eat 1 heaping teaspoon of peanut butter (plain or crunchy) and take your own sweet time swallowing it. As you chew and use

Curiosity Corner
"Like Things for Like Things"

Since the Middle Ages, one of the "laws" of folk medicine was based on the principle *similia similibus*—"like things for like things." When it came to medicinal plants, those whose characteristics match the body's organs were believed to have a curative effect, a belief that in time came to be called the Doctrine of Signatures and that eventually was proved utterly false.

As late as the nineteenth century, liverwort (*Hepatica* ssp.)—so named because its leaves are the shape of the liver—was used to treat liver ailments. Plants with red sap were applied to bleeding wounds, and the fuzzy burrs of the burdock plant were said to cure baldness. The Doctrine of Signatures was rooted in the belief of an inherent affinity, or sympathy, between living things and the forces of the universe—hence the reason it was often referred to as "sympathetic magic."

your tongue to clean the gooey treat off the roof of your mouth and your teeth, your breathing patterns are interrupted and may result in halted hiccups.

Oil and vinegar remedies

Grab some oil and vinegar from the kitchen cabinet when you need relief in a pinch. You can do a lot more than dress a salad with these staples.

- Vinegar takes the pain out of a bee or jellyfish sting. Scrape the stinger off with a credit card, and then pour undiluted vinegar directly on the sting.

- White vinegar dries up a cold sore when rubbed on the sore 3–4 times a day.

- White and cider vinegar take the burn out of sunburn. They also take the itch out of poison ivy rashes and insect bites.

- Olive oil is a good stand-in for shaving cream. Your skin will enjoy a nice moisturizing treatment as you wield your razor.

- Soaking in a bath to which you've added ½ cup olive oil and 2 cups baking soda will stop skin from itching and will soften it as well.

- Add 2–3 drops warm (not hot) olive oil to the ear to soften earwax. Drain your ear after 5 minutes. Do not do this if there's a chance you have a perforated eardrum.

Fight herpes with lemon balm tea

Lemon balm's volatile oil contains two substances that fight herpes simplex type 1 virus (HSV1), which usually affects the lips, mouth, and face, and HSV2, or genital herpes—the reason the herb is widely used in European over-the-counter herpes products. To make an infusion, pour 1 cup just-boiled water over 2–3 teaspoons minced lemon balm and let steep 10–12 minutes before straining into a jar. Soak a cotton ball in the solution and apply it to herpes blisters several times a day.

Remove splinters with an onion

Here's a pain-free (if rather smelly) way to get a splinter out of a finger or foot. Place a ¼-inch slice of onion over the splinter and wrap a bandage around the affected area to keep the onion in place. Leave the onion poultice on overnight, and by morning the skin should have shrunk and allowed the splinter to work itself out.

Cider vinegar tea for fatigue

Vinegar perks up a recipe, and it may perk you up, too. Every morning before breakfast, whisk together 1 cup warm water, 2 tablespoons apple cider vinegar, and 1 teaspoon honey. Sip the tea slowly until you've downed the last drop, and within a week you may find yourself feeling more energized.

Treat thrush with goldenseal

Thrush, or candidiasis—an infection of the mucous membranes of the mouth, vagina, or digestive tract—is made evident by a whitish, "furry" tongue. The dried root of goldenseal *(Hydrastis canadensis)* has a long history as a thrush treatment, and clinical trials have confirmed its efficacy. To treat thrush, make goldenseal tea by pouring 1 cup boiling water over 2 teaspoons powdered root; steep for 5–10 minutes. Let cool before using as a gargle or douche, or drink as a hot tea.

Chapter Seven

You're Looking Good

Every woman knows about fashion and grooming glitches: the runs in hosiery, the broken heels, the smeared makeup. The classic snafus for guys? Ketchup on khaki pants, no hair gel, gray ring around the collar. And for both sexes? The bad hair day, the broken zipper, the clothes as wrinkled as the face of Methuselah (who supposedly died at age 969). What, oh what, to do?

Just leaf through the next 23 pages for more than a hundred creative solutions to the often maddening grooming and clothing problems that plague us all, using items you most likely already have! Here, you'll learn how to recycle old garments and make them look brand new; make very cool jewelry from old-fashioned typewriter keys; whip up homemade skin treatments that will leave you glowing; revitalize your hair with beer and avocado; and even remove lipstick smears with bread! What's more, making your own grooming products is simple, environmentally friendly, and inexpensive. If our ancestors did it, why can't we?

Keep your straw hat
looking sharp with
hairspray!

Homespun Skin Care

Tape out that furrow

Is that furrow in your brow starting to become your own personal petite Grand Canyon? Smooth it out by putting tape on your brow overnight, every night for a month. Before going to sleep, rub moisturizer on the wrinkle and wipe off any excess. Now smooth the furrow with your fingers, hold it taut, and secure a piece of tape across the spot. Some folks recommend ouchless surgical tape, while other make do with any sticky tape. (Just make sure it extends beyond the moisturized area or it may not hold through the night.) Taping works by retraining the face muscles to relax—and, unlike Botox or plastic surgery, costs only pennies.

Look younger (and sweeter!)

Discourage wrinkling by applying a facial mask made of honey once a week, like Cleopatra did. Honey has properties that soften and hydrate skin and help it retain moisture, plus antioxidants and various compounds that can soothe irritations and inflammations. To make a honey mask, warm the honey. While it's heating, press a warm washcloth to your face to open the pores. Carefully spread the honey around the face, keeping it away from your eyes. Relax for 15 minutes and then rinse the mask off, using cold water in the final rinse to close the pores. Though your skin may not *look* like a baby's, it should feel almost as soft.

Soak in a hot tea bath

If a spot of tea in the afternoon is a calming break, a hot green tea bath in the evening after a tough day is a little touch of heaven. Place 2 tablespoons dried green tea leaves in the toe of an old nylon stocking, then bunch it up and close with a twist tie. Toss the bundle into a hot bath or tie it with string over the faucet opening so the water will run through. While you're enjoying the hot soak, the antioxidants of the tea will go to work, smoothing, soothing, and calming you both outside and in.

Chocolate body wrap

Love chocolate so much that you could bathe in it? Here's your chance. Just warm ½ cup of honey in a microwave or the top of a double boiler. Then stir in 1½ cups of unsweetened cocoa until it dissolves. If the mixture cools, reheat it, but don't let it get hot. Now spread the mudlike paste evenly over your body.

Here comes the good part: Wrap your legs, arms, and torso in plastic wrap to seal in the paste and sit tight (or lie down) for 20 minutes.

TURN A SOCK INTO A WASHCLOTH

Got yet **another mateless athletic sock**? (You're not the only one.) At bath time, simply turn it inside out (terry cloth on the outside), fit it over your hand like a mitten, and use it as an exfoliating scrubber.

Most of us take our skin for granted, but it is in fact the body's largest organ. Moreover, it grows faster than any other organ and continually replenishes itself. It's waterproof, flexible, generates all the hairs on the body, and can repair itself. And if you think that's amazing, read on.

• The average-size person's skin weighs about 9 pounds, or about 16 percent of body weight.

• An average-size person's skin would cover an area of about 17–21 square feet if laid out.

• Your skin has approximately 45 miles of nerves and more nerve endings than any other part of the body.

• The entire top layer of dead skin cells sloughs off and is replaced every month, yet we barely notice it.

• In the average person's lifetime, about 40 pounds of dead skin cells are shed and replaced.

• Within 1 square inch of skin are approximately 65 hairs, 100 oil glands, 650 sweat glands, 1,500 nerve receptors, and countless blood vessels.

• The average person has 5 million hairs on the body, with only about 100,000 growing on the scalp.

That done, peel off the wrap and wash away the paste in a warm shower or bath. Your skin should feel silky smooth, thanks to the hydrating and revitalizing antioxidants in cocoa and honey. And all without a single calorie!

Stomach medicine for a facial?

Strange but true: Over-the-counter stomachache medicines containing salicylic acid, like Pepto-Bismol, are beneficial to the skin. How so? Salicylic acid helps to slough off the top layer of dead skin cells and bring new healthy skin cells to the surface. Squash a few cotton balls together in your fingers, pour on some of the pink goo, and apply it to your face, taking care to stay clear of the eyes. Let it dry for about 15 minutes, then rinse and pat dry. Your skin will not only stomach this facial but will thank you!

Condition your legs

For a smooth leg shave without traditional shaving cream or gel, just substitute hair conditioner or an all-in-one shampoo-conditioner, both of which contain ingredients that soften, smooth, and moisturize hair. They'll do the same for hair and skin on your legs, underarms, and, for men, the face.

A summertime citrus body splash

Squeeze the juice from a lime, filter out the pulp, and pour the juice into a spray bottle. Add ½ cup rubbing alcohol and 3 teaspoons lemon or orange extract. Screw the lid on the bottle and shake well. Give yourself a spritz for a great way to cool down in the summer. Store the spray in the refrigerator with an identification label so no one will think it's safe to consume.

Prolong the scent

Add hours to the scent of your perfume by first dabbing a tiny bit of petroleum jelly on your wrists, neck, ear lobes, and anywhere else you apply the fragrance.

Three Ways to Slough It Off,
NATURALLY!

Many people use facials, masks, scrubs, and other methods to speed the natural process of shedding dead skin cells, called exfoliation. Sloughing off dead cells with exfoliants exposes new, plumper, cleaner, smoother cells that lie just underneath the skin's surface. Exfoliating also stimulates blood circulation, which brings a healthy glow to skin. There are lots of commercial products out there that exfoliate and stimulate skin renewal, and spas and salons charge a good bit of money for one session. You'll save a pocketful by sloughing off skin with items from your pantry and refrigerator. Just gently massage the exfoliants shown here into the skin, using circular motions. (When applying an exfoliating facial or mask, avoid the area around the eyes.) After rinsing and patting your skin dry, apply some moisturizer and feel renewed—literally!

1
Strawberry Scrub
Mash 5 or 6 strawberries, then mix in 1 tablespoon ground almonds and enough yogurt (about 2 tablespoons) for the mixture to be pasty enough to apply.

2
Oatmeal Ouster
Blend together 2 heaping teaspoons finely ground uncooked oatmeal with 1 teaspoon baking soda. Stir water in slowly until you have a spreadable paste.

3
Ginger Snapper
Blend together equal amounts of freshly minced ginger and brown sugar, then add vanilla extract or sweet almond oil to make an energizing body scrub. Ginger contains valuable antioxidants and is known to stimulate circulation.

The Eyes Have It

Bottoms up!

Models and performers have long held the secret to reducing puffiness and wrinkles no matter how late they were up the night before, and it's *not* an expensive eye cream. What is it? Hemorrhoid cream, which tightens puffy areas and wrinkles. If the odor of the cream is too strong, mix a bit of your moisturizer into it before applying. And do be careful not to get any of the cream into your eyes; after all, it's designed to be used much farther south.

Spoon 'em for energy

The next time your peepers need pepping, take two metal teaspoons from the kitchen drawer and hold them under very cold running water for a few minutes. Then lie down and place the bowls of the spoons over your eyelids for 30–60 seconds. The sharp cold of the metal will revive tired eyes and may boost your energy level at the same time.

Teething rings for tired eyes

Was the baby crying all night, leaving you with tired eyes? No problem. While baby naps, put two of his teething rings in the freezer until they're ice cold, stretch out on the sofa, and place the rings on your closed eyelids for about 10 minutes. The cold will not only reduce eye puffiness but invigorate you, too.

Lighten dark circles

For many people, tiredness causes dark circles under the eyes—"raccoon eyes" that add years to the appearance of men and women alike. If you can't catch up on your rest, place slices of ripe avocado under each eye or apply a paste

of ground almonds and milk to lighten the dark shadows.

Cool as a cucumber

When your eyes are all red and puffy (you party animal, you), cut a couple of slices of cold cucumber, lie down, and put a slice over each eye for 30 minutes. Once you're up, your eyes will be brighter and your body refreshed.

De-puff with tea

Caffinated tea—which contains natural tannins—is a mild diuretic and long-used by grandmothers and runway models alike for reducing eye puffiness. Soak two tea bags in warm water, and then chill the bags for a few minutes in the refrigerator. Place one tea bag on each eye for 5 minutes, and your peepers will be fresh as a daisy.

Makeup Tips

Firming up mushy lipstick

Purse sitting in the sun for too long? Instead of waiting for the air conditioning to firm up your softened lipstick, pop it into the fridge for a fast five-minute fix.

Emergency lip color

You can't decide if the new dress you're trying on is flattering to your face, and without extra color on your lips it's even harder to tell. So you dig into your handbag, and surprise! You've left both your lipstick and lip pencil at home. But you *do* have a brown eyeliner pencil. Press the eyeliner into service on your lips, and you may find that it looks fantastic!

A cheesy solution

Are you out of cotton balls and makeup remover pads and don't like to use tissues because of the residue they leave on your skin? Cut a few squares of cheesecloth for wiping off makeup. They're soft, porous, and absorbent. Use a bigger swatch as a covering for mushy facials so you don't drip goop on the floor or yourself; pat the cloth very gently over the mixture, just until it adheres.

A Surprising Cologne Corrective

Ever accidentally douse yourself with just a little *too* much cologne? (Haven't we all?)

If soap and water won't correct the problem, head to the liquor cabinet and grab a bottle of vodka. Dab a little on the places you applied the cologne or perfume, and the nearly odorless spirit will knock out the scent in short order.

No eye shadow applicator?

No problem. Use a cotton swab in its place: it's softer, the tip can be used to smudge and soften eye liner, and the best part? Toss it when you're done.

Makeup mistake?

If you go overboard with the mascara or sustain a smudge elsewhere during your makeup routine, just wipe off the slipup with a cotton swab dipped in petroleum jelly. Then start over with a lighter hand.

HOMEMADE LIP GLOSS

To make your own lip gloss, scoop the last bit of lipstick from the tube and blend it with a little **petroleum jelly.** Put the mix into an empty lip gloss pot, and voila!—it's ready to use. For a firmer gloss, refrigerate the mixture for an hour.

Home Hair Care

Instant dry shampoo

No time to wash your hair or are you caring for someone who can't step into a shower or bath? A dry shampoo will do the job. Take 1 tablespoon of cornmeal or cornstarch, and sprinkle the powder into the hair; massage it in section by section, and comb out any tangles. Brush well to remove all the powder, stopping often to shake out the brush. The powder absorbs dirt and excess oil, leaving hair clean and shiny.

Two-ingredient revitalizing conditioner

Give drab hair new life with this luscious conditioner—made with only two ingredients: take half of a ripe avocado, scoop out the fruit, and mash until smooth. Slowly stir in ¼ cup coconut milk; the mixture should look like a thick gel, so add more milk as needed. Work all of the mixture into your hair, then comb smooth. Wait 10–15 minutes before rinsing thoroughly. Your hair should feel thicker and look richer. (For an extra treat, use the other half of the avocado to whip up a little guacamole!)

Leave it to vinegar

Your hair has lost its luster, so you switched shampoos; that helped for a while, but now your hair has returned to dullsville. The reason? Buildup of the residue left by shampoo and other products. Vinegar will safely remove the residue and restore your hair's natural acidic pH balance, leaving it shinier, smoother, and easier to manage. Just mix 2–3 tablespoons apple cider vinegar with 1–2 cups of water in a jar. Then shampoo your hair as usual and rinse. Shake the vinegar solution and use it as a final rinse. Any vinegar smell will disappear as soon as your hair dries.

Run out of hair mousse?

You've shaken the can of mousse and turned it upside down, but not a drop comes out. Don't panic. Try a little shaving cream mixed with a drop of rubbing alcohol to keep your hair in place and moisturize at the same time.

SUPER (BOWL) HAIR

If you have a **six-pack of beer** left over from your Super Bowl party, use a little to make a hops shampoo that gives your hair body, shine, and volume. In an enamel-lined saucepan set over medium heat, bring ¾ cup beer to a boil, then simmer briskly until it reduces to ¼ cup. Cool, then mix with 1 cup of your regular shampoo. Transfer it to a jar with a lid and shake before using.

make your own
Hair Rinse

Herbal formulations have been used on hair for thousands of years, so something must be working. The bergamot in this herbal rinse helps control itching and dandruff, while the rosemary (used as a fragrance in soaps and perfumes) provides the nice scent.

Herbal Rinse and Shine

If the lid of the jar you use to steep the herbs is metal, place plastic wrap or wax paper between the lid and the jar to prevent the vinegar from corroding it.

  ¼ cup dried rosemary leaves
  ¼ cup dried bergamot
  2 cups cider vinegar
  2–3 cups warm water

1. Place the herbs in a heatproof, thick glass jar, such as one used for preserves.

2. Heat the vinegar until very hot but not boiling, then pour it over the herbs. Cool, then cover tightly.

3. Keep the jar in a warm spot for a week, shaking it once a day.

4. Line a funnel with cheesecloth and place the funnel over a jar. Strain the rinse into the jar and screw on the lid.

5. When ready to use, mix ⅓ cup of the rinse with 2 or 3 cups of warm water. Then pour over hair once or twice as a rinse.

Got mousse but out of gel?

Raid the pantry! Mix up a batch of flavorless Knox gelatin and you may never go back to the salon variety: dissolve ½ to 1 teaspoon unflavored gelatin in 1 cup warm water and refrigerate. Super hold, super price!

All set for gel but no hair spray?

No problem. Chop up 1 lemon and add it to a pan filled with 2 cups of water. Boil until reduced by half. Cool, strain, and pour into a spray bottle; add 1 ounce of rubbing alcohol. Stored in the refrigerator, the spray will keep for 3–4 weeks; unrefrigerated, it will last for 2 weeks.

Tame hairline frizzies

The hardest place to control frizzies is the area around your hairline. To show the frizzies who's boss, saturate an old toothbrush with hairspray and brush them back where they belong. Hold them in place with your fingers until the hairspray dries.

Panty hose scrunchies

Got long hair and can't find a scrunchie? Dig into that drawer with "emergency" panty hose—those with runs you've been saving to wear under slacks. Just cut the length you need, and you're ready to run for miles. Black and colored hose will look the most fashionable, but flesh tones will do in a pinch. Panty hose have the added advantage of not bruising or breaking your hair, as elastic sometimes does.

Eyeball those roots

If you're of a certain age, you may color your hair, and your white roots seem to peek out faster than a race car on the Indianapolis Motor Speedway. Here's a quick fix. Apply your mascara to the roots with an old toothbrush, blending it in as you go. This trick works best with dark hair—so what do you do if you're a blonde? Try beige or taupe eye shadow as temporary camouflage.

A sage decision for brunettes

Applied to brown or black hair, sage will darken gray hairs. Put ¼ cup dried sage into a bowl and pour 2 cups boiling water over it. Let the mixture steep for 3 hours or overnight before straining it into a bottle or jar. Shampoo your hair as usual, rinse, and then apply the sage tea to gray hairs one area at a time, dabbing it on with a cotton ball or a wad of cheesecloth. Air-dry or use a hair dryer, but *do not* rinse. You'll probably need to repeat the process once a week until you get the color you want.

Spike it with petroleum jelly

Feeling a bit funky (or, perhaps, punky) and want a new way to style your short hairdo? Use a drop or two of petroleum jelly to spike your locks into place. The bonus? When you wash it out, your hair will be softer and shinier!

Shelve the dye for darker locks

Leave chemical dyes on the shelf (where they belong!) and color your dark hair the way the ancients did: with rosemary! Pour a pint of boiling water over a cup of fresh chopped rosemary leaves, allow it to stand until cold, then bottle it and rinse hair after washing. Goodbye gray!

Household Superstar!
6 Quick Beauty Fixes with Lemon

Considering its size, the vitamin C powerhouse we know as the lemon provides an astonishing number of beauty benefits, six of which are listed below. (One word of caution: Lemons can cause skin to be extra-sensitive to sunlight, so don't expose yourself to the sun for too long after a skin treatment.)

1 Exfoliate dead skin and bring new skin to the surface by washing skin with lemon juice mixed with a little sugar.

2 Smooth wrinkles by boiling 1 cup milk, 2 teaspoons lemon juice, and 1 tablespoon brandy. Cool the mixture to room temperature, apply, and let dry before wiping it off.

3 Lighten age spots by dabbing them with lemon juice and rinsing off after 15 minutes. Repeat once later in the day.

4 Mix the juice from 1 lemon with ¼ cup olive oil or sweet almond oil for a facial that both exfoliates and moisturizes.

5 Fight dandruff with a daily scalp massage with 2 tablespoons lemon. Rinse with water and follow with a rinse of 1 cup water mixed with 1 teaspoon lemon juice.

6 Whiten and clean fingernails by soaking them in 1 cup lukewarm water and the juice of ½ lemon for 5 minutes, then rub the inside of the lemon rind against the nails.

Home Nail Salon

Why spend money at fancy nail salons when you can achieve the same look in the privacy of your own home? Here's how!

Cleaning nails

Soak dirty nails for 5 minutes in a bowl of water in which two denture tablets have been dissolved. While this method may seem odd, it stands to reason because teeth and nails are made of the same substance—keratin.

Caring for cuticles

Why waste money buying pricey, specialized cuticle creams? Instead, reach for the olive oil, sweet almond oil, baby oil, vegetable shortening, or even lip balm. Taking good care of cuticles will also discourage hangnails—a sign that both your nails and cuticles are too dry. As you massage oil into your cuticles, go ahead and oil the whole nail. No splits, no breaks, and less chance of an annoying hangnail.

Instant polish touch-up

Got a chip? Not on your shoulder, but on a polished toenail? If you're in a place where you can't repair it properly, dig into your purse and grab a lip pencil or lipstick and add color to the chipped spot. It won't hold for long, but it ought to get you through lunch or dinner or a movie. And you can always reapply your temporary fix in the ladies' room.

Freeze-dry your wet nails

You're late for your friend's wedding, but your nails are still too wet with polish to risk opening the car door. Quick! Open the freezer and stick your hands in. Your nails will be dry in a jiffy, and you can get on your way to the service.

YOU'RE LOOKING GOOD

Duds, Rags, Threads

Put a stop to static cling

Lack of humidity in the air is the main cause of static electricity in your clothes. Men have to worry only about trouser legs clinging to the skin, while women wearing panty hose experience the problem much more often. Try one of these methods to keep clothes static-free.

- **Spritz with hairspray** Spray a little hairspray along the underside of trousers or skirts. Or spray a paper towel and wipe the hairspray on the inside of the fabric.

- **Dampen with water** Wet a paper towel or your hand with water and run it along the exterior of panty hose and the interior of a skirt or pair of slacks. Or you could use a spray bottle to mist the inside of the clothing.

- **Separate with a coat hanger** Move a hanger up and down between the inside of clothes and panty hose or a slip.

The incredible shrinking waistband

It's not that unusual to find an elastic waistband has shrunk or expanded when you're putting on pants, shorts, or a skirt you haven't worn for months. Try this quick fix: open the waistband on the inside of the garment. Cut the elastic inside the band and insert a piece of taut elastic from the waist of an old pair of panty hose or a section of a stretchy headband. Attach the insert to one side of the cut elastic with a safety pin. Stretch the insert to the fit you want and safety-pin it to the other side of the original elastic. Cut off any excess for a flatter appearance and then smooth down the waistband with your fingers. You can cover any telltale bulge with a sweater, T-shirt, overblouse, or jacket.

Glue your bustin' buttons on

Buttons on new clothes will stay put longer if you dab the threads atop the buttons with white, clear-drying glue. Use a cotton swab to apply it neatly.

BLOWIN' IN THE WIND

Prevent skirts from flare-ups on windy days by sewing two or three small **mailbox keys or pennies** into the hem as weights. Wedding dress seamstresses use this trick to keep bridal veil hems hanging properly, choosing weights that can't easily be seen through gossamer fabrics—among them, the flat glass beads used in flower arrangements and fish bowls.

Iron-free wrinkle solution

Lay your wrinkled shirt on a flat surface (a countertop or dresser top will do). Hold a hair dryer a few inches above the shirt and aim the hot air at the wrinkle while smoothing it out with your other hand. After a few minutes the wrinkle should either be less noticeable or gone.

Serve musty clothes a cocktail

What do you do when you pull out an outfit to wear but are hit with a musty odor? Pour a little unflavored vodka into a spray bottle and lightly mist the outfit. The alcohol kills the odorous bacteria without adding an unwanted smell of its own.

Appliqués save the day

When a garment is beyond repair because of holes or stains, don't automatically shop for a new one. Consider hiding the damage with appliqués. They not only hide problem areas but also provide a decorative look. Most appliqués are iron-on these days, so you won't even need to sew.

Rid sweaters of pills

Pilling can ruin an otherwise perfect sweater. Use a razor or an electric shaver to cut the fuzzy pills off, taking care not to make a hole in the weave. Other handy de-pilling tools are an emery board, a pumice stone, and the rough side of a piece of Velcro. With any of these, rub lightly in one direction until the pills disengage.

Keep the zip in zippers

Stuck zipper? Take a closer look at the teeth. If they show lint or dirt between them, brush the teeth with dry toothbrush bristles, then rub them lightly with the stub of a beeswax candle. The zipper should now glide smoothly on its waxed track. If a zipper has *too* much zip and comes undone on its own (usually at the most embarrassing moments), use a cotton swab to coat the teeth with hairspray after you've donned the garment and zipped the zipper. Hairspray will hold both sides of the zipper together just enough to keep them from coming apart.

What's the Story?
It's a Cinch!

Nineteenth-century women were famous for their hourglass figures and for fainting—and one wonders whether they realized the two were related. Ladies owed their curvaceous figures to tight-fitting corsets that cinched in the waist and enhanced the bosom. The corsets were heavy and stiff, reinforced as they were with wood, whalebone, or steel ribs.

Once a woman was laced in, her posture was admirably erect. And no wonder: She couldn't bend! Worse, women often had trouble breathing. Corsets restricted normal movement of the diaphragm, the muscle below the lungs. When a diaphragm moves down, it allows the lungs to expand and take in fresh oxygen; when it moves up, the lungs contract and exhale carbon dioxide. In other words, the breath was actually being squeezed out of these figure eight, corseted ladies. Not surprisingly, as corsets disappeared, so did the smelling salts used to revive a person who fainted.

Putting Clothes Away

Perfume your lingerie

You've just dabbed the last drop of your favorite perfume on your wrist, and you're sorry you don't have anymore. But you can still enjoy its fragrance if you put the empty bottle in your lingerie drawer. The scent will waft up each time you open the drawer and will perfume your underclothes as well.

Eliminate pants creases with bubble wrap

How many times have you pulled on a pair of slacks only to take them off because unsightly coat hanger creases make them unwearable? Wrap the hanger bar in a layer of bubble wrap with the smooth side facing out (secure the wrap with duct tape). Other coverings that work just as well are strips of quilt batting or soft foam sheets used as filler in packing boxes.

Hang spaghetti straps securely

If your spaghetti strap tops and dresses are forever slipping off wire hangers, you've got lots of company. The easiest way to secure them is simply to clip both straps to the hanger with clothespins.

Stay-put scarves

A neat way to store scarves so that each is within easy reach is to attach a few shower curtain rings to a coat hanger's bottom bar, thread a scarf though each one, and then hang them on the closet rod—much easier than rummaging through a pile of scarves in your drawer to find the one you want.

Cedar scent

Cedar blocks have long been used as an alternative to strong-smelling camphor to keep moths from setting up shop in your clothes. If your cedar has lost its woodsy fragrance, don't spend money to replace it. Just use sandpaper or an emery board to rough up the wood and release the scent.

Moths also shy away from the scent of dried bay leaves, dried lavender, dried orange peel, cloves, and whole peppercorns. The feet of old panty hose make inconspicuous sachets for your closet or drawer.

DOUBLE YOUR HANGING SPACE

No need to redesign your closet or buy fancy hangers to increase your hanging space. Just slip a sturdy **shower curtain ring** over the necks of your hangers and hook a second hanger onto them. Presto! A hanger that takes twice the clothes.

Holey Hosiery!

What? In a book like this we're actually talking about *wearing* panty hose instead of using it as an emergency fan belt or dog leash!? Yes indeed. And these four hints about the hosiery itself have to do with keeping it in good condition.

1

Prevent runs

You'll get a lot more wear from panty hose if you first soak them for 30 minutes in a solution of ½ cup of salt dissolved in 1 quart of water. Rinse and drip dry. When you don't have time for pre-treating, soak the panty hose in salt water after use and then wash. Either way, the salt strengthens nylon fibers, making them less likely to tear.

2

Lengthen the life

Dampen a pair of panty hose and place them in a sealable plastic bag in the freezer. Remove the frozen hose, then defrost (not in the microwave please) and drip dry. Freezing the fibers hardens them, and your panty hose will last through many more wearings.

3

Soften to avoid runs

Rinsing panty hose with a drop or two of fabric softener in the water is a good anti-run tactic. The fabric softener makes the nylon mesh more stretchable and less prone to runs caused by tautness. To dry, roll the hose in a towel instead of ringing them out and hanging them.

4

Nip runs in the bud

If you don't have clear nail polish to stop a run in its tracks, rub a small amount of liquid soap along the run's top, bottom, and sides. The soap hardens into a barrier as it dries, preventing the run from continuing on its path. Rubbing a bar of wet soap over the run also works.

Saving Stained Clothing

Wash out makeup spills with baking soda

If you've spilled foundation makeup on your blouse, go to the kitchen and grab a box of trusty baking soda. Sprinkle the powder onto the stain until it's completely covered and press it gently into the fabric. Wet a nailbrush or a toothbrush and lightly brush the spot. If any makeup remains, repeat the process until all traces have disappeared.

Lipstick smear remover 1: petroleum jelly

Dabbing petroleum jelly on lipstick marks before washing a garment is a removal method used by stain specialists. If it's good enough for pros, let's hope it's good enough for you.

Lipstick smear remover 2: bread

Tear out the doughy center of the bread and knead it into a ball, then blot the smear repeatedly with the dough until the stain lifts from the fabric. Now wash the garment. The dough ball is also safe to use on lipstick marks on no-wash woolen clothing.

Soak out tomato sauce stains

It's a brave soul who eats spaghetti while wearing a white shirt without a big napkin tucked into his collar. (Even Emily Post says it's the sensible thing to do.) For an effective tomato sauce spot eradicator, combine ½ cup 3 percent hydrogen peroxide and 3 cups water in a dishpan, pot, or clean sink. Soak the stain in the solution for 30 minutes before laundering.

Shaving cream tomato sauce remover

Grab a can of non-gel shaving cream and spray it onto the stain, rub it in gently, and let dry before washing.

Foundation shaker

Blot up foundation makeup marks on washable fabrics with fresh white bread kneaded into a ball. The bread treatment should also erase pencil marks on woolen and washable clothing. Resist the temptation to use the pencil's eraser to rub out the marks, which in most cases will only make them look worse.

Milk an ink stain

To get rid of that nasty ink blotch on your shirt, put 2–3 tablespoons cornstarch into a bowl, and then stir in whole milk until you have a thick paste. Cover the stain with the paste and let it sit for 3–4 hours. Then brush off the paste and wash the shirt. Another paste to try is 2 tablespoons cream of tartar mixed with 2 tablespoons lemon juice.

Remove red wine stains

The wine tasted terrific last night, but the few drops on your slacks don't look all that great this morning. Club soda is a common antidote for red wine stains, but if that doesn't work, try one of these treatments:

- **Borax** Dissolve 1 tablespoon borax in 2 cups warm water. Submerge the stained part of the garment in the solution and soak for 1 minute, then toss the item in the washer.

- **Dishwashing liquid and vinegar** Dilute your favorite dishwashing liquid, and gently scrub it into the stain; rinse gently with water, then apply a drop of white vinegar. Pat dry, and rinse again with water.

- **Salt and boiling water** Pour a generous amount of salt on a still-wet stain and see if the salt turns pink as it soaks up the wine. If it doesn't, pour boiling water over the salt. In either case, wash the stained garment ASAP.

- **Baking soda** Heap baking soda on the stain and let sit for an hour or more to absorb the stain. Then shake off the baking soda and launder the garment.

Prevent perspiration stains

Spread baby powder or talcum powder along the collar and underarms of soiled clothing, and press gently with a warm iron. The powder should absorb the sweat and make it easier for the rest to come out in the wash.

Pop out bloodstains

You're nearing the end of a charity bike-a-thon when your front wheel hits a pothole, sending you and your bike clattering to the ground. Fortunately, all that's hurt is your pride and your bleeding elbow. You remember that a friend who knows about such things told you to soak bloodstains overnight in cola (yes, soda pop). You try it, and lo and behold, she was right!

make your own
Stain Remover

Vinegar, baking soda, and ammonia—a mighty trio beefed up even more by the addition of liquid castile soap. Even Lady Macbeth would've killed for this homemade cleanser, made for stains that have already dried.

Out-Darned-Spot Spray

Treat grease, coffee, fruit juice, and other common stains with this spray, shaking it well before using. Liquid castile soap is sold in natural products stores and some supermarkets.

> ½ cup white vinegar
> ⅓ cup clear household ammonia
> ¼ cup baking soda
> 2 tablespoons liquid castile soap
> 1½ quarts water

1. Combine all ingredients in a half-gallon container and stir well. Pour into a 16-ounce spray bottle.

2. Spray the solution onto a stain and let it set for 3–5 minutes.

3. Rub the stain gently with a soft cloth and then wash the garment as soon as possible.

A toast to club soda

The most successful way to get rid of stains is to treat them before they dry and become set in the fabric. If you're at a restaurant or a friend's home and food or drink drops onto your clothes, ask right away for a glass of club soda and a lint-free kitchen towel. Repair to the restroom with the soda and apply as much as you can. Wait 1 minute, then blot the stain gently with the towel.

Quick Fixes and Mends

Salvage discolored whites

Don't toss those drab and dingy whites just yet: dissolve 1 teaspoon cream of tartar in cold water in a clean plastic washtub or sink and soak the garment for a few hours before washing. (This is also a great way to restore old handkerchiefs.) To whiten yellowed clothes, soak the items overnight in a solution of ½ cup white vinegar and 6 cups warm water before washing.

Restore crispness to lace

If you have a lace scarf or shawl that's gone limp, wash it as you normally would and then dip it in a solution of 2 gallons warm water and 1 cup Epsom salt. The salt will cling to the fibers and add body.

No-snag, soapy thread

Anyone who's been sewing on a button when the thread tangles or knots knows how frustrating it is to have to start over when you can't free things up. To prevent frustration and time lost, run the thread lightly over a bar of soap before you begin sewing. The waxy coating will make thread easier to untangle and unknot.

Rethread a drawstring

Did the drawstring come out of your hoodie or favorite PJs? Attach a safety pin to one end of the string and use the closed pin to push the string back into place.

Use marbles to help mend gloves

Drop a marble into the fingertip of a glove that needs mending so you'll have a stretched, smooth surface on which to sew. Mend the toes

Undo a Scorch (Fast!)

It's your anniversary, and your first gift to your wife is to do the ironing before she awakens. Won't she be surprised! You bet, but not so much by your generous act as by the scorch on her pale blue blouse. Who knew the iron heated up so quickly?

Lucky for you, scorch marks don't have to be permanent. Here are four techniques to try:

- **For white cottons** Take a cotton cloth dampened with 3 percent hydrogen peroxide and dab at the scorch until it's gone.

- **For colored cottons** Wet a lint-free cloth with 3 percent hydrogen peroxide or white vinegar and lay it over the scorch. Press with the iron on low.

- **For all washable cottons** Cut an onion in half, rub it on the scorch, soak overnight in cold water, and then wash.

- **For woolens** Dampen the scorch with water and dab cornstarch onto it. Let sit for 20–30 minutes and brush off.

and heels of socks in the same way, using a tennis ball or billiard ball.

Sewing kit in a film canister

Your button falls off your blouse while you're en route to a potluck supper, but you're prepared. You have everything you need in a plastic film canister in your purse—a few shirt buttons, a set of sewing needles still stuck in their cardboard holder (don't want to get stuck!), thread, and different-size safety pins.

Especially for Guys

Hardworking hand lotion

Even if you take really good care of your finger-nails, hands with rough, dry skin take you down a notch on the "good grooming" scale. To take care of the problem as you sleep, whip up a thin paste by mixing together 2 table-spoons avocado oil, 1 tablespoon honey, and 2 teaspoons glycerin. Now stir in 1½ cups fine-ly ground rolled oats or almonds until you have the right consistency. "Wash" your hands and fingers in the paste, then slip on a pair of latex or cotton gloves before going to bed.

Skin pepper-upper

Diluted vinegar will not only tone your skin but help protect it from infections—and it's simple to make a vinegar-peppermint concentrate you can keep with your toiletries. Place 1 teaspoon dried peppermint (or 1 tablespoon fresh) in a sterilized bottle with a cap, then pour in ⅓ cup apple cider vinegar. Screw the cap on tight and set aside for 10 days.

Strain the mint-scented vinegar into a second sterilized bottle. To use, dilute 1 tablespoon of the scented vinegar with ½ cup boiled or dis-tilled water and splash it all over your face to pep up the skin.

Homemade aloe face mask

Men are no longer strangers to facials (in urban areas, at least), but you don't need to head off to a salon. Prepare a skin-friendly, moisturizing mask at home with an aloe vera leaf, an egg yolk, honey, and powdered milk. Start by slicing the aloe leaf open lengthwise and scraping 1 teaspoon gel into a small bowl. Beat in 1 egg yolk and 1 teaspoon warm (not hot) honey with a spoon, then stir in enough powdered milk to make a thin but spreadable paste.

Use your fingers to spread the paste from hairline to chin, steering clear of the area around your eyes. Leave the mask on for 20–30 minutes, then remove it with your fingers and a wet washcloth. Follow your facial with a splash or two of skin toner.

Experiment with aftershave

For a good-smelling antiseptic aftershave, play around with apple cider vinegar and the likes of orange flower water, witch hazel, and essential oils like bergamot and neroli. Experiment with different proportions until you find the formu-lation you like best, then store it in a sterilized bottle with a lid.

Double-duty scent for drawers

Drawers in a chest-of-drawers, that is—not your boxer shorts. Keeping a bundle of cedar shavings or pine needles in a drawer full of T-shirts, sweaters, or any other garments will not only give a nice, masculine scent to your clothes but also will keep moths and other insect pests at bay. (Oh, which reminds us: dried bay leaves are an excellent choice, too.) Just place a handful of the material in the cen-ter of a handkerchief, bunch the four corners together, and knot the bundle before tucking it into a drawer.

Keeping Shoes Shipshape

Bubble wrap for good form

You don't need expensive shoe trees to keep your shoes in good form: use bubble wrap. Cut two pieces small enough to roll up and fit into your shoes and boots. When packing a suitcase for a trip, remove the bubble wrap and stuff panty hose or socks inside the shoes to retain their shape and free up space in the suitcase. Now wrap the bubble wrap around the shoes so they won't dirty your clean clothes. True double duty!

Serving spoon shoehorn

Cinderella's stepsisters struggled to fit their feet into the glass slipper, but you needn't struggle if you find yourself without a shoehorn. Take an oblong-shaped serving spoon from the kitchen and place your heel into the bowl of the spoon as you work your foot into the shoe.

Instant shoeshine

You don't need to spend money on special shoe polish to get the shine you want on leather shoes. Just put a few drops of baby oil, olive oil, or even castor oil on the dull-looking leather and buff with a soft cloth. You'll not only have shiny shoes again, but softer ones, too. These oils lubricate the leather, softening stiff spots and creases. They also work on patent leather and leather boots, jackets, handbags, belts, and briefcases.

High-heeled wrinkles

They're the smart high-heel shoes you splurged on, and they still look as good as new—except for the ugly scrunched-up leather along the heel. Fix them yourself with a hair dryer and leather glue. Put your hair dryer on the warm setting and direct the air to the heel. The warmth will soften both the remaining original glue and the leather, allowing you to smooth the leather out from top to bottom. Glue down any loose edges, and you're ready for more high stepping!

Cover up spots with a marker

If your dark shoes are scuffed and you have no time to polish, pick a permanent marker that's a close match to the shoe color and "mark the spot."

Sock it to your shoes

Perhaps the worst thing about giving your bedroom a new coat of paint is the drips that splatter on your shoes, despite your best efforts to do the job neatly. A simple solution is to slip a pair of old socks over your shoes as protection. Then save the newly colorful socks for your next paint job.

Plain Janes to Fancy Janes

If you have a pair of plain Mary Janes, slip-on ballet shoes, or plain heels, why not dress them up with a pair of big clip-on costume earrings that you don't wear anymore? The extra color or glitter may be just the touch of glamour you want for that New Year's Eve party.

Handbags and Hats

Polish leather with a potato

Rub a cut potato across the surface of your dull leather handbag, give it a buff with a clean, soft cloth, and it'll look good as new.

Steam your suede

To clean stains and spots on a suede purse, first lightly rub the spots with fine-grained sandpaper or an emery board. Then hold the purse 6 inches away from a teakettle or pan with steaming water until the stain gets a little warm, making sure the steam doesn't saturate the bag. Brush with a suede brush or toothbrush, repeating the brushing once the suede is dry.

A space-saving handbag rack

If you've recently replaced a tall wooden stepladder, use the old one to store purses in your closet—especially helpful if you're short of shelf space. To make the ladder prettier, cover the steps with adhesive shelf paper or glue on decorative fabric swatches.

A new hat resizer

You've found the perfect hat at a yard sale, the type that's worn with the brim low on the forehead, but it's just a little too big for you. Go ahead and buy it anyway, then wear a sweatband under the hat to fill in the extra space. If the sweatband is too thick and makes the hat too tight, try a stretchy, thinner headband (surely one will work). Just remember to take the band and the hat off at the same time or you'll reveal your little secret.

About Those Lost Keys

You're not losing it when you lose your keys in your purse, and you are not alone. Who doesn't lose her keys in a handbag now and then? A simple solution to the problem: Attach a key line. Measure your purse from the bottom to the base of one of the handles and then add 4 to 6 inches. Now cut a piece of dental floss, fishing line, or a thin corded ribbon to that length. Thread your keys onto the line and knot the end. Place this end into your purse and wrap the other end around the base of the handle, knotting it tightly. Now, whenever you need your keys, just pull out the line. You won't have to fish for them anymore!

Restore shine to straw hats

Over time, straw hats lose their crisp, shiny look. You can spruce up yours in time for the rodeo or Easter Parade by spraying it with a light coating of hairspray and letting it dry. Be sure to spray in a well-ventilated area or outside.

Stuff hats to save their shape

Ever notice that the brims of hats in hat shops don't ever touch the shelves? Milliners know that brims resting on shelves will flatten out, so they overstuff the crowns with tissue paper to let the hats rest on the paper instead. If you don't have leftover tissue paper, use bubble wrap, dry-cleaning plastic, plastic grocery bags, old socks or panty hose, or a discarded sweater as stuffing.

Your Jewelry

Buttons for your wrist

If you're the type who likes to make your own bracelets and necklaces, alternating beads with some spare buttons you've got stashed away will make an unusual accessory. String buttons and beads of different colors and sizes onto two strands of dental floss, fishing line, or heavy-duty thread. Then experiment with a variety of combinations until you've fashioned a piece of jewelry worthy of a chic boutique.

Magnetic brooch holder

When it comes to silk blouses, dresses, or jackets, the last thing you want is to poke tiny holes in the smooth, expensive fabric with a pin. Instead, use magnets to attach the brooch. Remove the shaft of the brooch and attach one magnet to the back with super-glue. Make sure the glue dries completely before wearing the brooch. Place it in the desired location on the garment, holding it with one hand. With your other hand, place the opposing magnet behind both fabric and brooch. The magnets will lock the brooch in place, and you're ready for a no-pinholes night on the town.

Buttons for your toes

Don't think that adding a bit of glam to your plain pumps isn't jewelry ... it is! Rummage through your button collection for two that are oversized and interesting; glue gun them to the vamp of your (formerly) boring shoes, and give them a new life!

Wristwatch earring holder

If you've ever left your pierced earrings in a hotel room or had one mysteriously disappear from the nightstand never to be seen again, keep

Men's Jewelry, Then and Now

Some etiquette arbiters advise that a man should never wear more than a wedding ring and a watch, but these days they're crying in the wilderness. That's not to say understatement didn't have its heyday, which ran from the late 18th century to the 1970s—the decade famous for open shirts showing a chestful of medallions and chains. Little did the swingin' sideburned dudes of the '70s realize that they were bringing things full circle, in a way: Men of a certain rank were loaded down with jewelry until Louis XVI lost his head in 1793 and bedizenment went out of style.

Prehistoric humans adorned their bodies with beads and feathers, regardless of sex. Thousands of years later, King Tut's mummy was covered with so many amulets, pendants, bracelets, earrings, and other pieces of jewelry that the young pharaoh surely couldn't have borne the weight of them in life. In ancient Rome, jewelry was used to an extent never seen before, and the gold ring—once reserved for dignitaries—gradually appeared on the fingers of men of lower social rank and even soldiers. Men's jewelry flourished in Europe during the Renaissance among the upper crust, and portraits of King Henry VIII of England show his garments and hat brim studded with jewels.

Flash forward to the early 20th century, when men's jewelry was no longer associated with rank. Still, the common man's adornment was generally limited to a pocket watch and a ring. Only later did the love beads of the hippie era, the medallions of the disco days, and the bling of the hip-hop age bring flash to a man's wardrobe that rivaled (or outshone) that of early kings.

them safe and secure with another accessory: your wristwatch. After taking off your earrings, insert them into the holes of a leather or plastic watchband or between the links of an expandable metal band. You can now rest assured they'll still be there in the morning. No wristwatch? It's a cinch to use the holes of a belt as a temporary earring holder.

Unstick a stuck ring

Your one and only has just proposed marriage, and you want to slip on the engagement ring. But at this moment of a lifetime, you can't get your old ring off your finger! What to do? Fetch some mayonnaise and slather it on your finger. Romantic? No way. Necessary? Yes, in a (literal) pinch. Make a fist to help the mayo seep under the band of gold or silver. The ring should now slide off easily. Wash your hands and then mentally rehearse the funny family story you'll share with your grandchildren.

Bulletin board jewelry "box"

Tired of having to dump out all your precious jewels to find that one necklace you really want to wear today? Take a lesson from grade-schoolers, and buy an inexpensive bulletin board and some colorful push pins; paint the board your favorite color, and then hang each necklace and each ring to keep them from getting scratched and to keep them organized.

Fix those necklace knots with powder

It takes a lot of patience to untangle a knot in a necklace chain. How to complete the task in no time? Sprinkle the knot with talcum or baby powder, cornstarch, or vegetable oil and use a straight pin or two to pry the knot apart. The powder and oil lubricate the links, helping them to slide and separate more easily. Afterward, wash the untangled chain with a mild detergent, rinse, and pat dry.

Mind Your Specs

Protect eyeglasses from hair dye

Whether you're highlighting your hair at home or having it colored at a beauty parlor, it's possible that a little dye can drip onto the sidepieces of your glasses. To protect sidepieces, simply wrap them with plastic wrap until your new color "do" is done.

Got a screw loose?

The tiny screws holding your eyeglass frames together don't ever seem to stay tight for long, especially when the specs are reading glasses. One way to keep things tight is to dab the threads with a little clear nail polish when replacing a screw, then coat the screw heads once they're in place.

Tip: Don't spend money buying one of those extra-tiny eyeglass screwdrivers. A toothpick or the eraser end of a pencil will work just as well. To use the eraser, turn the pencil upside down, press the eraser against the screw, and turn.

Seeing is believing

Eyeglass cleaner is expensive these days, but some folks know that two common household products will clean and polish lenses just as well—try club soda or rubbing alcohol, the latter used either full strength or diluted with equal parts water. Keep your cleanser in a handy spray bottle and use a soft lint-free cloth to dry the lenses.

Clearing up foggy specs

Having your glasses fog up is no fun. It happens in cold weather when you go from outside to inside, when steam billows up from a pot of boiling water, or even when you're eating very spicy food. As a preventive, clean your specs with white foamy shaving cream, which will leave an invisible coating on the lenses that keeps water drops from sticking.

Shaving cream is also a fantastic cleaner for eyeglasses. If you've accidentally spritzed hairspray on your glasses and can't get the sticky stuff off, a dab of the white stuff on each lens will clean it right up.

Chapter Eight

Smart Ideas for Parents & Kids

Imagine this novel idea: parents today can pamper their children without buying them every electronic gizmo under the sun or the latest hot toy to hit the market. Likewise, they don't have to break the bank to keep kids happy, healthy, and clean. Is this truth, or is it fiction?

We're happy to say that it's true, and this chapter is chock-full of great ways to provide for your children's needs, teach them interesting and important things in fun ways, and keep them engaged and entertained ... all without having to take out a loan. Where do we even begin when it comes to the fun of sculpting with salt dough that you make from scratch (instead of its store-bought counterpart)? Best of all, you'll find simple suggestions for keeping children safe, secure, and happy, and keeping their stuff organized at little or no cost.

Store tiny toys in an empty *milk jug!*

Bath Time!

Baby in a laundry basket

When your baby can sit by herself but is still too wobbly for a regular tub bath, a plastic laundry basket—the kind with perforations in the sides—is a great solution. Set the laundry basket in the tub, add a few inches of water, and put your little one in this "bathtub playpen." Be sure the holes in the laundry basket are large enough not to catch your baby's fingers or toes and that all plastic edges are smooth and safe. And follow the number one safety rule: Never leave a baby or small child unattended when she is in or near water.

Infant seat in the tub

Need an extra pair of hands when bathing baby? Your plastic infant seat will make bath time safer and less stressful for everyone concerned. Remove the seat pad, buckle, and straps, and then line the seat with a soft towel folded to fit. To prevent slipping and sliding, lay another towel on the bottom of the bathtub and set the seat on the towel. Then put your baby in his place, and run just enough water into the tub for the bath. The infant seat supports your little one and lets you use both hands to easily bathe him.

Petroleum jelly = no tears

Babies can't stand getting anything in their eyes at bath time, be it shampoo or water. Whether you have no-tears shampoo on hand or have to make do with a bar of mild soap, dab a drop of petroleum jelly across your child's eyebrows, gently wiping off any residue with a soft cloth or tissue. The jelly will deflect water and shampoo from the eyes and keep baby happy and comfortable.

---

make your own
Kiddie Bubble Bath

Who can resist the appeal of a warm, frothy bubble bath? Not many adults and not even the grubbiest, most bath-averse child. Show a kid a bathtub piled high with bubbles, like whipped cream on a sundae, and you're likely to convert a diehard bath-hater into a happy bather. The trouble is, bubble bath liquid can be costly if used frequently. So why not make your own with this easy recipe?

No-Tears Bubble Formula

Though regular shampoo will work in this recipe, using a no-tears shampoo will eliminate the risk of irritating children's eyes. Add a mere capful or two to running water—more for more bubbles.

½ cup no-tears shampoo
   (clear or light in color)
¾ cup water
¼ teaspoon salt
Food coloring (optional)

1. Gently mix shampoo and water in a bowl or a 2-cup measuring cup with a pour spout.

2. Add salt and stir until the mixture is slightly thickened. (This takes a minute or so.)

3. If you want to color the solution, add a drop of food coloring and stir. Continue adding drops and stirring until you have the desired color.

4. Pour mixture into a clean bottle.

To make bath time pain free, pull on some *knee pads!*

Cotton gloves and slippery babies

A wriggling infant in a soapy bath can feel as slippery as a wet banana peel, but you can get a grip by wearing a pair of cotton gloves.

Padded knees

Anyone who has bathed a grandchild knows how tough kneeling on the cold hard floor can be. Remedy? Athletic knee pads!

Soap in a sock

Here's a good use for the mismatched socks your washing machine *didn't* eat. Fill a sock with soap fragments or a small bar and tightly tie the sock closed. Kids like to wash with sock-soap because it won't fly out of their hands.

Reusing novelty bottles

Tear-free shampoos and liquid bubble bath in colorful molded plastic bottles are popular gifts for youngsters, but they're expensive everyday products. If your child enjoys shampoo or bubble bath from a bottle shaped like a duck or a frog, save the bottle and refill it with less costly bath products. Your child will have his bath toy, you'll save money, and you'll do the environment a favor by reusing plastic.

Bath-time help from the kitchen

Set a kitchen timer to go off when it's time for a bath—and also time for a bath to end. For youngsters who are inclined to delay, setting the timer to buzz five minutes before bath time is an early warning system. If your child likes to stay in the bath until he gets pruny, the buzzer will remind him to get a move on. Using a timer can help children acquire a better sense of the time required for a specific task. Timers may also be useful when older siblings are competing for time in the bathroom.

Stop itching with baking soda

Adding half of a regular-sized box of baking soda to your child's bath will help relieve the itching caused by bug bites, poison ivy, heat rashes, sunburn, and even chicken pox. Allow the child to have a good soak and then gently pat her dry with a clean, soft towel.

Splashy Bath Toys

Personalized floaty toys

Teaching your little one to recognize letters or to spell her name? Get personal by picking up some inexpensive floating craft foam at your local craft shop. Available in bright colors, they can be cut to resemble every letter of the alphabet, making them perfect for bath-time learning! F-A-B!

Playthings from the kitchen cupboard

Many of the best bath-time toys are likely to be found in your kitchen. Plastic food containers like margarine/butter tubs, measuring spoons, large cooking spoons, funnels, colanders, cups, milk cartons—if it floats, pours, stirs, or drips, it will inspire your child's imagination. Plastic lids become floating platforms. Funnels create waterfalls. Plastic mesh berry baskets will create masses of bubbles in soapy water. (It's best to avoid wooden and metal items; wood will splinter and can mildew, and metal rusts.) Simple, sturdy plastic items are safe and easy to clean; just wipe down plastic bath toys routinely with a water and baking soda solution or run them through the dishwasher.

Go fish with a kitchen strainer

A small plastic vegetable strainer lets toddlers scoop up sponges or shapes cut from craft foam and promotes hand-eye coordination, too. An aquarium net also works. (Thoroughly wash and disinfect a used net first.) Help your toddler drop her "catch" into a plastic container, and

Cleaning Rubber Ducky

Molded plastic toys, such as a child's floating ducky, often have small holes that allow water to seep inside. Contaminated by sloughed-off skin cells and waste matter in the bath, this trapped water can breed unhealthy bacteria, so clean after each use. Here's how:

Squeeze the toy to remove as much bath water as possible. Then submerge it in a mild bleach solution (1 part household bleach to 15 parts water) and squeeze it to suck in the bleach solution. Shake the toy and then let it sit for 10 minutes before squeezing out the cleaning solution. In a separate container filled with clean water, rinse the toy using the same procedure and dry the now-safe toy for the next bath.

count the items together when he tires of fishing in the tub.

Commander of the fleet!

Save those wax-coated milk, cream, and half-and-half containers, snip the spout off, close the top with duct tape, and paint the little admiral's fleet in her color of choice, using water-insoluble paint. Add a name, numbers to the sides, and a Popsicle stick mast, and a no-cost bath-time armada is hers!

Throw in the sponge

Raid your kitchen drawers and storage cabinets for plain kitchen and utility sponges of all sizes and colors and cut them into different shapes. Your little one can play stacking games with floating circles, triangles, stars, crescent moons, leaves, keyholes, doughnuts, and whatever else your (and his) inventive mind can come up with.

Note: Before turning the playthings over to your child for the first time, disinfect used sponges by either 1) soaking them in a mild chlorine bleach solution and rinsing well or 2) wetting them and then microwaving on high for 1–2 minutes. *After* the bath, start a good habit by having your toddler help wipe the tub with a designated "clean-up" sponge.

Produce-bag storage

Turn a large-size, plastic mesh produce bag from the supermarket into a storage bag for bath toys. (Avoid string bags made of natural materials, which can become moldy and harbor germs.) If a plastic mesh bag has a paper label, soak it off in warm water. If the bag's drawstring isn't strong, replace it; a length of plastic-coated clothesline, knotted tightly, works well. Be sure to remove any metal staples or plastic tags. After your child's bath, put bath toys into the bag and rinse them under running water. Then hang the bag from a faucet handle or shower head so the toys can drip-dry.

Mesh produce bags are perfect for wet toys.

Simple Solutions from the Kitchen

Homemade bubbles

The ingredients for a homemade substitute for bubble-blowing liquid are right at you kitchen sink—dishwashing liquid and water. Pour 1 ounce dishwashing liquid into a clean 2-cup measure and fill with tap water (1 part dishwashing liquid to 15 parts water), then mix gently. This bubble solution performs best when left to sit overnight before use. Hard water will yield poor results, so test your tap water by making a small batch of solution. If you can't get bubbles, switch to distilled water.

Making salt sculptures

Why buy that colorful sculpting dough when you and junior can make your own from regular pantry staples? Here's how: mix 1 cup of salt together with 1 cup of flour. Using your fist, make a deep indent in the mixture, and pour in ¾ cup of water. To add color, simply use some nontoxic watercolor paint or food coloring. Knead well and shape into a ball. Roll out, and hand the little one some blunt-edged cookie cutters to cut out shapes, mold into sculptures, or make into holiday ornaments. Store in an airtight container, for tomorrow is another day!

Make slime with Metamucil

That nasty, gunky green favorite of kids everywhere is only a kitchen cabinet away and can save you at least 10 bucks worth of store-bought, kid-friendly YUCK. To make it, combine 1 teaspoon of Metamucil or psyllium husks (available at pharmacies everywhere) with 1¼ cups of water in a lidded jar, and shake vigorously for 3 minutes. Pour into a microwavable container, and add a few drops of hideous green food coloring. Microwave on high for 3 minutes; stop the process if the slime starts to ooze out the top of the container. Let rest for 3 minutes, and microwave for another 5 minutes. Remove carefully, and let cool for an hour. Store in an airtight container.

Kitchen cabinet toy box

Most babies know that the kitchen is where the real action is—it's full of shiny things, interesting sounds, yummy smells, and, oh yes, food. It's always important to childproof your kitchen, to install safety latches and plugs, and to make sure that anything even remotely dangerous is out of reach. Once done, you can designate one lower cabinet to be baby's kitchen toy box and stock it with a few specific items that your little one can play with: smaller pots and lids, a few plastic containers, a wooden spoon, a sturdy set of measuring spoons, and nesting metal measuring cups.

Shake, rattle, and roll!

Some metal and plastic food cans, like containers for coffee and stacked potato chips, come with plastic lids. Turn them into fun noisemakers by cleaning and drying an empty can, making absolutely sure that all sharp edges have been removed or filed down, and tossing in a small amount of dry pasta, cereal, hard candy, dried beans, or rice. Secure the plastic lid with duct tape, testing the noisemaker to be certain the top won't come off. A quieter alternative? Put crunchy cereal in a cardboard oatmeal box and secure the top with tape. When rolled on the floor, this homemade rattler makes a neat swooshing sound.

Milk jug to toy caddy

Too many tiny toys underfoot? No problem. You can bring some order to the tiny toy invasion by making a simple toy carrier from an empty gallon milk jug or household bleach container with a handle. With scissors or a utility knife, carefully cut a large opening out of the top third of the bottle, leaving the handle area and the plastic cap intact. Cover the cut edge with duct or masking tape (while the cut edge could be filed or sanded smooth, taping gives extra protection). Let your child decorate the carrier with permanent markers and then fill it with small toys. Arguing siblings can keep their treasures in separate carriers and perhaps avoid the usual arguments.

Invisible lemon juice "ink"

If your child has a taste for the mysterious, teach him the secret of invisible writing. All that's required is a small bowl of lemon juice, a

make your own
It's the Bomb!

Nothing makes kids happier at bath time than splashing around and creating some good, clean fun. Bath bombs, those expensive balls found in spa shops, are a literal blast to toss into the tub, but pricey. Here's how to make your own from scratch:

All-Natural Baking Soda Bath

> 2 teaspoons baking soda
>   (sodium bicarbonate)
> 1 teaspoon corn starch
> 1 teaspoon citric acid
> 20 drops glycerine
>   (available at pharmacies)
> Food coloring or liquid watercolor paints
>   (optional)
> Fragrance (optional)

1. Mix baking soda, corn starch, and citric acid in a medium bowl.

2. Add the glycerine, 3–4 drops of food coloring, and a few drops of fragrance (if desired).

3. Combine well until the mixture becomes crumbly.

4. Form and pack the mixture into golf ball-sized balls (or smaller), and set aside to dry, and harden overnight.

5. Place the child and baking soda bath bomb in the tub, and watch the fun!

cotton swab, and a piece of paper. Dip the swab in the juice and write on the paper. When the paper is dry, there will be no sign of the lemon juice "ink." Now hold the paper near to, but not touching, a hot lightbulb, moving the paper slowly over the heat. Magically, the writing will turn brown and legible. A trick worthy of the wizards of Hogwarts!

All-Time Favorite Play and Craft Recipes

You've probably run across some or all of the following recipes at one time or another, but they're not always easy to track down when you need them. All are basic to children's play and crafts—and luckily, all are easy to make.

Finger Paint

Keep containers of finger paint safely away from eager little hands. Finger painting is one of the kid activities that beg for supervision.

> ½ cup cornstarch
> 2 cups cold water
> Food coloring

1. Combine cornstarch and water in a saucepan and place over high heat.

2. Bring the mixture to a boil and cook until thickened, stirring constantly.

3. Remove from heat and cool to room temperature.

4. Divide mixture among containers and stir several drops of food coloring into each.

Storage. Pour the finger paint into small plastic containers with snap-on lids and store it at room temperature.

Craft Paste

This white paste is used for craft projects and making papier-mâché.

> 1 quart water
> ¼ cup salt
> 1½ cups white flour

1. Bring water to boil in a medium saucepan.

2. Remove from heat and stir in salt.

3. Add flour a little at a time, stirring constantly. Continue to add flour and stir until mixture is the consistency of thick gravy.

4. Cool to room temperature before using.

Storage. Store the paste in an airtight container in the fridge. It may keep as long as five days, but throw away immediately if it becomes moldy or has a bad smell.

Play Clay

Two kitchen staples—baking soda and cornstarch—are the basis of this easy-to-make clay.

> 2 cups baking soda
> 1 cup cornstarch
> 1¼ cups cold water
> Food coloring (optional)

1. In a medium-size saucepan, mix together baking soda and cornstarch.

2. Add water and stir. Add food coloring to the water, if desired.

3. Set over medium heat and stir continuously for 10 to 15 minutes. Do not overcook. Mixture should have the consistency of mashed potatoes.

4. Transfer the cooked mixture to a plate and cover with a damp cloth to cool to room temperature.

Storage. Between uses, store play clay in a self-sealing plastic bag or an airtight container. It keeps in the fridge for up to a week.

Hardening. Harden clay objects by air-drying overnight on a wire rack. Or place them on a cookie sheet in a preheated 350°F oven; then turn off heat and keep objects in the oven until it's cold. To microwave, place objects on a paper towel and microwave at medium power for 30 seconds. Turn objects over and heat for another 30 seconds, repeating as necessary until objects are hard and dry.

An egg carton game

Here's a fun activity that can help preschoolers master their counting and sorting skills. With a marker, write the numbers 1 through 12 in the egg sections. Then provide edibles such as shaped cereal, raisins, or nuts and have the child put the right amount in each numbered section. You can play a similar sorting game by having him separate different shapes and colors of cereal, dry pasta, or dried beans.

Alternatively, give the child a bowl of raw fruit and vegetable pieces—sliced carrots and apples, peas, grapes, mandarin orange segments, cherry tomatoes, broccoli, button mushrooms—whatever you have on hand. Then have him sort the food into the egg sections by type.

Food coloring to brighten snow-day play

After they've pelted one another with snowballs, kids can get antsy for more entertainment on a snow day, so try this: fill several plastic squirt bottles—ketchup and mustard bottles are ideal—with water and add a few drops of food coloring to each. Kids can "draw" designs on the snow with the colored water.

A carrier for precious papers

School children sometimes have important papers to take to school—like that world map your daughter has been working on for weeks for her geography class, or that book report your son keyboarded all by himself. Tubes from rolls of paper towels or standard-size plastic wrap, foil, or waxed paper are just the right size for 8½-by-11-inch and 11-by-14-inch sheets of paper. For larger projects, save longer tubes from wrapping or craft paper or oversized aluminum foil. Be careful not to cram too much into a cardboard tube or papers could be difficult to extract.

Household Superstar!

11 Things Kids Can Do with a Round Oatmeal Container

1 Store pencils, crayons, and rulers

2 Make sand-castle towers at the beach

3 Fill with small plastic toy soldiers

4 Fill with dried beans, seal with lid, turn on music, and use as a shaker

5 Seal with lid, turn on music, and use as a drum

6 Store secret jewelry

7 Have Mom cut a slice in the middle of lid, seal, and use as a not-quite piggy bank

8 Store favorite hand-me-down CDs and DVDs

9 Seal with lid, turn over, use as a stool

10 Fill with barrettes, scrunchies, and other hair accessories

11 Make a time capsule: have Junior write a small essay or draw a picture, add personal items, seal with lid, bury in yard, unearth next year!

Bubbles, Bubbles, Everywhere

Kids love bubbles. Big bubbles. Little bubbles. Clouds of bubbles. And your house is full of items that can make bubbles of all shapes and sizes. Many bubble-ologists swear by a simple blower made of two sheets of plain typing paper. Here's how to make what is prized for its humongous bubbles:

1

Stack the sheets and roll into a cone lengthwise, with the tip at the corner of the pages; the diameter at the large end of the cone should be about 1¼–1½ inches;

2

Tape the cone with masking tape starting about 2 inches above the large end (it's vital that the tape and bubble solution don't touch). Trim the small end of the cone to about ½ inch in diameter.

Try a straw!

3

To make the flat, smooth-rimmed opening essential for bubble blowing, trim the large end at a point where all layers of paper are overlapping. Cut off any rough spots on the bottom rim, testing for smoothness by running your finger over it; then test it for evenness by making sure the cone will stand upright on a smooth surface.

4

Dip the large end in bubble solution and blow slowly to make bubbles. Experts advise leaving the cone in the mix for 30 seconds the first time it's used; after that, a 2- or 3-second dip will do.

We used a metal coat hanger!

Plastic berry baskets work as well!

Playful Pantry Crafts

Glitter from salt

Bring some glitter and glitz to your little ones' projects, without the expense of buying the commercial stuff. Mix 1 tablespoon liquid watercolor with ¼ cup table salt or rock salt, then shake the salt and coloring in a plastic bag to distribute the color evenly. Spread the mixture on paper towels on a flat microwaveable plate and microwave on high for 2 minutes. Cool and break up any clumps with your fingers, then store in a dry, airtight container.

Play-dough hair with a garlic press

To make hair for play-dough figures, roll up a small ball of play dough, put it in a garlic press, and slowly press out the strands. Use a small paintbrush to dab a little water on the spot where a strand will be attached; then press the piece in place with a toothpick or the pointed end of a small-size knitting needle.

Pasta art

Even little kids can make beautiful abstract designs with this project that's old as the hills: poke around in your pantry for stray, half-empty boxes of dried pasta (we know they're in there!). Make different shapes and sizes by breaking up long strands of spaghetti and lasagna, add elbows or ziti, and color as desired with non-toxic food coloring. When dry, the possibilities are endless:

- Make a personal treasure chest by covering the top and sides of a shoe or cigar box with the pasta, using craft glue.
- Draw designs on folded construction paper or card stock and glue on pasta for a personal holiday or birthday card.

A Kitchen Christmas Tree

A star-shaped cookie cutter as a tree topper this Christmas? Yes, if you want to do something different and have a kitchen-themed tree. Decorating a holiday tree with kitchen items from your own cabinets and drawers can be a wonderful family project, especially when everyone enjoys cooking together. Almost anything but the kitchen sink can be used as ornaments—and herewith enough ideas to almost fill Old Saint Nick's toy bag:

- Your children's baby cups and spoons
- Cookie cutters attached with red ribbons
- Old salt and pepper shakers filled with silver and gold glitter
- Stainless steel spoons, attached with shiny ribbon to add sparkle
- Vintage tea strainers
- Vintage napkin rings
- Colorful pot holders
- Salt clay ornaments (see page 212)

To add pizzazz, string cranberries and popcorn or miniature marshmallows around the tree, and tuck colorful cloth or paper napkins into the branches. Finally, and most important, have fun creating a fond memory for everyone.

- String together colored elbows or any tubular pasta to make necklaces, bracelets, or anklets.
- Glue pasta shapes to barrettes, hairpins, and even belt buckles!

Paper Towel Tube Constructions

Paper towel tubes make super toy and craft materials and are usually stronger than toilet tissue rolls, so don't throw them out. Here are six kid-pleasing ideas that require little more than tubes, tape, glue, and scissors:

1

Make a fort by taping cardboard rolls together vertically to form a square and leaving an opening on one side to serve as a door. The size of the fort will depend on the number of tubes you have.

2

Fashion a log cabin by taping tubes together horizontally and taping ends together to form a square. Cut a door, then add a roof made of flat cardboard. Leave the roof unattached so that children can remove it and set their toy figures inside the cabin.

3

Make Easter egg holders by cutting cardboard tubes crosswise into 1½- to 2-inch-wide sections. Children can decorate the sections with poster paints or washable markers and then set their Easter eggs on the pretty rings. Use the same basic technique to let the kids create their own decorative napkin rings.

4

For sandbox play, supply toddlers and preschoolers with a selection of tubes cut in different lengths. They can stick tubes in the sand and build whatever they imagine.

5

Create a safe magic wand for a toddler by taping or gluing a construction paper star to one end of a cardboard tube.

6

Make music with a simple flute. Use a pencil to punch four holes about an inch apart in a cardboard tube. Secure wax paper to one end of the tube with a rubber band. A child can make music by humming into the open end of the flute.

Around the House

New use for an old aquarium

An old aquarium or fishbowl can be transformed into a fascinating 3-D decoration for a child's room—and your child can pick the theme and do much of the work. Start by cleaning and disinfecting the tank or bowl. Then paint the inside of the glass with a diluted mixture of water and water-soluble craft paint to create the look of ocean water, blue sky, billowy clouds, rainbows, green fields, or even abstract designs. The paint should be thin enough to see through, so test it for transparency and thin with more water as needed. On the bottom of the tank, spread a fairly thick layer (2 inches or more) of sandbox sand or fish bowl pebbles. Now let your child choose what goes inside.

Quick clean-ups

By their very nature, kids and dirt go hand-in-hand. Here are some easy ideas to keep your home clean using basic household supplies:

- **Plastic or painted wooden toys** Clean these with a paste made of 2 parts baking soda to 1 part dishwashing liquid. Apply with a soft cloth. Use a toothbrush to work the paste into small spaces. If the dirt is really stubborn, leave the paste on for a while. Remove it with a damp cloth or sponge.

- **Outdoor toys and kiddie vehicles** Rub with full-strength white vinegar, applied with a cloth. Remove residue with a damp cloth or sponge, or hose it off and dry with a clean cloth or towel.

- **Stuffed toys** Clean these unwashables by putting them in a plastic or paper bag, adding half or more of an 8-ounce box of baking soda, and shaking the bag for 30 seconds or so. When the toy looks and smells clean, remove baking soda residue by either vacuuming the toy with your machine's drapery attachment or shaking the toy in the open air, brushing off any residue with your fingers.

- **Crayon marks on washable wallpaper** Try warming the marks with a hair dryer. Give it a minute, then wipe the marks away with a damp cloth. Another idea is to apply a coat of rubber cement to the

BELLS ON THEIR TOES

Want to keep track of your little bundle of energy as she zips around the house? Poke around in your Christmas supplies, and tightly attach those **tiny bells** to each sneaker; not only will you know whether they're in the laundry room or racing around the den, they'll make music as they do it. Note: Bells should be attached only for children over the age of 3.

Household Superstar!
7 Kid-Friendly Uses for Tape

Tape is indispensable nowadays, especially in households with children. And the variety of tapes available, including easy-release painter's tape, make it simpler than ever to find the right tape for just about every need. Here are a few quick tape solutions for today's busy parents and active kids.

1 Use masking tape to secure disposable diapers when the sticky tabs fail.

2 Wrap the midsection of new crayons and chalk pieces with transparent tape to help keep them from breaking.

3 Wrap transparent tape tightly around the ends of string and ribbons to make stringing objects easier.

4 Attach address labels to children's pencils, pens, crayon boxes, and other school supplies with transparent tape or clear shipping tape.

5 "Laminate" library cards, bus passes, lunch tickets, and other paper take-alongs with clear shipping tape. Apply to both sides; then trim tape at the edge of card. Scanners are able to read bar codes through clear tape.

6 Can't find a bandage? Substitute a piece of gauze or tissue secured with transparent tape.

7 In a pinch, use masking or transparent tape as a temporary safety cover for electric outlets and switches.

marks, let it dry, and then gently roll off the rubbery glue.

- **Vomit or urine on a rug** First, wipe up what you can. Pour baking soda on the affected area, pat it in with a paper towel, and let it dry completely before vacuuming up the residue. Baking soda will clean, sanitize, and deodorize the spot. Use the same method to clean a wet mattress.

Dry a baby's cap on a balloon

Machine drying a baby's bonnet or cap, even on the delicate cycle, often leaves it looking wrinkled, limp, and less than adorable. Just inflate a balloon to the approximate size of the child's head, tie it securely, and attach it to a smooth surface with tape (away from baby's reach). Slip the washed and still-damp cap or bonnet over the balloon. With your hands, lightly smooth out wrinkles and gently shape the cap and brim. "Press" ribbons and ties by running them through your fingers and laying them out straight.

When the cap is dry, just pop the balloon and discard it. A few touchups with a warm iron will have the cap looking as good as new.

Secure sewing with dental floss

Tired of lost or dangling buttons on your kids' coats and jackets? Substitute dental floss for sewing thread to get a strong, longer-lasting hold. Also use dental floss when replacing buttons, eyes, and ears and stitching ripped seams in stuffed toys.

Tape your troubles away

Toy boxes, paperback book spines, and coloring books falling apart? Use clear shipping tape to reinforce corners, spines, and edges of books, game boards, and game and toy boxes.

Safety, Health, and Hygiene Hints

Cover dangerous corners with shoulder pads

A great way to safeguard new walkers and runners is with old shoulder pads—remember those? Cut open the long straight side and slip the pad over a corner so the inner padding encases the edges. Adjust as needed, and then tape the pad securely in place. Hiding these pads under an attractive cloth will not only please the eye but also stop curious youngsters from disturbing the pads.

Colorful bandages

Your little one just fell down and scraped his elbow/knee/fill-in-the-blank, and you're trying to console him, to no avail. Distract the little guy from his pain by having him color his own bandage while you gently clean the wound with a dab of soapy water and first-aid cream. While you're busy, make him busy: Give him a few plain bandages and a rainbow of nontoxic, water-based markers, and let his imagination run wild. He'll wear his bandage as a work of art!

Freeze stuffed toys for allergic kids

Forestall sniffles in allergic kids by giving their stuffed toys the deep freeze for three to five hours, once a week. Slip the toy into a freezer bag, stow it amidst the frozen peas and ice cubes, and any dust mites will be killed.

Bathtub appliqués = safe jammies

You can replace worn slip-preventive soles on an infant or toddler's footed pajamas with foot-shaped pieces or stripes cut from non-slip bathtub appliqués. Remove any loose bits from the old soles and sew on the new appliqués. Parents who don't sew can use fabric glue.

Two tip-to-toe uses for fabric softener sheets

If your child's sneakers smell like something died inside, stuff each shoe with a fabric softener sheet every night to lessen the odor. At the other end of the body, you can solve a flyaway hair problem by rubbing your child's hair with a dryer sheet to control static.

Ouchless Bandage Removal

Ouch! In the old days, parents were advised to rip bandages off of a child, causing many a boy or girl to do almost anything to postpone the inevitable. A quick rip didn't reduce the pain but merely got everything over with quicker.

A kinder, gentler, and generally pain-free approach is to carefully but thoroughly rub baby oil or dishwashing liquid along the edges and over the top of the bandage. Use enough to penetrate and lubricate the adhesive (but not the gauze), then slowly lift the bandage off, rubbing on a bit more oil or dishwashing liquid if you hit a sticking point. Your children will thank you, if only with an expression of relief.

In the Great Outdoors

Painting stones

Decorating medium-sized rocks with smooth surfaces is a longtime favorite kid's craft. Let their imaginations run wild when they find stones in different shapes. Wash them to remove dirt, grease, and any mossy patches, and then let the stones dry completely in the sun. Using poster or craft paints, youngsters can paint the tops and sides of the rocks however they like. When the paint is dry, seal the surface with several coats of spray-on, nontoxic, clear acrylic varnish, drying between coats. (Avoid brush-on varnishes because brushing is likely to smear the paint.) A sufficiently large stone would make a homey doorstop, while small stones could decorate a kitchen windowsill or serve as paperweights on a desk.

Cleaning outdoor equipment with vinegar

A simple, inexpensive solution of 1 part white vinegar to 1 part water makes a reliable cleaner for outdoor play equipment, kiddie cars, and bikes. For tough dirt, wipe with the vinegar solution; then rub the spot with baking soda on a damp rag or sponge and rinse. It's smart to wash swing seats and chains or ropes frequently. You can also use the vinegar solution to clean children's car seats.

Autumn leaf paintings for Junior Picasso

Nature offers us one of the most versatile and kid-friendly paintbrushes in fallen leaves. For a lovely way to spend an autumn afternoon with a child, take them on a walk in a park and ask them to collect leaves of various shapes and sizes. Bring them home, and using an old toothbrush,

Lessons from the Garden

Think about this, follow do it yourselfor: Teaching young children to garden can become a lesson in the joys of thrift and creative thinking. The child who decides to use a seen-its-day hockey stick as a stake for tomatoes, an old sneaker as a planter for kitchen herbs, or tape and a ballpoint pen to straighten a bent flower stem is a child who will learn to love the challenge of solving problems in imaginative ways—a budding member of the eminent DIY fraternity.

Equip your child with a small spade and bucket to begin, and let him get his hands in the dirt. Help him to plant a mix of flowers and vegetable seeds that will produce easy-to-tend compact plants, and let him learn by trial and error. Serve as an example by using as many ordinary household items in the garden as you can, and he'll soon follow your lead. Also be sure to let him help you compost kitchen waste and autumn leaves for the garden so he'll learn to think "outside the plot."

At the end of the growing season, leave plantings in place so your child can observe what happens in his garden in the fall and winter. Over the years, your child's plot can grow in size, and he can do more of the work on his own—hopefully as a full-fledged apprentice in the art of self-sufficiency.

gently remove any dust or dirt from their surfaces. Mix up a small batch of nontoxic finger paints (page 214) spread the table with a few pieces of newspaper, and top them with sheets of favorite, light-colored construction paper. Roll

Make a delicious homemade bird feeder with pinecones and **peanut butter!**

up your little one's sleeves, and using her index finger as a paint brush, have her paint one surface of each leaf; immediately press them down onto the paper, paint-side down. Count to 20 (another good lesson!), and remove the leaf by its stem. Instant (and free) art!

Pinecone bird feeders

The kinds of bird feeders you and your children can make from available materials are many, and this one is especially easy and fun. All you'll need: pinecones, sugarless peanut butter (the amount varies depending on the number and size of cones used), and all-purpose birdseed. Using a plastic knife, spread peanut butter over the cone, pushing it into the nooks and crevices. Now spread a layer of birdseed on a cookie sheet or a pie pan. Roll the cone in the birdseed, making sure it's covered, and gently shake off any excess. Tightly tie a length of string or yarn around the top or bottom of the cone, and hang it from a tree branch, fence, gatepost, balcony railing, or a secure plant hanger. How could any bird resist such a tempting feeder?

Organizing athletic equipment

Parents of young athletes are all too familiar with a house overflowing with a jumble of baseball bats, hockey sticks, tennis rackets, golf clubs, balls of every size and shape, sweatshirts, shoes, and stuff you can't even identify. Even one member of the junior varsity can create a major mess. Here are three suggestions for digging out of it.

- Put a tall plastic or metal garbage can in the garage or on the back porch to hold long items like bats, sticks, extra golf clubs, and volleyball posts. Weight the bottom of the can with bricks or heavy stones so it won't tip over.

- Install a pegboard and hooks (you may already have one in a work area) for hanging rackets, hats, gloves, protective padding, swim goggles and caps, wet clothes, and shoes.

- Designate one large laundry basket for athletic clothing—and do yourself a favor and lay down rules about who is to wash what, and when.

Chapter Nine

Pointers for Pet Lovers

Do you ever feel like Fluffy or Fido is the only one who really understands you? Do you ever find yourself talking to your fish or confiding in your parrot? If so, don't worry: you're definitely not alone!

Today, you can visit a canine bakery and buy cookies that a human would positively drool over—and you'll be paying that gourmet price for them. Or you can follow the recipe for Arlo and Scamp's Favorite Cookies in this chapter, using just a few simple and inexpensive ingredients to make your own delicious doggy delicacies. Likewise, you can buy your kitty a toy that costs as much as dinner for two at a fancy restaurant, or for a fraction of the cost you can recycle a belt to make a cat-sized collar, fashion a new pet bed by covering a pillow with fabric to match your décor, and turn an empty pill bottle into a rattling toy.

Read on, fellow animal-lovers, for great ideas on how to keep your pets well fed, clean, healthy, and happy, and your wallet full.

Instead of your slippers, puppies should teeth on *frozen bagels!*

Feeding Fido

Go bananas!

Add about a third of a soft banana to 1½ cups dry food. Slice it, mash it, and stir it into the pellets. Not only does it add variety and a bit of healthy sweetness (which pooches all seem to love), but a bit of banana also will settle your dog's stomach.

Healthy snacks

If you're on a diet, you know all about carrying around those petite peeled carrots to quell your appetite during snack time. The good news is that dogs generally love them, too. They're crunchy, sweet, and healthy enough to make them a regular part of Fido's diet in place of a biscuit.

Yogurt containers as doggie travel totes

Save those plastic yogurt containers with fitted lids; when you're taking Sparky along on a trip, they're the perfect size for your dog's favorite small treats. Though most dogs don't like to eat during travel, you can reward Sparky for his good behavior once you arrive at your destination.

Put the jerk back in the food

Is your faithful friend feeling finicky? Try this safe trick: put a stick of beef jerky in a new bag of dry dog food and reseal it for 24 hours. The scent will make the dry food more tempting to your canine, be he a purebred or a mutt.

Hydrogen peroxide for an upset stomach

If your dog has eaten something she shouldn't have (chocolate candy, echinacea, etc.) induce vomiting by forcing her to swallow 1–2 tablespoons of hydrogen peroxide mixed with a ¼ teaspoon of sugar. This medicine-cabinet staple will make her barf up anything that's bad for her in a hurry.

Pills for your pooch

No reason to wrestle your friend to the ground to try and get him to take a pill; this is what spray cheese is for. Avail yourself of a can, encase the medicine in a thick cloak of cheese, and it'll go down the hatch in a matter of seconds. (For a natural version, spread the offending pill with a heavy layer of peanut butter.)

Foods to Never, Ever Give Your Dog

Chocolate, which contains theobromine, a substance that is poisonous to dogs.

Onions, garlic, and other onion family members (leeks, shallots, scallions), whose ingredient thiosulfate can destroy your pet's red blood cells.

Add sweetness and flavor to dry dog food with a **banana!**

make your own
Gourmet Dog Biscuits

You can buy pricey dog biscuits in the grocery store and even pricier bakery-made dog biscuits at pet specialty shops. But if you like to bake, it does not cost much to create your own delicious treats. This vegetarian recipe comes from an upstate New York dog owner and is named for her two cockapoos.

Arlo and Scamp's Favorite Cookies

These wholesome treats smell so good coming out of the oven that you'll be tempted to sample one for yourself. (And you may!)

2 cups whole-wheat flour
1 tablespoon baking powder
1 cup natural peanut butter
1 cup skim milk

1. Preheat oven to 375°F.

2. Combine flour and baking powder in one bowl. In another bowl, whisk together peanut butter and milk.

3. Combine wet and dry ingredients and mix until a dough forms. Place the dough on a lightly floured surface and knead until the dough is pliant (about 5 minutes).

4. Roll dough to ¼-inch thickness, then use a dog bone–shaped cookie cutter to cut out shapes.

5. Place cutouts on a greased cookie sheet and bake for 20 minutes or until lightly browned. Cool the cookies on a wire rack and store in an airtight container.

Keeping Fido Groomed

File Scruffy's nails with sandpaper

Most dogs don't like having their nails filed, but doing so will keep their nails in generally good condition and keep them from splitting in colder weather. To ease your dog's stress about the big, mean, evil, nail-filing machine used by groomers, cut a half-dollar-sized round of 120-grit sandpaper, wrap it around your index finger, and *gently* go to it, stopping frequently to praise the little guy and reinforce his behavior with a favorite treat.

Tube socks for post-shampoo itchiness

Many dogs are skin-sensitive to shampoos, leaving them scratching and irritated after their bath (which they didn't want in the first place, in case you weren't sure). Keep any larger dog from scratching his neck and face by putting his back feet in cotton tube socks, and pulling them up as far as you can; if you have a smaller dog (with shorter legs), try a pair of cotton baby socks.

Use olive oil on matted hair

Loosen your dog's matted hair by rubbing a little olive oil into the knot. Then gently comb through the matted area with a wire brush until the brush teeth glide smoothly through Lucy's coat.

Oil away tar

Remove tar from your dog's foot pads by gently rubbing them with mineral oil or petroleum jelly. Then wash away the residue with a mild solution of soapy water. To help keep tar pickup to a minimum on your dog-walking expeditions, very carefully trim the hair that grows between your doggie's toes.

Dab off teary residue with baby oil

Some dogs' tear ducts create a residue that collects in the hair below the corner of the eye. This may stain the hair of light-colored dogs, and despite numerous products sold to "whiten" it, veterinarians say there is little you can do—so it's best not to fret. Still, you should remove it. Pour a little baby oil onto a cotton ball and gently work it into the area to loosen the residue and make it easier to dab off. You could also use a mild face-freshening astringent, in which case take care to keep it out of your dog's eyes.

Vinegar ear cleaner

All flop-ear dogs—especially water dogs like Labs and Retrievers—should have their ears gently cleaned at least once a week to prevent waxy buildup and infections (which result in both pain and odor). Mix 1 part white vinegar to 1 part water; dip a cotton ball into the mixture, and carefully wipe out your dog's ears, *without* inserting the cotton ball into the ear canal. Use a separate cotton ball for each ear to avoid cross contamination in case of infection.

Prevent dog hair clogs with a scrubber

At bath time, you can keep your dog's hair from clogging the tub drain if you place a nylon pot scrubber or a snipped-off section of kitchen sponge over the drain. This porous barrier will collect hair, which you can easily remove and discard.

Playtime for Pooch

Buying toys for your dog is a nice gesture, but it can get expensive. Fido may have great taste, but he'll be just as happy with homemade games, like these:

Blue jean baby

Tiny puppy teeth *should* chew—but not on your furniture, the cat, slippers, or fancy high heels or loafers. How to remedy this? Make sure your pup has plenty of toys to call her own. Make inexpensive, sturdy toys out of old denim jeans. Cut a double layer of denim into a square, stitch together on three sides, stuff with a few old tennis balls (not panty hose, which she can choke on if she tears the toy apart), and stitch up the fourth.

Softballs for small dogs

If your furry friend is tiny, he will have a blast chasing around an inanimate object larger than he is; an old softball is just the ticket to occupy his attention for hours.

Chase the flashlight

What could be more fun for a frisky dog than chasing a flashlight beam in a large, darkened room? Make sure not to shine the light in the little guy's eyes, and move the furniture to avoid the crashing that generally follows the careening.

Soda bottle toss

Punch two holes in the cap of an empty plastic soda bottle. Thread a thick string through the cap and knot it, then screw the cap back on tightly. Now toss the bottle toward your pup and draw it back. He'll enjoy chasing the elusive toy for hours, if you're willing to play along.

Walking the Dog

Panty hose leash

Your dog will appreciate the elasticity of a leash made from an old pair of panty hose. The idea is to knot it along every 4 or 5 inches and create a handle at the end by looping the hose and knotting it.

Cool wet T-shirt

Hot enough for you? Yes, and for your pooch, too! If you're walking him on a warm day, dampen a large (or small, depending on the dog's size) children's cotton T-shirt with cool water, wring it dry, and fit it over Buster's head, pushing his two front paws through the sleeves. Tie a knot on the side to take up the slack, making sure the shirt fits comfortably—neither too tight nor too loose. (Check it periodically to make sure it stays that way.) If the shirt dries out after a while, spritz it with water.

Glow-in-the-dark collar

Even a few regularly spaced strips of reflective tape along your dog's (or cat's) collar will help drivers see them if they happen to be out at night or at dusk.

Plastic bag pooper-scooper

Never throw away those plastic grocery store bags. They make prefect pooper-scoopers, and they're *free*. Just stick your hand into the bag, pick up the poop with your amply gloved hand, and turn the bag inside out before tying it off and disposing of it.

Cardboard cleanup tool

Cut a section from an empty cereal or cracker box to use as a disposable pooper-scooper whenever you walk your dog. Slide it under the pile of poop and put both the pile and your scooper directly into a plastic grocery bag. Tie the whole thing up, and it's ready to throw in the trash.

Soothe paws with petroleum jelly

Extreme temperatures can damage a dog's paws during a walk. Hot sidewalks, freezing paths, and road salts may irritate his foot pads and lead to cracking. To soothe Rex's feet and help initiate healing, rub a little petroleum jelly onto his paws. If Rex is a yard dog, no worries. If he's a house dog, be sure to wipe any excess petroleum jelly off his paws so that he won't track it onto carpeting or upholstery.

OLD BELT = TEMPORARY LEASH

Your dog's leash has been lost or stolen? **An old belt** will serve as a substitute until you can go to the pet center to buy a new one. Buckle the belt onto your dog's collar and use duct tape to create a handle at the other end. (Twist the tape into a "rope," loop it, and attach it to the end of the belt with several more layers of tape).

Cats and Their Litter Boxes

Foil litter box odors!

Once odor penetrates the bottom of a litter box, it's almost impossible to remove completely—a reason to whip up this easy-to-make aluminum foil odor barrier. Cut a piece of cardboard box to size, cover it with heavy-duty aluminum foil, and secure the foil to the cardboard with masking tape. When changing the kitty litter, don't toss out your homemade liner; instead, swab the foil with a wet sponge soaked in a solution of 2 parts vinegar to 1 part baking soda. If you treat the liner gently, you should be able to get at least three or four uses out of it.

Slice lemon, neutralize odor

Let's face it: There's nothing pleasant about eau de litter box—and here's a way to control odor in the area where the box sits. Place half a lemon, cut side up, on a saucer and set it on the floor a few inches from the box. (A scientist could explain to you why the smell of lemon in the air neutralizes unpleasant odors, but suffice to say that lemon gives baking soda a run for the money when it comes to odor control.) For tough odors, place several lemon halves on a paper plate or try a combo of orange, lemon, and lime halves.

Three ways to sweeten a litter box

If you're buying scented litter or the kind that neutralizes litter box odors, you're probably spending a lot every week on this kitty essential. Here are four suggestions that will help you achieve the same result at less expense:

- Add ⅓ cup baking soda to regular litter and mix well
- Sprinkle ⅓ cup baby powder onto the litter to keep it fresh
- Stir a handful of dried parsley or other aromatic dried herb into the litter.

No-cost litter box cleaners

Instead of using name-brand or off-brand cleaning products, choose one of these kitchen pantry or under-the-sink items to keep a litter box fresh as a daisy. After removing litter and liner, clean the box weekly with:

- Vinegar
- Household ammonia
- Lemon oil
- A solution of 1 part household bleach to 10 parts water

Finish the job by rinsing the litter box with plain water. Then wipe it dry with a clean cloth before refilling it.

A doormat for cats

To keep your cat from tracking dusty paw prints on the floor when she leaves her litter box, place a carpet remnant or an old place mat on the side of the box where Precious makes her exit.

Cats at Play

It never matters how expensive the toys are that you bring home for your little fluffball; they take pleasure in the extraordinary everyday objects that are found in every home. Case in point: aluminum foil. Simply ball up a piece, toss it, and watch your furry friend go skittering around the house after it. Other "free" toys include: plastic cap guards from bottled water jugs; empty wooden thread spools; old golf balls; plastic bottle tops; empty corrugated cardboard boxes; empty shoeboxes; empty plastic buckets (cleaned, please); and heavy gauge wire, with one end held in place by closing it in a door or drawer, and the other end looped, with a feather or some thread attached to it.

Rattlin' good fun

Use plastic medicine bottles or old film canisters to make toys for cats. Fill the vessel with coins, paper clips, or buttons—any small items that will rattle when shaken. Roll the toy out on the floor and watch as your kitty delights in batting it around.

Sock it to 'em

Clean an old sock, stuff the toe-end with some catnip, and tie it off tightly. Dangle the tempting toy from a string, and you've got a game going with your cat. Alternatively, tie the filled sock to a doorknob and let Kitty bat it about on his own. A sock isn't the only thing to use: You could also stuff a baby bootie with catnip or cut off the sleeve of a worn-out blouse or shirt and turn it into a catnip holder.

"You're pulling my leg!"

That's the name of the game you'll play with your cat when you stuff a leg of old panty hose, and a feline-human tug of war ensues. Cut off one panty hose leg and fill the toe with catnip. Knot the hose above the filled area and make several more knots along the length of the leg. A catnip-free version of the toy uses old rags or wadded-up panty hose as stuffing; in this case, you'll want to engage your cat in a game of "chase the snake" as you wiggle the toy around on the floor.

Watching your own Wild Kingdom

Have an active bird feeder and a video camera? You've got the makings for hours of unbridled entertainment for your little indoor hunter. Video the birds in action, pop in the DVD or tape where your kitten can see the television, turn it on, and watch the fun unfold. Marlin Perkins never had it so good!

Food and Drink for Pets

Healthful stir-ins

When cooking, save the rich liquid from steamed, oil-free vegetables and the drippings from meat and stir a spoonful or two into your pet's food bowl, adding a little warm water to thin the juices if necessary. If your cooking session doesn't coincide with pet-feeding time, put the juices in a jar and store in the fridge for later use. Heat the stir-ins in the microwave to warm, not hot, before sharing them with Sadie.

Panty hose Kitty's brush

For easy brush cleanup, slip a small piece of panty hose over the head of the brush *before* grooming. Make sure the bristles poke through. Once grooming is done, remove the panty hose, which should be laden with cat fur, and discard.

A mouse pad for Tomcat's bowl

When you replace your computer mouse pad, use the old one as a place mat for your pet's food bowl. It's perfect for keeping it from skidding and for catching spills.

Ant-proof your pet's food

When you feed dogs or cats outdoors, keep ants out of the food bowl with this neat trick: Set your pet's bowl in the center of a baking pan filled with water.

Mineral oil = fewer hairballs

Just add 1 teaspoon mineral oil or petroleum jelly to your cat's daily feedings to help ease hairballs through the digestive tract. (Note: Vegetable oils and other oils won't work because your cat will absorb and digest them.) To get a jump on hairballs, give your cat a good brushing every day.

make your own Cat Treats

Rolled oats are the basis of these cookies made just for cats. They're more healthful than their commercial equivalents because they contain nary a trace of preservatives and artificial ingredients—well, if you make your own stock, that is. Even if you use canned broth or stock cubes, your treats may be more "natural" than the store-bought equivalent.

Miss Kitty's Oatmeal Cookies

Note that your cookies can be chicken-, beef-, or tuna-flavored. If you choose tuna, you could substitute the liquid in a can of water-packed tuna instead of oil; if the liquid doesn't amount to half a cup, just thin it with tap water.

> 1½ cups rolled oats
> ¼ cup vegetable oil
> ½ cup all-purpose flour
> ½ cup chicken broth, beef broth, or oil
> or water from canned tuna

1. Preheat oven to 350°F.

2. Mix all ingredients into a dough.

3. Dust your hands with flour and shape dough into ½-inch thick round cookies. Set the cookies on a greased baking sheet.

4. Bake 30 minutes or until the cookies are lightly browned, then cool for 30 minutes on a cookie rack. Once cool, break them into bite-sized pieces for your little friend.

Keeping Pets Bright-Eyed and Bushy-Tailed

A kitchen staple bed freshener

Between washings of your pet's bedding, sprinkle it with baking soda and let it sit for about an hour. Shake off the baking soda outdoors, then vacuum off the rest.

Quick 'n' simple panty hose pet bed

Stuff the seat of a pair of old panty hose with soft material that your pet will happily sink into—cotton balls, chicken feathers, orphan socks, store-bought pillow stuffing (synthetic or all-natural), or even wadded-up panty hose. Just knot the legs and snip off the excess hose. To smarten up the bed, cover it with an attractive pillowcase and stitch the case closed.

Shrink an old sweater for Sweetums

To keep your dog warm during cold-weather walks, provide her with a sweater by shrinking one of your old round-necked or v-neck, pullover woolen ones to pooch-size. (Use a child's sweater if your dog is small.) First, measure the sweater against your dog; if it's at least three times too big, you've got a winner. Toss it into the washing machine with ¼ cup mild detergent and set the

What's the Story?
Old Wives' Tail

Have you heard that adding tomato juice, apple cider vinegar, or baking soda to a dog's diet will neutralize the acidity in dog urine? The urine that kills your grass? Well, that turns out to be a spurious piece of folklore. Adding any of these ingredients to your dog's diet won't prevent dog pee from killing grass—and anyway, it's not the acidity that does the damage but rather the high concentration of nitrogen in dog urine.

What's worse, following this discredited advice may be quite harmful. According to the Web site for the University of Wisconsin's Cooperative Extension Service, "Veterinarians warn that feeding pH-altering supplements such as tomato juice, vinegar, or baking soda [to dogs] could result in urinary tract diseases, bladder infections, crystals, and bladder stones." Read all about it at http://polk.uwex.edu/hort/lawnanddogs.html.

water temperature to hot; set the machine for a large wash, even though the load consists of a single sweater. After removing the sweater, press it between two towels to squeeze out as much water as possible. While the sweater is damp, it's time for a fitting. Reshape the sweater so that the neck is wide enough to fit easily over your doggie's head. (If it doesn't, cut a slit and bind the edges with seam binding to prevent fraying). The arms of the sweater should fit over the dog's two

Store pet supplies in **shoe bag pockets!**

front legs, and the body of the sweater should reach about halfway down her back. Lay the sweater on a drying rack and let it dry in a well-ventilated room. Now let Sweetums strut her stuff in her new winter outfit—which didn't cost a cent.

Recycle a belt as a collar

Save a few dollars by making a pet collar from a small leather belt. (A grosgrain belt is suitable for smaller, lightweight pets, but only if it has a binding along its length). Cut the belt to the desired length for your little dog or cat or rabbit. Place the new collar on a block of wood and poke holes in it with an awl, then buckle it around your pet's neck to make sure it fits comfortably.

Shoe bag pet-stuff organizer

A hanging shoe bag placed inside a closet door or in your laundry room can help you get a handle on all your pet stuff. Use the pockets for storing toys, treats, cloths—even your pet's vital health statistics, including the vet's name and number. With everything in one place, you'll have an easier time locating what you need whenever you need it.

Polish makes pretty (easy to find)

Glow-in-the-dark pet-safe nail polish dabbed onto your cat or dog's collar—and on his claws or toenails—will make your pet easier to spot when he's out after dark. Available at pet stores.

Keep basic info handy

Place all important papers having to do with your pet in a small lidded box (a cigar box is ideal) so you can easily grab it if you have to run to the vet's office in an emergency. Likewise, a pet sitter will be able to easily find everything in one place if he needs to.

Don't throw away that old comb!

Use it as a belly scratcher for your dog or cat. Your fingernails will do the job, too, but pets seem to love the feel of a fine-toothed comb digging into their fur.

Skin and Coat Care

Eggs make coats shine

A weekly scrambled egg added to your cat or dog's food helps keep her coat shiny, and it's a healthy treat your pet will love. Raw eggs are off limits, of course, because they could be contaminated with salmonella.

Unsticking something sticky

That sticky something in your pet's fur could be pine sap, mud, or something unmentionable. Before you get out the scissors and cut away the icky patch, leaving your dog or cat with a bald spot, try this: Mix 1 teaspoon mild shampoo or liquid dish detergent with ¼ to ½ cup warm water and whisk it well. Wearing rubber gloves, apply some of the solution to your pet's sticky spot, rubbing it in with your fingers. Then comb the spot with a wire-toothed brush. Once you've removed the sticky stuff, wash away any soapy residue with fresh warm water.

De-skunk your pet with vinegar

Many people have heard of using tomato juice to rid a pet's coat of skunk odor, but here's a less expensive and neater way to remove the scent: Deodorize your pet with a bath of 50/50 white vinegar and warm water. Keep rinsing and washing until all odor is gone. Your pet is a water-wary cat, you say? Consult cat care guides or browse the Internet for ways to bathe a cat, which involve enlisting a helper, using a hand-held shower nozzle, staying patient and calm, and reassuring Missy repeatedly that everything's going to be okay.

An under-the-sink itch stopper

Dry skin isn't a problem for humans alone. If you notice your dog or cat scratching more than usual, gently rub a little Murphy's Oil Soap into his coat.

Mouthwash for skin problems

You may think mouthwashes are for oral hygiene only. But they're also a good all-around disinfectant for your dog or cat (and for *you*, for that matter). Use one of the stronger mouthwash brands as an astringent on your pet's skin to disinfect wounds, clean cuts and scrapes, and cool down boils and other hot spots. Just moisten a cotton ball with mouthwash and dab it on the affected area to help a banged-up dog or cat heal more quickly.

REVITALIZE DRY HAIR WITH TEA

If your pet's coat is looking a little less than lustrous, shampoo Fluffy or Fido as you usually do, then complete the wash by rinsing the coat with a quart of **warm unsweetened tea.**

Chasing Away Fleas

Mix your own repellants

Homemade flea repellents are easy to mix and bottle, so why not give them a try?

Use them to spritz your dog or cat *almost* all over, especially under the "armpits," behind the ears, and around the head, taking care to shield the eyes. When you spray at the base of the tail, avoid spraying the pet's genitals. Herewith, two quick and easy recipes:

- **Lemon Lash-Out** Cut 2 lemons into small pieces, toss the pieces into a saucepan holding 1 quart water, and boil the pieces for 1 hour. Remove the pan from the heat and let the mixture stand overnight. Strain the lemony liquid into a spray bottle and spritz your pet as directed above.

- **Vinegar Vamooser** Repel fleas with a solution made from 10 parts water to 1 part white vinegar. Pour it into a spray bottle and spray your pet as directed above.

Pine scent in the doghouse

A pile of fresh pine needles placed underneath your doggie's bed will discourage fleas.

Draw a line in the salt

Pour table salt around all the crevices of the doghouse to keep fleas out of your dog's cozy abode.

Cedar deterrents

Add cedar chips or cedar sawdust to the stuffing for you pet's pillow or bedding. If your dog has a doghouse, hang or nail a cedar block inside. The odor of cedar repels fleas as well as other nuisance insects, including moths.

Scent flea collars with essential oils

Store-bought flea collars often carry an unpleasant odor, and you may hesitate to put a chemical-laden collar so close to your pet's skin. Fit your pet with a natural, pleasant-smelling flea collar instead. Rub a few drops of essential oil of tea tree, citronella, lavender, eucalyptus, or scented geranium into an ordinary webbed or rope collar or a doggy bandana, and then refresh the oil weekly.

Kill eggs with salt, too

This flea killer takes a little time to work its magic. Sprinkle salt on your carpets to kill flea eggs; let it sit for a day, then vacuum. Repeat the process a few days later to make sure you haven't missed any flea eggs. Each time you vacuum the salt, be sure to tie up and discard the vacuum cleaner bag.

A Systemic Flea Repellent

Who says fleas can be repelled only with topical treatments? Not your vet. He or she probably knows that brewer's yeast works as a systemic flea repellent when your pet ingests it. If you use the powdered form, sprinkle 1 teaspoon into your cat or small dog's food daily (a 50-pound dog will need a tablespoon).

That this treatment is systemic doesn't mean you can't use brewer's yeast topically as well; just rub it directly into your pet's fur. But take note: Some animals develop a skin allergy after eating or being rubbed with yeast. If your pet is one of them, discontinue use of this repellent immediately.

Pet-Related Housecleaning

Prevent chewing with oil of cloves

Puppies do chew—even on the legs of tables and chairs. Discourage chewing by dabbing the most attractive spots (your shoes, a cardboard box, and anything wooden your pup can get his teeth around) with oil of cloves. The bitter odor and taste are a deterrent to nibbling.

Frozen teething bagels

Not just for teething human babies, this traditional method for soothing painful gums is perfect for pups, too; freeze a few baby bagels until they're rock solid and ice cold. Let the little one chew on those to ease his painful choppers. When the bagel gets mushy, take it away before he eats it, and replace with a dog toy.

Odor-eating vinegar

Accidents do happen, especially with new pets.

Eliminate that unpleasant urine smell from carpeting with a 50/50 solution of white vinegar and warm water. Pour it onto the affected area so that it soaks through to the padding, then allow it sit for half an hour. Wash the affected area with cool water until the vinegar is rinsed out, then pat the carpet dry with towels. Cover with a ½-inch-thick layer of dry, clean white rags, towels, or paper towels, weight them down with heavy objects (bricks, paperweights, door stops, and the like) and let the absorbent material sit for several hours to soak up the moisture.

Clear the air with coffee beans

Some pet owners have found they can remove pet odors from a room by heating a cupful of freshly ground coffee beans in a cast iron skillet over low heat. As soon as the scent is released, remove the pan to the smelly room and set it on a trivet. By the time the ground beans are cool, much of the pet odor should have dissipated.

Cats Gotta Scratch

So your cat has ripped one side of that new (and not exactly cheap) chair to shreds? While you're having it reupholstered, make him a simple and inexpensive scratching post by stapling or gluing a carpet remnant to a log or a section of 2-by-4 board. Attach the post vertically to a ½-inch thick section of plywood by hammering nails though the bottom of the plywood and into the log or board.

If you saved the leftover sections of carpet last time your den was carpeted, your new scratching post should cost nothing. If you don't have any carpet remnants, pick one up at the local home supply or hardware store.

Away with pet hair!

It's embarrassing when guests don't want to sit on your sofa because they don't enjoy "wearing" your pet's coat on their clothing. Here are some ways to remove dog and cat hair from your furniture and clothing—and preventing pet hair from getting there in the first place.

- Lightly mist your hair-covered garment with water, then put it in the dryer with a damp towel and a fabric softener sheet. Dry on the air cycle for a few minutes.

Keep Fido off
the furniture with a
shower curtain!

- Gently rub upholstered furniture and your clothing with a slightly damp kitchen sponge to remove pet hair.

- Wrap your hand with masking tape or duct tape, sticky side out. Run both your palm and the back of your hand over furniture or your clothing to collect pet hair.

- Slip a rubber glove onto your hand and rub your fingers back and forth over your upholstered furniture until pet hair balls up and you can lift it off.

Kill carpet odor with baking soda

If a musty smell has infiltrated the carpet, as often happens with recently cleaned pet urine spots, use baking soda to neutralize the odor. Once the carpet has thoroughly dried, sweeten the area by working 1/8 to 1/4 cup of baking soda into the carpet pile. Wait 15 minutes before vacuuming it up.

- Cover a sponge, a blackboard eraser, or your hand with a fabric softener sheet and rub away pet hair.

- Try vacuuming your pet, using the brush attachment on your vacuum. If she doesn't mind the noise, make this a weekly task that will collect loose hairs before they start flying around the house. If your pet doesn't like being vacuumed, try holding the vacuum brush about 2 inches away from her fur.

Foil as a noisy deterrent

Noise deters pets from jumping on furniture. To train cats to stay off upholstered couches and chairs, top the cushions with aluminum foil.

If cats jump onto the furniture, the crunching sound of foil under their paws will send them scurrying in a hurry.

Recycle a shower curtain liner

Covering your furniture with an old shower curtain is likely to keep pets at arm's length. It isn't comfortable to lie on, and the crunchy plastic makes an unpleasant noise when your pet climbs onto it.

If You Own a Horse...

Make a tube sock snood

Rather than buying a tail bag, or snood, make one from a tube sock—a thrifty way to protect your horse's tail on your way to a show. Here's how:

1. On each side of the sock cuff, cut a strip that will remain attached to the sock—each one about 3 inches in length and 1 inch wide.

2. Braid your horse's tail, and slip the tube sock over it.

3. Interlace one of the loose sock strips with the top of the braid, then tie the second sock strip to the first one, knotting it tightly.

Bleach it away

Rain rot is a common skin infection affecting horses. Mix 1 part household bleach to 10 parts water, and pour the solution into a spray bottle. Use it to clear up the affected area. Just be sure not to spray near the horse's eyes.

Shine her up

After hosing off your horse, sponge on a solution of white vinegar and water (1 part vinegar to 10 parts water). This simple mixture will remove soap residue, repel flies, and shine the coat.

Alternatives to store-bought hoof dressing

Keeping your horse's hooves in good condition is essential to his well-being. While many products are found on the market, here are three dressings you already have at home:

- Vegetable shortening
- Aerosol cooking spray
- WD-40

In winter, it's important to apply dressing to the hooves to prevent "snowballing." This occurs when snow freezes in a hoof and makes it hard for a galloping horse to place it flat on the ground, often leading to sprains. Just remember that any of these dressings may make the hoof and shoe slippery, so be sure not to apply too much in winter or apply too frequently.

Freeze factor

Smear petroleum jelly inside your horse's water bucket in winter before filling it with water. When it ices over, you'll find it much easier to slide out the ice as it coasts along a coat of slippery gel.

Fight those flies!

Keep flies away from your horse's eyes by dabbing a little petroleum jelly around each eye. During the summer, smear zinc oxide ointment in and around Angel's ears to repel flies.

Shine up your saddle

Clean and polish your horse's chrome bits, buckles, and straps with toothpaste. This handy and inexpensive polish works wonders on a saddle's shiny parts.

Flies and gnats

These pesky creatures are notoriously annoying when it comes to horses. Help your friend Flicka keep her cool by shading her eyes and giving her a spritz of bath oil spray.

Saddle smarts

When you take apart your saddle for cleaning, it's easy to forget which stirrup strap is left and which is right. Take two empty toilet paper tubes and mark one *Left*, one *Right*. As you remove each strap, lace the strap through the correct paper tube and buckle it.

Hair gel keeps manes tidy

Forget fancy grooming techniques and tools; if hair gel works for you, it'll work for your horse, too. Use a dollop to make braiding easy and to keep stray hairs from popping out of place on show day.

Spray stalls with vinegar to keep nibbles at bay

To keep stalls from being chewed on by nickering nags, mix a spray that's half white vinegar, half water; horses hate the taste of anything tart, so they'll leave the real estate alone.

make your own
Hoof Dressing

A horse's hooves can easily become dry and cracked, especially in dry climates. This simple homemade hoof dressing, made from equal parts lard and pine tar, will work as well as any store-bought product to keep Stardust's hooves in good shape. Pine tar is available at farm supply stores and online.

Pine Tar Hoof Soother

This concoction has a thick consistency in warm weather and hardens to a paste in the winter, when you may have to microwave it to make it easy to apply.

1 pound lard
1 pound pine tar

1. Put lard in a large microwave-safe container and microwave on low power until the lard melts.

2. Add pine tar and stir with a large wooden spoon until the dressing is well mixed.

3. Apply the dressing to your horse's hooves with a soft 2½-inch-wide paintbrush.

Rabbits, Hamsters, and Other Creatures

Give rabbits plenty of paper

Rabbits are burrowers, and a pet bunny with something to burrow into will be a happy camper. Offer Bunny shredded newspaper, balled-up phone book pages, or other similar paper, placing it in the bottom of his cage so he can dig away.

Cardboard hidey-hole for Bunny

Rabbits enjoy the comfort of a "cave." Remove the lid from a cardboard box and cut out a door shape. Turn the box upside down in the rabbit cage and your pet will use it as a cozy hideaway. Choose a shoebox or a larger cardboard box, depending on your pet's size.

A roll to gnaw on

It seems almost all animal pets—dogs, cats, rabbits, chinchillas, mice, gerbils, guinea pigs, hamsters, ferrets, and the like—enjoy gnawing on an empty paper towel or toilet tissue roll. So do some birds, like cockatiels, so put some rolls aside for your furry or feathery charges. They also like to gnaw on cardboard tissue boxes. Just make sure to remove the thin plastic liner attached to a tissue box's dispensing slot.

Let hamsters branch out

Hamsters like fresh branches to climb on and gnaw. Choose small willow or fruit wood branches. Make sure they're pesticide-free.

Coconut gerbil house

Gerbils and other rodents are active creatures and like to stay occupied. A coconut shell suspended from the top of the cage makes a great climb-in, climb-out toy. First, clean the shell well, removing all coconut meat. Then use a jigsaw to cut an opening in the shell, filing down the rough edges. Boil the shell in water for 10 minutes and let it air dry. Insert an eye hook into the shell so that when you suspend it from the cage ceiling, the opening will be on the side (not pointing downward). Hang the shell low enough for your pet to reach.

Nibble, nibble, nibble

Sure, your pet rodents enjoy those expensive chew toys. But you can provide just as much munching pleasure for free. Besides all those empty cardboard rolls and small cardboard boxes, give your nibblers small blocks of wood left over from woodworking projects. Do not, however, give them any treated wood.

"SO WHERE'S THE HINT FOR MY FERRET?"

Right here. **Ping-Pong balls** and tennis balls make great toys for ferrets, and guinea pigs will find them rather amusing as well. Ferrets and guinea pigs understand that not every toy has to be a chew toy.

Turtles, Snakes, and Other Reptiles

Save your turtle's gravel

Don't throw away the gravel or aggregate in your turtle's bowl every time you clean it. Dump the gravel, aggregate, and any other bowl materials into a colander. Place the colander over a bucket and pour pitchers full of water over the contents until the gravel is clean. Next, pour household bleach over everything. Finally, run water over the colander contents until the bleach smell dissipates.

Your pet snake is lost?

It happens, but don't panic. Here are two good ways to find your missing pet:

- Place foil or crinkly plastic packing material around the room in potential hiding places, so you can hear the snake moving around.

- Sprinkle some flour on the floor in areas where you suspect your pet might be hiding.

Bring the outdoors in for a pet lizard

Your pet lizard will enjoy having fresh small tree branches in his cage. Lizards like to climb and hang out on the branches you can collect from your yard.

Lazin' lizards!

Caged lizards like to relax, so make your pet a little hammock. String a section of old pillowcase or a bandana between two corners of the cage, and you'll soon see your lizard resting comfortably in her new piece of furniture.

A reptile cage catchall

Keep the area around a reptile's cage neat by placing an old shower curtain liner or plastic tablecloth beneath the cage. When it's time to straighten up, bundle up the plastic liner, brush sand or crumbs or any other bits of detritus into the trash, and then wipe the liner with a sponge before returning it to its original spot.

Curiosity Corner
Girl Turtle or Boy Turtle?

Want to give your pet turtle a gender-appropriate name? Finding the answer to the question of female vs. male is easier than you might think. Just turn the turtle over and examine its undershell—which, by the way, is called the plastron.

If the plastron is convex (curved outward), the turtle is female; if it's concave (curved inward), the turtle is male.

Because the curves are slight, you may have to hold the turtle horizontally before your eyes to determine which way the undershell curves.

Creatures of the (Not So) Deep

Tape fish food dispensers

Some fish food containers have big open tops; others have way too many large holes—and both can lead to overfeeding your aquarium or goldfish-bowl fish. Cover half of the container mouth with masking tape to better control the dispersal of fish flakes.

Panty hose tank cleaners

Save an old pair of panty hose for yet another household use! Once you've removed the fish, the water, and any ornaments from an aquarium tank, you can turn panty hose into a cleaning tool in two ways: 1) Fit a leg over your arm so you have the foot over your fingers, like a mitten. 2) Ball the panty hose up and use it as you would a sponge. No matter which method you choose, make a simple vinegar and water solution (1 part white vinegar to 1 part water) and use panty hose to wipe down the sides and bottom of the tank.

Put aquarium water to good use

When you change the water in your tank, don't pour it down the drain! It's excellent for hatching brine shrimp (the favorite food of sea horses, if you keep a sea horse or two in your aquarium), and it makes an excellent fertilizer for houseplants and outdoor ornamentals alike. The nutrients in the water make flowering plants and vegetables thrive like few other fertilizers. And don't be put off by the smell—it will dissipate about an hour after you water your plants.

Pep up Goldie with salt

Treat your goldfish to a swim in the ocean. Well, a *simulated* ocean. Stir 1 teaspoon marine salt into 1 quart room-temperature water and pour it into a wide-mouthed container. Let Goldie swim for about 15 minutes in this slightly salty mix and then return her to her bowl. The saltwater will put a little pep in her step. (Caution: Do not use table salt because the pH is too high.)

Tasty treats for hermit crabs

Enhance your hermit crab's diet by adding bits of any of the following to its food dish. The list is long, so take a deep breath and jump in: mango, papaya, coconut, apples, applesauce, bananas, grapes, pineapple, strawberries, melons, carrots, spinach, leafy green lettuces (not iceberg), broccoli, grass, leaves, strips of bark from deciduous trees (no conifers), unsalted nuts, raisins, unsalted crackers, unsweetened cereals, and plain rice cakes. A wide-ranging crustacean menu indeed!

Eggshells for hermits

Hermit crabs need a lot of calcium, a mineral available in various forms in pet stores. To provide calcium to your pet crawler for free, boil an egg, dry and crush the shell, and add it to your crab's regular food once a week.

Our Fine Feathered Friends

Lights-out drapes

An attractive small tablecloth or a pillowcase or scarf can become a nighttime cover for your bird's cage. Covering the cage will help your bird relax.

Natural decor for Tweety

Clip a small tree branch for your cockatiel's cage. He'll be able to climb and reclimb and also will peck it to sharpen his beak.

Clean house with vinegar

A 50/50 mixture of white vinegar turns a birdcage into a sparkling clean home and does a good job of cleaning plastic bird toys. After wiping on the mixture, rinse with fresh tap water and then dry the cage with a clean cloth.

Paper bag fun for Polly

Open a brown paper bag and set it on a table or other surface. Your bird will enjoy peeking in and out.

Let your bird play peck-the-spools

Make a hanging toy for your bird's cage by stringing wooden spools on a leather cord and tying it diagonally near the top of the cage. Your bird will enjoy pecking at it and making the spools sway back and forth.

Use your imagination!

It's easy to keep a bird occupied. While pet stores sell a ton of toys for caged birds, you can easily entertain your pet with items you have around the house. Milk jugs, mop heads, and

Baubles for Birdie

Make use of old jewelry to occupy your pet bird. Suspend an old bracelet, necklace, or ring from the top of the cage—Patty the parakeet doesn't give a hoot what's in fashion as long as she has something shiny to play with. Just be sure not to use anything with gems or parts that your bird could pry off and swallow. For safety's sake, place the item on the outside of the cage so your bird can peck at it but can't pull it into the cage.

whisk brooms are good toys for birds that like to pluck feathers.

- Plastic bottle caps
- Plastic milk jugs, with the top cut off and the edges frayed with scissors
- Wads of newspaper
- Shredded computer paper
- A natural-bristle whisk broom
- Wireless clothespins
- Small wooden balls

A fun (or frustrating?) toy

Add a new dimension to a clear plastic beverage bottle by putting beads, plastic clothespins, or other brightly colored objects inside and recapping the bottle. Your bird will spend hours on end trying to figure out how he can get to the objects inside.

Chapter Ten

Tips for Travelers

Vacations have always been our chance to relax, to unwind, to learn, and to have fun. But in a time when flights are canceled at the drop of a hat and highway traffic can slow to a snail's pace, you may find yourself worrying more about controlling your rocketing blood pressure than the relaxation that used to be synonymous with the word "vacation."

That said, there are plenty of things you can do to make your trip run more smoothly. Ordinary transparent tape and plastic bags take up no space in your suitcase but go a long way toward solving and preventing problems. Then there's panty hose, which help keep your clothes wrinkle free and your bags organized. Whether you're setting off on a camping trip or a big-city adventure, put on your traveling duds and browse the information-packed pages to come.

For safety, cover your luggage zippers with *duct tape!*

Practical Packing

Take tape along for the ride

Throw a roll of tape into your suitcase and see how useful it is when you're on the road. Use transparent tape to:

- Reseal the caps of any liquids you open, like shampoo and hair gel
- Make emergency repairs on torn hems
- Fix torn maps
- Tape postcards and other mementoes into your travel journal
- Tape together earrings, cufflinks, or any other tiny items that might go astray
- Remove lint from dark clothes
- Tape driving directions to the dashboard for quick reference
- Tape stray buttons to their respective garments for repair upon returning to your hotel room

Save those newspaper bags!

The long plastic bags your morning newspaper comes in offer protection in your suitcase as well—and they're just the right shape for shoes and hairbrushes. To keep dirt or hair from marring your other belongings, slip shoes and brushes in, one to a bag.

Pack jewelry in hose toes

It can be hard to handle jewelry when you're on the move; small items can easily get lost in your suitcase, and necklaces and other dangly jewelry tend to become tangled up and snag clothing. Old pairs of panty hose provide an easy solution. Just cut out the feet, place a single piece of jewelry in each one, and tie off the little bags with twist ties. Your jewels and bangles will be readily at hand and in good condition when you need them.

Make a suitcase divider

Take a tip from smugglers: the old false-bottom suitcase trick. You'll keep packed items separated and be spared the annoyance of digging through layers of clothing to get to your toothbrush. Just take some sturdy cardboard and cut out a piece that matches the width and length of

CHUCK IN SOME CLOTHESPINS

Clothespins—the lightweight, plastic clip-on type—don't take up much room in a bag, and they earn their freight. Use clothespins to hang up the socks and dainties you wash out in the bathroom sink, clip together maps and other documents, and draw draperies tightly for privacy and to keep out light.

Organize your
luggage with
sturdy cardboard!

your suitcase interior—and voila: You have a portable divider. Put items you aren't going to need until later on the bottom of the suitcase, lay the cardboard on top, and place toiletries, a change of clothing, and the other items you'll use right away on the cardboard. Or place shoes and other heavy items on the bottom, then put lighter clothing on top to make it less likely to wrinkle.

Tote some tubes

Before hitting the road, save a few toilet-paper tubes, and then put them to work when you pack for a trip. Here are three ways empty rolls will come in handy:

- Stuff one or two tubes with socks and use them as shoetrees to keep leather shoes from becoming crunched and creased.

- Wrap necklaces and chains around a tube to prevent tangling.

- Tape small pieces of delicate jewelry inside a tube for protection.

A bit o' baking soda

You already know that baking soda keeps your fridge smelling fresh—and it can do the same for the contents of your suitcase. There's no need to tote a whole box, though. Just fill a pill bottle or film canister with baking soda and poke a few small holes in the top. A little might spill out in the course of your travels, but baking soda is unlikely to harm anything in your bag. (To keep any spillage contained, tuck the container into one of the open sleeves found in the interior of most suitcases.) Baking soda does more than just help control odor. While on the road, you can dip into your stash to do anything from soaking your tired feet to cleaning a thermos. Caution: Baking soda may arouse suspicion when traveling by plane, so make sure to remove prior to checking in for your flight.

Smooth out wrinkles

When it comes to packing clothing, rolling beats folding. Why? Because rolled clothes are less likely to wrinkle—and they take up less room in

Household Superstar!
12 Amazing Uses for Plastic Bags

You can hardly have enough self-sealing plastic bags with you when on a road trip or wilderness vacation. Bags of various sizes allow you to:

1 Carry guidebooks and other sightseeing gear in the rain

2 Make an instant rain bonnet

3 Wear as a rain poncho (you'll need a large-size trash bag for this)

4 Wrap your feet to keep them dry

5 Store dirty laundry

6 Store cotton balls and other toiletry items

7 Organize clothing in a suitcase

8 Store liquids that might spill

9 Collect trash

10 Save leftovers

11 Carry MP3 players and other electronic portables

12 Carry crayons, pencils, and other kids items

the suitcase to boot. They wrinkle even less if you roll them in:

- **Plastic dry-cleaning bags** Your dry cleaner returns your clothing in sheer plastic bags because plastic prevents fabric from rubbing against fabric and creating tiny creases. You, too, can minimize creases by wrapping garments in the bags and rolling them up.

- **Panty-hose legs** Simply cut off the legs of a pair of panty hose and slip a rolled garment into each one. If you leave the panty-hose foot sections on, use these pouches as secure compartments for cameras, MP3 players, and other valuables; with a piece of clothing stuffed into a hose leg, there's no way such items are going to fall out and play hide-and-seek in your bag.

Roll up your tie

A creased tie really puts some wrinkles in the smooth business look—but here's a way to ensure ties are wrinkle free every time you pull one from the suitcase. First, lay the tie out full length. Beginning with the narrow end, roll it into a coil. Take a sock and gently stuff the rolled-up tie inside. If you're the forgetful type, pin a note to the sock so that when you're rummage through your suitcase for your tie you won't think you accidentally left it behind.

Pack a lunch box

Not with sandwiches but with toiletries and other items that might spill or leak when jostled. Stashing cosmetics and toiletry items in such a compact, sturdy, and separate case will also make it easier to get your hands on them. Of course, the lunch box will come in handy when it comes time to pack some snacks and beverages to take along on a picnic or day of sightseeing.

Instant Travel Totes

A plastic-bag filing system

Various sizes of self-sealing plastic bags provide an easy way to stay organized when you're on the move—small sandwich bags for receipts and large freezer bags for pamphlets, brochures, maps, and other memorabilia you collect along the way. The more bags you bring, the more organized you'll be. For instance, you might want to use separate bags for each place visited; for each type of receipt (restaurants, hotels, shops); or for each day of your trip.

Pack trash bags

Common sense alert: You can fill up trash bags with dirty laundry when you travel. Heavy-duty bags are especially handy because you can just toss them over your shoulder and head out to a laundromat. On a picnic or car trip, the trash bag will come in handy for—you guessed it—trash. And if you don't fancy yourself a fashionista, you can even cut a couple of slits for your arms and one for your head and don a trash bag as an improvised raincoat. (Just hope you don't run into anyone you know from back home!)

Note: If you forget to pack trash bags, the plastic laundry bags you'll find in many hotels will serve the same purposes (except for the raincoat).

A handy coin holder

Don't discard torn panty hose, which can come in handy as a coin holder when you're on the move. To keep all those coins you get as change from cluttering the bottom of your purse or weighing down your pockets, tuck them into the foot of a pair of old panty hose, tie the top in a loose knot, and store this money bag in your suitcase. You won't have to lug around a lot of extra coinage, and since the loose change will all be in one place, you can easily dip into your coin reserves as needed.

Little moneybags

Foreign currency can flummox even the world-liest traveler, considering how long it takes to start feeling comfortable with unfamiliar coins and bills. For easier sorting, stash bills and coins of various denominations in self-sealing plastic bags—a different bag for each denomination. When it comes time to pay for something, you won't have to sort through a pile of confusing currency.

The case for taking a pillowcase

Nothing adds a homey touch to strange quarters like laying your weary head on one of your own pillowcases. This nice touch of home takes up little room in your suitcase, and it can do double duty as:

- **A protector** To keep knitted garments like sweaters from snagging on other items in you suitcase, slip them into a pillowcase.

- **A laundry bag** When the pillowcase becomes soiled, stash your dirty clothes in it. Clothing will be less prone to mold and mildew when kept in a pillowcase than it will in a plastic bag, and you can just empty the case and throw it into the wash when you come upon a laundromat.

Picnic-in-a-Bag

Traveling overseas can be costly, but one of the best (and most delicious) ways to be both clever *and* tastefully frugal whether you're in Boston or Brighton is to pack yourself a picnic in a bag. Tuck a few self-sealing plastic bags into your pocket, purse, or backpack, and visit a local bread bakery, a cheese shop, and a meat shop; then, head to a park or courtyard, and enjoy your feast in the out-of-doors. Use your imagination, and fill a bag or two with any combination of the following:

Hard cheese:
Cheddar, Parmesan, swiss, gruyere, and Gouda are all cheeses that travel well. If you're in a foreign country, ask for advice from the cheese monger. Stay away from ultrasoft cheeses that may not survive a long walk to a picnic area or park.

Bread:
Baguettes, rolls, or thick slices of fresh bread are ideal for out-of-doors picnicking, and local bakers will often lend their advice on great places to enjoy your meal.

Meats:
Cured meats—smoked turkey and smoked ham, for example—will withstand not being refrigerated for up to 2 hours and are delicious accompaniments to hard cheeses.

Remember to carry a bottle opener, a small picnic knife, a napkin, and something to sit on (other than the ground), and enjoy your out-of-doors feast more than the priciest restaurant meal. When you're done, put your trash in another sealable plastic bag, and go on your way.

Handy Helpers

Three ways duct tape eases life on the road

Like to read in bed but need some light on the subject? Tape a small flashlight to the wall above your pillow (but not on wallpaper). Want to come and go without the door locking behind you every time you step out? Place a small strip of tape across the bolt. Prefer to sleep past sunrise? Tape the draperies shut to keep out the light.

Put toilet-paper tubes to good use

You'll find some nifty uses for toilet paper tubes in a hotel room—so save a few empty tubes at home to take on your trip. Or, in the hotel, you could stash empty tubes before the chambermaid has a chance to discard them. Read on for some ways to use them.

- If your laptop computer power cord is unruly or takes up too much desk space on your worktable, loop the cord in a loose coil and stuff it into the tube to keep it contained.

- Pamphlets, small prints, and other fragile paper mementoes almost never make it back home without a crease or two—so roll them carefully and insert them into the tube for safekeeping. For larger papers, you might need to tape two tubes together or bring along a tube from a roll of paper towels.

- Mosquitoes are annoying roommates. If they appear unexpectedly and you're unprepared with spray or other

Household Superstar!
11 Duct-Tape Favors for Travelers and Campers

When you run up against a problem while driving down the highway, hiking, or camping, a roll of duct tape can bail you out in a flash. Here are 11 ways you could make use of the shiny silvery stuff.

1 Tape your pants tightly around the ankles to keep ticks and other bugs off your legs.

2 Tape your pants tightly around the ankles to keep cloth from getting caught in bike pedals.

3 Twist tape into a "rope" to use as a clothesline or to lash things together.

4 Twist it into an emergency shoelace.

5 Repair a rip in a tent.

6 Tape a flashlight to a wall or tree.

7 Reseal bags of potato chips and other road food.

8 Trap flies by cutting the tape into strips and laying them out, sticky side up.

9 Tape up purchases wrapped in newspaper or bubble wrap.

10 Patch a hole in a canoe, inner tube, or air mattress.

11 Tape curtains shut to keep out light and prying eyes.

A beanbag *will steady your camera as well as a fancy tripod.*

repellants, make your own "flypaper." Just wrap some adhesive tape around the tube, sticky side out, and set it upright on a flat surface.

Buffer sore bums

Long car rides can take their toll on your rear end and lower back. So why not turn bubble wrap into a comfy seat cushion? Just place a long double layer of bubble wrap, bubble side out, against the back and bottom of your car seat. Your body will conform comfortably to this cushy padding. And consider this: If you do some shopping along the way and come across a fragile item you just can't resist buying, you'll have some packing material right at hand!

Aromatherapy at 35,000 feet

We all know how stressful air travel can be, so why not bring along some sniffable relaxants? Before you leave home, drip some lavender oil or clary sage oil onto cotton balls. (Herbalists have long prescribed both as calmatives.) Pack the cotton balls in a small, self-sealing plastic bag or pill bottle and take them out for a good whiff when you want to unwind or doze off. You might also want to dab a dose of these oils onto your skin as you would perfume to make sure you'll arrive at your destination smelling fresh.

Cap your camera

When shooting a picture in the wet, slip a disposable shower cap over the body of your camera so that the lens pokes out of the cap opening. You'll be able to press any buttons you need to, thanks to the thinness of the plastic.

A beanbag camera steadier

If you want to shoot pictures from a speeding car, a train, or a boat, you'll find it almost impossible to keep your camera steady. The answer? A makeshift beanbag. Just pop into a supermarket and buy some dried beans or rice, pour them into the foot of a panty-hose leg, tie it closed, and rest your camera on the beanbag to keep it from vibrating as you snap your picture.

Quick Fixes on the Road

Hole in the sole?

Make a temporary sole-hole fix with duct tape; the backing is waterproof, so your repair might hold up through a couple of downpours. If a broken shoelace is slowing you down, cut off a strip of tape that's about as long as your lace, roll it tightly (lengthwise) with the sticky side in, and thread your new "lace" through the holes.

Tape a broken car hose

You can use duct tape to fix gas-powered locomotion, too: Tear off a strip to make a quick repair on your car's broken water hose—but don't rely on your handiwork to get you any farther than the nearest garage.

Damp umbrella holders

Hate toting around a wet umbrella? Make sure you always have a plastic grocery bag with you; simply stuff the closed umbrella in the bag, roll it tightly like a sausage, and stow it in your purse or pocket.

Plastic bag galoshes

Rain can really dampen your enthusiasm for walking or hiking—but you needn't let bad weather get in the way of your fun. Before pulling on your boots, wrap each foot in a plastic bag. Your feet will stay warm and dry all day, and you can put your wet footwear in one of the bags when it's time to pack and move on.

Wick water from wet shoes

To speed air-drying, stuff water-soaked shoes and boots with crumpled newspaper, which will wick out the moisture. Speed the drying even more by placing the shoes or boots on their sides, turning them over from time to time, and replacing the newspaper as it becomes damp.

Duct-Tape Fixes at the Tumbledown Inn

It's midnight. A severe ice storm has forced you into an unintended overnight stay in a motel. And the only one with a vacancy looks like it might fall down around your ears. Duct tape to the rescue!

Broken window? Tape a broken pane of glass to keep out the breeze or a ripped screen to keep out mosquitoes.

Cracked toilet seat? Skittish about sitting on it? Wrap the break for the sake of comfort and safety.

Torn shower curtain? Tape up a rip in a shower curtain with duct tape. Or use the tape to repair a torn shower-curtain eyelet that won't keep a curtain ring in place. Just fold a piece of tape and slip it over the eyelet, cut a hole through the tape, and place the ring through it.

Freshen car air

The air in your car is getting a bit stale, and those little cardboard pine trees that hang from the rear-view mirror aren't what you have in mind as a solution. The trick is to plan ahead and bring a plastic bag filled with cotton balls soaked in pure vanilla extract, tea tree oil, or eucalyptus oil. Take out a couple, put them in the car's ashtray or cup holder, and enjoy a natural scent that's subtler than that of over-perfumed or synthetic commercial air fresheners.

Safety Measures for Travelers

An improvised money belt

You can save some of the green stuff you stash in a money belt by making your own out of a pair of panty hose. Put your money, passport, and other valuables into the foot of the hose and tie the top around your waist. Your makeshift (and free) accessory will be concealed by your clothing.

Point your shoes toward the emergency exit

When you check into a hotel, take a few minutes to study the fire-exit diagrams posted on the inside of your door. Then place your shoes by the door before you retire for the night, pointing them in the direction of the emergency exit in your corridor. This way, if an alarm goes off in your hotel room and you wake up and smell smoke, you won't panic trying to remember which way to turn to escape.

Seal luggage latches

When you check your bags on a flight these days, you'll probably be told to leave them unlocked in case security decides to inspect them. You then proceed to visualize your luggage being tossed about and the latches popping open—and your belongings suddenly vulnerable to thieves. Allay your concerns by covering the latches of your suitcase with just enough duct tape to fit over the fastenings. Security will then be able to inspect the bag by peeling back the tape, and they'll more than likely retape the fasteners once they're done. Use tape that matches the color of your suitcase so that your quick fix won't be obvious to watchful wrongdoers.

Thwart pickpockets

A simple safety pin can make your wallet a lot more secure. Put your wallet in a pocket of your trousers or your jacket and close the opening with a safety pin in such a way that you can still squeeze the wallet out—but just barely. The pin is sure to thwart an unsuspecting thief who tries to pickpocket you, since you'll doubtlessly notice the tug.

A fine-toothed wallet protector

If you're a man, a wallet and a comb are two items you're likely to carry at all times. But did you know you could use them in tandem to prevent pickpockets from nabbing your wallet? Place your comb in the fold of your wallet so the teeth extend beyond the open edge; then double-loop a rubber band around the wallet through the comb teeth. When you put the wallet in your pants pocket or the breast pocket of your jacket, the teeth will catch on the fabric when moved. The upshot? When a thief tries to slip the wallet from your pocket, the comb will act as both a barrier and an alarm.

Hidey-Holes
to Outwit Thieves

Burglars break into buildings, but garden-variety thieves look for loot anywhere they can find it—like your suitcase, whether it's en route to the cargo hold of a plane or perched on the luggage rack in your hotel room. One way to protect your valuables from theft is to conceal them in unexpected places. Three safe carriers for expensive items are:

1

An empty film canister
The size and shape of these containers make them especially convenient for rings and earrings.

2

A tampon box
Leave some of these products in the top part of the box and stash valuables at the bottom.

3

A tennis ball
Make a slit along one of the seams and put jewelry and other small valuables inside the ball.

Traveling with Kids

Keep baby essentials organized

Pack a separate self-sealing bag with the essentials little Zack or Zoe will need each day—a set of clothing, a change of clothing, and some disposable diapers. If you have more than one child in tow, prepare a separate bag for each of the little ones. The payoff? You won't have to dig through suitcases to put outfits together when dressing the troops every morning.

Save that empty dishwashing liquid bottle!

If you've traveled with kids before, you know the sorts of messes they can create. Prepare yourself for the inevitable by saving an empty (but unrinsed) bottle of dishwashing liquid. Fill the bottle with water before you set out, and tuck it away in a leak-proof, self-sealing plastic bag, along with some paper towels or washcloths. Use this cleaning kit to wipe faces after snacks, wash hands after bathroom stops, and clean up spills and smudges in the car and hotel room.

A petite plastic tote

Young travelers will like keeping their small personal items—coins or gum—in a tote they make

themselves. All you need is an empty film canister or pill bottle and a key ring with a plastic spring-lock clip that attaches to belts or backpacks (the clips are sold in hardware stores and locksmith shops). Help a young craftsperson cut two holes near the top of the canister to accommodate the metal ring, then let her choose beads and ribbons and glue them on for extra pizzazz.

Map fun for little navigators

One way to keep kids busy on a car trip—and teach them about geography as well—is to help them follow your route on a map. While planning the trip, cut out and color photocopy the portion of a map that corresponds to your route for each day of travel. Attach the segments to a clipboard, give the kids some washable markers, and have them chart your course and check off towns and landmarks as you go. Who knows? If you need directions, you might be able to get some help from the back seat.

Double duty for fruit and veggie bags

Apples, onions, and other fruits and vegetables often come in mesh bags. Once the kids have eaten their way through these healthy staples, stash the bag for a day of outdoor fun. Mesh bags are ideal for carting toys to the beach or anyplace else where gear is likely to become sandy and dirty. At the end of the day, just stick the playthings in the empty bag and rinse the whole kit and caboodle out under the hose. If you can't get your hands on a mesh bag, take a plastic bag and punch holes in it—just enough holes to allow the water to run out.

Bag it

Family car trips can be a wonderful experience—and even more so when you're equipped with a good supply of self-sealing plastic bags in various sizes. Use them to:

- Store crayons, pencils, and other items that can easily go astray.

- Stash trash that collects en route (tape a bag to the back of one of the front seats so it's handy, and kids get accustomed to using it).

- Save leftovers when the kids refuse to eat.

- Serve snacks you can pull out when the crew starts whining, "I'm hungry."

- Sock away soiled garments until you have a chance to launder them.

Backseat snack tray

Little appetites always seem to get bigger on car trips. This fun way to dish up snacks may be eggs-actly what you need to keep the kids satisfied. Thoroughly wash an empty Styrofoam egg carton with warm soapy water. After it dries, fill each compartment with a different treat—cheese cubes in one, breakfast cereal in another, M&Ms in another. When the gang in the back seat chimes in with a chorus of "I'm hungry," pass the carton around.

Delicious pre-trip prep

A great way to prepare your young travelers for the sights, smells, and tastes they'll experience on your family excursion is to have a living room picnic with foods that are indigenous to your destination. While your intrepid kids are eating, take the opportunity to educate them on the history of the location, its geography, and other interesting facts that they'll retain once they get where they're going!

Crafty Diversions

"Mine!" "No, *mine!*" scream the kids from the backseat when they're not robotically asking, "Are we there yet?" Junior road warriors inevitably get bored and restless, but less so if you keep those little hands busy with a travel activity kit they help create. Before leaving home, have your kids decorate a paper bag or shoebox of a size that won't take up too much space in the car or on a plane, then pack it with materials for activities kids can do on the move. Use your imagination, but consider bringing along:

- Coloring books and crayons
- A blank book for writing
- Stickers
- Colored pipe cleaners
- Plastic safety scissors
- Colored construction paper
- Transparent tape
- Roll-on glue or glue sticks

Spray-bottle play

On a hot summer's day, a simple spray bottle can be a godsend for young travelers—and their parents, too. Recycle a couple of spray bottles from the laundry or cleaning closet, clean them well, fill them with water, and keep them on hand. Use them to:

- Spritz the kids for a cool-down while sitting on a beach, hiking, or hitting the hot city sidewalks. Turn the spray in your direction, too.

- Dress the kids in their swimsuits and set them loose in a park or other public outdoor spot with a couple of spray bottles. Drenching one another with parental approval might be the highlight of your children's trip.

Outdoor Survival

Scrounge around for old film canisters

If you still use a film camera, horde your film canisters for use when hiking or camping out. These convenient, waterproof containers with their snap-on, leakproof lids are great for storing matches, small batteries, or other small items that could leave you high and dry or in danger if they become wet and unusable. If you've made the switch to a digital camera and don't have easy access to film canisters, use old pill bottles instead.

Zap sap with butter

Sticky tree sap is one of the more harmless hazards you'll encounter in the wild, but that hardly means it isn't really annoying to find sap on your skin. To get rid of it, just open your cooler, take out some butter or margarine, rub a little into the sap wherever it happens to be, and wash the area with soap and water. This gentle treatment will not only be easy on your skin but has another application for campers: It will waterproof tent canvas and other outdoor equipment fabrics.

The Compass on Your Wrist

A compass is the standard tool for guiding your way in the wild, but you don't always have one at hand. And that's a bit of a pain when you want to find your way out of the wilderness before a bear or bobcat finds *you*. Luckily, your wristwatch and the sun can come to your rescue, so hope to high heaven it's not cloudy, and then use them to get your bearings. Here's how:

1. Point your watch so that the hour hand faces the direction of the sun.

2. Find the midpoint of the smallest section on the watch face between the hour hand and 12 o'clock—and you've found due south.

An example: If it's four o'clock, due south is midway between the four and the 12, at the two; if it's 10 o'clock, due south is midway between the 10 and the 12, at the 11.

When daylight savings time is in effect, add an hour. So, if it's four o'clock, point the five at the sun, and you'll see that the midpoint between the two and the three points due south.

A nifty tin-can fire starter

It's cheaper and more eco-friendly to start a campfire without lighter fluid. Instead, try building a fire with this homespun, fluidless charcoal starter.

Cut both ends off an old one-gallon can. Punch several holes near the bottom of the can, then punch two holes near the top and insert a length of coat hanger wire through them to form a handle. When it comes time to start a fire, set the can in the fire pit, place a piece of crumpled newspaper in the bottom, and lay briquettes on top of the newspaper. Light the paper through the holes punched at the bottom. When the briquettes are glowing, lift the can away with the wire handle—which will be hot as blazes, so be sure to wear gloves or use tongs when grabbing it.

Tin-can candleholder

Don't curse the darkness. Instead, make a reflective candleholder. When opening a large can of cat food or tuna, be sure to keep the lid partially attached. Once Felix has made meals of the contents, wash out the can and bend back the lid so it faces straight up. Put a candle inside and then place the can so the lid blocks the wind. The candle will burn steadily—and seem all the brighter because the lid will reflect the light.

Great (cotton) balls o' fire

Nothing's more frustrating than trying to start a fire when the wood is damp and won't ignite, so here's a trick to warm an outdoor enthusiast's heart. Pack a dozen or so cotton balls heavily saturated with petroleum jelly in a plastic bag. When a fire just won't get going, place several of the balls among the paper scraps and kindling and light them. Then get those marshmallows ready, since the petroleum jelly usually burns long enough to get even the most reluctant campfire blazing.

Repurpose breath-mint tins

Once you've finished your breath mints, save the tin for your next outdoor outing. A tin with a tight lid is great weatherproof carryall for:

- Fishing hooks and artificial flies
- Matches
- Aspirin
- Packets of sugar and artificial sweeteners
- Safety pins
- Loose change and keys you don't want to carry in your pockets while fishing, hiking, or doing other outdoor activities.

Floss it in the wild

Your dentist will applaud you for flossing when you're roughing it, and floss is useful for many other purposes around the campground as well. Such as:

- **Hanging stuff** Floss is so strong you can use it to hang a small lantern, shaving mirror, and other gear from a branch.

- **Repairing canvas gear** Floss is slender enough to thread through the eye of a needle, yet sturdy enough to hold canvas in place, making it ideal for mending tents, backpacks, and tarps.

- **Cutting and slicing food** Hold a piece of floss taut and slice your way through cheese, cake, and other soft foods.

What's the Story?
Mr. Nelson's Backpack

In the spring of 1920, Lloyd Nelson, inventor of the modern backpack, set off to explore the Alaska wilderness for oil. After an Indian lent him a sealskin pouch stretched across willow sticks strapped to the back, Nelson decided his fortune might lie instead in designing a pack that could be carried over the shoulders for support and comfort. Soon he was sitting in his basement in Bremerton, Washington, sewing together canvas packs and mounting them on wooden boards.

Before too long, forest rangers and Boy Scouts were toting what was then known as Trapper Nelson's Indian Pack Boards. In the 1960s backpacks began showing up in college bookstores, where they were an instant and enduring hit with students setting off to explore the world.

Shampoo to the rescue

Though shampoo may seem like a luxury item when camping, it's well worth putting some into a small plastic container you can easily fit into a backpack or bag. Not only will you keep your locks squeaky clean, but you can also use shampoo to:

- Lubricate a tent zipper

- Remove sap and other sticky stuff from your hands

- Stand in for shaving cream when you decide to get rid of wild-man stubble.

Vinegar at your campsite

Vinegar adds some zest to your campsite meals, of course, but it also:

- **Repels gnats and mosquitoes** Just dab some white vinegar on your exposed skin.

- **Traps flies and mosquitoes** Pour some apple cider vinegar into a container and place it on the picnic table, in the camp kitchen, or anywhere else these pests tend to congregate.

- **Helps kill bacteria in water** Add a few drops of apple cider vinegar to your water bottle or canteen.

Wave bye to beach sand

You'll probably come home from a day at the beach with an unwanted souvenir: plenty of sand in the car, in your shoes, on your clothes, and even around the house. Leave the sand where it belongs—on the beach—by bringing along a plastic bag you've partially filled with baby powder. When you're ready to call it a day, dip your feet and hands into the soft white stuff, and then dust more powder over the rest of your body. When you brush the baby powder off, the sand will go with it.

The Many Merits of a Walking Stick

The humble piece of gear known as the walking stick is easy to come by and needn't cost you a penny. It can also make you feel like, oh, the lord of the manor moseying about his estate or one of those stalwarts who hike the entirety of the Appalachian Trail.

How to obtain one? Just find a suitable piece of wood that's not too heavy, easy to hold on to, and, so that it won't be unwieldy, no taller than you are—a broomstick, a fallen branch, a dowel, or a piece of thick molding. If you want to get fancy, carve convenient hand grips in the stick and sand the wood down and varnish it. Or visit your local vintage shop and walk away in style.

Among the stick's many merits are these:

A stick helps you keep your balance when you're out walking, especially when you cross streams and rocky terrain.

It reduces stress on your knees, legs, hips, and back as you climb uphill.

It's a handy poking-stick for checking crevices, ledges, tall grass, and underbrush for snakes and other creepy-crawly creatures.

The stick needn't sit idle when you aren't walking. You can use it to lean against when you want to stop and enjoy the scenery; as a pole to hold up a tent or tarp; and as a prop to keep a heavy backpack from falling over when you set it down.

Creature Comforts in the Wild

Take a drop cloth along

Been spending your spare time painting the house and doing other messy home repairs? Finally getting a chance to go camping? Well, leave the work behind but do bring some of the painter's drop cloths you used to protect floors and furniture. Choose one that more or less matches the dimensions of your tent floor and pitch the tent on top of it. The drop cloth will prevent dampness from seeping in and keep the tent cleaner in the bargain.

You might want to bring another drop cloth (a new plastic one—they're cheap!) to use as a tablecloth; campsite tables are often covered with pitch, sap, bird droppings, and other unappetizing debris.

Pill-bottle salt and pepper shakers

No need to eat bland food just because you're roughing it. Pour salt, pepper, and any other spices you like into separate small screw-cap pill bottles and label them with an indelible marker—preferably on a piece of masking tape so you'll be able to reuse them. Because these containers are airtight, moisture won't cause the contents to dampen and congeal. For a taste of the comfort of home, take two lids from another set of pill bottles and punch small holes in them with an ice pick. When you set the camp table, put one of the holey lids on the salt and the other on the pepper, and then shake away to suit your taste. Be sure to replace the solid caps at the end of the meal to keep moisture at bay.

Staying Clean in the Wild

The great outdoors smells great, but *you* won't smell so good after a few days of roughing it. Here are some ways to clean up in comfort:

Wash up with sun-warmed water Fill a large plastic bottle with water and leave it in the sun; after a few hours you'll have warm water for a soothing sponge bath.

Bathe in a wading pool For a bit of luxury, pack a small inflatable wading pool. Find a sunny spot, inflate the pool, fill it with water, wait a while for the sun to do its job, then step into your warm bath.

Shower with a holey bucket Poke sieve-like holes in the bottom of a plastic bucket, then stack it inside a larger (and solid) plastic bucket. When it's time for a shower, hang the bucket with the holes from a branch and fill the bucket without holes with warm water. Stand beneath the hanging bucket, pour warm water into it, and enjoy the brief sensation of warm water rushing over you.

Save those plastic bottles!

Before you pitch plastic bottles into the recycling bin, consider the ways you can put them to good use on camping trips and picnics. When you're in the great outdoors, you can use a plastic bottle to:

- **Make a bowl** Cut off the bottom portion to make a bowl of any depth you want;

keep your sleeping bag
smelling fresh with a
bar of soap!

you might want to sandpaper the edges to make them less rough.

- **Dispose of liquids** Pack out used cooking oils and other liquid trash.

- **Create an ice pack** Fill a bottle with water, freeze it, and use it to keep a cooler cold. Or put it in a backpack to keep food cool on a day hike.

- **Serve as a makeshift latrine** Keep it just outside the tent so you don't have to wander into the woods in the dark. (This works at least for the males in the family.)

And those plastic tubs, too!

Dig into your plastic butter or yogurt container supply the next time you go hiking or camping for many practical outdoor uses. Plastic containers make it easy to:

- **Snare stingers** To keep bees and wasps from invading your outdoor meals, fill a container with water, add a little sugar, poke a hole in the lid, and place this sweet trap off to one side of your dining area. The pests will fly in but won't be able to fly out.

- **Feed Fido** Fill a container with kibbles so the dog's dinner is ready when he's hungry, and use a second container for water.

- **Block ants** Fill four plastic containers with water and put one under each leg of a table. Ants won't be able to get through your makeshift moat and crawl up the table legs to ruin your picnic.

Freshen sleeping bags with soap

Sleeping bags tend to become a bit musty after a couple of uses, but you can freshen a bag by putting a bar of soap or a fabric softener sheet inside. Do it after you crawl out of the sleeping bag each morning, then zip the bag shut. The next time you slip in, remove the bag freshener and put it aside to use again, then drift off into sweet-smelling dreams.

Bubble-wrap mattress

Pack a 6-foot length of bubble wrap and lay it under your bag before you crawl in. Those air pockets are not only soft, they'll also protect your sleeping bag from dampness.

Hula-hoop privacy protector

Maybe it's happened to you—you head out to get away from it all with a group of like-minded outdoor enthusiasts, only to find yourself in a crowd and yearning for a little privacy. If you have a hula hoop, some rope or twine, an old shower curtain or table cloth, and a few large metal binder clips, bring them along—to build your own portable cubicle that's great for changing, washing up, even showering under a bucket (see "Staying Clean in the Wild," on page 264). Suspend the hula hoop from a branch with the rope or twine. Drape the shower curtain or tablecloth over the hula hoop, fastening the material on the hoop with binder clips or any other fasteners you might have. While your creation probably won't be a thing of beauty, you'll welcome the chance to disappear inside it whenever modesty is in order.

A bug-shooing hanky

Fabric softener sheets aren't as cool-looking as a lot of outdoor gear, but you'll be glad to have some along when mosquitoes start swarming around the campsite. Just pin or tie one to your clothing to keep the pests away.

Foil dampness and grime

For a little extra campsite comfort, take some aluminum foil from the kitchen when packing your gear. Here are three ways to use it:

- Wrap your matches in aluminum foil to protect them from moisture.

- Lay a large piece of foil under your sleeping bag to prevent dampness from seeping in.

What's the Story?

The Amazing Swiss Army Knife

It's hard to imagine a piece of travel gear handier than a Swiss Army Knife. Depending on the style, this pocket-sized gadget might contain, in addition to a couple of blades, a ballpoint pen, bottle opener, file, magnifying glass, nail file, pliers, saw, scissors, toothpick, tweezers, and often lots more. Some recent models are even equipped with USB flash drives, digital clocks, and laser pointers.

The first Swiss Army Knife was introduced to the Swiss Army in 1891 and was a relatively simple implement: a pocket knife with a wooden handle that contained a blade, a screwdriver, a can opener, and a punch; an improved version with an extra blade, a corkscrew, and a special spring mechanism appeared in 1896. In Switzerland, the device was known as Offiziersmesser (officer's knife)—too much for U.S. soldiers to pronounce when they became familiar with the knife during World War II and dubbed it "the Swiss Army Knife."

By the way, there are two Swiss Army Knives: the Genuine Swiss Army Knife and the Original Swiss Army Knife. That's because the Swiss government once allowed two companies—Wenger and Victorinox—to produce them. In 2005, Victorinox acquired Wenger, and a year later produced a knife with 85 devices and 110 functions: The Giant, a nearly 9-inch-wide collector's item that costs around $1,200.

- Wad some foil into a ball to use as a scouring pad. Foil is great for scraping off barbecue-grill grime and blackened residue from the bottom of pans you set over an open fire.

Traveler's Rx

Balloon therapy

Balloons lift your spirits, and they can be good for the body, too. Pack a durable, uninflated balloon in your traveling medicine kit and use it to make a cold or hot pack to soothe a sprain or muscle soreness. Just fill the balloon with very cold water or very hot water and lay it over the afflicted area. If you have a freezer and want to go all out, make an ice pack by freezing a water-filled balloon.

Chest rub for barking dogs

If a day of sightseeing leaves you with pleasant memories but sore feet, rub a little medicated chest rub on your feet before going to bed (put on a pair of socks to keep the rub from marring the sheets). Your feet will feel like new in the morning.

Presoaked bug repellents

You never know when bug spray might come in handy, but cans and bottles can take up a lot of room in your portable medicine kit. Here's a way to leave those bulky containers behind: Before leaving home, soak cotton balls in repellant and store them in a self-sealing plastic bag. When pests make an appearance, just pull out a cotton ball and dab some of the defensive liquid on your skin.

Pill-bottle toothbrush protector

Ever opened your travel kit to find your toothbrush soaked in shaving cream? An easy and tidy way to keep up with dental hygiene on the road is to make a toothbrush holder kit out of an old plastic prescription drug bottle. Cut a slit in the lid and slide the lid over the handle of

Baking Soda: Don't Leave Home Without It!

You might not devote much time to thinking about the marvels of baking soda, but throw a plastic container into your suitcase and you'll be surprised at how often you reach for it. Use baking soda to:

Treat burns Add 1 tablespoon baking soda to 1 cup cold water, dip a cloth in the solution, and lay the wet cloth on the burned area until it no longer feels hot.

Take the itch out of poison ivy Apply a paste made from 3 teaspoons baking soda and 1 teaspoon water to the rash.

Take the sting out of a bee sting Apply a paste made from 1 teaspoon baking soda and 1 teaspoon of water and let it dry.

Brush your teeth and gargle Dip a wet toothbrush in a small amount and brush as you normally would. Finish your dental hygiene routine by mixing 1 teaspoon of baking soda with ½ cup water and then gargling the solution.

Soothe sore feet Fill a receptacle—say, a tub, wastepaper basket, or large ice bucket—with about a quart of warm water, add 1 tablespoon baking soda, and soak your tired tootsies until the water cools.

your toothbrush; then replace the lid so the bristles of the toothbrush are inside the container, where they'll remain clean.

Chapter Eleven

Hints for Home Gardeners

The typical family throws out a surprisingly large amount of food. But what's unfit for you to eat may very well be the perfect food for your plants! It turns out that many kitchen staples can either be composted into the perfect plant food or can be fed to plants as is.

And that's just the start. Your cupboards are *filled* with natural, nontoxic gardening aids, from bananas and bath soap to peanut butter and pine needles. Not only will using them save you time and money, but you'll officially join the ranks of "green" gardeners who switch away from factory-made, often-toxic fertilizers, pesticides, and weed killers.

Gardening creatively with what you already own is a rewarding endeavor—a money-saving, eco-friendly approach to one of our favorite hobbies. So whatever color your thumb is, get out in the yard and get growing!

Start your garden by
growing seeds in
paper cups!

Starting Seeds, Rooting Cuttings

Make seed holes with chopsticks

Instead of buying a dibbler—the wooden garden tool used to poke seed holes in the soil—why not use a chopstick or pencil? Same holes, no cash outlay. A third choice: A full-size folding nail clipper, the blunt arm of which you can poke into the soil and twist. Later, when it comes time to transplant seedlings, use the same arm of the file to work a seedling and its root ball from the seed flat.

No dibbling (or watering) required

An alternative to dibbling holes into the soil of a seed flat is to wet the soil, lay the seeds on the surface, and then cover the seeds with another thin layer of soil. Shrink-wrap the flat with plastic wrap, and your job is done. Condensation on the wrap will drip down to keep the seeds moist until germination.

Spice jars as seed sowers

When sowing seeds directly into a garden plot, put them in an empty dried herb or spice jar—the kind with a perforated plastic top. Then shake them over the bed or along a row. This improvised sower works best for medium-sized seeds.

Sowing tiny seeds

Seeds of impatiens, lobelia, carrots, lettuce, and a few other flowers and vegetables are so miniscule that they're difficult to sow evenly. To remedy the problem and make seedlings easier to thin out once they sprout, combine the seeds with grainy foodstuffs like semolina, couscous,

Keep It Clean

Dirty gardening equipment can carry molds, plant diseases, even bugs. So don't underestimate the need to sanitize clippers and pots when rooting or otherwise propagating plants. Guard against plant disease with this two-step washing:

1. Scrub any pre-used propagation equipment with a brush dipped in mild dishwashing liquid.
2. Fill a big galvanized washtub or your bathtub with a solution of 1 part household bleach to 9 parts water. Then submerge containers or tools for about 5 minutes.

Once they're completely dry, your germ-free, spore-free implements are ready for their respective jobs.

grits, or dried herbs, all of which will put some space between diminutive seeds.

Easy-free-sey plant markers

To label your seeds flat by flat so you won't risk confusing, say, your Better Boy tomatoes with your Early Girls, turn empty yogurt cups, bleach jugs, or other white plastic containers into plant markers. Cut strips from the plastic, trim the ends to a point, and use an indelible felt-tip marker to write the plant name (variety included) on each. Stick the strips into the flats as soon as you plant seeds so you'll know which plant is which from the start.

Transport cuttings to a friend's house in a *sliced potato!*

Paper cup seed starters

Small paper drinking cups—the kind dispensed at water coolers—make excellent seed starters. They're the right size, you can easily poke a drainage hole in the bottom, and they're easily cut apart when it comes time to plant your seedlings. Note that we specify *paper* cups: Plastic-foam cups might sit in your local landfill until your great-great-grandchildren have come and gone.

Dry-cleaning bag humidifier

To provide the humidity needed to root a flat of cuttings, lay a dry cleaning bag over the cuttings, making sure it doesn't touch the plants. (Ice cream sticks or pencils can serve as "tent poles.") Clip the bag to the rim of the flat with clothespins or small metal clamps.

Root rose cuttings under glass

An easy way to root a cutting from your favorite rosebush is to snip off a 4–6-inch piece of stem and plant it in good soil, whether in the garden or a pot. Then cover it with a large fruit jar to create a mini-greenhouse.

Willow tea rooting preparation

Soaking six or eight willow twigs in water gives you a solution of indolebutyric acid (IBA), a natural plant-rooting hormone. Start by snipping the twigs from a willow (any species will do), then split them with a few hammer blows. Cut the twigs into 3-inch pieces and steep them in a pail filled with 4–5 inches of water for 24 hours. Use the tea either to water just-planted cuttings or as an overnight soaker for cuttings.

A rolling seed flat

Turn a child's wagon into a seed flat on wheels. Poke holes in the wagon bottom with a screw-hole punch and hammer, then fill the wagon with peat pots or expandable peat pellets, labeling them as you go.

Potatoes as transporters

If you need to take cuttings to another town, use a potato as a carrier. Slice a large potato in half crosswise, poke three 1-inch deep holes in each cut side with a chopstick or pencil, and insert the cuttings, which will stay moist for 3–4 hours.

Caring for Trees and Shrubs

Papery protection for young trees

If you've put out tree seedlings that look a bit spindly, wrap the trunks in newspaper pages to protect them from the elements. Secure this newsprint sleeve with double-knotted dental floss or twine.

Lichens: Love 'em or hate 'em?

Lichens are the ruffled, funguslike organisms that grow on stones, brick walls, and tree trunks. Many gardeners love the natural look lichens lend to trees—but if you don't count yourself among them, here's a simple way to make lichens disappear: Scrub them with a stiff brush dipped in a solution of 2 tablespoons household bleach and 1 quart water. Just make sure none of the runoff comes into contact with your garden plants.

A warm sleeve for tree rose grafts

Tree roses, also called standard roses, are really just regular rosebushes grafted onto long rootstock trunks. To protect the graft over the winter, cut the sleeve off an old sweater or sweatshirt. Prune back the bush's top growth in late fall so you'll be able to slip the sleeve over the branches and around the graft scar. Stuff the sleeve with dry leaves, peat moss, or straw for insulation, then tie a plastic bag over it for protection from snow and ice. When you remove the sleeve come spring, your tree rose will grow more vigorously.

Speed rose-blooming with foil

In late May or early June, place sheets of aluminum foil on the ground beneath your rosebushes and anchor the foil with stones. Sunlight reflecting off the foil will quicken blooming, whether your roses are hybrid teas, floribundas, or climbers.

Feed bananas to roses

Most gardeners know that banana peels make a good fertilizer for tomatoes, peppers, and their solanaceous cousins, but roses love them too. Chop banana peels (three max) into small pieces

SOAP YOUR SAW

When trimming tree branches or shrubbery with a garden saw, run the blade through a bar of **antibacterial soap**. The soap will not only give the blade more glide but will help reduce a branch's wound-threatening bacterium population as well.

and dig them into the soil beneath a rosebush. The peels provide 3.25 percent phosphorus and more than 10 times that amount of potassium, spurring sturdier stems and prettier blooms.

A grassy boost for azaleas

After mowing your lawn, lay some of the grass clippings out to dry. Then spread a thin layer of clippings around the base of azalea plants. As the grass decays it leaches nitrogen into the soil, supplementing regular feedings. Many gardeners find this "something extra" speeds the growth of azaleas and darkens the leaves. Be careful, though: Piling grass clippings too thickly may make them slimy and, in turn, expose the plant's stems to disease.

Cola and tea for gardenias

Occasionally watering a gardenia bush with your favorite cola will increase the acidity of the soil, while the sugar will feed microorganisms and help organic matter to break down. And tea? Place tea bags around the base of a gardenia and cover them with mulch. Whenever you water the plant, the ascorbic acid, manganese, and potassium present in tea leaves will trickle down to the shrub's hungry roots.

Sappy post-job cleanup

Taking saw or shear to tree branches usually leaves stubborn sap on the tool. Use a clean cloth to rub any of the following substances onto the blade(s), and say "so long" to sap:

- Nail polish remover
- Baby oil
- Aerosol cooking spray
- Suntan oil
- Peanut butter
- Vegetable shortening

Lubricate pruning shears

Rubbing petroleum jelly or spraying WD-40 on the pivot joint of your shears will have you snipping away at shrubs so smoothly you'll feel like a pruning pro.

Growing Annuals, Perennials, and Bulbs

A seed-starting secret

You've just sown flower seeds in a planting bed and are pleased with the spacing and soil coverage. But did you know that one extra step will warm the soil and speed germination, keep the earth moist, and thwart birds foraging for seeds? It will—and all it takes is spreading a layer of clear plastic wrap over the seeded area. Anchor the plastic with rocks and remove it as soon as the seeds sprout.

A salt flowers crave

Epsom salt is magnesium sulfate—which, as a supplement to your plants' regular feedings, will deepen the color of blooms and help fight disease. Every three or four weeks, scratch 1 teaspoon Epsom salt into the soil around an annual or perennial's stem and water well. Alternatively, dissolve 1 tablespoon Epsom salt in 1 gallon water. Every two weeks or so, pour some of the solution into a spray bottle and spritz the leaves of your flowers.

Prop up tall perennials

Peonies, delphiniums, and gladiolus are among the tall perennials that generally need support. A wooden stake is the usual answer, but a less obtrusive option is an old lampshade frame. Place the metal frame, narrow side down, amid seedlings when they're about 6 inches tall, working the frame into the soil to a depth of about half an inch. As the seedlings grow, tie them loosely to the top of the frame with twist ties. The leaves will obscure the frame as the blooms above stand tall.

Bromeliads like fruit

To encourage a potted bromeliad's rosette of leaves to sprout its pretty flower, place the plant in a plastic dry cleaning bag with a ripening banana or three or four ripe apples. The ethylene wafting from the fruit will stimulate flower production.

Splints for bent stems

If any of your flower stems are bent, pick one of these common items to use as a splint: For thin stems, a toothpick or cotton swab; for thicker stems, a drinking straw, pencil, ballpoint pen, or ice cream stick. Affix splints to stems with transparent tape, but not too tightly.

Ties for stakes

Panty hose "ropes" have long been used to tie snapdragons, hollyhocks, tomatoes, and other tall flowers and viney vegetables to stakes (they're soft and pliable), but panty hose is hardly the only household item that will serve the purpose. Try these ties:

- Gift-wrapping ribbon left over from birthday parties
- Broken cassette tapes
- Plastic interlocking trash bag ties
- Dental floss (tape size)
- Velcro strips
- Fabric strips cut from old sheets
- Yarn from your knitting basket

Dry Flowers with Cat Litter

All you need to dry those roses, cornflowers, or peonies you're so proud of is cat litter, a microwave oven, and a deep microwave-safe bowl. How to? Read on.

Drying flower heads

Pick the flowers when they're dry (no dew or raindrops) and snip off the flower heads. Pour 4–5 cups litter into the bowl and scoop out space for one or two flowers at most. Nestle the flowers into the litter and gently spoon on more until they're covered. Microwave on high for 2 minutes and then let the litter cool completely—not so much because it's hot to the touch but because the drying continues at this point. Once you remove the dried flower head(s), blow off any dust or brush it away with a small paintbrush.

Drying long-stemmed flowers

To dry snapdragons, statice, or other long-stemmed flowers for dried arrangements, pour cat litter into an airtight container large enough to accommodate the stems. Arrange the flowers on top so that there's a little space between them, then cap the container. After 7–10 days, your flowers should be dried and ready to display.

Flowerdome

Get creative and use an old umbrella—stripped of both its handle and fabric—as a frame for a flowering climber or vine. In your spot of choice, drive a 5-foot metal pipe wide enough to accommodate the handle into the ground about a foot deep, then slide the umbrella stem inside. Plant seedlings of morning glory, trumpet creeper, or any other thin-stemmed flowering vine next to the pipe. Over the next few weeks a unique garden focal point will take shape.

Scrape some soap

If your garden gloves have gone missing but you need to work in the soil of your flower beds post haste, just scrape your fingernails over a bar of soap beforehand. The dirt will come out from under your nails more easily when you scrub your hands.

Bag bulbs to prevent rot

Brown paper grocery bags filled with sawdust or peat moss are the easy answer to winter storage of tender crocus, tulip, daffodil, iris, and other bulbs and rhizomes. Put a 2-inch layer of sawdust or peat in the bottom of the bag, and then arrange bulbs of the same type on top, making sure they don't touch. Continue layering the bulbs and organic material until the bag is about three-quarters full. Clip the bag closed with clothespins or metal clamps, and use a marker to label each bag with the name of the bulbs therein.

Plastic bulb protectors

To keep rodents from nibbling on newly transplanted bulbs, seal bulbs off in wide-top plastic containers. Before planting, punch drainage holes in the bottom and sides of a large plastic jug or carton (think laundry bleach with the top cut off or economy-size yogurt), bury it in the soil up to the open top, and fill it with soil and humus. Plant two or three small bulbs in the container or one or two larger bulbs.

Old plastic storage boxes are more space efficient—and who knows what kinds of potential bulb protectors you might find if you go rummaging through your basement or attic?

Flavor food with scented geraniums

Scented geraniums (*Pelargonium* cultivars) have edible leaves that release a fragrance when rubbed. Among the varieties to grow in pots (or in warmer climes, flower beds) are those with the aroma of rose, lemon, apple, apricot, mint, cinnamon, ginger, or nutmeg. Foods benefiting from the addition of finely chopped scented geranium leaves include fruit compotes, cookies, cakes, and poached pears.

Flowers You Can Eat

Eating flowers is nothing new. In fact, it dates from the days of the Roman Empire and ebbed in popularity only after the Victorian age. Edible flowers are enjoying a revival, and you can join the trend by putting some of the cut flowers from your garden not only in a vase but also on serving platters and dinner plates.

A warning: *Never* use flowers that have been sprayed with pesticide of any sort. Also avoid such toxic plants as azaleas, bleeding hearts, crocuses, chrysanthemums, daffodils, hydrangeas, lilies-of-the-valley, oleanders, rhododendrons, and sweet peas.

Bee balm These red flowers, said to taste like oregano with a hint of mint, are most often used in fruit dishes and leafy green salads.

Calendulas The golden-orange calendula, a marigold cousin, resembles saffron in taste. Sprinkle petals on pasta and rice dishes.

Dandelions Dandelion flowers should be eaten only when very young and just-picked; try the honeylike petals as a garnish for rice dishes. The leaves are a great addition to salads, but be aware that dandelions grown in a flower bed are tastier than those that pop up on the lawn.

Johnny-jump-ups The mild wintergreen flavor of these flowers is a refreshing complement to salads and soft cheeses.

Nasturtiums Nasturtium blossoms have a sweet-and-spicy taste reminiscent of watercress, and the leaves add a peppery tang to salads.

Sage blossoms Sage flowers have a subtler taste than the sage-leaf kitchen herb and add a nice touch to bean, corn, and mushroom dishes.

Roses Use larger petals to sprinkle on desserts or salads, smaller petals as a garnish. Rose petals are also used to make syrups and jellies.

Squash blossoms Fried squash blossoms are an Italian specialty beloved the world over. A typical recipe calls for dipping the blossoms in beaten egg white, then in bread crumbs and grated Parmesan cheese before frying.

Houseplant Hint-o-Rama

Free houseplants!

Every time you eat an avocado, save the pit and grow a houseplant. Just scrub the pit clean and insert three sturdy toothpicks into it just above the base. Fill a drinking glass with water and set the toothpicked pit on the rim. Change the water often and top it off as necessary.

After several weeks, the pit will sprout a shoot and roots, at which point you can pot your fledgling houseplant. Keep the pot in a sunny window and pinch off appropriate new shoots to make the plant bushier. Pinching off the shoot of the central stem after the stem grows about 6 inches tall will result in an even fuller plant.

Coffee filter soil guard

When potting plants in flowerpots, put a small coffee filter in the bottom of the pot first, then add drainage material and soil. This way, excess water will leak out of the drainage hole while the soil stays put.

Cleaning fuzzy or corrugated leaves

Smooth-leaved houseplants can be cleaned by wiping with a damp paper towel, but fuzzy or corrugated leaves require special care.

- **Brush dust away** An effective way to clean African violets, bertolonias, and other fuzzy-leaved houseplants is with a soft-bristled toothbrush, a paintbrush, or a pipe cleaner. Brush gently from the base of each leaf toward the tip.

- **Breeze dust away** Dust plants with corrugated leaves, like peperomias, with a hairdryer. Set the appliance on cool or low and blow air on every leaf.

The cloth glove trick

Wearing an old cloth glove lets you clean houseplant leaves in half the time. Just run each leaf through your gloved fingers from bottom to top, and presto! You've dusted both sides.

Go one size larger

To prevent houseplants from becoming rootbound (and dying quickly), replant them in a container larger than the one they originally come in. Add extra dirt, and your plants will grow faster and live twice as long.

A when-to-water pencil gauge

Houseplant manuals tell you to water whenever the soil dries out, but determining dryness is easier said than done. Not so with a pencil. Push a pencil deeply into the soil and then pull it out. If bits of dirt cling to the bare wood point, the soil is still moist. If the pencil comes up clean, it's time to water your houseplant.

Water with ice cubes

Place ice cubes atop the soil of potted plants, making sure they don't touch the stem. The ice will melt slowly, releasing water gradually and evenly into the soil.

Pot within pot

Use a stockpot, Dutch oven, or large saucepan to water cacti and succulents. Just pour a few inches of water into the pot, put in the houseplant, and leave it there until no more air bubbles come to the water's surface. Drain the plant well before putting it on a saucer. Other houseplants that benefit from the pot-in-a-pot method include anthuriums and grassy-leaved sweet flag (*Acorus gramineus*).

Going Away for Awhile?

When you leave home for a few days, you needn't ask a neighbor to water your houseplants. Try one of these three methods.

1

Plastic bottle/Paper towel waterer

Slice the bottom off a 2-liter plastic soda bottle and stuff three paper towels into it up to the neck. Turn the bottle upside down and stick the neck into the soil of a houseplant you've just watered. For support, insert a chopstick alongside the bottle and fit two rubber bands around the items. Right before you leave home, fill the bottle with water, which will trickle through the towels and into the soil for about a week.

2

Plastic bag greenhouse

A large plastic bag can become a greenhouse for small houseplants like African violets. Water the plant well and let it drain. Spread a layer of peat moss on the bottom of the bag, then place the plant on top (the peat will absorb excess moisture). Tie the bag loosely with a twist tie, leaving a small gap for ventilation. When the bagged plant is placed in indirect light, the soil will stay moist for two weeks.

3

Bath towel soaker

Dampen a plush bath towel and spread it out in a sink or bathtub near a sunny window. Turn on the cold water tap just enough so that water drips slowly onto the towel. Arrange houseplants (sans saucers) on the towel, making sure the drain holes and towel are in contact. Leave the tap on while you're away, and the moisture in the towel will be drawn up by the plants' roots.

Smart Tricks for Better Vegetables

Sun boxes for veggie seedlings

When you're starting vegetables indoors near a normally sunny south-facing window but the early spring sun won't cooperate, maximize the rays with aluminum foil–lined sun boxes. Cut out one side of a cardboard box and line the three inner "walls" with foil. When you face the boxes toward the outside, sunlight will reflect back on your vegetable seedlings. Plants will not only catch more sun, but their stems will grow straight rather than bending toward the light.

Foil pesky cutworms

Before setting out a tomato, pepper, or eggplant seedling, wrap each stem with a 4-inch-square collar of aluminum foil, leaving it loose enough to allow the stem to grow as it expands. Plant the seedlings with 2 inches of foil above the soil and 2 inches below so that cutworms won't be able to penetrate the shiny armor.

Nighttime warmers

If you wake up to the weatherman's prediction of an unseasonably cold night, get outdoors as early as possible and flank your vegetable plants with something that will absorb the heat of the sun all day and radiate it at night. That "something" could be large, flat stones or those terra cotta tiles left over from your bathroom renovation. Another solution is to bend wire coat hangers into wickets, secure them over the plants, and drape them with black plastic trash bags for the night.

Safeguard your ears (of corn) with mineral oil

Are corn earworms and black beetles targeting your ripening ears of corn? Protect the ears by squirting mineral oil at the base of the silk, using a medicine dropper. Repeat the process every few days as the plant grows. The right timing is essential: Apply the oil only after the silks have begun to dry and turn brown; if you start earlier, less pollination will occur and the kernels won't develop properly.

What about those pesky birds looking for a fresh meal? Keep them from pecking ripening corn by enclosing the ears in paper bags and tying the bags closed with twine.

Secure trellis-grown melons with panty hose

If you grow your melons on a trellis, a sling made from panty hose will keep growing melons from falling to the ground. Cut off a hose leg, slip it over a melon, and tie the hose to the trellis.

Keep root vegetables straight with pipe

To prevent horseradish and heirloom varieties of carrots and parsnips from forking or getting bent out of shape, grow them in PVC pipe sections placed vertically in the ground and filled with rich soil and humus. When you harvest the roots in the fall, you'll be surprised how straight and thick they've grown.

Prevent melon rot with tile

Cantaloupes, honeydews, and other melons will eventually rot if they grow heavy enough to rest on the soil and are left to sit there. If you slip a large travertine tile or slate roof tile under a melon, the tile will absorb heat during the day and keep the melon cozy on cool evenings. No tiles on hand? Substitute a panel cut from a cardboard box.

Hang a bag of mothballs

Mothball haters include rodents and insects (duh!), so consider putting some of the smelly orbs in your vegetable garden. Just don't let them touch the soil, or the toxic chemicals mothballs contain (usually naphthalene or dichlorobenzene) could contaminate it. (If you think you can simply place mothballs on lids, tiles, or other flat surfaces to keep them off the ground, think again. In no time at all, wind and garden invaders will knock them off.) For safety's sake, put a few mothballs in small mesh bags and hang them from a cornstalk or a beanpole trellis.

Grow onions through newspaper

Here's some headline news: One of the easiest ways to grow healthy onions is through newspaper mulch. Why? Because onion stalks cast a very slim shadow at best, letting in the sunlight that will sprout weed seeds. A lights-out mat of newspapers will stop sprouters short.

In early spring, wet the soil of the onion patch. Then spread three or four sections of newspapers over the area, hosing down each one. With one or two fingers, punch holes about 5–6 inches apart through the wet mat and place an onion set within each. Firm moist soil around the sets and cover the mat with shredded leaves and grass clippings. Weeds won't stand a chance as your onions grow and thrive.

Household Superstar!
10 Garden Uses for Panty Hose

Among the many places panty hose have been used around the house are the yard and garden—with the following a mere selection.

1 Slip panty hose "caps" over unpicked produce to thwart birds, squirrels, and insects.

2 Tie plant stems and vines to stakes with panty hose, using a figure-eight loop.

3 Tie climbing roses to a trellis with panty hose—white hose for a white trellis, neutral-colored hose for natural wood.

4 Use panty hose as bags to hold human hair clippings or soap slivers, which when tied to stakes around the garden plot may repel deer.

5 Keep coiled garden hose from coming loose by tying it with panty hose.

6 Cover a watering can spout with panty hose when watering delicate flowers.

7 Store bulbs in panty hose in winter—different varieties in different legs, labeled.

8 Prevent soil loss in patio plants by laying a piece of panty hose over the drainage holes of pots.

9 Use as a tea bag for manure tea.

10 Use to strain liquid fertilizer (including manure tea), pesticide, or fungicide into a sprayer.

A tire tower for potatoes

Increase your potato yield by growing potatoes in a stack of tires. Fill a tire with soil and plant two whole or halved seed potatoes about 2 inches deep. Once the potatoes have sprouted 6–10 inches of foliage, place a second tire atop the first and fill with more soil, leaving 3–4 inches of foliage exposed.

Repeat the process again, and your three-tire tower will triple your potato crop. Potatoes sprout on the underground stems—and the taller the stems, the greater the number of tasty tubers.

Two sprays for pumpkins

Ward off fungus diseases in the pumpkin patch by spraying each pumpkin with this homemade mix: 1 teaspoon baking soda and ½ teaspoon corn oil stirred into 1 quart water.

Fungus diseases aside, some gardeners claim they can enrich a pumpkin's color with a different spray: aerosol whipped cream, applied around the base of each plant every three weeks.

Grow your own luffas

The luffa, or loofah, gourd (*Luffa cylindrica*) is a purely practical choice for gardeners: It's grown primarily for its dried pulp, which we know as the exfoliating beauty sponge of the same name. Just plant and cultivate luffas as directed on the seed packet—though if you live in a climate zone with a growing season shorter than seven months you'll need to start seeds indoors.

When a gourd lightens in weight and its skin begins to brown, peel it. Wet it thoroughly and squeeze out the seeds with both hands, then set the gourd on a rack to dry for two to four weeks, or until hard. (Placing gourds near a heating vent will speed the process.) Use a sharp knife to slice the dried luffa crosswise into rounds, and *ta-dah!*—homegrown skin scrubbers for the whole family.

Tomato-Tending Tips

Fertilize with banana peels

Grow stronger tomato plants by placing three or four banana peels in the bottom of each planting hole. (Note: No need to eat all the bananas at once! Freeze peels in freezer bags until you have enough to work with.) When you plant a tomato seedling, top the peels in the hole with a mixture of dry leaves, manure, and soil. Banana peels act as a kind of time-release fertilizer, leaching potassium and trace minerals into the soil.

A corny hot-climate moisturizer

Save corncobs and shucks to help tomatoes thrive in arid climates. Place 4–5 inches of corn waste at the bottom of each planting hole and cover with a layer of cow manure. Then refill the hole with soil as you plant the seedling, taking care not to mix the three layers. The spongy corn waste will conserve moisture for the roots on hot, dry days.

Tin foil root-cooler

On really hot days, lay sheets of aluminum foil around the base of your tomato plants, shiny side up, and anchor them with a few stones. The foil will reflect the sun's rays upward, reduce soil temperature by about 10 percent, and help keep the tomatoes' root zones from drying out.

An ornamental yet practical support

If you grow tidy determinate tomato plants, which grow only so big and then stop, consider painting a stepladder in bright colors and using it as an ornamental A-frame trellis. Plant one seedling 3–4 inches from each leg, then tie the

What's the Story?

The Tomato: Fruit or Vegetable?

You're probably aware that the tomato is technically a fruit, which botanists define as the reproductive body of a seed plant, usually having edible sweet pulp. (Actually, it's a berry, but we're not about to bore you with a botany lecture.) Yet for all intents and purposes, the tomato is a vegetable because of the way it's used: as a savory side dish, in green salads, and as a base for the red sauces bequeathed to the world by the Italians.

Indeed, in 1893 the United States Supreme Court declared the tomato a vegetable. Why? Because U.S. tomato growers claimed they were being hurt by a flood of tomatoes imported from Mexico and Cuba, and at the time fruits were not subject to tariffs. Vegetables *were* taxed, and the Court ruled that because the tomato is eaten with the main part of a meal rather than with dessert, it should legally be classified as a vegetable. With imported tomatoes now taxed, the U.S. tomato industry flourished as growers planted thousands of acres more of everyone's favorite fruit, um, we mean berry … oh yes, *vegetable*.

stems loosely to the ladder as they grow. As the plants mature, they'll be supported by the ladder's brackets and slats, and no ripening tomatoes will have to rest on the soil and risk rotting.

"Just a spoonful of sugar ... " makes what? Your tomatoes sweeter.

When your tomato fruits start to show color, add a spoonful of sugar to your watering can—especially when you've found a variety you like but that seems a bit too acidic. (That old-time tomato taste we all long for results from an optimum balance of acidity and sweetness.) Your tomatoes will not only be sweeter but juicier.

Prevent blossom end rot with Epsom salt

The bane of many a tomato grower, fruit-spoiling blossom end rot is often caused by a calcium deficiency. Stop the disease before it starts with this simple addition to your tomato bed: ½ cup Epsom salt poured into the bottom of each planting hole. Cover the salt with a thin layer of soil before putting in your seedlings.

Epsom salt is magnesium sulfate, which aids the transport of calcium to the tops of tomato plants and the fruit. As a bonus, Epsom salt helps the plants absorb phosphorus and sulfur.

Grow rooftop tomatoes in hay

Live in an urban apartment and have no place to grow tomatoes? If building regulations permit, haul a bale of hay up to the roof and you have a nitrogen-rich medium that heats up like a compost pile. (Plenty of big-city garden centers sell hay, especially in the fall.) Starting in very early spring, give the bale a daily hosing to activate the heating process. Once the bale decays into fertile compost (usually seven to eight weeks), it's cool enough for planting. Stand two stakes in the bale and nestle a tomato seedling into the hay next to each one. A daily watering will keep the plants growing well for the rest of the season.

PAINT YOUR SMALL TOOLS

To make small tools easier to spot when you're working in the tomato patch, **paint their handles** bright colors—say, fluorescent orange. This way, you won't waste time searching for the trowel you left under the sprawling Golden Jubilee tomato plant two rows away.

Secrets for Fruit Growers

Rake-it-up pine tree mulch

Money doesn't grow on trees. But if you're a blueberry grower, free mulch does—if you have pine trees in your yard. Naturally acidic pine needles will not only leach the acid blueberries crave into the soil but also will help protect the plants' shallow roots. Just rake up needles and spread them beneath the blueberry plants to a height of about 2 inches.

Aluminum peck-peck prevention

If you grow productive fruit trees and enjoy making fruit pies for friends and neighbors, don't throw away those aluminum pie plates! Use them to scare away blackbirds, starlings, and other fruit-loving birds. Poke a hole in the rim of each plate, thread a 2-foot piece of dental floss or string through the hole, and triple-knot it tightly. Hang a couple of plates on the branches of each fruit tree, and that's it. Shiny reflective objects swinging in the wind are more effective bird repellents than stationary plastic owls and scarecrows.

Toss thread, thwart birds

You don't always have to buy netting at the garden center to protect ripening cherries and other tree fruit from birds. Just buy two or three spools of black thread. Stand beside the tree, grab the loose end of the thread, and toss the spool over the tree to a helper. (If you're thinking this activity would be great for kids, you're right.) Continue tossing the spool back and forth until it is empty. The invisible thread won't seal birds off from the tree, but once they hit it a time or two they'll look for their ripe fruit lunch elsewhere.

The Value of Netting

Serious fruit growers will almost certainly need netting if they're to keep tree fruits and berries safe from birds, squirrels, and other pests. Available at garden centers and home stores, netting is usually made of nylon or polypropylene and comes in various dimensions and assorted mesh sizes, from about 1/8 inch to 2 inches.

Is there an around-the-house alternative to store-bought netting? Not really, unless you want to sew lots and lots of fishnet T-shirts or supermarket onion bags together. Or maybe you're in possession of a racy "peek-a-boo" mesh shower curtain, which at least is large enough to cover a couple of raspberry bushes.

Ant stick-ups

Ants won't be able to climb your fruit trees and have their way with ripe fruit if you wrap the trunks with one of these stick-'em-fast materials:

- Contact paper, folded in half with sticky-side out
- Two-sided transparent tape, wrapped around the trunk in a 3-inch-deep band
- Sheets of newspaper secured with masking tape and spritzed with an adhesive insect spray
- Cardboard sleeve taped shut and smeared with petroleum jelly

Cacti and Succulents, Point by Point

Cacti and succulents are some of the most popular houseplants because they're (mostly) very easy to care for.

An old hose for heavy lifting

If you live in cactus country, you may well landscape with large cacti.

Whenever you need to move a particularly heavy one for any reason, do not drag or roll it. Hold it by the roots, loop a 6-foot section of old garden hose underneath, and lift the cactus with both hands. Of course, you'll need a helper for the largest varieties, including saguaro and cardón cacti.

A gripping newspaper

Protect your fingers when repotting a spiny cactus by making a gripper, or pincer, from a couple of sheets of newspaper. Fold the sheets from top to bottom into a 3-inch paper band. Wrap the band around the middle of the cactus and grip the ends tightly. Then gently tug upward until the plant comes free of the pot.

Dust gently with a soft brush

Gentle is the way to go when dusting potted cacti, so brush them lightly with an old soft toothbrush or shaving brush. In summer, spray the plants lightly with water after brushing.

Rub out pests with alcohol

First, two diagnoses: 1) White wooly spots on your potted cactus or succulent mean mealybugs are doing their thing; 2) small beige or brown bumps on the plant's stems are actually scale insects. If you spy only a small number of either of these pests, kill them by wiping them up with a cotton swab soaked in rubbing alcohol. For heavier infestations, spray the plant with a solution of 1 cup water, 1 teaspoon corn oil, and 1 teaspoon dishwashing liquid.

Take out the sting with tape

Remove tiny cactus prickles from the fingers by firmly pressing adhesive tape on the affected area and then ripping it off. For larger or more stubborn prickles, resort to a pair of tweezers.

Pencil as pusher

Easily remove a small cactus or succulent from a pot by pushing a pencil into the drainage hole, eraser end first. As long as the soil is fairly dry, the root ball should emerge from the pot in one clump.

The All-Important Lawn

Lawn tonics

Some "my-grass-is-greener-than-yours" lawn growers achieve great success with homemade lawn tonics made from ordinary items. Add any of the following ingredients to the reservoir of a 10- or 20-gallon hose end sprayer and water your lawn with the mixture every three weeks or so. Adding 1 cup dishwashing liquid each time will help spread the solution more evenly and make it stick to blades of grass.

- A 12-ounce can of non-diet cola or beer. The sugar in both stimulates microbes that help to break up the soil.

- 1 cup corn syrup or molasses. See note on sugar, above.

- 1 cup household ammonia. Ammonia adds nitrates, the primary ingredient in most fertilizers.

- ½ cup mouthwash. The alcohol in mouthwash kills bacteria and spores and helps deter some pests.

Shoo off skunks and raccoons with camphor

These two furry pests like to raid your lawn at night for grubs, worms, and insects, especially after a rain. The evidence they leave behind? Little round holes. To make your lawn unattractive to the foragers, sprinkle the grass with camphor crystals—an all-natural alternative to toxic moth crystals.

Recycle that grass!

Take a cue from public parks and golf courses and "grasscycle" when you mow your lawn—which means leaving clippings on your lawn

The Lawn Alternative

Ground covers are the low-maintenance alternative to lawns, but don't think you can just plant them and forget them. All plants need watering and fertilizing, though not as often as a picture-perfect lawn. Here's where ground covers really come into their own:

- On hard-to-mow slopes or in tight spaces
- When you want a "natural" garden
- When you're an indifferent mower who's tired of hearing the neighbors complain about your unkempt lawn

English ivy and pachysandra are typical all-green ground covers, but you can also choose flowering vines or spreading plants like aubrieta, periwinkle (*Vinca* spp.), and sun rose (*Helianthemum* spp.).

when you finish. Just mow often enough to make sure no more than one-third of the length of the grass blades is lopped off each time. The resulting clippings serve as beneficial mulch and keeps yard waste out of community landfills.

Three temporary trunk protectors

If you have any fragile tree seedlings that would suffer if you accidentally rammed one with your mower, wrap them up before you mow. Wrap slender trunks in bubble wrap or several sheets of newspaper secured with masking tape or duct tape. An old towel pinned with two or three large safety pins will also work. All three wraps are a snap to put up and take down.

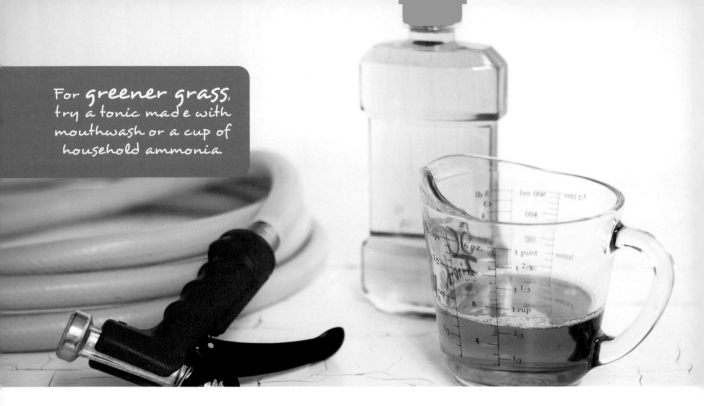

For **greener grass**, try a tonic made with mouthwash or a cup of household ammonia.

Oil your mower blades

Spraying lawnmower blades and the underside of the lawnmower housing with aerosol cooking oil or WD-40 will keep cut grass from building up in your mower, so whip out a can and spray away before you rev up the machine.

Panty hose for your power mower?

Believe it or not, yes. A few layers of panty hose (or, alternatively, two fabric softener sheets) will protect the air intake opening on your power mower—specifically, the carburetor intake horn. Just cut the material to size and secure it to the horn with duct tape.

Coat hanger topiary for ground covers

If you take the low-maintenance route and choose ivy, pachysandra, or ivy over lawn grass, you can ornament the expanse with a mini-topiary or two. Turn wire coat hangers into frames in your shape of choice: a circle, a heart, even your child's initials. Anchor the frame in the soil and train strands of the plants to cover it, using clippers to neaten the growth as necessary. Who knew topiary could be so simple?

Kiddie pool to garden pond

Think it's too expensive to install a small decorative pond in the corner of your lawn? Not if your liner is a child's plastic wading pool. To start, dig a hole to the depth and diameter of the kiddie pool, and make sure the pool sits flat on the bottom of the hole and its top is level with the lawn. To allow drainage during heavy rains, punch holes in the sides of the pool.

Now position the pool in the hole and pack dirt around the sides. Layer the bottom of the pool with a 50/50 mixture of coarse sand and peat moss, and place flat stones around the top edge to camouflage the pool's plastic lip. After using a garden hose to fill the pond, set pots of water plants inside—marsh marigolds, Nymphaea (water lilies), royal ferns—and your pretty new garden feature is complete.

Watering Your Garden

A toothpick time-to-water test

Just as you test a baking cake for doneness by sticking it with a wooden toothpick, you can do the same to see whether a garden bed needs watering. Stick the toothpick into the soil as far as it will go, then examine it. If it comes out clean, it's time to water. If any soil clings to the pick, you can forgo watering and test the soil again the next day.

Milk jug tricklers

Tomatoes aren't the only garden plants that like lots of water. Others with a big thirst include squashes, melons, and rosebushes. How to keep them quenched? Bury plastic milk-jug reservoirs alongside. Start by perforating a jug in several places. Dig a planting hole large enough to accommodate both plant and jug, and bury the jug so its spout is at soil level. After refilling the hole and tamping down the soil, fill the jug with water. Then top it to overflowing at least once a week, and your plant's roots will stay nice and moist.

Water ferns with weak tea

Also, when planting a fern, put a used tea bag in the bottom of the planting hole to act as a reservoir while the fern adapts to its new spot; the roots will draw up a bit more nitrogen. Another drink ferns like: a very weak solution of household ammonia and water (1 tablespoon ammonia to 1 quart water), which also feeds them a little nitrogen.

Borax for sun-sensitive plants

To keep direct sunlight from burning the leaves of ferns, azaleas, yews, hollies, hostas, and herbs such as thyme and chives, add borax to your watering can—1 tablespoon dissolved in 1 gallon water. Wet the leaves of the plants and soak the soil with the solution a couple of times in the spring (more than two treatments is overdoing it), and your plants will be better able to stand up to the sun's hot rays in summer.

Recycle unsalted cooking water

Boiled foods release nutrients of one kind or another, so why pour their cooking water down the drain? Let the water cool, and then use it to give a garden plant or two a healthful drink. But take note: When you cook any of the following, do *not* add salt to the water because salt is harmful to plants.

- **Eggs** Hardboiled eggs leave calcium in the cooking water, so use the liquid to water calcium-loving solanaceous garden plants: tomatoes, potatoes, eggplants, peppers, chayote squash, tomatillos.

A Homemade Rain Gauge

A large plastic soda bottle, preferably the kind *without* a black plastic base, may not be the spiffiest-looking rain gauge in the world—but hey: It doesn't cost a cent, and it works. Just cut off the top third of the bottle, turn the top upside down, and fit it into the larger piece to act as a funnel. Then use waterproof tape to tape the pieces together at the rim.

Lay the bottle on its side and use a ruler and indelible marker to mark off lines ¼ inch apart. Set the gauge in an open area in the yard when you expect rain, then check to see how high the water rises—a clue to how long you should hold off watering your plants.

- **Spinach** Plants need iron, too—and spinach water gives them not only iron but also a decent dose of potassium.
- **Pasta** Starchy water will spur the release of plant nutrients in the soil, meaning starch may be better for plants than for you.
- **Potatoes** Ditto.

A penny splashed ...

You could either take that jar holding six dollars and 21 cents worth of pennies to the coin-roller at the supermarket or use the coins as a splashguard in a window box. Watering plants in window boxes often splatters mud onto windowpanes, as does a driving rain. To solve the problem, simply spread pennies over the soil surface.

Hose punctured?

If water is leaking from a tiny hole in your garden hose, stick a wooden toothpick into the hole and then break it off at surface level. Wrap electrical tape or duct tape around the hose to secure the toothpick, and the leak is history. The wet wood will swell and form a tight seal.

Improving Soil, Making Compost

Hair, hair!

Human hair is by far one of the best nitrogen sources you can add to your compost heap. Six or seven pounds of hair contain a pound of nitrogen—the same amount yielded by *200 pounds* of manure. Check with barbershops to see if they'll give you a boxful of hair; you'll find that many will do so gladly.

Help from Fluffy

Sprinkle unused, alfalfa-based kitty litter onto your compost pile and toss well. Alfalfa is high in nitrogen—an excellent compost activator—which will ultimately hasten decomposition.

Attract earthworms with coffee grounds

The larger the number of earthworms wriggling about in your soil, the better its tilth. Attract the worms to planting beds or other garden areas by digging coffee grounds into the soil.

Solarize soil with clear plastic

What free resource will kill weed seeds, most plant diseases, and nematodes in your soil? The sun. Till the soil and water it, then lay a sheet of clear plastic over the area (a split-open dry cleaning bag will do nicely) and anchor the edges with stones. After four to six weeks, the sun's heat should have rid the soil of most plant menaces.

Composting in a leaf bag

Turn autumn leaves into compost by storing them over the winter in large black plastic leaf bags. When filling the bag with leaves, add a small shovelful of soil and a handful of 10-10-10 fertilizer as an activator. Then direct a stream of water from your garden hose into the bag to saturate the leaves.

Tie the bag closed and bounce it on the ground a few times to mix the contents. Store the bag in a sunny place so that it absorbs the heat of the sun. By spring the leaves will have rotted into rich compost.

COFFEE, TEA, OR COLA?

So your compost pile seems a bit slow in producing the fertile organic matter you want to dig into your garden beds? Speed decomposition of the contents by pouring on **coffee, tea, or non-diet cola**—all three of which will increase the bacterium population that help both soil and compost break down.

Feeding Your Plants

Matchbooks as fertilizer?

Yes! But *only* when you want to add sulfur to the soil to lower the pH for acid-loving plants. Tear out the matches from several matchbooks and toss them into the bottom of planting holes for impatiens, hydrangeas, azaleas, and gardenias.

Fireplace freebie

Hardwood ashes from your fireplace will supply potassium and phosphorous to garden plants. Just make sure not to use wood that has been treated with preservatives or anything else. To fertilize plants, spread a half-inch layer of ashes a few inches from the stem and dig it into the soil.

A couple of caveats: 1) If you store ashes outside, protect them from the rain or their nutrients will be depleted; 2) don't use ashes around potatoes, since ash can promote potato scab.

Limit your plants' coffee consumption

It isn't the caffeine in coffee grounds that garden plants like azaleas and rosebushes and evergreens love but rather the acidity and aeration the grounds provide—not to mention nitrogen, phosphorous, and trace minerals. Just be sure to dig the grounds into the soil to keep them from becoming moldy.

How much to use? Dig about ¾ cup of grounds into the soil near the roots, repeating once a month. And don't overdo it. Fertilizing even acid-loving plants with coffee grounds too frequently could increase soil acidity to undesirable levels.

Tree-feeding drill

To make sure fertilizer reaches a tree's feeder roots, put your power drill to work on something besides wood: the soil. Use a bit at least 1 foot long and 1½ inches in diameter, and bore holes in the soil around the drip line—the imaginary circle beneath the outermost tips of the tree canopy. Space the holes about 2 feet apart, then bore a second ring of holes about 2½ feet from the tree trunk. Funnel a slow-release fertilizer into all of the holes, and then plug them with soil and water well.

Finding Free Manure

Not surprisingly, a lot of farmers and stable owners are more than happy for you to haul manure away from their property for use in your garden (after drying and aging, of course). Also, if your city has a zoo, call the administrative office to see if manure is supplied to gardeners. And when the circus rolls into town … well, you get the picture. A caveat: *Never* use manure from pets as a fertilizer; it often contains roundworms and toxic parasites.

Add sawdust and leaves to aging manure

Fresh, or raw, manure must be aged so that it won't burn your plants' roots—and only the most committed home gardeners will wait for the six months it takes. If you're one of those gardeners, water a fresh manure pile, cover it with a tarp so the nutrients won't leach out during a rain, and turn the pile with a pitchfork every 10 days or so. To control the odor (especially in summer), add sawdust, dead leaves, or wood chips, forking them evenly into the pile.

Mulches and Such

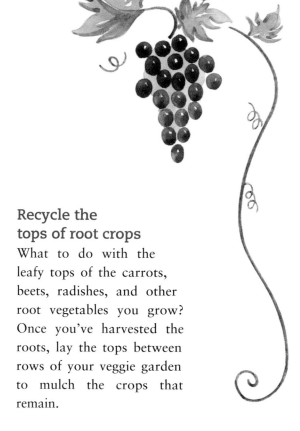

Free mulch quest

Mulch is usually there for the taking if you know where to look for it. Besides the dead leaves and grass clippings you can collect from your own yard, check with local agricultural businesses and local governments to see if they would like for any waste material to be taken away. In particular, ask for chippable bark, salt marsh hay, prairie hay, pine straw, wheat straw, pecan shells, peanut shells, or cotton burrs or hulls.

Strawberries like sawdust

A sawdust mulch benefits strawberries in two ways: it gives them the acidity they crave and keeps snails and slugs at bay. Raise the foliage of each plant and mound sawdust 2–3 inches high around the stem. But know what you're using: Sawdust from black walnut, cedar, or chemically treated wood contains toxins that do garden plants no favors.

Foil and paper heat-beaters

A single-layer mulch of aluminum foil or brown paper (the latter sprayed with clear shellac) decreases soil temperature because both materials reflect the sun's rays. On very hot days, keep the roots of a favorite specimen cool by laying foil or paper around the base of the plant.

Recycle the tops of root crops

What to do with the leafy tops of the carrots, beets, radishes, and other root vegetables you grow? Once you've harvested the roots, lay the tops between rows of your veggie garden to mulch the crops that remain.

Black plastic for a small space

If you have a tiny garden—say a 4-by-5 foot patch of soil in a paved courtyard—don't bother to buy the black plastic mulch sold at garden centers. (Black plastic is the standard weed-eliminating underlay for bark chip mulches.) Plain black plastic trash bags will do the job equally well. Just spread out the bags side to side—and when it comes time to restyle your small garden months or years later, you can use the bags for their original purpose: to hold trash.

Waging War on Weeds

A pinpointed salt zap

Salt will kill many weeds that can't be pulled up from the roots. Use a garden fork to scrape the soil away from the base of the weed and then cut the stem as close to the ground as possible. Pour salt onto the wound, trying your best not to spill any into the soil.

Drive weeds from cracks with vinegar and salt

If weeds or grass sprout from cracks in your driveway, sidewalk, or any other outdoor paved surface, squirt them with a vinegar and salt solution. To make it, combine 2 cups vinegar, ¼ cup salt, and 2 drops liquid dish detergent in a jar, screw the cap on tightly, and shake well. A simpler alternative is pouring boiling salted water into the cracks. When applying either weed killer, make sure no runoff reaches your garden plants.

Newspaper and plastic smotherers

If part of your garden seems a little too weed-friendly, try one of these mulches to keep undesirable plants from sprouting:

- **Newspapers** Wet several sheets of newspaper so that they cling together, and then set the mat over a patch of weeds. Camouflage the mat by topping it with wood chips or other mulch. Remove it once the weeds are kaput.

- **Trash bags** Split the seams of black plastic trash bags to double their size and use them to blanket the problem spot. Spiff the plastic up with wood chips or such and leave it in place 10–14 days—by which time the weeds should be dead and gone.

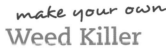

make your own
Weed Killer

Chemical-laden weed killers do the job, all right, but so do greener alternatives that are easy to make at home. Whatever your views of conventional vs. organic gardening, it's always wise to try weed killers with low toxicity before using harsher poisons.

Vinegar Weed Beater

The acetic acid in vinegar kills the leaves of a weed, not the root—but if you apply this spray often enough it will deplete the weed's stored energy reserves and kill off the intruder.

    2 cups water
    1½ cups vinegar (white or cider)
    ½ cup dishwashing liquid

1. Using a funnel, pour all of the ingredients into a 1-quart spray bottle.

2. Shake well to mix.

3. Spray the solution directly on weeds, taking care not to spray any surrounding grass or desirable plants.

A poison ivy–killing cocktail

Poison ivy is one weed you don't want to mess around with. An easy way to kill it? With a spray of vodka and water. Combine 2 tablespoons vodka with 2 cups water and pour the solution into a spray bottle. Vodka's dehydrating action will kill poison ivy soon after the leaves are saturated.

Frost Busters

Coat hanger cold frame

To protect seedlings in heavy planters that you're unable to bring indoors, straighten out two coat hangers and then bend the wire into arcs. Cross them and insert the ends into the planter just inside the rim, leaving headroom for the seedlings. Cover this wire frame with a plastic dry cleaning bag, securing the plastic to the planter by wrapping it with loosely tied twine. Temporarily remove the plastic whenever the seedlings need watering.

Extra insulation

If you're keeping seedlings or hardening off young plants in a cold frame and a hard frost is forecast, line the inside of the frame with sheets of newspaper. Newsprint is a first-rate insulator.

A newspaper blankie

When the weather forecaster predicts a frosty night, tent thinnish sections of the newspaper over seedlings and weight them down at the edges with stones. They'll keep your plants nicely insulated from the cold until the temperature climbs the next day.

Bushels of warmth

In cold climates, old-fashioned bushel baskets make excellent plant protectors, keeping cold winds out while letting in some light. At night, drape the baskets with black plastic for extra protection.

Improvised cloches

The French came up with the idea for the glass cloche, or bell jar, to protect seedlings from frost. Cloches line the shelves at garden centers, but a household substitute will do the job equally well. Some ideas for impromptu plant protectors:

- A tall flower vase, placed upside down over the plant
- A large glass fruit jar
- A 2-liter soda bottle. Slice the bottom off with a sharp knife and place the bottle over the seedling.
- A 1-gallon milk jug, used in the same way as the soda bottle

Warm cozy glow

If frost threatens to damage a large container plant on your patio or perhaps a citrus tree that's bearing young fruit, string incandescent Christmas lights through the branches. Cover the plant with a sheet or drop cloth and turn on the lights. Your plant will stay warm through the night.

Feathered (or Furred) Friends 'n' Foes

Help birds build nests

To attract birds to your yard (they happily feast on leaf-eating insects when not eyeing your veggies or fruits), hang some nest-building materials in a tree. Fill a large-mesh onion bag with dryer lint, hair from your hairbrush, fabric scraps, and short pieces of string or yarn. Then watch your feathered visitors fashion a new home.

A plastic-plate hummingbird feeder

Attract hummingbirds with a fake-flower feeder. Cut a red plastic plate in the shape of a hibiscus flower and poke a hole in the center large enough to accommodate a hamster water bottle. Fill the bottle with sugar water tinted with red food coloring and insert it into the hole, securing it on the back of the "flower" with duct tape. Hang the feeder on a rhododendron bush or a trellis laden with flowers—and even after the real flowers fade, hummingbirds will stop by for a drink.

A real flap

If your property is windier than most, try this trick for keeping birds away from garden plants. Cut plastic garbage bags into "flags" or long strips and staple them to tall wooden stakes with a staple gun. When the plastic whips around in the wind, birds will be scared away by both the movement and the noise.

Scarecrow stuffers

If you decide to put a traditional stand-up, hatted scarecrow in your vegetable plot (as much for nostalgia as anything else), be aware that the stuffing materials for his shirt and pants are probably already in your closet or storeroom.

Anything soft and pliable will do as long as you seal it into a plastic trash bag to keep it dry: old pillows, rags, wadded-up newspaper, bubble wrap, packing peanuts, shower curtains, or drop cloths. And don't forget the old-timey originals: hay, straw, and dead leaves.

Hummingbirds are attracted to the color red!

Guard garden plants with garlic

Encircling a flower bed or vegetable plot with garlic plants will discourage squirrels and other furry pests—including voles, shrews, and field mice—from making a meal of your plants. Space the garlic plants about 6 inches apart to ward off hungry intruders.

Make moles run

Run away from their tunnels, that is. Shoveling used cat litter into the tunnel will announce loud and clear that their territory has been invaded, and moles will leave your yard in a hurry.

Bonus hint: To tell whether holes in your lawn were dug by gophers or moles, "read" the soil mounds alongside. Gophers leave soil piled in a fan or horseshoe shape, while mounds made by moles are more pyramidal.

Oily gopher-and-mole chasers

Soak rags, paper towels, or facial tissues in peanut oil or olive oil and stuff them into gopher or mole holes. The oils will quickly become rancid and stink the critters out of house and home. Or take this less smelly tack: Stick children's pinwheels around the yard and garden; moles and gophers don't like steady clickety-clicking and may escape to a quieter spot.

Go Gophers! (Please)

So your lawn can't compete with Larry's across the street because gophers keep digging tunnels? Maybe Larry knows something you don't: To repel the pests (and their partners in crime, moles) with household ammonia. Do it one of two ways:

- Make a solution to pour down into the tunnel (recipe: 1 cup ammonia to 2 gallons water) and then shovel in some dirt.

- Soak an old dishcloth with undiluted ammonia and stuff it into the tunnel opening.

Rabbit rebuffers

Plenty of repellents will turn rabbits away from your garden plants. Among those to try:

- Talcum powder, dried red pepper flakes, or garlic powder, dusted on and around plants

- Hair from humans, dogs, or cats

- Bars of strong-smelling bath soap placed in vegetable garden rows

- Lemon peels scattered among the plants

Flag down deer

The movement of something white mimics the deer's warning signal that predators or other dangers are imminent: flashing the white underside of its tail. Wind-whipped white "flags" that could keep deer out of your vegetable garden are white plastic grocery bags, rags, or strips of old T-shirts.

Hammer 2- to 3-foot stakes around your plot at 6-foot intervals. Tack plastic grocery bags to the stakes so they'll billow in the wind, or affix white fabric strips long enough to flutter. If you're lucky, deer will run the other way when the white flags fly.

Bring Down Winged Insects

Fool coddling moths with fake apples

The larvae of these moths attack fruits, but you can make sure coddling moths never lay eggs by luring them with fake apples—red Christmas tree balls hung in fruit trees. Start by threading a 12-inch loop of twine through the ball holder, then knot it two or three times. Spray the "apples" on all sides with an adhesive insect spray and hang three or four on fruit tree branches. Coddling moths will zero in on the red targets and get stuck.

Bottle up wasps

Wasps follow their noses to sugar, so set them a sweet trap. Slice the top 3 inches off the top of a large plastic soda bottle and set the necked piece aside. Create a hanger by poking holes on either side of the base near the top. Thread an 18- to 24-inch string through the holes and triple-knot the ends. Place the necked piece into the bottle upside down to form a funnel, taping it tightly.

Pour sugar water into the bottle (use 4 parts water to 1 part sugar, dissolved), and hang your contraption on the branch of a tree favored by wasps. Wasps trying to reach the liquid will either drown or be unable to escape from the bottle.

Repellents in your herb rack

We love our herbs and spices, but most garden pests find them unpalatable or even lethal. Sprinkle any of the following examples around your plants and watch leaf-hungry pests go in search of another spot to dine.

- Powdered cinnamon
- Powdered cloves
- Cayenne pepper
- Black pepper
- Chili powder
- Hot curry powder
- Garlic powder

SUCK 'EM UP

Use a battery-operated **handheld vacuum cleaner** to rid your plants of small leaf-eating insects. Run the vacuum over both sides of the leaves of the affected plant to suck up red spider mites, flea beetles, aphids, white-flies, and other tiny pests.

- Dried lemon thyme
- Dried bay leaves, crumbled

An aspirin two-fer

The active ingredient in aspirin, salicylic acid, is produced by plants as a natural protection—and that works to the gardener's advantage. Experiments have shown that plants watered with a weak aspirin/water solution not only repel aphids and other sucking insects but also promote strong plant growth.

To make a systemic solution, fill a bucket with 5 gallons water and drop in 3 aspirin tablets (use regular strength, or 325 mg). Stir until the tablets dissolve. Water garden plants as usual with the solution or pour it into a spray bottle to spritz the plants' leaves and stems on all sides. Thereafter, apply the aspirin water every two weeks.

Send bugs to the mothball chamber

If whiteflies, mealybugs, or any other insect pests are attacking your houseplants, sentence them to death by mothball. Put an affected plant (pot, saucer, and all) into a clear plastic dry-cleaning bag. Water the plant and drop five or six mothballs into the bag.

Now tie the bag closed with a twist tie, then move the bagged plant to a bright, though not directly sunlit, spot. Let it sit for a week before taking the plant from the bag and returning it to its usual place. If necessary, repeat the treatment until all of the pests have given up the ghost.

Trap grasshoppers with molasses

To keep grasshoppers from munching on your ornamentals and vegetables, fill several wide-mouth jars half full with a water/molasses solution (8 parts water to 1 part molasses) and place them in problem areas. The pests will be attracted by the smell, dive in, and drown.

make your own
Insecticide

Rid garden plants and houseplants of aphids, whiteflies, and other insect pests with this garlic-based spray. If you don't have a sprayer, use a well-rinsed cleaning product spray bottle. No matter your equipment, be sure to cover both sides of the leaves.

Chase-'Em-Off Garlic Spray

Use only dishwashing liquid in this recipe (not laundry or dishwasher detergent) and store the spray as you would any insecticide: in a capped and labeled bottle kept in a childproof cabinet.

    10 garlic cloves, unpeeled
    1 tablespoon vegetable oil
    3 cups hot water
    1 teaspoon dishwashing liquid

1. Puree the garlic (peels and all) in a blender.

2. Strain the mixture through a fine sieve into a quart jar. Add oil, water, and dishwashing liquid, screw the jar cap on tightly, and shake gently to mix. Pour the mixture into a spray bottle.

3. Apply every 3 days for a week to control hatching insect eggs. Repeat as needed after rains or when new infestations occur.

Attract pests with warm colors

Paint milk cartons or plastic dishpans red or orange or yellow, coat with an adhesive insect spray, and set at 12-foot intervals in the garden. Flying insects zoom to them and get stuck fast. To kill aphids in particular, forgo the adhesive and simply fill a yellow container three-quarters full of water. The little green ones will zip straight to the container and end up in a watery grave.

Let toads do it

Toads are among the most insect-hungry garden visitors. Attract them by placing a broken flowerpot or two in a shady spot, then sink a pan filled with water and rocks into the soil so any visiting toads will stick around.

Get a jump on squash borers with kerosene

You can prevent squash borers from attacking squash and melons even before you seed these plants. How, pray tell? By soaking the seeds in kerosene overnight. The seedlings and mature plants will repel borers—but, as you'll no doubt be happy to hear, the kerosene won't infiltrate the fruits.

Eradicate earwig with corn oil

Earwigs are partial to clematis, chrysanthemums, dahlias, and gladiolus—so how do you give the little buggers the brush-off? Not with a whiskbroom but with oil, an earwig non-botanical favorite. Pour a pool of corn oil onto a saucer, set it on the ground amid your flowers, and the pests will crawl into the saucer and drown.

Three Ways to Slay Slugs and Snails

The gastropod gourmets we know as slugs and snails have a special taste for dahlias, delphiniums, hostas, lupines, marigolds, zinnias, and almost any flower or veggie seedling. Luckily, there are ways to deprive them of their meals. Use:

- **Beer** Bury shallow containers (a jar lid is the usual choice) so that the rim is level with the soil, then fill it with beer. Slugs and snails love the yeast in beer and overindulge until they drown.

- **Ashes** Sprinkle wood ashes along garden rows. Like salt, the ashes shrivel the skin of slugs and snails.

- **Fruit rinds** After enjoying half a grapefruit for breakfast, put the rind upside down in the garden. Slugs and snails will gather under it, at which point you can smash the rind with the back of a shovel and add it (and the dead crawlers) to your compost pile. Other citrus rinds work, too.

Protective fabric softener hankies

Keep mosquitoes from dive-bombing you as you work in the garden by tucking a few fabric softener sheets into your clothing. Pin a sheet to a shirt pocket, loop one through a belt loop, and tuck one under the rim of your cap. Once mosquitoes get a whiff of the scented sheets, they'll buzz off in a flash.

Thwart Creepy-Crawlers and Diseases

Repel caterpillars with onion juice

Spray cabbage and other vegetables targeted by caterpillars with onion juice, and watch the pests take a detour. To make a spray, peel 2 medium-size onions, grate them into a large bowl, and add 1 gallon water. Let the mixture sit overnight, then strain it into a spray bottle. To make the plants smelly enough to repel the pests, you may need to spray the leaves twice.

Hunt down hornworms with the hose

While hornworms are the largest of the vegetable garden caterpillars, they're also among the hardest to spot; their pale green color camouflages them as they chomp on the leaves of tomato, potato, and pepper plants. To find hornworms, turn your garden hose nozzle to the fine spray setting and direct the spray to a plant. Any hidden hornworms will thrash about and reveal their whereabouts, at which point you can pick them off and drop them into a bucket of water. The hotter the day, the more of a shock the cold spray will be to a hornworm's system.

Soup can stockades

To keep cutworms and other crawlers from reaching newly planted seedlings, use soup cans as barriers. Cut the top and bottom out of a can, wash it well, and place the can over a seedling. Twist it until the bottom is 2 inches underground, and tender seedlings will gain protection from all directions.

Fight fungus with baking soda

Keep powdery mildew, black spot, and other fungus diseases from infecting your fruit trees, vegetables, gardenias, roses, and such with a baking soda solution. In a large spray bottle, combine 1 teaspoon baking soda, 1 teaspoon dishwashing liquid, and 1 quart warm water. Shake well and spray plant leaves and stems on both sides to discourage fungus diseases from taking hold.

Poison rose black spot with tomatoes

It's long been known that roses grown next to tomatoes are less likely to fall victim to black spot. Make a fungicide by snipping tomato leaves from a plant and whirring them in a blender with a little water; use enough leaves to make 2 cups of slurry. Combine with 1½ quarts water and 2 tablespoons cornstarch and mix well. Store the solution in the fridge, marking it with a warning label. Spray your rosebushes once a week with the fungicide.

On the Patio

Bleach out pots
When repotting patio plants, sterilize flowerpots and planters to keep those newly purchased pygmy roses or Kurume azaleas from succumbing to fusarium wilt or leaf curl. First plug the drainage holes with clay or putty. Then scrub off caked debris with a scrub brush or toothbrush. Rinse the pots and fill with a solution of 1 part household bleach to 4 parts water. Let stand for 2 to 3 hours. Discard the bleach in a laundry room sink (not the yard), rinse the pots with fresh water, and let them air dry.

A bubble wrap warmer for camellias
Camellias grown in containers are particularly sensitive to the cold because of their shallow roots. When winter comes, wrap the pot with thick plastic bubble wrap or several sheets of newspaper and secure the wrap with duct tape. You'll want to turn the pot so the tape is out of the sight line of visitors.

Packing peanuts + plants = smart substitute
Instead of putting rocks or pot shards in the bottom of a patio planter to aid drainage, fill the bottom quarter with packing peanuts. What do they have over rocks? They make the planters lighter and allow you to use less potting soil. And, if the peanuts are made of Styrofoam, you're keeping them out of your local landfill. (Green tip: Biodegradable packing peanuts made from cornstarch can go straight into your compost pile.)

Plastic raincoats for exposed furniture
A big rain is forecast, and you don't have enough indoor space to bring patio or lawn tables and chairs inside. What to do? Cover them with plastic dry cleaning bags. Split the bags lengthwise to double their size, drape them over the furniture, and weight them down with bricks or firewood. Of course, you'll need to save bags in advance; they won't take up much space if you store them folded on a shelf in the garage or garden shed.

---

make your own
Moss

Want to make a new patio look like it's been around for a while? Whip up a mixture to paint on brick or stone walls or some of your masonry or terra cotta patio planters. First, though, you'll have to go in search of moss and collect a few patches to use as a starter.

Do-It-Yourself Mossifier
A handheld blender works best to puree this mixture, but a long whisking session will do the job in a pinch.

> 8–12 ounces moss
> 12 ounces beer
> ½ teaspoon sugar

1. Put 8–12 ounces of moss in a pail.

2. Add beer and sugar and puree the mixture until smooth.

3. Using a paintbrush, spread the mixture about ¼-inch thick on masonry planters on the areas you want to mossify. The moss should appear in 4 to 7 days.

Help your pots drain faster with **packing peanuts!**

Bubble away rust with vinegar and baking soda

If you have a concrete patio and metal furniture is leaving rust stains, try this: Pour full-strength white vinegar on the stains, top the puddle with a little baking powder, and leave it for about 10 minutes before wiping it off with an absorbent cloth. Older rust stains may need two or three more applications before they disappear.

Wicker basket to hanging plant

Finally, a use for that wicker basket you've had stuck in the back of the closet for three years! Dig up four or five of the plants in your flower bed and transfer them to the basket—and voila: a hanging plant for the patio. First, though, use an aerosol varnish to weatherproof the basket and line the inside with clear plastic wrap poked with a few drainage holes.

Veg out mosquitoes

To stop mosquitoes and other insect larvae from breeding in birdbaths or rainwater barrels, put a few drops of vegetable oil on top of the water. The oil spreads to form a film over the surface, ensuring that mosquito larvae won't be able to breathe through the water surface. Renew the oil every week through the summer. Light mineral oils also work, but they can make the water unsafe for avian and human consumption.

Herbal mosquito repellents

Steep pennyroyal or fleabane leaves in hot water and let sit for 4–6 minutes. Strain the solution into a spray bottle and spray on patio plants to repel mosquitoes. Or do the same with garlic. Simply simmer 8 to 10 peeled garlic cloves in 2 cups cooking oil for about an hour. Cool, strain into a spray bottle, and spritz away.

Chapter Twelve

Ladies and Gentlemen,
Start Your Engines!

Once upon a time not so very long ago, small-town and suburban streets were lined with car owners at the curb washing their pride and joy—a '48 Nash in Racing Green, or a '57 Chevy in Dusty Pearl—in a glorious Saturday afternoon ritual. Automatic car washes have put a dent in this "analog" practice, but this doesn't mean you can't try some old-fashioned car-care tricks, especially if you like saving money.

Forget expensive car-care contraptions and concoctions and read on: Peanut butter to clean your car? Yes. Vodka? Absolutely. You'll also find ways to keep your wheels in great running condition, be you a driver or a cyclist, and save tons of time (not to mention dough) in the process.

What common, if smelly, substance will eliminate the need for a post-wash waxing? Which baby care item will clean windshields in a jiffy? What fizzy beverage in your fridge has more than one use under the hood? The next 21 pages hold the answers to these questions and more, so let's get on the road.

Cheers to a great
windshield cleaner—
vodka!

Solutions for Car Washers

Baking-soda car cleaner

Prepare in advance for your next few car washes by making your own condensed cleaner base. Pour ¼ cup baking soda into a gallon-size jug, then add ¼ cup dishwashing liquid and enough water to fill the jug almost to the top. Screw on the cap, shake well, and store the concentrate for later use. When it comes time to wash the car, shake the jug vigorously and then pour 1 cup of the cleaner base into a 2-gallon water pail. Fill the pail with warm water, stir to mix, and your homemade cleaning solution is ready to use.

A surprising no-wax washer

Add 1 cup kerosene to a 3-gallon pail filled with water and then sponge the solution over your car. You won't have to spray the car before washing or rinse or wax it once you're done. And the next time it rains, rainwater will bead up and roll off the car, lessening the likelihood of rusting.

Hair conditioner for shine

Wash your car with a hair conditioner containing lanolin. You'll become a believer when you see the freshly waxed look and when you find that the surface will repel rain.

You can see clearly now

Add ¼ cup household ammonia to 1 quart water, pour it into a plastic bottle with a watertight cap, and keep it in your car for washing the windshield and windows. As soon as your windshield begins to get dirty, take out the solution and apply it with a sponge; then dry the windshield with a soft cloth or paper towels.

Banish back-road dirt

In many rural areas, so-called oil roads (some unpaved, others semi-paved) are sprayed with oil to control blowing sand and dust. If you find yourself driving along one of these back roads, your windshield may end up coated with oily grime. To cut through the muck, sprinkle cream of tartar over the windshield, and then wipe the glass down with soapy water, rinse well, and dry.

A one-step window cleaner

Clean your windshield and car windows by rubbing them with baby wipes stored in your glove compartment. What could be easier?

Clean your blades

If your windshield wiper blades get dirty, they'll streak the glass instead of keeping it clean and clear. Make a solution of ¼ cup household ammonia to 1 quart cold water. Gently lift the blades, and wipe both sides with a soft cloth or paper towel soaked in the solution. Then wipe the blades with a dry cloth before lowering them into place.

Fizz windshields clean with cola

When it rains after a long dry spell, a dirty windshield turns into one big mess. Get rid of streaks and blotches by pouring cola over the glass. (Stretch a towel along the bottom of the windshield to protect hood paint.) The bubbles in the cola will fizz away the grime. Just be sure to wash the sticky cola off thoroughly or your cleaning efforts will end up *attracting* dust and dirt.

Vodka on the job

When your windshield-washer reservoir needs filling, raid the liquor cabinet to make your own washing fluid. In a screw-top gallon jug, mix 3 cups vodka (the cheapest you can find) with 4 cups water and 2 teaspoons liquid dishwashing detergent. Screw on the cap and shake well, then pour as much fluid as needed into the reservoir.

No windshield washing fluid?

If the reservoir is empty (and doesn't it always seem to be?), use an unlikely substitute to clean your windshield: feminine hygiene maxi-pads, a box of which you could stash in the trunk. Hold a pad on the sticky side and rub the windshield vigorously. The glass will really shine once you've wiped it to the max.

Shine those car lights

Keep your headlights polished (and yourself, safe) by applying window cleaner and rubbing vigorously with an old pair of panty hose.

---

make your own
Windshield Washer Fluid

Under the hood sits the windshield-washer fluid reservoir that occasionally needs to be topped. And why use a store-bought cleaning fluid when you can mix up your own? With this recipe, you'll not only let your car do the work of keeping the windshield clean, but you may save a few cents.

Keep-It-Bright Windshield Wash

The alcohol in this solution will speed the drying process when the fluid is sprayed onto the windshield—and it helps prevent icing in cold winter weather in the bargain.

  1 tablespoon liquid dishwashing detergent
  3 cups rubbing alcohol
  10 cups water

1. Pour detergent into a clean gallon-size plastic jug with a watertight cap.

2. Add the alcohol and then the water. Cap the bottle and shake it vigorously.

3. Pour as much of the fluid as needed into your car's windshield washer reservoir. Save the rest for later or use it to wash the windows in your house.

Make Metal Gleam

Rid chrome of wax

It's easy to get so excited about waxing your car that you go too far: Wax mars your shiny chrome bumper with smudges that harden and won't come off. WD-40 to the rescue! Spray a little of the lubricant over the dried wax, then wipe it off with a clean soft cloth. The wax will dissolve like magic.

Get wax off rubber with peanut butter

If you're waxing your car and accidentally get white wax on black rubber trim or moldings, wipe the area with peanut butter. The rubber will revert to its original blackness.

De-wax metal trim with ammonia

Car wax mistakenly applied to metal trim can spoil the effect a keen car cleaner strives for. To rid the trim of wax, wipe it with a rag dampened with household ammonia. In a jiffy the trim will sparkle like new.

Baby the trim

Metal trim on your car still not shiny enough for you? Squirt a little baby oil onto a paper towel and polish the metal for a shine worthy of a sterling silver baby cup.

Make chrome glisten

Brighten chrome trim on your car by wiping it with nail polish remover. (Just keep it away from the paint!)

"Let It Shine, Let It Shine, Let It Shine..."

So goes the famous song. If you want to give the chrome on your car a shine to end all shines, simply dampen a clean soft cloth with full-strength white vinegar and gently polish the surface to bring out the natural shine of the chrome.

Two other shine-it-up methods will have the same effect:

- Dampen a pad of ultrafine steel wool (grade 0000), dip it into a little baking soda, and squeeze it until it makes a paste. Then use the pad to scrub the chrome a small section at a time, working with small circular movements. When you've finished, rinse the chrome well and dry it with a clean soft cloth.
- Wash chrome with a cloth soaked in apple cider vinegar. After you've dried it, polish the chrome with baby oil.

Bugs, Smells, and Sticky Stuff

Counterattack on bug splats

If you're at war with the zillions of bugs that seem attracted to the front of your car, plan a little battle strategy. The next time you clean off the bugs, get preventive and spray the front of your car with nonstick cooking spray or vegetable oil or wipe it down with baby oil. Most bugs won't stick around, and the ones that do can be hosed or wiped off more easily.

Mesh away bug messes

Get rid of the bug corpses on your car by squirting a little dishwashing detergent over the spot and scrubbing with a mesh bag—the kind supermarket onions are sold in. The mesh is rough enough to remove bugs, yet not so rough it'll scratch your car paint or windshield. Once you've scrubbed away the bugs, wipe the surface with a clean cloth.

A nutty debugger

To get rid of dead bugs on your windshield or bumper, smear the area with peanut butter (no jelly, please) and let it sit for a while to soften the bug splatters. Then wash off the mess with a cloth soaked in soapy water.

Fight skunk odor with mustard

Get rid of skunk stink by dissolving 1 cup dried mustard in 3 gallons water and splashing the solution over the car's tires and undercarriage, using a spray wand to clean the latter.

Take-It-Easy Bumper Sticker Removal

You say you just can't seem to get around to removing that "Honk if you love whatever" sticker from your back bumper? Once you finally stop slacking off, you may be surprised by how many sticker removers are squirreled away in your cabinets and fridge. Just paint the bumper sticker with one of these four substances and let it soak in for 3 or 4 minutes. Then gently scrape off the sticker with the edge of a credit card.

- Brush the sticker with nail polish remover.
- Apply a thick layer of cold cream.
- Drench the sticker with a citrus-based cleaner.
- Smear it with mayonnaise.

Wax (paper) your radio antenna

If grime clogs your antenna and gets it stuck in an up or down position, extend the antenna to its full height and rub along its length with wax paper. It will be so smooth it'll glide up and down like the arm on a trombone.

Rub Christmas tree sap off the car roof

Got a fresh Christmas tree strapped to the roof of your car? You'll probably end up with sap stuck to the finish—and soap and water won't do the job. Pour a few drops of rubbing alcohol over the sap and rub it with your fingertips.

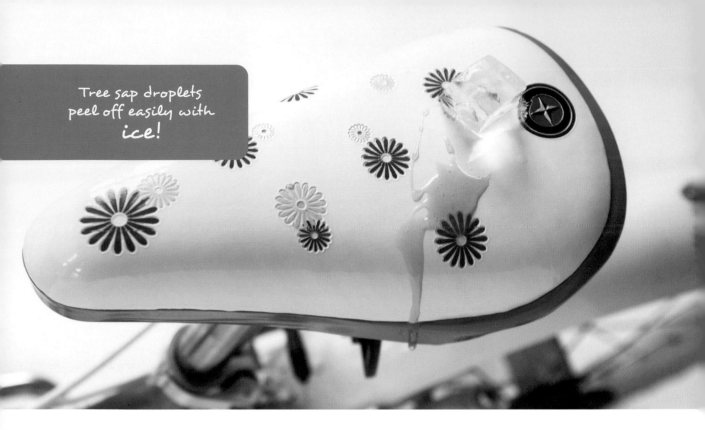

Tree sap droplets peel off easily with *ice!*

Then wipe it off with an alcohol-dampened rag and let the area air-dry.

Freeze the sticky stuff
Another way of getting rid of sap is to press an ice cube over it for a minute or so. When the sap hardens, simply peel it off of your car, bicycle, or other surface.

Oil away a decal
To remove a decal or sticker from your windshield, spray it with vegetable oil or WD-40 and let the spray soak in for a while. Then scrape the decal off with the edge of a credit card. If bits of it stay stuck, heat the area with a hair dryer and try again.

Take down tar
Road tar can be difficult to remove from your car, but you'll win the battle over black goo fast when you try one of these removal methods, rinsing and drying after each one.

- Try spraying the tar with a laundry pre-wash stain remover. Let it sit for 10–15 minutes and then wipe it off.

- Wet a cloth with linseed oil and apply it to the tar spots. Let the oil soak in for about 10 minutes. Once the tar softens, douse another cloth with linseed oil and wipe the tar away.

- Rub the tar with peanut butter, leave it on for 10 minutes, and then wipe it away with a soft cloth.

- Spray the spots with the old standby WD-40 and let it soak in for 5 minutes. Then wipe the tar away with a soft cloth.

- Pour a cup of carbonated cola on a clean cloth and rub the tar off the car surface.

- Mix 1 cup kerosene with 1 gallon water and scrub the tar away with a rag soaked in the potent solution.

Dealing with Dents and Scratches

Pop goes the dent

If the body of your car is dented, you may be able to pull out the dent with a little suction. Look around your house and find anything with a suction cup attached—for example, the base of an automatic pencil sharpener or a plunger. Place the cup directly over the dent and push it in straight so that the suction engages the metal. Then pull outward gently and firmly. If you're lucky, you'll hear the popping sound that happily tells you the dent is gone.

White out scratches

If your white car gets scratched, use typewriter correction fluid for a touch-up. If your car is another color, try to find a correction fluid or nail polish color to match and apply it as a temporary fix.

Brush out scratches

You can often polish out small scratches in a car's finish with your dental hygiene staples. Squeeze a dollop of toothpaste onto an old toothbrush and work the paste into the scratch. Buff the area with a clean cloth.

Brighten old paint with scouring powder

If your car is old and painted with oxidized paint that's looking dull, try washing it with low-grit bathroom souring powder. Apply the cleanser, wet it with a light spray, and then rub gently with your car-washing mitt. (Test this first on a small area of the car body that isn't front and center.) When you've finished, rinse the car well and wax it.

Wintertime Worry Chasers

Gain traction with bleach

If your car is stuck on an icy patch and can't get enough traction, pour a small amount of undiluted chlorine-based bleach over the tires. The bleach will react chemically to soften both the ice and the rubber, thereby improving traction. Wait for a minute to let the chemical reaction take place, and then try driving away. You can also supply traction by spreading sand, salt, or cat litter over the snow in front of the tires. (Because bleach accelerates tire tread wear, you should only do this in emergency situations.)

Shovel snow with a hubcap

If your car gets mired down in snow, ice, or mud, and you don't have a shovel handy, take off a hubcap and use it to dig the car free.

Use oil to prevent stuck doors

Prevent car and trunk doors from freezing shut in the winter by spraying or wiping the rubber gaskets with a coating of WD-40 or vegetable oil. The oil will seal out any water that could later freeze, while causing no harm to the gaskets.

Tape your door lock at the car wash

Put a strip of tape over your car's door lock before going through a car wash in cold weather. This will keep out water that could later freeze and make the lock inoperable. Once you're out of the car wash, remove the tape.

Thaw door locks with a straw

If the lock on your car door freezes and you can't insert the key, don't get left out in the cold. Try blowing your warm breath into the keyhole through a soda straw. The ice should melt in short order, after which you can unlock the door with ease.

Flame frozen locks

If the lock on your car door is frozen, hold the key in your (preferably gloved) hand and heat it with a match or cigarette lighter. Press the key into the lock and turn it gently without forcing. After a few seconds, the hot metal key will melt the ice, and you'll be able to open the door. Bet-

START YOUR CAR WITH A HAIR DRYER

If you get up one cold morning and your car won't start, connect a **hair dryer** to a long extension cord and direct hot air at the carburetor. Then fire up the engine with ease.

Spray Away Road Salt

Don't you just love the snowfall that makes your town look like the set for a Christmas movie? And don't you hate with a passion the slush your car's wheels throw up as you drive the city streets? You know that the slush is full of the salt the city used to clear the roads, but did you know that salt could rust your car's undercarriage? Not to worry: A cleanup is easier than you think.

All you need is an old garden hose and an ice pick to give your car's undercarriage a salt-cleansing shower. Punch holes in a section of the hose that equals the width of the car body. On a day when the temperature is above freezing, put the hose beneath the car, turn the water on full blast, and let it spray the underside of the car for 10 minutes or so. Move the hose and repeat the process until the entire undercarriage has had a good shower.

ter still, if you have electrical power handy, use a hair dryer to direct hot air into the lock to melt the ice.

A panty hose tree tie

When you buy your Christmas tree, the trick is to get it home without having it scratch the roof of your car or fall off it. Simply line the roof with an old blanket to protect the roof from sap and scratches, then tie the tree in place with a rope made by twisting an old pair of panty hose. Panty hose are strong enough to hold the tree in place, yet soft enough to protect it and the car roof from damage.

Keep ice off wipers

To keep ice from forming on the blades of your car's windshield wipers and hampering their operation in cold weather, wipe each blade with a soft cloth soaked in full-strength rubbing alcohol.

Raw onion windshield rub

No one enjoys scraping ice off the windshield on a freezing cold morning. To avoid the tedious job, slice an onion in half and rub the cut sides against your windshield and car windows the night before a freeze to keep frost from forming.

Shield your windshield with rubber bath mats

To keep your windshield from frosting overnight, position inexpensive rubber bath mats over the glass. Hold them in place with the windshield wipers.

Yogurt cup scraper and scooper

Scrape ice from your windows and windshield using an empty yogurt cup. When you scrape with the edge of the rim, the cup will scoop up the ice. As you scrape, empty the ice onto the ground with a quick flick of the wrist.

Bag your side mirrors

On cold nights, slip plastic bags over your car's side mirrors and hold them in place with clothespins. In the morning, simply remove the bags and your mirrors will be ice-free.

Don't get steamed

Driving can be frustrating in the winter when the inside of your windshield keeps fogging up—not to mention dangerous. Following are three ways to deal with foggy glass:

- Use a clean chalkboard eraser to wipe the inside of the windshield clean.
- Squirt a little shampoo onto a cloth and wipe the glass with it.
- Use "outside air" instead of "recirculated air" and run the defroster.

Checking Under the Hood

Two ways to prevent corrosion

It's not unusual for a car's battery posts to get so corroded that you can't get a proper connection to jump-start the car. So take a little preventative action: Occasionally coat the posts with a bit of petroleum jelly to keep them from corroding. Alternatively, tape a copper penny to the top of the battery so that the corrosion is drawn to the penny and not the battery posts.

Clean corrosion with baking soda

If you fail to keep your battery posts clean, you'll have to deal with corrosion. To clean them, stir 1 tablespoon baking soda into 1 cup water, then pour the solution over the posts. After 4 or 5 minutes, rinse the posts with clear water.

A fuzzy shock protector

When you're working on your car and have to disconnect the negative battery cable, don't let the cable come into contact with the car's metal frame or you'll suffer a nasty shock. One safe way of handling the cable is to make a slit in a tennis ball and push the ball over the end of the cable.

Foot powder leak-spotter

If oil is leaking from your engine and you can't find the leak's source, clean the engine with an aerosol degreaser—say, a silicone spray like WD-40—and then spray its sides and bottom with spray-on foot powder. The leak will reveal itself by turning white.

Dislodge a stubborn oil filter

If you like to change the oil filter yourself but this time it won't budge, a screwdriver and hammer are your saviors. Hammer the screwdriver right through the filter about 2 inches from the engine block. Then grab the screwdriver and use it as a lever to turn the filter counterclockwise. Once you get it started, remove the screwdriver and spin the filter off, making sure there's a pan underneath to catch the leaking oil.

Gum up the works

If the radiator hose in your car springs a leak while you're on the road, chew some gum and stick the wad over the leak. Secure it with adhesive tape. It will hold until you can have a proper repair made (but don't dawdle).

First aid for a fan belt

If the fan belt in your car grows dry, lubricate it with a bit of petroleum jelly. With the engine off, dab the inside edges of the belt with the jelly, then start the engine and let it idle for a couple of minutes. Not only will the petroleum jelly lubricate the belt and keep it from cracking but it will eliminate squealing and slippage.

A cola loosener-upper

If nuts and bolts under the hood refuse to budge, pour a little carbonated cola over the connection or loosen them with a few squirts of WD-40. Give either substance 2–3 minutes to penetrate, after which you should be able to loosen the hardware with a wrench.

Extend a wrench handle with pipe

For a reason known only to toolmakers, some lug wrenches are so short it takes a muscleman to turn them. If you'd prefer not to waste a lot of energy when you tighten a bolt under the hood, slip a short length of slender PVC pipe over the wrench handle and you'll get more than enough leverage to use the tool without strain.

Tape that noisy horn!

If your car horn gets stuck and won't stop bleating, tap the horn button a few times. If that doesn't stop the din, a piece of tape is your solution. Open the hood, disconnect the wire to the horn, and tape down the terminal screw. You'll enjoy blessed silence until you have the horn repaired.

Wash Those Grimy Hands

After working for a good while on a car, your hands are probably as dirty as the hands of a six-year-old kid who's been making mud pies. To get them good and clean, make use of any number of simple household items.

- Before washing your hands, rub them with salt to get rid of any strong odors, including the smell left by gas fumes.

- Pour a little olive oil over your hands and rub them together to dislodge the grease. Then wipe them with paper towels and wash as usual.

- Pour a little laundry presoak stain remover into your palms and work it into a lather. Rinse off the lather, dry your hands with paper towels, and wash them again with soap and water.

- Mix together ½ cup vegetable shortening, ⅓ cup cornmeal, and ¼ cup powdered soap. Then grab a small handful of the mixture, wash your hands under the tap, and rinse with clear water.

- Wet your hands, sprinkle them with dry baking soda, and then wash them as usual with soap and water.

- Pour a bit of vegetable oil over your hands (a tablespoonful will do) and rub it in. Then wash your hands as usual.

- Add a little sugar to some liquid hand soap and wash away.

- To get greasy muck out from under your fingernails, sprinkle baking soda over a damp nailbrush and brush your nails from every angle. If that doesn't do the job, soak your hands in lemon juice for about 10 minutes and then resume the baking-soda brushing.

Wheel and Tire Care

Wheels do make the world go round! Here's how to keep yours in working order.

Oven-cleaner sidewall whitener

To rejuvenate your whitewall tires, spray them with oven cleaner, then thoroughly hose it off. The tires will be sparkling white once more.

Spiff up hubcaps with oven cleaner

Use oven cleaner to remove brake dust, dirt, and grime from your car's aluminum hubcaps. Spray the cleaner onto the hubcap, let it stand for a minute to do its thing, and then rinse it off with a garden hose. Don't use oven cleaner on painted hubcaps, though, since it may take off the paint along with the grunge.

Check for loose wheels

There's a way to see whether vibration has caused the nuts and bolts on your car's wheels to loosen. Simply put a dab of paint on each fastener and another dab right next to it. Then check the dots from time to time. If they're no longer aligned, the fastener is loose. Tighten them all to keep your wheel safe and sound.

Check your tires with a penny

To check the tread depth of a tire, insert a penny into the groove in the tire, head first. If you can see the top of Lincoln's head above the tread rubber, it's worn down to less than $\frac{1}{16}$ inch. Time to replace the tire!

A bubbly hubcap unsticker

If you have trouble removing a hubcap, open a bottle of carbonated cola, hold your thumb over the opening, and shake it up. Then spray the cola around the hubcap's rim. After the cola has soaked in for 2–3 minutes, the hubcap should come off with ease.

Inside Your Car

An odor-eating pair

Deodorize the interior of your car by sprinkling baking soda over everything but the electronic equipment. Take a soft-bristled brush and work the baking soda in well. Close the car up for an hour or so, and then thoroughly vacuum the interior. To keep the car smelling fresh and clean, place a small open container filled with freshly ground coffee beans where it won't get knocked over. The grounds will absorb any strong odors you bring into the car—the smell of fast foods, to name one.

No butts about baking soda

Make good use of the ashtrays in your car by placing about an inch of baking soda in the bottom of each one. If you smoke, it will keep cigarettes from smoldering and stinking up the car even after you've put them out. If you're a nonsmoker, the baking soda will absorb other stale smells.

Baby-wipe your dash

If your car dashboard gets sticky from spilled drinks or greasy hands, clean it with baby wipes. Once it's clean, you can bring a shine to the dashboard with a little baby oil.

Sweeten bad smells with vinegar

To remove the odor left when someone gets carsick, wipe down vinyl upholstery (all of it) with a cloth soaked in a solution of half white vinegar and half water. Then place a bowl of vinegar on the car floor and keep the car closed up tight overnight. In the morning, wipe everything down with a damp cloth.

Upholstery Upkeep

Yes, you *can* make your own cleaners for car seats (and perhaps put the money toward a fun road trip). Here are two recipes, one for vinyl upholstery and the other for leather.

Vinyl Shiner. Mix together ¼ cup liquid soap, ½ cup baking soda, and 2 cups warm water. Dip a clean cloth in the mixture and wipe the seats and trim, then rinse with clear water. If you encounter any tough spots, rub them with a paste made from baking soda and water; let the paste soak in for an hour or more, then wash the entire area with the cleaner and rinse it.

Leather Luxuriator. Mix together ½ cup rubbing alcohol, ½ cup white vinegar, and 1½ cups water. Soak a soft cloth in the solution and clean the upholstery with a circular rubbing motion before buffing it dry. To keep the leather from drying out and tearing, occasionally wipe it with a thin layer of baby oil.

Hold taping sessions

Carry a roll of tape in your glove compartment and use it for the following jobs, among others:

- Tape your garage door opener to the underside of the visor on the driver's side of the car. It will be handy, yet out of the way, and it won't fall into your lap as you drive.

- Tape a pen to the dashboard just in case you need one; taping it will keep it from rolling around and getting lost.

- Attach permit stickers to the inside of the windshield instead of using the adhesive on the back. Taping will make the stickers easier to remove.

- Whenever you park at a busy shopping mall, temporarily tape a distinctive paper or cloth pennant to the top of your car's antenna. When you come out laden with packages, you'll be able to spot the car right away.

Magic carpet cleaner

No matter how meticulous you are, you'll eventually end up with greasy stains on the carpet inside your car. When the inevitable happens, mix equal parts of salt and baking soda and sprinkle the mixture over the grease spot. Use a stiff brush to work the powdery white stuff into the spot, and let it sit for 4 or 5 hours. Vacuum it up, and no more stain!

Stop battery drain with a tennis ball

If for some reason you need to keep a car door open for a good while—and the dome light is one of those that won't allow you to switch it off—rely on a trusty tennis ball. Just wedge the ball between the door and the switch. The switch will stay off, your battery will stay charged, and your jumper cables will remain where they belong—in the trunk. If you can't put your hands on a tennis ball, substitute any soft-surfaced small object, like a triangular wedge of scrap wood padded with rags.

Bag a steering wheel

If you have to park in the sun on a really hot summer day, tear a 12-inch strip from one side of a brown paper grocery bag and slip it over the top of the steering wheel, securing it with a piece of tape if necessary. When you return to your car, you'll grab hold of a friendly-to-the-touch wheel.

Adjust air temp with tape

If you have trouble keeping your heat or air conditioning from blowing directly into your face, cover the part of the air vent that's directed at you with duct tape. Just be careful not to cover the entire vent.

Along for the Ride

Laundry basket hold-all

If you tend to collect things in your car and risk drowning in the clutter, here's the simplest way to tidy up: Keep a small plastic laundry basket on the floor behind the driver's seat and use it to hold all those magazines, videos, cleaning supplies, catalogs, maps, and anything else you accumulate. Your clutter will be confined to one spot, and when you give someone a ride, you won't have to scurry to make space for your passenger. You also won't have to fib about how you've been "meaning to clean up all this mess."

Get a (panty-hose) leg up on record storage

It's important to keep your car's registration and the records of mileage, maintenance, and repair warranties where you can put your hands on them quickly. If they regularly get lost in the mess in your glove compartment, store them in the cut-off leg of a pair of panty hose or a self-sealing plastic bag.

Pillbox coin holders

Store spare coins in a used pill bottle and keep it in your car's cup holder. This way, you'll always have the right change ready for paying tolls or using in drink or candy machines along the way. No more, "Can you please give me change for a 20?"

Stock up on trash bags

Keep a number of 30-gallon plastic trash bags in your car for unexpected uses. You never know when you'll need a container for things you acquire on the road or when you'll need to wrap something greasy to keep it from soiling your

The Old Bag

If you're a woman who likes to hold on to her old handbags, you could stash an old oversized one with lots of pockets and zippered compartments in the trunk as an emergency kit. Pack it with a container of motor oil, a can of WD-40, a wrench, bottled water, and any other odds and ends you might need. You could also tape labels to the compartments to let you see at a glance what's where.

upholstery. Likewise, if you spill something on your driver or front passenger seat, simply pull a trash bag over the seat if you have to drive before the offending spill dries. The bags can also protect your upholstery and carpet if your kids or pets pile in the car wet or muddy.

Briefcase to toolbox

If you have a worn briefcase, don't throw it out; put it to good use. Fill it with the tools you need to carry in your car and store it in the trunk. If you get a flat tire or engine trouble on the road, the tools will be neatly packaged and readily at hand.

Take a toy shovel

If you're likely to be driving through snowy areas, keep a shovel handy in case you have to dig out your car. Your best bet? A child's sturdy toy shovel, which works better than you may think for digging out your car—and of course will take up less room in the trunk than a cumbersome full-size snow shovel.

A drink tray for auto fluids

Make a convenient carrier for the various fluids you need to keep on hand for your car, like bottles of motor oil and transmission fluid. Simply take one of those multiple drink carriers from a local fast-food joint and reinforce the bottom with duct tape. It will ensure all of the containers are in one place and keep them from sliding around in the trunk.

Laundry detergent as air freshener

Keep your trunk smelling fresh even on hot summer days when trunks can turn into ovens. Simply snuggle an open box of laundry detergent against the spare tire, and the trunk will smell fresh in any weather. Naturally, you'll want to keep the box no more than half full to prevent spills.

Put on some weight

If you have a pickup truck or a car without four-wheel drive, you'll need to keep something heavy in the trunk to prevent slipping and sliding on icy roads. If your trunk isn't full of heavy tools or the like, fill a couple of pairs of panty hose with bricks and store them in the trunk over the car's rear wheels. The hose will keep the bricks from sliding around, making noise, and scattering dust through the trunk.

Drive a Pickup Truck, SUV, or RV?

"Carpet" a pickup bed

Line the bed of your pickup truck with an old carpet remnant to keep your cargo from rattling or being knocked around and damaged. It'll be easier on your cargo and gentler on your ears.

Shower-curtain rod dividers

A good way to keep things in place in the back of your pickup truck is to set up movable barriers. Fit spring-loaded shower curtain rods at strategic points, wedging them between the sides of the truck bed. You can then move them around to push against any cargo to keep it from rattling or breaking as you rumble along rough roads.

On board catchalls for SUVs

Sometimes the amount of stuff that rattles around in an SUV accommodating a big family knows no bounds. Keep it under control by wedging a plastic milk crate (with padded rim, if the kids are young) or laundry basket in a central spot in the vehicle and urging little riders to keep their playthings and books there when not using them—a long shot, maybe, but worth a try.

Keep a hamper handy in an SUV garage

If you're a parent with young children, how many times have you had to juggle the baby in one arm and shopping bags in the other once you get home? You could make two or three trips between SUV and house, but an easier solution is to keep a laundry hamper handy in the garage. Drop all of your bags (including supermarket bags holding nonperishable goods) into the hamper as soon as you exit the vehicle. Then, once the kids are settled, you can retrieve everything in the hamper at your leisure.

Carry-along car wash for RVs

If you travel in an RV and stay at parks where water to wash your vehicle isn't available, make a batch of washing fluid and carry it with you. Pour ⅓ cup fabric softener into a 1-gallon jug and fill it almost to the top with water. Cap the jug and shake well. When you're ready to wash your RV, put the liquid into a spray bottle and spray the vehicle one 3-foot section at a time. Let it sit for 10 seconds or so, then dry the area with paper towels or a chamois. You can also rely on this mixture during a water shortage, since it uses far less water than standard washing.

Keep mice out of RVs with steel wool

The access slots where you hook up your RV to a cable or hose are "step this way" entries for mice and other small critters. To take up the welcome mat in one fell swoop, wrap the cable or hose in steel wool before connecting it, making sure the scratchy material seals the surrounding gap. With their entry barred, varmints will leave you in peace.

In the Garage and Driveway

Nix nicks with carpet

If your garage is cramped and you tend to bump your door on the sidewall when you get out, attach carpet scraps to the garage wall where the door hits. The carpet will soften the blow and prevent nicks and dents.

Install a bumper bumper

If you need to pull your car all the way into the garage until it almost hits the back wall, affix an old tire on the wall at bumper height. If you do pull in a little too far, your bumper will hit the pliant tire and save the car and the wall from damage.

A combo work seat and tool caddy

If you're tinkering with something on a low part of your car, you'll find it hard to keep squatting or kneeling as you work. But you don't have to. Instead, make an easily constructed combo seat–tool caddy out of a sturdy plastic crate or wood box. Bolt a 1-by-3-inch wood strip onto two parallel sides of the underside of the box or crate. At the ends of each strip, attach screw-cap casters. You can now store your tools inside the crate or box—and unless you weigh three tons you can sit on top of the contraption as you work (just be sure to put the lid on—or top the box with a sheet of plywood). No more achy legs!

Slide right under on vinyl

You don't have to buy a creeper to work under your car. Simply place a 4-by-5-foot scrap of vinyl flooring on your garage floor or driveway pavement—shiny side up—and park the car over it; keep a foot or so of the vinyl protruding from under the car. Lie on your back on the vinyl, and you've got a slippery mat that lets you easily slide underneath the car.

Out, damned spot!

Many garages and driveways are marred by unsightly—and sometimes dangerously slippery—grease stains from oil leaks or greasy tools. Prevent stains when you work by covering the area with newspapers or paper grocery bags. If your car is leaking even a little oil, place an unopened brown paper bag or a flattened cardboard box under the leak. Or scatter cat litter in the area; sweep it up whenever it gets saturated, and replace it with fresh litter as needed.

Contain dust with newspaper

Before you sweep out a really dusty area of your garage, shred a bunch of old newspaper, dampen it with warm water, and scatter it around the area. The soggy paper will keep the dust from rising and resettling as you're sweeping.

Stop garage door seepage with WD-40

If water seeps in through your garage door during a heavy rain, spray the seal on the door with WD-40. The seepage should stop even if the rain doesn't.

Grease Blotters Galore

They're smelly, they're ugly, and they're the automotive equivalent of the banana peel (and not in a good way): the grease spots on the garage floor or driveway. Happily, the self-sufficient methods for making them disappear are many.

Newspaper
Spread several thicknesses of newspaper over spots, thoroughly soak the paper with water, and weight it down. When the paper is dry, remove it—and the stain should come up with it.

Cornmeal
Mix together equal parts of baking soda and cornmeal and sprinkle the mixture over the spot. Let the powder sit and soak up the grease for a couple of hours, then sweep or vacuum the mess away.

Soda
Pour carbonated cola over the spot and hose it off with water.

Baking Soda
For tougher grease spots, sprinkle on baking soda and let it stand for about 3 or 4 hours, then scrub it with warm water and a stiff brush.

Laundry Stain Remover
Spray the area with laundry prewash stain remover. Let sit for about 10 minutes, then sprinkle with powdered detergent and scrub with a broom or stiff brush. Rinse with a hose.

Sawdust, Cat Litter, and Sand
Sprinkle the area with sand, sawdust, or cat litter and leave it 4 or 5 hours to absorb the grease. Then sweep it up.

Paint Thinner
For really tough spots, pour a little paint thinner over the spot and the surrounding area, sprinkle baking soda or cat litter on top, and then cover it with newspapers and let everything sit overnight. In the morning, remove the newspaper and sweep up the mess.

Hints for Cyclists

Shine your bike with furniture polish

Once your bike is nice and clean, you'll want to shine it up and show it off. Instead of using liquid or paste wax and spending time applying the wax to the bike's various tubes, joints, and hard-to-reach spots, all you really need to do is spray the bike all over with a furniture polish that contains wax—something you probably already have around the house.

Salt-and-lemon juice rust buster

Salt can cause metal to rust—yet it can also be used to *remove* rust. (Go figure.) If any rust spots appear on the handlebars or wheel rims of your bike, try this home remedy. In a small container, mix ⅓ cup salt with 2 tablespoons lemon juice to make a paste. Apply the paste to the rusted area with a dry cloth and rub it in. Rinse and dry it thoroughly, and then step back and admire your rust-free bike.

Maintain your chain with WD-40

The hardest part of a bicycle to clean is the chain. But you can make the job easier with WD-40. Turn the bike upside down and spray some WD-40 onto a soft, clean cloth. Rub the chain with the cloth a few links at a time. Move the pedals forward to work on a new section of chain.

Once the entire chain is clean, carefully dislodge it from the chain ring (the metal toothed wheel that engages it) and use a screwdriver or dull knife to remove any gunk that's lodged between the chain ring's teeth. That done, use a cloth to polish between the teeth with a back-and-forth flossing motion, and then reseat the chain.

Proving a Bike Is Yours

You know how susceptible bikes are to theft—and even though your bicycle has a serial number engraved on its frame, thieves can easily file it off. To make sure you can identify your bike should you ever find it in someone else's possession, remove the seat of the bike, roll your business card or a similar ID around a pencil, and push it inside the pipe supporting the seat. Once the seat is back in place, no one will think to look there. And won't the new bike "owner" be surprised when you disassemble the bike seat and pull out your ace in the hole!

Spray for a smooth ride

To keep the chain of your bicycle well lubricated, spray it with WD-40 and wipe off any excess with a soft cloth. You can also spray WD-40 into the cables and bearings to drive out moisture, and then on the springs in the seat to eliminate squeaking. Finally, spray the frame of the bike to keep dust from sticking to it.

Repair a slash with a dollar bill

If a sharp rock or anything else in the roadway slashes your tire, you can patch the puncture in the inner tube—but it will bulge out through the slash in the tire when you try to ride. How to prevent the bulge? After patching the inner tube, fold a dollar bill in quarters and tuck it between the inner tube and the tire slash—a quick fix that should hold you for the ride home.

Bent bike wheel?

If one of your bicycle's wheels gets bent and you don't have any tools at hand, try this temporary fix: Remove the wheel and smack it against a nearby tree. Check it for alignment, and then smack it again if necessary. When the wheel looks reasonably straight, put it back on the bike and, if feasible, ride to the nearest bike shop to have the wheel repaired or buy a new one.

Let Mother Nature help you with a flat tire

If you get a flat tire while cycling and don't have a repair kit with you, completely deflate the tire, turn the bike upside down, and pull one side of the bad tire out from the rim of the wheel. A good way to work it out is with the wide end of a house key, but any dull metal object will do. Once the tire is loose around one side, find some leaves and moss along the roadside and stuff them inside the rim. Then squeeze the tire back into place and ride straight home. The repair will let you ride (carefully) for a while, but not for long—so repair the flat properly as soon as possible.

Baby powder for motorcyclists?

Yes indeed. If you're a motorcyclist who likes to deck yourself out in leather before taking to the highway, sprinkle the seat with baby powder before you mount. The fine powder will make it easier for you to slide freely from side to side on the seat, assuring you of a smooth ride.

Keep your visor unfogged

To keep a motorcycle helmet visor from fogging up on the road, put a drop of dishwashing liquid on the inside, then rub it over the whole surface with your finger until it's no longer visible. Then kiss misty visors good-bye as you mount your bike and speed off.

Motorbike wash-time protectors

If your motorcycle gets caked with mud and road grease, you'll want to hose it down. When you do, be careful to keep the pressurized water stream away from the cables and controls. The easiest way is to cover them with plastic. Save the plastic sleeves that protect your morning newspaper and slip them over the handlebars at wash time. To keep water out of the ignition lock, fix a piece of masking tape over the keyhole.

Chapter Thirteen

Home Repairs Made Easy

In the last few years, do-it-yourself repairing (or upgrading, for that matter) has taken on a status that has elevated it from drudgery to sheer fun, with money-saving and often down-right stylish results. But when push comes to shove, do-it-yourselfers (DIYers, for short) like to fix and upgrade things for two reasons: pure unadulterated enjoyment and savings.

In the coming pages, we'll take everyday DIY-ing to the next level, and show you how you can save even more of the green stuff by using common household items to help you work faster, safer, and more efficiently. You don't have to be particularly handy to make use of our advice: These are basic, simple procedures, whether you're resetting a hinge screw or doing a little plumbing.

Though the emphasis here is on nontoxic alternatives to commercially available chemicals, we recommend you wear gloves, eye protection, and take other safety precautions as necessary.

Silence that squeaky hinge with **shaving cream!**

Window Insights

Rub out window scratches with toothpaste

Squeeze a small amount of toothpaste onto a soft cotton cloth and vigorously polish the scratch for a minute or two. Wipe off the excess with a damp rag and presto! The scratch is gone. Be sure to use plain, white paste—no gels or striped varieties. You can use an extra-whitening toothpaste; most have higher amounts of abrasive.

Stop cracks in their tracks with nail polish

You can buy yourself some time before replacing a cracked window by applying a couple of coats of clear nail polish to both sides of the crack. Once dry, the polish will seal any holes in the glass and contain the damage.

Stifle a rattle with a matchbook

A rattling window is sure to rattle your nerves, especially when you're trying to sleep. How can you ever silence that racket? Easily, with a book of matches. Slide the thin end of the matchbook in between the sash and the loose corner of the window frame. Wedge it in as far as you can, but leave at least a third of the book exposed for easy removal. Then give the window a few light tugs to make sure it won't shake on blustery nights. Sweet dreams!

Plug a drafty window leak

That drafty window is guaranteed to suck out precious heat from your home and raise your fuel bills. What can you do if it's wintertime and the caulk gun is all dried up? Simple. Once you've located the source of the draft (it's often along the top of the lower sash or in a corner between the sash and window frame) take two paper towels, sandwich them together, and fold them up from the bottom an inch at a time until you have a thick padded strip. Lay the pad over the air leak and secure it on all sides with masking tape.

Clip a busted slide

Is a broken corner slide preventing you from opening that window screen or aluminum storm window? Don't scrape your fingers trying to reach the spring. Reach for a paper clip instead. Partly open the clip, then use needle-nose pliers to bend the last ¼-inch of the wire to form a right angle. Slide the hook under the sash and use it to grab the slide from below. Push toward the center of the window to free it.

Fast fix for a major screen tear

A window screen is no match for a big dog's big paws. If you can't replace the screening material right away, make a temporary repair by attaching the loose screen to the frame with duct tape. First, clean the area with a cotton ball soaked in rubbing alcohol. Let it dry, then attach two facing strips of tape to the edge of the torn screen, leaving some excess tape along the bottom. Press the strips together, and attach the excess to the inside of the frame with another piece of duct tape. Be sure not to leave any gaps that can allow mosquitoes and other insects to enter.

Repair a Torn Screen

Why replace a whole window screen when its only defect is a few tiny holes?
Here's an easy three-step way to seal those small tears:

1

If possible, remove the screen and lay it on a flat surface on top of a few sheets of newspaper.

2

Use a toothpick or your fingertips to straighten out the torn threads and reduce the gaps between them.

3

Spread a small amount of epoxy, model airplane glue, or clear nail polish over the threads with a match or a piece of a matchbook cover; use the toothpick to open any clogs before the glue hardens.

4

Repeat the process until the glue has saturated the area around the tear. Give it 24 hours to dry, and your screen will be as good as new.

Open Sesame: DIY Door Fixes

Get the lead in

Forget about oil, which can do more harm than good to a stuck lock. The best lubricant for a lock's inner mechanism is graphite, and a good source of graphite is pencil lead. Rub a sharpened, soft lead pencil (No. 1 or No. 2) repeatedly against the companion key, and insert it several times into the lock. Perform this trick twice a year to keep locks in top working condition.

Remove a broken key

It happens all the time: Keys get old and bent and wind up breaking off inside the lock. If you can't enter your house or apartment through another door, run to a neighbor to borrow a couple of items before calling a locksmith. First, try removing the broken piece with tweezers. If that won't work, apply a drop of super glue to the end of the piece that's still on your key chain.

Line it up with the part inside the lock, and carefully insert it. Hold it in place for 40–60 seconds and then slowly pull out the key.

Light up your lock

You know what it's like to come home to a dark porch and have to feel around for the lock on your front door. If you never want to go bump in the night again, dab a few drops of glow-in-the-dark paint around the keyholes of your exterior locks with a cotton swab or small paintbrush. Do the same for any dead-bolt locks on the inside of your house as well, which will make exiting much easier in the event of a power outage or other emergency.

Polish a loose doorknob

A wobbly doorknob is often the result of a loose setscrew (a tiny screw found on the doorknob shank), which keeps the knob firmly in

SILENCE A PERSISTENT SQUEAK

If a freshly oiled door hinge continues to squeak and squawk, the most likely cause is rust, dirt, and other debris on the hinge pin. To silence it for good, use a heavy book to prop the door closed and then remove the offending hinge pin. Give it a good scrubbing with fine-grade **steel wool**, and then blow off any dust or loose steel threads, then rub it with some oil. Tap the hinge pin back into place, then relish the quiet that ensues.

place on the spindle. Everyday usage can cause setscrews to loosen, but you can keep them in place by brushing on a little clear nail polish right after you tighten them.

Pamper a noisy hinge

Is that squeaking door hinge making *you* unhinged? A few drops of baby oil applied around the pin should solve the problem. Can't find the oil, and you're out of WD-40? A bit of cooking spray, petroleum jelly, or even shaving cream can be used to quiet a squeaky hinge.

Reset a hinge screw

A loose hinge will cause a door to stick or become difficult to open or close. Tightening the hinge screws usually solves the problem, but if an undamaged screw won't grip, it means the hole is stripped or stretched out.

To fix it, slide a magazine or two to prop the opened door, if necessary, and then remove the hinge. Loosely fill the screw hole with wooden toothpicks or matchsticks soaked in wood glue. Keep them flush with the frame by carefully trimming off any protruding ends with a utility knife. When you screw back the hinge, the extra wood should hold the screw firmly in place.

Pop goes the rusted bolt

Loosen a rusted bolt by rubbing it with a few tablespoons of carbonated soda.

Unstick a stuck door

If your front door sticks because it rubs against the floor or threshold, try this simple fix. Duct-tape all four edges of a coarse sheet of sandpaper to the floor where the door rubs, then open and close the door over the sandpaper until it swings smoothly.

Curiosity Corner
And You Think *You* Have an Old Door!

It may not be the world's oldest door, but a battered, seldom-used storeroom door in Westminster Abbey was recently declared the oldest door in Great Britain.

According to a dendro-chronology test (the scientific analysis of tree-ring growth patterns), the door's five vertical planks came from a single tree that was felled between 1032 AD and 1064 AD. That date establishes it as part of the original abbey built during the reign of Edward the Confessor and further distinguishes it as the only surviving Anglo-Saxon-era door in England. Some experts additionally believe the door's 6½-foot-high-by-4½-foot-wide size and double-sided form would have made it unique among the Saxon abbey doors, and that it might have even secured the entrance to Edward's chapter house.

Warwick Rodwell, Westminster Abbey's consultant archaeologist, credits the late timber expert Cecil Hewett with inspiring the project. Upon seeing the old door in the 1970s, Hewett observed it could be "very early." Very early indeed!

Walls and Ceilings

Find a wall stud with a razor

Don't have a stud finder? Use an electric razor instead. Switch on the razor and place it flush against the wall. Move it slowly over the wall, and note the sound of its hum. When the razor moves over a stud, the pitch of the buzz will rise.

White-out wall and ceiling flaws

If you've ever used a typewriter, you know how valuable a small bottle of white correction fluid can be. What you may *not* know is that it's even more useful around the home for covering up small stains and blemishes on white walls, moldings, and ceilings. Simply dab it on the defect, and it's gone. When touching up glossy surfaces, coat the dried correction fluid with a little clear nail polish.

Wipe away wallpaper paste

Removing old wallpaper can be a pain, but what's even worse is contending with old wallpaper paste. A window squeegee can make the job a lot easier (and neater). Dip the squeegee in a bucket of very hot water (add 1 cup of vinegar for extra-strength paste). Use the spongy side to apply the solution to the wall; then flip it over and use the blade to remove the glue. Wipe the goop off the blade frequently with a damp rag.

Cover nail holes without spackle

Out of spackle? Before you head over to the hardware store, look in your medicine cabinet—a bit of plain white toothpaste should do the job. You can also fill small holes in plaster and drywall with a paste of equal parts baking soda and white glue. Or you could mix 2 tablespoons salt and 2 tablespoons cornstarch with just enough water to make a stiff putty.

Stick on a patch

Some people think the lack of wall studs makes it far more difficult to patch a hole in drywall. But they're wrong. In fact, all that's needed to set the patch is a couple of paint-mixing sticks (free at most hardware stores)—or, if it's a small hole, Popsicle sticks. Glue the sticks to the back of the wall or attach them with drywall screws. Once the sticks are secure, add the drywall plug, tape, and joint compound.

Secure a screw

An unanchored wall screw may work loose over time as the hole surrounding it expands. Take up the slack by cutting one or two twist ties (the

Find the stud with an **electric razor!**

kind used on bread bags) into strips, equal in length to the screw. Bunch them together in your fingers, stuff the hole, and then reset the screw. If the hole has significantly widened, use steel wool, small pieces of cardboard, or a cotton ball soaked in carpenter's glue or white glue. Let the glue dry for at least 24 hours before placing any weight on the screw.

Banish ceiling stains

Get rid of ugly ceiling stains by donning a pair of goggles and aiming a long-handled sponge mop moistened with equal parts water and chlorine bleach at the ceiling. Then scrub away, keeping at it until the stains are gone.

Fix small cracks

Don't replaster a ceiling just to cover up a few small cracks. Try this instead: Make a paste of equal parts baking soda and white glue and use it to fill in the gaps. It's easier, and it really does the job—but it only works with white ceilings, of course.

Match a patch

When plastering a section of ceiling, it's worth putting in the extra effort to do the job right. Once the plaster is level, try to match the texture of the surrounding ceiling. You can usually come pretty close by applying some gentle touches with a small scrub brush, a pocket comb, or a dry abrasive sponge.

Simple (and Safe) Wallpaper Removal

You don't have to rent a commercial steamer or use toxic chemicals to strip your old wall covering. Here are two easy methods that are not only nontoxic but surprisingly inexpensive, too.

1

Fill two-thirds of a spray bottle with hot water and one-third with liquid fabric softener. Spray a section of wallpaper until it's saturated. Let the solution soak in for 15–30 minutes, peel or scrape off the covering, and repeat. Keep the bottle warm by storing it in a pot of hot water between uses.

2

Use a garden sprayer or a paint roller to apply a solution of equal parts white vinegar and hot water. Saturate an area of wallpaper, wait 10 minutes, then peel it off. For extensive jobs, work with the windows open; vinegar is nontoxic but has a strong odor.

Flooring Fix-Ups

Give scratched floors the boot

Light scratches in wood flooring can often be successfully camouflaged with shoe polish. Just be sure to shop around and find the best color match for your floor. Apply the polish with a soft cloth, let it dry, then buff with a slightly dampened rag. Now that's a quick 'n' easy cover-up!

Dealing with dents

An easy repair for shallow dents on wood floors is to fill them with clear nail polish or clear shellac. Allow at least 24 hours for it to dry. The wood's natural color will show through, causing the blemish to vanish.

Iron off a broken tile

To lift a damaged vinyl tile, cover it with a cloth, then give it a rubdown with a clothes iron on a medium setting. Use slow, even strokes. The heat from the iron will eventually loosen the glue and the tile, making it easy for you to pry it up with a putty knife. If you don't have an iron at hand, try using a hair dryer.

Wash away carpet glue

Removed your carpet only to find old glue stuck to the subfloor? Don't scrape it off; instead, mix a solution of 3 parts hot water and 1 part vinegar. Spread the mixture over the subfloor and let sit for 30 minutes. The softened glue will come right off with a putty knife.

Stick up a rug

If your favorite braided rug is coming apart at the seams, grab the epoxy or hot glue gun. Apply a small amount of adhesive to the outside edges of the separated braids and pinch them together until the glue dries. A similar approach is used to repair slight pulls in a Berber carpet. Squeeze a bit of glue into the base of the loose stitch and push it back into place. If the pulled stitch is very long, you can trim it down with a sharp knife or scissors before gluing. The weaves of looped Berbers may require you to thread a toothpick through a loop to keep it free of glue.

Renew a burned carpet

To remove slight burns and singes from carpeting, use a tweezers to lift the threads and then carefully slice off the charred tips with a sharp scissors, razor blade, or utility knife. Trim the threads as little as possible to avoid leaving an indentation. The longer and denser the material, the better your results are likely to be.

Stone-cold clean

Tools covered with flooring adhesive can be a royal pain in the neck to clean. So instead of scrubbing and scouring, place them in a plastic bag and put it in the freezer overnight. In the morning, the glue will be rock solid and easily chipped off with a hammer and wedge. Just be sure to wear goggles to protect your eyes from any airborne shards.

A GRATER FIX FOR GASHED VINYL

Gash in your vinyl floor? Find a small, spare piece of vinyl and grind it down with a **cheese grater**. Remove any chunks and mix the gratings with clear nail polish. Use the mixture to fill in the dent.

Heating Up, Cooling Down

Do like Grandma used to do

Increase the warmth and moisture inside your home on bitterly cold days by just simmering a large pot of water on the stove. Don't forget to periodically check the pot, and refill the water as needed. Toss a few cloves, some orange peel, and one or two cinnamon sticks into the pot, and you'll have a delightful air freshener as well.

Get incensed about drafts

To pinpoint the often mysterious source of house drafts—and where you'll need to add or renew your weather stripping—wait for a windy day, then light a stick of incense. Start with the window or door nearest the draft. Hold the incense in a bottom corner of the frame and slowly raise it. The smoke should travel up in a straight line; when it moves sharply in one direction or another, you've located a leak. Repeat the process for all the sealed openings around the house.

Block door drafts

A drafty door can raise your fuel bills all year round. Until you can replace the weather stripping, try blocking the air leak with a homemade draft shield. Get an old tube sock, or cut a sleeve off an old shirt or jacket, and fill it with sand, rice, or foam padding weighed down with a few small stones. Sew the open ends and keep it against the crack at the bottom of the door. For safety's sake, prevent stumbles by spray-painting the draft-blocker a bright color.

Free Window Insulation (and More)

Hold on to the soft foam packing material used for toys, sporting goods, and electronics items. It can come in handy when insulating the gaps around window fans and air-conditioning units.

Even your air conditioner's old foam filters can be called back into duty as insulation material; just be sure to wash them well in some soapy water and let them dry completely before using.

Also, don't forget to recycle those large pieces of rigid foam packing from major appliances and other products. When you store your air conditioner for the winter, place sections of foam under the corners to protect floors from gouges and scratches.

Straighten a bent fin

Bent condenser or evaporator fins restrict air circulation and cause room air conditioners to operate less efficiently. The problem is easily preventable, however. Remove the outside grille and inspect the foil-like fins on the machine at least once a year. Straighten any bent ones by inserting a spatula or pocket comb alongside and running it up and down.

Keep air conditioners running clean

A dirty filter obstructs a room air conditioner's airflow, which decreases cooling, increases power consumption, and results in higher utility bills. Check your air conditioner filters every four weeks and clean them when most of the surface is matted with dust. You can clean "slide-out" mesh filters simply by spraying them with a garden hose. Wash pliable soft foam filters in a bucket of warm water mixed with 2 tablespoons baking soda. Wring filters out well when done and let them air-dry thoroughly before reinserting them.

Degrease a dirty fan

Even occasional use can cause a rotating fan to collect dust and grime on its blades and grilles. Besides spreading allergens throughout your home, the built-up dirt reduces the fan's air output and places unwanted stress on the motor.

To clean a dirty fan (which you should do twice a year), unplug the power cord, and remove the housing. Vacuum off any loose dust using a soft brush attachment, then wipe down the blade and grilles with a rag or sponge dipped in solution of ¼ cup household ammonia and ¼ teaspoon dishwashing liquid in 1 gallon warm water. Make sure all the parts are dry before you reassemble them.

Household Superstar!

12 Neat Home Repair Uses for Nail Polish

1 Mark off liquid measurement levels (pint, quart, etc.) inside a bucket.

2 Mix with ground vinyl dust to repair a gash in vinyl flooring.

3 Fill in light dents in wood floors and wooden furniture.

4 Fill in imprinted numbers on hand tools to make them easier to read.

5 Keep knobs on dressers and cabinets from loosening by dipping screws into clear nail polish before tightening.

6 Coat brass handles and knobs with clear nail polish to prevent tarnish.

7 Paint the buttons of a remote control or the edges of a keyhole with glow-in-the-dark nail polish to make them easier to spot.

8 Stop rust from forming on screws, nails, and fasteners by covering them with clear nail polish.

9 Coat scratches on metal appliances to prevent rust.

10 Apply to the bottoms of shaving cream cans and other metal containers to keep them from leaving rust marks.

11 Indicate measurements on the handle of a hammer.

12 Use clear nail polish to seal small tears in window shades and window screens.

Finessing Furniture

That light through yonder window is damaging

Sunlight can wreak havoc on your furniture, but you can restore it to its former luster with plain old petroleum jelly. Use a soft cloth to rub a good amount into the wood until the finish perks up. Remove any leftover ointment with a clean cloth, and then polish the wood to renew its shine.

Tea time for grime

To remove accumulated grime on wooden furniture, put two tea bags in a quart of boiling water, and let it cool. Dip a soft cloth into the solution, wring it out, and then test it in an inconspicuous area on the table. If you're pleased with the results, wipe down one section of the piece at a time. Continue dipping, wringing, and wiping until all the old polish has been removed. Let it dry, buff with a soft dry cloth, then stand back and watch it glow.

Steam out a dent

You can usually repair a small, shallow dent in wood furniture with a warm, damp cloth and a steam iron. Fold the cloth and place it over the dent, then press down with the tip of a warm iron for several seconds. If the dent doesn't swell, repeat the process, but don't overdo it. The idea is to provide just enough moisture to swell the wood back to its original size.

Repair veneer edging with an iron

If veneer stripping or edging is bulging or popping up from the surface of a piece of furniture, lay a warm, damp cloth over it, and press down with the tip of a warm iron for several seconds. Once it's flattened, roll it with a rolling pin.

Unstick a drawer

Wooden drawers can become stuck for all sorts of reasons, but the most common cause is excessive humidity. Although you can't see it, the wood fibers actually swell from the extra moisture in the air. To shrink them back to their original size, use a hair dryer on a warm setting, directing it to the drawer slides and the drawer itself—which should open with ease after a few minutes. For stubborn stuck drawers, try rubbing the sides, bottom edges, and slides with lip balm, a bar of soap or paraffin wax, or beeswax.

Lubricate metal drawer runners

Rust and other deposits can cause metal drawer runners to lock up or to move unevenly. Keep them running smoothly and rust-free by lubricating them occasionally with petroleum jelly or WD-40.

Hassle-free hardware

Want to keep the shine in your decorative brass handles and knobs? Give them a coat of clear nail polish or clear lacquer. This simple task will provide years of protection against skin oils and tarnishing.

Revive sagging cane seats

The more use it gets, the more a cane seat is likely to sag. To tighten it, first soak two or three dishtowels in hot water and wring them out lightly. Now turn the chair over and lay the hot towels on the bottom of the seat for about 30 minutes. Remove the towels and let the seat air-dry, and then give the cane at least 12 hours to shrink back into place.

Wipe Out Water Rings

All it takes is one sweating glass or steamy plate and you'll be forever reminded of it in the form of an ugly white water ring on your wood tabletop.

You can often dry up a fresh ring using a hair dryer on a low setting. Most established rings, however, require some form of abrasion. Here are five time-tested methods.

Ashes and Mayonnaise

Mix the ash from one cigarette in a tablespoon of mayonnaise. Dip a rough cloth in the mixture and rub it vigorously into the ring. Polish when done.

Salt and Lemon Oil

Pour a little lemon oil onto a rag and dip it in ½ teaspoon of salt. Gently rub the rag over the spot. If the ring starts to lighten, repeat the process using vinegar instead of lemon oil. (Not recommended for shellac finishes.)

Lemon Oil and Steel Wool

Lightly rub the stain with #0000 extra-fine–grade steel wool dipped in lemon oil. Once the ring is gone, polish the table with lemon oil and buff with a clean cloth.

Salt and Corn Oil

Mix equal parts of corn oil and salt, rub it into the ring, and then polish it off with a clean cloth.

Baking Soda and Toothpaste

Mix equal amounts of white toothpaste and baking soda and apply it to a rag. Rub in the paste moving parallel to the wood grain, wipe it off, and then polish with lemon oil.

Tighten loose joints

A bit of wood glue is usually all you need to secure a wobbly chair leg or rail. If the joint is too loose, however, glue alone may not do the job. An easy way to solve the problem is to increase the width of the tenon (the contoured end of the loose piece) by coating it with wood glue and wrapping it with cotton thread or a wood shaving. (If you decide on the latter, choose a shaving that's uniformly thick for a consistent fit). Let it dry, then glue the tenon back into the mortise.

Reglue it right

Most wobbly furniture can be fixed by simply regluing the parts back together—but since new glue won't stick to old dried glue, the key is to get rid of the old stuff. One of the best tools for getting rid of dried glue is the small wire-bristle brush you use for cleaning battery posts and terminals. The external brush (shaped like a pine tree) is ideal for removing glue from mortises and holes, while the internal brush (shaped like a cup) is perfect for scraping dried glue from tenons and dowel ends.

Paste over a minor burn

Although fewer people smoke in their homes these days, burn marks on wooden furniture are a more common problem than you might think. If the scorch doesn't go below the finish, you can usually rub it out with a paste made of fine firewood ash and lemon juice (2 parts ash to 1 part juice). Wipe the area clean, then polish and wax.

Sticky Business

The list of items that can wind up stuck on a tabletop is as long as it is varied. About the only thing that's true in all cases, though, is that you should never simply yank off the offending object, because you may wind up damaging the tabletop's finish. To unstick something, follow these instructions:

- A piece of paper placed under a wet or hot object can stick like glue. First, carefully peel off as much of the paper as possible, then dab the remainder with a rag dipped in some olive oil. Let the oil soak in several minutes, and wipe away the residue with the dry side of the rag.

- If the youngest member of the family has decorated your tabletop with stickers or postage stamps, cover them with a coat of petroleum jelly and let it sit for 2–4 hours. Use an old credit card to gently scrape off the stickers. Repeat if necessary; polish when done.

- If said child parks her lollipop on the table, scrape away as much of the candy as you can, then squirt a little baby oil on top of what's left. Give it a few minutes to soak in before sliding off the residue. Buff it to a shine. Baby oil also works well for bubble gum, stuck glassware, and candle wax.

- Dried airplane glue, epoxy, and other types of household cement are notoriously difficult to remove, but they can sometimes be softened with an application of cold cream, peanut butter, or vegetable oil.

Scratch Begone!

Instant fix for scratched woodwork

Your guests will be walking through the door any minute when you happen to notice several fresh, light scratches on your dark-wood wall unit. What can you possibly do on such short notice? Rush to the kitchen, fetch a small cup or container, and mix 1 teaspoon of instant coffee in 1 tablespoon vegetable oil or water. Apply the mixture with a cotton ball and let it dry. (Not recommended for valuable antiques or shellac finishes.)

Cover scratches in leather

Camouflage those unsightly scratches in leather furniture with a like-colored permanent marker. Before you start, test the marker on an inconspicuous part of the couch to make sure it's a good match. Work slowly and carefully when tracing over the scratch. Medium or fine-point markers work best overall; extra-fine tips may deepen a scratch while thick markers often leave a visible "edging" around repairs.

Fill cracks with coffee

Is that small crack, nick, or gouge all you can see each time you look at your dark wood dresser? Reach for the instant coffee. Mix 2–3 tablespoons with just enough water to make a thick paste; for wood with red tones, add a few drops of iodine. Put the paste on a small putty knife or a disposable plastic knife and use it to fill the crack. Remove any excess around the edges with a barely damp cloth. Let the paste dry completely, then buff with furniture wax.

"Homeopathic" scratch care

Most light scratches on wood can be repaired without a trip to the hardware store. That's because masking a scratch is simply a matter of covering it up or adequately lubricating the exposed wood fibers. What's truly amazing is the number of items you probably already have around your home that can get the job done.

---

make your own

Leather Rejuvenator

Heat, sunlight, and simple wear and tear can cause leather furniture to dry out and crack. Restore some of the lost pliability and prevent the cracks from spreading by cleaning, oiling, and polishing.

Liven-It-Up Leather Lotion

Olive oil rubbed into the leather is left to soak in overnight before you restore leather upholstery to its original shine.

- 1 cup water
- 1 cup white vinegar
- 1 teaspoon household ammonia
- ½ to 1 cup olive oil
- Furniture cream

1. Combine water, vinegar, and ammonia in a pail and stir to mix. Pour olive oil into a small bowl.

2. Dip a sponge into the water and vinegar solution, wring it out, and use it to wet a section of upholstery.

3. Rub oil into the wet leather with your fingertips, a rag, or a cotton ball. Let soak in overnight.

4. The next day, shine leather with furniture cream and buff with a soft cloth.

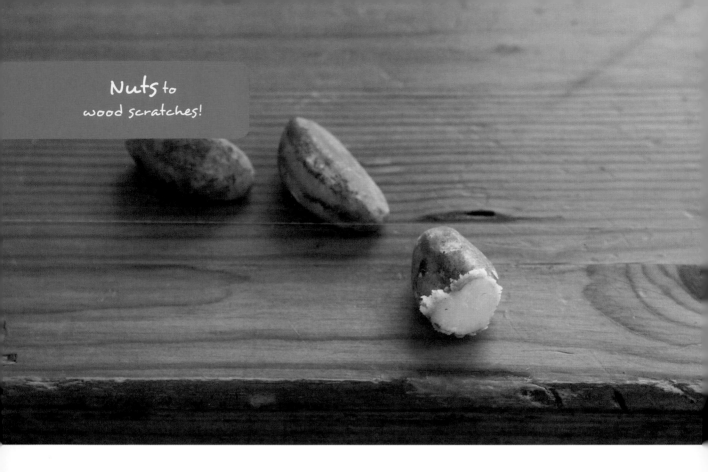

Nuts to wood scratches!

Regardless of which method you use, wax the surface when done.

- Conceal scratches with closely matched shoe polish, a melted crayon, a permanent marker, or some iodine.

- Use the meat of a Brazil nut, walnut, or pecan. Rub the nut over the scratch several times, then vigorously massage the oil into the scrape with your thumb.

- Can't find the nutcracker? Rub in a little peanut butter or mayonnaise instead. Wipe it off with a damp rag after 30 minutes or so.

- If that's too messy, try a little baby oil, or mix 1 tablespoon olive oil or vegetable oil with 1 tablespoon lemon juice. Apply it with a soft cloth, then buff it off after 30–45 minutes.

- Cover scratches with a generous amount of petroleum jelly. Let it soak for 24 hours, then remove the excess with a soft cloth.

Wax away hairline scratches

High-gloss lacquer finishes are prone to developing hairline scratches when dishes or other items are slid across the surface. You can often get rid of these light scratches with car wax, which contains a light abrasive. Test the wax first on a bottom edge or other inconspicuous area to make sure it won't discolor or damage the finish. Once you're set, apply the wax to a soft cloth and polish using a steady circular motion.

Woodworking Tips

Make customized wood putty

When working with specific types of wood, save some of the finest sawdust produced by your sanders. Mix a handful of the sawdust with ordinary white wood glue until it becomes a thick paste, then overfill the crack. Let dry, then lightly sand. Note: Cracks filled with adhesive-based putty will not accept stain the same way that solid wood does.

Instant wood putty

Need some wood putty in a hurry for an emergency repair on an inexpensive piece of furniture? Mix a couple tablespoons of spackling paste with instant coffee until you achieve the desired shade of brown. Fill in the crack and smooth with a damp rag.

Pluck some putty

An old guitar pick makes a great tool for applying small amounts of putty to fill nail holes and small cracks in wood. An easy solution with no strings attached!

Soften wood filler

Acetone-based cellulose wood fillers (one being Plastic Wood) are designed to dry quickly. If you notice that your acetone filler has started to stiffen in the can, you can soften it by adding a little acetone nail polish remover. Stir in just enough to bring the filler to the right consistency or it will become too runny to use. Note: There's no saving filler that's already hardened.

Get rid of glue with vinegar

Don't despair when you get a hardened glob of glue on your woodwork. Cover it with a rag soaked in warm white vinegar and leave it overnight. The glue will slide off with ease in the morning. Vinegar will also soften old glued joints—and even that last bit of white or yellow glue that's hardening in the bottom of the bottle. Just add a few drops of vinegar to the bottle and let it sit for an hour or two. Shake well, drain the vinegar, and repeat the process as necessary.

How to Identify Finishes

If you're about to strip a piece of furniture but don't know how it's finished, do this test to see which solvent to use. (Note: Test solvents first on a hidden section if you don't intend to strip the whole thing.)

1. Start by moistening a rag with some rubbing alcohol and rubbing vigorously. If the finish softens, it's shellac.
2. If the finish is unaffected, brush on one or two coats of turpentine. If the turpentine loosens the finish, it's varnish.
3. Still not budging? Try a coat of lacquer thinner. If that does the job, it's a lacquer finish.
4. If alcohol, turpentine, and lacquer thinner won't work, the piece has a polyurethane finish and requires a chemical stripper.

The last straw for glue spills

Keep a bunch of plastic drinking straws nearby when working in the wood shop; they come in handy when working with adhesives and lubricants. If you use too much wood glue along a seam, for instance, simply fold a straw in half and use the folded edge to scoop up the excess.

Stop stripper drips

The next time you need to strip a table or a chair, place the legs inside recycled tuna cans or aluminum pie pans. The containers will catch the drips, which, besides keeping your workspace cleaner, will let you recycle the stripper for a second coat.

Flip a stripped finish

Stop off in the kitchen before stripping that next piece of furniture. The flat, flexible blade on an old plastic spatula is exactly what you've been looking for to scrape off used stripper. Hold the spatula from the blade in a reverse position and push it in a straight, steady motion to remove the old finish.

Better ways to stain

Put those old pairs of panty hose to work when staining furniture. A rolled up piece of nylon hose makes a great alternative to a cotton cloth or a rag. Not only does it drip less, but it won't leave behind any lint.

A leftover paint roller also makes a terrific stain applicator. Cut a 9-inch roller into three equal pieces. Whether affixed to an applicator or held in your hand, a roller holds more stain than a brush and applies it more evenly than a rag.

Baby the end grain

Want to save a few dollars? Don't spend them on a commercial sealer when finishing your next woodworking project. Instead, seal the end grain with baby oil (or its unscented cousin, mineral oil). It will work just as well as the stuff you get from the hardware store when it comes to keeping the color uniform by preventing the end from soaking up too much stain.

Rust Busters

In the workshop …

Remove rust from knives, screwdrivers, and other tools by rubbing them with a slice of **raw potato** dipped in salt.

Scour rusty tools and machine parts with a steel wool soap pad dipped in **turpentine**.

Dip a rag into a paste made from 4 tablespoons **salt** and 2 tablespoons **lemon juice** to remove rust spots on chrome and other metallic surfaces.

Apply a thin coat of **WD-40** or **petroleum jelly** to wrenches, saw blades, screwdrivers, shears, or pliers to keep them rust-free during extended periods of non-use.

Rub down tools with **hair conditioner** to help prevent rusting.

Drop in a few recycled **silica gel packs** (the kind found in a new pair of shoes and other leather products) to keep rust out your toolbox. Ditto a few pieces of **blackboard chalk** or **charcoal briquettes** wherever you store tools in your workshop.

Around the house …

Rub rust marks on stainless steel with **lighter fluid**, then scrub with a damp sponge sprinkled with scouring powder. Rinse thoroughly.

Plunge a rusty kitchen knife into a large **onion** a few times, and it may end up rust-free.

Brush rust stains on porcelain with **toothpaste** (tool of choice: old toothbrush).

Mix **salt** with **turpentine** to remove rust on most surfaces.

Remove rust stains left by metal furniture on patio paving stones by wetting the stain and topping it with **powder** used to make citrus-flavored drinks (think lemon or orange Kool-Aid).

Coat a nick on a metal appliance with clear **nail polish** to keep it from rusting.

Rub rust rings from metal cans off of kitchen and bathroom countertops with **car wax**.

Put a **coffee filter** in a cast iron skillet to absorb moisture and prevent rust.

Help Around the Kitchen

Rub out scorch marks

If you spot a scorch mark on your laminate countertop, don't reach for the abrasive cleanser; chances are you'll only remove the finish. If the burn isn't too deep, buff it out with car wax or a mixture of toothpaste and baking soda.

A fast fix for dents

If the color hasn't been altered, you can disguise dents and scratches on practically any kitchen surface—including wood, glass, and even some types of tile—with clear nail polish. Brush on the polish in thin coats, letting it dry between applications. When you're done, smooth the polish with a piece of very fine grit sandpaper, then buff the area with a soft cloth.

Save a rusty dishwasher rack

But how? With pieces of flexible, clear plastic tubing sold at hardware stores. For most racks, tubing with an inside diameter of ⅛ inch works best. Cut the tubing into ¼-inch lengths and slip them over the rack tops.

Check the fridge gasket

If your frost-free refrigerator/freezer is more than five years old, inspect its rubber gaskets for leaks at least once a year. The easiest method is to place a bill of currency halfway inside, shut the door, and tug on the bill. Repeat the process in several spots around the seal. The bill should hold firmly; if it's easy to pull out, the gasket needs to be repaired or replaced.

Add ballast to your freezer

Freezers work at maximum efficiency only when they are at least two-thirds full. If you

---

What's the Story?
The Mother of All Dishwashers

Homeowners the world over owe a debt of gratitude to Josephine Garis Cochrane of Shelbyville, Illinois. In 1886, Cochrane, a Victorian-era socialite, invented the first automatic dishwasher to prevent her servants from breaking the family china when they hand washed it. Interestingly, Cochrane was not the first inventor in her family; her maternal great-grandfather, John Fitch, received a patent for the steamboat in 1791. (The "father of steam navigation," Robert Fulton, didn't build his first steamship until nine years after Fitch's death in 1798.)

At a time when women were all but shut out of commerce and trade, Cochrane's hand-operated Garis Cochrane Dishwashing Machine was the hit of the 1893 World's Columbian Exposition in Chicago and subsequently became a staple in many hotels and restaurants.

It wasn't long before Cochrane's invention spawned numerous imitators and competitors, both in the United States and overseas. Yet, her Crescent Washing Machine Company continued producing dishwashers according to her designs well after her death in 1913. In 1926, Crescent was purchased by Hobart Manufacturing Co., which later sold dishwashers under the KitchenAid name, a brand now owned by Whirlpool.

Test the seal on your refrigerator door with a *dollar bill!*

don't have enough food to freeze, add some bulk by filling a few plastic soda bottles or milk jugs with water and placing them in your freezer. You can easily remove the ice ballast when you get food to replace it.

No-stick kitchen drawers

Most kitchen drawers work on a guide-and-track system. That is, rounded guides on the drawer keep it moving back and forth on tracks mounted inside the cabinet. Accumulations of dust and other impediments can slow down drawers or cause them to stick. Keep them moving freely by spraying the tracks and guides with a little WD-40 once or twice a year.

Cabinet doors banging?

If your wooden cabinet doors always close with a bit of a bang, soften the blow by sticking bumpers at each door's top and bottom corners. Inexpensive door bumpers are one solution, but perhaps a little too obvious for the creative do-it-yourselfer. Instead, try pressing small circular bandages (also called spot bandages) into service, testing to see if you need a double layer for each bumper to silence the bang.

Repair instead of replacing

If you've ever bought a replacement part for a kitchen appliance, you're probably still recovering from sticker shock. The truth is many nonmechanical parts can be easily repaired for just pennies. For instance, a broken handle on a microwave oven or a cracked dishwasher arm can often be easily reattached with some two-part epoxy. Likewise, a little caulk can be used to patch a small crack in your refrigerator's rubber gasket, while a few strips of duct tape can usually mend a busted tab on a refrigerator door shelf. Remember: Replace only that which can't be fixed.

Plumbing Secrets

No plunger, no problem

Use a rubber ball or tennis ball instead. Secure the ball in a vise and cut it in half with a hacksaw or a utility knife. Fit the concave side over the drain and press down with your palms or the base of your thumbs to create suction.

Clamp down on loose plungers

A plunger with a loose handle makes every job more difficult and can even be dangerous if the handle slips out or breaks off. If your plunger handle is easily separated from the suction cup, tighten it by placing an adjustable hose clamp around the base of the cup.

Saucer as sink shield

Don't let your work go down the drain! Before you take apart a faucet or nearby fixture, take a small plate or saucer out of the kitchen cabinet. Then simply place it upside down over the sink drain to prevent any small pieces from getting lost.

Loosen a stuck faucet

You've tried everything, but that faucet handle won't budge. Relax and have a cool soft drink. After a few sips, pour out several ounces over the faucet. Give the carbonation 5–10 minutes to loosen any rust or corrosion around the faucet—followed by a few gentle strikes with a mallet. Mission accomplished.

Plug pipes before soldering

It's almost impossible to solder a crack in a copper water pipe; the heat turns the dripping water to steam, which keeps solder from adhering. An easy way to overcome the problem is to stuff a piece of white bread 8–10 inches down

---

make your own
Drain Cleaner

Even if you clean out your dirty pots and pans before washing them, grease can still collect inside the drain. Ditto for conditioners and other hair products used in the shower. Use this potent nontoxic mixture twice a month in your kitchen and bathroom drains to help keep them clog-free.

Aunt Ida's Grease Buster

This powder gets its powerful punch from the chemical reaction between the alkalinity of the baking soda and the acidity of the cream of tartar. Be sure to keep your face pointed away from the drain when adding the water, which triggers the reaction.

  1 cup baking soda
  1 cup salt
  ¼ up cream of tartar
  1 cup boiling water

1. Put baking soda, salt, and cream of tartar in a glass canister, put the lid on tight, and shake well to mix.

2. Pour ¼ cup of the mixture down a dry drain and follow it with 1 cup boiling water.

3. Wait for the bubbles to subside, then flush with cold water for 3–4 minutes.

Blow-dry a *frozen water pipe* to get things moving.

the pipe before you start. The bread will soak up the water, giving you time to solder the pipe. It will also break up and be flushed away once the water is turned back on.

Hose off pipe leaks

Need a quick patch for a leaking water pipe? Cut off a section of old garden hose or rubber tubing that's several inches wider than the affected area of pipe. Slice it lengthwise, then wrap the hose around the leak. Attach it with three hose clamps: one on each end and one in the middle.

Blow-dry a frozen pipe

If a water pipe freezes in the winter cold, close the shutoff valve and open the nearest faucet. Then, starting at the faucet, use a hair dryer on a medium setting to thaw the pipe. Be sure to keep the dryer moving so the pipe won't get too hot in one spot; a sudden shift in temperature can cause pipes to crack. After it thaws, wrap the pipe in fiberglass or foam insulation to keep it from freezing in the future.

Prevent pipes from freezing in winter

Cold snap on the way? You can keep pipes from freezing during the winter months by pouring 1 cup of salt followed by 1 quart of boiling water down your drains once every week or so.

Bathroom Basics

Fix scratched surfaces

Scratches in your acrylic bathtub? Pick up some metal polish. Apply it with a soft cloth using a circular motion. The light abrasive in the polish lifts out most fine scratches. To smooth out deeper nicks and scrapes, dampen them with a bit of water and then gently rub with a piece of very fine wet-dry sandpaper before polishing.

Scratches on enamel tubs and surfaces can be covered with a few thin coats of epoxy-based touch-up paint (available at most hardware stores) or liquid paper. Clean the damaged area with some rubbing alcohol on a cotton ball. Let the alcohol thoroughly evaporate before applying the paint.

Fill tubs before caulking

Before you caulk a seam around a bathtub, fill the tub with water. The extra weight will widen the gap in the joint between the tub and the wall, which makes for a thicker seal that's less likely to crack or tear later on. Just make sure you can reach all the way around the tub before turning on the water.

A smarter, simpler way to save water

Some folks put bricks inside their toilet tanks to reduce the amount of water per flush. It's a good way to conserve water, but it can be lousy for the toilet because bricks submerged in water often break up and cause leaks. A better option is to use recycled plastic bottles filled with sand or water. Remove any labels and check that the bottle is tightly sealed before placing it in the tank.

Detect Toilet Tank Leaks

A continuously running toilet is telling you that something is leaking, so don't ignore it. It might be annoying, but it's also wasting up to 2 gallons of water per minute and can cost you plenty in higher water bills.

To check for leaks, lift off the tank cover and make sure the water level isn't too high. Gently bend the float arm downward (or use a screwdriver to turn the ballcock adjustment screw counterclockwise). If that doesn't stop the water from running, you can easily pinpoint the source of the leak by adding 1–2 teaspoons of food coloring to the tank water. Don't flush the toilet for an hour or two.

- If the food coloring appears in the water inside the bowl, the leak is coming through the valve—in which case the flapper needs to be repaired or replaced.

- If the water collects outside the bowl, look in the tank and make sure the refill tube is properly attached (a loose or misdirected tube can shoot water under the lid). If the tube isn't the problem, the tank itself is leaking. Eureka!

Down in the Basement

Sound off on circuits

Labeling the breaker box is often one of those perpetual chores on homeowners' to-do lists—and for good reason, since an unlabeled breaker box forces you to locate circuits by trial and error. Here's a trick to speed the process: Before heading down to the basement, plug a radio into an outlet on the same circuit you need to switch off. You'll know you've found the right one when you hear the radio go silent. (Give that song a 10!) A vacuum cleaner will also work as a noise source.

Touch up a scratched washer or dryer

Metal buckles, zippers, and clasps can leave dings and scratches on both washing machines and clothes dryers—marks that will surely rust when exposed to moisture and wet clothing. Don't wait to repair the damage, or you'll regret it. First, clean the area with a cotton ball dipped in rubbing alcohol. When the alcohol has dried (a few seconds at most), cover the scratch with a thin coat of clear nail polish or like-colored auto body touchup paint, available from auto supply stores.

Catch the ripper

If your clothes come out of the wash with small rips or snags, it's likely that something inside the washer is the guilty party. Rub a wad of recycled panty hose over the agitator and tub to detect any coarse edges that snag. Then smooth over the rough spots with a piece of very fine grit sandpaper or epoxy.

Keep washer lint at bay

Does it seem like you're forever clearing washer lint out of your basement sink drain? There's an easy way to solve the problem: Make a lint catcher. Place an old tube sock or the foot section from an old pair of panty hose over the end of the washing machine's drain hose. Attach it

PILOT, WE HAVE IGNITION!

Do you wince at the mere notion of having to rekindle the pilot light on your gas burner? A match-holder could make the job a lot less stressful. Get an old telescoping radio or TV antenna and cut off the tip. Then use pliers to crimp an alligator clip onto the end. You could also straighten a **wire hanger** and use needle-nose pliers to form a small loop at the end, or attach a small spring from a pen at the end to hold the match.

with thick rubber bands or tie it with sections cut from the panty hose's elastic waistband. Leave enough slack in the catcher to prevent the lint from clogging the hose.

A great stand-up routine

Why go through a balancing act every time you need to stand up a mop, duster, or broom? Cut off the finger sections from some old latex gloves and slip them over the ends of all those long wooden handles. The rubber provides enough traction to stop a pole from sliding whenever you lean it against a wall.

Air out a basement

You don't have to live with that musty-smelling basement. Once you've taken care of the source of the moisture, combat any lingering odor by mixing 4 pounds kitty litter with 2 pounds of baking soda in a large container. Then fill several coffee cans to the brim and place them around your basement. Replace with fresh mixture as needed.

Hang up insulation

When insulating the floor above an unheated basement or crawl space, use wire strips cut from recycled metal hangers to keep the fiberglass batts in place. Cut pieces slightly wider than the batt, and place them about 17 inches apart between the floor joists. Although the wires should hold the batts firmly in place, make sure they don't compress the fiberglass.

Exterior Repairs

Get a better handle on glass

Need to move a large pane of glass? Wish there were some way to get a better grip on the big sharp slab? Well, there is. Cut off two short sections from an old garden hose (four sections for a two-person job). Use a sharp knife or scissors to slit each piece down the middle, and then slip them onto the top and bottom edges of the glass.

Bag a lock

Give your outside padlocks some needed protection in winter by covering them with plastic sandwich bags. The plastic wards off rust and prevents damage when moisture seeps inside the lock and repeatedly freezes and thaws.

Bonus hint: When a lock does ice up, you can usually open it by warming the key for several seconds with a match or lighter before inserting it. (Whack forehead and say, "But of course!")

Juice out those concrete patio rust stains

Unsightly orange rust stains defacing your concrete or stone patio? Remove them with the citric acid found in powdered lemonade, lemon-lime, or orangeade drink mixes. Wet the surface with water, then pour the powder over the stain. Cover it with a sheet of plastic to keep the moisture from evaporating, and put a weight on top to hold it in place. After 30 minutes or so, remove the plastic, scrub with a stiff-bristled brush, and rinse. Repeat if necessary.

Weather shingles with soda

Worn or broken wooden roof shingles should be replaced as soon as possible, but it may be years before the new shakes blend in with their

Save the Chlorine for the Pool

Forget what "they" say: Skip the chlorine bleach when removing moss or algae from roofing shingles. Chlorine can strip the color from some materials and corrode metal gutter parts, and the runoff will kill any vegetation growing down below. Oxygen bleach powder, on the other hand, is completely nontoxic and much gentler on roofing materials—yet it's just as effective as chlorine bleach, if not more so.

Following the manufacturer's directions, mix enough powder and water to make 2 to 4 gallons of bleach solution (less for spot treatments). Apply it with a bristle brush on a pole, moving in a downward motion; the bleach will foam up as it's working. Keep the surface wet for 20 minutes, then hose off the debris. (Caution: Working on a roof is dangerous. Be sure to wear appropriate footwear and take all necessary precautions.)

This same procedure can be used to clean algae, moss, or mildew off a wooden deck. It's also an excellent way to prepare a deck for sealing.

New Life for an Old Garden Hose

Don't throw out that leaky old garden hose. Instead use a thin drill bit to punch a few more holes, crimp the end, and presto!—a terrific soaker hose. Don't need a soaker hose? There are still lots of terrific uses for a retired hose around the house.

Slice open a section of hose and use it as a protective cover for a chain saw's teeth or a circular saw blade between uses.

Cut a piece long enough to cover the tines of a metal rake. (Use a utility knife to slit the hose, but don't cut through to the ends.) Slip it over the rake and use as a squeegee to clear away puddles on decks, patios, and walkways.

Use it to cover a fraying length of rope to keep it from getting worse.

Staple small, diagonally sliced pieces to the overhead joists in your basement workshop to keep power cords out of your way.

Slit a short piece down the middle and put it over the shoulder of a shovel blade to cushion your foot and improve traction as you step down on it.

Slip a small section over a wire bucket handle for a more comfortable grip.

surroundings. One way to speed things up is to "age" them beforehand using a solution of water and baking soda. In a large bucket, mix 1 pound of baking soda in ½ gallon of warm water. Either dip the shingles in the bucket, or apply the solution with a paintbrush. Let them dry for a few hours, and they'll take on a weathered, gray appearance. Don't forget to coat your new "old" shingles with a wood preservative before installing them.

Make a gutter scoop

The next time you need to clean the leaves out of your gutters, don't waste your money on a new gutter scoop. Instead, take a plastic oil container and cut the bottom off diagonally. It's the perfect width for any gutter, and it comes equipped with a spout that serves as a handgrip.

Foil a leaking gutter

If your steel gutter has sprung a leak, patch the hole by applying a generous coating of roofing cement to the hole or crack and then covering it with a piece of heavy-duty aluminum foil. Repeat the process and finish off the job with a top coat of cement. Now that's a seal!

Chisel with care

Cushion your hand while chiseling cracked concrete. An ordinary sponge ball wrapped around the chisel makes a handy shock absorber. To shield your eyes and face from any stray fragments, push the chisel through a piece of window screen before you start chipping away.

Quick fix for a loose brick

You don't need to mix up a fresh batch of mortar just to replace a single loose brick in a retaining wall, porch step, or outdoor grill. Simply get out two-part epoxy and apply it to the sides of the brick where the mortar has come loose. Let it cure for 24 hours, then seal any remaining gaps with urethane or silicone caulk.

Instant aging for new mortar

If you think those new mortar joints are going to stand out like a sore thumb against the old cement, "age" them to match by dabbing the wet mortar with a damp black tea bag. (You may need to experiment a bit to obtain the right shade.)

Pour your own stepping-stones

Looking to put that leftover cement to good use? Why not make a few concrete stepping-stones? Your molds? A couple of garbage can lids. Coat the inside of the lids with a thin, even layer of motor oil so the cured concrete will slide out. You can even add your own decorative touches by etching shapes in the wet cement using leaves or other objects.

Cover cement with hay to keep it from setting up

Every builder who works out-of-doors has had the frustrating experience of working with cement when the temperature dips. To minimize problems, keep the area covered with hay before the pour, then after the concrete is placed and smoothed, cover it with plastic sheeting followed by hay.

Insider Tool Tips

Sharpen blades with a matchbook
Don't have a whetstone? You can still restore a dull blade on a small craft or utility knife by rubbing it a few times on the striking surface of a matchbook or, if one is handy, an emery board. Be sure to sharpen both sides of the cutting edge.

Be carpet scrap happy
As handy as they are for repairing tears and burns in carpeting, carpet remnants may be even more useful around the workshop. You can:

- Glue them to the inside of your toolbox to cushion tools in transit.
- Tack them to the tops of sawhorses and workbench surfaces to prevent scratching furniture finishes.
- Staple several remnants inside a narrow cabinet to form cushy cradles for drills and other power tools.
- Staple remnants (one at a time) to a small block of wood to make a reusable contact-cement applicator.

Hands-on handles
You'll get a firmer (and more comfortable) grip on hammers, wrenches, screwdrivers, and other tools if you wrap the handles with adhesive tape or flat foam weather stripping. Hard tools, now soft to the touch.

Extend an oilcan's reach
Need to lubricate a difficult-to-reach gear or joint? Tape a piece of broom straw to the oilcan's spout. The drops of oil will travel along the straw to their distant destination.

Nail-pulling protectors
Have you ever pulled a nail out of a piece of wood only to discover the hammerhead marred the grain? You can easily prevent it from happening by slipping the brim of a baseball cap under the head of the hammer before you start pulling. Can't find a cap? A plastic spatula or a large guitar pick will work just as well.

Shield wood from hammers
Protect wood from accidental hammer blows with this homemade hammer guard. Take the lid from a small plastic container and cut a small hole (one large enough to fit over the nail head) in the center. Place the lid over each nail before hammering it in. To prevent wood from splitting, blunt the tips of your nails with a hammer before using them.

Pliers as flashlight holder
Trying to hold a flashlight and work at the same time is a juggling act you don't want to perform. But you can still get the illumination you need if you don't have a helper to hold the light. Just place the flashlight between the jaws of a pair of pliers and position it at the required angle. Slip a thick rubber band around the handles of the pliers to keep the flashlight from slipping.

Fizz away corrosion
Loosen a rusty nut or bolt by covering it with a rag soaked in hydrogen peroxide, vinegar, or club soda. Let it sit for an hour to give the liquid time to work into the corrosion. The carbonation in club soda or soft drinks has another workshop application as well: It will unfreeze a rusted padlock or cabinet lock.

Caulking and Adhesives

Cold weather caulking

Need to do some caulking on a crisp, cool day? Keep your caulk pliable and running smoothly by wrapping the tubes in a heating pad for 30–45 minutes before using them. Trap the heat by wrapping each tube in plastic wrap before inserting it into the caulk gun.

Stick it to caulk

Don't use your finger to tool a bead of silicone or butyl rubber caulk unless you don't mind wearing it for a while. A Popsicle stick or the back of a plastic or old teaspoon is a much better way to go about it; both have smooth, rounded edges and are easy to hold without getting the caulk on your skin.

Improve your aim

It can be difficult to maneuver a caulk gun in a tight spot or to properly seal a crevice that's out of reach. But an effective extension tool may be as near as a kitchen cabinet or drawer: a plastic drinking straw. Attach the straw (or any plastic tube of the right size) to the nozzle of the caulk tube. Keep your impromptu extender from slipping off by securing it with duct tape.

Mix it up

Recycled bottle caps and jar lids are ideal for mixing two-part epoxy. The raised edge keeps the adhesive from spreading out as you're mixing it, and the limited interior space prevents you from using too much.

In the bag

Looking for an easy way to mix *and* apply two-part epoxy? Venture no farther than the pantry. Grab a plastic sandwich bag and pour as much adhesive as you'll need into a corner section. Tie off the rest of the bag and mix the epoxy by rolling it between your fingers. Use a pin to put one or more small holes in the bag and gently squeeze the epoxy out.

Undo the glue

You shouldn't have to fight to get glue out of a bottle or tube. Declare a truce by dabbing a little petroleum jelly on the inside of the glue lid or on the tip of the tube before replacing the cap. It will prevent the glue from sticking to the cover, and you'll have one less frustration to face.

TAPE A TUBE

Wrapping caulk tubes in **duct tape** can help you work more neatly and efficiently. The tape helps tubes fit more snuggly in the caulk gun and prevents the sticky mess that follows when tubes swell and collapse as the plunger squeezes out the caulk.

Clamping and Sanding

Clamps from the car

Got an old beat-up jumper cable that's just lying around collecting dust? Cut off the battery clips and bring them down to your workshop. They make dandy spring clamps and can accommodate widths up to 1½-inches thick. You could also use an automotive hose clamp to secure a cracked wooden leg or spindle. Just be sure to put a piece of cloth between the clamp and the wood so you won't risk gouging the surface.

Pour on the pressure

It's impossible to clamp some irregularly shaped items and fragile objects to do repairs, but you can still provide adequate pressure. Fill a small plastic bag with sand to weigh down repairs on small, fragile items; use a larger bag for big, sturdier items.

True grit

Want to extend the life of your sanding belts and get the most use out of each sheet of sandpaper? Then back either with strips of duct tape. The tape will prevent the paper from tearing and take some of the stress off the belts. Write down the grit of the paper and the direction of the belt on the tape using a permanent marker.

Resizing sandpaper

There's no rule that says you have to use a whole sheet of sandpaper for every job. In fact, many sanding jobs require you to cut the paper to odd shapes or sizes. Figuring out what to use in place of a block is the tricky part. Here are a few common household items you can use to get the job done (some will require you to glue or tack on the sandpaper):

What's the Story?
Sandpaper's Sojourn

The first recorded use of sandpaper took place in thirteenth-century China, when ancient artisans used natural gum to bond crushed shells, seeds, and sand to parchment. Still, up until the nineteenth century most woodworkers and cabinet-makers relied on dried sheets of sharkskin to smooth their wooden wares.

In the 1800s the fish skins were replaced by "glass paper," made by gluing small particles of glass by hand onto sheets of paper. Commercial production of glass paper began in London in 1833 when John Oakey, a onetime piano manufacturer's apprentice, developed a way to mass produce it. A year later, Isaac Fisher Jr. of Springfield, Vermont, obtained four patents for coating and manufacturing what he called "sandpaper."

Sandpaper jumped in popularity in 1921 when 3M introduced Wetordry, the world's first waterproof sandpaper, after purchasing the patent from its unsung inventor. The product, first used for repainting automobiles, is still sold today—a case of "if it ain't broke, don't fix it."

- A box of playing cards
- Pencils and pencil erasers
- Section of garden hose
- Kitchen sponges
- Wooden clothespins
- A wood block secured to a sponge mop holder (for walls and ceilings)

Ladder Lowdown

Stuck on top

Few things are quite as vexing as dropping a
needed screw or tool from the top of a ladder.
One way to put the kibosh on such mishaps is to
glue a magnet strip to the top rung of your ladder. It will safely hold on to all your fasteners
and small tools until you need them. When it
comes to larger tools, secure them to the ladder's
tool shelf with large rubber bands or tubing.

Off on the right foot

A scrap of outdoor carpet wrapped around the
bottom rung of a ladder makes a handy mat for
wiping the soles of your shoes before you
ascend. It will also let you know you've reached
bottom when climbing down. Secure the carpet
scrap with duct tape and replace with a fresh
piece when needed.

Boot up a ladder

Set the feet of a ladder in a pair of old rubber
boots to give it a skid-free footing on smooth
surfaces.

Don't leave your mark

Cushion the tops of a ladder's rails with an old
pair of socks, gloves, or a couple of bunched up
T-shirts to prevent it from damaging vinyl siding
and wood shingles or leaving marks or scratches on interior walls. One less thing to repair!

The Clever Homemaker's
crisis center

When a grease splatter burns your hand, the advice in emergency guides (and this book) is to race to the nearest faucet and hold the burn under cold running water for 15 minutes. But what about all those other problems we encounter in daily life? The kind that aren't necessarily emergencies but need a quick fix nonetheless. Ants taking over the kitchen, a makeup spill on your white silk blouse, diaper rash causing your baby dire distress—you can take care of them all by using the common household items and suggestions that fill the previous chapters in this book. This section, however, will provide you with emergency fixes that will help you quickly avert virtually any crisis that may come up in your home. Culled from a vast well of folk remedies and ages-old common sense, it speaks to the imagination of ordinary do-it-yourselfers possessing an extraordinary knack for solving problems great and small.

Body Repairs

A cold is coming on like gangbusters.
Set your hair dryer to warm, hold in front of face, and breathe in the warm air. (*Fire up the hair dryer, page 154*)

You have a **cold or allergy,** and your stuffy nose feels like it may explode.
Peel and halve a clove of garlic and hold it on your tongue as long as you can, taking fumes into throat and lungs.

Inhale a pinch of ground pepper to precipitate sneezing and clearing.

Add ¼ cup vinegar to the water in a vaporizer.

Your head is pounding like a steel drum.
Soak your feet in hot water laced with mustard powder to calm a vascular headache. (*Head-to-toe headache remedy, page 161*)

Tie a scarf, bandana, or necktie tightly around your head at forehead level. (*Wear a headband, page 161*)

You're coming down with the flu.
Drink a cup of elderberry tea or a glass of water with 20–30 drops of elderberry tincture. (*Swat the flu bug with elderberry, page 156*)

A painful toothache or gum infection is killing you.
Mix 2–3 teaspoons of table salt in a glass of warm water; vigorously swish in mouth. (*Saltwater rinse for toothaches, page 163*)

Clamp down on a cotton ball wetted with several drops of clove oil and get to the dentist. (*Clove oil to the rescue! page 163*)

Make a pain-relieving mouthwash with 6 ounces water, ¼ teaspoon salt, and 6–8 drops clove oil. (*Ditto*)

Your ear aches.
Use a clean eyedropper to drop 3 percent hydrogen peroxide into your ear and let it bubble for 3–5 minutes. (*Bubble away ear trouble, page 162*)

You have a **cold sore** that looks (and feels) terrible. Dab it with yogurt or vinegar throughout the day.

You overdid it, and now your **back muscles are screaming.**
Position a cold, unopened soft drink can between a wall and the painful area, and then move from side to side to massage it. (*Tin can massage, page 164*)

Leg cramps wake you and send you out of bed hopping like a frog. Stand on a cold stone or ceramic tile floor to slow blood flow and relax tightened, cramped muscles. *(Painful leg cramp relievers, page 164)*

You burned your tongue on that first bite of hot pizza. Sprinkle a pinch or two of sugar on your tongue to ease the pain.

Constipation— 'nuff said. Take 1 tablespoon blackstrap molasses before bed. *(Grease the skids with blackstrap molasses, page 166)*

Take 1–2 teaspoons castor oil for relief in about 8 hours. *(Old-timey constipation cure, page 166)*

Diarrhea is keeping you on the run. Make an infusion from the berries or dried leaves of blackberry, blueberry, or bilberry plants. *(Treat diarrhea with berries, page 166)*

Puree a whole lemon in a blender, add salt, and take 1 teaspoon two or three times a day.

An upset stomach is upsetting your day. Brew infusions from angelica, anise, caraway seed, chamomile, cinnamon, fennel seed, ginger, marjoram, oregano, or peppermint. *(Stomach soothers, page 165)*

Drink cold club soda with a dash of bitters.

Your hiccups aren't responding to the usual cures. Eat some peanut butter and take your time before swallowing it. *(Peanut butter for hiccups, page 180)*

You need a quick treatment for an ordinary skin cut. Place a peeled, bruised half-clove of garlic over a cleaned cut, secure with a bandage, and leave for up to 10 minutes. *(Treat a cut with garlic, page 171)*

Use mouthwash to disinfect the cut.

Apply a substantial amount of black pepper directly to the cut. *(Black pepper stops bleeding, page 171)*

You banged your arm or leg so hard it's going to bruise. Immediately press an onion on the spot for 15 minutes to reduce discoloration. *(Lessen bruising with an onion, page 171)*

Don't Scratch That Itch!

Whatever the cause—animal, vegetable, or mineral—itchy skin can drive you nuts. But scratching can result in infections and scarring. Control your instinct, and try one of these itch-stopping remedies instead.

Mosquito and other insect bites Saturate a clean cloth with white or cider vinegar or rubbing alcohol, and dab bites. A few drops of ammonia or a generous dab of chest rub applied directly to the bite (not bleeding or open sores) will also quell itching.

Chigger bites Soothe itching with a saltwater soak; then coat the rash with vegetable oil or lard.

Poison ivy or poison oak Apply a paste of 3 teaspoons baking soda and 1 teaspoon water to the rash. Vinegar also takes the sting out.

Athlete's foot Soak the affected foot in a saltwater footbath. (Beat athlete's foot, page 170). Dust feet, socks, and shoes with baking powder to dry the infection. For stronger relief, make a salve of 1 teaspoon baking soda and ½ teaspoon water; rub between toes and leave for about 15 minutes. Rinsing feet with undiluted cider vinegar three or four times daily will also calm itching.

Itchy sunburn Make a lotion of 1 part powdered milk, 2 parts water, and a couple pinches of salt, and dab on burned areas. Or treat sunburn with strong green tea. (Soothe sunburn with green tea, page 171)

Apply a banana peel, inside down, on the bruise and secure it with a bandage.

Apply cotton gauze soaked in cider vinegar for an hour.

An inflamed boil needs draining. Cover boil with a wet tea bag and secure with a bandage, then leave on overnight.

A wasp or bee sting threatens to ruin a day in the sun. Apply a paste of 2 parts baking soda to 1 part vinegar. *(Double-duty paste for bee stings, page 172)*

Pour on undiluted vinegar and scrape away stinger with a credit card.

Dab on a paste of meat tenderizer and water. *(Papaya milk [sort of] for stings, page 172)*

Place an onion slice over the sting.

Spray the sting with WD-40 or a window cleaner containing ammonia.

Your toddler has a sudden nosebleed. Set her on your lap, leaning slightly forward, and gently pinch her nostrils closed. *(Stopping Baby's nosebleed, page 179)*

Baby has a sudden, painful case of diaper rash. Apply honey, which will absorb liquid and keep skin dry. *(Diaper rash soothers, page 178)*

Quicken healing by sealing out moisture with petroleum jelly or vegetable shortening or toasted cornstarch. *(Ditto)*

Apply the spice fenugreek. *(A spicy baby powder substitute, page 178)*

Nothing seems to help your colicky infant get comfortable. Give him several sips of fennel seed or peppermint tea to help expel gas and relieve cramps. *(Two herbal teas for colic, page 179)*

Your baby gets a cut or scrape. Use a baby wipe or hand wipe to clean a dirty cut or scrape when no water is available.

Squeeze lemon juice, mouthwash, vinegar, or hard liquor directly on the injury, cover with a napkin, and hold in place for a minute or two to stop bleeding.

Your child's baby tooth just came out, and the blood is flowing. Squeeze excess liquid out of a cool used tea bag and press the bag onto the empty tooth socket. Hold for 1–2 minutes, then reapply as necessary to stop bleeding.

Those beautiful new shoes gave you an ugly new blister. Slice open an aloe leaf and scoop out the gel. Apply gel and bandage blister. *(Aloe for blisters, page 174)*

Household Help Line

A water pipe in the basement is leaking. Make a temporary patch using a garden hose or rubber tubing that's larger in diameter than the pipe. *(Hose off pipe leaks, page 349)*

You arrive at your country cabin to find the water pipes frozen. Blow warm air from a hair dryer on a pipe until it thaws. *(Blow-dry a frozen pipe, page 349)*

You forgot to cover the outdoor faucets, and a freeze is predicted. Shut off valves and then open taps and drain remaining water. Wrap spigots and any exposed pipe in several sheets of newspaper to insulate against cold, and cover with plastic bags secured with duct tape.

A tear in a window screen is letting the bugs in. Apply a few dabs of clear epoxy glue, model

10 Grooming and Clothing Mishaps

Appearance matters, and keeping yourself looking good means knowing what to do when trouble rears its not-so-pretty head.

1. **Too much scent** You went a little wild with the cologne, and the scent is overpowering. Dab a little vodka on the spots where scent was applied.

2. **No lipstick** When you changed purses, you forgot it. Use a brown eyebrow pencil to add a little color to your lips. *(Emergency lip color, page 188)*

3. **No mousse** There's no hair mousse in the bottle, and you're not one to wear bangs. Mix a little shaving cream with a drop of rubbing alcohol and rub into the hair where needed. *(Run out of hair mousse? page 189)*

4. **Paint in hair** While you're painting the ceiling, paint drips onto your hair. Rub olive oil on the spots until all paint traces are gone.

5. **Chlorine-damaged hair** Swimming in the pool turns your blonde tresses green. Massage ketchup or undiluted tomato juice into your hair. Cover with a shower cap (not a towel) and leave on for 10–15 minutes before rinsing.

6. **Blood on clothes** You cut your hand, and the blood drips onto your khaki pants. Soak stained portion overnight in carbonated soft drink, then wash as usual. *(Pop out bloodstains, page 198)*

7. **Chocolate stains** Your three-year-old smears chocolate on her shirt to wipe her hands. Cover the stain with meat tenderizer, leave for an hour, brush away powder, and wash.

8. **Lipstick marks** Lipstick stains mar your shirt or blouse. Remove the center from a piece of white bread and knead into a ball. Blot the stain with the bread ball until lipstick is mostly gone. Wash as usual. *(Lipstick smear remover 2: Bread!, page 197)*

9. **Scorch marks** Your favorite white cotton shirt has a prominent scorch mark. Dab the mark with a white cotton cloth moistened with 3 percent hydrogen peroxide, then wash as usual.

10. **Stuck ring** You tried on your friend's new ring and can't get it off. Apply mayonnaise liberally to ring and finger to aid the ring's slide. *(Unstick a stuck ring, page 204)*

airplane glue, or nail polish over and around the hole. *(Repair a Torn Screen, page 329)*

Use duct tape for temporary repairs

when a screen has detached from the frame or has large rips and tears. *(Fast fix for a major screen tear, page 328)*

Your house key broke off in the **lock.** Try to extract the broken part with tweezers or needle-nose pliers. Use Super Glue to join the key's two parts. *(Remove a broken key, page 330)*

Someone very young left pencil or ink doodles on **your wall.** Rub pencil marks with a piece of rye bread or a clean art gum eraser.

For ink marks, dab on white vinegar with clean cloth or sponge, then continue until marks are gone.

Your child decorated your wall with crayons. Rub lightly with a clean fabric softener sheet. Rub vigorously with a clean art gum eraser.

Scrub with shaving cream and a soft toothbrush or nailbrush.

Soften marks with a hair dryer and remove with baby oil on a cloth. *(Erasing crayon marks from walls, page 72)*

Scrub gently with a damp cloth dipped in baking soda or white toothpaste.

For crayon on wallpaper, very lightly

skim the surface with a steel wool soap pad, stroking in one direction, until marks disappear.

You've **spilled paint** on your beautiful wood floor.

Stir 1½ teaspoons vinegar and 1½ teaspoons laundry detergent into 2 cups warm water and sponge up remaining paint. *(Clean up paint spills with vinegar, page 74)*

You spot a glob of butter or **sour cream on your rug.**

Scoop up with a spoon, blot with a paper towel, and pour on baking soda, talcum powder, cornstarch, or cornmeal. Leave for up to six hours to absorb grease, then vacuum and repeat as needed.

You dropped a **contact lens** or earring stud on the rug and can't find it.

Tightly attach a couple layers of cheesecloth, a piece of panty hose, or a fabric softener sheet over the crevice tool of your vacuum cleaner with a rubber band or tape. Slowly and carefully vacuum the rug, checking the covered nozzle until the lost item appears.

You just noticed an ugly white **water ring** on your wooden table.

If the ring is still wet, use a hair dryer on low to dry it quickly.

For darker woods, mix ashes from one cigarette in a tablespoon of mayonnaise and rub into the spot until color is restored. *(Wipe Out Water Rings, page 339)*

For a nonshellac finish, pour a little lemon oil on a rag, dip it in salt, and gently rub the spot. *(Ditto)*

Lightly rub the ring with fine (#0000) steel wool dipped in lemon oil. *(Ditto)*

Mix equal amounts white toothpaste and baking soda and rub in, going with the wood grain. *(Get rid of water rings and spots, page 76)*

Coming to Your Pet's Rescue

Kitty, Rover, and assorted other pets have their own share of problems—among them, these five plights.

Your DOG swallowed something that wasn't food. Induce vomiting by giving Poochie 1–2 tablespoons of hydrogen peroxide. *(Hydrogen peroxide for an upset stomach, page 226)*

FIDO's doghouse is Flea City. Wash down interior walls, plus dog bed and any bedding, with strong salt water. Repeat treatment every few weeks to keep your best friend's home flea-free.

Fluffy the CAT rolled in some sticky stuff. Mix 1 teaspoon mild shampoo or dishwashing liquid with ¼ to ½ cup warm water, massage it into the sticky patch and remove residue with a wire-toothed brush. *(Unsticking something sticky, page 236)*

***Pee-yew!* Your pet had a run-in with a SKUNK.** Wash your pet in a bath of equal parts white vinegar and water. *(De-skunk your pet with vinegar, page 236)*

Your pet SNAKE is not where he's supposed to be. Lay sheets of aluminum foil, bubble wrap, or crinkly cellophane in potential hiding places so that you can hear him moving. *(Your pet snake is lost? page 243)*

Guests are coming, and you notice scratches on your serving table.

Apply 2-3 tablespoons instant coffee mixed with just enough water to make a thick paste. *(Instant fix for scratched woodwork, page 341)*

See "Homeopathic" scratch care *(page 341)* and proceed as directed.

A vinyl or cork **tile is about to pop out** of the kitchen floor. Cover the tile with aluminum foil and iron with a hot iron to heat the glue. Weigh down tile with books, bricks, or other heavy flat object until the glue resets.

Your interior decorator uncle is due for an overnight stay, and a piece of **wood furniture** in the guest room somehow got gouged. Make ersatz wood putty by adding instant coffee to 2 tablespoons spackling paste to get the desired color. (*Instant wood putty, page 343*)

The kitchen **sink is clogged, and you have no plunger.** Use a tennis ball or small rubber ball cut in half as a suction cup. (*No plunger, no problem, page 348*)

Put any of the following into the drain, let sit for 10–15 minutes, and then flush with boiling water:

1 cup baking soda and 1 cup hot white vinegar.

½ cup borax, then boiling water added slowly.
2 Alka-Seltzer tablets or 3 denture tablets followed by 1 cup vinegar.

1 cup salt, 1 cup baking soda, and ½ cup white vinegar to rid drain of hair clogs.

Your **washing machine** is doing the shake, rattle, and roll. Use a flashlight to peek under the machine when it's in action. If one of the washer feet isn't resting firmly on the floor, place a wood shim, small carpet scrap, or piece of linoleum tile under the unsteady foot.

A **drinking glass crashed** to the bathroom floor, and you're worried you'll miss the tiniest pieces. First, wear gloves to pick up large pieces. Then choose one of these methods:

Press the area with wet newspaper to take up tiny bits of glass.

Press a slice of bread or a wad of adhesive tape over tiny slivers and glass dust to remove them from the floor.

Ants are swarming over your kitchen counters.

Sugar Make an ant trap by dissolving 2–3 teaspoons sugar in 1 cup water, moisten paper towels or sponges in sugar water and set out overnight. Next morning, sweep trap and ants into a dustpan. (*Lure ants with sugar, page 90*)

White vinegar Spray windowsills, door thresholds, counters, cabinets, and other surfaces with a mixture of equal parts white vinegar and water. (*Repel ants with vinegar, page 90*)

Cayenne pepper and cinnamon Sprinkle these substances on surfaces where ants gather. (*Spicy ant repellents, page 52*)

Grits, flour, or ashes Spread over ant trails, and ants will soon find somewhere else to walk. (*Ants hate grits, page 51*)

Lemon juice, etc. Outside the house, pour lemon juice on thresholds, sills, cracks, and holes where ants can enter. Scatter lemon rinds around door entrances. Or use borax, powdered chalk, salt, talcum power, cream of tartar, powdered sulfur, or oil of clove in the same way.

Petroleum jelly Apply around the rims of pets' food bowls to keep ants at bay.

Roaches. Anywhere, anytime.

Mix equal parts baking soda and sugar and scatter where roaches are seen.

Making sure there's no danger to children and pets, sprinkle boric acid powder into cracks and crevices and under appliances where roaches lurk.

Seal off roach entrances with equal parts corn-starch and plaster of Paris mixed with enough water to make a thick paste.

If you're fast, you can kill a scurrying roach with a spray of WD-40.

Your house is invaded by fleas.
If the invasion isn't too severe, place bowls of salt in areas where fleas are to attract and trap them.) Set a plate containing a little water and a few drops of dishwashing liquid on the floor, place a gooseneck lamp alongside, and bend the bulb close to the water to attract fleas.

Wash floors with the juice and rinds of 4 lemons in ½ gallon water to repel fleas.

Vacuum rugs often to remove flea eggs.

On the Road

It's a cold morning, and the car won't start.
Get your hair dryer and a long extension cord. Pop the car hood. Now blow hot air directly at the carburetor to warm the engine for easy ignition. *(Start your car with a hair dryer, page 312)*

The fan belt just broke. Help!
For a temporary fix, twist a pair of panty hose into a long rope, thread it around the fan pulleys, and knot tightly.

Your auto horn won't shut up.
Stop the incessant blaring by raising the hood and taping down the terminal screw. *(Tape that noisy horn! page 315)*

You backed into a post, and your taillight cover cracked.
If the light itself is okay, you can temporarily repair the translucent cover with red or yellow duct tape. Cut tape and adhere to cover cracks, then turn on the light to be certain it's clearly visible.

It's a dark and stormy night, and your headlight goes out.
Covering the dead headlight with reflector tape will help get you home safely.

Your wheels are spinning on an ice patch.
Pour undiluted chlorine bleach over your tires. *(Gain traction with bleach, page 312)*

Lay a large piece of scrap carpet or a thick pad of newspaper (two or three sections of the average daily) where the wheel hits the icy road.

Your car wheels are bogged in snow or mud.
Make a shovel dig more efficiently by spraying it with WD-40.

Your car's temperature gauge suddenly goes into the danger zone.
Check under the hood after the engine cools. If you see a cracked or broken water hose, you can probably make a short-term repair—just long enough to get to an expert—by wrapping the hose with duct tape.

Acknowledgments

The writers and editors who produced this book wish to thank the following people and organizations, all of whom graciously shared their knowledge or expertise. American Society of Travel Agents; Arizona Cooperative Extension, Mojave County; Larry Buchwald; Jim Buie; Andrew R. Byers; Trevor Cole; Vicki Coombs; Pat Courtney; Marilyn Dale; Marianne Dervish; Polly DuBose; Carolyn Jackson; Dan Janssen; Pamela Johnson; Marilyn and Gene Kalet; Barbara Kaye; Madelon Konopka; John J. Ligon; Dr. Sandra McCurdy; Marty Malone; Men's Garden Club of America; Montana State U. Extension Service, Park County; North Carolina Cooperative Extension, Henderson County; Maurice Ogutu; Oregon State U. Extension Service, Lane County; Penn State Cooperative Extension, Indiana County; Mary Kay Pleyer; Bob Pollock; Angela Ponce; Julia Pryor; Jack Reagor; Linda Renslow; Derek Scasta; Barbara Scott; Aliza Schiff; Hannah Schiff; Mary Skinner; Martha A. Smith; Jim Sorrenti; John Teague; Texas AgriLIFE Extension Service (Texas A & M System), Navarro County; Diane Turner; Sara Beth Warne; Sean Whalen; U. of Illinois Extension, Countryside Extension Center; U. of Nebraska Extension-Lincoln, Lancaster County; U. of Tennessee Extension, Bedford County

Index

Page numbers in *italics* refer to illustrations.

for skin maintenance, 582–83
for sore throats, 553
honeydews, 679
hoof dressing, 638, 639
hooks, 537
hops pillows, 574
hops shampoo, 587
horns, car, 713
hornworms, 699
horse care, 638–39
horseradish, 555, 678
hostas, 698
hot feet, 568
hot pepper, 449, 554
houseplant hints, 676–77
hubcaps, 710, 714
hula hoops, for portable cubicles, 664
humidifiers, odor removal from, 478
hummingbird feeders, 694, *694*
hydrangeas, 675
hydration drinks, 578
hydrogen peroxide, 484
  clearing earwax with, 560
  corrosion removal with, 754
  for dog's upset stomach, 624
  for scorch marks, 597
  for tomato sauce stains, 595
hygiene tips, for children, 619
hypericin, 574
hypnotic suggestion, 573
hyponatremia, 566

I
ibuprofen, 558
ice cream, 415, 439
ice cubes, 440
  baking bread with, 428
  candle wax removal with, 474, *475*
  for cleaning of garbage disposals, 447
  sap removal with, 708, *708*
  skimming fat with, 413
  storing of, 439
  watering plants with, 676
ice cube trays, for storage, 497, 503, 513
ice packs, 663, 665
ice picks, 711
ice scrapers, 453
icing, 430
incense, locating drafts with, 734
indigestion, 558, 563, 564, 565
indolebutyric acid (IBA), 669
infant seats, as bathing aid, 606

infusions, 557, 563, 565
ink, "invisible," 611
ink stains, 492, 595
insect bites, 565, 579, 607
insecticide, *see* bug repellents
insects, 701
  cleaning car splatters of, 707
  gardening and, 679, 683, 684, 696–98
  trapping of, 488, 662–63
  see also bug repellents; *specific insects*
insomnia, 565, 574–75
instant dry shampoo, 587
insulation, for windows, 734
interior decoration, *see* decorating, home
invisible ink, 611
iris bulbs, 674
iron, cast, 460, 470
iron, hot, 470, 471, 537
  cleaning of, 482, 491
  lifting vinyl tiles and, 733
  scorches due to, 597
ivory, shining of, 482
ivy, 686

J
jars, 536, 610, 688
  as candleholders, 535
  as greenhouses, 669
  for homemade hair rinse, 588
  making snow globes out of, 549
  for paint leftovers, 527
  as roach motels, 450
  as seed sowers, 668
  for storage, 503, 513
jaundice, 578
jellyfish stings, 579
jewelry, 601–2
  packing of, 646, 647, 655
  storing and organizing of, 497, 503, 504, 601, 602, *602*, 613
joint pain, 558, 562, 565
juice, fruit, stain removal of, 473
juicers, cleaning of, 459
juniper, for gastrointestinal distress, 563
junk mail, curtailing of, 498

K
Keep-It-Bright Windshield Wash, 705
keepsake boxes, 496
kerosene, 698, 704, 708

keyholes, 735
key rings, 512, *512*, 656
keys, 499, 600, 659
kiddie pools, as decorative ponds, 686
kidney health, 566, 567, *567*
kitchen tools, 415, 435
knee pads, for bath time, 607, *607*
knives, *506*, 507, 754
knots, 521
Knox gelatin, 588
Kool-Aid, 743
kosher salt, 455

L
labeling, 497, 505, 508, 520, 521, 527, 540, 717, 749
labor, induction of, 564
lace, restoring crispness to, 597
lacquer finish, 740, 741
ladders, 511, 522, 529, 600, 681, 757
lamination, with tape, 618
lamps, 530–33, *531*, 546
lampshades, 530–31, *531*, 546, 672
lard, 639
latrine, makeshift, 663
laundry bags, substitutes as, 649
laundry baskets:
  for athletic equipment storage, 621
  as baby baths, 606
  managing car clutter with, 717, *718*, 719
  as pillow nest, 524, *525*
  as shoe catcher, *495*, 499
laundry detergent, 453, 475–76, 718
laundry prewash stain remover, 708, 713, 721
laurel, 449
lavender, 571, 574, 593, 635
lavender oil, 652
lawn care, 685–86
laxatives, 564
leaf curl, 700
leash substitutes, 628
leather, 476, 715, 739
leaves, 642
  centerpieces of, 536
  in children craft projects, 620–21
  cleaning of, 676
  in gardening maintenance, 689, 690
  as printing stamps, 541

for soot removal, 478, 480
stained clothing removal and,
   596
stone and brick cleaning with,
   469
for toenail fungus, 568
for toy cleaning, 617
vinyl upholstery deodorized
   with, 715
wallpaper removal and, 732
for walls and floors, 446, 470
as weed-killer, 692
for window washing, 486
for yellowed clothes, 597
vinegar, apple cider, 474, 564,
   568, 632
in aftershave, 598
bacteria killed with, 660
for fatigue, 579
for hair revitalization, 587, 588
polishing chrome with, 706
for skin maintenance, 598
for trapping flies and mosquitoes, 660
Vinegar Weed Beater, 692
vinyl, 720
cleaning floors of, 446, 468–69
cleaning upholstery of, 475,
   715
repairing floors of, 733, 735
visors, unfogging of, 723
vodka:
as cologne or perfume correc-
   tive, 586
killing poison ivy with, 692
for musty clothes, 592
as windshield cleaner, 702, *703*,
   705
volatile oil, 557
vomit stains, 618

W
wagons, as seed flats, 669
waistbands, fixing of shrunken,
   591
walking sticks, 661
wallet protectors, 654
wallpaper, 534, 544
for bookcases, 527–28
cleaning of, 446, 470, 617–18
glazing of, 522, 529
removal of, 730, 732
for storage boxes, 541
whitewashing of, 522
walls, *445*, 446, 470, 730–32
warm baths, 575
warts, 572–73

wash (herbal preparation), 557
washcloths, socks as, 582
washer, clothes, 749–50
washing, of cars, 704–5
wasps, 663, 696
wasp stings, 570
watering, of gardens, 687–88
watermarks:
in bathroom, 478, 485
on leather, 476
on shower doors, 478
on stainless steel, 446
on wood tables, 482
water-packed tuna, 417
water rings, removal of, 474–75,
   737
wax, car, *see* car wax
wax paper, cleaning antennas
   with, 707
waxy buildup, on floors, 468
WD-40, 453, 454, 458, 463,
   465, 469, 638, 671, 686, 717,
   736, 743, 745
bicycle chain maintenance with,
   722
car care uses for, 706, 708,
   712, 713
garage door seepage and, 720
weeds, killing of, 689, 692
Wenger, 664
Westminster Abbey, 729
Wetordry sandpaper, 756
wheel and tire care, 702, 714
for bicycles, 722–23
Whirlpool, 744
whiteflies, 696, 697
white noise, as sleep aid, 575
white-out, 709, 730
white vermouth, 414
white vinegar, *see* vinegar
whitewashing, 522, 545
whooping cough, 556
wicker baskets, 701
wicker furniture, 482
willow tea rooting, 669
window boxes, 547, 688
windows, 653, 726–27, 734, 735
window treatments, 482, 486–
   87, 524
windshields:
bug repellents for, 707
cleaning of, 702, *703*, 704,
   705, 707
fog prevention for, 711
preventing frost on, 711
removing stickers or decals
   from, 708

wine, 440–41, 443
wine, red:
carpet stains of, 473
clothing stains of, 595–96
dyeing Easter eggs with, 548
making dressings with, 440
as meat tenderizer, 441
wine, white:
for carpet stains, 473
chilling of, 443
as lemon substitute, 433
making dressings with, 440
wine bottles, 415
wine boxes, for storage, 496
wiper blades, 704–5, 711
wire racks, 506
witch hazel, 550, 571, 598
wood ashes, 477
wooden slides, 506–7
wood-paneled walls, cleaning of,
   470
woodpeckers, 671
wood tables, watermarks on, 482
woodworkers, 756
woodworking tips, 741–43
Worcestershire sauce, 461
workshop, 511–13, 525
wounds, 565, 575, 578, 634
   see also cuts and scrapes
wreathes, 537, 546
wrinkles, 582, 589
clothes and, 592, 647–48
around eyes, 585
on high-heel shoes, 599
wristwatches, 601, 658

Y
yellowed clothes, 490, 597
yews, 687
yogurt containers, 624, 663, 668

Z
zinc oxide cream, 571, 576, 639
zinnias, 698
zippers, 592, *645*, 654, 660